Lecture Notes in Computer Science   11271

Commenced Publication in 1973
Founding and Former Series Editors:
Gerhard Goos, Juris Hartmanis, and Jan van Leeuwen

Marco Kuhrmann · Kurt Schneider
Dietmar Pfahl · Sousuke Amasaki
Marcus Ciolkowski · Regina Hebig
Paolo Tell · Jil Klünder
Steffen Küpper (Eds.)

Product-Focused Software Process Improvement

19th International Conference, PROFES 2018
Wolfsburg, Germany, November 28–30, 2018
Proceedings

 Springer

Editors
Marco Kuhrmann (ID)
Technische Universität Clausthal
Goslar, Germany

Kurt Schneider
Leibniz University Hannover
Hannover, Germany

Dietmar Pfahl (ID)
University of Tartu
Tartu, Estonia

Sousuke Amasaki
Okayama Prefectural University
Okayama, Japan

Marcus Ciolkowski (ID)
QAware GmbH
Munich, Germany

Regina Hebig (ID)
Chalmers | University of Gothenburg
Gothenburg, Sweden

Paolo Tell (ID)
IT University of Copenhagen
Copenhagen, Denmark

Jil Klünder (ID)
Leibniz University Hannover
Hannover, Germany

Steffen Küpper (ID)
Clausthal University of Technology
Goslar, Germany

ISSN 0302-9743 ISSN 1611-3349 (electronic)
Lecture Notes in Computer Science
ISBN 978-3-030-03672-0 ISBN 978-3-030-03673-7 (eBook)
https://doi.org/10.1007/978-3-030-03673-7

Library of Congress Control Number: 2018960431

LNCS Sublibrary: SL2 – Programming and Software Engineering

This Springer imprint is published by the registered company Springer Nature Switzerland AG
The registered company address is: Gewerbestrasse 11, 6330 Cham, Switzerland

Preface

The 19th International Conference on Product-Focused Software Process Improvement (PROFES 2018) brought together software researchers and industrial practitioners to Wolfsburg, Germany, during November 28–30, 2018. The hosting institutions were Clausthal University of Technology (TUC) and Leibniz Universität Hannover (LUH) in Germany. In the spirit of the PROFES conference series, PROFES 2018 provided a premier forum for practitioners, researchers, and educators to present and discuss experiences, ideas, innovations, as well as concerns related to professional software process improvement motivated by product and service quality needs.

PROFES 2018 had an international committee of well-known experts in software quality and process improvement carefully peer-reviewing the scientific submissions. This year, we received 65 submissions for the scientific paper track of which 16 were selected as full papers and eight as short papers resulting in an overall acceptance rate of 37%. Scientific papers in the PROFES conference received three to four reviews each. Continuing the open science policy initiated by PROFES 2017, we encouraged and supported the authors of all accepted papers to make their papers and research data publicly available.

The scientific contributions presented at PROFES 2018 cover a number of topics, which seem to manifest themselves as constantly relevant in the community, also reflecting industrial needs and agendas. The topics included

1. Measurement and monitoring
2. Empirical studies
3. Processes and methods
4. Global software engineering (GSE) and scaling software development
5. Software testing

Further relevant topics were added by the events co-located with PROFES 2018, the "2nd International Workshop on Managing Quality in Agile and Rapid Software Development Processes (QUASD)" and the "3rd Workshop on Hybrid Software and System Development Approaches (HELENA)", and three tutorials. Complementing the main scientific program, these events were included in the program to bring together researchers and representatives from industry by providing researchers with the opportunity to attend industry tutorials and providing practitioners with the latest research.

The role of an Industry Paper Co-chair was added to the Organizing Committee. Responsibilities included developing the new Industry Days in which we ran the tutorial "The Human Factor in Agile Transitions – Using the Personas Concept in Agile Coaching" as an open space event. The tutorial was enriched with lightning talks, mostly given by industry delegates. The Industry Days allowed industry delegated to peer up with researchers and to establish new collaboration networks with other companies. The mix of practice-oriented and scientific events attracted additional participants from local industry and fostered discussion and knowledge exchange between industry and academia.

The keynote talks this year were once again of high quality. The first keynote entitled "The Hitchhiker's Guide to Engineering AI-Infused Applications" was given by Dr. Andrew Begel, who is Senior Researcher in the Ability Group at Microsoft Research in Redmond, WA, USA. He received his PhD in Computer Science from the University of California, Berkeley, in 2005. Andrew Begel studies the communication and collaboration effectiveness of software engineers in collocated and distributed development. His most recent work has been to help tech companies learn how to work more effectively with autistic software engineers, to understand evolving job roles in the software industry, and to study and facilitate the growing impact of AI technologies on software engineering.

The second conference day was opened by the keynote entitled "Architecture – Key to Digital Transformation" given by Prof. Manfred Broy who was Full Professor in Computer Science at the Technische Universität München where he headed the Chair for Software & Systems Engineering from 1989 to 2015. In 2008, he established *fortiss* – the research institute of the Free State of Bavaria for software-intensive systems and services. From January 2016, he is Founding President and Scientific Director of the Bavarian Center for Digitization (Zentrum Digitalisierung.Bayern).

We are thankful for having had the opportunity to organize PROFES 2018 in Lower Saxony supported by Clausthal University of Technology (TUC) and Leibniz Universität Hannover (LUH). The Program Committee members and additional reviewers provided excellent support in reviewing the papers. We are also grateful to all speakers, authors, and session chairs for their time and effort that made PROFES 2018 a success. We are especially thankful to our sponsors and partners. We would also like to thank the PROFES Steering Committee members for the guidance and support in the organization process.

Finally, we owe thanks to Silke Kenzler and her team from Kenzler Conference Management and Manuela Laqua and her team from the WMG Wolfsburg Wirtschaft und Marketing GmbH for the significant support in setting up the local arrangements in Wolfsburg. Also, we thank everyone in the organization team as well as the student volunteers for making PROFES 2018 an experience that will live on in the participants' memory for years to come.

November 2018

Marco Kuhrmann
Kurt Schneider
Dietmar Pfahl
Sousuke Amasaki
Marcus Ciolkowski
Regina Hebig
Paolo Tell
Jil Klünder
Steffen Küpper

Organization

Organizing Committee

General Chairs

Marco Kuhrmann	Clausthal University of Technology, Germany
Kurt Schneider	Leibniz University Hannover, Germany

Program Co-chairs

Dietmar Pfahl	University of Tartu, Estonia
Sousuke Amasaki	Okayama Prefectural University, Japan

Industry Paper Chair

Marcus Ciolkowski	QAware, Germany

Short Paper Co-chairs

Regina Hebig	Chalmers | University of Gothenburg, Sweden
Paolo Tell	IT University of Copenhagen, Denmark

Workshop and Tutorial Co-chairs

Jürgen Münch	Reutlingen University, Germany
Krzyszstof Wnuk	BTH Karlskrona, Sweden

Proceedings and Web Co-chairs

Jil Klünder	Leibniz University Hannover, Germany
Steffen Küpper	Clausthal University of Technology, Germany

Social Media and Publicity Co-chairs

Silverio Martínez-Fernández	Fraunhofer IESE, Germany
Marcos Kalinowski	Pontifical Catholic University of Rio de Janeiro, Brazil

Local Arrangements

Silke Kenzler	Kenzler Conference Management, Germany
Andreas Rausch	Clausthal University of Technology, Germany

Program Committee

Full Paper Program Committee

Andrea Janes	Free University of Bolzano, Italy
Andreas Birk	SWPM, Germany
Anh Nguyen-Duc	University College of Southeast Norway, Norway
Ayse Tosun	Istanbul Technical University, Turkey
Bruno Da Silva	California Polytechnic State University, USA
Bruno Rossi	Masaryk University, Czech Republic
Carmine Gravino	University of Salerno, Italy
Daniel Graziotin	University of Stuttgart, Germany
Daniel Mendez	Technical University of Munich, Germany
Daniel Rodriguez	The University of Alcalá, Spain
David Ameller	Universitat Politècnica de Catalunya, Spain
Davide Fucci	HITeC, University of Hamburg, Germany
Dietmar Pfahl	University of Tartu, Estonia
Dietmar Winkler	Vienna University of Technology, Austria
Edson Oliveira Jr.	State University of Maringa, Brazil
Ezequiel Scott	University of Tartu, Estonia
Fabian Fagerholm	University of Helsinki, Finland
Frank Houdek	Daimler AG, Germany
Gerardo Canfora	University of Sannio, Italy
Giuseppe Scaniello	University of Basilicata, Italy
Gleison Santos	UNIRIO, Brasil
Guilherme Travassos	COPPE/UFRJ, Brasil
Hajimu Iida	Nara Institute of Science and Technology (NAIST), Japan
Hironori Washizaki	Waseda University, Japan
Janne Järvinen	F-Secure, Finland
Javier Dolado	University of the Basque Country, Spain
Jens Heidrich	Fraunhofer, Germany
Jingye Li	Norwegian University of Science and Technology, Norway
Juergen Muench	Reutlingen University, Germany
Kari Smolander	Lappeenranta University of Technology, Finland
Kenichi Matsumoto	Nara Institute of Science and Technology (NAIST), Japan
Klaus Schmid	University of Hildesheim, Germany
Luigi Buglione	Engineering.IT/ETS, Italy
Makoto Nonaka	Toyo University, Japan
Maleknaz Nayebi	University of Toronto, Canada
Marco Torchiano	Politecnico di Torino, Italy
Markus Ciolkowski	QAWare, Germany
Martin Solari	Universidad ORT Uruguay, Uruguay
Maurizio Morisio	Politecnico di Torino, Italy

Michael Felderer	University of Innsbruck, Austria
Michael Stupperich	Daimler AG, Germany
Michal Dolezel	University of Economics, Prague, Czech Republic
Noriko Hanakawa	Hannan University, Japan
Oscar Pastor	Universitat Politècnica de València, Spain
Paolo Panaroni	INTECS, Italy
Petri Kettunen	University of Helsinki, Finland
Rini Vansolingen	Delft University of Technology, The Netherlands
Risto Nevalainen	Spinet Oy, Finland
Rudolf Ramler	SCCH, Austria
Sousuke Amasaki	Okayama Prefectural University, Japan
Stefan Wagner	University of Stuttgart, Germany
Steffen Küpper	Clausthal University of Technology, Germany
Stephen MacDonell	University of Otago, New Zealand
Tomi Mannisto	University of Helsinki, Finland
Vahid Garousi	Wageningen University, The Netherlands
Yoshiki Higo	Osaka University, Japan

Short Papers Program Committee

Anh Nguyen Duc	University College of Southeast Norway, Norway
Beatriz Marín	Universidad Diego Portales, Chile
Filomena Ferrucci	Università di Salerno, Italy
Jil Klünder	Leibniz University Hannover, Germany
John Noll	Lero – the Irish Software Engineering Research Centre, Ireland
Jose Luis de La Vara	Carlos III University of Madrid, Spain
Monalessa Barcellos	UFES, Brazil
Renato Novais	IFBA, Brazil
Steve Counsell	Brunel University, UK

Keynotes

The Hitchhiker's Guide to Engineering AI-Infused Applications

Andrew Begel ⓘ

Microsoft Research, Redmond WA 98052, USA
andrew.begel@microsoft.com

Keynote Abstract

Artificial intelligence and machine learning (AI/ML) are some of the newest trends to hit the software industry, compelling organizations to evolve their development processes to deliver novel products to their customers. In this talk, I will describe how Microsoft software teams develop AI/ML-based applications using a nine-stage AI workflow process informed by prior experiences developing early AI applications (e.g. search and NLP) and data science tools (e.g. application telemetry and bug reporting). Adapting this workflow into their pre-existing, well-evolved, Agile-like software engineering processes and job roles has resulted in a number of engineering challenges unique to the AI/ML domain, some universal to all teams, but others related to the amount of prior AI/ML experience and education the teams have. I will tell you about some challenges and the solutions that teams have come up with.

I believe there are three challenges in the AI/ML domain that make it fundamentally different from prior software engineering application domains:

1. Discovering, managing, and versioning the data needed to power AI/ML is much more complex and difficult than other types of software engineering,
2. AI/ML model customization and reuse practices require very different skills than are typically found in software teams, and
3. AI components do not modularize like software components – models may be "entangled" in complex ways and experience non-monotonic error behavior.

The lessons that Microsoft has learned can help other organizations embarking on their own path towards AI and ML.

Architecture – Key to Digital Transformation

Manfred Broy(iD)

Institut für Informatik, Technische Universität München,
D-80290 München, Germany,
broy@in.tum.de
http://wwwbroy.in.tum.de/~broy/

Abstract. The digital transformation is changing our world, our economy and society more and quicker than any other technology before. There are many publications which describe the disruptive changes due to digitization and, in particular, due to new business models. However, it is most interesting to understand the details of the technology behind digitization. Looking at the economy, the key to digitization is software and abilities of companies to evolve systems and software in a way that accelerates their specific businesses. One of the crucial issues there is system and software architecture design. Choosing the appropriate architecture and the appropriate methodology to design and rearrange architecture is the basis for handling digitization successfully.

Keywords: Specification · Design · Contracts · Assumptions · Commitments System specification · Interface · Architecture

1 Introduction

Digitization changes our world by technology with a speed never seen before. The reasons are quite obvious. One of the key drivers of this rapid development is Moore's law. Since nearly 60 to 70 years, we observe that the power of hardware with respect to communication, computation, memory, and user interfaces including sensors and actuators grows exponentially. As a result, in many application areas the usage of digital technology is getting cheaper and cheaper such that it is used for everything (see [7]). Due to the increasing power of hardware software can be used for high performance jobs such as in data analytics. Software is eating the world (see [1]).

As a result, new companies enter the market and grow in a surprisingly short time span to global enterprises. At the same time, existing established enterprises run into the risk losing their market, no longer being able to sell their well-established products and, in particular, run short in reaching their customers by new innovations introduced by their competitors being digital companies. These new enterprises are more agile, closer to the customers and use all the different digital channels to reach their market. In addition, they use digital technologies everywhere, be it in the design of the product, their co-operation with partners, the production, their offering of services, observing and providing service to the customers. For many of those companies, software is the main instrument to run their business. In order to do that, they develop and operate enormous software systems. Often, they are platform companies applying specific techniques to organize their software development and, in particular, the relationship between software development and business development.

2 The Main Drivers

Certainly, one of the main success factors in the disruption caused by the digital transformation is understanding the market, understanding the customer, and serving the customer by services and products over digital channels. This requires quick reactions to meet customers' expectations. Since everything in the digital company is run on the basis of software, at least for the successful companies of today, a key issue is to be able to run software systems with all the quality needed, and all the services required.

This way, product management including requirements engineering by experienced product owners who on one hand know the market and on the other hand understand how to organize innovation is success critical. However, it is not sufficient just to understand what the customers and the market need. At the same time, one has to be able to address these needs by software systems that support exactly what is needed with sufficient quality and a very short time to market. If this is done on a basis of a well-developed design approach, perhaps using a kind of software platform, an essential capability is to modularize and reuse services and microservices in a very modular, well-understood way. This needs a deep understanding of the design of software and system architecture.

3 System and Software Architecture as a Key

What is needed is a software and, as long as physical products are involved, a system architecture that is organized in a way such that it is easy to implement changes and supports a very systematic system evolution. Depending on the business, there is a number of very different aspects that have to be supported by software architecture.

In particular, the following things have to be kept in mind.

- Quickly designing new services out of predesigned sub-services
- Understanding and documenting the feature interactions between different services
- Guaranteeing the right expected quality with respect to functional and quality-concerned issues
- Being able to make quick changes in the functionality of services
- Reusing existing services
- Managing compatibility.

Essential competencies here are classical methods and principles from architectural design including *modularity, capsulation,* and *information hiding* as well as *modular composition* and clear interface-driven descriptions of dependencies between architectural elements.

Components and Features One of the very basic understanding of architecture is the decomposition of systems into a set of services with their documented feature interaction (see [4]) and decomposition of systems into architectures composed of a set of elements, often called *components* (see [3, 10]) that interact to achieve a certain goal.

Interfaces There, a principle is that we do not have to understand all the technical implementation details of components but concentrate on their interface behavior as specified, where this specification is enough to describe the functioning of the architecture and the overall functionality and services delivered to the outside. This requires what we call a *modular design specification* approach (see [3]) based essentially onto the notion of interface.

Modularity The essential here is that we only need to know the interface specifications of components to be able to use them as components inside of architectures and to predict the architectural behavior. This is what modularity is about. Knowing the interface specification of components and how the components are connected and composed is enough to predict the overall behavior of the architecture and, in particular, the interface behavior of the architecture to the outside.

Encapsulation and Information Hiding The classical concept of encapsulation and information hiding is directly related to this idea. Interface specification means encapsulation where the only way to interact with the component is via their interface which means that the elements inside the components cannot be accessed freely from the outside but only over the interface. This is the key idea of encapsulation. In fact, an interface describes an abstraction from the implementation details of a component. To understand the effect of a component as part of an architecture, it is enough to understand the interface specification.

Design by Contract This is what is also addressed by the famous idea of design by contract. The interface specification is the contract (see [9]). The contract is enough for the implementer of a component to have all the requirements that have to be observed in the implementation.

Interface Specification The interface specification is all what is needed for the user of a component to understand how the component can be used correctly in the design of the architecture.

4 How to Specify Interfaces

Today, at least in software systems, interface design is often done in an object-oriented style. Then the interface of an object-oriented component, represented by a class or a set of classes, consists

- of all the methods that can be called and are offered by the component and in addition also in
- the description of all the methods the component wants to call and therefore are methods that are assumed such that a component can work correctly.

Unfortunately, however, the idea to describe interfaces at in object oriented design by classes and methods using design by contract as suggested by Bertrand Meyer runs into severe difficulties. Following the idea of design by contract, each method is characterized by its effects on the attributes of the class in which the method is defined giving an assertion called a pre-condition that describes the state of the attributes under which a method can be called safely, and an assertion called post-condition which describes the effect of a call in a state which fulfills the pre-condition.

Destruction of Information Hiding We meet a first problem in such a methodology. In the assertion, we have to talk about attributes. However, attributes are part of the implementation. At least, as far as we talk about the local attributes clearly for a class with exactly the same interface behavior, we can use quite different concepts of attributes. Attributes are part of the implementation, and therefore, should be hidden according to the principle of information hiding. Clearly, being forced to formulate assertions in terms of attributes is in conflict to the principle of information hiding. Another difficulty is that a method call cannot only change the attributes of a class in which it is defined. In the body of a method, generally there are method calls of methods from other classes which in course change the attributes of these other classes. Therefore, the description of the effect of method calls by pre- and postconditions requires not only to refer to the attributes of the considered class in which the method is defined but, in the general case, also to talk about attributes of other classes as long as within the considered method other methods of those classes are called.

Insufficient Expressiveness A third problem is the order in which forwarded method calls are executed and, in particular, callbacks. In those case, usually, pre- and post-conditions do not offer enough expressive power of expressing all what we want to express in interface specifications.

Problems with Concurrency and Parallelism Fourth and finally, if we deal with concurrent parallel systems, we have to enter a thread concept and using threads, assertions become even more difficult, and practically it is impossible to describe the interface behavior by assertion on state attributes in sufficient detail. As a result, we see that interface specification following the design by contract idea runs into difficulties.

Services are more than Method Calls However, there is an additional methodological problem, if we want to describe in interface behavior services. A service does not consist of just one method call. Services offered by a sequence of method calls, in some cases even unbounded sequences of method calls, and services are delivered in an interaction between the service provider and the service user. Therefore, method specification by design by contracts does not really describe services. They rather describe atomic steps as part of services. To derive a service description from a design by contract description is a rather difficult puzzle because then we have to find out just looking at the assertions what are meaningful orders in which method calls are executed to form services.

As a result, we believe that we need a more powerful, more expressive description of services by interfaces. This is a goal of the design method FOCUS (see [3, 5]) which describes interfaces with interface specifications in terms of data streams and communication histories. It specifies services this way. Thus, we get a very straightforward concept of architecture design specification which is modular and supports concepts of encapsulation and information hiding very directly.

5 Service-Oriented Architecture Specification

In a service-oriented architecture specification concept (see [2]) we describe services in terms of interfaces. In full generality, a component offers a number of services over different interfaces. A component may also use services. Therefore, in a component specification its behavior is specified by specifying the services offered over certain sub-interfaces by the component and also which services are required by the component that have to be offered to the component over certain other sub-interfaces.

The second interesting issue is how these services are related. Thus, we need concepts to define the relationship between those services. This finally leads into a concept of a service-oriented architecture.

Assumed and Guaranteed Services Layered architectures have to be described in terms of components that assume certain services to be able to guarantee certain services (see [6]). This leads to a very powerful scheme of designing architecture: architectures are designed by composing components. A very specific and very powerful way of composition is the connection of components certain specify assumed services with components that guarantee theses services, more precisely, services that have all the properties of the assumed services. This leads to a very powerful way of composing systems in layers where the correctness of an architecture is shown by showing that all interfaces which require assumed services are connected to interfaces that provide guaranteed services.

Following the idea of design by services, services that logical are defined by interface specifications with required and provided services, we easily can build layered architectures (see [8]). Given in such specifications of components of microservices being building blocks we can put layer after layer on top of layers which guarantee the assumed services to compose layers.

Platforms When building platforms in the case where a lot of similar software systems have to be developed by putting them together from given microservices, we have to deal with two challenges.

Layers as Building Blocks First of all we have to provide a well-chosen selection of components with microservices so we can quickly develop composed services from them and therefore support the rich variety of such services and on the other hand we have to be able to manage software evolution meaning that we have to develop microservices, however, in a way that changes and corrections in microservices can be done in a way that the improved microservices are still compatible with the microservices used before, at least in most cases and where we have a clear understanding which changes can be done effecting the correctness of product architectures done before and how we can guarantee that things still fit together.

Architectural Government This requires, of course, a well-chosen governance for the development carried out by architects, both for the platform of microservices as well as architects which design from the microservices the products. What is needed, in addition, is a methodology which allows us to decide under which circumstances certain changes can be done within the given microservices without effecting the correctness of produced products and in which cases this cannot be guaranteed and therefore the product owners and architects have to be informed that whenever they wish to see improved components certain incompatibilities are involved and therefore certain changes have to be done inside the product design.

6 Conclusion

We did not give any formal definitions of architecture specifications along the lines we have described. However, such a formalism exists (see [3, 4, 6]). What we are interested in is understanding how to design a software methodology which has the expressive power and the right concepts to support in a digital company what is needed to run the company and to change software systems as quickly as required and at the same time as reliable as needed such that correctness is improved by further steps and we do not run into the classical problems of legacy systems: systems with a lot of compatibility problems, difficult to maintain, nearly impossible to evolve.

References

1. Andreessen, M.: Why Software is Eating the World. http://www.wsj.com/articles/SB10001424053111903480904576512250915629460
2. Broy, M., Krüger, I., Meisinger, M.: A formal model of services. TOSEM - ACM Trans. Softw. Eng. Methodol. **16**(1), February 2007
3. Broy, M.: A logical basis for component-oriented software and systems engineering. Comput. J. **53**(10), 1758–1782 (2010)
4. Broy, M.: Multifunctional software systems: structured modeling and specification of functional requirements. Sci. Comput. Program. **75**, 1193–1214 (2010)
5. Broy, M.: A logical approach to systems engineering artifacts: semantic relationships and dependencies beyond traceability—from requirements to functional and architectural views. Software and Systems Modelling (to appear)
6. Broy, M.: Theory and Methodology of Assumption/Commitment Based System Interface Specification and Architectural Contracts (to appear)
7. Geisberger, E., Broy, M.: agendaCPS – Integrierte Forschungsagenda Cyber-Physical Systems (acatech STUDIE). Springer Verlag, Heidelberg u.a. (2012)
8. Herzberg, D., Broy, M.: Modeling layered distributed communication systems. Formal Aspects Comput. **17**(1), 1–18 (2005)
9. Meyer, B.: Applying "Design by Contract". Comput. (IEEE) **25**(10), 40–51 (1992)
10. Szyperski, C.: Component Software: Beyond Object-Oriented Programming. 2nd Edn. Addison-Wesley Professional (2002)

Contents

Workshop: HELENA 2018

Processes and Methods

On the Tasks and Characteristics of Product Owners: A Case Study in the Oil and Gas Industry

Carolin Unger-Windeler[1,2(✉)] and Jil Klünder[1]

[1] Software Engineering Group, Leibniz University Hannover, Hanover, Germany
{carolin.unger-windeler,jil.kluender}@inf.uni-hannover.de
[2] Baker Hughes, a GE Company, Research and Development, Celle, Germany

Abstract. Product owners in the Scrum framework – respectively the on-site customer when applying eXtreme Programming – have an important role in the development process. They are responsible for the requirements and backlog deciding about the next steps within the development process. However, many companies face the difficulty of defining the tasks and the responsibilities of a product owner on their way towards an agile work environment.

While literature addresses the tailoring of the product owner's role in general, research does not particularly consider the specifics of this role in the context of a systems development as we find for example in the oil and gas industry. Consequently, the question arises whether there are any differences between these two areas. In order to answer this question, we investigated on the current state of characteristics and tasks of product owners at Baker Hughes, a GE company (BHGE).

In this position paper, we present initial results based on an online survey with answers of ten active product owners within the technical software department of BHGE. The results indicate that current product owners at BHGE primarily act as a nexus between all ends. While technical tasks are performed scarcely, communication skills seem even more important for product owners in a system development organization. However, to obtain more reliable results additional research in this area is required.

Keywords: Agile software development · Product owner
Systems engineering · Systems development

1 Introduction

Nowadays, it is a competitive advantage to develop and distribute high-quality software at a high pace [7]. Consequently, software process improvement is a topic many companies have to deal with [1]. For example in the oil and gas industry (but also in other domains such as in the automotive [7]), safety-critical systems are developed that need to be tested thoroughly before they can be rolled out.

© Springer Nature Switzerland AG 2018
M. Kuhrmann et al. (Eds.): PROFES 2018, LNCS 11271, pp. 3–11, 2018.
https://doi.org/10.1007/978-3-030-03673-7_1

As a consequence, working software needs to be delivered at an early stage of the system development phase while it still remains flexible and adaptable to changes. Agile software development is a promising possibility to satisfy those needs [4,6,10]. However, integrating agile software development practices is often reported as difficult [5]: Introducing agile is not just the introduction of a development method, it is also about changing people by establishing a new mindset [9]. Becoming agile often goes along with fundamental changes that are facing a lot of barriers [5,7]. Regardless of the industry or the company's motivation – the dilemma is always the same: while the decision of doing agile is made easily, actually becoming agile is not [9]. Nevertheless, a lot of companies across all industries strive for it [8].

This is also the case at *Baker Hughes, a GE Company (BHGE)*. BHGE combines capabilities across the full value chain of oil and gas activities – including the development of digital solutions combining hardware technologies with software products. While hardware engineering has always been one of the company's core businesses, software engineering is relatively new to them.

In daily business, BHGE develops safety-critical systems based on reliable software. To deliver adaptable but high-quality software at an early stage of the system development phase, the management decided to integrate agile development practices. However, BHGE faced difficulties while becoming agile. A previous internal interview study identified the tailoring of the Product Owner (PO) role as the main issue. While becoming agile the main difficulty was – and still is – to understand what skills really are required of a PO in this context.

In this contribution, we shed light on the PO at BHGE in order to analyze their tasks and characteristics. To identify the adjusting screws to tailor this role in this context eventually, now tasks and characteristics of active POs are analyzed to asses their current-state and to compare the role of the PO in this context to the PO role described in the literature. In this paper, we present preliminary results based on an online survey conducted at BHGE.

2 Reference Model of Tasks and Characteristics of Product Owners

Tailoring the PO role in a system development context is not particularly addressed in current literature. So we looked into the adjacent area of agile software management in large-scale scrum.

2.1 Related Work: Characteristics of Product Owners

Pilcher [11] attempted to generate a practical guide that enables new POs to apply agile product management techniques effectively in Scrum. Furthermore, he describes five desirable characteristics of POs, addresses common mistakes when applying this role and suggests a team of POs when it comes to scale this role to large projects. The described characteristics are as follows:

(1) **Communicator & Negotiator.** The PO communicates with and aligns different parties including customers, users, development and engineering, marketing, sales, service, operations, and management.
(2) **Visionary & Doer.** The PO envisions the final product and sees it through to completion. This includes requirements description, closely collaborating with the team, accepting or rejecting work results, and steering the projects by tracking and forecasting its progress.
(3) **Leader & Team Player.** The PO is responsible for the product's success, provides guidance for everyone involved and makes tough decisions. He needs to be a team player, rely on close collaboration with other Scrum team members, yet has no formal authority over them.
(4) **Available & Qualified.** Being a PO is usually a full-time job. Project's progress suffers when the PO is overworked. Being adequately qualified usually requires an intimate understanding of the customer and the market.
(5) **Empowered & Committed.** An empowered PO is essential to bring the product to life. The PO must have the proper decision-making authority – from finding the right team members to deciding which functionality is delivered as part of the release.

These characteristics are quite high-level and are not sufficient to be checked in the current state analysis at BHGE. To close this gap, the following tasks need to be put in consideration as well.

2.2   Related Work: Tasks of Product Owners

Bass [2] describes how PO teams scale agile methods to large distributed enterprises. To do so, he identified the following nine PO tasks:

(1) **Intermediary.** Act as an intermediary person between all stakeholders.
(2) **Traveller.** Spend time at client site as well as on all geographical locations of the team to get to know them and disseminate information.
(3) **Communicator.** Be available and communicative to all team members to connect teams.
(4) **Techncial Governor.** Provide a technical governance framework to project teams in order to ensure usage of common tools and technologies for the project.
(5) **Release Master.** Manage and approve release plans and schedules.
(6) **Prioritizer.** Prioritize requirements in the backlog to ensure immediate value to the customer.
(7) **Groom.** Gather requirements, translate them into user stories and ensure an evolving backlog.
(8) **Risk Assessor.** Evaluate technical complexity and potential shortcomings in the development teams' skills and capabilities.

(9) **Technical Architect.** Design, implement and disseminate a reference architecture between the scrum teams.

Bass [2] states that all those tasks should be split on multiple product owners that collaborate in a team. However, in this case study each participating PO is asked about the individual performance regarding each task.

2.3   Reference Model of Tasks and Characteristics

Based on the previously described tasks and characteristics, the reference model shown in Fig. 1 is proposed. It is applied to classify the characteristics of the PO at BHGE in terms of the corresponding tasks. As Pilcher [11] and Bass [2] do not rate the entities, all of them are considered as equally important. However, some of the characteristics are seen more related to certain tasks (e.g. Communicator & Negotiator), while others are required on the full range (e.g. Visionary & Doer).

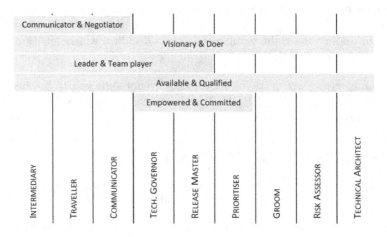

Fig. 1. Product Owner Characteristics and Tasks

3   Product Owner Analysis at BHGE

BHGE develops high-end drilling tools for more than a century. With less accessible oil and gas reservoirs, the drilling process and its tools become increasingly complex. To cope with the increased complexity, digitalization found its way into the drilling technology and the integration of a software development process was needed. To deliver high-quality software at an early stage of the system development phase, the technical software group decided to follow agile practices. The Scrum framework was chosen, teams were formed, roles were introduced and all other guidelines adhered. Though, the integration of an agile software group into a traditional system development environment is challenging at all ends – a previously conducted internal interview study at BHGE identified the tailoring of the PO role as their main issue from a software development perspective. Understanding the required skills of a PO that fit in this context is still the hardest part. Unfortunately, no literature is particularly discussing this issue. However, related work in the adjacent area of large scale scrum describes required skills of POs in the form of characteristics and tasks. This description is used as a starting point to assess current state of actual POs at BHGE, to distinct the role of a PO in the system developement and to tailor this role in this context eventually.

3.1   Data Collection

In order to get an overview of the current tasks and characteristics of POs at BHGE, we conducted an online survey with ten active POs within the technical software department. The participants are located in Germany, the Netherlands, India, USA and do not necessarily work on the same product. They were asked to answer questions that would give some indications about their role in terms of the above mentioned characteristics and tasks. The most considerable part of the survey was structured as a multiple-choice question: *"How would you describe your current role?"* Two possible predefined answers were *"I act as an intermediary person between all stakeholders"* and *"I prioritise the backlog"*. To get more detailed information about certain tasks additional questions had a 4-point Likert-scale or were open-ended.

3.2   Data Analysis

With the quantitative method of the survey, the statements of the POs regarding their tasks can be summarized in a bar chart. Additionally, based on how many POs performed each task, we divided the tasks into the equidistant intervals summarized in Table 1. The results are shown in Fig. 2.

Table 1. Division of the tasks

Scarce	0–33% of the POs perform that task
Moderate	33–66% of the POs perform that task
Common	66–100% of the POs perform that task

According to the reference model in Sect. 2 the characteristics of the POs at BHGE can be evaluated as well. Therefore, we again divided the characteristics into the equidistant intervals summarized in Table 2. The results are shown in Fig. 3.

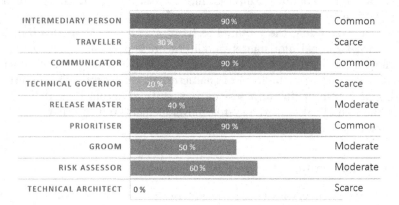

Fig. 2. Product Owner Tasks @ BHGE

Table 2. Division of the characteristics

Weak	0–33% of the related tasks are performed scarcely
Moderate	33–66% of the related tasks are performed moderately
Strong	66–100% of the related tasks are performed commonly

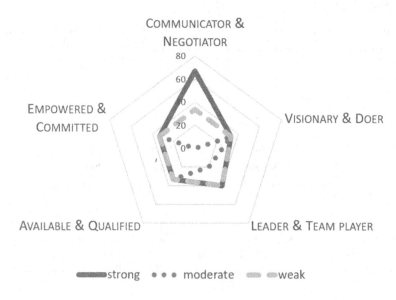

Fig. 3. Product Owner Characteristics @ Baker Hughes, a GE Company

4 Results

Commonly performed tasks. The POs at BHGE often act as an intermediary person between all stakeholders and disseminate information across teams, as 9 out of 10 PO would describe their role accordingly. Prioritising the backlog is also something they describe as a common task.

Moderately performed tasks. Managing the releases, groom the product backlog, as well as assessing risks are identified as moderately performed tasks as some POs perform those tasks, while others do not.

Scarcely performed tasks. The absence of technical decision making is striking. They do not act as a technical governor nor as an architect. Additionally, the POs do not travel much.

Considering the tasks, it gets clear that the Product Owners at BHGE are highly communicative but do not make any technical decisions.

Strong Characteristics. With 2 out of 3 tasks that are mapped to the characteristic of *Communicator & Negotiator* the POs can be considered as strong communicators and negotiators.

Moderate Characteristics. All other characteristics are present in a moderate way as most of the mapped tasks are performed moderately. The POs do have a vision, lead the scrum team, are available and qualified, have decisional power and are committed.

Weak Characteristics. The POs at BHGE do not lack a characteristic according to the reference model.

Overall, POs at BHGE are highly communicative and are empowered to prioritize the backlog according to the stakeholders needs and mostly act as the nexus between all ends.

The system development organization asks them to communicate and negotiate with all stakeholders – including the end user of the overall product, leaders of other departments that are involved in the system development as well as the scrum teams. The communicative effort mainly results in the prioritization of the backlog. They are not empowered enough to master the releases as there are too many dependencies to the overall system development plan. POs at BHGE do not make any technical decisions – neither as a technical governor nor as an architect. A reason is that the currently developed software is replacing legacy systems gradually. Hence, the framework is already set. All architectural decisions are made by a designated architecture team. Another conspicuously scarce performed task is traveling. This is due to the fact that representatives of all involved departments as well as the POs and the end users are co-located.

5 Conclusion and Future Work

When BHGE first introduced the role of the PO, they needed to tailor this role to the context of their system development organization. While literature addresses the tailoring of the product owner's role in general, research does not particularly consider the specifics of this role in the context of a system development organization. Consequently, the question arises whether there are any differences between these two areas. In order to answer this question, we investigated on the current state of characteristics and tasks of product owners at Baker Hughes, a GE company (BHGE). Inital results show that there are differences indeed: being a Product Owner in a traditional, top-down system development organization requires strong communication skills, while technical decisions do not number along the task of a PO as they are made by designated teams. According to this findings, the current descriptions of the general PO role is not sufficient as some tasks are obsolete while others are missing. Also, a recent study of Bass et al. [3] identified two more tasks which should be further discussed in this context. However, to obtain more reliable results additional research in this area is required.

We hypothesize that a more detailed description of this role will help companies defining the tasks and responsibilities of a product owner on their way towards an agile work environment. In future research we will focus on adjusting the tasks and characteristics of PO in a system development context to provide a better understanding of this role.

Acknowledgement. This work was supported by Baker Hughes, a GE Company. We commit to upholding the highest ethical standards and complete legal compliance in all we do. Since no data of our employees should be distributed, our data is archived internally for future reference.

References

1. Proceedings of the 2018 International Conference on Software and System Process - ICSSP 2018. ACM Press, New York (2018)
2. Bass, J.M.: How product owner teams scale agile methods to large distributed enterprises. Empirical Softw. Eng. **20**(6), 1525–1557 (2015)
3. Bass, J.M., Beecham, S., Razzak, M.A., Canna, C.N., Noll, J.: An empirical study of the product owner role in scrum. In: Proceedings of the 40th International Conference on Software Engineering Companion Proceeedings - ICSE 2018, pp. 123–124. ACM Press (2018)
4. Begel, A., Nagappan, N.: Usage and perceptions of agile software development in an industrial context: an exploratory study. In: First International Symposium on Empirical Software Engineering and Measurement (ESEM 2007), pp. 255–264. IEEE, 20–21 September 2007
5. Boehm, B., Turner, R.: Management challenges to implementing agile processes in traditional development organizations. IEEE Softw. **22**(5), 30–39 (2005)
6. Dybå, T., Dingsøyr, T.: Empirical studies of agile software development: a systematic review. Inf. Softw, Technol. **50**(9–10), 833–859 (2008)
7. Hohl, P., Münch, J., Schneider, K., Stupperich, M.: Forces that prevent agile adoption in the automotive domain. In: Abrahamsson, P., Jedlitschka, A., Nguyen Duc, A., Felderer, M., Amasaki, S., Mikkonen, T. (eds.) PROFES 2016. LNCS, vol. 10027, pp. 468–476. Springer, Cham (2016). https://doi.org/10.1007/978-3-319-49094-6_32

8. Klünder, J., Hohl, P., Schneider, K.: Becoming agile while preserving software product lines. In: Proceedings of the 2018 International Conference on Software and System Process - ICSSP 2018, pp. 1–10. ACM Press, New York (2018)

9. Klünder, J., Schmitt, A., Hohl, P., Schneider, K.: Fake news: simply agile. In: Projektmanagement und Vorgehensmodelle 2017 - Die Spannung zwischen dem Prozess und den Mensch im Projekt, pp. 187–192. Gesellschaft für Informatik, Bonn (2017)

10. Laanti, M., Salo, O., Abrahamsson, P.: Agile methods rapidly replacing traditional methods at nokia: a survey of opinions on agile transformation. Inf. Softw. Technol. **53**(3), 276–290 (2011)

11. Pichler, R.: Agile product management with Scrum: Creating products that customers love. The Addison-Wesley signature series, Addison-Wesley, Upper Saddle River (2010)

Agile Manifesto and Practices Selection for Tailoring Software Development: A Systematic Literature Review

Soreangsey Kiv[1]([⊠]), Samedi Heng[2]([⊠]), Manuel Kolp[1]([⊠]),
and Yves Wautelet[3]([⊠])

[1] LouRIM-CEMIS, Université catholique de Louvain, Louvain-La-Neuve, Belgium
{soreangsey.kiv,manuel.kolp}@uclouvain.be
[2] HEC Liège, Université de Liège, Liège, Belgium
samedi.heng@uliege.be
[3] KULeuven, Leuven, Belgium
yves.wautelet@kuleuven.be

Abstract. Agile methods have been largely used for many years to provide developers with a flexible software development process leading to software quality improvement. To get the best results and eliminate unnecessary efforts, the development team should select the most appropriate methods and techniques. The fundamental core of an agile method has to be well-understood before deciding which parts of the method need to be adopted. We believe that the quickest way to do so is to understand the prescripts of the Agile Manifesto. Many researches have proposed different tailoring approaches based on the relation and straight-forward interpretation between each agile practice and agile values or principles. We however have observed that agile practitioners do not dedicate the necessary attention to the Agile Manifesto before adopting agile methods or practices and directly use them. It is because the importance of Agile Manifesto in tailoring context is not obvious enough to the community. This study aims at doing a systematic literature review on the existing case studies, to verify the relation between the Agile Manifesto and agile practice selection.

Keywords: Agile manifesto · Agile methods
Agile methods adoption · Partial agile adoption
Systematic literature review

1 Introduction

Representatives from eXtreme Programming (XP), Scrum, Dynamic Systems Development Method (DSDM), Adaptive Software Development (ASD), Crystal, Feature-Driven Development (FDD) and Pragmatic Programming met in 2001 to discuss and establish common ground for an alternative to structured and traditional heavy software development life cycles. They eventually emerged with a

© Springer Nature Switzerland AG 2018
M. Kuhrmann et al. (Eds.): PROFES 2018, LNCS 11271, pp. 12–30, 2018.
https://doi.org/10.1007/978-3-030-03673-7_2

manifesto for Agile Software Development, commonly known as the *Agile Manifesto* (http://agilemanifesto.org/), defining values and principles to be respected to be defined as *agile*.

No method can, of course, be a one-size-fits-all solution. Likewise, simply choosing a particular agile method and following every rule is also inconsistent and inefficient. Instead, software development teams apply agile methods differently, i.e., depending on their problems, resources, and goals or expectation [1]. For instance, the development team will choose to adopt concepts and building blocks that are the most suitable to them based on their specific situation, goals, problems, constraints, etc. This selection makes the method more adherent to the development context; it is known as software methods tailoring [16].

Choosing agile concepts, or more concretely agile practices, to adopt requires a sufficient knowledge of the concepts and the impacts these could have to the team. Understanding all the details of agile concepts could be a time consuming and complicated task so that many approaches have been proposed in order to simplify agile methods tailoring.

One of the interesting topics in agile methods tailoring is the relation and straight-forward interpretation between each agile practice and agile values or principles [3,8,18,22,25,27,32]. On this basis, different ideas for agile methods tailoring have been suggested. For instance, Ahmed and Sidky [3] proposed the road-map to adopt agile practices based on five values, considered as the most essential to agility. According to Madi et al. [27], knowing the most important values is the key to follow the best set of practices as agile values are fundamental. They analyzed papers and books to explore the key agile values and the relationships between them. Our previous works [22,23] illustrated the strong relationship between the Agile Manifesto (values and principles) and agile practices, together with an approach for practices selection using an intentional modeling framework.

Even though the ideas seem so rational and reliable, to the best of our knowledge no formal verification on the relation between agile practices and values or principles has been performed yet. Their relations were assumed based on the assumptions or beliefs of authors. Moreover, although their relations have been supported by many researchers, we have observed that agile practitioners do not seem to agree that Agile Manifesto is useful for the adoption. This has led to the claim that *"Agile is Dead"* raised by Dave Thomas, one of the Agile Manifesto authors [35]. In many cases [5,7,9,12,34], development teams do not dedicate any effort to understanding any agile value or principle before adopting any agile method; they simply adopt the specific agile methods or practices which have been known as popular. These reasons motivated us to study and verify, from a statistical point of view, the relation between the agile values, principles and practices in tailored agile methods adoption, by mean of a systematic literature review. Indeed, value and principle are subjective concepts that vary greatly from one method to another. Gathering all the values and principles in literature and categorizing them would require enormous time and efforts. We leave thus this question for future research. Also, our aim is to ease the selection process, having a limited number of concepts would definitely be helpful and efficient. Consequently, we decided to focus on the fundamental 4 values and 12 principles defined in the Agile Manifesto.

In this research, we conducted a systematic literature review to extract key information from the case studies such as: (1) *How has the Agile Manifesto and its importance been discussed in tailored agile methods adoption?* And (2) *Can the Agile Manifesto and agile practices selection be related?* We believe that this study will help to enhance the value of the fundamental ideas of the Agile Manifesto and make its importance more obvious to the community.

The rest of this paper is structured as follows. First, literature reviews related to agile methods adoption are briefly discussed in Sect. 2. Our research methodology, including details on research questions, search strategy, and data extraction is discussed in Sect. 3. Then, the results of our literature review are presented in Sect. 4 followed by the threads to validity in Sect. 5. Finally, our conclusion and findings are summarized and discussed.

2   Related Work

Over the last decade, many agile methods have been proposed based on the Agile Manifesto to meet specific requirements and situations. For instance, Scrum is proposed with the objective to put more focus on project management organization while XP is designed to be more responsive to customer requirement changes [28]. Although agile methods are flexible, they may not be easy to adopt. To ease the process, various meta-models have been proposed [14,26,28,31,33,37,38], serving as a road-map for agile adoption. We note, for instance, the situational method framework [31], development process [28], goal-oriented meta-model [14,26], Agile Unified Process [4], Goal-Net theory [33], etc.

Another research direction focusing on selecting agile practices during adoption is agile methods tailoring [1,3,10,15,24,27]. Campanelli and Perreiras [10] analyzed methodological and practical aspects of research on tailored agile methods and the criteria used for agile methods tailoring. Their results show that practice selection is based on internal environment such as project type, communication, culture and management support and objectives. Qumer and Henderson-Sellers [29] also acknowledged the impact of organizational culture and technical aspects. Abbas et al. [1], Esfahani et al. [15], Kurapati et al. [24] and Madi et al. [27] provided a formalized answer on how to select agile practices for tailored agile methods adoption but admitted that no final academic solution was found on practice selection in tailored agile methods adoption.

Alongside the aforementioned approaches that depend mainly on the business goals, the culture and the resources of the organization, there exists a new group of methods based on agile values and principles [3,22,27]. Madi et al. [27] identified 10 key agile values and show how frequently they were mentioned in the literature. Their identified agile values are: *flexibility, customer-centric, working software, collaboration, simplicity, communication, natural, learning, pragmatism* and *adaptability*. According to them, these 10 values constitute the most important influence on practitioners in practice selection. The Sidky Agile Measurement Index (SAMI) [3] showed the adoption of agile practices based on an agile maturity model. SAMI is a 5-step road map to guide adopting teams based on five values considered essential to agility: (level 1) *enhancing communication and collaboration*; (level 2) *delivering software early and continuously*; (level 3) *developing high quality, working software in an efficient and integrated manner*; (level 4) *respond to change through multiple levels of feedback*; and (level 5) *establishing an environment to sustain agility*. SAMI is not based on any specific agile method such as XP, Scrum or Crystal, but instead, uses agile values and principles to define the path to agility. However, the framework was built just based on assumptions of the author as mentioned in [3]. Lee and Yong [25] also claimed that each agile practice should help accomplish agile principles in a method and can be grouped into management practices, software process practices and software development practices. Similarly, we defined in [22,23] the relation between agile value, principle and practice in the goal perspective where principle contributes to value and practice is used to achieve the principle. We also proposed a framework which can be used to help selecting practices. In all these references, agile value and principle are seen, directly and indirectly, as the set of goals that the development team needs to achieve in order to be agile and practice is used to help them accomplish these goals.

Motivated by these methods, we strongly believe that there is a relation between agile value, principle, and practice in a goal perspective. In other words, when it comes to selecting agile practice, by understanding the Agile Manifesto, practitioners should be able to effectively and quickly distinguish the outcome of different practices more easily. Although such idea has been confirmed by many researchers [3,22,25,27], its usefulness in supporting a practitioner to select an agile practice remains unclear.

Many systematic literature reviews have been performed with respect to many different aspects in agile methods, from the general concept such as [2,11,13] to the specific topics like [10,17,30]. Among all, the more closely related to our work is [10], a systematic literature review of 56 research papers on agile methods tailoring. It provides a detailed literature on agile methods tailoring and a deep understanding on how the researches on agile methods tailoring were conducted. The authors identified also the research community view on agile method tailoring, and the research gaps on the theme. The result, however, does not prove anything about the relation between agile value, principle and practice.

3   Research Methodology

This paper adopts a Systematic Literature Review (SLR) approach [19] to study and verify the relationships between the Agile Manifesto and agile practices, in the context of tailored agile methods adoption. An SLR allows us to adopt a formal and systematic approach to identify, select and synthesize recent literature relevant to our research questions [19]. It consists in defining (1) research questions, (2) search strategy, (3) study selection, (4) data extraction, and finally (5) data analysis. Each step will be explained hereafter. Figure 1 illustrates the process we have followed.

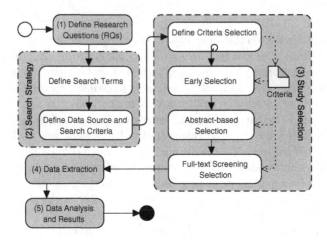

Fig. 1. Research protocol.

3.1 Research Questions

The main aim of this research is to confirm the relationship between the Agile Manifesto and agile practices, more specifically *whether or not the Agile Manifesto (i.e., the 4 values and 12 principles) is still the core concept that teams should understand before choosing an agile practice or method to adopt.* To answer this, we have formulated two fundamental Research Questions (RQs) in this research:

RQ1: How Has the Agile Manifesto and Its Importance Been Discussed in Tailored Agile Methods Adoption? This first question is to verify whether or not the Agile Manifesto has lost its attention and importance. Answering this question allows us to know about the state of the art of the Agile Manifesto from a practitioner's point of view; it includes:

- *RQ1.1: How often has the Agile Manifesto been discussed by agile practitioners during their adoption?*
- *RQ1.2: In which manner has the Agile Manifesto been discussed, as a whole or only part of it, just as a reminder or in detail?*
- *RQ1.3: Has the Agile Manifesto been recognized as important by practitioners for their adoption or not? If it has, how often and how has it been described?*

RQ2: Is the Agile Manifesto Related to Agile Practices Selection? This question verifies whether or not there exist relations between the Agile Manifesto and practices, as mentioned by many researchers. As pointed out in the related work (see Sect. 2), agile values and principles have been regarded as a set of goals to achieve for a method to be agile. This set of goals is said to be accomplished by adopting agile practices.

We seek to answer this question by comparing the development team's goals of adopting agile methods with what is described in the Agile Manifesto. The results would allow us to confirm whether or not the Agile Manifesto could be related to agile practice selection, from the practitioner's point of view.

Based on our observation, development team's goals in adopting tailored agile methods can be described in three situations: (1) sometimes, development teams decide to change their development process based on *problems* they encountered. Their goal is to solve these problems by using a set of agile practices or methods; (2) some other cases, *problems* are not the root cause of the adoption. Knowing that agile methods are the most popular nowadays, some development teams decide to follow them with the hope of improving their current processes. They have their predefined goals or *expectation* to achieve by adopting specific agile practices or methods; (3) regardless of the *problem* to solve or the *expectation* to fulfill, in many cases, result from adopting agile methods are described as *benefits*. These benefits can be seen as the accomplished goals.

Hence, in order to know whether or not the Agile Manifesto could be related to agile practice selection, we defined three other sub research questions:

– *RQ2.1: Is the Agile Manifesto relevant to the team's problems that led to tailored agile methods adoption?*
– *RQ2.2: Is the Agile Manifesto relevant to the team's expectations from tailored agile methods adoption?*
– *RQ2.3: Is the Agile Manifesto relevant to the team's benefits of tailored agile methods adoption?*

If the development team's goals of agile methods adoption in most situations are relevant to the Agile Manifesto, then the description in the manifesto can still cover the core goals of this methods creation. Understanding the Agile Manifesto would allow the development team better defining their goals in adopting agile methods and consequently better selecting the set of agile practices.

3.2   Search Strategy

Search Terms. Our objective is to understand the importance of the Agile Manifesto in tailored agile methods adoption. Software method tailoring is the process that makes the method more adherent to the development context [16]. Various terms are used in the literature as a synonym for *tailor*, i.e., *partial, customize*, and *practice selection* [1,6,14,22,24]. Based on the research questions, we defined search terms as the combination of various words referring to tailored agile methods including *partial, tailor, customize, practice selection* and the name of the most popular agile methods (according to the 11th VersionOne survey [36]). Since we want to find out the *expectations/goals* of adopting agile methods, we thus also added the word "goal" into the search terms. We summarize the search terms as follows: "*(Agile OR Scrum OR XP OR Kanban OR ScrumBan OR Lean OR DSDM OR AgileUP OR FDD OR Iterative Development) AND ((practice AND select) OR tailor OR customize OR partial OR adopt OR expectation OR goal)*".

Search Engines and Search Criteria. We only consider formal data sources, i.e., papers that were published in peer-reviewed conferences and journals from the four well-known digital libraries in the field of software engineering: IEE-EXplorer (http://ieeexplore.ieee.org), ScienceDirect (http://sciencedirect.com), SpringerLink (http://link.springer.com) and ACM Digital Library (https://dl.acm.org). We did not consider GoogleScholar since it provides also unpublished and non peer-reviewed papers.

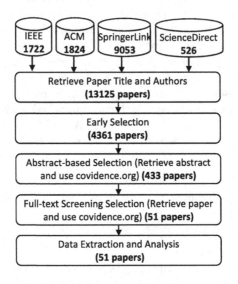

Fig. 2. Papers selection.

For each search engine, we used advanced search options to ensure our dataset quality. In general, we set the publication years between 2000 and 2017, the field of Software Engineering, and the search terms matching title of the paper, keywords or abstract. Basically, we found 13125 papers in total: 1722 papers in IEEEXplorer, 526 papers in ScienceDirect, 9053 papers in SpringerLink, and 1824 papers in ACM Digital Library (see Fig. 2).

3.3   Study Selection

We defined a 3-step paper selection process due to the number of papers found: *Early Selection, Abstract-based Selection* and *Full-text Screening Selection*. Each step, described in the following subsections, has a well-defined selection criteria. Figure 2 provides the results of selected papers of each step.

Early Selection. The goal was to have a consistent list of papers. All the search results were merged into a single file listing 13125 papers in total. We then eliminated redundant papers or papers not published in the 2000–2017 period. This step allowed us to discard about two-thirds of the papers to finally retain 4361 papers.

Abstract-Based Selection. The goal was to determine whether or not the article relates to our research questions based on its abstract which was carefully read by three reviewers. Before we started the real selection process, we defined and refined several times the criteria for inclusion and exclusion to gather the maximum possible relevant articles and effectively reject irrelevant papers. The final criteria are summarized in Table 1:

Table 1. Inclusion and exclusion criteria for Abstract-based selection.

Inclusion criteria	Exclusion criteria
-Tailored/partial/customized agile methods or agile practices selection;	-Agile usage/implementation/adoption not for software development;
-Empirical/research on adopting agile methods for software development;	-Agile usage in theory;
-Literature review/survey on agile framework;	-Simulation model;
-Challenge/issue in agile methods adoption;	-Article from workshops;
-Approach, model, framework, introduction or guide to agile methods adoption;	-Use of a specific practice/technique (daily meeting, pair programming, etc.);
-Integration of agile methods to other methods;	-Agile method which has not been introduced in one of the most popular agile methods
-Transformation from other to agile methods;	
-Agile practices usage	

We used Covidence (www.covidence.org), a collaborative tool for facilitating the SLR process.

To get started, we needed to upload the title and abstract of the 4361 papers into Covidence. However, since SpringerLink and ACM Digital library do not allow downloading multiple abstracts at once, we therefore developed a third-party program for help. We then started the review process.

Each reviewer read the title and abstract of each paper and voted individually (Yes/No/Maybe) based on the above criteria. Papers with three 'Yes' votes were included for the next step, those with three 'No' votes were eliminated and papers with three 'Maybe' or conflicted votes were solved by a face-to-face discussion. 433 papers were selected for next step.

Full-Text Screening Selection. The goal was to do a full-text screening of each paper and determine if it still relates to our research questions. We followed the same process as in the previous step and used the same tool.

First, we downloaded manually the full-text in PDF format and uploaded it to Covidence. 399 papers were successfully uploaded, and 4 papers were rejected for technical and format reasons. In addition to the abstract-based selection, we extended our inclusion criteria to the real case study which:

– describes the influence of agile value or principle over agile methods or practice selection;
– describes how they adopt some set of practices or methods based on their problems or expectations;
– describes the benefits they gained from adopting some set of agile practices or agile methods.

As long as one of the criteria is found, the article is included. At the end, 383 papers were eliminated and only 51 papers were selected in this study.

3.4 Data Extraction

Each paper was read carefully and data was extracted by only one reviewer. We divided the 51 papers into three sets and each reviewer took care of one set. For each paper, we extracted the following information:

– **Conference or Journal name and year of publication:** It allows us to determine if the dataset is representative for our study;
– **Type of agile:** It allows us to know in which environment the tailored agile methods are adopted;
– **Type of institution:** It allows us to know in which sector agile methods are tailored and adopted;
– **Mention about Agile Manifesto:** It allows us to answer RQ1.1 and RQ1.2. We denoted the findings as 'Yes' when the paper explicitly mentioned the word Agile Manifesto and we extracted values or principles and denoted them otherwise;
– **Agile Manifesto influence on partial agile adoption:** Basically, we tried to find a clear statement of influence by the authors. We denoted 'Yes' if author simply refers 'Agile Manifesto' as influential, or we extracted the values and principles if any of them were described as influence. It allows us to answer RQ1.3;
– **Problem:** We read very carefully to understand the cause behind the agile methods tailoring. For any mentioned problem that led to agile practices or methods adoption, we extracted the specific statements without any modification and stored them in a list. Mapping this list to the 4 values and 12 principles of the Agile Manifesto allowed us to determine whether or not the Agile Manifesto is relevant to the team's problems and to answer RQ2.1;

- **Expectation:** We followed the same process for extracting problems. Instead of looking for the team's problems, we tried to understand their expectations from specific practices or agile methods before the adoption. This allows us to answer RQ2.2;
- **Benefit:** Again the same process was followed. Instead of looking for the team's problems, we tried to understand the team's benefits after the adoption. This allows us to answer RQ2.3.

4 Results

As seen in Fig. 3, we found that more than 60% of the selected papers were published in the field of agile methods and in highly ranked conferences (A- or B-based on Core Portal Conference—http://portal.core.edu.au/conf-ranks/) including ICSE, HICSS, XP, AGILE and PROFES. In addition, most of these papers were published less than 10 years ago. We also noticed that more than 70% of the studies in the dataset were conducted in IT companies while the rest were in the IT sector of a non-IT company. Furthermore, it is noticeable that agile methods are tailored and used mainly in normal agile environment (51%), distributed environment (23%), and Scaled Agile (8%). As a result, we can conclude that our dataset is representative for our study.

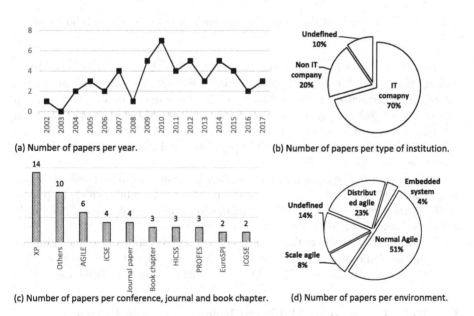

(a) Number of papers per year.

(b) Number of papers per type of institution.

(c) Number of papers per conference, journal and book chapter.

(d) Number of papers per environment.

Fig. 3. Dataset information.

4.1 RQ1: How Have the Agile Manifesto and Its Influence Been Discussed in Tailored Agile Methods Adoption?

Figure 4 summarizes the result of our analysis from the 51 papers.

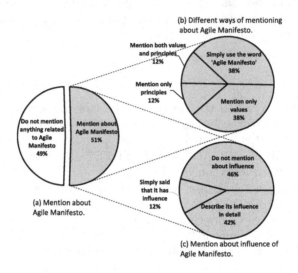

Fig. 4. The influence of the Agile Manifesto in tailored agile methods adoption.

Overall, 51% (26 papers) of the papers mention the Agile Manifesto when evoking the tailored agile methods adoption (see Fig. 4a). Furthermore, all the papers do not discuss the Agile Manifesto in the same way. 38% of them (10 papers out of 26) simply mention the word "Agile Manifesto" without even referring to neither a value nor a principle. The other 38% refer to only the values, 12% (3 papers) refer to only the principles and the rest 12% refer to both values and principles (see Fig. 4b).

With respect to the influence of the Agile Manifesto on tailored agile methods adoption (see Fig. 4c), it is only discussed in 14 papers among which 11 papers (42%) acknowledge it with a clear explanation while the other 3 (12%) only acknowledge without further details.

The result of RQ1 shows that the interest of the development team in understanding the Agile Manifesto is not significant. Overall, out of 51 case studies, 51% talk about it while only 21% (11 papers) acknowledge its influence.

4.2 RQ2: Is the Agile Manifesto Related to Agile Practices Selection?

In order to answer RQ2, our intuition was to compare the problems, expectations and benefits extracted from the 51 selected papers with the Agile Manifesto, i.e., the 4 values and 12 principles. Since we had already provided the mapping

Table 2. Mapping agile values and principles.

Value	Principle
Value1: Individuals and interactions over processes and tools	**Principle_5:** Build projects around motivated individuals. Give them the environment and support they need, and trust them to get the job done
	Principle_6: The most efficient and effective method of conveying information to and within a development team is face-to-face conversation
	Principle_8: Agile processes promote sustainable development. The sponsors, developers, and users should be able to maintain a constant pace indefinitely
	Principle_11: The best architectures, requirements, and designs emerge from self-organizing teams.
	Principle_12: At regular intervals, the team reflects on how to become more effective, then tunes and adjusts its behavior accordingly
Value2: Working software over comprehensive documentation	**Principle_1:** Our highest priority is to satisfy the customer through early and continuous delivery of valuable software
	Principle_3: Deliver working software frequently, from a couple of weeks to a couple of months, with a preference to the shorter timescale
	Principle_7: Working software is the primary measure of progress
	Principle_10: Simplicity–the art of maximizing the amount of work not done–is essential
Value3: Customer collaboration over contract negotiation	**Principle_4:** Business people and developers must work together daily throughout the project
Value4: Responding to change over following a plan	**Principle_2:** Welcome changing requirements, even late in development. Agile processes harness change for the customer's competitive advantage
	Principle_9: Continuous attention to technical excellence and good design enhances agility

among the 4 values and 12 principles in [23] (see Table 2), we only compared them (problems, expectations, and benefits) with the 12 principles.

From the data extraction process, we gathered 3 lists of statements, one for the problems[1], one for the expectations[2], and one for the benefits[3]. As a result, we have 42 statements describing problems, 155 statements describing expected results and 205 statements describing benefits.

---

[1] Problems were extracted from 12 papers that described the problems they encountered which led them to tailored agile adoption.

[2] Expectations were extracted from 27 papers that discussed the team's expectations.

[3] Benefits were extracted from 37 papers that discussed the benefits of tailored agile methods adoption.

The mapping process was carried out manually by one author and double-checked by another, in the form of a Cartesian product. This means that for each list, we compared every statement to the 12 principles of the Agile Manifesto. They are mapped when they have a close relation to one another. For instance, the problem "delivery pains" is closely related to both Principle_6 "Our highest priority is to satisfy the customer through early and continuous delivery of valuable software" and Principle_7 "Deliver working software frequently, from a couple of weeks to a couple of months, with a preference to the shorter timescal". This problem is thus mapped to both the Principle_6 and the Principle_7. The result of the mapping is exposed in Fig. 5a. Figure 5b provides the mapping of problems, expectations and benefits to the 4 values. The number of problems, expectations and benefits, which were mapped to the values, is the result of the union between the different principles contributing to each value.

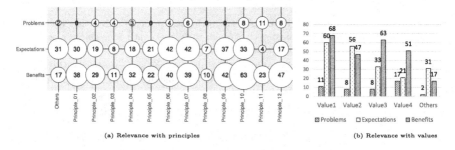

(a) Relevance with principles   (b) Relevance with values

Fig. 5. Mapping of problems, expectations and benefits with Agile Manifesto.

The final lists of problems, expectations, benefits and the result of mapping with Agile Manifesto is available online at https://goo.gl/rrghEH.

The correlation ratio between the Agile Manifesto and agile methods adoption goal (problems, expectations, and benefits) is defined by the number of problems, expectations and benefits that can be mapped to at least one agile principle over the total number we found. For instance, 40 out of 42 problems can be mapped to at least one of the principles. The correlation ratio between problems and the Agile Manifesto is thus 95%.

RQ2.1: Is the Agile Manifesto Relevant to the Team's Problems that Led to Tailored Agile Methods Adoption?

As seen in Fig. 5a, most of the problems (95%) can be mapped to the 12 principles. The top line in Fig. 5a shows the distribution of problems in line with related principles. The three most relevant ones are Principle_10, Principle_11, and Principle_12. The reason is that most problems faced by the development team are customer-based and the change-oriented ones that motivate tailored agile methods adoption. Four principles are not mapped with any problem. However, at the value level, we can see in Fig. 5b that all the values are relevant.

We can summarize that the Agile Manifesto and team's problems are closely related to one another. However, the number of problems is not significant; it leads us to conclude that problems faced by the development team are not the main reason for tailoring agile methods for adoption.

RQ2.2: Is the Agile Manifesto Relevant to the Team's Expectations from Tailored Agile Methods Adoption?

We extracted 155 expectations in total from the selected papers. Figure 5a (second row) and Fig. 5b present the detailed statistics of agile principles and values respectively. The majority of the expectations (80%) can be mapped to at least one principle. The three most relevant principles are Principle_6, Principle_7 and Principle_9 which contribute to Value2 "working software over comprehensive documentation" i.e., having a working software is always what people expect the most. More precisely, Principle_6 and Principle_7 describe a very similar idea on software delivery and thus they both have slightly different numbers of "expectations". At the value level, Value1 "Individual and interaction over process and tool" is the most relevant. In contrast to the "problems" section, Principle_11 and Value4 are the least relevant. While the differences between the two most relevant values (Value1 and Value2) are not significant, a big gap exists between the most and the least relevant values (Value1 has 60 related expectations and Value4 just 21).

Briefly speaking, we can conclude that the Agile Manifesto is relevant to the team's expectations when tailoring agile methods for adoption. However, agile principles are not all equally important. This corresponds exactly to the motivation of tailored agile methods adoption, i.e., adopting only the most relevant principles or practices instead of full adoption.

RQ2.3: Is the Agile Manifesto Relevant to the Team's Benefits of Tailored Agile Methods Adoption?

The mapping results between the benefits extracted from the papers and the elements of Agile Manifesto are presented in Fig. 5a for the principle level and Fig. 5b for the value level. We found that the majority of the benefits (92%) could be mapped to at least one principle. At the value level, Value3 and Value1 are the most relevant among all. This proves that agile methods allow development teams to improve their communication both between team members and to customers. Globally, the number of "benefits" mapped to each value does not change much from one value to another. Also, it is noticeable that there is a strong correlation between expectations and benefits.

The overall results show that 95% of problems, 80% of expectations and 92% of benefits can be mapped to principles and values of the Agile Manifesto. It means that the Agile Manifesto is highly related to the real development of team's goals in every situation: problems, expectations and benefits.

5   Threats to Validity

Kitchenham [20] states that the systematic process involved in SLR is designed to avoid bias. Thus, in every step of our SLR process, we manage the limitations and the bias as much as we can.

Starting from data source, Kitchenham et al. [21] claim that researchers should collect from at least 4 different sources. Inspired from this idea, we collected our data from four different sources: IEEEXplore, ACM Digital Library, SpringerLink and ScienceDirect.

For the keywords used in search engines, we used multiples terminologies (synonyms) used by both researchers and practitioners. We only consider papers published between 2000 and 2017, since the Agile Manifesto could not be mentioned before 2000. Therefore, we unavoidably missed some papers. However, we believe that we have retrieved a large and representative sample for this review.

Regarding the inclusion and exclusion criteria, we defined and refined them several times before starting the real selection to collect the maximum relevant papers and effectively reject irrelevant ones. According to Kitchenham [20], this can greatly minimize the possibility of bias.

To address the problem of quality, in accordance with Campanelli and Parreiras [10], we only considered peer-reviewed papers from conferences and journals. There is no explicit definition of "quality" criteria, instead, we assume that all conference papers/journals reach an acceptable level of quality. However, this could be a limitation of this study.

Next, in the data extraction and classification stages, we applied standard classifications defined in the current literature based on shared and common definitions. We had multiple face-to-face discussions when there were misunderstandings in some concepts. Nevertheless, the data extraction about the influence could be considered as a limitation of the study. In fact, the influence was not always explicitly mentioned and some data may consequently have been missed or misunderstood.

Another final type of bias is the publication one. Based on Kitchenham and Charters [19], they refer to the problem that positive results are more likely to be published than negative results. In fact, very few case studies have reported failed case of adoption, instead, they have been focusing more on the benefits of the adoption.

To summarize, despite some limitations, we consider the internal validity of this research to be acceptable. Most of the bias encountered are inherent and we aimed to manage them as much as we could.

6   Discussion and Conclusion

The primary aim of this paper was to verify the relation between the Agile Manifesto and agile practices selection through an SLR approach. We first tried to find out *how the Agile Manifesto has been discussed in tailored agile methods adoption*. Then, we tried to see *whether or not agile practices selection can be related to agile values or principles defined in the Agile Manifesto* by comparing them with team's problems, expectations and benefits.

The result of RQ1 shows that our observation is true, the Agile Manifesto has really lost attention from the development team. Among the 51 selected papers, only about half of them (51%) mentioned the Agile Manifesto (detail and not detail). Agile practitioners tend to follow only the rules of a specific methodology such as Scrum, XP, etc., and completely ignore the manifesto.

On the contrary, the results of RQ2.1, RQ2.2 and RQ2.3 show that the 4 values and 12 principles of the Agile Manifesto are highly relevant to team's problems, expectations and benefits. 95% of problems, 80% of expectations and 92% of benefits can be mapped to principles and values of the Agile Manifesto. It means that the Agile Manifesto still covers fundamental aspects of any agile method. Therefore, development teams should spend some time to understand the Agile Manifesto before adopting any agile method including a tailored one. In addition, as can be seen in Fig. 5, there is a strong correlation between expectations and benefits (except for the principles Principle_10 and Principle_12). This high correlation can explain that, by tailoring agile methods to meet their expectations, the team can of course obtain the benefits accordingly.

As a conclusion, even though a lot of research supports the idea that the Agile Manifesto (values and principles) allows defining the set of practices, yet software development teams tend to neglect the Agile Manifesto when tailoring agile methods for adoption. We found however that the Agile Manifesto should be more valued and draw more attention from the development team; it deserves to be a guideline for the development team to tailor any agile method and select the right features for adoption. Having a deep knowledge of the Agile Manifesto gives advantages for better tailoring agile methods to maximize the team's expectation and eventually the benefits.

Finally, this study provides a more insightful validation on the relation between the Agile Manifesto and agile practices which was always made based on the assumptions or beliefs of the researchers. This validation can be used as the evidence to create a more complete framework for tailored agile methods adoption in an alternative perspective. For the next step, we aim at building a repository through a systematic review of the empirical studies to gather the relationships between the Agile Manifesto and each practice. Using this repository, the practitioner can then identify easily the related practices to fulfill fully or partially principles and values of the Agile Manifesto.

Acknowledgments. Authors would like to thank Benjamin Croix for his involvement in the Systematic Literature Review, i.e., the papers selection process and data extraction.

References

1. Abbas, N., Gravell, A.M., Wills, G.B.: Using factor analysis to generate clusters of agile practices (a guide for agile process improvement). In: AGILE Conference, pp. 11–20. IEEE (2010)
2. Abrahamsson, P., Salo, O., Ronkainen, J., Warsta, J.: Agile software development methods: review and analysis. arXiv preprint arXiv:1709.08439 (2017)
3. Ahmed, E.M., Sidky, A.: 25 percent ahead of schedule and just at "step 2" of the sami. In: Agile Conference, AGILE 2009, pp. 162–169. IEEE (2009)
4. Ambler, S.: The Agile Unified Process (AUP). Ambysoft (2005). http://www.agilealliance.hu/materials/books/SWA-AUP.pdf
5. Auvinen, J., Back, R., Heidenberg, J., Hirkman, P., Milovanov, L.: Software process improvement with agile practices in a large telecom company. In: Münch, J., Vierimaa, M. (eds.) PROFES 2006. LNCS, vol. 4034, pp. 79–93. Springer, Heidelberg (2006). https://doi.org/10.1007/11767718_10
6. Ayed, H., Vanderose, B., Habra, N.: A metamodel-based approach for customizing and assessing agile methods. In: Quality of Information and Communications Technology (QUATIC), pp. 66–74. IEEE (2012)
7. Bass, J.M.: Scrum master activities: process tailoring in large enterprise projects. In: 2014 IEEE 9th International Conference on Global Software Engineering (ICGSE), pp. 6–15. IEEE (2014)
8. Beck, K., et al.: Manifesto for agile software development (2001)
9. Bowers, J., May, J., Melander, E., Baarman, M., Ayoob, A.: Tailoring XP for large system mission critical software development. In: Wells, D., Williams, L. (eds.) XP/Agile Universe 2002. LNCS, vol. 2418, pp. 100–111. Springer, Heidelberg (2002). https://doi.org/10.1007/3-540-45672-4_10
10. Campanelli, A.S., Parreiras, F.S.: Agile methods tailoring-a systematic literature review. J. Syst. Softw. **110**, 85–100 (2015)
11. Cohen, D., Lindvall, M., Costa, P.: An introduction to agile methods. Adv. Comput. **62**(03), 1–66 (2004)
12. Derbier, G.: Agile development in the old economy. In: Proceedings of the Agile Development Conference, ADC 2003, pp. 125–131. IEEE (2003)
13. Erickson, J., Lyytinen, K., Siau, K.: Agile modeling, agile software development, and extreme programming: the state of research. J. Database Manage. **16**(4), 88 (2005)
14. Esfahani, H.C., Cabot, J., Yu, E.: Adopting agile methods: can goal-oriented social modeling help? In: 2010 Fourth International Conference on Research Challenges in Information Science (RCIS), pp. 223–234. IEEE (2010)
15. Esfahani, H.C., Eric, S., Annosi, M.C.: Towards the strategic analysis of agile practices. In: CAiSE Forum, pp. 155–162 (2011)
16. Fitzgerald, B., Russo, N., O'Kane, T.: An empirical study of system development method tailoring in practice. In: ECIS 2000 Proceedings, p. 4 (2000)
17. Hummel, M.: State-of-the-art: a systematic literature review on agile information systems development. In: 2014 47th Hawaii International Conference on System Sciences (HICSS), pp. 4712–4721. IEEE (2014)
18. Jalali, S., Wohlin, C.: Global software engineering and agile practices: a systematic review. J. Softw. Evol. Process **24**(6), 643–659 (2012)
19. Kitchenham, B., Charters, S.: Guidelines for performing systematic literature reviews in software engineering (2007)

20. Kitchenham, B.: Procedures for performing systematic reviews. Keele, UK, Keele Univ. **33**(2004), 1–26 (2004)
21. Kitchenham, B., Brereton, O.P., Budgen, D., Turner, M., Bailey, J., Linkman, S.: Systematic literature reviews in software engineering-a systematic literature review. Inform. Softw. Technol. **51**(1), 7–15 (2009)
22. Kiv, S., Heng, S., Kolp, M., Wautelet, Y.: An intentional perspective on partial agile adoption. In: Proceedings of the 12th International Conference on Software Technologies - Volume 1: ICSOFT, pp. 116–127. INSTICC, SciTePress (2017)
23. Kiv, S., Heng, S., Wautelet, Y., Kolp, M.: Towards a goal-oriented framework for partial agile adoption. In: Cabello, E., Cardoso, J., Maciaszek, L.A., van Sinderen, M. (eds.) ICSOFT 2017. CCIS, vol. 868, pp. 69–90. Springer, Cham (2018). https://doi.org/10.1007/978-3-319-93641-3_4
24. Kurapati, N., Manyam, V.S.C., Petersen, K.: Agile software development practice adoption survey. In: Wohlin, C. (ed.) XP 2012. LNBIP, vol. 111, pp. 16–30. Springer, Heidelberg (2012). https://doi.org/10.1007/978-3-642-30350-0_2
25. Lee, S., Yong, H.S.: Agile software development framework in a small project environment. J. Inform. Process. Syst. **9**(1), 69–88 (2013)
26. Lin, J., Yu, H., Shen, Z., Miao, C.: Using goal net to model user stories in agile software development. In: 2014 15th IEEE/ACIS International Conference on Software Engineering, Artificial Intelligence, Networking and Parallel/Distributed Computing (SNPD), pp. 1–6. IEEE (2014)
27. Madi, T., Dahalin, Z., Baharom, F.: Content analysis on agile values: a perception from software practitioners. In: 2011 5th Malaysian Conference on Software Engineering (MySEC), pp. 423–428. IEEE (2011)
28. Mikulėnas, G., Butleris, R., Nemuraitė, L.: An approach for the metamodel of the framework for a partial agile method adaptation. Inform. Technol. Control **40**(1), 71–82 (2011)
29. Qumer, A., Henderson-Sellers, B.: A framework to support the evaluation, adoption and improvement of agile methods in practice. J. Syst. Softw. **81**(11), 1899–1919 (2008)
30. Schön, E.M., Thomaschewski, J., Escalona, M.J.: Agile requirements engineering: a systematic literature review. Comput. Stan. Interfaces **49**, 79–91 (2017)
31. Schwaber, K.: Agile Project Management with Scrum. Microsoft Press, Redmond Wash (2004)
32. Séguin, N., Tremblay, G., Bagane, H.: Agile principles as software engineering principles: an analysis. In: Wohlin, C. (ed.) XP 2012. LNBIP, vol. 111, pp. 1–15. Springer, Heidelberg (2012). https://doi.org/10.1007/978-3-642-30350-0_1
33. Shen, Z., Miao, C., Tao, X., Gay, R.: Goal oriented modeling for intelligent software agents. In: Proceedings. IEEE/WIC/ACM International Conference on Intelligent Agent Technology, (IAT 2004), pp. 540–543. IEEE (2004)
34. Shu, X., Turinsky, A., Sensen, C., Maurer, F.: A case study of the implementation of agile methods in a bioinformatics project. In: Concas, G., Damiani, E., Scotto, M., Succi, G. (eds.) XP 2007. LNCS, vol. 4536, pp. 169–170. Springer, Heidelberg (2007). https://doi.org/10.1007/978-3-540-73101-6_28
35. Thomas, D.: Agile is dead (2014). https://pragdave.me/blog/2014/03/04/time-to-kill-agile.html
36. VersionOne: 11th annual state of agile development survey (2017)

37. Wautelet, Y., Heng, S., Kiv, S., Kolp, M.: User-story driven development of multi-agent systems: a process fragment for agile methods. Comput. Lang. Syst. Struct. **50**, 159–176 (2017). https://doi.org/10.1016/j.cl.2017.06.007

38. Wautelet, Y., Heng, S., Kolp, M., Mirbel, I.: Unifying and extending user story models. In: Jarke, M., et al. (eds.) CAiSE 2014. LNCS, vol. 8484, pp. 211–225. Springer, Cham (2014). https://doi.org/10.1007/978-3-319-07881-6_15

Agile Meets Assessments: Case Study on How to Do Agile Process Improvement in a Very Small Enterprise

Jakob Diebold[1]([☒]), Philipp Diebold[2,3] [iD], and Arthur Vetter[4]

[1] store2be Gmbh, Oranienstraße 185, Berlin, Germany
jakob.diebold@store2be.com
[2] Fraunhofer IESE, Fraunhofer-Platz 1, Kaiserslautern, Germany
philipp.diebold@iese.fhg.de
[3] Bagilstein GmbH, Elbestraße 40, Mainz, Germany
[4] Karlsruhe Institute of Technology, AIFB,
Kaiserstrasse 89, Karlsruhe, Germany
arthur.vetter@partner.kit.edu

Abstract. Smaller software companies, such as start-ups do not often follow an explicit process, but rather develop in a more or less unstructured way. Especially when they grow or customer involvement increases. This development without any structured process results in problems. Thus, our objective was the improvement of the current development process of one software start-up by introducing appropriate agile practices and eliciting their effects. For this reason, we performed a pre and post process assessment using interviews. Based on the initial assessment, agile practices were selected and implemented. Finally, the post assessment and additional code metrics served as controlling mechanism to check whether weak points are addressed. The comparison of the two assessments showed that 13 ISO 29110 base practices have been improved by the introduced eight agile practices. Thus, even more aspects have casually been improved than initially planned. Finally, the additional retrospective with company employees showed how the introduced agile practices positively influenced their work.

Keywords: Agile development · Agile practices · Assessment
ISO 29110 · VSE

1 Introduction

Development processes have shown to be important in the area of software development, even when it appeared to be an engineering discipline [1]. In the area of development processes, the way of development tremendously changed with the publication of the agile manifesto [2] from a traditional plan-based way to a more agile way.

Regularly, Software Process Improvement (SPI) initiatives are often considered for the sake of addressing existing problems of improvement goals, such as increasing quality or shorten time-to-market [3]. Especially the two mentioned issues are crucial

© Springer Nature Switzerland AG 2018
M. Kuhrmann et al. (Eds.): PROFES 2018, LNCS 11271, pp. 31–47, 2018.
https://doi.org/10.1007/978-3-030-03673-7_3

for Very Small Enterprises (VSE) or Small Medium-sized Enterprises (SME) due to the fact that they often focus on one single product that needs to have a high quality and always new features within updates.

Compared to larger companies, these smaller ones normally provide a higher flexibility on different levels, e.g. dealing with customer changes. However, they also often work in an informal way without a structured process. To provide these companies with structured processes, common software process models like SPICE (ISO 15504) or CMMI were tailored to their needs, resulting in the ISO29110 [5], a process assessment and improvement standard for VSEs. Similar to the mentioned standards [4], the ISO 29110 is presenting the "What" to do. Thus, it does not contradict with agile processes, covering the "How".

For this reason, our work combines both aspects, assessments with ISO 29110 as well as process improvement using agile practices. Our overall research goal is to identify which agile practices to select for improving the process and how do these changes influence process covered by assessments. Within a case study of a VSE, improvement suggestions, namely agile practices, are derived from the pain areas identified during the initial assessment. Based on a second assessment we were able to compare both and get a good impression of what the different agile practices improved or affected.

The remainder of this paper is structured as follows: Sect. 2 provides some background and related work. This is followed by the design of the case study (Sect. 3). The main section contains the results of both assessments, the implementation of the agile practices as well as the retrospectives (Sect. 4). Finally, we discuss the threats of this study (Sect. 5) and conclude the paper (Sect. 6).

2 Background and Related Work

Agile. Different studies [6, 7] showed that agile development is the leading style of development approaches, especially in information systems. Even if Scrum is the dominating method within this development area, Diebold et al. [8] showed that it is common to not use any of the methods as given by books but adapting it to the specific (companies' or projects') context. For this reason, there is a little shift from the introduction of complete agile methods to smaller elements of the methods, the agile practices. Besides the usage of Scrum as common method, VersionOne [6] also provides a list of commonly top-used agile practices (they call them techniques) mentioned by their participants: Daily standup, Prioritized backlogs, Short iterations, Retrospectives, Iteration and Release planning, Unit testing, Team-based estimation, and Taskboard.

ISO 29110. The ISO 29110 was developed based on the ISO 12207 as well as CMMI and adapted to the needs of VSEs. This assessment standard is broken down into the common five parts: overview (part 1), framework and taxonomy (part 2), assessment guide (part 3), different profiles (part 4), and management guide for these profiles (part 5). Parts 3 and 5, which are also most important for our work, address the improvement of the company itself. Due to the context of VSEs, the standard only considers two processes in the process assessment model (PAM), "Project Management" (PM) and "Software Implementation" (SI). These processes are refined into base practices (BPs), similar to common assessment models, to evaluate the fulfillment.

Laporte et al. [9, 10] performed several case studies in different VSEs with this PAM. Within the first study [9] all ISO 29110 work products and BPs were introduced, focusing on documentation. The second study [10] with two cases focused on documentation of the architecture and tests. Besides the mentioned case studies that deal specifically with ISO 29110, many case studies were performed by adapting the common standards for assessments of smaller companies [11, 12].

Agile in Start-Ups and VSE. After the ISO 29110 related work, we now describe studies dealing with (very) small enterprises and start-ups as a subset of them, similar to our case study. In a grounded theory study [13], Coleman and O'Connor explored how software development processes of start-ups look like. They identified that start-ups as well as agile methods focus on products and are considered for smaller teams so that they fit together. However, he identified that many agile methods could not be applied due to the fact of a very small number of developers (even lower than suggested by Scrum or so) [14]. Even if they are applied, it is impossible to use them as dogmatic as given by the book. Instead they have to be adapted to the company's context [8].

O'Donnell and Richardson [15] introduced practices from Extreme Programming (XP) in an Irish SME without adapting them to their specific context. They identified faster improvements and higher adaptability. Nonetheless, they also recognized that the small team-size, the customer being the project manager, and less documentation, results in problems, e.g. making and understanding decisions without the necessary documentation in their case. Finally, they conclude that it is necessary to analyze which elements are appropriate for the specific context before introduction.

3 Study Design

In general, our study is a case study according to [16, 17] with interviews in an assessment-mode as data collection method. We first present the objective of this study with its research questions, followed by the study procedure. Finally, the company's context is roughly presented.

3.1 Research Questions

The overall objective of this study was the elicitation of the current state and its improvement. This is typical for case study and action research, inducing improvements. This study goal was refined into the following three research questions (RQ):

> **RQ1:** Which agile practices are appropriate for this specific VSE context?
> **RQ2:** How does the usage of agile practices improve the development process according to common assessment standards, in this case ISO 29110?
> **RQ3:** How do these improvements improve quality and time-to-market?

3.2 Study Procedure

The overall procedure of the case study included the following four steps: After the Pre-Assessment (beginning July 2016), the Agile Practices were identified and introduced (Mid of August 2016), and finally the Post-Assessment was conducted (End of October).

Step 1 - Pre-Assessment: Within this assessment, two interviews (each 90 min) and one self-assessment (by the first author, being one of the three company employees; also 90 min) were conducted according to the ISO 29110 PAM [5]. All authors iterative defined a semi-structured interview guideline following the PAM with its base practices of the two process areas. Before starting with the interview questions[1], the interview purpose was stated. For the analysis of the interviews, we used the commonly used **N**(one)**P**(artially)**L**(argly)**F**(ully)-scale (cf. Table 1), defined for different assessment approaches such as SCAMPI [18].

Step 2 - Identification of Appropriate Agile Practices: First, we identified the improvement spots, based on the rating of the base practices in the pre-assessment, focusing on "not achieved" (N) and "partially achieved" (P) practices (see Sect. 4.1). This complies with the first step of the Agile Deployment Framework [19]. Based on Literature [6, 7] and our experience, mainly coming from Fraunhofer IESE as applied research institute [8, 20], the agile practices that might address the previous none or bad covered base practices, were selected (see Sect. 4.2 for more details). These ideas were discussed in the author-team before bringing them up as final suggestions to the development team of the company.

Step 3 - Implementation of Selected Agile Practices: Based on [19], the next step was the preparation of the implementation of the agile practices. This included also necessary adaptions of these practices [8], which is important in our company's context due to the small size of the team (which is less than suggested by Scrum). Even if literature suggests to perform process improvements in a step-wise or iterative approach [20], in our case all agile practices were implemented together due to time limitations. Besides the agile practices and their adoptions, we also documented difficulties and problems that appeared during the introduction.

Step 4 - Post-Assessment Including Retrospective: At the end of the case study, we performed another assessment, similar to the initial one (two interviews and one self-assessment with the same participants). Thus, we were able to trace the change of BPs within the ISO 29110-PAM. Since we mapped the improvement actions, the introduction of the agile practice, to the BPs which we wanted to improve, we were able to check whether it worked or not. In addition to this assessment, a retrospective with all study participants was performed to identify further advantages and disadvantages of this process improvement. Finally, besides the subjective manner of the assessments, we were interested in checking the implemented improvements objective measures. This is especially interesting for RQ3 regarding the quality of the software.

---

[1] Interview questions can be found here: http://doi.org/10.13140/RG.2.2.17706.93120.

Table 1. Results of pre- (row 2 "PM/1" and 4 "SI/1") and post-assessments (row 3 "PM/2" and 5 "SI/2") (N = not achieved, P = partially achieved, L = largely achieved, F = fully achieved according to the SCAMPI approach [18])

Process / Assessment	BP1	BP2	BP3	BP4	BP5	BP6	BP7	BP8	BP9	BP10	BP11	BP12	BP13	BP14	BP15	BP16	BP17	BP18	BP19	BP20	BP21	BP22	BP23	BP24	BP25	BP26	BP27
PM / 1	P	L	L	N	P	L	N	P	P	P	N	N	N	F	P	P	L	F	F	F	P	L	P	P	F	L	
PM / 2	P	L	L	F	P	L	P	F	P	P	P	L	N	N	F	L	L	L	F	F	F	P	L	P	P	P	F	-
SI / 1	P	N	L	L	P	P	L	N	N	P	L	P	F	N	L	L	L	L	N	L	L	N	F				
SI / 2	F	F	L	F	P	L	L	P	N	P	L	L	F	N	L	L	L	L	N	L	L	L	F				

3.3 Company Context

The company studied within this case study is a software start-up located in Karlsruhe Germany. With being founded in 2015 by three students they are a very-small enterprise (VSE) according to the European commission. These three were the main employees (including the first authors of this paper) supported by up-to two additional working students. At the beginning, all employees were working as developers, with the time being, some focused more on sales/marketing, consulting, or customization of the product for specific customer needs. Regarding their process, they were aware of the fact of having almost none or no structured one, just coding some kind or refactoring due to architecture and design and final testing. Before starting with this improvement initiative, no dedicated Agile Practices were used in their company respectively the process.

Their product is a project monitoring software for very large companies, developing large and complex products. Thus, the software provides a hierarchical dashboard with a flexible configuration of the specific project and/or customer needs. As an Excel-Add In it is completely integrated in the Microsoft Office-environment, written in Visual-Basic.NET. The software code was managed by GitHub. As support ticketing system, a self-hosted instance of osTicket was used.

4 Study Results

Within this section, we present the results of the overall case study, structured according to the parts of the presented procedure.

4.1 Pre Assessment

The pre and post assessment results are structured according to the two ISO 29110 processes. We evaluated each BP with the NPLF-scale of the SCAMPI approach [18].

Project Management. This process of the ISO 29110 includes 27 BPs that need to be checked for creating the companies' profiles. The overall objective of this process is the systematic project management of all software implementation activities during the life-cycle. All the ratings of the single BPs are presented in Table 1 (row 2) with the NPLF-scale. In the following paragraphs, we are going to provide some example descriptions of BPs, their ratings as well as reasons for the ratings.

BP1 of Project Management deals with the "Review of the statement of work". In our case, the company has no statement of work. Instead, it only has the customer offer, including the customers' requirements. This offer is informally and none-structurally reviewed. Thus, our rating resulted in a "partially". The second one (BP2) "Define with the customer the delivery instructions of each one of the deliverables specified in the statement of work" is "largely achieved" because the deliverables are included in the initial offer but not in a separate document for traceability or something else. The "Identification of tasks […] to produce the deliverables specific in the statement of work" (BP3) is done using either issues in GIT or the tool Asana (for changes that are not directly software-related). Since not all issues are specified on the same level of detail, it is "largely achieved". Since at this point in time, no "estimation of the duration to perform each task" (BP4) is performed, this BPs is obviously "not achieved".

Other examples are BP12-14 which all deal with the project plan as work product, from describing, verifying, to review. Since the company does not have a formal project plan, we need to rate all these three as "not achieved". This is exactly the opposite compared to BP20-21, which are both dealing with backup aspects and are both rated as "fully achieved". The company has a code-repository on GIT as well as a network drive, which both include an automatic backup mechanism.

Software Implementation. Compared to Project Management, this process only implements 23 BPs for the company's profile. This process targets the systematic performance of analysis, construction, integration, and testing activities of a new or changed software product. All the ratings of the single BPs are presented in Table 1 (row 4) with the NPLF-scale. In the following paragraphs, we are going to provide some example descriptions of BPs, their ratings as well as reasons leading to the ratings.

The first three BPs within the Software Implementation deal with the requirements, from documenting (BP1), verifying (BP2), to validation (BP3). For the first one, it is necessary to use all possible information sources and cover the feasibility as well as scope. Since all these aspects should be covered in a document, which is only in a task in GIT in the company's case (also BP4), we rated BP1 with "partially achieved". Most often the degree of detail is varying and the details are only known to the owner of the requirement, which increases communication. Since no review of the requirements is conducted, BP2 is easily rated as "not achieved". The validation is covering the customers' expectations. Either most requirements come directly from the customer and are thus later validated or are discussed within the team of the company's founders, which also communicates with the customers. Thus, a "largely achieve" is feasible.

Within the area of testing, ISO 29110 requires "Design or update unit test cases and apply them to verify that the Software Components implements the detailed part of the Software Design" (BP12). In our case the company does not have a lot of module tests so only very few modules are completely tested (2.99% of the lines of code, cf. Table 4). For this reason, we need to rate it as low "partially achieved". Following the created tests, it is necessary to "correct the defects found until successful unit test" (BP13). In the cases where the tests are existing in our case, this is "fully achieved". We decided to rate it like that due to the fact that the missing tests were already rated down before.

Overall. When considering the overview of the first assessment, it shows some very good covered areas as well as some gaps. Out of the 50 BPs of the ISO 29110, 12 (24%) were rated as "not achieved", 15 (30%) as "partially achieved", 16 (32%) as "largely achieved", and 7 (14%) as "fully achieved".

4.2   SPI Using Agile Practices (RQ1)

After the pre assessment, we could identify a set of ISO 29110 BPs which we wanted to improve with agile practices. For this, we first need to find the appropriate agile practices that would help in improving the identified issues. Thus, we used common literature about existing agile practices and went into some details for those that seem to be helpful. We categorized the BPs that might be addressed with one or a set of agile practices, verified this, and named these categories according to the appropriate ISO 12207 processes (cf. Table 2, column 1 and 2). In addition to the agile practices, we also analyzed who is involved in the processes that are impacted by these improvements as well as how the agile practices need to be adapted to the specific company's context. Most of the adaptions, that will be presented when going through the different improvement areas, appeared during the implementation or usage of them.

Project Planning. The major findings within this area are the lack of a project plan as well as managing requirements. These issues directly affect several BPs within both processes. Since we focus more on the engineering part, we identified the practice of User Stories [21] for managing requirements. This is also an ideal element for starting some kind of planning, per iteration as well as long-term. Furthermore these stories were arranged in a product backlog in which they were prioritized together with the customer. For a better effort estimation, which is strongly connected with the planning, we introduced the concept of story points [22] together with the planning poker practice [23]. This seems to be appropriate due to the fact that you do not need to think in concrete timings, e.g. hours or days, but gives a rather abstract comparison-mechanism.

We defined the user story to (1) need to bring value, (2) formulated actively, (3) allocated to a user group (as specific as possible), and (4) self-contained. Since the case company did not make the benefits/value explicit, following template was used (similar to common user story templates): *As a < user type >, I want to < function >.* An example is: *As a meeting organizer, I am able to allocate a user group to the action management.*

The backlog was created based on the set of user stories, written on post-its and stuck on the office wall. The final backlog also included some elements from story mapping since categories and clusters were included in a second dimension (besides the priority). After defining the initial set of stories, the team started the estimation with story points. They considered half a working day as one story point and not the

Table 2. Identified improvement BPs, mapping to ISO 12207 processes (as improvement areas) and solutions

ISO 12207 processes	ISO 29110 BPs	Addressing Agile Practices
Project planning	PM.BP 4, 7, 11-14, SI.BP1,2	User stories, Backlog, Planning poker with story points
Project assessment and control	PM.BP 16, 22	Burn-Down-Charts
SW Construction	SI.BP 11	Coding standards
SW Qualification testing	SI.BP 5, 10, 12	Test-driven development
SW Implementation	SI.BP 12, 17	Definition-of-Done
SW Architectural design and SW documentation management	SI.BP 9, 14, 19	User stories and their connections

recommended one day [21], due to their part-time development. Planning Poker was performed as stated in common guidelines [23].

During the implementation and usage of these agile practices belonging to project planning, no adjustments were necessary, so that the team kept them from the beginning of the case study up to the end and further.

Project Assessment and Control. The identified main issue here was the missing transparency of the project status during the development. Therefore, we selected the burn-down-chart as the appropriate agile practice to improve the project monitoring. Together with the Definition-of-Done (which we describe later in detail) we wanted the chart to show the already "done" stories and story points as well as the still open ones.

During the usage of this concept, the team recognized a distortion of the performed work. This is due to the necessarily performed reviews and updated regression-test list. Since these two activities were often forgotten, it resulted in less "done" stories during the sprint and, instead, many at the end. Additionally, this also has the effect of conducting a lot of reviews in a short time before finishing the sprint, product, or release. This results in less benefits of the burn-chart, such that often the team members did not update it. To overcome this problem, the team decided to conduct reviews of the already completely implemented user stories regularly (once a week). For that reason a specific column "to review" was integrated in their already used Github-Kanban-Board. Finally, they also found a mechanism within their analog backlog to order the user stories.

SW Construction. Even if the assessment did not show a large amount of improvement potential, we decided to introduce coding standards for new or refactored code. They focus on guidelines how the code should be structured and look like. This practice should simplify the communication, due to a common understanding [24], and further influence the (collective) ownership of the code [25].

To not burden the developers, we tried to keep the coding guidelines as small and easy as possible. The concrete conventions, which were defined by the team: (1) Variables are written in CamelCase; (2) Variables are declared at the beginning of a method (if possible); (3) Methods are named on the schema: verbNoun (Adjective); (4) Each method is commented with an XML-comment.

During the definition and usage of the coding guidelines, the necessity of some aspects was questioned, e.g. the XML-comments that take a lot of effort. The major problem that appeared with the practices was falling into oblivion, because they needed to be removed from the office whiteboard. To overcome this, the team made the guidelines visible on a project-wiki page and additionally pinned them printed on an office wall.

SW Qualification Testing. The major issue regarding testing was the lack of existing (module or unit) tests. To not just start implementing more of these tests, but using an agile practice, we decided to implement test-driven development (TDD), another important practice from XP. We and the team were aware of the fact that this practice is one of the most effort-intensive practices, since it needs to be established and often results in an intervention of the current development procedure. For this reason, it was decided to use this new way of testing and development only for new features and not for changes, which are normally quite small in their case.

During performing TDD a very specific problem appeared with their software product: Since it is an Excel-Add In which interacts with a lot of third-party products (mainly from MS Office), the testability of some modules or classes is very hard. After this finding, the team tried to decouple the single internal functionality from the interfaces. So, that it is easy to implement test at least for these internal functionalities.

SW Implementation. Besides the previous mentioned quality assurance activities, like testing and reviews, other aspects need to be considered such that a specific requirement or user story is finished. To overcome this issue and establish the things that need to be done, the Definition-of-Done (DoD) was selected to be introduced as agile practice. Since we already mentioned the specification of requirements as user stories, the defined list of criteria is applicable to every story: (1) Code is implemented, working, commented, and refactored; (2) Code is complying with coding guidelines; (3) Code is reviewed by another developer (4-eye principle); (4) Module-Tests are implemented (if possible), (5) UI-test with a set of specified inputs; (6) (New) functionality is part of the test-checklist considered for regression-testing; (7) All used Excel-versions are tested.

One issue that appeared during the usage of the DoD was already mentioned in the project monitoring: Stories without the code review are not "done". Furthermore, the maintenance of the test-checklist for the regression testing was not updated for every story. The team put that down to the fact that the DoD was not present enough to all the developers, similar to the Coding guidelines. This was resolved similar to the Coding guidelines with a wiki-page as well as a printout in the office.

SW Architectural Design and SW Documentation Management. The main aspect in this area that appeared in the assessment was the missing traceability record. To overcome this missing piece of documentation between the parts in the software (e.g. module or class) and the requirements, the idea was to establish a reference to the specific user story in the code.

During the implementation of this, the team recognized that this is not realizable due to the fact that modules could not be referenced one-by-one to a single user story. Further they assume that it would be to effort intensive to reference all connected stories.

4.3   Post Assessment

Now we are going to present the second assessment results.

Project Management. Similar to the first assessment, Table 1 (row 3) with the NPLF-scale presents the results for all BPs of this ISO 29110 process. We are not providing the reasons behind all ratings, but rather on some examples that could be later used for the comparison of the first and second assessment.

The "assignment of roles and responsibilities" (BP6) is done implicitly for all employees (between the co-founders) because they strictly clarified their responsibilities within the team. Since this makes project-specific roles obsolete, it was rated as "largely achieved". The following two BPs deal with some effort estimation aspects, first "assigning start and completion date [...] in order to create the Schedule of the Project Tasks" (BP7) and second "Calculate and document the project Estimated Effort" (BP8). With regard to the first one, the company did not consider the two dates and thus cannot create a schedule out of it. Nevertheless, the estimated duration of performing the tasks and the priorities give a rough indication. This duration also can be used for the other BP, due to the fact the overall project effort/duration can be calculated. Thus, we are ending in the first case with a "partial" and in the second with a "fully achievement". Similar to the first assessment, there are no changes with regard to the project plan such that all BPs connected with this (BP13, 14) need to be rated with "not achieved".

Software Implementation. Similar to the first assessment, Table 1 (row 5) with the NPLF-scale presents the results for the BPs. We are not providing the reasons behind all ratings, but rather on some examples later used for the comparison.

Through the usage of GIT as version and configuration system, "incorporate the requirements specification to the software configuration" (BP4) is "fully achieved". For the "Document or update the Software Design" (BP5) the developer of a story suggests (design) solutions, of which one is selected by the team. Since the decision is not (formally) documented, we could only rate it with "partially". Nonetheless, the "Verify and obtain approval of the Software Design" on technical level is performed during the implementation. Furthermore, the code review (included in the DoD) does also consider the design. Thus, this BP is rated as "largely achieved".

Since no traceability record is created (BP9), similar to the pre-assessment, it is rated as "not achieved". The functionality behind the traceability record is covered to some extent by the management of branches and pull-requests in the version control system, including the unit test in the repository. But since there is no document for the design BP10 is rated as "partially achieved".

Overall. When considering the overall results of this second assessment, it shows that the company is on a good way. Out of the 50 BPs, 5 were rated as "not achieved", 12 as "partially achieved", 20 as "largely achieved", and 12 as "fully achieved". With these new results, the company achieved quite good improvements (which will be stated and discussed in the next sub-section) and learned a lot.

4.4   Comparison of Both Assessments (RQ2)

On the high-level view, the integration of the agile practices could show improvements: Out of the 50 of the ISO 29110, 26% were rated better in the second one (13 BPs, cf. Table 3): 7 increased by 1 level (14%), 4 increased by 2 levels (8%, PM.BP8 & 12, SI. BP1 & 22), 2 increased by 3 levels (4% PM.BP4, SI.BP2). None got worse (only one could not be assessed in the second case) that means ¾ stayed the same.

When considering our processes (areas) from ISO 12207 we could see most improvements within project planning with six BPs from PM and three from SI. This is followed by Software Implementation with two SI BPs as well as Monitoring and Testing each with one. Five out of these 13 improved BPs were not expected (cf. Table 3, column 3) because of positive side-effects of the agile practices, such as User stories that provide input, help and support to many BPs. But besides that, we also had ten BPs which should be improved through our agile practices, where we could not achieve any changes (cf. Table 3, column 4).

The improvements on project planning result on the one hand from user stories with a story board and backlog and on the other hand from planning poker with story points for estimation (PM.BP4). PM.BP7 and 8 are based on the combination of both. Within PM.BP11 and 12 the board with the prioritized stories replaces the functions of a project plan. Even if it is no formal project plan, it enables easier changes in the project progression (PM.BP17). The usage of the stories template also standardizes the management of requirements for the implementation (SI.BP1, 2, 4). Within the monitoring area, the burn charts could improve PM.BP16 especially through the visualization. The testing especially improved through the higher importance of creating unit tests in the practice TDD (SI.BP12). Even if not initially expected, the DoD influenced two BPs (SI.BP6, 22) through the manifestation of some activities, e.g. code reviews.

As seen in Table 3, some BPs could not be improved even if planned. Even if the user stories improved the project planning, they could not replace a formal project plan, which is the reason for not improving all expected ones. For the monitoring, there is not that much improvement since the team did not consequently track their effort so that a comparison is impossible. For some of the practices the "formal" documentation is missing (SI.BP5) and this also results in none-improvements in others (SI.BP10). In the architecture and documentation area, as mentioned during the introduction of the agile practice, it was not considered as useful to create a specific document.

4.5   Retrospective (RQ3)

We additionally decided to perform a retrospective with all the founders of the company regarding our improvement initiative with the two assessment. Thereby, we could identify the following positive as well as negative aspects.

As main positive aspect, the participants mentioned planning, effort estimation, and identification of dependencies. In general, the people internalized the importance of (development) processes and mentioned that now they are "really" performing the activities correct, e.g. managing requirements. Highlighted was the usage of user stories due to a clear definition and scoping of requirements resulting a better overview. Even if we believe, that the customer value of the single functionalities could be stated within

Table 3. Improved ISO 29110 BPs after the introduction of the agile practices

ISO 12207 processes	Expected, improved	Unexpected, improved	Expected, unimproved
Project planning	PM: 4, 7, 11, 12; SI: 1, 2	PM: 8, 17; SI: 4	PM: 13, 14
Project asses. & Control	PM: 16		PM: 22
SW Construction			SI: 11
SW Qual. Testing	SI: 12		SI: 5, 10
SW Implementation		SI: 6, 22	SI:17
SW Arch. Design and SW Docu.			SI: 9, 14, 19

the user stories template, they mentioned that just through the usage of their user story template, the connection to the customers' value improved.

The major learning of the improvement initiative was how companies could benefit from structured processes, such as some internal standards, e.g. programming style-guides. Furthermore, they could recommend others, to use all the practices which they implemented during the case study.

Besides these benefits, also some negative issues were mentioned, which were not that generic, as the positive ones, but rather specific for some practices. For example, the burn-down chart did not bring the expected results, due to the realization and team size. Furthermore, the temporarily absence of the visual representation of the coding guideline or DoD (in the office) showed a disadvantage. This was recognized quite early and resulted directly in an improvement.

4.6   Measurement (RQ3)

We further compared some code metrics before and after the introduction of the agile practices. They were collected within their common IDE using Add-Ons. We used these metrics for a better objective view to evaluate whether the quality of the software product improved, compared to the previous subjective results. We selected seven common code metrics (cf. Table 4) due to the suggestion of IESE-colleagues working on quality modelling and measurement:

With the test coverage, as first metric, that increased by more than 2% for all lines of code (cf. Table 4, row 2), the objective measure confirms the subjective feeling that test-driven development (in our case study only for new features) increases the coverage of the tested code. Since this should probably result in finding bugs and improving the product, the quality increases.

Compared to all other metrics, the comments are the only one that got worse (cf. Table 4, row 3). The only reason for explaining we could imagine are the introduced coding conventions/style guides as well as lower (average) size of methods such that things do not need to be commented any more due to meaningful names. Contrary to that, the documentation within the code increased (cf. Table 4, row 4). Which was part of the coding conventions which was checked within code reviews.

Table 4. Comparison of Pre- and Post-Assessment code metrics

Metric	Pre- &	Post-Assessment
Test coverage[a]	2.99%	5.21%
Comments/code	6.2%	5.3%
Documentation[b]	7.2%	7.8%
Lines/file	183.77	173.60
Methods/class	13.57	13.19
Average complexity [26]	2.53	2.47
Max. complexity [26]	42	39

[a]Percentage of lines of code executed by all unit tests
[b]Percentage of specific documentation comment lines

Due to the introduction of the coding guidelines, that include some conventions of file, class, and methods lengths, the lines per file as well as the method per class ration could be decreased (cf. Table 4, row 5 & 6). Furthermore, several rations of the different metrics were also considered. Especially the lines per file could be significantly reduced by 10 lines on average.

Finally, the last group of metrics covers complexity. McConnell's complexity metrics [26] showed an improvement (cf. Table 4, row 7 & 8). The average complexity could be improved slightly, which is the reason due to a large number of untouched code between the two assessments. Nonetheless, the maximum complexity, measured as possible paths through one methods, could be decreased.

Even if the time interval between the two measurements was quite short, except one metric, all showed an improvement; some more some less. Nonetheless, it is hard to generalize an improvement of the quality from these measures in this short interval.

5 Threats to Validity

Within this section we are going to discuss the threats regarding the validity of our study results according to [28] and how we tried to deal with them.

First of all, we are aware of the fact that our case company is not representative for all VSEs and much less for SMEs, mainly due to the fact that they are 1.5 years old and working with a small team. This also influences their daily work in the way, that they could not spend the same amount of time in the (further) development of their product every day or even over weeks, because of other activities such as sales, marketing, etc.

Regarding the case study execution, the time interval of four months between the two assessments and measurements were fixed by the company because of their product or customer times. For implementing and adapting the agile practices as well as obtaining an effect, it is a quite short interval. Even if we would have liked to have a longer time frame in between, we believe that our results indicate at least a trend. Further, we hope to conduct another measurement (including assessment) at a later point in time. Additionally, and also caused by the short timing, we needed to introduce the agile practices for the improvement all in parallel as big-bang and could not perform a step-by-step introduction which could be more beneficial for the company [20] as well as for research for measuring the effects of the single agile practices. This makes it also harder to identify the impacts, benefits, and drawbacks of the singe agile practices.

Furthermore, with performing assessments with interviews, we are facing common threats to validity that are common to these studies. Conducting interviews, always includes some possible bias from the interviewer, especially in our case were the interviewer was one of the company's founders. We tried to minimize this threat by using the ISO 29110 BPs as a standardized (and externally given) interview guideline. But we only focused on the BPs of the ISO and thus only implicitly considered the mentioned work products. The interviews were conducted with all founders (being the employees) of the company to overcome the threat of having subjective individual viewpoints. Finally, the notes which we extracted from the audio tapes, were provided to the interview participants for a review, which increases the objectivity of the results. Nevertheless, all interviews or assessments done with interviews are at least to some extend subjective because of the personal skills and interpretations of the assessor. Asking for evidences in an assessment in the only way of trying to get some more objective results or statements on that.

For the analysis of both assessment results, besides the main author another researchers with assessment experience reviewed the results, provided input, and within a final discussion we ended up with the above rating. Similar for the selection of the appropriate agile practices, which was discussed among all authors.

Ending to the threats to validity, some more information on the possibility of replicating this study in a different context. For sure this is only possible in SME or even VSE for which this specific ISO-standard is developed for. Using the created interview guidelines that are based on the PAM with its base practices (BR) the replication of the interview can be done quite easily. The hardest part for a replication is the identification of the agile practices as improvement suggestions. This is the case because it requires experiences in agile development with knowing the single practices (even if having and using an existing experience base) as well as understanding the given context of the company. With that knowledge/experience and the information given above on the procedure the study can be replicated.

6   Conclusions

Within this paper we describe our case study in a software start-up. It comprises two ISO 29110-assessments with the implementation of agile practices in between as process improvement. Based on the two assessments with the same interview participants in both assessments, a good pre- and post-comparison was possible. This was supplemented by a retrospective and comparing objective measures of the product quality.

Based on all the results, the introduction and implementation of the eight agile practices (RQ1) showed significant improvements in the daily development of the case company. From the 50 base practices of the selected assessment standard, 13 were improved through the introduction of the agile practices (RQ2), whereas eight of them were expected to be improved and five additional ones improved. Based on the assessments and the retrospectives, user stories seem to be the most powerful agile practice in this case study. Nonetheless, we also expected ten to be improved that did not change, which we trace back to several aspects, e.g. missing agile culture/mind set, missing documentation-awareness in agile. But overall, the results were very positive.

Besides the concrete results presented in the previous paragraphs, we learned a lot during this study and would like to share these lessons such that other companies could benefit from:

- A pre-post-comparison is very helpful for evaluating the effects of the implemented (process) improvements
- External interviewers are better to provide objective results
- Some agile practices are easier to be established than others, for example UserStories can be integrated independent of most context issues. Whereas other practices, especially meetings, have the problem that they involve several people
- Experience in agile is necessary to suggest (appropriate) agile practices
- especially to fill the identified gaps from the initial analysis
- Often the practices do have more effects than expected, especially when considering some of them in combination

Even if the study gives a good idea of how software process improvement works by integration in agile practices, we have some ideas of how to further proceed within this study and topic in general. The future work on the one hand deals with the study itself, which would mainly focus on a long-term check of how the agile practices influence the daily development. This would mean another assessment (if necessary including a retrospective) after some more months of using the new way of developing. Furthermore, we could address some of the mentioned limitations regarding the generalizability (cf. Section 5), e.g. performing similar studies with different companies from different domains. If we would have had more time for this overall improvement, we would even have implemented the single agile practices after each other.

Regarding the overall initiative, our idea would be to combine the elicited findings, what and how the single agile practices improve, with other existing data to come up with some kind of knowledge for goal-oriented process improvement using agile practices. Finally, another aspect for future work might be the integration of aspects from the agile development (e.g. agile methods or practice) into the used standard ISO 29110. However, this is a generic lack which research is currently trying to overcome, e.g. in the medical domain by creating a technical report [27].

Acknowlegements. We would like to thank all interview participants for their time and the openness. Furthermore, we thank Prof. Oberweis and Mr. Zehler for providing feedback on the paper.

References

1. Sommerville, I.: Software Engineering. vol. 9. Pearson Studium (2012)
2. Agile Alliance: Manifesto for Agile Software Development (2001). http://agilemanifesto. org/
3. Schmitt, A., Diebold, P.: Why do we do software process improvement? In: Abrahamsson, P., Jedlitschka, A., Nguyen Duc, A., Felderer, M., Amasaki, S., Mikkonen, T. (eds.) PROFES 2016. LNCS, vol. 10027, pp. 360–367. Springer, Cham (2016). https://doi.org/10. 1007/978-3-319-49094-6_23
4. Turner, R., Jain, A.: Agile meets CMMI: culture clash or common cause? In: Wells, D., Williams, L. (eds.) XP/Agile Universe 2002. LNCS, vol. 2418, pp. 153–165. Springer, Heidelberg (2002). https://doi.org/10.1007/3-540-45672-4_15
5. International Organization for Standardization: ISO/IEC 29110: Systems and software engineering - Lifecycle profiles for Very Small Entities (2015)
6. VersionOne: The 9th Annual State of Agile™ Survey Report. VersionOne, Inc. (2015)
7. Kumos, A.: International Study: Status Quo Agile 2014. University of Applied Science Koblenz (2014)
8. Diebold, P., Ostberg, J.-P., Wagner, S., Zendler, U.: What do practitioners vary in using scrum? In: Lassenius, C., Dingsøyr, T., Paasivaara, M. (eds.) XP 2015. LNBIP, vol. 212, pp. 40–51. Springer, Cham (2015). https://doi.org/10.1007/978-3-319-18612-2_4
9. Laporte, C., O'Connor, R.: Systems and software engineering standards for very small entities: implementation and initial results. In: Proceedings of QUATIC 2014, pp. 38–47 (2014)
10. Laporte, C., O'Connor, R., Paucar, L.: Software engineering standards and guides for very small entities: implementation in two startups. In: Proceedings of ENASE 2015 (2015)
11. Brodman, J., Johnson, D.: A software process improvement approach tailored for small organizations and small projects. In: Proceedings of ICSE 1997, pp. 661–662 (1997)
12. Johnson, D., Brodman, J.: Applying CMM project planning practices to diverse environments. IEEE Softw. 17(4), 40–47 (2000)
13. Coleman, G., O'Connor, R.: An investigation into software development process formation in software start-ups. J. Enterp. Inf. Manag. 21(6), 633–648 (2008)
14. May, B.: Applying lean startup: an experience report - Lean & lean UX by a UX veteran: lessons learned in creating & launching a complex consumer app. In: Proceedings of Agile 2012, pp. 141–147 (2012)
15. O'Donnell, M.J., Richardson, I.: Problems encountered when implementing agile methods in a very small company. Softw. Process Improv. 16, 13–24 (2008)
16. Runeson, P., Höst, M.: Guidelines for conducting and reporting case study research in software engineering. Empi. Softw. Eng. 14(2), 131–164 (2009)
17. Runeson, P., Host, M., Rainer, A., Regnell, B.: Case Study Research in Software Engineering: Guidelines and Examples, 237 p. Wiley, Hoboken (2012)
18. SCAMPI Team: CMMI Institute: Standard CMMI Appraisal Method for Process Improvement (SCAMPI) Version 1.3b: Method Definition Document for SCAMPI A, B, and C. 277 p, December 2014
19. Pikkarainen, M., Salo, O., Still, J.: Deploying agile practices in organizations: a case study. In: Richardson, I., Abrahamsson, P., Messnarz, R. (eds.) EuroSPI 2005. LNCS, vol. 3792, pp. 16–27. Springer, Heidelberg (2005). https://doi.org/10.1007/11586012_3
20. Diebold, P., Zehler, T.: The right degree of agility in rich processes. Managing Software Process Evolution, pp. 15–37. Springer, Cham (2016). https://doi.org/10.1007/978-3-319-31545-4_2

21. Cohn, M.: User Stories Applied: for Agile Software Development. Addison-Wesley, Boston (2004)
22. Cohn, M.: Agile Estimating and Planning. Prentice Hall, Upper Saddle River (2006)
23. Mahnic, V., Hovelja, T.: On using planning poker for estimating user stories. J. Syst. Softw. **85**(9), 2086–2095 (2012)
24. Newkirk, J.: Introduction to agile processes and extreme programming. In: Proceedings of ICSE 2002, pp. 695–696 (2002)
25. Beck, K.: Extreme programming explained: Embrace change, 1st edn. Addison-Wesley Professional, Boston (2000)
26. McConnell, S.: Code complete: [a practical handbook of software construction], 2nd edn. Microsoft Press, Redmond (2004). http://swbplus.bsz-bwde/bsz113031793cov.htm
27. Association for the Advancement of Medical Instrumentation: AAMI TIR45: 2012 - Guidance on the use of Agile practices in the development of medical device software (2012)
28. Feldt, R., Magazinius, A.: Validity Threats in Empirical Software Engineering Research - An Initial Survey (2010)

Implementation of a DevOps Pipeline
for Serverless Applications

Vitalii Ivanov[1] and Kari Smolander[2(✉)]

[1] Dream Broker Oy, Helsinki, Finland
vitalii.ivanov@dreambroker.fi
[2] Lappeenranta University of Technology, PL20, 53851 Lappeenranta, Finland
kari.smolander@lut.fi

Abstract. Context: The term "serverless" defines applications that use elements of Function as a Service or Backend as a Service cloud models in their architectures. Serverless promises infrastructure and operations cost reduction, faster software development, and automatic application scalability. Although many practitioners agree that Serverless simplifies operations part of DevOps, it still requires a new approach to automation practices because of the differences in its design and development workflow. **Goal:** The goal of this paper is to explore how Serverless affects DevOps practices and demonstrate a DevOps pipeline implementation for a Serverless case project. **Method:** As the method, we use the design science research, where the resulting artefact is a release and monitoring pipeline designed and implemented according to the requirements of the case organization. **Results:** The result of the study is an automated DevOps pipeline with an implementation of Continuous Integration, Continuous Delivery and Monitoring practices as required by the Serverless approach of the case project. **Conclusions:** The outcome shows how strongly the Serverless approach affects some automation practices such as test execution, deployment and monitoring of the application. In total, 18 out of 27 implemented practices were influenced by the Serverless-specific features of the project.

Keywords: DevOps · Serverless · Design science research
Continuous integration · Continuous delivery

1 Introduction

Over the last decade, DevOps has become an important part of the software engineering culture in many successful companies. This term defines the combination of practices, tools and principles aiming at faster feature release, improved quality assurance, and enhanced collaboration within the team [1]. DevOps has been influenced by the wide adoption of microservices, containers and cloud computing [2]. A recent step in the evolution of the cloud-based and microservice architecture is the serverless computing – a code execution model where the cloud provider takes total responsibility for the operating system and hardware management. The purpose of the serverless computing is to simplify an operations part of DevOps, and to provide a

M. Kuhrmann et al. (Eds.): PROFES 2018, LNCS 11271, pp. 48–64, 2018.
https://doi.org/10.1007/978-3-030-03673-7_4

scalable execution architecture and a predictable pricing model, where platform users pay only for the computing that they use without the need to pay for idle resources.

Despite the large number of materials investigating the serverless use cases [3], scalability [4], cloud providers, platforms [5] and success stories of this new cloud computing model [6], fewer studies are focused on the DevOps practices supporting Serverless applications. Even if the serverless computing is by design aimed at the simplification of operations processes, it still requires making some changes in the DevOps practices, for example in the test execution, deployment and monitoring. How exactly should these practices be implemented depends on the specific use case of the serverless computing and the particular project. In general, the serverless concept is the same regardless of the provider and the platform, so the experience from one project might be useful for many other applications.

This paper describes an implementation of a DevOps pipeline for the Serverless application that includes Continuous Integration (CI), Continuous Delivery (CD) and Monitoring practices implemented according to the requirements for the case project, such as the technology stack and the software architecture. The pipeline design and implementation decisions are based on interviews with the experts from the case company and its operating environment.

This paper tries to answer the following research questions related to the requirements for the DevOps pipeline for Serverless applications:

- RQ1. What are the requirements for the DevOps pipeline for Serverless applications?
- RQ2. How does the Serverless architecture affect DevOps practices such as CI, CD and Monitoring of the application?
- RQ3. How well does the implemented DevOps pipeline fulfil the business requirements?

The rest of this paper is organized as follows. Section 2 reviews the existing literature about DevOps and Serverless applications, as well as describes how to combine them together. Section 3 describes our research method. Section 4 provides the results of the interviews and the detailed description of our DevOps pipeline implementation. Section 5 discusses the results and Sect. 6 concludes the study.

2 Background and Related Work

2.1 DevOps

DevOps is a relatively new term that appeared a decade ago [7]. Initially it was a word to explain the need of collaboration between development (DEV) and operations (OPS) teams. DevOps does not have a single generally adopted definition and many companies understand it differently [8]. For instance, possible definitions are "a way of collaboration in which processes are automated as much as possible", "aspect of organizational culture in which DEV and OPS personnel work together closely" or "the principles and practices which are needed to create a scalable service infrastructure" [9].

From the software architecture perspective, DevOps has an impact on the development cycle including build, test, deployment, and monitoring phases [10]. In addition, DevOps literature usually includes source control practices because they play a crucial role in code sharing and team collaboration [11, 12]. Most of the DevOps automation practices can be grouped into CI, CD and Monitoring categories.

CI can be defined as a software development practice where developers merge their code changes into the shared code base as often as possible and these changes are validated by running code quality tools, building the project and running automated tests [13].

CD is the next step after CI that makes sure that a project is ready to be released at any time by request. It can be released to development, staging or production environments. Continuous Deployment is another similar term, which means that the deployment of successful builds to the chosen environment happens automatically after every commit to selected branches [11].

Continuous Monitoring is the set of practices used to monitor applications' runtime behaviour for early detection of problems, such as performance degradation or business logic errors [14].

CI and CD practices together can be called a release engineering pipeline [8]. This pipeline can also be called with a broader term – the DevOps pipeline - especially if it includes additional practices such as Continuous Monitoring.

2.2   Serverless Applications

The term "serverless" first appeared in the context of cloud-based computing in 2014, when Amazon launched its AWS Lambda service [15]. AWS Lambda allows deploying individual functions to the cloud and paying only for their execution, while avoiding unnecessary expenses for the idle resources. This model is called Serverless Computing or Function as a Service (FaaS), a cloud computing execution model where the logic runs in stateless containers that are event-triggered and fully managed by third party platforms [16]. The term "serverless" also defines the Backend as a Service (BaaS) model that relies on an extensive use of backend services such as databases or authentication managers provided by external vendors [15]. The term "serverless" does not mean that there is no server-side logic or servers in general. It emphasizes that developers can delegate to the cloud provider most of the operational tasks related to the server maintenance such as operating system updates, fault-tolerance, scalability and monitoring [17].

The combined use of BaaS and FaaS allows building the applications while minimizing expenses for infrastructure and server maintenance [4]. The applications that use BaaS, FaaS or both of them are called Serverless Applications or applications with Serverless Architecture [16].

Serverless applications promise *low cost, enhanced scalability* and *decreased time to market* [3, 15]. They also have their weaknesses and limitations such as *latency of code execution, limited life-span* [3, 15], and potential *vendor lock-in* because the code running in a serverless environment is usually dependent on other services such as database, logging or API mapper provided by the same platform [4].

The common use cases of Serverless applications include websites, chatbots, triggered processing, scheduled events and big data processing. CPU-intensive long running tasks and real-time processing such as multiplayer-intensive games should not use a Serverless architecture [18, 19].

2.3 DevOps for Serverless Applications

The analysis of the existing literature allows to reveal a common pattern that cloud-based architectures encourage the use of DevOps through the decomposition of the system into smaller and more manageable components which leads to smaller teams and simplifies the process of decision making related to every single component, compared to large monolithic systems [2, 20]. Serverless computing, the next step in the evolution of cloud services, is sometimes even described even as the No-Ops solution [21], but in practice, it still requires a CI/CD pipeline and maintenance operations [22].

The Serverless architecture brings advantages to the DevOps process. From the very beginning, it offers operability, as the serverless approach already combines DEV and OPS and even erases the difference between DEV and OPS specialists [23]. The DevOps challenges for Serverless applications include complicated local debugging because the applications are executed in a cloud and usually tightly coupled with other cloud services [17]. Serverless platforms provide limited access to the execution infrastructure. Developers no longer have access to the servers needed for monitoring the behaviour of applications on the operating system level [17].

Serverless applications make CI and CD practices "a new normal" [23]. The resulting infrastructure can be easily modified because Serverless computing implies that configurations and business logic are stored together in the same repository. This close connection between the business logic and the infrastructure together with the atomic nature of serverless functions makes deployments and rollbacks simple with the help of Infrastructure as Code (IaC) tools that help to provision cloud platforms and data centres through the declarative description of used services and their interconnections.

To summarize, there are not many academic research papers on DevOps for Serverless applications but there are much more practical applications in the industry. This confirms the observation made by Dingsøyr and Lassenius that DevOps topics are industry rather than research driven [24].

3   Research Process

The method used in this paper is the design science research method described in the guideline by Peffers et al. [25]. This method was chosen because the expected outcome of the work had to be an artefact – the designed and implemented DevOps pipeline. The design science research methodology (DSRM) process model is shown in Fig. 1. The result artefact is the DevOps pipeline created in accordance with the DSRM guidelines using four iterations of improvements. Every iteration was a two-week Scrum sprint. In the beginning of the first sprint and at the end of the last sprint, special workshops were organized to gather experiences and observations that contribute to the research questions of this work.

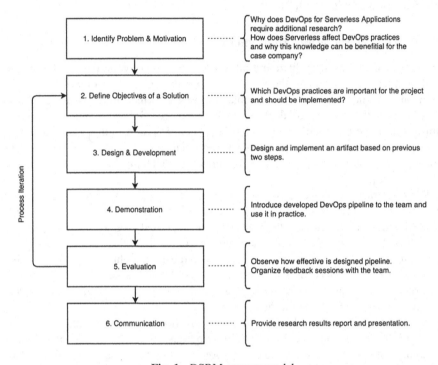

Fig. 1. DSRM process model

3.1 Data Collection

The problem and motivation identification (Step 1) was based on the practical need of the case project and supported by a preliminary literature review. The identified problem and motivation were discussed and approved by the stakeholders within the case company. In order to gather requirements, define the objectives (Step 2) and evaluate the solution (Step 5), a series of workshops was organized. The first workshop focusing on defining the objectives lasted four hours. The workshop was attended by a DevOps engineer, a team lead, two developers and a QA engineer. The participants discussed CI, CD and Monitoring practices, evaluated their importance, the amount of efforts required for their implementation, and answered the question of how does Serverless architecture affects these practices. Based on the results of the first workshop, the first version of the pipeline was designed (Step 3) and discussed with the development team (Steps 4 and 5). After the discussion, it was modified and introduced into the project workflow. After this, the process was repeated in an iterative way: first, the evaluation and objectives definition discussion (Step 2), then the design and development (Step 3), then the demonstration and use (Steps 4 and 5). These steps were repeated four times with an interval of two weeks. The final review session was organized as a workshop that was attended by the senior DevOps engineer, the team lead, two developers and the QA engineer. The goal of the final workshop was to get feedback about the implemented DevOps pipeline. The content of the workshop was organized in the following way: the organizer presented the architecture of the project, noted the Serverless parts of it and described all the steps of the DevOps pipeline execution. The participants were free to ask their questions and give the suggestions during the presentation. At the end of the presentation, the participants answered the questions of what the best parts and risky parts of the pipeline are and also went through the initial list of the selected DevOps practices to discuss how exactly each of them was implemented.

In addition to the workshops within the company, two developers and one QA engineer outside of the case company were interviewed to get their opinion about the influence of Serverless architecture on DevOps automation practices. All interviewees participated in development and maintenance of the Serverless projects.

The data gathered from the workshops was mostly qualitative. Every new review session provided more qualitative data about the current version of the DevOps pipeline. For the final pipeline, the authors made an estimation of the costs based on the pricing model of AWS cloud platform.

3.2   The Case Description

The case project is a web service for processing binary files. For authentication, it uses a third-party authentication service. This paper does not describe the domain field and the exact features of the case project. The architecture is shown sufficiently to present the DevOps pipeline designed and implemented into the project. The project was designed using Amazon Web Services including AWS Lambda. The project design decisions were accepted as an input data to this study.

The container diagram of the project is shown in Fig. 2 which uses a C4 model [26]. All containers except for the web client are hosted at the Amazon cloud platform and use particular AWS services. The icons inside the blocks are official icons of Amazon Web Services, which correspond to the container names. The case project uses the following Amazon services: API Gateway, AWS Lambda, S3, DynamoDB and SNS. The web client is a web application running in a browser.

The container diagram demonstrates that all the backend logic of the application is stored in AWS Lambda functions. Solutions used for data storage, such as DynamoDB and S3 buckets, may also be considered as Serverless, because they are provided by the cloud platform and do not require any server configuration. It means that the case project can be considered as a project with a clean Serverless architecture using FaaS and BaaS services. Serverless patterns used in the application are the following: *the use of AWS Lambda with AWS services as event sources* where S3 bucket triggers a function when a file uploading is finished, *on-demand Lambda function invocation over HTTPS* (Amazon API Gateway) where the gateway is configured to map incoming requests to the particular functions, *fan-out pattern* to distribute a message over multiple subscribers and finally *custom authorizer pattern* where all requests to the API Gateway are validated by the AWS Lambda function with the authentication logic.

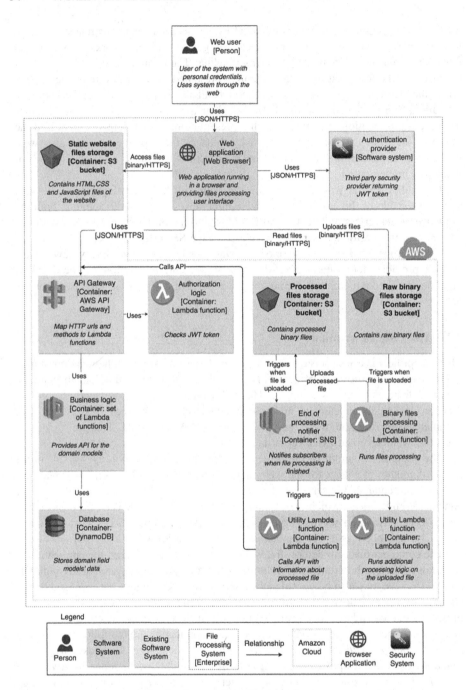

Fig. 2. Case project container diagram

4   Results

4.1   Influence of Serverless Architectures on DevOps Practices

To elicit requirements for a DevOps pipeline a series of workshops and interviews was organized. They helped to identify and select which CI, CD and Monitoring practices are required for the case project and to gather opinions of the participants on how Serverless architecture affects these practices. Based on the popular DevOps literature analysis, 27 practices were selected for the discussions [10–12]. The results of the workshops and interviews are summarized in Table 1. The column "Importance" answers the question "How important is implementation of the practice for the case project". The result value is the average of the grades given by the participants of the workshop where 0 means "no need to implement" and 10 means "must be implemented". The column "Affected by Serverless" answers the question "Is the implementation of this DevOps practice affected by Serverless architecture", meaning to ask if the implementation of the practice is impacted by the use of FaaS/BaaS platforms or if it requires Serverless-specific tools. For instance, the practice "Fully scripted deployments" is impacted by Serverless approach because it requires special tools to deploy an application to the external platform such as AWS Lambda. In this case, a tool can be for example CloudFormation or Serverless Framework. If more than a half of the interview participants answered "yes", the column "Affected by Serverless" was marked as "Yes".

The results of the workshop and interviews showed that 18 out of 27 DevOps automation practices selected for this research are affected by the Serverless architecture. It influences 2 out of 6 *source control*, 2 out of 5 *build process* and 5 out of 7 *testing and QA* practices. The results showed that all 4 selected *deployment* and all 5 *monitoring* practices are affected by Serverless. The practices that have a grade of Importance of 5 or more were considered worth implementing in the pipeline. This criterion was based on the estimation of available human resources and deadlines of the case project. In general, during the workshop it was emphasized that the company requires a reliable DevOps pipeline to guarantee high quality of the code through build process, QA and deployment automation, source control and monitoring.

A constraint for the DevOps pipeline was the use of the GitLab Community Edition. The AWS-based architecture of the case project also included some constraints for the future DevOps pipeline such as the use of certain IaC tools and AWS cloud platform by itself. Choosing Node.js as the project implementation technology affected the choice of unit testing frameworks and mocking libraries. No limitations for the cost of the pipeline execution were declared. The research plan covered two months of work on design and implementation of DevOps pipeline.

4.2   Design and Implementation of the Pipeline

The DevOps pipeline components are shown in Fig. 3. When the engineers push the code to the GitLab Server, it triggers the GitLab Runner (#3). The GitLab Runner executes CI and CD pipelines that consist of jobs. The Job is the GitLab term that describes an activity in a CI/CD pipeline. The jobs are run using Docker containers

Table 1. Influence of Serverless on DevOps practices and importance for the case project

#	Practice	Category	Importance (0–10)	Affected by Serverless (Y/N)
1	VCS is used to store code history and share the code	Source control	10	Yes
2	Log aggregation	Monitoring	10	Yes
3	Build process is run automatically on commit	Build process	9	No
4	Build artefacts are managed by purpose-built tools, no manual scripts	Build process	9	Yes
5	Dependencies are managed in a repository	Build process	9	No
6	Automatic unit testing with every build	Testing & QA	9	No
7	Automated end-to-end testing	Testing & QA	9	Yes
8	Fully scripted deployments	Deployment	9	Yes
9	Standard deployments across all environments	Deployment	9	Yes
10	Finding specific events in the past	Monitoring	9	Yes
11	Active alerting according to the user-defined heuristics	Monitoring	9	Yes
12	Branches are used for isolating work	Source Control	8	No
13	Peer-reviews	Testing & QA	8	No
14	Mockups & proxies used	Testing & QA	8	Yes
15	Large scale graphing of the trends (such as requests per minute)	Monitoring	8	Yes
16	Tracing	Monitoring	8	Yes
17	Pre-tested merge commits	Source Control	7	No
18	All artefacts have build versions with commit or CI build number	Build Process	7	Yes
19	Build environment based on VMs	Build Process	7	No
20	Code coverage and static code analysis is measured	Testing & QA	7	Yes
21	Integrated management and maintenance of the test data	Testing & QA	7	Yes
22	Automated performance & security tests in target environment	Testing & QA	7	Yes
23	Auto deploy to the test environment after tests pass	Deployment	7	Yes

(*continued*)

Table 1. (*continued*)

#	Practice	Category	Importance (0–10)	Affected by Serverless (Y/N)
24	All commits are tied to the tasks	Source control	6	No
25	Database deployments	Deployment	6	Yes
26	Release notes auto-generated	Source control	3	Yes
27	Version control DB schema changes	Source control	0	No

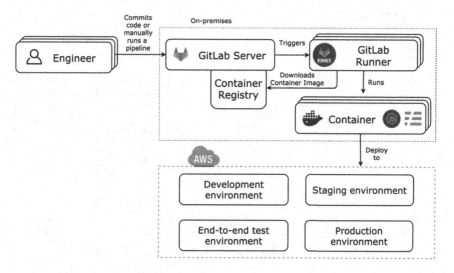

Fig. 3. DevOps pipeline components

with the required build environment, including the following tools: npm, Node.js, and Serverless Framework (#19). The images of the Docker containers are stored in GitLab Container Registry that is also a part of GitLab suite.

Figure 3 shows that the GitLab suite, including Runner instances, is deployed and works on the company's premises. However, the case project, having a cloud-oriented architecture, is deployed on the AWS cloud infrastructure (#9).

The case project was split into three subprojects and each of them is stored in a separate VCS repository: "API-service", "files-processing-service" and "static-website". The separation was based on the purpose of the Lambda functions following the best practices provided by Munns [27]. One of the practices says, "Unless independent Lambda functions share event sources, split them into their own code repositories". Each of these subprojects has its own Serverless Framework definition file that enables their independent maintenance and deployment.

GitLab requires the use of Git as the version control system (#1). A Git branching model described by Driessen [28] was chosen as the development workflow (#12). The model uses so-called feature branches. There are a develop branch with the latest development changes merged from feature branches, release branches with the version ready for internal testing and a master branch with a stable production-ready version.

All commits to develop, release and master branches should be done through merge requests. The merge request feature is supported by GitLab. A code review should be conducted after submitting a merge request and before merging. GitLab provides a user interface for reviewing the code of the merge requests (#13).

Figure 4 shows CI and CD pipeline of the case project using Ståhl & Bosch notation [29].

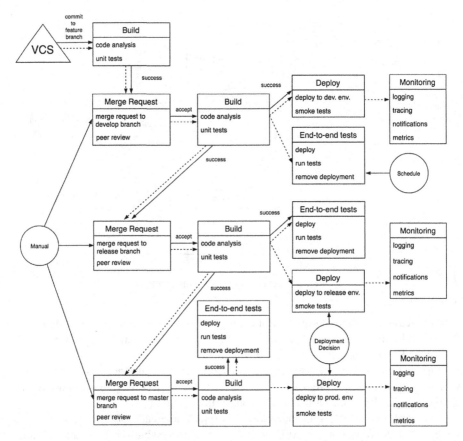

Fig. 4. CI, CD and monitoring pipeline

The Git workflow model suggests that the developer checks out the code and creates a feature branch. The input to the pipeline is a commit to the feature branch. After the local development and testing, the changes from the branch are committed into the repository. The commit triggers the build process in GitLab that runs the code analysis and unit tests (#6, 20). The choice of the libraries and code analysis tools depends on the developer's preferences and can be changed, but Serverless architecture requires special tools to mock external dependencies such as cloud databases (#14).

The merge request from the feature branch triggers the build in the develop branch. After the build is successfully finished, code is deployed to the cloud platform using a development account. End-to-end tests of the development pipeline are run nightly to minimize the cost of the pipeline execution (#7).

The changes in the develop branch can be committed to the release branch. Again, the commit again runs the build but this time it triggers the end-to-end tests automatically (#7, 23). The reason for this is that commits into the release branch are done less often than to the develop branch. It is assumed that the develop branch will receive five merge requests per day and the release branch only one merge request per two weeks. The changes in the release branch are deployed for internal testing conducted by the end users within the company.

After the release version has been tested and all of the bug fixes have been applied, the changes can be committed to the master branch and deployed to the production environment. Committing to the master branch is also done through a merge request and is followed by the build process.

All deployments are done with the help of the Serverless Framework (#4, 8). After the deployment is done, smoke tests are executed to check that the application was successfully deployed and its most important functions work normally. The Serverless Framework configuration file also describes the monitoring infrastructure and activities that should be applied to the running application. The data received from the deployed service is an input to the monitoring tools that also run in the cloud.

This pipeline can be scaled up for implementing new services. The approach with atomic deployments of the services assumes that every service can follow its own release roadmap and be deployed independently.

End-to-end tests for Serverless applications require a deployment of the services in the cloud to achieve a production-like environment. This approach requires a cloud infrastructure description that can be done with specific IaC tools such as Serverless Framework and AWS CloudFormation.

Monitoring of the application is implemented using the AWS tools: CloudWatch (#2, 10), Alarms (#11), Metrics (#15), and X-Ray (#16). AWS Lambda functions write the logs to the CloudWatch Logs, where they are aggregated by function names. Metrics that were chosen for the pipeline implementation are AWS Lambda function duration, invocations, errors and throttles, S3 buckets number of objects and size, DynamoDB provisioned write and read capacity units. They can be easily changed in the future depending on the criteria that engineers will find important.

5   Discussion

5.1   Answers to Research Questions

RQ1 What are the Requirements for the DevOps Pipeline for Serverless Applications?
25 out of 27 suggested DevOps automation practices were marked as important for the case project. These practices were related to source control, build process, deployment, testing & QA, deployment and monitoring. The most critical DevOps automation practices were the use of VCS (#1) and log aggregation (#2). The team found "release notes auto-generation" (#26) as one of two least important practices among suggested. "Version control DB schema changes" (#27) was called as an important practice for relational databases but in the context of the case project and its schemaless database this practice was also marked as not important.
DevOps pipeline requirements correspond to findings in existing studies about implementation and adoption of DevOps automation practices [30, 31]. No unusual expectations from CI, CD and Monitoring practices were identified even if it was clear that their implementation will be affected by Serverless features.

RQ2 How Does the Serverless Architecture Affect DevOps Practices such as CI, CD and Monitoring of the Application?
18 out of 27 DevOps automation practices were affected by Serverless. There was no group of DevOps automation practices that would not be influenced by this new cloud computing model. Monitoring practices were most significantly influenced by the Serverless (#2, 10, 11, 15, 16). This can be explained by the close connection of Serverless computing services with cloud platforms and by the fact that the monitoring services are provided on the same platform. The least impact Serverless makes on the source control practices. However, Serverless influences the important decision of how to organize the code in the VCS repositories (#1). Serverless functions can be placed each one into a separate repository or several functions into one service according to their purpose or domain field. This decision can influence all other decisions in the DevOps pipeline.

The implementation of the pipeline showed that the Serverless architecture strongly affects the choice of the tools, for instance, IaC solutions and mocking libraries (#14). The close connection of Serverless applications with the cloud infrastructures usually requires the deployment of the application to the cloud platform and a heavy use of the cloud platform services. The existence of Serverless-oriented tools such as Serverless Framework shows that developers and DevOps engineers have realised the high demand of specialized tools to maintain Serverless applications.

Lack of research on the interconnection between the Serverless architecture and DevOps practices makes it difficult to compare our results with previous studies. However, our results match the observations made by practitioners in the software development industry. For instance, design of Serverless applications makes the local deployment environment unnecessary but requires the developers to have knowledge about operations [23]. In addition, extensive automated testing and full-scale CI/CD are important, and the risk of a vendor lock-in becomes higher [32].

RQ3 How well does the Implemented DevOps Pipeline Fulfil Business Requirements?

The implemented DevOps pipeline fulfils all the requirements identified in RQ1. The pipeline includes all of the practices selected in the workshop on DevOps automation of the case project and ensures high quality of the code through unit tests, code quality check tools and end-to-end testing [33]. It allows separating the stable production version from a release candidate and the version that is under active development.

Stakeholders had positive expectations for Serverless applications and they were mostly related to the scalable execution model without a server configuration. Some of the concerns about this new cloud computing model were directly related to the DevOps, such as the use of IaC and the lack of experience with the Serverless approach. These problems were solved using the Serverless Framework - the tool that forms the core of the implemented pipeline. Although the tool was new for the team, it allowed reducing the risk of unexpected problems and lack of knowledge about Serverless application development.

There were no initial requirements regarding the costs of the pipeline execution, but the estimated costs were called by the participants of the final evaluation workshop as 'very low' for the enterprise company especially considering the comprehensive test coverage ensured by the designed pipeline. The estimated expenses for the end-to-end testing are just $50.49 per month with turned on CloudWatch alarms and metrics and $10.49 without them. These numbers include expenses for API Gateway calls, AWS Lambda functions requests and computing, CloudWatch logs storage, X-Ray tracing, DynamoDB and S3 reads and writes. Even with 20 times more intensive testing, the price will be only $249.83. The cost of the Lambda functions execution only is $12.08 for 1000 test set executions. The affordable pricing model of Serverless computing is confirmed by existing research [3]. The price of production and release execution was not calculated because it is not related to the DevOps pipeline and mostly depends on the popularity of the project and the expected intensity of its use.

5.2   Threats to Validity

The designed pipeline presented in this paper has been validated only in the case project. The implemented DevOps practices might not be fully applicable to every Serverless application. The factors that might affect the DevOps decisions include the size of the project, its architecture and technology stack, the size and experience of the team, culture within the company and requirements from the tools and processes used in the team.

However, interviews with the software engineers outside of the case company helped us to build less biased picture about the influence of Serverless architecture to DevOps practices.

6 Conclusions

All of the 27 identified DevOps automation and monitoring practices could be used in our Serverless case project. 18 out of 27 practices were affected by Serverless. The use of design science as the research method produced an artefact, the DevOps pipeline for Serverless applications that illustrates these practices and their automation. The qualitative data, design, and implementation of the pipeline showed that some of the practices are strongly affected by this new cloud computing execution model. These practices included, for instance, standard deployment to all environments, use of mock-ups in unit testing and all monitoring practices. The high popularity of serverless-oriented tools that are aimed to simplifying debugging, deployment to multiple environments and declarative definition of the infrastructure for the applications such as Serverless Framework, suggests the importance of solving these challenges in practice.

The results of the study do not contradict the results of existing research on Serverless computing, such as expected benefits and concerns about Serverless applications. Inexpensive pricing model and simpler environment configuration were described as the benefits of the Serverless computing. The concerns, such as vendor lock-in and complicated debugging were also noted also in the case project. Interviewees in the study also agreed that Serverless architecture requires knowledge of both DEV and OPS practices and might raise the popularity of a new role of Cloud Engineer that would combine DevOps Engineer and Software Developer skills.

Future research in this field should include deeper studies regarding the impact of Serverless architectures on testing & QA practices, such as performance and security testing. Security of Serverless applications can also be an additional research direction since the vendor of the host environment applies some privacy control limitations on the execution of the system.

Acknowledgements. We wish to thank all participants for their time and contributions.

References

1. Riungu-Kalliosaari, L., Mäkinen, S., Lwakatare, L.E., Tiihonen, J., Männistö, T.: DevOps adoption benefits and challenges in practice: a case study. In: Abrahamsson, P., Jedlitschka, A., Nguyen Duc, A., Felderer, M., Amasaki, S., Mikkonen, T. (eds.) PROFES 2016. LNCS, vol. 10027, pp. 590–597. Springer, Cham (2016). https://doi.org/10.1007/978-3-319-49094-6_44
2. Balalaie, A., Heydarnoori, A., Jamshidi, P.: Microservices architecture enables DevOps: Migration to a cloud-native architecture. IEEE Softw. **33**(3), 42–52 (2016)
3. Adzic, G., Chatley, R.: Serverless computing: economic and architectural impact. In Proceedings of the 2017 11th Joint Meeting on Foundations of Software Engineering, pp. 884–889. ACM, Padeborn (2017)
4. Sbarski, P., Kroonenburg, S.: Serverless Architectures on AWS: With examples using AWS Lambda. Manning Publications Company, Shelter Island (2017)
5. Rodgers, J.: Serverless Hosting Comparison. https://headmelted.com/serverless-showdown-4a771ca561d2. Accessed 03 Jun 2018

6. Montiel, I.: How We Migrated our Startup to Serverless. https://read.acloud.guru/our-serverless-journey-part-2-908d76d03716. Accessed 03 Jun 2018
7. Kim, G.: Top 11 Things you Need to Know about DevOps. https://www.thinkhdi.com/~/media/HDICorp/Files/White-Papers/whtppr-1112-devops-kim.pdf. Accessed 03 Jun 2018
8. Dyck, A., Penners, R., Lichter, H.: Towards definitions for release engineering and DevOps. In: Release Engineering (RELENG), IEEE/ACM 3rd International Workshop, pp. 3–3. IEEE (2015)
9. Erich, F.M.A., Amrit, C., Daneva, M.: A qualitative study of DevOps usage in practice. J. Softw. Evol. Process **29**(6), e1885 (2017)
10. Bass, L., Weber, I., Zhu, L.: DevOps: A Software Architect's Perspective. Addison-Wesley Professional, Boston (2015)
11. Humble, J., Farley, D.: Continuous Delivery: Reliable Software Releases through Build, Test, and Deployment Automation. Pearson Education, London (2010)
12. Kim, G., Debois, P., Willis, J., Humble, J.: The DevOps Handbook: How to Create World-Class Agility, Reliability, and Security in Technology Organizations. IT Revolution (2016)
13. Fowler, M.: Continuous integration. https://martinfowler.com/articles/continuousIntegration.html. Accessed 03 Jun 2018
14. Fitzgerald, B., Stol, K.J.: Continuous software engineering and beyond: trends and challenges. In: Proceedings of the 1st International Workshop on Rapid Continuous Software Engineering, pp. 1–9. ACM, Hyderabad (2014)
15. Chapin, J., Roberts, M.: What is Serverless. O'Reilly Media Inc., Sebastopol (2017)
16. Roberts, M.: Serverless architectures. https://martinfowler.com/articles/serverless.html. Accessed 03 Jun 2018
17. Baldini, I., et al.: Serverless computing: current trends and open problems. In: Chaudhary, S., Somani, G., Buyya, R. (eds.) Research Advances in Cloud Computing, pp. 1–20. Springer, Singapore (2017). https://doi.org/10.1007/978-981-10-5026-8_1
18. Zambrano, B.: Serverless Design Patterns and Best Practices. Packt Publishing, Birmingham (2018)
19. Zanon, D.: Building Serverless Web Applications. Packt Publishing, Birmingham (2017)
20. Cukier, D.: DevOps patterns to scale web applications using cloud services. In: Proceedings of the 2013 companion publication for conference on Systems, programming & applications: software for humanity, pp. 143–152. ACM, Indianapolis (2013)
21. Claburn, T.: From DevOps to No-Ops: El Reg Chats Serverless Computing with NYT's CTO. https://bit.ly/2waLJXz. Accessed 03 Jun 2018
22. Becker, T.: A Production-grade CI/CD Pipeline for Serverless Applications (2018). https://bit.ly/2PjPN0m. Accessed 03 Jun 2018
23. Gancarz, R.: Serverless takes DevOps to the Next Level (2017). https://www.infoq.com/articles/serverless-takes-devops-next-level. Accessed 03 Jun 2018
24. Dingsøyr, T., Lassenius, C.: Emerging themes in agile software development: Introduction to the special section on continuous value delivery. Inf. Softw. Technol. **77**, 56–60 (2016)
25. Peffers, K., Tuunanen, T., Rothenberger, M.A., Chatterjee, S.: A design science research methodology for information systems research. J. Manag. Inf. Syst. **24**(3), 45–77 (2007)
26. Brown, S.: Software Architecture for Developers, vol. 2. Visualise, document and explore your software architecture. Leanpub (2018)
27. Munns, C.: Serverless architecture patterns and best practices by Chris Munns. https://www.youtube.com/watch?v=_mB1JVlhScs. Accessed 03 Jun 2018
28. Driessen, V.: A Successful Git Branching Model. https://bit.ly/197szRP. Accessed 03 Jun 2018

29. Ståhl, D., Bosch, J.: Automated software integration flows in industry: a multiple-case study. In: Companion Proceedings of the 36th International Conference on Software Engineering, pp. 54–63. ACM, Hyderabad (2014)
30. Rejström, K.: Implementing continuous integration in a small company: A case study. Master's thesis, Aalto University, School of Science, Espoo (2016)
31. Udd, R.: Adopting continuous delivery: A case study. Master's thesis, Aalto University, School of Science, Espoo, Finland (2016)
32. Buckholz, G.: The pros and cons of a serverless DevOps solution. https://www.agileconnection.com/article/pros-and-cons-serverless-devops-solution. Accessed 03 Jun 2018
33. Ståhl, D., Bosch, J.: Experienced benefits of continuous integration in industry software product development: A case study. In The 12th iasted International Conference on Software Engineering, pp. 736–743. Innsbruck, Austria (2013)

Iterative Prototyping Methodology for the Development of Innovative and Dependable Complex Embedded Systems Through SPC&KPI Techniques

Patricia López[1(✉)], Jon Mabe[1], Leire Etxeberria[2],
and Eneko Gorritxategi[3]

[1] IK4-TEKNIKER, 20600 Eibar, Spain
{patricia.lopez,jon.mabe}@tekniker.es
[2] Mondragon Unibertsitatea, 20500 Mondragón, Spain
letxeberria@mondragon.edu
[3] Atten2 Advanced Monitoring Technologies, 20600 Eibar, Spain
egorritxategi@atten2.com

Abstract. In recent years, the use of complex embedded systems in critical domains has become increasingly widespread, driven by the emergence of Industry 4.0, Smart Grid or Smart Health Care paradigms. These latest trends require the development of smart, innovative and dependable complex systems, that combine multiple engineering disciplines, to achieve their challenging goals. In order to assist developers, researchers and designers in this development process, this paper presents a iterative prototyping methodology focused on facing challenges derived from: (i) uncertainties and risks entailed while generating new products based on novel technologies, (ii) unforeseeable interactions intrinsic to system complexity and heterogeneity (e.g.: software, hardware, chemistry, photonics, mechanics, etc.), (iii) operation dependability and regulatory requirements, and (iv) increasing importance of reducing time to market and project cost. The proposed methodology provides a complete solution based on New Product Development processes, dependability and safety standards, and Statistical Process Control (SPC) and Key Performance Indicator (KPI) techniques. Special attention is paid to the adaptation and integration of SPC and KPI techniques in the development process, as a mechanism to improve the system's functionality and dependability. Finally, the development of an innovative real-time photonic sensor for analysing lubricant quality in industrial critical applications is presented as a case study.

Keywords: Complex systems · Embedded software · Design methodology
Product development · Research and development · Dependability management

1 Introduction

In the last years, the use of complex embedded systems in critical domains such as industry, energy, manufacturing, health, etc. has increased mainly motivated by the emergence of the Industry 4.0, Smart Grid, Smart Health Care, etc. paradigms. To

© Springer Nature Switzerland AG 2018
M. Kuhrmann et al. (Eds.): PROFES 2018, LNCS 11271, pp. 65–80, 2018.
https://doi.org/10.1007/978-3-030-03673-7_5

cover these new cases, innovative, smart and dependable complex embedded systems are required. The development of such systems entails technological, scientific and operational challenges that derive from:

- Uncertainties and risks related to the generation of new products based on novel technologies and innovative ideas. A preliminary exploration and testing of intermediate solutions are necessary to specify the requirements of the final solution. Thus, understanding and specifying requirements are part of the solution-finding [1, 2].
- Unforeseeable interactions among the system components intrinsic to system heterogeneity and complexity (e.g., software, hardware, chemistry, photonics, mechanical, etc.), which need expertise in multiple engineering disciplines to be correctly designed [3, 4].
- Operation dependability and regulatory requirements imposed by critical domains such as industry or energy [5]: high sensitivity, reliable and autonomous operation, harsh environments, almost zero maintenance, minimum failure rates, etc.
- The increasing importance of time to market (TTM) and project costs reduction to be competitive [6]. In the Industrial Internet of Things context, the boundaries between traditional industry and internet companies are becoming increasingly blurred, and connectivity is opening up new business opportunities for sensor manufacturers, which require swift reaction times once the opportunity has been identified [7].

It is not trivial to find a development methodology that thoroughly covers all the above challenges. This paper presents a development methodology that adapts and combines three development approaches to support the process of bringing innovative design ideas to real dependable complex products, with limited resources (time and budget) for project execution.

On the one hand, New Product Development (NPD) processes generally cover the stages from opportunity identification to product launch. They propose a structured development process that will help in shaping the system and identifying changes and deviations at relatively early phases. Consequently, changes and deviations will impact much less on projects' cost and time, since late-stage design iterations are avoided [8]. However, this type of approach does not generally go into detail about how systems should be developed (specification, design, implementation, verification and validation phases), neither consider safety nor dependability issues.

On the other hand, there are standards that support the development of dependable and safety critical systems. Those standards require a very rigorous development process based on requirements specification and risks identification and analysis. Also, to ensure that system risks are at an acceptable level, it must be demonstrated that all prescribed activities listed in the standard have been performed. Due to the intrinsic novelty and lack of previous experience, it is not possible to accurately specify the requirements of the innovative and dependable complex embedded systems, and consequently, it is not possible to directly apply these standards in their development. However, a partial consideration of the additional demands that safety certifications impose from the beginning of the development process, could help to reduce re-design, re-verification, re-validation and refactorization effort needed to obtain a dependable and certifiable final product, as well as mitigate the problems that could appear when a novel technology drives the development of a new product [9].

Finally, to face the uncertainties regarding how the system will work, Statistical Process Control (SPC) and Key Performance Indicators (KPI) concepts are adapted and integrated into the presented methodology. These techniques are successfully applied, for instance, in industrial manufacturing to monitor and control processes. The adaptation of SPC and KPI techniques to the development of innovative and dependable complex embedded systems will help in monitoring the performance and, therefore, acquire a higher knowledge about it. This knowledge will help in identifying risks, faults, weaknesses, etc. and, consequently, improve the system's functionality and dependability.

In summary, the development process of an innovative and dependable complex embedded system starts from the identification of an idea that could not be directly translated into accurately specified systems, including risks and limitations analysis. The proposed methodology will support this process and enable the complete specification of the system while reducing and limiting the resources (time and money) invested in obtaining a certifiable final product.

The rest of the paper is organised as follows: Sect. 2 provides an overview of prior research on NPD processes, dependable and safety critical systems' development, and SPC and KPI techniques. Section 3 discusses related work. Section 4 includes a detailed description of the proposed methodology and Sect. 5 shows a case study which illustrates its applicability. Finally, Sect. 6 concludes this paper.

2 Background

This section provides a brief introduction to NPD processes, dependable and safety critical systems' development, and KPI and SPC concepts, and highlights their main contributions relevant to the work presented in this paper.

2.1 New Product Development (NPD) Processes

Regarding NPD, there are different strategies or conceptual models that might be applied to the formulation of new products development. Those models capture all development aspects: ideation and early concept validation, design and development, testing and validation, manufacturing and product launch.

Traditional NPD approaches, such as Stage-Gate [10], propose a linear or sequential process that may lack from the flexibility needed to accommodate to fast changing scenarios, with evolving and emerging requirements, uncertain environments, unforeseeable risks, etc., which is the case of the development scenarios addressed in this paper. Lately, this weakness has led to the generation of new hybrid models, such as Agile [8], Triple A [11] or Open Innovation [12] Stage-Gate, which are based on a Stage-Gate model and incorporate looping approaches (Agile development, Spiral approach, etc.). The core idea of those methods is a staging and gating process, where the stages represent the development of the project, executed by multidisciplinary teams, and the gates symbolise intermediate assessment points. At each gate, the continuation of the project is decided based on the information generated within the previous stages, including not only the technological progress but also the business case, risk analysis, and availability of necessary resources. The NPD processes are focused on the unknown, uncertain and risky parts of the project, to clarify them as early as possible with the aim of minimising project development time and cost [13]. However, this type of approaches does not cover into detail the specification, design, implementation, verification and validation development phases, nor dependability and safety concerns.

2.2   Dependable and Safety Critical Systems' Development

Dependability and safety are mainly achieved by effective planning and implementation of dependability and safety activities throughout the complete system life cycle. To develop such systems, it must be demonstrated that potential risks are at an acceptable level and that all prescribed activities listed in an applicable standard have been performed.

The generic IEC-61508 [5] and derived safety standards are based on a V-model approach for system development. First, the system must be analysed for its specific hazards and risks in its particular environment, to determine safety requirements. After that, system requirements must be traced throughout the whole development cycle, including design decisions, implementation, test cases, and final validation. To assist this process, the IEC-61508 standard proposes a combined utilisation of a set of measures and techniques to prevent and control system failures at each stage of the system's lifecycle. The effectiveness and precision with which these techniques and measures should be applied will depend on the safety level to be achieved. The main challenge of safety critical systems is to design the system in such a way as to prevent dangerous failures and to control them when they arise. This requires a good knowledge of both the system and its specific environment as well as a long and expensive development process. However, the knowledge of the system is usually minimal for innovative systems.

2.3   Statistical Process Control (SPC) and Key Performance Indicator (KPI)

Both SPC and KPI concepts are successfully applied for example in industrial manufacturing plants to monitor and control processes. On the one hand, SPC is a method of quality control which employs statistical methods to monitor, control and increase the knowledge of a process [14, 15]. Process control is mainly based on deciding and determining when a variation is natural and when it requires correction. This control is principally oriented to manufacturing processes, to prevent and detect early problems that could generate poor quality products. However, it could also be applied to non-manufacturing processes, such as software engineering processes.

On the other hand, KPIs are metrics or performance measurements used to evaluate the results of an action or strategy based on predetermined objectives. Those metrics show how a process or product progress as well as help in determining any deviation from the final objectives and defining corrective actions [16, 17].

Therefore, since verifying and validating a complex and heterogeneous system could imply more than just checking that inputs and outputs are correct, the combination and adaptation of both SPC and KPI approaches to system development could be of great value. The visualisation of the system as a plant aims to identify and statistically analyse possible deviations in the KPIs that may eventually result in more important impacts on system outputs. The application of those concepts in the development of innovative complex embedded systems, especially in design and validation phases, will help monitoring system performance and therefore acquire a higher knowledge about it. This knowledge will assist in identifying risks, faults, weaknesses, etc. and consequently adjust and improve system functionality and dependability.

3 Related Work

This section collects several scientific references, regarding hybrid approaches that try to cover the development of innovative safety and dependable systems. In general terms, those researches propose the use of agile methods for safety-critical software development and establish that if safety-critical systems require greater emphasis on activities like formal specification and requirements management, then an agile process will include these as necessary activities to methodologies [18–20]. Although those hybrid development approaches cover the innovative and the dependability and safety aspects of the proposed systems, they are mainly focused on software development and the management of the complexity and uncertainties due to system components heterogeneity (e.g., software, hardware, chemistry, photonics, mechanical, etc.) are not addressed.

4 Development Methodology

The proposed methodology combines the three approaches presented in the previous section: (i) NPD processes, (ii) dependability and safety standards, and (iii) SPC and KPI techniques. This combination offers a complete solution to assist the development of innovative and dependable complex embedded systems, with limited resources (time and budget) for project execution. The development process starts with the identification of an idea that could not be directly translated into an accurately specified system, with risks and limitations identified. The proposed methodology will support the process of bringing this idea into an utterly specified system, with identified risks and limitations and trying to limit the invested resources (time and money) to obtain a dependable and certifiable final product.

Figure 1 shows the structure of the proposed methodology. It is based on the Stage-Gate NPD model and provides a clearly defined development process that covers the stages from (i) product opportunity identification and (ii) proof-of-concept validation, through (iii) iterative prototypes development and (iv) real field validation stages and, finally, (v) product launch. The final stage (product launch) is not covered in this paper because it is more related to marketing and manufacturing than to development.

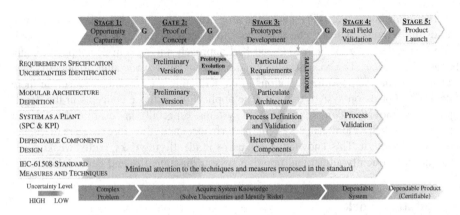

Fig. 1. Structure of the methodology in which three approaches presented are combined.

As described in the background section, in the NPD approach, all the stages are separated by gates, which are considered a crucial decision point where the continuity of the project should be evaluated based on the results obtained in previous gates and the feedback received from the client. This approach proposes a structured development focused on the unknown, uncertain and risky parts of the project, promoting the early identification of errors and deviations and, consequently, changes will have a reduced impact in projects' cost and time. Also, additional demands imposed by safety and dependability standards are partially considered in all the stages to reduce re-design, re-verification, re-validation and refactorisation effort needed to obtain a dependable and certifiable final product. On the one hand, special attention is paid to documentation and the use of specific measures and techniques for designing and testing. On the other hand, in the prototypes development stage, an iterative V-model development process is proposed. Finally, the adaptation of SPC and KPI techniques is proposed for prototype design and validation to help in monitoring system performance and, therefore, identifying risks, faults, weaknesses, etc. and, consequently, improve the system's functionality and dependability.

4.1 Opportunity Identification Stage

The first step towards a new product is to envisage an idea, vision, or concept that looks promising for a particular application. Once the problem-to-solve has been defined, and the potential solutions have been identified, the objective of this stage is to briefly determine technical, economic, intellectual property and business advantages that will help in the detailed evaluation of the suitability of the idea in the next gate.

4.2 Opportunity Identification Gate

The primary activity to accomplish at this first gate is to authorise (or not) the initialisation of the project. The decisions to be taken are related to the evaluation and acceptance of the results of the activities carried out during the opportunity identification stage. The unsuccessful results will stop the development at this point before undesired deviations could impact much more on projects' cost and time.

4.3   Proof-of-Concept Validation Stage

The primary objective of this second stage is to confirm the feasibility of the envisaged system. As in NPD approaches, it is recommended to parallelise as much as possible the required proof-of-concept developments to favour early identification of technological and functional risks, integration problems, technology, etc. Based on the results of the proof-of-concept developments, a preliminary set of requirements and a system architecture must be proposed (see Fig. 1). At this point, it is important to start identifying the requirements that cannot be accurately specified due to uncertainties. It is also recommended to assign a priority level to each identified requirement and uncertainty. Mainly, it is essential to prioritise requirements and uncertainties that have a high impact or that are more critical to the basic functionality of the system.

4.4   Proof-of-Concept Validation Gate

The main activity in this gate is to authorise (or not) the prototype(s) development. The results of all the previous stage's activities will be taken into consideration to make this decision. Additionally, if the continuity of the project is authorised, the previously mentioned prototype evolution plan must be drawn up. As shown in Fig. 1, this plan will guide the iterative prototype development during the next stage and will help in shaping the system. The plan should be focused on gradually solving identified uncertainties and add functionality (considering the assigned priorities) to favour early identification of risks and undesired deviations.

4.5   Prototype Development Stage

In this stage prototypes are iteratively designed and developed until a completely defined physical system is achieved. The resulting system will have all the heterogeneous subsystems efficiently integrated, be functional and dependable, and be ready for real field validation. The iterations follow the prototype evolution plan defined in the previous stage to gradually resolve the identified uncertainties, acquire an adequate level of understanding of both the system and its possible environment, and identify risks and weaknesses. It is important to note that some requirements will evolve and emerge during development due to the innovative nature of the system and new customer requirements. This issue is addressed in the prototype development gate.

The prototype development stage is further divided into different sub-stages corresponding to the phases of the V-development model. These sub-stages include (i) requirements specification, (ii) architecture definition, (iii) detailed design, (iv) implementation, (v) verification, (vi) integration and (vii) validation. The most relevant sub-stages for this paper are described below. Nevertheless, it is recommended to document in all the sub-stages the activities performed, decisions taken, techniques and measures used, etc. so they are shown as evidence of development and system dependability. Finally, it is important to maintain traceability between system specifications and subsystems, architecture, design and testing, along with the versions of the documents being generated. All the activities and documentation should be updated and completed as the development of the prototype(s) progresses with each of the iterations.

Requirements Specification. The main objective of this sub-phase is to specify prototype requirements and the heterogeneous subsystems that compose it (mechanics, electronics, optics, embedded software, etc.), making a concretion of system requirements identified in the proof-of-concept gate as it is shown in Fig. 1. Each of the prototypes to be developed should meet a subset of those requirements until all the system requirements are precisely defined and met. Taking into consideration safety and dependability demands it is recommended to make a structured specification to manage prototype's complexity. Additionally, the prototype validation plan that will be carried out in the last sub-phase of the V-development should be defined.

Architecture Definition. The objective of this sub-stage is to define the architecture of the prototype and its heterogeneous subsystems (mechanical, optical, software, etc.), making a high-level description of the components that compose it. As it is shown in Fig. 1 a concretion of system architecture described in proof-of-concept gate may be performed. Taking into consideration safety and dependability demands the definition of a modular architecture is recommended to favour and facilitate the management of the complexity of the system and reuse components between iterations. On the other hand, regarding SPC and KPI techniques, the concept of a system as a plant must be applied at this point (see Fig. 1. In this context, the processes performed by the system (i.e., measure, calibration, etc.) should be defined. These processes will be defined as a sequential succession of physical system components to provide specific functionality. Due to the system heterogeneity, these processes will establish dependencies between components of different nature (software, hardware, photonics, mechanical, fluidics, etc.) that may affect the output value of the process (measurement result, calibration, etc.). Besides the dependencies, it will be important to identify if possible, potential propagation errors, weaknesses, risks, etc. In this context and related to "system as a plant" concept, it is recommended to identify KPIs of the components involved in the process to get information regarding intermediate results related to the performance of the process. Also, as far as possible, it is necessary to establish thresholds and confidence ranges associated with the KPIs, to determine during validation whether the behaviour of the process (system) is faulty or as expected. The monitoring of those parameters together with the established thresholds during validation will allow to detect changes in the performance and to identify in an early way possible failures and errors. All this information will be refined and adjusted as development progresses. For example, in the first iteration of development it will be difficult to establish thresholds for KPIs due to lack of knowledge of the system. However, as development progresses, these thresholds can be defined more and more precisely. Finally, as in the previous sub-stage and regarding safety and dependability concerns, it is also recommended to define the integration tests that will be carried out in the integration sub-stage.

Detailed Design. The purpose of this sub-stage is to make a detailed description of the design of the components defined in the architecture, decomposing them into smaller sub-components until a sufficient level of detail is achieved. Moreover, regarding safety and dependability concerns, depending on the risks identified and the criticality of the component, the design should include fault tolerance and risk reduction and mitigation techniques (redundancy, diversity, automatic self-testing). It is of great interest to apply Verhulst's proposal [14] (described in the Background section). On the other hand, it must be considered that the detailed design of the components could require completing KPI definition to obtain a better performance monitoring coverage. In this context, it is recommended to make the design based on a white-box approach. This results from the fact that internal parameters of the components must be accessible from the outside, and the analysis of the execution paths will help to increase validation coverage. As in previous sub-stages, all the information related to this sub-phase should be completed and updated as system design progresses. Finally, to comply with safety and dependability demands, the tests to be performed in verification sub-stage should be defined to ensure that the component meets the defined specifications and the required dependability level.

Validation. The purpose of this final sub-phase is to determine if the prototype meets the specified requirements. The tests will validate the behaviour of the prototype under controlled conditions and environment, that will be progressively updated and completed in each iteration until almost working conditions are reached. As it is shown in Fig. 1, to validate the prototype's performance it is recommended to apply "system as a plant" concept. In this context, KPIs and components' outputs identified in the architecture definition and detailed design sub-stages and must be monitored and statistically analysed using SPC techniques to identify undesired variations in the prototype's performance. At this point, it should be identified whether a particular component or set of components of a process within a test population is running at the expected confidence level based on the quantitative analysis of its parameter values against its thresholds and the statistical response of previous tests. Then, determining the causes of these variations will help to adjust and improve system functionality and dependability in each iteration. The control and reduction of the detected variations will bring the process, and therefore the performance, to a stability condition maintaining the variations within desired upper and lower control limits (UCL, LCL). As far as possible, the trend to be followed by the data to be analysed (outputs and KPIs) or system response should be known. This trend will determine the real confidence range of the analysed data. As it is shown in Fig. 2, for the same data value, the real confidence range varies considerably depending on the system response (linear or exponential) and the defined UCL and LCL.

4.6   Prototype Development Gate

The main activity of this gate is to control the prototype evolution, authorise the transition to real field validation if the prototype's evolution plan is finished and all the uncertainties are solved, or cancel the continuation of the project if unexpected or undesired deviations have occurred (see Fig. 1). According to NPD approaches, this control will minimise the deviations' impact on projects' cost and time.

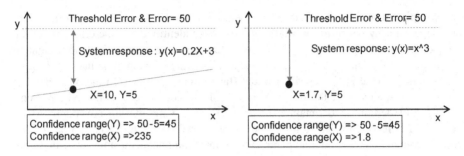

Fig. 2. Confidence range determination for the specified UCL.

On the one hand, if the prototype evolution plan is not finished, validation results are successful, and the customer agrees, the development continues with the next iteration. If the validation results are unsuccessful or the customer demands new requirements or suggestions and, consequently, changes or modifications are required, these changes must be identified and included within the next prototype iteration. In this case, taking into consideration safety and dependability demands, it is recommended to perform an impact analysis to identify all the subsystems and components affected by the change. On the other hand, if the plan is finished and there aren't new requirements, it is the moment to determine the suitability of moving forward to the real field validation stage.

4.7   Real Field Validation Stage

This stage represents the validation of the system concept against real working conditions, real users and real samples. Testing in a real environment, where all working conditions impact the system at the same time, can reveal hidden weaknesses in system design, and even new and unpredictable requirements that will contribute to improving system's functionality and dependability. As in validation sub-stage, it is recommended to monitor identified KPIs and components' outputs, and afterwards statistically analyse them to detect unexpected system performance.

4.8   Real Field Validation Gate

At this point, thanks to the combination of approaches of the presented methodology, all the uncertainties are solved, and weaknesses and risks identified and controlled. If there is a client already involved in the development process, there should not be a problem on moving into the product launch stage. Note that the described methodology will allow migrating the final system or prototype, and new versions based on it, to a certifiable product with limited time and resources, since many of the certification demands have already been considered.

5   Case Study

This section presents a generic description of the application of the methodology to real development. The attention is mainly focused on the resolution of uncertainties, as well as risks and weaknesses identification for achieving an accurate and complete system requirements' specification. The proposed case study compresses the development of an autonomous sensor for the oil degradation (OD) level monitoring of industrial lubricating oils, which can be installed in non-oil recirculating systems, such as robotic arms in automotive plants. The continuous monitoring of industrial lubricant fluids allows detecting the optimum oil change moment, consequently reducing maintenance downtime, increasing components and consumables life and reducing the incidence of catastrophic failures with crucial economic impact.

The proposed sensor is based on an innovative measurement principle that consist of illuminating the sample to be measured with a white led. An RGB control sensor is used to receive the reflected rays, in both the fluid and a back-reflection element to quantify a series of physical and chemical parameters related to oil degradation.

Once the market opportunity has been identified, its feasibility evaluated (technical, market, etc.) and approved in the opportunity capturing stage and opportunity capturing gate, the next step in the methodology is to enter the proof-of-concept validation stage. In this stage, a test set-up with commercial components (emitters and receivers) is built to validate the real feasibility of the measuring principle. Unsuccessful results in this proof of concept will stop the project or require some changes in the measuring principle. In both cases, thanks to the Stage-Gate approach, this issue is detected in a very early development phase, thus, minimising negative impact.

In this case, the success of the preliminary tests supports transferring the concept of the measurement principle to a real system. Thus, an initial set of requirements and system architecture are defined. The proposed solution is composed of electronic, mechanic, optic, fluidic and embedded software subsystems that will interact with each other to provide the expected functionality (see Figs. 3 and 4). Due to the innovative nature of the system, it is not possible to accurately define the architecture and some of the requirements. Some of the most important of these uncertainties are listed below:

- Fluidic and hydraulic subsystems architecture that supports sample renovation.
- Fluidic subsystem architecture that supports air evacuation from the measurement cavity.
- Optical subsystem architecture that maximises dynamic measurement range (oil type and degradations).
- Measurement stability.

Next, during the proof-of-concept validation gate, those uncertainties and their priority are evaluated to define the prototypes evolution plan. This plan focuses the development effort on the main points that contribute to the final system functionality while favouring rapid failure identification and the consequent reduction in the impact (time and cost). In this case, the prototype evolution plan that guides the iterations of the prototype development stage includes the iterations listed below:

76   P. López et al.

- A prototype with configurable fluidic sample cavity height and interchangeable optic back elements to solve uncertainties regarding sample renovation, air evacuation and measurement resolution and to determine the impact of external conditions (e.g. temperature) in the measurement stability.
- A prototype with the final mechanic, hydraulic and optic design that include "additional" functionalities (data and alarms log, configuration, calibration and oil references management, firmware update, etc.).

Figure 3 shows an overall description of the final system architecture where the physical interconnection of the heterogeneous components is detailed. On the other hand, Fig. 4 shows the measurement process together with the sub-processes in which it is divided and its dependencies with physical components, external factor and identified KPIs for performance evaluation.

In the first development iteration components depicted in black in Figs. 3 and 4 are designed, implemented and validated. The analysis of identified KPIs and sub-

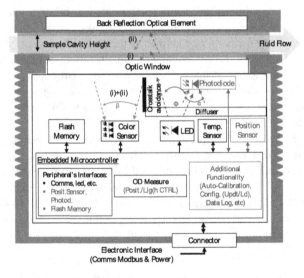

Fig. 3. System architecture.

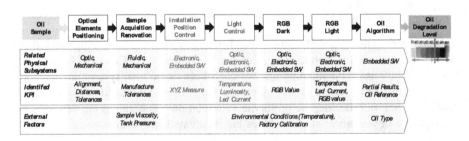

Fig. 4. Oil Degradation (OD) measurement process definition.

processes' outputs using SPC techniques will help to identify dependencies, risks and weaknesses that will contribute to improving prototype's functionality and dependability. In this context, Fig. 5 shows the dependency between the sample cavity height and the RGB measurement (including the led and the RGB colour sensor), for various oil degradations. This analysis allows to determine the impact of the sample cavity height on the RGB measurement resolution and therefore on the oil degradation measurement. Consequently, it is required to integrate verifications into mechanical manufacturing and assembly, to ensure that sample cavity height is within a confidence range that guarantees the resolution and dependability of the measurement. After analysing the trend of the graph data and as a first estimation, a margin of approximately 0.125 mm can be established. This value will be adjusted as the development progresses and more sensors are built and tested, and therefore system performance is better understood.

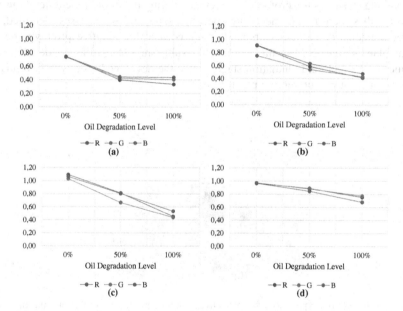

Fig. 5. RGB measurement resolution for different fluidic cell heights: (a) 2 mm; (b) 1.5 mm; (c) 1 mm; (d) 0.5 mm.

Then, the evaluation in prototype development gate of the obtained validation results authorises the continuation of the development. The conclusions obtained from this evaluation (including client's feedback) are listed below:

- Fluidic sample cavity height and optical back reflection element material are specified.
- Better light control is required, and the integration of a photodiode to implement a closed-loop control is proposed. This change will impact both electronic and software embedded subsystems.

- A smaller hydraulic fitting is required. This change will mainly impact the mechanic design, but the optical design will also be modified, and re-validation needed.

At this point, a new iteration is added to the initial plan but is motivated by the conclusions of the previous gate. The structured development process of the methodology, based on NPD approaches, favoured the integration of new requirements and modifications. Also, thanks to the structured specification and modularity required by safety and dependability standards, the rest of the components from the previous prototype are reused, so the impact of the changes is minimised. Required changes in this iteration are in red in Figs. 3 and 4. After modifications, the evaluation of the validation results in prototype development gate is successful, and no new requirements are required from the client, so development progress to the next iteration.

In the final iteration system's functionality is completed and only embedded software implementation is required. Changes in this iteration are in blue in Fig. 3. Furthermore, Fig. 6 shows the prototypes developed during the development iterations. At this point, all system requirements are specified, risks and weaknesses identified, no new requirements or particular demands required, and the iterative prototype development plan is finished. As the validation results are successful, the development continues to the real field validation stage, where the developed prototype is validated in robotic arms at an automotive plant.

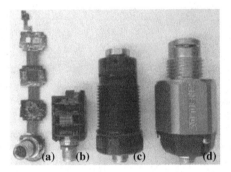

Fig. 6. Developed prototypes: (a) custom electronic subsystem; (b) custom electronic subsystem into the mechanical housing; (c) Prototype 1 (1st iteration); (d) Prototype 2 (2nd and 3rd iterations).

Finally, although it could be considered that additional safety and dependability demands could slow down the prototypes' development process, the application of these demands contribute to reduce required time and cost to obtain a certifiable final product. Generated documentation and used measures and techniques for designing and testing are used as safety and dependability evidences.

6 Conclusions and Future Work

This paper is motivated by the lack of approaches able to support the process of bringing innovative design ideas to real dependable complex embedded products, specially in situations hindered by limited resources in time and budget. The proposed methodology adapts and combines three development approaches to offer a complete solution ((i) NPD processes, (ii) dependability and safety standards, (iii) and SPC and KPI techniques). The structure of the methodology is based on the Stage-Gate NPD model and covers the stages from (i) product opportunity identification and (ii) proof-of-concept validation, through (iii) iterative V-model prototypes development and (iv) real field validation stages. Particular attention is paid to the adaptation and integration of SPC and KPI techniques to monitor and analyse the system's performance. Finally, all the stages in the development process include additional dependability and safety demands.

As it is shown in the case study, the proposed methodology enables the complete specification of the system (requirements specification, and risks and weaknesses identification), despite the high level of uncertainty at the beginning of the development. All the problems encountered due to these uncertainties and evolving requirements are detected at relatively initial stages, so the impact of the required changes and modifications in the project's cost and time is minimised. Also, generated documentation and the use of specific measures and techniques for designing and testing contribute to reducing the effort for re-design, re-verification, etc. required to obtain a certifiable product. Nevertheless, it is difficult to present a precise quantification of the cost and time reduction during project execution. It is not possible to compare the same development applying and not applying the proposed methodology, as once the system is developed all the problems encountered due to uncertainties and evolving requirements disappear. Comparing the presented case study with a system with similar characteristics developed without applying the proposed methodology, an approximate 17% cost and time reduction is estimated to obtain a certifiable product.

Finally, the next steps will focus on specifying precisely how system uncertainties and evolving requirements impact on safety aspects. Safety issues have been considered very broadly in the methodology, and it would be of great interest to detail more precisely how these aspects are integrated during iterative system specification.

References

1. McGrath, R.G., Macmillan, I.C.: Discovery-Driven Growth: A Breakthrough Process to Reduce Risk and Seize Opportunity, 1st edn. Harvard Review Press, Boston (2009)
2. Loch, C.H., DeMever, A., Pich, M.: Managing the Unknown: A New Approach to Managing High Uncertainty and Risk in Projects, 1st edn. Wiley, New Jersey (2006)
3. Golden, B., Aiguier, M., Krob, D.: Modeling of complex systems II: a minimalist and unified semantics for heterogeneous integrated systems. Appl. Math. Comput. **218**(16), 8039–8055 (2012)
4. Marwedel, P.: Embedded System Design. ES. Springer, Cham (2018). https://doi.org/10.1007/978-3-319-56045-8

5. IEC 61508:2010 Functional safety of electrical/electronic/programmable electronic safety-related systems. The International Electrotechnical Commission (2010)
6. Xianhong, L., Munir, Z.: Key Concepts in Innovation. Palgrave, Basingstoke (2011)
7. Resenhoeft, T.: The fast track to success with agile product development. Bosch Press Release. https://bit.ly/2vr4A0J. Accessed 24 Feb 2018
8. Karlström, D., Runeson, P.: Integrating agile software development into stage-gate managed product development. Empir. Softw. Eng. 11(2), 203–225 (2006)
9. Ruth, H., Silvestri, L.J.: Good Development Practices (GDPs). The Regulatory Forum Sponsored by AccuReg. http://www.regulatory.com/forum/article/gdps.html. Accessed 24 Feb 2018
10. Soenksen, L.R., Yazdi, Y.: Stage-gate process for life sciences and medical innovation investment. Technovation 62–63, 14–21 (2017)
11. Cooper, G.R.: What's next?: after stage-gate. Res.-Technol. Manag. 57(1), 20–31 (2014)
12. Grönlund, J., Rönneberg, D., Frishammar, J.: Open innovation and the Stage-Gate process: a revised model for new product development. Calif. Manag. Rev. 52(3), 106–131 (2010)
13. Vedsmand, T., Kielgast, S., Cooper, R.G.: Integrating Agile with Stage-Gate – How New Agile-Scrum Methods Lead to faster and better innovation. InnovationManagement.se (2016). https://bit.ly/2cQkziz. Accessed 24 Feb 2018
14. Qiu, P.: Introduction to Statistical Process Control, 1st edn. Chapman and Hall/CRC, Boca Raton (2014)
15. Škulj, G., Vrabič, R., Butala, P., Sluga, A.: Statistical process control as a service: an industrial case study. In: Cunha, P.F. (ed.) Forty Sixth CIRP Conference on Manufacturing Systems 2013, vol. 7, pp. 401–406. Elsevier, Amsterdam (2013)
16. Antolić, Z.: An example of using key performance indicators for software development process efficiency evaluation. R&D Center Ericsson Nikola Tesla (2008). https://bit.ly/2LYAvju. Accessed 27 Aug 2018
17. Chae, B.K.: Developing key performance indicators for supply chain: an industry perspective. Supply Chain Manag. 14(6), 422–428 (2009)
18. Gary, K., et al.: Agile methods for open source safety-critical software. Softw. Pract. Exp. 41(9), 945–962 (2011)
19. Ge, X., Paige, R.F., McDermid, J.A.: An iterative approach for development of safety-critical software and safety arguments. In: Proceedings of the 2010 Agile Conference, pp. 35–43. IEEE Computer Society, Washington (2010)
20. Kuhrmann, M., et al.: Hybrid software and system development in practice: waterfall, scrum, and beyond. In: Proceedings of the 2017 International Conference on Software and System Process, pp. 30–39. ACM, New York (2017)

HAVOSS: A Maturity Model for Handling Vulnerabilities in Third Party OSS Components

Pegah Nikbakht Bideh[1]([⊠]), Martin Höst[2], and Martin Hell[1]

[1] Department of Electrical and Information Technology, Lund University, Lund, Sweden
{pegah.nikbakht_bideh,martin.hell}@eit.lth.se
[2] Department of Computer Science, Lund University, Lund, Sweden
martin.host@cs.lth.se

Abstract. Security has been recognized as a leading barrier for IoT adoption. The growing number of connected devices and reported software vulnerabilities increases the importance firmware updates. Maturity models for software security do include parts of this, but are lacking in several aspects. This paper presents and evaluates a maturity model (HAVOSS) for handling vulnerabilities in third party OSS and COTS components. The maturity model was designed by first reviewing industry interviews, current best practice guidelines and other maturity models. After that, the practices were refined through industry interviews, resulting in six capability areas covering in total 21 practices. These were then evaluated based on their importance according to industry experts. It is shown that the practices are seen as highly important, indicating that the model can be seen as a valuable tool when assessing strengths and weaknesses in an organization's ability to handle firmware updates.

Keywords: Maturity model · Software security
Software maintenance · Firmware updates · Vulnerabilities

1 Introduction

Software maintenance focuses on issues such as adapting systems to changed functionality requirements, changed environments and corrections of faults. Identified security vulnerabilities can be seen as one type of fault that has received more attention in the last decade, following a number of attacks impacting large organizations, customers, and the society. Attacks have also become more sophisticated and the increasing number of software intensive systems, in IT systems and in the shift towards cloud computing and IoT devices, have resulted in more attack targets. The number of security vulnerabilities reported and recorded in the NVD CVE (National Vulnerability Database, Common Vulnerabilities and Exposures) database has for many years been relatively stable, ranging

M. Kuhrmann et al. (Eds.): PROFES 2018, LNCS 11271, pp. 81–97, 2018.
https://doi.org/10.1007/978-3-030-03673-7_6

between approximately 4,200 to 7,900 between 2005–2016 [15]. In 2017 the number increased to about 14,700. New companies producing connected devices, as well as older mature companies adjusting their products to the current trend of connectivity, increases the competition on the market. Meeting this competition requires high functionality and fast time-to-market. Using open source software (OSS) instead of developing all code in-house decreases development time, and software maintenance for OSS can focus more on updating the software when new versions are released. However, urgent updates as a result of security vulnerabilities can be very costly for the organization. Thus, it is important to handle the process of identifying and evaluating new vulnerabilities, and subsequently update the software, in an accurate and efficient way.

A maturity model can be seen as a tool that helps organizations improve the way they work, typically by introducing and implementing changes in the organization. This is often a slow process, requiring efforts and resources throughout the organization. The change, to be effective, must have support both from management and the work force, and internal communication processes must be well implemented in order to support the change management required for implementing improvements. The maturity model will help the organization identify the issues in need for improving and prioritizing the efforts. It will also help the organization in ensuring that no important aspects are neglected. However, it will typically not in detail describe *how* the changes should be implemented since this can vary widely between organizations and depend on size, type of organization, business domain, regulations etc.

The goal of this paper is to define, evaluate, and present a maturity model (HAVOSS – HAndling Vulnerabilities in third party OSS) focusing on managing vulnerabilities in third party libraries and code, and the subsequent software update activities that are required to limit a product's exposure to attacks. We target all practices related to this aspect of software maintenance for embedded systems. The model builds upon existing models for software maintenance and security, interviews with industry, and recently published guidelines and recommendations for security in IoT devices. An initial version has been iterated using feedback from industry representatives, and has then been evaluated by industry. The evaluation shows that the proposed practices are highly relevant.

The paper is organized as follows. In Sect. 2 we first present related work and maturity models focusing of secure software. In Sect. 3, we describe the methodology used when defining and evaluating the model, and in Sect. 5 the different maturity levels are defined. Then we present the results of our evaluation in Sect. 6 and the paper is concluded in Sect. 7.

2   Related Work

The Capability Maturity Model for Software, CMM, and CMMI (e.g. [18]) have been very influential in how to support process improvement in software engineering. The models guide an organization through five maturity levels where process standardization (level 3) is seen as more mature than project level processes (level 2), and experience based improvement (level 4 and level 5) is a natural continuation after that type of standardization. The idea of standardizing approaches in the organization, and after that to improve through experiences, has influenced the model presented in this paper. There is also the Software maintenance maturity model (SMmm) [1] addressing unique activities of software maintenance, and there are maturity models for process improvement implementation [14].

There are several well-known maturity models focusing on software security and the software development life cycle.

The Building Security in Maturity Model (BSIMM) [10] is based on actual practices in a large number of companies. It thus represents the current state of software security. It can be used to assess the Secure Software Development Lifecycle (SSDL). BSIMM covers 12 practices divided into the four main domains *Governance*, *Intelligence*, *SSDL Touchpoints*, and *Deployment*.

OWASP Software Assurance Maturity Model (SAMM) [2] is an open framework developed by OWASP, with the aim to help organizations evaluating their existing software security practices throughout the whole organization. SAMM is a flexible model that is designed to be utilized by both small, medium, and large companies. SAMM is built on business functions of the software development life cycle, and each business function is tied to three security practices. The business functions are *Governance*, *Construction*, *Verification*, and *Operations*.

The Systems Security Engineering – Capability Maturity Model (SSE-CMM) [9] is intended to be used as a tool to evaluate and assess security engineering practices. It allows organizations to establish confidence in their own capability, but it also helps customers to evaluate a provider's security engineering capabilities. The model is based on the idea that organizations need a repeatable, efficient and assured mechanism to improve their security engineering practices. SSE-CMM has been developed to address these needs by reducing the cost of delivering secure systems. The model contains a number of base practices which are organized into in total eleven process areas.

The Microsoft Security Development Lifecycle (SDL) [12] is another security assurance process focusing on secure software development. The purpose of SDL is to reduce the number and severity of vulnerabilities in software and it aims to guarantee security and privacy during all phases of the development process. Education, continuous process improvement, and accountability are three main concepts of SDL which emphasizes ongoing activities within the whole software development lifecycle. SDL is built upon five capability areas which correspond to different phases of the software development lifecycle, and each area consists of a collection of security activities. SDL defines four levels of maturity for these areas, namely Basic, Standardized, Advanced, and Dynamic. The basic level means little or no processes related to the activity, while dynamic level corresponds to complete compliance across an entire organization.

The Cybersecurity Capability Maturity Model (C2M2) [3] is designed to help organizations of any type and any size to evaluate and improve their cybersecurity programs. The model can be used to strengthen cybersecurity capabilities and also to prioritize actions to improve organization's cybersecurity processes.

The model is organized into 10 domains and each domain has a set of cybersecurity practices. Practices in each domain will help organizations to achieve more mature capability in the domain.

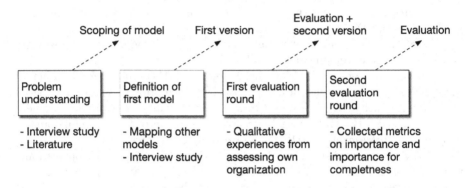

Fig. 1. Research steps

The most important features for vulnerability handling such as vulnerability identification, vulnerability assessment, vulnerability tracking and disclosure policy are included in some of mentioned maturity models. Vulnerability identification through software development process exists in BSIMM [10], SAMM [2], SDL [12] and SSE-CMM [9] and only in SMmm [1] it exits in maintenance phase. Assessing vulnerabilities only includes in SSE-CMM [9]. Vulnerability tracking by incident response team exists in almost all of them. None of them has any communication or disclosure policy except C2M2 [3]. We tried to gather all of these vulnerability handling features in our maturity model and make a complete maturity model for vulnerability handling. Being highly focused on handling vulnerabilities in third party code, our proposed maturity model should not be seen as a replacement for the other models. HAVOSS is intended to be used as a complement to other, more general, maturity models.

3   Methodology

The model has been designed iteratively based on feedback from presenting it to practitioners in the field. A first problem-understanding was achieved through an interview study with practitioners [8] where it was clear that there is a need to support these processes in industry. In that study, 8 companies in the IoT domain were interviewed about how they handle vulnerabilities in OSS and COTS code in their developed and maintained products, and what challenges they see in that. It was clear that there is a need to support these activities, meaning that the scope of the model was decided to include all activities that are relevant to identifying and solving vulnerabilities in third party (OSS and COTS) code. A literature study with a comparison to available models also showed the need for this type of model.

3.1   Research Steps

The maturity model was defined through a series of research steps as described in Fig. 1. Based on the identified need, a first version was designed. One important source was the previously conducted interview study with industrial practitioners on how they handle vulnerabilities [8]. In that study it was clear that many organizations do not have defined processes, neither for identifying, analyzing, or taking care of vulnerabilities in third party code in the products they develop and support. Another input source was already available models, as presented in Sect. 2. Many of the models include aspects that are related to the capability areas in our model. However, the available models are more general and not as complete in managing third party software vulnerabilities as this model. For example, BSIMM [10] includes "Software Environment" which is related to product knowledge in our model, and it includes "Configuration Management & Vulnerability Management" which is related to evaluating and remedy of vulnerabilities in our model. It is similar for the other models. They include relevant areas, but they are not as focused on vulnerability management for included third-party software where sources of vulnerabilities must be identified and monitored. Based on these input sources, a first version of the model was defined.

The model was decided to consist of *capability areas*, each consisting of a set of *practices* that can be used to identify improvement proposals in assessments. Each practice is represented as a *question* in order make it easier to interpret in an assessment. The final resulting capability areas and questions are presented in Sect. 4.

When the first version was available it was iteratively improved through evaluations with practitioners, in two main evaluation rounds. Helgesson et al. [6] identify three ways of evaluating maturity models when they are designed, either off-line by the authors alone, off-line by including practitioners, or on-line, i.e., in actual process improvement. Both evaluation rounds in this study can be classified as off-line by including practitioners, since all evaluations are carried out based on practitioners' opinions and experiences of trying to assess their organization. However, at this stage we have not actually conducted any improvement activities guided by the model where a before/after scenario could be analyzed.

In the first evaluation round, refinement of the model was conducted through feedback from practitioners. This was done in several sub-steps, where we in each sub-step sent the model to a contact person in industry who individually assessed their own processes with the model. When they had done that we had a meeting with the organization where we discussed general feedback on the model and we discussed a number of feedback questions, e.g. about if there were any misconceptions from researchers, if the questions were hard to answer, if there were any questions missing, and if the respondent had any thoughts about the answer alternatives. All meetings were held in a way resembling a semi-structured interview where audio was recorded, so the information could be accessed in the analysis. This type of feedback was obtained from two companies, which resulted in a number of adaptions of the model.

In the second evaluation round, feedback was received with other feedback questions than in round 1, now focusing more specifically on every practice of the model. As in the first evaluation round, the model was sent to practitioners, but in this step they were asked to consider not just the answer of each question, but they were also asked to assess the practice with respect to the following two dimensions:

- *Importance of practice:* For each question the participant was asked to judge how important the practice described by the question is in management of vulnerabilities. Possible answer alternatives were 1–5.
- *Importance for completeness:* For each question the participant was asked to judge how important it is to include the practice for the completeness of the questionnaire. Possible answer alternatives were 1–5. The given motivation was that some practices can be overlooked if they are not included in a model like this. A high score represents that the practitioner thought that it is easily overlooked if it is not included in the model. In the same way a low score means that the practice would probably be solved also without a model like this, i.e. the practice can be considered "obvious".

For each question in the model the participants were allowed to give free text comments in a separate field in the form they received.

The conducted research was influenced by design science. Compared to the framework according to Hevner et al. [7] it identified the needs and the problems in the environment e.g. through the interview study, and the evaluations were conducted with people from the same environment. The developed model was, as described above, based on available models and it represents a contribution to the available knowledge base.

3.2   Participating Companies and Practitioners

The participants in evaluation round 1 and evaluation round 2 are summarized in Table 1. The second row shows if the company participated in evaluation round 1 (✓ = yes) and the third row shows how many practitioners from each company who individually answered the questions on importance and importance for completeness in evaluation round 2. The companies are working with software engineering and they represent different size, age, and maturity. Companies A, D, and F are large companies, while the other are smaller. Company E is an example of a startup while the other companies are more traditional companies. Company G offers consultancy services to other companies, while the

Table 1. Participating practitioners

Company	A	B	C	D	E	F	G
Evaluation round 1	✓	✓					
Participants in evaluation round 2	12	2	4	1	1	1	2

other companies work with traditional in-house development. All companies but company C are working in the area of embedded software for IoT systems. All involved practitioners were in some way responsible for security and/or working with security-related questions in the organization. In company A most communication was held with the main security responsible. Other persons were working within development roles.

3.3 Validity

The goal has been to obtain good validity of the research by considering typical threats to validity (e.g., [17]). Construct validity denotes to what extent the operational constructs are interpreted in the same way by the researchers and the involved practitioners. Care was taken to use as general terms as possible, not to focus on wrong specific meanings of terms in the organizations. This risk can never be ruled out completely, but it can be noticed that some terms in the model were changed in the first evaluation round, in order to not give too specific (and not completely right) meaning to the company practitioners.

Reliability denotes to what degree the analysis is dependent on the specific researchers. This is always a threat, but care has been taken to do the analysis in the whole group of researchers. The analysis has also considered feedback from members of the industrial participants. For example, both company A and B were involved in both the first end second evaluation round.

Internal validity denotes the risk that other factors than the ones known by the researchers affect the result. This is not a typical controlled study where factors are controlled, but still there may be some factors that affect the results such as ongoing and general improvement attempts with respect to security. Care has been taken to understand the situations of the participating organizations, and many of them have been involved in previous research studies with the researchers. Basically, we see the situation of the participating companies as typical examples of industrial organizations, and no major internal threats.

External validity denotes the possibility to generalize the results. All organizations are Swedish or has a Swedish origin and all participants are employed in Sweden, but they operate on an international market and most of them have mainly international customers. We do not classify them as particularly typical, but more as general examples of organizations in general, at least in the area of embedded systems and IoT systems, when it comes to their approach to managing vulnerabilities. However, in this type of study care must be taken when generalizing to other organizations.

4   Capability Areas and Practices

In this section our proposed vulnerability management maturity model is presented in detail. The six capability areas consist of in total 21 practices. In the assessment sheet, the practices are formulated as questions, e.g. A1, "Tracking maintained and used products" is formulated as "How do you keep track of

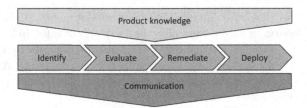

Fig. 2. The capability areas included in the proposed maturity model.

which type of products are maintained and/or used?"[1]. The capability areas are *product knowledge, identification and monitoring of sources, evaluating vulnerabilities, remedy of vulnerabilities, delivering updates* and *communication*. The areas and the relation between the areas is depicted in Fig. 2. Product knowledge is a prerequisite for the other areas and practices. Without this, it is not possible to efficiently, or even at all, handle vulnerabilities. Identifying, evaluating, and remediating vulnerabilities, as well as deploying updates, can be seen as areas of practices that are carried out in sequence. Finally, communication of vulnerabilities and related information can, and often should, be done in parallel with the practices and activities in the other areas. In the following subsections, each capability area and the practices are given in more detail.

4.1   Product Knowledge

Product knowledge assesses companies' knowledge of their products' components. A higher maturity level in this area indicates higher knowledge about the components. This capability area is divided into five practices:

A1. Tracking maintained and used products. Organizations should track maintained products by themselves and also products used by customers regularly, in order to be able to identify their active products.

A2. Tracking included third party OSS and COTS components included in products. Developing companies use many OSS components. This reduces the time-to-market and allow a more cost-efficient development and maintenance organization. Development is largely reduced to selecting the appropriate component to use, while maintenance is reduced to updating it when needed.

A3. Tracking used OSS or COTS versions in the included components. In addition to tracking used OSS and COTS components, it is also of importance to track the versions used in released products and firmware. Version tracking allows an efficient identification of potential vulnerabilities.

A4. Tracking possible threats that products are facing. Threats are possible dangers that might exploit a vulnerability in software products. To avoid

---

[1] The assessment sheet, together with evaluation data are available at https://zenodo.org/record/1340623#.W2wP7RixWkB.

critical dangers, and to facilitate correctness in the evaluation of vulnerabilities, it is necessary to track possible threats in software products.

A5. Specifying product usage, operating environment, and end-of-life. By specifying intended usage and operating environment, customers can better understand the intended use of a product, and it also provides important parameters when evaluating the threats and identified vulnerabilities. Specifying an end-of-life informs customers the duration for which they can expect feature and security updates for products. Note that end-of-life for feature updates and security updates can differ.

4.2   Identification and Monitoring of Sources

New vulnerabilities are found on a daily basis and there are several sources for information regarding these. A well defined and efficient process for identifying and monitoring sources of vulnerability information allow both faster and more robust management of vulnerabilities and maintenance of products and devices. The practices in this capability area focus on three aspects.

B1. Determining external sources to use for identifying new vulnerabilities. New vulnerabilities are typically recorded and identified through the CVE numbering scheme [13] and further detailed in NVD [15]. While this centralized database contains most vulnerabilities, and some other information related to them, it is also worthwhile to monitor new academic results through conference proceedings and journals, as well as monitoring security advisories and the most well-known mailing lists where software security and vulnerabilities are discussed.

B2. Receiving and following up on vulnerabilities reported to the company by external parties. In some cases, new vulnerabilities are disclosed directly to the organization. This can be the case if a third party researcher or professional analyzes the product and reports the results to the manufacturer through a responsible disclosure process.

B3. Monitoring the identified sources of vulnerabilities. Having a well defined process for monitoring vulnerability sources will help minimize the exposure time for products and devices. Often, there are exploits widely available either at the time of disclosure or very shortly after [19].

4.3   Evaluating Vulnerabilities

The goal of this capability area is to help organizations assess their maturity in evaluating the severeness and relevance of identified vulnerabilities. This has direct impact on the next area (remedy of vulnerabilities). Accurate and efficient evaluation, as well as well-founded and correct decisions regarding vulnerabilities, are prerequisites for timely and cost-efficient remediation. The practices in this area thus focus on the following two aspects.

C1. Evaluating severity and relevance of vulnerabilities. After identifying a potential vulnerability, it must be evaluated with respect to product configuration, operating environment, and threat assessment. Unused component functionality, network configuration or unrealistic exploit requirements might render the vulnerability unexploitable. Methods for ranking vulnerability severity might aid in the evaluation. A well-known metric is the Common Vulnerability Scoring System (CVSS) [5,11], which gives a rating on the scale 0–10.

C2. Making decisions for handling and reacting to identified vulnerabilities. Firmware and software is often updated on a regular basis in order to include new functionality and patch bugs. Severe security vulnerabilities might need immediate attention and result in updates that are not within the planned cycle. Such updates are very costly and often engage large parts of the organization. It is thus very important to only perform out-of-cycle updates if necessary.

4.4 Remedy of Vulnerabilities

Based on the severity, vulnerabilities can be divided into three basic categories, namely those that need urgent changes, those that can be patched in the next planned release, and those that need no changes or updates. This capability area assesses the maturity level of organizations for handling these categories.

D1. Handling vulnerabilities that need urgent changes. Urgent changes require immediate action and will impact several processes within the organization. The organization should have an action plan for handling this event in order not to cause unnecessary and unforeseen problems.

D2. Handling vulnerabilities that are updated in a planned release. Here, the maintenance organization must make sure that the affected component is patched in the next release.

D3. Handling vulnerabilities that need no changes. When vulnerabilities have been evaluated, and the results show that attacks are impossible or very unlikely, the organization must make sure that this is well documented. If the component is not updated to a patched version, the vulnerability will always be present, so the organization must make sure that it is not unnecessarily evaluated over and over. Moreover, new information might affect the status of a vulnerability. In that case, it must be re-evaluated since updated information (e.g., new exploits), might affect the decision.

4.5 Delivering Updates

After updating the used components with the latest version, or applying patches to the software, the new firmware or updated software must be deployed to the actual devices. This does not only require a communication channel to the devices, but the channel must also be secure, including verifying the authenticity of new software. However, verifying authenticity is not enough, it is also important to make sure that updates are actually installed on devices [4]. This capability area is divided into two activities.

E1. The process of delivering and applying upgrades to deployed products. The update process can be done fully automatically if the devices support that. In some cases, users will be notified of new updates but needs to go through manual steps to apply them. In other cases, new firmware or software is posted on a website, and it is up to the user to identify and apply these patches. Exactly which process is used can be situation dependent. Although a fully automatic approach is typically preferred, requirements on system or device availability, and also privacy concerns, can render such an approach infeasible in some cases. It can be noted that a recent survey [16] based on 2205 users, reported that only 14% have ever updated their router's firmware.

E2. The process of protecting the integrity of patches while they are delivered and deployed. Integrity protection, typically through digital signatures or MACs, is needed to protect from malicious updates being installed on devices. This in turn will require a PKI or pre-shared keys.

4.6   Communication

Communicating vulnerability and security information, internally and externally, and have structured ways of doing this, allow a more robust and transparent process. It will make the security awareness more visible and contribute to more secure products. This capability is divided into six practices.

F1. Communicating internally when vulnerabilities are identified and resolved. Informing everyone within the company that is somehow affected by the vulnerability, its evaluation, remediation and deployment, allow a well-managed and structured process for updating the software.

F2. Communicating externally when vulnerabilities are identified and resolved. External communication here means e.g., producing advisories that inform the public that the vulnerability has been identified and solved. It also includes forwarding new information to other manufacturers or providing OSS patches upstream.

F3. Communicating with media when vulnerabilities are handled. Widespread and critical vulnerabilities will often come to the attention of media. Well defined processes for communicating with media can improve how the security work within the company is perceived by the public.

F4. Communicating with important customers about critical vulnerabilities. Very large and important customers might be particularly affected by some vulnerabilities, requiring a heads-up when new vulnerabilities are found. Moreover, attacks that affect important customers can have significant impact on the manufacturer's business. At the same time, such communication is resource consuming, for both parts, so it should only be practiced if necessary.

F5. Informing customers about the patching status of products. In order for customers to verify the security of their products, it should be easy to see which software, versions, and patch levels products have. This is part of what is sometimes referred to as a bill of materials. Processes for delivering such information, perhaps together with specific information related to patched vulnerabilities can ease the burden for the support team.

F6. Transferring other security related information while delivering patches. Attaching information on patched vulnerabilities and also providing information on how the patch should be applied, or which additional configuration settings should be applied, can help the customer understand why the patch is applied.

5   Maturity Levels

The intention of the maturity levels is that they should represent an increasing maturity for the assessed organization when it comes to their processes for working with third-party vulnerability updates. This type of maturity can, of course, be defined in different ways, but as described in Sect. 2, we have chosen a way of viewing maturity that is inspired by the approach in CMMI for software development. This means that an increasing maturity implies an increased definition and standardization of approaches in the organization. We argue that this standardization is necessary in order to be able to learn from experiences and also to be effective in managing vulnerabilities. If different parts of an organization have individual responsibility to define and manage their processes for this it will not be effective. This means that we can formulate the basic contents of the levels as follows.

The first level is *level 0*, which means that no effort is spend at all on the activity. It may be that an organization does not work with vulnerabilities at all. Then they are assessed at this level. The next level, resembling level 1 in CMMI, *level 1* means that the process is carried out in some way but it is often unclear how it is done, and the responsibility is often left to developers who happen to find the need and have the right competence and resources for it. At the next level, *level 2*, there are defined approaches and routines, although there is not a standardized approach in the organization. The next level, *level 3*, represents a state where there is a standardized process in place for the practice. That is, the same, defined, procedures are used in all teams and projects. At the most advanced level, *level 4*, experiences are collected from using the standardized procedures, and these experiences are used when constantly improving the processes.

In the model presented to the participants, the maturity levels were presented as described in Table 2. When performing an assessment of the maturity, the intention is that every question is assessed. That is, there is one assessment result (level 0 – level 4) for each question. The results can then be presented either as one result for each question or a summary for each area of questions.

Table 2. Maturity levels used in the assessment

Level	Description
0	We don't do this
1	We do this in an ad-hoc way based on individual's own initiatives
2	We know how we do this, but we do it in different ways in different teams/products
3	We have defined processes for this that are common to all teams/products
4	We collect experience and/or metrics from our approach and base improvements on that

When improvements are identified based on an assessment it is possible to identify improvements based on the questions with low scores. When this is done there are some dependencies that can be identified. It is, as described in Sect. 4, possible to see that capability area A about product knowledge is a pre-condition for the other capability areas, see Fig. 2. It is therefore recommended to start with capability area A in an improvement programme.

6 Results of Evaluations

In this section the results of carrying out the evaluations are presented.

6.1 First Evaluation Round

In the first evaluation round a number of adaptions were made. In the discussions it was clear that the practitioners thought that there were no major misconceptions, and that the model included the major important aspects according to them. However, it was clear that some terminology that was used could be changed to terms that are more general in order to lower the risk of confusion about company specific terms. There were also some questions, especially in capability area A that were refined in order to be more understandable. Concerning the completeness, new questions about how to communicate with external sources, such as customers, were added. Also, based on the question about answer alternatives, i.e. the maturity levels, they were presented in a clearer way and the two highest levels in that version of the model were combined into the current most advanced level. In the original version there was one level for collecting experience and another level for using the experiences for improvement. These changes resulted in the model that is presented in this paper (Sects. 4 and 5).

6.2 Second Evaluation Round

In the second evaluation round the focus was on understanding the important of the questions and to what extent the questions would be handled without any model. The results with respect to *importance of activity* and *importance for completeness* of each question are shown in Figs. 3 and 4. Median values have been explicitly given to avoid ambiguity in the plots.

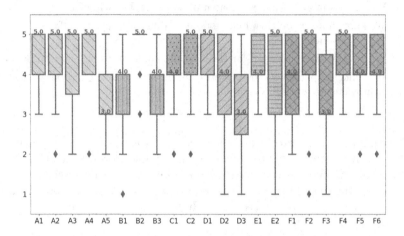

Fig. 3. Importance of activity

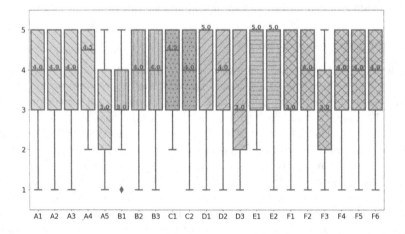

Fig. 4. Importance for completeness

It can be observed that almost all questions are seen as important by the practitioners. The freetext answers reveal some more detailed perceptions. One comment on D3 (Handling vulnerabilities that need no changes) was that this might be easily overlooked. This captures the importance of the question but also indicates why it has received slightly lower score overall. It is not seen as important as vulnerabilities that do require changes. Question F3 (Communicating with media), which also had a relatively low score, was not present in the initial version. It was added after interviewing company A, who viewed this as an important aspect that was not covered by the other questions. One comment on this question (from another company) was that this is mostly relevant for larger companies.

Some freetext answers also suggested adding more questions. One suggestion was to add security assessment, in which assets are identified. The importance of such a question will depend on to which extent the company knows which assets are actually protected. Another suggestion was to also consider how third party components are selected. Components, and in particular their maintainers must be trusted not to e.g., add malicious code into the software. To see if there are differences between the capability areas, we aggregate the answers to these areas, see Fig. 5. Again, it can be seen that the values are high, and there are only minor differences between the areas. A Kruskal-Wallis test (non-parametric alternative to one factor, n-levels, ANOVA) shows that no significant difference could be found between the areas ($p = 0.23$ for importance), which can be expected from the graphs.

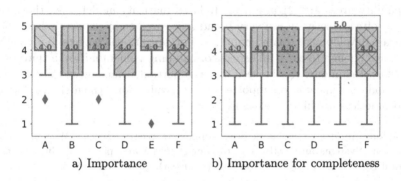

a) Importance   b) Importance for completeness

Fig. 5. Grouped results

Approximately half of the evaluation answers were from company A. We compared the results from company A to the results from the other companies by looking at box-plots and it seems they are not different. This is a motivation why we analyze the results from every respondent without considering the company. These differences were also analyzed for each question with Mann-Whitney tests, but as expected no significant differences were found. Company A was shown a summary of their responses and asked if they think their result would have differed 2 years back or 2 years from now.

Not significantly different. If we look back a bit further, say 5 years, most activities have definitely increased in importance. Some activities will probably increase a bit further in the future, especially the F-section where laws and regulations might play a part, but overall the activities are already perceived as important. Reduced importance is unlikely in the foreseeable future.

They were further asked if the similarity between Company A and other companies were expected.

It's expected. It indicates the increased attention to security issues is not restricted to specific businesses and this is what we have perceived as well.

That is, it can be seen that company A are working with improvements that are in line with the model.

7   Conclusions

The presented maturity model aims to help organization assess their maturity in handling software vulnerabilities in third party OSS and COTS components. The importance of such a model is due to the increasing number of vulnerabilities that are being reported, and the growing number of connected devices that are bound to change the society in the near future. The model is based on six capability areas and 21 practices. Related maturity models, i.e., those that focus on software security are very broad and cover many aspects related both to software development, maintenance, and organizational aspects, but they are not detailed enough to cover all aspects of handling vulnerabilities in third party code. Thus, this model can be seen as an important complement to other well-known models. This is also supported by our evaluation, which shows that the defined practices are highly relevant.

Acknowledgements. This work was supported partly by the Wallenberg AI, Autonomous Systems and Software Program (WASP) and partly by Swedish Governmental Agency for Innovation Systems (Vinnova), grant 2016-00603.

References

1. April, A., Hayes, J.H., Abran, A., Dumke, R.: Software maintenance maturity model (SMmm): the software maintenance process model. J. Softw. Evol. Process. **17**(3), 197–223 (2005)
2. Chandra, P.: Software assurance maturity model - a guide to building security into software development. Technical report, OWASP (2017)
3. Christopher, J.D.: Cybersecurity capability maturity model (C2M2). Technical report. Rhodes University (2014)
4. Cui, A., Costello, M., Stolfo, S.J.: When firmware modifications attack: a case study of embedded exploitation. In: Network & Distributed System Security Symposium (2013)
5. FIRST: Common vulnerability scoring system v3.0: Specification document. https://www.first.org/cvss/specification-document. Accessed 06 Mar 2018

6. Helgesson, Y.L., Höst, M., Weyns, K.: A review of methods for evaluation of maturity models for process improvement. J. Softw. Maint. Evol. Res. Pract. **24**, 436–453 (2011)
7. Hevner, A.R., March, S.T., Park, J., Ram, S.: Design science in information systems research. MIS Q. **28**(1), 75–105 (2004)
8. Höst, M., Sönnerup, J., Hell, M., Olsson, T.: Industrial practices in security vulnerability management for iot systems - an interview study. In: Proceedings of Software Engineering Research and Practice (SERP) (2018)
9. ISO/IEC: Information technology - security techniques - systems security engineering - capability maturity model. Technical report, International Organization of Standardization (2008)
10. McGraw, G., Migues, S., West, J.: Software security and the building security in maturity model (BSIMM). J. Comput. Sci. Coll. **30**(3), 7–8 (2015)
11. Mell, P., Scarfone, K., Romanosky, S.: A complete guide to the common vulnerability scoring system version 2.0. In: Published by FIRST-Forum of Incident Response and Security Teams, vol. 1, p. 23 (2007)
12. Microsoft: Simplified implementation of the Microsoft SDL. Technical report, Microsoft Coporation (2010)
13. Mitre: Common vulnerabilities and exposures. https://cve.mitre.org/. Accessed 15 May 2018
14. Niazi, M., Wilson, D., Zowghi, D.: A maturity model for the implementation of software process improvement. J. Syst. Softw. **74**(2), 155–172 (2005)
15. NIST: National vulnerability database. https://nvd.nist.gov/. Accessed 15 May 2018
16. Powell, M.: Wi-fi router security knowledge gap putting devices and private data at risk in UK homes. Technical report (2018). https://www.broadbandgenie.co.uk/blog/20180409-wifi-router-security-survey
17. Runeson, P., Höst, M.: Guidelines for conducting and reporting case study research in software engineering. Empir. Softw. Eng. **14**, 131–164 (2009)
18. SEI: Capability Maturity Model Integration, Version 1.2, vol. CMU/SEI-2006-TR-008(2008). Carnegie Mellon Software Engineering Institute (2008)
19. Shahzad, M., Shafiq, M.Z., Liu, A.X.: A large scale exploratory analysis of software vulnerability life cycles. In: Proceedings of International Conference on Software Engineering (ICSE), pp. 771–781 (2012)

Towards a Digital Ecosystem for Rural Areas: Experiences from Three Years of Development

Frank Elberzhager[(⊠)], Matthias Koch, and Balthasar Weitzel

Fraunhofer IESE, Fraunhofer Platz 1, Kaiserslautern, Germany
{frank.elberzhager,matthias.koch,
balthasar.weitzel}@iese.fraunhofer.de

Abstract. Software and software systems are increasingly connected today, and the trend is continuing. The development of such systems requires competencies that go beyond classic software engineering. Key challenges are cross-domain work, increasing complexity with shorter time to market, shared responsibility and control across multiple companies, as well as the ever-increasing demands regarding security, user experience, and other qualities. In this publication, we share our software development experiences from the Digital Villages project. The major goal in this project is to support rural areas with digital services running on a platform. While typical software engineering activities such as design, implementation, or testing are, of course, necessary further on, evaluation and incorporating feedback from users play a far more important role when going towards digital ecosystems. Our results are based on a current project runtime of three years, and might provide background for others who want to shift towards developing such systems.

Keywords: Software engineering · Digital ecosystem · Experiences

1 Introduction

The world we live in today is becoming increasingly networked. Connected cars, homes, and factories, smart and mobile devices, and even combinations of these are only some examples. This trend permeates both the private and the business sector and is often called the digital transformation nowadays. For companies, new possibilities for offering their products and services in such connected systems emerge, and the chances for innovative products and new businesses increase. In this context, terms such as the Internet of Things (IoT), digital ecosystems, or cyber-physical systems among others have become established.

While such connected systems provide enormous opportunities for companies on the one hand, there are several challenges regarding the development and operation of such systems on the other hand. The development of embedded or information systems as such is often characterized by high complexity, but the integration into increased connected systems raises this complexity greatly. Challenges are, for example, the high heterogeneity, organizational issues such as conflicting motivation of players, evolution aspects, or contradicting qualities. In addition to such challenges, the pressure to be on the market more quickly is increasing; in other words, a common business goal is to

© Springer Nature Switzerland AG 2018
M. Kuhrmann et al. (Eds.): PROFES 2018, LNCS 11271, pp. 98–105, 2018.
https://doi.org/10.1007/978-3-030-03673-7_7

achieve short time to market to remain competitive. Furthermore, quality plays a decisive role in user acceptance, but also regarding the innovative strength and thus the future viability of such systems.

In this paper, we share experiences from a platform developed in the Digital Villages project, which started in 2015. The goal of this project is to support the daily life of people living in rural areas by means of digital innovation. Since the availability of services is constantly decreasing in such areas (e.g., fewer stores, doctors, or transportation possibilities), the goal of the project is to create new digital services that allow residents to use the available services in a much more efficient way. In addition to that, the actual social integration of people is intended to be enhanced. The major focus for us is what are good software engineering practices during the development of a platform and services running on the platform in (software) ecosystems.

We present our software engineering methodology and report concrete experiences regarding how we cope with selected challenges. Practitioners may get several ideas about what to consider when building or participating in a digital ecosystem with their software systems, and researchers will get new ideas for future research.

This paper is structured as follows: Sect. 2 provides an overview of related work regarding software engineering in the IoT and digital ecosystem development. Section 3 provides our context. Section 4 describes development activities including their adaptations and related experiences, including a discussion of the experiences. Section 5 concludes our publication.

2   Related Work

Software engineering (SE) is concerned with the creation of large and complex software systems. A look at the increasing number of publications that correlate SE to IoT or digital ecosystems clearly reveals the need for dedicated consideration of the specific challenges in this type of systems.

Jansen et al. [1] illustrate in an early publication challenges from the practical perspective of software vendors, who potentially become part of a software ecosystem. A key challenge is how to gain insights into the ecosystem, i.e. understanding how it works and who its participants are, as well as the development of strategies for vendors aimed not only how to initially take part in the ecosystem, but also how to survive in the ecosystem.

One big topic that research focuses on are technical aspects. They include, for example, challenges w.r.t. energy consumption or the distribution of nodes; in other words, network and communication challenges, along with research on security and privacy. Furthermore, a major topic is the consideration of open source (software) ecosystems, where the specificities of such systems is investigated. In addition, the application of other concepts in IoT and software ecosystems such as cloud computing, artificial intelligence, or Big Data is an active area of research.

Research in the area of SE is focused mainly on architecture challenges; however, requirements engineering as well as ecosystem modeling, including the monitoring and managing of an ecosystem's health beyond technical functionalities, are found as well. Santos and Werner [2] determined three dimensions along which SE methods can be distinguished: an architectural, a business, and a social dimension. The authors propose an initial approach for the architectural dimension, focusing on the establishment of the ecosystem's central platform. Morkevicius et al. [3] comment on linking requirements and design artifacts to an ecosystem's architecture. Due to the lack of formal techniques, traceability between these is typically missing. Therefore, they suggest the usage of the Unified Architecture Framework (UAF) and combining it with the Industrial Internet Reference Architecture (IIRA) to enable traceability and provide SE support in the construction of IoT systems. According to Coutinho et al. [4], modeling an ecosystem on a high level of abstraction is still an open issue today.

The area of quality assurance in such connected systems is another research focus where several publications emerged during the last five years. Main topics are testing network protocols [5], considering qualities such as performance or interoperability [6], or describe technical means such as testbeds or frameworks [7]. However, a high level of heterogeneity can be observed with special solutions, but an overall consideration of the SE activities is basically missing.

3 The Project

Digital Villages is a research project that focuses on the digitalization of rural areas. The main objective of the project is to acquire knowledge about how the attractiveness of rural areas in Germany can be increased by means of digital services. So far, these services focus on logistics and mobility as well as communication mechanisms among residents and between residents and municipalities. In the first two years of the project, the foundation has been laid to connect local vendors and producers with interested residents as purchasers of goods. Additionally, residents can act as voluntary carriers by picking up ordered goods from vendors and delivering them to a local pooling station or directly to the buyer's home (Fig. 1). To realize this, a central platform linking all actors and technical systems is required.

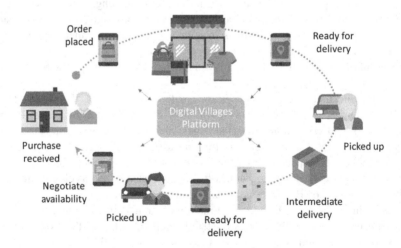

Fig. 1. Ordering and delivering goods in digital villages

The central platform takes on a mediating role, for example by allocating the purchase made by a resident in the online shop, i.e., the delivery of the goods, to the right persons with the right device, in this case users of the mobile apps. This procedure is concretely triggered by an order placed by a resident in the corresponding online shop. The respective vendors prepare the incoming orders. Subsequently, the central platform informs all the users of a mobile application that open deliveries are waiting to be transported from vendors to buyers. Via the application, residents can volunteer to take over a delivery. The delivery can be made in person to the recipient, or the carrier can deliver the package to a pooling station, from where the recipient can pick it up him-/herself. During the whole process, the central platform coordinates all the events, such as informing the recipient about the necessary onward transport to the destination if a package is dropped off at an intermediate pooling station.

Since the third year of the project's runtime, activities concentrate on extension of the platform by adding further services companying the delivery scenario sketched before. These services mainly address communication among residents and communication with the local administration.

In the context of this project, we assumed the roles of the initiator, developer, and operator of the central platform. We involve additional partners as service or data providers contributing to the digital ecosystem, such as payment providers or content providers for products in the online shop. In the future, we plan to include further parties to develop and offer services with our platform.

4 Experiences

In this section, we describe our main software engineering activities in the project. While they are based on established and proven activities, we identified the need to adapt them to the specificities of the project context. We share our experiences and highlight lessons learned for our engineering and development activities.

4.1 Requirements Engineering

Due to the end-user-centric focus of the system, **we performed the development in close contact with the relevant stakeholders**. This allows the elicitation of problems and improvement potentials as well as concrete requirements on the one hand, and early evaluation of concepts and prototypes on the other hand. Therefore, we aimed at identifying the relevant stakeholders and derived dedicated activities for including and involving them in the project. In contrast to traditional requirements engineering (RE) activities, we could not rely on simply asking the stakeholders about their requirements. Instead, due to the novelty of this type of system, we largely "invented" our own requirements and verified their correctness together with the stakeholders. For this purpose, we conducted separate workshops that typically consisted of an informative part where we presented current work results as well as a feedback and discussion part where we gathered the stakeholders' opinions and new ideas.

Within the stakeholder groups, **we faced a heterogeneity of people in terms of knowledge and experience with technical systems as well as openness towards**

such systems. To deal with the skepticism of the rural area residents, the workshops largely consisted of building trust and listening to people's worries and doubts instead of being classic requirements workshops. However, we benefited from the conversations with the residents since they revealed underlying needs and wishes, which formed the basis for the formulation of hypotheses about their actual requirements.

4.2   Architecting

The architecting activities were mainly triggered by new or changed requirements. The typical basis for our architecting activities was a business-process-oriented requirements specification. On this basis, we created a data model consisting of client entities and more complex backend entities. Using this model and the business process, a separation into processing units responsible for subsets of the data entities could be performed. Since the main communication mechanism was based on events, we used sequence diagrams to define communication protocols with events as messages between the processing units. A textual description of the expected response of each processing unit when receiving an event accompanied these diagrams. Automated consolidation of these communication protocols into behavioral descriptions of each processing unit was done to ease the realization of these modules. The formal definition of the data model, events and communication protocols reduced the number of integration faults. We can confirm this effect in our project since in cases where we did not have such a definition, the number of such faults drastically increased.

The use of event-based communication supported the flexibility required in the project. It enabled to attach new functionality easily, since new components can subscribe to events emitted by existing ones. Furthermore, the event-based communication method turned out to be beneficial for offline functionality of clients. User interaction not directly requiring a response from the backend could be queued locally and transferred to the backend later. The downside of the event-based internal communication was the increased complexity. The event-processing units needed to be organized both according to the events that come in and according to the state of the entity concerned. The effort required to reconstruct communication paths was higher due to missing support in IDEs for tracing the sending and consuming of events.

4.3   Design and Implementation

The rollout of applications to **end users with non-technical backgrounds implied the need for creating appealing user interfaces and focusing on a positive overall user experience**. Based on knowledge acquired from the requirements engineering activities, we created concepts for the visual design of the user interfaces. For this purpose, we started with pen-and-paper and wireframe prototypes to discuss the workflows the application is used in as well as the layout and content of the interfaces. After deciding on the screen designs from a conceptual perspective, we created visual designs that reflect the actual look and feel of the intended devices. Since such decisions can affect architectural decisions, user experience designers and architects often met to align the concepts. **Our development benefited from the decision to use different prototypes for different purposes**, so early decisions could be made with prototypes that were easy to change, while more elaborated prototypes were created to enable the implementation activities. We used the definition of architecture and visual designs to derive implementation tasks and feed them into a development stack set up for each application and the platform individually. A task for a developer is composed in such a way that one person can complete it within at maximum two days.

4.4 Testing and Evaluation

As one of our main challenges was to deliver flexible software with high quality within a limited period, our testing and quality assurance activities needed to ensure, on the one hand, that few defects were introduced, and, on the other hand, that defects were detected quickly. We introduced **automated unit and integration tests** that were automatically run in the continuous integration and deployment pipeline and would break the build if they failed. **All failing builds triggered notifications in the team chat**, so there was also a bit of social pressure to not commit code that contains faults. After a successful commit, a manual code review by a second person was required before the changes were merged to the master branch. Thus, code quality flaws were also detected. When all tasks of a user story had been implemented both on the backend and the client, we performed manual system tests that included clients and backend following a test plan created based on the implemented workflows.

Our **project results were evaluated in practice in two municipalities** in the state of Rhineland Palatinate, Germany. To get more condensed results, the residents could use our solutions during three test phases of one month each. Before the actual field tests could be carried out, there was a phase of promoting our solution in the municipalities. This was mainly done by the local administration, supported by our staff. Workshops with residents helped to raise attention for the topic. In addition to that, advertisements were put up in important places within the municipality. **While the field tests were running, our team offered continuous support via easy to use feedback channels**. During the very first test run, the whole team even stayed at the municipality to offer quick solutions for challenges that arose. This enabled us to create fixes for urgent issues found during the field tests to be able to roll them out directly.

4.5 Discussion

In its core, the development approach pursued in the Digital Villages project consists of a combination of known and established software engineering principles, which we brought together and tailored or extended them selectively to address the specific challenges of developing an innovative ecosystem in rural areas. The high number of stakeholders, which led to organizational challenges, were mainly addressed by involving them early and continuously during requirements engineering activities as well as during the evolution of prototypes and finalized products. To handle the complexity of the overall system and the high level of quality required of the product, emphasis was placed on the architecting and quality assurance activities. We focused on the definition of a detailed data model and its early verification with different roles in the development team, including designers and requirements engineers. This included the commitment to consistent naming conventions agreed on by the whole development team to facilitate communication.

Furthermore, the formal definition of the (technical) communication mechanisms with the help of graphical support in the form of sequence diagrams allowed representing and handling the system's complex relationships. Using custom extensions for Enterprise Architect, we additionally generated dedicated views on the event-based communication to ensure the architecture documentation covers all aspects necessary for its implementation. The quality assurance activities ranged from unit tests via automated integration tests to extensive internal system tests to cover technical or programming-related issues, including design and usability defects. To enable early detection of relevant and critical issues on all these levels, we did not rely on pure coverage of lines or even single user stories, but instead needed to consider the set of requirements as a whole to define appropriate and representative test scenarios. Finally, we decided to welcome external feedback early in the project and encouraged users to share their view on the provided functionalities by performing joint evaluation phases, in which actual users used the project's results in the real world while being supported and supervised by members of the development team. Since this perspective revealed issues that the team had never thought of, a significant contribution to the overall quality of the system could be provided by these non-IT experts and their occasionally unexpected usage of the applications.

We are aware of some threats to validity. The development approach has only been applied in the context of the Digital Villages project to date; hence, its applicability as well as its efficiency and effectiveness have not yet been evaluated in the context of other domains. However, because we rely on practices that have proven their utility in contexts beyond the one described in this paper, we are convinced that their combination in the setting of any ecosystem will show similar positive effects. The challenges experienced in the Digital Villages project are typical for such kinds of systems and can be observed in industrial projects, too. At the same time, the selected practices are independent of the specific domain "rural areas", which is why we expect them to be applicable in other domains.

5 Conclusion

In this publication, we introduced the Digital Villages project as an example for developing a platform and services for a software ecosystem. Based on the challenges encountered in our environment, we provided experiences with the software and systems engineering activities we applied throughout the past three years.

Regarding the research question we formulated, we could derive lessons learned for typical software and systems engineering activities. They had to be adapted to a certain extent, which was influenced by the concrete challenges we faced in the Digital Villages project. Such experiences might help practitioners when they plan to develop ecosystems.

We are aware that our results basically show that many established software engineering activities are applicable in the ecosystem development context while some activities were needed to adapt to handle new requirements. Such results may not reinvent the (software engineering) wheel, but provide a certain confidence when companies shift towards such digital ecosystem or IoT development. To the best of our knowledge, not many of such experience reports already exist. The application of the development approach is scheduled for upcoming ecosystem projects in which we aim to investigate the need for making adaptations, which we plan to share.

Acknowledgments. Parts of this work have been funded by the project "Digitale Dörfer", funded by the Ministry of Internal Affairs and Sports of the state of Rhineland-Palatinate (grant no. "56:382 Digitale Dörfer"). Additionally, parts of this work have been funded by the "EnStadt: Pfaff" project (grant no. 03SBE112D and 03SBE112G) of the German Federal Ministry for Economic Affairs and Energy (BMWi) and the Federal Ministry of Education and Research (BMBF).

References

1. Jansen, S., Brinkkemper, S., Finkelstein, A.: Business network management as a survival strategy: a tale of two software ecosystems. In: First Workshop on Software Ecosystems (2009)
2. Santos, R.P.d., Werner, C.M.L.: A Proposal for Software Ecosystems Engineering (2011)
3. Morkevicius, A., Bisikirskiene, L., Bleakley, G.: Using a systems of systems modeling approach for developing industrial internet of things applications. In: System of Systems Engineering Conference (2017)
4. Coutinho, E.F., Viana, D., Santos, R.P.d.: An exploratory study on the need for modeling software ecosystems: the case of SOLAR SECO. In: 9th International Workshop on Modelling in Software Engineering (2017)
5. Che, X., Maag, S.: A passive testing approach for protocols in internet of things. In: IEEE International Conference on Green Computing and Communications and IEEE Internet of Things and IEEE Cyber, Physical and Social Computing (2013)
6. Bellagente, P., Ferrari, P., Flammini, A., Rinaldi, S.: Adopting IoT framework for energy management of smart building: a real test-case. In: International Forum on Research and Technologies for Society and Industry (2015)
7. Nikoletseas, S., Rapti, M., Raptis, T.P., Veroutis, K.: Decentralizing and adding portability to an IoT test-bed through smartphones. In: International Conference on Distributed Computing in Sensor Systems, DCOSS (2014)

Software Processes Analysis with Provenance

Gabriella Castro Barbosa Costa[1,2](✉), Humberto L. O. Dalpra[1],
Eldânae N. Teixeira[1], Cláudia M. L. Werner[1], Regina M. M. Braga[3],
and Marcos A. Miguel[4]

[1] COPPE - Federal University of Rio de Janeiro, Rio de Janeiro, RJ, Brazil
{gabriellacbc,humbertodalpra,danny,
werner}@cos.ufrj.br
[2] Computing and Mechanics Department, Federal Center for Technological
Education of Minas Gerais, Minas Gerais, MG, Brazil
[3] Computer Science Department, Federal University of Juiz de Fora,
Juiz de Fora, MG, Brazil
regina.braga@ufjf.edu.br
[4] Projetus Information Technology, 36120000, Juiz de Fora, Brazil
marcos@projetusti.com.br

Abstract. Companies have been increasing the amount of data that they collect from their systems and processes, considering the decrease in the cost of memory and storage technologies in recent years. The emergence of technologies such as Big Data, Cloud Computing, E-Science, and the growing complexity of information systems made evident that traceability and provenance are promising approaches. Provenance has been successfully used in complex domains, like health sciences, chemical industries, and scientific computing, considering that these areas require a comprehensive semantic traceability mechanism. Based on these, we investigate the use of provenance in the context of Software Process (SP) and introduce a novel approach based on provenance concepts to model and represent SP data. It addresses SP provenance data capturing, storing, new information inferencing and visualization. The main contribution of our approach is PROV-SwProcess, a provenance model to deal with the specificities of SP and its ability in supporting process managers to deal with vast amounts of execution data during the process analysis and data-driven decision-making. A set of analysis possibilities were derived from this model, using SP goals and questions. A case study was conducted in collaboration with a software development company to instantiate the PROV-SwProcess model (using the proposed approach) with real-word process data. This study showed that 87.5% of the analysis possibilities using real data was correct and can assist in decision-making, while 62.5% of them are not possible to be performed by the process manager using his currently dashboard or process management tool.

Keywords: Software process analysis · Software process improvement
Data provenance

M. Kuhrmann et al. (Eds.): PROFES 2018, LNCS 11271, pp. 106–122, 2018.
https://doi.org/10.1007/978-3-030-03673-7_8

1 Introduction

During the software process (SP), many different types of data can be generated and collected [11], such as: (i) Product Data: source code, configuration management data, documentation, executable codes, test suites, testing results, and simulations; (ii) Process Data: explicit definition of a software process model, process enactment state information, data for process analysis and evolution, history data, project management data; and (iii) Organizational Data: ownership information for various project components, roles and responsibilities, and resource management data. Then, it is not a novelty that software development companies started to adopt data-driven practices in parts of their business over time [4]. However, the use of SP data remains a challenging topic for software engineers. Considering that engineering education "tends to focus on formulas, clear cause effect relations and predictable behaviors of the systems built by engineers, the notion of statistical behavior, analysis of large data sets and the use of averages and deviations feels less tangible, or, if nothing else, requires an alternative mindset from the people working with the data" [4]. Besides that, over time, the records accumulate, and the volume of data makes it difficult to conduct SP data analysis.

One possible way to support the analysis and verify the quality of SP generated data is by using provenance techniques and models. Data provenance can be defined as the description of the origins of a piece of data and the process by which it arrived in a database. It brings transparency and helps to audit and interpret data. Provenance has been successfully used in complex domains, like health sciences, chemical industries, and scientific computing [14]. The emergence of technologies such as Big Data, Cloud Computing, E-Science, and the increasing complexity of information systems further emphasize that traceability and provenance can be promising approaches.

Based on these facts and considering that SP is also a complex domain, the goal of this paper is to improve the process manager's understanding about the SP execution, providing analysis and decision-making possibilities using process data and provenance concepts. Then, our main research question is: *How can the use of provenance models and techniques in the SP domain support process managers analysis and data-driven decision making?* Then, we investigate the usage of provenance in the context of SP and propose a novel approach with a provenance model (called PROV-SwProcess) to deal with the specificities of SP. This approach addresses SP provenance data capturing, storing, new information inferencing and visualization. A difference of the proposed approach is its ability to infer new information, since it is ontology-based and uses an inference machine. In order to support process managers analysis and data-driven decision making, a set of SP analysis possibilities (e.g. process structure identification, possibilities for its redesign, understand stakeholder's involvement in process execution) were derived from PROV-SwProcess model and some insights of how to use them in decision-making are detailed. The current version of PROV-SwProcess model presented in this paper was carefully evaluated by three experts in process and provenance. Moreover, a case study was conducted in collaboration with a development company to instantiate PROV-SwProcess model (using the proposed approach) with real-word process data and the SP analysis possibilities were discussed.

The research methodology was undertaken in four steps (1) Research problem definition and a *quasi*-systematic review analyzing the use of provenance in SP. (2) The approach was specified and some studies to evaluate its viability were performed ([6, 8]). (3) The core of the approach, PROV-SwProcess model, was defined and an evaluated by three experts in provenance and SP. (4) The approach was implemented with its tool support and a case study was performed.

This paper is organized as follows: A brief background considering SP and provenance is presented in Sects. 2 and 3 describes some related works. PROV-SwProcess model is presented in Sect. 4, with a discussion about the analysis possibilities derived from it. The approach that supports the model instantiation, new information inferencing and data visualization is presented in Sect. 5. Section 6 describes the model evaluation and a regular case study with a real-world process. Section 7 presents the paper conclusions.

2 Background

A well-defined SP should indicate the activities to be executed, the required resources, produced and consumed artifacts, adopted procedures (methods, techniques, models of documents, etc.), and the criteria for carrying out the activities [2]. The essential elements of SP considered in this approach are [12]: (i) **Activity**: deals with the process activities used to create and/or maintain software and how they compose the SP; (ii) **Stakeholder**: refers to organizations, persons, projects, or teams acting or interesting in the software process activities; (iii) **Resource**: involves hardware equipment and software products used by the activities; (iv) **Procedure**: relates to methods, techniques and document templates adopted by the software process activities; and (v) **Artifact**: represents different types of objects produced, changed, and used in process activities.

During the process execution, SP data are captured and analyzed during the process evaluation. Process analysis (or evaluation) can be of two different types [26]: (i) Deductive Analysis: considers an abstract specification of a process in some formal logic, aiming to discover inconsistencies or anomalies that would be present in enactments of the process; or (ii) Retrospective Analysis: analyze empirically gathered data from several enactments of a process, to discover patterns of anomalous behavior. Our approach focuses on retrospective analysis, i.e., on SP execution data.

Data provenance can be defined as the origins description of a piece of data and their processing history [14]. Provenance differs from traditional data items and metadata considering that it is an immutable directed graph, incrementally captured at runtime [23]. Nevertheless, process data provenance capturing does not interfere in the SP execution and allows the process managers or process data analysts to refine the applied filtering rules for data process collection [15].

According to Freire *et al.* [14], when we have provenance from computational tasks, it can be divided into two types: (i) prospective provenance, that captures a computational task's specification and corresponds to the steps that must be followed to generate a data product, and (ii) retrospective provenance, that captures the steps executed as well as information about the environment used to derive a specific data product.

To obtain the benefits of provenance information, data provenance should be captured/stored in an integrated manner to allow queries on that data. In this vein, there are two main models proposed in the literature: Open Provenance Model (OPM) [20] and, more recently, W3C PROV model [18]. In this paper, PROV was chosen and extended, considering that it is a standard model provided by W3C and it has causal relationships that are not explicit in OPM. PROV model [18] aims to express data provenance through the description of entities, activities, and agents involved in producing or delivering an object, and the causal relationships between them. The seven main PROV causal relationships are: (1) used, (2) wasGeneratedBy, (3) wasAssociatedWith, (4) wasAttributedTo, (5) actedOnBehalfOf, (6) wasDerivedFrom, and (7) wasInformedBy.

3 Related Work

Our approach differs from the other process analysis approaches based on process execution logs [1, 2, 5] since it addresses the possibility of deriving implicit knowledge, using an ontology, inference rules, and an inference machine. In this vein, causal relationships between the process execution data can be automatically inferred, even if it has not been provided (e.g., artifacts creation and modification by stakeholders, derivation between artifacts, usage of specific procedures to develop an artifact). Considering this fact, related work is analyzed through two different perspectives: (a) provenance data models that are extensions from PROV (considering that PROV-SwProcess model[1] is an extension of PROV), and (b) the use of provenance in the context of SP.

Considering that PROV model is generic and presents several possibilities of causal relationships, there are in the literature some proposals to adapt this model to specific domains, such as D-PROV [19] and ProvONE [7]. D-PROV extends PROV to represent the process structure, i.e., to enable prospective provenance storage and query. D-PROV was a previous incarnation of ProvONE, which is a model for scientific workflow provenance and extends PROV with its specific structure elements. Although these models are useful in scientific workflow domain and process in general, it does not suffice for capturing and analyzing provenance in the SP domain. For example, in ProvONE, the workflow execution corresponds to the execution of computational tasks only by software agents but, in the SP, we need to express different types of agents, such as, persons, teams, and organizations. Besides, ProvONE does not have specific types of procedures and artifacts and does not propose new rules to derive implicit provenance information. Considering the gaps of ProvONE and the fact that PROV does not capture the specificities of SP, extensions in this model should be made. An initial effort in this regard was made in previous works [6, 8].

---

[1] It is detailed in Subsect. 4.1.

Considering the use of provenance in SP, it was found in a previous literature review, that the application and use of provenance data in the SP domain were mentioned for the first time in 2005 [27] and all others were published from 2007 onwards. One of the possibilities regarding a greater number of publications appearing after 2007 is due to the emergence of the Provenance Challenge, started in 2006 [21]. However, it should be considered that this event addressed the provenance challenges in the general scope and not specifically in the SP domain. The results dating from only 2005 also shows the lack of maturity of this research field and the need, as underscored by some authors [9, 10, 16], for more scientific papers about using provenance in the context of SP.

A code provenance management tool called Ariadne is proposed in [9]. It tracks the provenance of source code and generates provenance reports to facilitate the management of its intellectual property. Other works, such as [10, 16], motivate the need to model and extract software artifacts provenance. Davies et al. [10] explore the recovery of the provenance of software artifacts by a broad set of techniques (signature matching, source code fact extraction, software clone detection, call flow graph matching, string matching, historical analyses etc.) and Godfrey [16] cites the PROV model specification and shows a motivating example that uses hashing to quickly and accurately identify version information of embedded Java libraries. Although these works deal with provenance in the context of software development, they do not address the provenance of SP as a whole. They focus on software artifacts or source code. In PROV-SwProcess, we treat not only the artifacts, but the activities, agents and the various relationships that can be established in SP. A technique called PRiME [17] also adapts projects to interact with a provenance layer. Based on PRiME, Wendel et al. [25] present a solution to failures in software development processes, using the Open Provenance Model and SOA architecture. However, the last two works do not specify how data provenance can be inferred and used to support SP analysis and data-driven decision-making as done in our approach. The most recent publication in this scenario [13] starts a discussion of using complex networks concepts (besides an ontology) to help in SP data interpretation aiming to support in SP improvement. However, it does not address specific concepts of SP as we have done in PROV-SwProcess Model (it uses ProvONE) and does not provide the analysis discussed in our work.

4   Provenance in Software Processes

Based in a previous literature review (whose main points were presented in Sect. 3), there is no consensus regarding the most appropriate provenance model to be used specifically in SP domain. The model most used in the provenance area is PROV. However, the direct application of this model to SP domain lacks in capturing some SP specificities such as Resources and Procedures used or adopted by the activities, different types of SP artifacts (e.g., software product, software items and models), as well as new possible relationships between them. To overcome this gap and considering the existence of different systems that can be used during SP execution (e.g., version control system, issue trackers, and documentation management systems) without a standard model to capture the provenance of these processes execution, PROV-SwProcess model was defined and described in the next subsection.

4.1 PROV-SwProcess: A PROV Extension Data Model for Software Processes

PROV-SwProcess model was developed to be a standard for SP provenance representation. It was defined as a PROV extension, aiming to capture and infer relevant information about SP data.

A preliminary proposal of PROV-SwProcess (called PROV-Process) was published in 2016 [8]. It is an initial approach to apply the PROV model in SP domain. PROV-SwProcess aims to incorporate the basic ideas of this work, as well as additional contributions, to derive an adequate standard that can be used in SP.

PROV-SwProcess covers prospective and retrospective provenance [14] and the essential aspects of SP: activities, stakeholder, resource, procedure, and artifact [12]. It is divided into (i) associations (or relations), (ii) classes, and (iii) specific inference rules. Figure 1 describes PROV-SwProcess[2], focusing its Retrospective Provenance[3] part and using a diagram to represent its conceptual model. The following points should be considered regarding it: (1) Constructs and associations presented between "≪≫" were derived from PROV. For example: the ≪Activity≫ class corresponds to the Activity PROV type. Newly PROV-SwProcess associations/relations and classes appeared without "≪≫"; (2) Elements in ellipses are specializations of the Entity PROV type and elements in pentagons are specializations of the Agent PROV type; (3) Associations with solid lines are used to capture Retrospective Provenance and associations with dashed lines can be inferred by PROV-SwProcess approach and their respective provenance rules, that is, they do not necessarily need to be captured or informed in the SP provenance data. The data are transformed into an ontology that enables to make inferences into the data using a reasoner; (4) All PROV-SwProcess relations have a related inverse relation (for example: the inverse relation of Used≫ is the relation ≪WasUsedBy≫), however, these were not explicit in the figures aiming to facilitate the understanding of the proposed model; (5) When there is more than one SP instance to be analyzed, the relation WasComposedBy can also be inferred, allowing to obtain all the stakeholders, resources, artifacts, and procedures involved in a SP instance.

PROV-SwProcess Ontology and Inference Rules

PROV-SwProcess model has also an ontology that extends PROV-O ontology [18] and is specified using Ontology Web Language (OWL2)[4]. We adopted an ontology to support our model and approach, considering that it addresses the possibility of deriving implicit knowledge, using some inference rules and an inference machine or

---

[2] The complete model specification can be accessed at: http://bit.ly/provswprocess.

[3] PROV-SwProcess defines both Retrospective and Prospective Provenance, however, due to space restrictions, we focused on its Retrospective part in this paper.

[4] http://bit.ly/provswprocessontology.

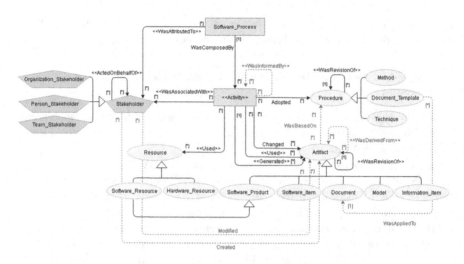

Fig. 1. PROV-SwProcess model (Retrospective Part) (Color figure online)

reasoner (as an example, in Fig. 1, all the associations with red dashed lines are inferred even it was not provided in the process data execution).

An inference rule can be applied to PROV-SwProcess instances to add new PROV-SwProcess statements, bringing implicit information. The inferences rules have been defined and specified using the Semantic Web Rule Language (SWRL), specifically to the SP domain. They can be divided into 8 groups: (1) *Created*, (2) *Modified*, (3) *WasBasedOn*, (4) *WasAppliedTo*, (5) *WasDerivedFrom*, (6) *WasInformedBy*, (7) *WasComposedBy*, and (8) *HadRole*. All the proposed inferences have the form:

IF A1 and … and Ap THEN there exists y1 … ym such that B1 and … and Bk

That means: $\forall$ x1, …. ,xn. A1 $\wedge$ … $\wedge$ Ap $\Rightarrow$ $\exists$ y1 … ym . B1 $\wedge$ … $\wedge$ Bk, where x1 … xn are the free variables of the inference.

As an example, an inference rule of the *Created* group is[5]:

IF wasAssociatedWith(_ass; ac,sta,_attrs1) and generated(_gen; ac,art,_attrs2) THEN there exists _id such that created(_id; sta,art,[]).

This inference states that if an activity *ac* was associated with a stakeholder *sta* and this activity *ac* generated an artifact *art*, the relation *created* between the stakeholder *sta* and the artifact *art* can be inferred. Figure 2 shows an example to explain PROV-SwProcess model possible inferences (the inferred associations appear in red). Even if there is no explicit and direct relation in the provenance data between Mary and Payment_Test_Cases, we can infer, using the rule presented, that *Mary* created *Payment_Test_Cases*.

In order to achieve the main objective of the approach (improve the process managers' understanding about the SP execution, providing analysis and decision-making possibilities using process data and provenance concepts), some specific goals were derived from PROV-SwProcess model and are described in the following.

---

[5] All the inferences rules are detailed in the complete PROV-SwProcess model specification.

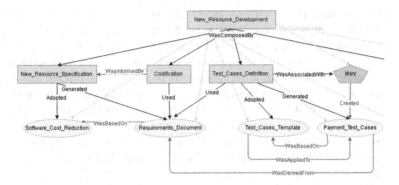

Fig. 2. PROV-SwProcess inferences example (Color figure online)

4.2   Software Process Analysis Goals

Aiming to support process managers' analysis and data-driven decision making, a set of SP analysis possibilities, divided into specific goals, was derived from PROV-SwProcess model and some insights of how to use it in decision-making are detailed. Due to space restrictions, these analyses represent an initial set of how to apply the resources provided by the approach, and do not cover the whole model.

- **Goal 1: Process Structure Identification and possibilities for process redesign**
  - **Question 1.1**: What are the process activities, artifacts, resources, procedures, stakeholders, and the relations among them?
    - **How to answer the question?** Using a list or a graph with the executed activities, artifacts, resources, procedures, and stakeholders with its relations.
    - **Analysis**: It is possible to identify all the process elements that participated in process executions (or in some process instance) and the relations among them.
    - **Decision-Making Possibility**: After identifying the process elements and the relations between them it is possible to find gaps (elements without association or inadequate relation established) in the analyzed data and try to correct it in next process executions.
  - **Question 1.2:** Which procedures are used by the process?
    - **How to answer the question:** Using the number of procedures used to the develop the process artifacts and a list or graph with them.
    - **Analysis**: It is possible to check which procedures influenced an artifact development; Verify the procedures most useful in the analyzed instance(s), when a procedure is used by artifacts in a number greater than the average; Check procedures useless, i.e., although existing, these procedures were never used during the execution of the processes carried out by the organization.
    - **Decision-Making Possibility**: When verifying that procedures influenced an artifact development, the process manager can evaluate if this fact was really planned/expected (in process modeling phase) or not; if this information is

not specified in the process model, the process manager may include it; Being aware that a procedure is widely used by the process instances, the manager can better plan any changes in this procedure, since this can have a great impact on future executions; If a procedure has not been used during process execution, this in-formation may be valid for the process manager to evaluate whether this procedure needs to be changed/reshaped to be used as planned or if it should be removed from the process. Another point of analysis would be the impact of not having a standard for the development of some artifacts – it could impact the quality level of generated artifacts, as well as cause errors by the difficulty of understanding some information in these artifacts, etc.

- **Question 1.3:** Which activities has a high complexity?
  - **How to answer the question:** Using the number of Artifacts, Stakeholders, Procedure and Resource associated to a specific activity or a graph showing these relations.
  - **Analysis**: It is possible to check when activities are associated with many stakeholders, artifacts, procedures, and resources, when compared to the other activities, indicating that an activity could be more complex than others.
  - **Decision-Making Possibility**: With the information provided by the analysis presented above, the process manager can evaluate if this fact was really planned/expected (in process modeling phase) or not; if this information is not specified in the process model, the process manager may change the process model to better represent the process that was in fact executed; A possible evaluation of the activities detected as more complex can be performed, aiming to divide it into less complex sub activities.
- **Question 1.4:** Which activities has a high dependency?
  - **How to answer the question:** Using the number of dependent activities of each executed activity and a list of them or some graph representation showing these dependencies.
  - **Analysis**: It is possible to analyze the dependency between two activities, i.e., when occurred the exchange of some artifact by two activities, one activity using some entity generated or changed by the other. It is also possible to discover which activity occurred before or after another during execution time and to identify possible bottlenecks based on activities dependency.
  - **Decision-Making Possibility**: From the previous analyzes, the process manager can confront the activities (and its flow) specified in the process model and how they occurred during execution. If there are any discrepancies, he can make changes in the process model, according to what he verified that, in fact, it was executed. Another decision is trying to make changes in the process model to avoid bottlenecks, if it were identified in the previous analysis.

- **Goal 2: Understand stakeholder's involvement in process execution**
  - **Question 2.1**: What is the activities distribution among stakeholders?
    - **How to answer the question**: Number of activities each stakeholder is involved and a list or some graph representation with them.
    - **Analysis**: It is possible to discover, from a stakeholder, all the activities (and the total of these activities) in which he/she participated, allowing to understand the activities distribution among stakeholders in the process execution.
    - **Decision-Making Possibility**: When verifying that a stakeholder is participating in much activities than others, the process manager can evaluate if this fact was really planned/expected (considering, for example, that a stakeholder was associated to a high number of activities because him/her always is attributed to activities with a lower level of complexity) or if it has been occurring due to an inadequate activity distribution during the process instantiation.
  - **Question 2.2**: Which artifacts are known by a stakeholder, considering that in some process execution he/she created or modified such artifact?
    - **How to answer the question**: Number of artifacts each stakeholder is involved in its creation or modification and a list with them or some graph representation showing stakeholders x artifacts.
    - **Analysis**: It is possible to discover all the artifacts that were created and/or modified by a stakeholder, allowing to understand about what artifacts this stakeholder has some knowledge, considering he/she manipulated this artifact in some process execution. Considering the artifact view point, it is possible to discover all the stakeholders that has some knowledge about it, considering it was created or modified by them.
    - **Decision-Making Possibility**: in a future instantiation of the analyzed process, if a certain task is associated with a specific artifact, the process manager (or the responsible for the process instantiation) can allocate to this task a stakeholder with greater or less knowledge about the artifact to be manipulated during this task execution, according to the project objectives/goals.
  - **Question 2.3**: What are the relationships among stakeholders?
    - **How to answer the question**: Number of responsibility relation among stakeholders and a list of them or some graph representation showing stakeholders responsibility relations.
    - **Analysis**: It is possible to know the responsibility between the stakeholders during a process instance execution, detecting whether one stakeholder is responsible for many others or not.
    - **Decision-Making Possibility**: After analyzing the responsibility among stakeholders in executed instances, the process manager can use this information when allocating the responsibilities between stakeholders when a new instance of this process is created, according to the project objectives / goals.

– **Question 2.4**: Which roles each stakeholder assumes?
  - **How to answer the question:** Number of roles performed by a stakeholder and a list of them or some graph representation showing stakeholders x roles.
  - **Analysis**: It is possible to analyze all the roles played by a specific stakeholder as well as, from a role, to verify which stakeholders can accomplish it.
  - **Decision-Making Possibility**: In a next instantiation of this process, if the process manager needs to allocate some person stakeholder in a specific activity that needs some pre-defined role, he can evaluate who can perform this role, based on stakeholders' skills. On the other hand, he can also decide who should participate in a training programming in order to be able to accomplish more roles during process execution.

Considering the presented model and its analysis possibilities, next section presents the approach that supports the model instantiation.

5 Approach

In our vision, the best way to capture the SP provenance data is adapting the process execution engine or the workflow engine used by the organization to collect provenance data (as it is done in cases of scientific workflows). However, most small and medium-sized companies, in the initial levels of software maturity models, do not use such tools to execute their software processes, but rather a set of different tools (e.g., version control system, issue trackers, and documentation management systems). Considering the diversity of such tools, a wrapper should be developed to structure all the recorded execution data according to PROV-SwProcess Model. This is the initial effort required to use our approach. Considering this fact, the approach that supports the model instantiation, new information inferencing and data visualization is composed by three main elements: (i) SP provenance data capture and storage; (ii) Deriving SP implicit information using inference mechanisms; (iii) Converting SP provenance data into a graph format aiming to facilitate process manager in a decision-making activity. These three main elements use as basis PROV-SwProcess model presented in Subsect. 4.1.

Approach execution has five activities: (1) Process execution and provenance data capture; (2) Data transformation according to the PROV-SwProcess model; (3) Data storage and ontology generation; (4) Inference machine execution; and (5) Data visualization and analysis. These activities must be carried out sequentially. Considering the first activity, a set of execution data is requested for each of the analyzed processes:

1. *Performed SP instance with its name and responsible (a Stakeholder);*
2. *Performed activities of the SP instance with its name, start, and end time;*
3. *Stakeholders associated with the performed activity and their respective roles;*
4. *Artifacts changed, used, or generated by the performed activity;*
5. *Procedures adopted for the execution of the performed activity (optional);*
6. *Hardware and/or Software resources used by the performed activity (optional);*
7. *Process model to capture prospective provenance (optional).*

Although data from items 5 and 7 are optional, it is important to note that to achieve a more accurate and specific data analysis, it is important to report as much data and information as possible. If the data captured in the first activity are not previously organized according to the PROV-SwProcess model, they must be manipulated and organized/stored according to this model. After storing the SP data, an ontology is generated with them and an inference machine is executed. Lastly, a graph visualization using all the data and new inferred information is generated to allow process manager analysis and support data-driven decision-making. A tool that supports the execution of the proposed approach was implemented as a web application.

Finally, we should point that some training about the visualization tool support is required, to show to the process manager how to use it to obtain the proposed analysis. SP should not be changed to use the approach and it could be used to any kind of software process.

6 Evaluation

Initially, an evaluation in a survey format was made with experts in provenance and software processes, to verify and correct PROV-SwProcess concepts, relations, and inferences possibilities (Subsect. 6.1). After that, a case study was conducted in collaboration with a software development company to instantiate PROV-SwProcess model (using the proposed approach) with real-word process data (Subsect. 6.2).

6.1 Evaluation with Experts

PROV-SwProcess model presented in this paper is in its third version. It was generated after two rounds of an evaluation with specialists in SP and data provenance.

In the first round, two experts in software process and data provenance with PhD degree evaluated the first version of PROV-SwProcess model. The evaluation was performed based on a questionnaire containing 32 Discrepant Cases (DCs) to be analyzed. DCs are issues suggesting defects or general situations in which defects can be detected [22] and making explicit for the reviewers the perspectives to look for defects. The definition of DCs to compose the questionnaire intended to cover all the PROV-SwProcess elements follows a defect taxonomy [24]. A question example from the questionnaire is: "Is some association needed to describe a performed software process (in addition to *wasAttributedTo* and *wasComposedBy*) omitted from the model?". The specialists could answer *Yes*, *No*, or *I don't know/I am not sure*. *Yes* as an answer means that the expert has found some semantic defect in the model. In these cases, a justification was requested. Then, based on this explanation, some alteration in PROV-SwProcess was evaluated, trying to solve the defect. When the expert answers *No*, it means that the element in evaluation has no semantic defect. *I don't know/I am not sure* was applied when the expert had doubts about some specific element. After receiving the expects questionnaire, a direct conversation with the specialist was conducted to understand the expert reasoning and what could be done in the model to eliminate errors found and uncertainties. During this round, 'Participant 1' found 9 defects (out of 32 DCs) and presented 2 uncertainties, while 'Participant 2' found only

1 defect. Analyzing these numbers, it is possible to note that the percentage of defects found was much lower than the number of correct elements in the model (81% of correct items versus 16% of defects and 3% of uncertainties), however, we considered the need for a re-evaluation of the model generated after this first evaluation round.

The second round follows the same format of the first, with a different expert (with PhD degree and good knowledge in provenance and SP). Some adjustments were made to the form to accommodate the model corrections, e.g., new added relations/concepts. This evaluation form has 38 questions and the expert pointed out 32 correct points and 6 defects (2 omissions and 6 incorrect facts). We corrected these points and generated the version presented in this paper. Although a new analysis of this third version was not performed by a fourth expert, we chose to evaluate this last version through an instantiation of the model with real data, as will be presented in next subsection.

6.2 Evaluation Using Real-World Data

Considering the proposed approach, we are interested in evaluating its feasibility in real world contexts. In this vein, a case study was conducted in collaboration with a development company to instantiate PROV-SwProcess model (using the proposed approach) and check SP analysis goals (presented in Sect. 4.2) using real-word process data.

Study Definition
The evaluation scope was defined based on GQM method [3]: **Analyze** the proposed approach and PROV-SwProcess provenance model to evaluate its feasibility **for the purpose of** supporting data analysis and data-driven decision making **with respect to** provide relevant information **under the point of view of** process managers **in the context of** software process. From the scope definition, the research question is as follows: *How can the use of provenance models and techniques in SP domain support process managers analysis and data-driven decision making?* Our study proposition is: *PROV-SwProcess model (and its tool support) can improve the process manager's understanding about the SP execution, providing analysis and decision-making possibilities.*

Planning
Context Selection: The study was based on real process execution data, collected from a development process in a medium software development company. This company is specialist in developing accounting systems and solutions and has been acting in a national market for 25 years.

Data Collection: The data were collected using a direct observation. Researchers had a direct contact with the subject using a semi-structured interview and a questionnaire to check the results when using the approach with collected process execution data.

Instrumentation: The following instruments were selected: Consent form from the company and the subject, to allow the publication of the collected data in this work. Profile subject background questionnaire. Questionnaire used during the interview to evaluate the correctness/usefulness of the approach analysis possibilities.

Study Execution

Goals: This experiment aims to evaluate PROV-SwProcess model (and the proposed approach) in supporting SP analysis and decision-making using process execution data from ten random instances of a real-world SP.

Subject Characterization: The subject is a male, 40 years old, who works in company as a SP manager for ten years and has a broad knowledge of the analyzed process.

Scenario: The analyzed data is from a process that deals with error handling and the implementation of new features in an ERP Project. It is performed by six different roles (Client, Test Team, Support, Support Manager, Development Manager, and Programmer) and has five activities: *System Error Report, New Feature Request, Case Registration, Case Resolution,* and *Close the Case.*

Execution: The following steps were conducted: (1) process execution data extraction and structuring according to PROV-SwProcess model (a wrapper was developed for Mantis and a proprietary VCS); (2) data upload in the tool support; (3) using approach data visualization module to generate the visualizations that assist in the SP analysis, and (4) validation of the obtained analyzes with the process manager, through a semi structured interview and a questionnaire. As an example, considering SP Analysis Goal 2 (*Understand stakeholder's involvement in process execution*), the generated provenance graph to assist in answering question 2.4 *(Which roles each stakeholder assumes?)* is shown in Fig. 3. Stakeholders are represented by the orange pentagons, activities are the blue rectangles, and the roles are the yellow ellipses. Using this figure, we can see all the stakeholders that acts as a *Programmer*, as *Support* or as a *Client* (their names were omitted for confidentiality reasons). The group of roles in the lower corner of the figure corresponds to three roles informed in the process model which had no associated stakeholder. According to this figure, we can see, for example, that the most versatile stakeholder is *Person_1*, that acts as *Programmer* and as *Support*. Considering the decision-making possibilities about this question, in a next instantiation of this process, if the process manager needs to allocate a *Programmer* or a *Support* person in a specific activity, he knows who can perform these roles. In addition, he can verify why there are three roles not performed during the analyzed instances. All the other questions (proposed in Sect. 4.2) were analyzed during the interview.

Results and Discussion: All the SP analysis goals and questions were performed. Table 1 presents a summary of the obtained results during the interview (87.5% of the analysis possibilities was correct and can assist in decision-making, while 62.5% of them are not possible to be performed by the process manager using his currently dashboard or process management tool). Considering these results, we can see that only the analysis of question 1.3 was not considered correct (the subject said that activities complexity is not easy to measure and other aspects should be considered, like activities time duration).When checking question 1.1, the subject said that without our approach he can obtain all the process elements, however, the relations among them are not explicit in his currently process dashboard as in our approach or he takes much time to obtain it using complex SQL queries. Considering question 2.2, he mentioned that he can do this analysis using some SQL query, however, he could not obtain a visualization that facilitates the analysis, as in our approach.

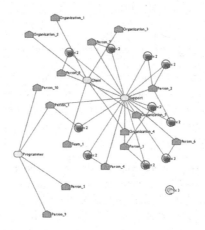

Fig. 3. Provenance Graph to support Question 2.4. (Color figure online)

Table 1. Evaluation of the goals and analysis using SP data

Goals	Questions	(1)	(2)	(3)
1	Question 1.1	Yes	Yes	Partially
	Question 1.2	Yes	Yes	No
	Question 1.3	Partially	No	No
	Question 1.4	Yes	Yes	No
2	Question 2.1	Yes	Yes	Yes
	Question 2.2	Yes	Yes	Partially
	Question 2.3	Yes	Yes	No
	Question 2.4	Yes	Yes	No

(1) Is the provided analysis correct? (2) Can the provided analysis assist in decision-making? (3) Does your current process management tool/dashboard provide this kind of analysis?

6.3   Threats to Validity

Considering the evaluation with experts, they were defined according to their knowledge in the approach related areas (SP and provenance) and not using a random selection. In addition, their evaluation was performed offline, without any follow-up from the researchers. Considering the case study, it can be considered as a first step of the approach evaluation in real scenarios, since the number of case study and subject are not ideal, especially from a statistical point of view. Further study is already being conducted and could provide additional evidence that was not observed. Despite of that, additional evaluations are still necessary, considering other SP contexts and larger cases, aiming to extend the validity of the approach to SP in general. Additional aspects such as non-functional requirements, e.g., performance and scalability, were not considered in the presented study, however, they show preliminary evidence of the approach benefits in SP analysis and decision-making.

7 Conclusions

Considering the research question *How can the use of provenance models and techniques in the SP domain support process managers analysis and data-driven decision making?*, our main goal consists in providing an approach that *uses provenance models and techniques in SP domain to support process managers analysis and data-driven decision making*. PROV-SwProcess model and an approach to support its instantiation and process data analysis was presented and evaluated by experts and using a case study. An initial set of eight questions was defined based on process goals and some analysis and decision-making possibilities were discussed. While the expert's evaluation allowed corrections and improvement points on the provenance model, the case study showed that 7 out of 8 analysis using real data was correct and can assist in decision-making, and 5 of them are not possible to be performed by the process manager using his currently dashboard or process manager tool. Based on this study, we obtained preliminary evidences that *PROV-SwProcess model (and its tool support) can improve the process manager's understanding about the SP execution, providing analysis and decision-making possibilities*. Future researches can arise from this work. Initially, further studies should be performed to analyze the approach using other process/scenarios, as well as the definition and evaluation of SP analysis goals and questions using prospective provenance. Improvements in the visualization mechanism can be done aiming to consider other information, e.g., activities execution ordering and spent time.

References

1. Aversano, L., et al.: Managing coordination and cooperation in distributed software processes: the GENESIS environment. Softw. Process. Improv. Pract. **9**, 239–263 (2004)
2. Avrilionis, D., et al.: A unified framework for software process enactment and improvement. In: Proceedings of Software Process, pp. 102–111. IEEE Computing Society Press (1996)
3. Basili, V., et al.: Goal question metric paradigm. In: Marciniak, J.J. (ed.) Encyclopedia of Software Engineering, pp. 528–532. Wiley, New York (1994)
4. Bosch, J.: Speed, Data, and Ecosystems: Excelling in a Software-Driven World. CRC Press, Boca Raton (2017)
5. Cook, J.E.: Software process analysis. ACM SIGSOFT Softw. Eng. Notes. **25**(1), 44 (2000)
6. Costa, G.C.B., Werner, C.M.L., Braga, R.: Software process performance improvement using data provenance and ontology. In: La Rosa, M., Loos, P., Pastor, O. (eds.) BPM 2016. LNBIP, vol. 260, pp. 55–71. Springer, Cham (2016). https://doi.org/10.1007/978-3-319-45468-9_4

7. Cuevas-Vicenttín, V., et al.: ProvONE: A PROV Extension Data Model for Scientific Workflow Provenance (2016). https://purl.dataone.org/provone-v1-dev. Accessed July 2018
8. Dalpra, H.L., et al.: Using ontology and data provenance to improve software processes. In: Brazilian Ontology Research Seminar, São Paulo, Brazil, pp. 10–21 (2015)
9. Dang, Y.B., et al.: A code provenance management tool for ip-aware software development. In: Proceedings of the 13th International Conference on Software Engineering, pp. 975–976. ACM (2008)
10. Davies, J., et al.: Software bertillonage. Empir. Softw. Eng. **18**(6), 1195–1237 (2012)
11. Derniame, J.C., et al.: Software Process: Principles, Methodology, and Technology. Springer, Heidelberg (1999). https://doi.org/10.1007/3-540-49205-4
12. Falbo, R.D.A., Bertollo, G.: A software process ontology as a common vocabulary about software processes. Int. J. Bus. Process. Integr. Manag. **4**(4), 239–250 (2009)
13. Falci, M.F., et al.: Software process improvement through the combination of data provenance, ontologies and complex networks. In: Proceedings of the 20th International Conference on Enterprise Information Systems, vol. 2, pp. 61–70 (2018)
14. Freire, J., et al.: Provenance for computational tasks: a survey. Comput. Sci. Eng. **10**(3), 11–21 (2008)
15. Ghoshal, D., Plale, B.: Provenance from log files. In: Proceedings of the Joint EDBT/ICDT 2013 Workshops, New York, pp. 290–297. ACM, NY, USA (2013)
16. Godfrey, M.W.: Understanding software artifact provenance. Sci. Comput. Program. **97**, 86–90 (2015)
17. Miles, S., et al.: PrIMe. ACM Trans. Softw. Eng. Methodol. **20**(3), 1–42 (2011)
18. Missier, P., et al.: The W3C PROV family of specifications for modelling provenance metadata. In: Proceedings of the 16th International Conference on Extending Database Technology, pp. 773–776. ACM (2013)
19. Missier, P., et al.: D-PROV: extending the PROV provenance model with workflow structure. In: Proceedings of the 5th USENIX Workshop on the Theory and Practice of Provenance (TaPP 2013). USENIX Association, Berkeley, CA, USA, pp. 9:1–9:7 (2013)
20. Moreau, L., et al.: The open provenance model core specification (v1.1). Futur. Gener. Comput. Syst. **27**(6), 743–756 (2011)
21. Moreau, L., et al.: Special issue: the first provenance challenge. Concurr. Comput.: Pract. Exp. **20**(5), 409–418 (2008)
22. Shull, F., et al.: How perspective-based reading can improve requirements inspections. IEEE Comput. **33**(7), 73–79 (2000)
23. Sun, L., et al.: Engineering access control policies for provenance-aware systems. In: Proceedings of the Third ACM Conference on Data and Application Security and Privacy, pp. 285–292. ACM (2013)
24. Teixeira, E.N., et al.: Verification of software process line models: a checklist-based inspection approach. In: Proceedings of XVIII Ibero-American Conference on Software Engineering, Peru, Lima (2015)
25. Wendel, H., Kunde, M., Schreiber, A.: Provenance of software development processes. In: McGuinness, D.L., Michaelis, J.R., Moreau, L. (eds.) IPAW 2010. LNCS, vol. 6378, pp. 59–63. Springer, Heidelberg (2010). https://doi.org/10.1007/978-3-642-17819-1_7
26. Wolf, A.L., Rosenblum, D.S.: A study in software process data capture and analysis. In: Proceedings of the Second International Conference on the Software Process-Continuous Software Process Improvement, pp. 115–124. IEEE (1993)
27. Xu, P., Sengupta, A.: Provenance in software engineering - a configuration management view. In: Proceedings of the Eleventh Americas Conference on Information Systems (AMCIS), Omaha, NE, USA, pp. 3103–3107 (2005)

The Essence Theory of Software Engineering – Large-Scale Classroom Experiences from 450+ Software Engineering BSc Students

Kai-Kristian Kemell[1]([⊠]) [iD], Anh Nguyen-Duc[2] [iD],
Xiaofeng Wang[3] [iD], Juhani Risku[1], and Pekka Abrahamsson[1] [iD]

[1] University of Jyväskylä, 40014 Jyväskylä, Finland
{kai-kristian.o.kemell, juhani.risku,
pekka.abrahamsson}@jyu.fi
[2] University of Southeast Norway, Notodden, Norway
angu@usn.no
[3] Free University of Bozen-Bolzano, 39100 Bozen-Bolzano, Italy
xiaofeng.wang@unibz.it

Abstract. Software Engineering as an industry is highly diverse in terms of development methods and practices. Practitioners employ a myriad of methods and tend to further tailor them by e.g. omitting some practices or rules. This diversity in development methods poses a challenge for software engineering education, creating a gap between education and industry. General theories such as the Essence Theory of Software Engineering can help bridge this gap by presenting software engineering students with higher-level frameworks upon which to build an understanding of software engineering methods and practical project work. In this paper, we study Essence in an educational setting to evaluate its usefulness for software engineering students while also investigating barriers to its adoption in this context. To this end, we observe 102 student teams utilize Essence in practical software engineering projects during a semester long, project-based course.

Keywords: Software Engineering · Method · Practice · Essence
SEMAT · Education · Software process engineering

1 Introduction

Software Engineering (SE) work out in the field is diverse, with practitioners employing a myriad of different methods and practices in equally diverse SE endeavors [5, 10]. As little consensus exists in terms of best practices and methods, practitioners have taken to using what they consider to be the best option(s) for their own SE context, often tailoring them by omitting some suggested practices or rules [5]. Though e.g. Agile methods are currently widely employed out on the field, the practices and methods that are understood as being Agile are numerous [1]. Especially software startups use a diverse mix of agile methods and practices, with some simply opting to use ad hoc SE methods [17].

M. Kuhrmann et al. (Eds.): PROFES 2018, LNCS 11271, pp. 123–138, 2018.
https://doi.org/10.1007/978-3-030-03673-7_9

This diversity in the SE industry has, alongside other factors such as technological advances, resulted in a gap between education and practice in SE [2, 13]. As it is not possible to teach university students all the methods and practices employed by practitioners, curriculum-makers are faced with choices on what to focus on. General theories and methods that can be taught to students to support them in the adoption of new practices in the future are one option in attempting to tackle this gap. One such theory is the *Essence Theory of Software Engineering* (Essence from here-on-out), proposed by the SEMAT initiative[1] [10].

Created to address the vast range of methods employed in the field, Essence is a method-agnostic progress control tool for SE. Essence is modular in nature and can be used to model any existing methods, practices, or combination of such [15]. Thus, Essence is designed to suit any SE possible context [9], making it a potentially powerful tool. However, its flexibility is also a potential a downside: in order to use Essence, resources have to be devoted towards modeling the practices and methods being used, as well as learning how to do specifically by using Essence.

Presently, Essence has yet to see widespread adoption among practitioners, although it has seen some traction among the academia [21]. It is possible that its rather resource-intensive adoption is one barrier for its adoption, as has been discussed in extant research [8, 18]. For this purpose, some tools have been suggested to aid practitioners in its adoption and in using it: e.g. [8] presented SematAcc to help users visually track the alpha states while using Essence and [11] presented an Essence-themed board game to make learning Essence easier. However, more tools and further studies specifically focusing on its supposedly difficult adoption are also required to better understand the barriers of its adoption and to consequently be able to tackle them. Additionally, an educational perspective on Essence is interesting because Essence can help address the gap between education and industry needs. For example, [2] report that SE graduates are often perceived by the industry as lacking in e.g. the ability to follow processes and project management skills, both of which Essence can help teach.

In this paper, we study Essence in a large-scale classroom setting. We observe over one hundred project teams consisting of second year SE students employ Essence during course projects mimicking a field SE endeavor. The teams carry out a complete SE project, from requirements formulation to a finished software product, using Essence to manage their project. Then, based on their projects, the students reflect on their experiences with Essence in a written experience report. With the data collected from these experience reports, we seek to understand:

RQ1: How useful do bachelor level students find Essence?
RQ2: What are the challenges in adopting Essence, specifically for inexperienced software developers, and what could be done to make its adoption easier?

The rest of this paper is structured as follows. In the next section, we discuss the Essence specification and extant research on it in further detail. In the third section, we present and discuss the study design. In the fourth section, we analyze the data and present our findings. We then discuss the practical and theoretical implications of our

---

[1] semat.org.

findings in the fifth section, as well as the potential limitations of the study and directions for future research. The sixth and final section concludes the paper.

2 The Essence Theory of Software Engineering

Essence is a modular, method-agnostic progress control tool for SE endeavors. Proposed by the SEMAT initiative to address the myriad of methods and practices employed by industry practitioners, Essence is a framework into which any combination of existing methods or practices can be inserted. In practice, Essence consists of a kernel and a language. The kernel [14], its authors argue [10], contains all the elements present in every SE endeavor, while the language can be used to extend the kernel to fit any specific SE endeavor. I.e. Essence, in its base form, contains the elements required to track progress in a generic SE endeavor, but it is intended to be tailored for specific SE contexts.

The Essence kernel consists of three views: *alphas*, *activity spaces*, and *competencies*. In the kernel, there are seven alphas (Fig. 1), "things to work with": opportunity, stakeholders, requirements, software system, work, team, and way of working [10]. These alphas, Jacobson et al. [10] posit, are present in every SE endeavor. Alpha is an acronym for an "Abstract-Level Progress Health Attribute" [14]. For the project to progress, these alphas need to be worked on. To this end, the kernel contains activity spaces. Activity spaces may contain 0 or n activities, or "things to do". The activity spaces in the kernel, much like the alphas, are elements Jacobson et al. [10] argue are found in every SE endeavor. Finally, the kernel contains a set of competencies: skills needed to carry out the endeavor [10]. These alphas, activity spaces, and competencies are further split into three areas of concern: *endeavor*, *solution*, and *customer*.

The alphas of the kernel serve as a way of tracking project health. *Alpha states* offer a way of tracking progress on the various areas of the endeavor. Each of the seven base alphas has a set of states that describe the progress made on each individual alpha. For example, the states for the requirements alpha range from conceived, where the requirements have only just been formulated, to fulfilled, where they have been implemented into the system in a manner satisfying the stakeholders.

Jacobson, Stimson and Hastie [9] suggest Essence as a solution to what they call method prisons. In speaking of method prisons, they refer to the idea of organizations being stuck following one method or set of methods regardless of their suitability in the current context at any given time. However, they posit, the SE practitioners often present methods as monolithic for example by using very varied presentation styles to describe them. By presenting methods in a uniform manner, by e.g. using Essence, and by simply promoting a method-agnostic idea, Jacobson et al. [9] argue that organizations could escape method prisons and potentially improve their work processes by creating better methods specifically suited for their SE context.

Though its modular and extensible nature is the greatest strength of Essence, it can also be its greatest weakness. Whereas it makes Essence a powerful tool, it also makes it both resource-intensive and potentially difficult to adopt. Perhaps consequently, Essence has not gained widespread recognition among practitioners, although it has gained some traction among the academia [21]. Graziotin and Abrahamsson [8] suggest

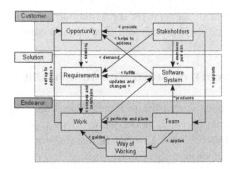

Fig. 1. The essence kernel alphas

that the modest attention Essence has received among practitioners may well stem from the steep learning curve of the specification. Even though Jacobson et al. [9] make a potentially interesting case in promoting the idea of tailoring methods more actively, it may seem easier for practitioners to get started by simply using an existing method.

3   Research Design and Methodology

In this section, we describe the methodology of the classroom study on Essence in the context of student SE projects. In the first sub-section, we discuss the course from which the data was collected. The role of Essence in said course is then discussed in the second sub-section. The third and final sub-section discusses our data collection and analysis methodology in detail. The data is then analyzed in the following main section.

3.1   The Course

The study presented in this paper was conducted using data from the *TDT4140 – Software Engineering* course at the Norwegian University of Science and Technology (NTNU). More specifically, all data for this study was collected during the 2017 spring iteration of the course during which the students utilized Essence in their projects. In this instance of the course, each project team was to engineer a functional software by carrying out a real SE project in a university setting. The theme of the projects was to radically improve university education by means of software robots. The exact goal of the projects was to "make a bot to replace Prof. Abrahamsson at his course on SE".

Following the first lecture of the course, the students were instructed to form project teams consisting of 4 to 5 students. The teams were formed by having the students give a subjective evaluation of their own programming skills in terms of programming confidence and then form teams with individuals with similar evaluations. This was done to negate any potential internal issues (e.g. workload distribution issues) within the teams arising from skill differences in programming. Starting from the first lecture, these teams were to work on their projects until the end of the course. The teams were first tasked with interviewing university teaching staff in order to discover tangible needs that could be addressed through their software. Stakeholders were involved in this fashion to make the project mimic a real SE endeavor more closely.

After gathering needs through the interviews and selecting the one(s) they wished to address, the students were to plan their development methodology and start utilizing it. During the course and the projects, weekly two-hour-lectures continued to offer relevant information and to support the project teams. The project work itself was carried out largely independently by each team.

3.2   The Role of Essence in the Course

Essence was introduced to the teams in the first lecture. The first lecture focused on discussing SE work in practice, specifically from the point of view of projects. During the lecture, Essence was discussed primarily in relation to its seven alphas, which were underlined to present the essential elements of an SE endeavor. In terms of methods, the students were instructed to initially work in whatever fashion they thought was best. The reasoning behind this line of action was to create fertile ground for the later adoption of Essence: by letting the teams first work in a rather unsystematic or even ad hoc fashion, they would likely be more receptive to tools that could help them systematize their way of working. I.e. having experienced unsystematic SE project work, they would better understand the need for more structured approaches to SE.

This approach, in practice, resulted in the teams largely working with various "ScrumBut"[2] approaches for the first three weeks. Their use of Scrum was likely to have stemmed from a previous course at the university having introduced them to Scrum. After three weeks of working as they saw fit without outside assistance from the teaching team, the teams were introduced to the Ivar Jacobson Practice Library[3]. They were tasked with using the practice cards (Fig. 2) from the library to re-construct their way of working and to modify it as they saw fit based on their experiences so far.

Fig. 2. A project team showing their practice cards

---

[2] ScrumBut refers to using Scrum while omitting some parts of it, "We use Scrum, but…" (refer to: https://www.scrum.org/resources/what-scrumbut).

[3] https://practicelibrary.ivarjacobson.com/start.

In this fashion, the teams were introduced to both the progress control aspect of Essence and its method-agnostic philosophy during the course. After the introduction of the practice cards, the use of Essence was not enforced during the project work and there were no regular check-ups to confirm its utilization. Full and correct utilization of Essence was not mandatory, and its utilization or lack thereof did not affect the grades given to the teams. All teams were instructed to utilize it to what extent they felt they could, but this was not supervised in practice. This approach was chosen to gather more unbiased data on the possible barriers of adoption in the case of Essence.

3.3 Data Collection and Analysis Methodology

The data for this study was collected through written reflective reports provided by each team at the end of their projects[4]. In their report, each team was instructed to reflect on their experiences with Essence, along with other content unrelated to this study. As for Essence, they were to describe how they utilized it and how they felt about having done so. More specifically: (1) what they thought was good about Essence, (2) what they thought was bad about Essence, and (3) how they utilized Essence during their project.

Ultimately, 102 project teams of 4–5 students finished the course and delivered a written project report. Our data analysis is based on these 102 reports. The teams were not given a strict format to follow in the sections of their reports describing Essence, which led to the data being somewhat diverse in presentation. Each report was to discuss the afore-mentioned three topics related to their use of Essence, but past these general guidelines the Essence sections of the reports were freeform. In practice, this largely just meant that teams that had utilized Essence relatively little wrote little about it whereas teams that had utilized it fully wrote far more about their experiences.

Thematic analysis was chosen as the method of analysis for this study due to the large volume of the data, as well as the lack of pre-determined assumptions of how the students possibly perceived the use of Essence in this context. Both the final themes and the initial codes used to formulate them were generated from the data in an inductive fashion. The analysis process was iterative and reflexive.

Initially, the author conducting the thematic analysis went through the data and recorded key points for each report, both by directly quoting the reports and by making summarizing remarks, in a separate text document. During this process, initial codes were formulated based on recurring sentiments in the reports. E.g. many reports turned out to describe various initial difficulties in adopting Essence. The analysis process was iterative, and reports and the recorded key points and quotations were regularly re-read as further codes were generated. This phase was concluded once all reports had been analyzed and the final set of codes had been applied to each of them where applicable.

Finally, the themes were generated inductively from the coded data. Codes were arranged into matching themes, with each theme encompassing one or more codes. In

---

[4] A book showcasing the results of the projects can be found on Figshare: https://figshare.com/articles/100_Open_Sourced_Software_Robots_for_Tomorrow_s_Education_Revolutionizing_the_University_Learning_Experience_with_Bot_Technologies/5597983.

determining the themes, the research questions were used as a framework for organizing the data under the themes as well as determining the relevance of the codes and what was to ultimately be included into the study. In presenting the results in the next section, some of the direct quotations used in the analysis process were also included.

Additionally, in our first research question we speak of *usefulness*. Usefulness is a construct often used in relation to evaluating software systems designed especially for work-related use (e.g. [4]). In the context of this study, we define usefulness to be related to either learning something new about SE or SE progress control (educational usefulness) or providing help in SE project work (practical usefulness). These two seemingly separate types of usefulness are nonetheless closely linked together, however. E.g. a learning experience related to SE project work may simultaneously result in practical usefulness through the application the newly-learned information into practice, which may also take place at a later point in time. In our analysis, we thus speak of usefulness while referring to usefulness in both senses.

4   Results

The reports showed a very varying degrees and success of utilization of Essence among the 102 project teams. Whereas some of the teams had clearly utilized Essence in its entirety and reflected upon it in depth, some of the teams had done the bare minimum of selecting different practices to use while forgoing the progress control aspect of Essence. However, despite the varying degree and success of Essence utilization among the teams, the reports discussed similar themes across the spectrum.

4.1   Theme 1: Difficult or Resource-Intensive to Learn

The reports indicated that the majority of the teams considered Essence difficult to learn to some extent. Even most of the teams that ultimately utilized Essence successfully considered it to have been difficult to initially grasp. As the course involved only a general introduction to Essence and its principles, the teams were to study and use Essence on their own using what resources they would find on the SEMAT website or the Internet in general. This resulted in most teams feeling that Essence was difficult to learn, or "hard to get a grasp on when first introduced" (Report 048). The teams generally considered to be a direct result of the types of resources available online:

> ...we felt that almost anywhere we went to read about SEMAT we were either drowned with information (the Essence Kernel PDF has 308 pages) or the information was too abstract that we felt left confused after reading. (Report 041)

> The web page material, the articles and the academic resources about SEMAT are filled with many new terms, but few clear definitions. It would be easier for the next years students to grasp what SEMAT really is, if there existed some sort of document on blackboard explaining the SEMAT terminology. (Report 016)

Largely in line with the quotation above, though Essence was considered difficult to learn, the teams almost uniformly cited the lack of good tutorial resources as the main reason for this. The existing ones were considered either too lengthy or to simply be written in a needlessly complex manner, failing to offer a good initial touch to the specification. This is also supported by some reports directly stating that past the initial barrier of adoption, Essence was a useful tool. However, due to its resource-intensive adoption, many felt that they wanted to focus on the practical SE work instead:

> We just wanted to get on with the programming and it seemed like it was just one more unnecessary thing we needed put effort into when we already had quite a lot with learning new technologies and languages. (Report 044)

Past the self-reported issues related to learning Essence, it was also occasionally possible to determine that a team had not managed to internalize Essence based on the contents of their report. It was evident that some teams had only utilized the practice cards, as they had been directly instructed to do, and ignored the kernel and its alphas and other views, i.e. the progress control aspect of Essence. It is likely that this was caused by the perceived difficulty of learning the specification: some of these teams likely felt that they had understood Essence despite only grasping parts of it. Though the difficulty of learning Essence was primarily blamed on the lack of good tutorial resources, one of the teams did specifically state that they felt Essence itself was too abstract for them.

Despite Essence being considered somewhat difficult to initially learn by the teams, it was generally considered to have been a positive experience. Even the teams that reported having particularly struggled with learning it, or having been unwilling to initially devote resources towards doing so, felt that it had ultimately been useful:

> In retrospective, perhaps we would have had even greater progress with our project and higher learning outcome from the course if our understanding of SEMAT had improved at an earlier stage (Report 062)

> When we later, a bit too late probably, actually sat down and studied what it meant and how to use it, it seemed kind of genius. (Report 044)

4.2   Theme 2: Inexperience

Another recurring theme present in the reports was inexperience in relation to SE. In their reports, the teams often discussed their own perceived inexperience with SE in relation to Essence. The inexperience of the teams evidently had a multifaceted significance to their experiences with Essence.

On one hand, the teams felt that Essence was *more* useful because they were inexperienced. They felt that, being inexperienced developers, Essence helped them (1) structure their way of working, (2) learn about new methods and practices, and (3) manage their projects better. In conjunction with the practice library, Essence was perceived to have been very educational in relation to SE methods and practices.

> While still being on our own and with little experience, SEMAT provided us guidelines that allowed us to improve and learn while planning and working on the project. Resulting in a much better experience with projects than before and a concept we are proud of. Knowledge we absolutely will include in future projects and programming. (Report 078)

...our experience with the ESSENCE kernel has been almost exclusively positive. Given that is prevents overlooking parts of the software development cycle, we perceived it as more beginner friendly than other competing, more fragmented approaches to software development methodology. (Report 047)

On the other hand, some teams felt that their inexperience with SE might have also had a negative impact on the usefulness of Essence. As Essence encourages one to develop their own way of working, these teams felt they could not make the most of Essence due to their lack of knowledge about practices:

A team of beginner developers such as ourselves might get locked up in the [practice] cards already made, resulting in using methods that is ineffective for us since we wouldn't make up any new techniques that isn't "available". We think that with a little more experienced team that hasn't made their own method yet, this would be extremely helpful. (Report 013)

Not all teams considered this to be a negative situation, however. Some teams felt that the way Essence encouraged them to experiment with new practices and to learn by working as a team was helpful, even though they initially did not have a clear idea of what practices might work for their team. Essence, they felt, challenged them to actively think about what they were doing and why, and even though it did not provide direct answers to those questions, it facilitated learning in a positive manner. Thus, the general sentiment among the groups was that Essence, as well as the practice library related to it, had been very useful for them as inexperienced developers. As a concluding remark, it is worth noting that while not all of the teams comprised of individuals with little or no past experience with practical SE work, the resounding majority of them nonetheless did, being comprised of second year SE students. This was also evident in the way the teams actively reflected on their own inexperience in various ways in their reports.

4.3   Theme 3: Way of Working and the Method Prison

One of the most discussed positive aspects of Essence perceived by the teams was its method-agnostic approach. The ability to freely choose between methods and practices was considered both new and highly positive, letting them, in the words of Jacobson et al. (2017), escape the "method prison":

Our team really liked the freedom SEMAT gives you in defining the way you develop something and how you can customize it, choose the practices you want and not be forced to use practices you don't want to use (Report 036)

There were many positives of applying the kernel to our project, like choosing what we wanted to implement in our regular work day allowed us to use only what we wanted and thought we could benefit from. This level of freedom created a higher level of productivity than for example Scrum, where we are forced to use all aspects of the framework that do not necessarily benefit us. Not being forced to do things that we feel would slow us down and not benefit us really made us appreciate the SEMAT Essence Kernel (Report 071)

As many of the students in the course had previously taken a course on Scrum, many of the reports consequently also included reflections related to Scrum. These teams discussed how they had initially started using Scrum or ScrumBut but had then begun to reflect on what they were doing and why, resulting in them refining their own way of working by using Essence. Used in conjunction with the practice card library, Essence provided them with new alternative practices to utilize. This resulted in the teams experimenting with different practices. On a more general level, they felt that the method-agnostic approach of Essence prepared them for different ways of working in the future.

Additionally, the teams reported positive experiences with actively reflecting on their way of working. Aside from initially tailoring a method for themselves, some of the teams reported having found Essence useful in facilitating the idea of continuously improving their work processes based on their experiences. Furthermore, some teams also noted that Essence had made it easier to communicate their way of working to the team as well as to discuss it within the team:

> *This overview of all practices really benefited us when we put together our way of working and made it easy to visualize our workflow. Whenever a team member was unhappy with any aspect of our work methodology we reviewed the cards and added or removed any if needed.* (Report 060)

Finally, the teams discussed having learned much about new methods and practices simply by browsing through the practice cards available in the Ivar Jacobson practice library. This serves to underline the importance of tools related to adopting Essence. In this case, the practice cards helped teams of inexperienced developers tailor methods using Essence despite not having any previous experience with different SE practices.

4.4   Theme 4: Progress Control

The Essence kernel provides a framework upon which to build a project-specific tool. However, even without any modifications, the kernel already serves as a basic progress control tool. This was also reflected in the reports. Most teams that had properly utilized the kernel had positive experiences using Essence to manage and track progress:

> *Selecting and using the alpha state cards that were relevant to our circumstances to assess our progress proved extremely effective. When we used them for the first time we were surprised to learn that we had not made as much progress as we thought. The cards were useful in seeing where we wanted to be in terms of progress in the different alphas, and thus facilitated the process of fixing our impediments.* (Report 005)

> *The team then agreed to purchase a cork board and print out the Alpha State Cards in order to quickly and easily get an overview over the team's overall progress. This proved valuable, as none of the team members had partaken in any projects of this scale previously. The clear visualization the cards provided gave a much clearer picture of the project's progression overall than what the team found orally.* (Report 055)

Although Essence did clearly facilitate the idea of tailoring methods and choosing the methods that work best, this may not always be preferable. If the alternative to being locked in a "method prison" is the use of ineffective ad hoc methods, following an established method by the book may well be the more effective option. However, the teams felt that Essence helped them *formalize* their way of working aside from also facilitating the idea of tailoring it to suit their context-specific needs.

In relation to the inexperience of the teams discussed in a preceding sub-section, many of the teams felt that the Essence kernel provided a good overview of a software engineering endeavor *especially* because they had little experience with SE project work. Even though not all teams that utilized the kernel extended it, they nonetheless felt the Essence kernel in its base form was already useful in tracking their progress – except for one. One of the teams felt that they had a solid understanding of the state of their project prior to using Essence and that "it didn't help us anything to convert it into cards and more complicated sentences" (Report 059). This is not surprising as tools are just that: tools. Similarly, though formal methods and practices are typically preferred, it is quite possible to carry out SE endeavors using ad hoc methods, as e.g. a notable number of software startups chooses to do [17].

4.5 Summary of Findings

Having discussed the results through the themes present in the data set, we now turn back to our formal research problem. Below, we provide summarizing answers for the two research questions posed in the introduction before going into more detail:

RQ1: Do bachelor level students find Essence useful?

Results: Essence was considered useful by the students, for varying reasons

RQ2: What are the challenges in adopting Essence, specifically for inexperienced software developers, and what could be done to make its adoption easier?

Results: The largest challenge in adopting Essence was the lack of good tutorial resources, which consequently could be addressed by creating better such resources.

Though the student teams nearly universally considered Essence useful, there were differences between the teams in terms of *why* they considered it useful, largely based on the extent to which they had utilized it. Essence was considered useful for (1) teaching new methods and practices, (2) teaching a method-agnostic approach to SE, (3) helping the team properly structure their way of working, and (4) providing a useful framework for managing an SE project, depending on the degree of its utilization among each team. Few teams had anything negative to say about the specification itself, with most of the negative feedback relating to difficulties in adopting Essence.

Indeed, though Essence was considered useful by the teams, it was nonetheless evidently difficult for them to adopt. Many teams, even those that did utilize it the most, considered it to have been difficult to initially learn. The reports that discussed the reasons behind its perceived difficult adoption all cited the lack of good tutorial resources as the main problem. The teams felt that the resources they could find online were either hundreds of pages long or did simply not describe Essence simply enough for beginners. This resulted in some teams opting to focus their efforts elsewhere by e.g. focusing on learning to program and use programming tools, leaving Essence for later.

Having discussed our findings in relation to our research questions, we present a further, visual summary of how the themes discussed earlier in this section are interlinked (Fig. 3). It is organized in a manner similar to how Giardino et al. [6] summarized their findings and depicts the adoption of Essence among students as a process. The student teams, as developers, were inexperienced. This inexperience resulted in a

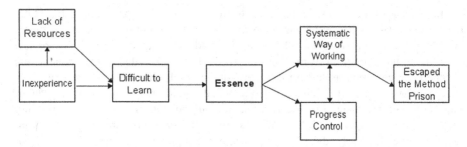

Fig. 3. Adoption process of essence among SE students

lack of resources as they had to divide their resources between e.g. learning to program, learning to use the programming tools, and learning Essence. In this situation, Essence often took on a lower priority, consequently becoming more difficult for the teams to learn. However, once the teams began to understand and utilize Essence, they began to work more systematically. All teams utilized Essence and the practice cards to work in a more systematic fashion, and many, but not all, teams grasped the kernel and began to use it as a progress control tool. For the teams that understood how to fully utilize Essence, its use ultimately resulted in an escape from the so-called method prison [10]. These teams actively reflected on their way of working and saw Essence also as a tool to facilitate learning in order to (attempt to) work in an efficient fashion in any given context in the future.

Based on our findings, we therefore argue that SE students find Essence useful for multiple reasons. Furthermore, we confirm that Essence is considered difficult to learn, and our data suggests that the largest challenges in adopting Essence currently stem from a lack of tutorials and guides aimed at beginners. The current resources available online were considered too lengthy or advanced to be of use for new users of Essence.

5   Discussion

As extant literature has suggested [8], our findings confirm that Essence is indeed considered difficult and resource-intensive to adopt. However, our findings indicate that stems from a lack of good tutorial resources as opposed to Essence being difficult to use as such. The current manuals and other resources available were considered by the student teams to be too complex for beginners. Thus, the most direct solution to this issue would simply be the creation of better tutorial resources specifically aimed at new users of Essence.

As a solution to making Essence easier to adopt, [8] suggested the development of tools that could be used to make the practical use of Essence easier. This was not confirmed by our findings as none of the teams voiced explicit wishes for more tools to help utilized Essence. However, given that the practice card library, an external tool as well, was very positively received among the teams, it is likely that further tooling would also make Essence either easier to adopt and possibly more useful.

In terms of the usefulness of Essence for bachelor level students, our data indicates that Essence was indeed considered useful by the resounding majority of the project teams we studied. Less than ten teams out of 102 reported having found the use of Essence an outright negative and useless experience. In this light, we argue that Essence is useful for bachelor level students. More specifically, it was found useful in terms of (1) teaching new methods and practices, (2) teaching a method-agnostic approach to SE, (3) helping the team properly structure their way of working, and (4) providing a useful framework for managing an SE project.

From the point of view of SE education in universities, Essence is interesting as, based on our experiences, it can potentially provide a common ground for SE education through its method-agnostic nature. Such common ground is currently missing. We have showed that it can simultaneously teach students SE progress control as well as practical SE work. It also prepares SE students for working with different methods and practices out on the field. Essence could therefore be used to provide students with a higher-level understanding of the way SE work is structured. Essence can serve as a basis upon which SE students can build a general understanding of different SE methods as opposed to learning about single methods one at a time.

Learning to construct a method out of practices is an important learning goal for software engineering education. Based on our observations during the course, it was noted that some teams also learned to include so called anti-patterns or bad practices explicitly in their process description. This is a novel thought and should be further elaborated in future studies. By labeling a practice as a bad-practice, the team in question explicitly communicated about their improvement needs. Manual testing is an example of such practice as it indicates lack of automated test suite, which slows down the development and is thus not a sustainable solution.

Additionally, in terms of generalizing our findings, we suggest that our findings could also be interesting for future research from the point of software startups. SE students, like startup practitioners [3, 12], are often more inexperienced developers, and it is also not uncommon for university students to participate in software startups during their studies. Most software startups fail [7] for various reasons, and Kon et al. [12] posited that specifically younger, more inexperienced startup practitioners are considered more prone to failure among investors. Software startups face various challenges across their life cycles [22], including challenges with "building product", "staying focused & disciplined", and "over capacity/too much to do", which Essence could potentially be used to aid in solving. Finally, it has been established that software startups, like mature organizations, should concern themselves with structuring their work processes [19], which is something we found Essence to be useful for among SE students. Relating these past studies to our findings here, we suggest that future studies could investigate Essence from the point of view of software startups. Our findings, however, do not offer direct support to this link between these two contexts. In possibly pursuing this line of research, it could be useful to also evaluate the suitability of the Essence kernel in the context of software startups, as software startups have been shown to develop software in different ways than mature organizations [10], and their business aspect is linked with their SE process in a unique fashion.

Finally, while we have studied perceived difficulties in adopting Essence in the context of SE students, future studies may wish to study impediments to its adoption among practitioner organizations. As Essence has yet to see widespread practitioner adoption [21], the reasons behind this situation are worth investigating. Similarly, it is likely that more experienced practitioners find Essence useful or not useful for different reasons than the SE students studied in this paper.

5.1   Limitations of the Study

The primary limitations of the study are associated with the data collected during it. In collecting the data, we chose to rely on self-reported use of Essence over observation and regular check-ups. From this results that the validity of the reported utilization of Essence among the teams cannot be directly confirmed. However, the student teams seldom failed to report problems in utilizing Essence, with most teams that failed to utilize Essence fully reporting so themselves. In other cases, it was also largely possible to determine whether a team had understood the specification or not based on the way they reported on its utilization. We thus argue that this does not present a major threat to the validity of our data in such a large data set (102 teams).

Additionally, while the use of students as subjects for scientific studies is a long-standing topic of discussion across disciplines, including SE, the aim of this study was to study Essence specifically in relation to SE students and education. The use of students as subjects in this context is therefore not an issue.

6   Conclusions

In this paper, we have studied the Essence Theory of Software Engineering in a large-scale bachelor level course through experience reports. We introduced Essence to 102 project teams in a project-based SE course at a Norwegian university and observed its use during the projects. Based on 102 project reports discussing, among other things, the Essence use experiences of project teams of 4–5 individuals, we described the barriers of adoption of Essence and its usefulness for SE students.

We discovered that while Essence was considered difficult to learn by the teams, these difficulties largely stemmed from the lack of good tutorial resources. Some teams failed to fully utilize Essence, forgoing its progress control aspect partially or entirely, primarily due to its difficult adoption. There is thus a clear need for better introductory guides to Essence that are specifically designed for new users.

Past its difficult adoption, Essence was nonetheless nearly universally considered useful by the project teams. Even the teams that had not fully utilized Essence considered the method-agnostic approach and the practice cards to have been useful for planning out and formalizing their way of working during their projects. Additionally, the teams that had grasped the Essence kernel (except for two teams) also reported Essence having been useful in tracking progress during their projects. They felt that Essence gave them a good general understanding of SE project work through the alphas and that the alpha states helped them keep track of progress on their endeavor.

We therefore argue in favour of using Essence in SE education. By helping SE students gain a better understanding of SE project work and by preparing them for future adoption of various practices and methods, Essence can help tackle gaps [2, 13] between SE education and practice. To summarize our findings:

(1) Essence can teach students new methods and practices by encouraging them to study them in order to tailor their own methods using Essence
(2) Essence encourages students to adjust their way of working based on the SE context at hand as opposed to following existing methods by the book
(3) Essence helps students structure their way of working in a practical setting
(4) Better tutorial resources for Essence are needed to make it easier to adopt.

References

1. Abrahamsson, P., Salo, O., Ronkainen, J., Warsta, J.: Agile Software Development Methods: Review and Analysis, p. 478. VTT Publications, Otamedia (2002)
2. Almi, N.E.A.M., Rahman, N.A., Purusothaman, D., Sulaiman, S.: Software engineering education: the gap between industry's requirements and graduates' readiness. In: 2011 IEEE Symposium on Computers & Informatics (ISCI) (2011)
3. Crowne, M.: Why software startups fail and what to do about it – evolution of software product development in startup companies. In: Proceedings International Engineering Management Conference (IEMC), pp. 338–343 (2002)
4. Davis Jr., F.D.: A Technology Acceptance Model for Empirically Testing New End-User Information Systems: Theory and Results. Massachusetts Institute of Technology (1985)
5. Ghanbari, H.: Investigating the causal mechanisms underlying the customization of software development methods. Jyväskylä Studies in Computing, vol. 258. Uni. of Jyväskylä (2017)
6. Giardino, C., Paternoster, N., Unterkalmsteiner, M., Gorschek, T., Abrahamsson, P.: Software development in startup companies: the greenfield startup model. IEEE Trans. Softw. Eng. **42**(6), 585–604 (2016)
7. Giardino, C., Wang, X., Abrahamsson, P.: Why early-stage software startups fail: a behavioral framework. In: Lassenius, C., Smolander, K. (eds.) ICSOB 2014. LNBIP, vol. 182, pp. 27–41. Springer, Cham (2014). https://doi.org/10.1007/978-3-319-08738-2_3
8. Graziotin, D., Abrahamsson, P.: A web-based modeling tool for the SEMAT essence theory of software engineering. J. Open Res. Softw. **1**, e4 (2013)
9. Jacobson, I., Stimson, R., Hastie, S.: Escaping Method Prison (2017). https://www.infoq.com/articles/escape-method-prson. Accessed 15 May 2018
10. Jacobson, I., Ng, P., McMahon, P.E., Spence, I., Lidman, S.: The essence of software engineering: the SEMAT kernel. ACMQueue **10**, 40–52 (2012)
11. Kemell, K.O., et al.: Gamifying the escape from the engineering method prison - an innovative board game to teach the essence theory to future project managers and software engineers (2018). (to be published in the proceedings of ICE 2018)
12. Kon, F., Cukier, D., Melo, C., Hazzan, O., Yuklea, H.: A Panorama of the Israeli Software Startup Ecosystem. SSRN (2014). https://ssrn.com/abstract=2441157
13. Lethbridge, T.C., Díaz-Herrera, J., LeBlanc Jr., R.J., Thompson, J.B.: Improving software practice through education: challenges and future trends. In: Proceedings: FOSE 2007 Future of Software Engineering (2007)
14. Object Management Group: Essence – Kernel and Language for Software Engineering Methods. Version 1.1. http://semat.org/essence-1.1. Accessed 28 May 2018

15. Park, J.S., McMahon, P.E., Myburgh, B.: Scrum powered by essence. ACM SIGSOFT Softw. Eng. Notes **41**(1), 1–8 (2016)
16. Parnin, C., et al.: The top 10 adages in continuous deployment. IEEE Softw. **34**(4), 86–95 (2017)
17. Paternoster, N., Giardino, C., Unterkalmsteiner, M., Gorschek, T., Abrahamsson, P.: Software development in startup companies: a systematic mapping study. Inf. Softw. Technol. **56**, 1200–1218 (2014)
18. Pieper, J.: Discovering the essence of software engineering – an integrated game-based approach based on the SEMAT essence specification. In: Proceedings of the 2015 IEEE Global Engineering Education Conference (EDUCON), pp. 939–947 (2015)
19. Ries, E.: The Lean Startups: How Today's Entrepreneurs Use Continuous Innovation to Create Radically Successful Businesses. Crown Books, New York (2011)
20. SEMAT: SEMAT and Essence – What is it and why should you care? http://semat.org/what-is-it-and-why-should-you-care. Accessed 20 May 2018
21. SEMAT: Great pick up of Semat. http://semat.org/news/-/asset_publisher/eaHEtyeuE9wP/content/great-pick-up-of-semat. Accessed 13 May 2018
22. Wang, X., Edison, H., Bajwa, S.S., Giardino, C., Abrahamsson, P.: Key challenges in software startups across life cycle stages. In: Sharp, H., Hall, T. (eds.) XP 2016. LNBIP, vol. 251, pp. 169–182. Springer, Cham (2016). https://doi.org/10.1007/978-3-319-33515-5_14

Empirical Studies in Industry

An Exploratory Study on Software Products and Development Organizations in New Zealand

Di Wang[1] and Matthias Galster[2(✉)]

[1] Lentune Software Solutions, Christchurch, New Zealand
di.wang@outlook.co.nz
[2] University of Canterbury, Christchurch, New Zealand
mgalster@ieee.org

Abstract. The types and characteristics of software products as well as the characteristics of development organizations that build those products contribute to the *context* in which software development professionals operate. To better understand this context in the software development sector, we explored the context of software development professionals in New Zealand, an example of a small but growing and vibrant software industry. In this paper, we present preliminary findings of a questionnaire-based survey with professionals. In contrast to other studies on software development in industry (which tend to focus on processes and practices), we explore non-technical product-related and organizational characteristics. We found that software development professionals in New Zealand mostly work on long-living (but frequently released) products for specific customers (rather than products developed for a broader market). Also, software development professionals mostly work in organizations that have existed for quite a while and that aim at a global customer base. Very small and very large organizations are uncommon. Based on these characteristics, we can compare different software industries. Also, this concrete characterization of *context* allows researchers and practitioners implement more focused process improvement initiatives.

Keywords: Software products · Software development organizations
Descriptive survey · New Zealand

1 Introduction

The software sector worldwide faces challenges in delivering quality products on time and within budget. Therefore, understanding the types of products (and services) produced and the characteristics of organizations which develop those products is important. As argued by Basili et al., domain and organizational factors define the *context* in which software methodologies and technologies are used [1] and in which software professionals operate. Therefore, we empirically

© Springer Nature Switzerland AG 2018
M. Kuhrmann et al. (Eds.): PROFES 2018, LNCS 11271, pp. 141–149, 2018.
https://doi.org/10.1007/978-3-030-03673-7_10

investigated types of software products produced in the New Zealand software industry and by whom (i.e., by what types of organizations). We picked the specific context of New Zealand's software industry as one example of a relatively small but vibrant and fast-growing software industry [7] and a region where software became a major export factor [7], similar to regions like Turkey [4], Estonia[1], Brazil and Chile [8]. In contrast to previous studies that investigate software development in industry and which usually focus on development processes and practices (i.e., *how* software is developed), we research the *what* and *where* of software development:

- **RQ1: What types of software products do software professionals develop?** This question investigates *what* software development professionals produce and offers insights into the outputs (and characteristics of those outputs) produced by software development professionals. Therefore, RQ1 is not aiming at investigating any technical or technological aspects of software products (or any development artifacts created by developers, e.g., source code, documentation), but rather "customer-related" aspects (e.g., types of products, payment models).
- **RQ2: In what types of organizations do software professionals develop products?** This question investigates *where* professionals operate. We investigate characteristics of organizations in which software development professionals produce their outputs. In contrast to statistics or industry sector reports published by national governments or professional bodies (e.g., about the size and number of organizations in a sector), this question investigates more detailed characteristics (e.g., size of teams in organizations, age of organizations, target markets).

Understanding the context in which products are developed helps plan and implement focused process improvement initiatives. Our "unit of analysis" are individual software development professionals. This means, we report on individual professionals and what they work on as well as where they work (rather than on software development organizations per se). The work presented in this paper is part of a larger effort to better understand the software development industry in New Zealand. The overall goal of this effort is to analyze various facets of the industry, including the types of organizations, the types of products and services these organizations produce, characteristics of the workforce, and the processes and practices applied in organizations. In this paper, we only cover the first two facets (products and organizations) and present preliminary findings regarding these two facets.

2   Research Method

We conducted a *descriptive* survey based on the guidelines suggested by Ciolkowski et al. [2] and Pfleeger and Kitchenham [9]. Our **target population** included software development professionals in technical roles in industry.

---

[1] https://investinestonia.com/business-opportunities/software-development/ [last access: August 4, 2018].

Given our study goal, we did not restrict the target population with regards to business domain, company size or number of years of practical experience. For **sampling**, we used purposive sampling [11], because respondents needed to hold a software development role in the New Zealand software industry. To recruit participants, we advertised the survey in our personal local and national networks, through industry contacts and by postings in online communities (e.g., regional and national LinkedIn, Facebook and meet-up groups, newsletters). We also branched out into chain referral sampling [3]. The sample size was restricted with regard to the responses that we could obtain and there is no simple way to define the size of the sample. For **data preparation and collection**, we used a self-administered online questionnaire (Qualtrics software) [5]. The online questionnaire was active from late 2017 to early 2018. The questionnaire included questions about the educational and professional background of respondents. We asked respondents to refer to their current or most recent position. If participants had more than one position, we asked them to refer to the one that they spent time in most. This made it easier for participants to answer questions and reduced the probability of "it depends" answers. The questionnaire was reviewed by others from the target population not involved in the research. It was also evaluated through a series of pilots with representatives from the target population and revised accordingly. The questionnaire and the raw data are available online (https://bit.ly/2ovSTlL). For **data analysis**, we used descriptive statistics and quantitative analysis. In particular, we used frequency analysis and cross-tabbed answers to questions in contingency matrices. Below we only report findings that led to relevant insights.

3   Results

3.1   Demographics

We received 101 complete responses for analysis.

- **Industry experience:** Almost one quarter of respondents (24%) had more than 20 years of industry experience. Nineteen percent had 16–20 years of experience. Only 7% had 1–2 years of experience (22%: 11–15 years; 12%: 6–10 years; 16%: 3–5 years).
- **Employment status and seniority:** Most respondents (76%) held a full-time (rather than part-time) position. Also, most respondents held a senior position (65%), rather than an intermediate or junior position.
- **Educational background:** Most respondents (95%) held a university degree, while the rest entered the software industry with a high school qualification. Furthermore, 73% of respondents had a software engineering/computer science related degree.

3.2   RQ1 – Software Products

We characterize software products based on four criteria:

Table 1. Life spans, release frequencies and payment models of software products.

Life span	%	Release frequency	%	Payment model	%
0–6 months	0%	Daily or less	18%	Free	18%
7–12 months	1%	Weekly	10%	Free with ads	6%
1–3 years	14%	Fortnightly	12%	Optional purchases	1%
3–5 years	17%	Monthly	14%	Subscription	42%
5–10 years	25%	Quarterly	30%	One-off payment	28%
10+ years	30%	Bi-annually	5%	Event-based charges	19%
Other	0%	Annually	3%	Other	13%
I don't know	13%	Other	0%	I don't know	0%
		I don't know	8%		

1. **Main product:** Most respondents (54%) worked on custom software (i.e., software solutions specifically designed for a particular user/customer), followed by respondents (28%) who developed market software, i.e., products not for a specific customer, but for a particular market. Complete system solutions (i.e., hardware and software, e.g., embedded systems, medical devices) were developed by a minority of respondents (19%). Similarly, few respondents were involved in offering consulting services, such as IT consulting (17%), IT services (10%) or IT training (1%). Two percent of respondents indicated "Other" (e.g., education). Note that respondents could indicate more than one type of product (i.e., the total percentage exceeds 100%). The most frequent combination of types of products/services mentioned by respondents were custom software and IT consulting (6%).
2. **Product life span:** Most respondents worked on products with a life span of more than 10 years, see Table 1. Overall, respondents worked on long-living products. Many respondents did not know the life span of their products. We did not find any relationship between the life span and other questions.
3. **Release of products:** As can be seen in Table 1, most respondents worked on products that are released to customers quarterly. Interestingly, daily deployments are also quite frequent, whereas long release cycles of half a year or a year are not common.
4. **Product payment models:** Most respondents worked on products with a subscription-based payment model, see Table 1[2]. One-off payments for products are also quite common. Event-based charging (e.g., charges for product support or new features) and "free" software (e.g., online selling platforms are developed "for free" while revenue is generated though selling items) were less common. Interestingly, ad-based payment was also less common. Most respondents who indicated "Other" commented on payment models that are similar to a subscription-based model (e.g., consumption-based billing, billing

---

[2] Responents could indicate more than one option, i.e., the total exceeds 100%.

based on the number of users or annual maintenance contracts). The most common combination of payment models was subscription-based and one-off payments (9%). We did not find correlations with other questions.

3.3   RQ2 – Software Development Organizations

Diversity of Products. We describe the diversity of products offered by software development organizations based on two aspects:

1. **Domains:** In term of domains that software development professionals worked in, the top three domains were: (1) Primary industry (27%), (2) Finance/ banking/insurance (25%), and (3) Information technology (24%). The least common domains included: (1) Social media, Defense/military, and Publishing (6% each), and (2) Art (4%). However, most respondents (53%) worked in organizations which do not target *one* domain, but *multiple* domains.
2. **Number of products:** We found that most respondents (70%) worked in organizations that offer 2–10 products. On the other hand, few respondents (10%) worked in organizations that offer one single product. Similarly, few respondents worked in organizations that offer a large number of products and services (11–25 products: 9% of respondents; more than 25 products: 9% of respondents). Two percent of participants were not sure about the number of products and services produced by their organization.

We did not find any significant relationship between the diversity of products and the domain of organizations.

Globalization of Development Organizations. We characterize the degree of globalization of software organizations based on the following aspects:

- **Geographical distribution:** Regarding geographical distribution, 55% of respondents worked at international companies which also have offices and branches overseas. On the other hand, 45% worked for domestic companies which only have branches and offices within New Zealand. This could indicate that there is a large number of "home-grown" organizations in New Zealand.
- **Target markets:** We found that 48% of respondents work on products sold to the Australian market, 38% for North America and 33% for the European market. The global market is addressed by organizations of 29% of respondents, whereas Asia (16%), South America (7%) and Africa (6%) appeared less frequently. One percent of respondents indicated "Other" (e.g., stating that country is not relevant). Furthermore, 78% of respondents also indicated New Zealand as their target market. Since this was a multiple choice question, the total exceeds 100%. This partially confirms the trend of producing locally and selling globally and also highlights software as an export factor, while still supplying the domestic market.

Structural Characteristics of Organizations. We defined structural characteristics of organizations as follows:

1. **Company type:** Most respondents (48%) worked for software product providers (i.e., organizations who own/develop their own software product). On the other hand, 14% of respondents worked at pure software development organizations, i.e., organizations that do not own products, but offer development to external clients. Nineteen percent worked at organizations that were a mix of software development organization and software product provider. Finally, 15% of respondents worked at organizations that perform in-house development (i.e., the core business of the organization is not software, but software teams serve internal clients), and 4% worked at consulting companies.

2. **Company size:** Most respondents (16%) worked at organizations with 26–50 employees, while 13% worked at organizations with 51–100 employees (see Table 2). Few respondents worked in very small or large companies.
   The size of development organizations appears correlated with the number of products an organization offers: Large organizations tend to offer more products ($\chi^2 \approx 91.45, df = 64, p = 0.01$). Similarly, pure software development organizations tend to be smaller compared to software product providers and organizations with in-house development ($\chi^2 \approx 100.1, df = 80, p = 0.01$).

3. **Team sizes:** Most respondents (50%) worked in organizations with teams of 2–5 people, followed by respondents who worked in teams of 6–9 people (32%), and respondents that work in rather large teams (7% of respondents worked in teams of 10–15 people; 6% of respondents worked in teams with more than 15). Only 5% work on their own and no respondent worked in a team with more than 30 people. Interestingly, there is no relation/correlation between team size and any of the other questions.

4. **Company age:** In term of company age, most respondents (35%) worked at organizations that had existed for more than 20 years, followed by respondents from organizations that have existed 6–10 years (18%), 11–15 years (15%), 16–20 years (15%) and 3–5 years (12%). Two percent worked at companies that had only existed for 1–2 years or less. The remaining 3% indicated that they did not know the age of their organization. This indicates that there might be few "real" start-ups in New Zealand founded recently.

Table 2. Size of organizations (number of employees).

Employees	%	Employees	%	Employees	%	Employees	%
Less than 5	7%	5–10	7%	11–15	7%	16–20	2%
21–25	7%	25–50	16%	51–100	13%	101–150	6%
151–250	11%	251–500	7%	501–1,000	3%	1,001–2,0000	5%
2,001–5,000	1%	5,001–10,000	4%	10,000+	6%		

4 Discussion

4.1 Key Findings

Understanding the context in which software is developed is important in order to further explore process improvements in specific contexts. In this short paper, we aimed at characterizing the context of software development in New Zealand based on the products developed and the organizations in which these products are developed.

Regarding RQ1 (types of products), we found that software development professionals mostly work on custom software for specific customers rather than products geared towards an "anonymous" market. Also, the life span of products is quite long, but still releases happen frequently. Subscription-based payment models appear to dominate. For process improvement this may imply that a focus should be on providing tools and practices for maintaining software over a long period. Also, these findings may explain if requirements engineering and analysis practices used in New Zealand differ compared to other countries.

Regarding RQ2 (types of organizations), we found that there is a balance between international and domestic organizations, but this does not limit the markets that organizations target. Also, mosts software development professionals work in organizations that offer more than one product and products for multiple domains. This means that developers need to constantly update their domain knowledge. Furthermore, products are produced mostly by organizations who own that product (i.e., develop and sell it). In contrast to what one might expect in a fast moving industry, most respondents worked in rather "old" organizations where the size for most respondents ranged between 26 and 250 employees, i.e., small and very large organizations were uncommon. Typical team sizes in these organizations of 2–5 are what one would expect from an industry in which agile software development practices are common. Some of our findings may not be surprising. However, our survey takes a picture of reality, and as argued by Torchiano and Ricca, reality is rarely surprising or controversial [10].

4.2 Limitations and Threats to Validity

Threats to *construct validity* are about the appropriateness of the measures used in the study. Our respondents might have interpreted questions differently than intended. This could have led to misleading findings. Although we reviewed and piloted the survey instrument, it is possible that our selection of questions either excluded important topics our could have been misunderstood by respondents. Threats to *internal validity* are about confounding factors that could have impacted our results and causal relationships and the appropriateness of the conclusions drawn from our study. It is possible that we were biased in the interpretation of the answers. We avoided this threat as much as possible by having two individuals involved in the evaluation of the data. Also, by giving options to respondents, we did not need to determine what respondents might have meant in their answer. A related issue is self-selection bias, i.e., more senior or mature professionals might have been more interested in participating. *External validity* is about the generalization of our findings. Our sample included 101 respondents from New Zealand. Since we advertised the survey through mailing lists, etc. we cannot compute the response rate. We cannot claim that those who participated are representative of the entire (New Zealand) software industry.

5   Conclusions

We presented findings related to characteristics of software products and software development organizations. While our findings are specific to New Zealand (i.e., provide context-specific insights), they also contribute to the larger body of knowledge on software businesses to help draw a map of software development sectors. Furthermore, this research could provide insights for countries where the software industry has grown rapidly and where domestic software companies have taken a major role in developing products not only for the domestic market. Also, this study can be replicated in other contexts and countries. This would allow benchmarking different regions regarding their development industries as a first step towards understanding intrinsic differences in software industries (i.e., contexts) and understanding why software development processes, practices and techniques differ between various regions. For example, in the past New Zealand's software industry has been characterized as "implementation-centric, with a culture of informality and reliance upon personal capability" [6], while other software industries might be more strict in their applications of processes and practices.

References

1. Basili, V., Briand, L., Bianculli, D., Nejati, S., Pastore, F., Sabetzadeh, M.: Software engineering research and industry: a symbiotic relationship to foster impact. IEEE Softw. (in press)
2. Ciolkowski, M., Laitenberger, O., Vegas, S., Biffl, S.: Practical experiences in the design and conduct of surveys in empirical software engineering. In: Conradi, R., Wang, A.I. (eds.) Empirical Methods and Studies in Software Engineering. LNCS, vol. 2765, pp. 104–128. Springer, Heidelberg (2003). https://doi.org/10.1007/978-3-540-45143-3_7
3. Creswell, J.: Research Design: Qualitative, Quantitative, and Mixed Methods Approaches. Sage Publications, Thousand Oaks (2014)
4. Garousi, V., Coscuncay, A., Betin-Can, A., Demirors, O.: A survey of software engineering practices in Turkey. J. Syst. Softw. **108**, 148–177 (2015)
5. Gray, D.: Doing Research in the Real World. Sage Publications, Thousand Oaks (2009)
6. Kirk, D., Tempero, E.: Software development practices in New Zealand. In: 19th Asia-Pacific Software Engineering Conference (APSEC), pp. 386–395. IEEE (2012)
7. Ministry of Business, Innovation and Employment (MBIE) New Zealand: ICT sector report (2017)

8. Ochoa, S., Robbes, R., Marques, M., Silvestre, L., Quispe, A.: What differentiates Chilean niche software companies: Business knowledge and reputation. IEEE Softw. **34**(3), 96–103 (2017)
9. Pfleeger, S., Kitchenham, B.: Principles of survey research - part 1: turning lemons into lemonade. ACM SIGSOFT Softw. Eng. Notes **26**(6), 16–18 (2001)
10. Torchiano, M., Ricca, F.: Six reasons for rejecting an industrial survey paper. In: 1st International Workshop on Conducting Empirical Studies in Industry (CESI), pp. 21–26. IEEE (2013)
11. Vogt, P.: Dictionary of Statistics and Methodology - A Non-technical Guide for the Social Sciences. Sage Publications, Thousand Oaks (2005)

Software Professionals' Attitudes Towards Video as a Medium in Requirements Engineering

Oliver Karras[(✉)]

Software Engineering Group, Leibniz Universität Hannover,
30167 Hannover, Germany
oliver.karras@inf.uni-hannover.de

Abstract. In requirements engineering (RE), knowledge is mainly communicated via written specifications. This practice is cumbersome due to its low communication richness and effectiveness. In contrast, videos can transfer knowledge more richly and effectively. However, video is still a neglected medium in RE. We investigate if software professionals perceive video as a medium that can contribute to RE. We focus on their attitudes towards video as a medium in RE including its strengths, weaknesses, opportunities, and threats. We conducted a survey to explore these attitudes with a questionnaire. 64 out of 106 software professionals completed the survey. The respondents' overall attitude towards video is positive. 59 of them stated that video has the potential to improve RE. However, 34 respondents also mentioned threats of videos for RE. We identified the strengths, weaknesses, opportunities, and threats of videos for RE from the point of view of software professionals. Video is a medium with a neglected potential. Software professionals do not fundamentally reject videos in RE. Despite the strengths and opportunities of video, the stated weaknesses and threats impede its application. Based on our findings, we conclude that software professionals need guidance on how to produce and use videos for visual communication to take full advantage of the currently neglected potential.

Keywords: Requirements engineering · Video · Attitude · SWOT Survey

1 Introduction

One of the most widely used documentation options to convey stakeholders' needs is a written specification as suggested by standards such as ISO/IEC/IEEE 29148:2011 [1]. However, the supposedly simple handover of a written specification insufficiently supports the rich information and knowledge transfer which is necessary to develop an acceptable system [9,15]. Abad et al. [2] found the need for improving requirements communication by exceeding pictorial representations in written specifications. The authors proposed to invest more efforts in

© Springer Nature Switzerland AG 2018
M. Kuhrmann et al. (Eds.): PROFES 2018, LNCS 11271, pp. 150–158, 2018.
https://doi.org/10.1007/978-3-030-03673-7_11

addressing interactive visualizations such as storytelling, for example with videos [2]. In the last 35 years, several researchers [5,7,8,12,14] proposed approaches that use videos in RE to support requirements communication. Despite all this research, video is still not an established documentation option in terms of RE best practice [10]. In our recently published position paper [13], we discussed video production in RE. In accordance with the aforementioned researchers [2,5,7,8,12,14], we also concluded that software professionals could enrich their communication and RE abilities if they knew what constitutes a good video for visual communication. As future work, we proposed to develop a quality model for videos to encourage and enable software professionals to produce effective videos on their own [13].

However, our future work and probably the existing approaches [5,7,8,12,14] are based on the assumption that software professionals perceive video as a medium that can contribute to RE. In this paper, we investigate this assumption by conducting an explorative survey focusing on the following research question:

Research question:
What are software professionals' attitudes towards video as a medium in RE?

Based on the attitudes, we expect to achieve insights that either substantiate or refute the assumption. By answering this research question, we can understand if software professionals fundamentally reject video as a medium in RE. Such a rejection would be reflected in a negative attitude including the mention of weaknesses and threats of videos. Otherwise, we assume a neutral or even positive attitude towards video including the mention of strengths and opportunities. Therefore, this information provides insights into the current perception of videos in RE by software professionals. We contribute the following insights.

Software professionals have generally a positive attitude towards video as a medium in RE. Although 59 respondents state that video can improve RE, this medium has a neglected potential. The identified strengths and opportunities of videos such as *richness*, *simplicity*, improved *communication*, and improved *understanding* indicate the benefits of video as a powerful and simple documentation option for communication. However, the mentioned weaknesses and threats such as high *effort*, technical *constraints*, *misuse*, and *intimidation* impede the application of videos in RE. Furthermore, they indicate a lack of knowledge by software professionals on how to produce and use good videos.

2   Documentation for Communication: A Challenge of RE

Different studies investigated RE practices in terms of documentation and communication [2,3,6,10,16]. All of them indicate that a written specification is (1) the most common medium for requirements communication and (2) a crucial RE challenge due to its low communication richness and effectiveness.

In a field study, Al-Raws and Easterbrook [3] found that written specifications insufficiently support communication due to the inherent restrictions of available notations. They conclude that specifications need to be enriched in order to turn them into an effective means of communication. Fricker et al. [10] also conducted a survey on RE practices. Their results show that all applied and established documentation notations consists only of pictorial or textual representations. Lethbridge et al. [16] performed a study on the use of documentation. Their findings indicate that software professionals often perceive documentation as too complex. The authors conclude the necessity to focus on power and simplicity of documentation to increase its relevance. Carter and Karatsolis [6] reported lessons learned from developing a robust documentation. Based on their experiences, they suggest to include multimedia documentation, such as videos, in RE. The authors believe that adding such multimedia documentations to the RE palette of notations can produce a significant value. Abad et al. [2] conducted a systematic literature review on visualization in RE. One of their key findings is the need for a better support of requirements communication that exceeds pictorial representations in written specifications.

All previously mentioned studies indicate a still existing need for improving documentation for communication in RE. Several researchers [5,7,8,12,14] addressed this problem by focusing on the use of video as a documentation option in RE. They followed the line-of-thought of Lethbridge et al. [16] as well as Carter and Karatsolis [6]. Despite its communication richness and effectiveness, video is still not an established documentation option in RE. Therefore, we conducted a survey on software professionals' *attitudes towards video as a medium in RE.*

3   Survey – Video as a Medium in RE

We aligned the survey design by following the steps and guidelines for carrying out a questionnaire survey as proposed by Robson and McCartan [18, p. 244 ff.].

Design: We iteratively refined the questionnaire design consisting of 6 closed (demographics and attitude) and 4 open-ended (strengths, weaknesses, opportunities, and threats) questions. We performed the initial testing by using the checklist provided by Baum et al. [4] to review every single question. This was followed by 5 rounds of pre-tests. In each pre-test, a software professional completed the survey and we discussed how the questionnaire could be improved.

Data Collection: In late 2017, we conducted the survey implemented in LimeSurvey. We relied on a number of communication channels to reach suitable participants, e.g. LinkedIn, ResearchGate, a mailing list of a German RE professionals group, and advertisement at the *25th IEEE International Requirements Engineering Conference.* Our target population included practitioners and researchers since both groups have relevant attitudes towards video as a medium in RE. While practitioners report an industrial, project-oriented point of view, researchers state a scientific, project-oriented one.

Analysis: We analyzed the open-ended questions with manual coding [19]. This is a qualitative data analysis consisting of two consecutive coding cycles of which each can be repeated iteratively. The first cycle includes the initial coding of the data. The second cycle focuses on classifying, abstracting, and conceptualizing categories from the coded data. In the first cycle, we applied *in vivo coding* which assigns a word or phrase found in a response as a code to the respective data. In the second cycle, we performed *pattern coding* which groups the coded data into categories. We iterated three times through each cycle.

3.1 Survey Results

Demography: The respondents worked in 11 countries: 40 in Germany, 16 in other European countries, 6 in North America, and 2 in Asia including the Middle East. Of 64 respondents 34 were from industry and 30 were from academia. 8 practitioners stated their job as *requirements engineer*, 7 as *project manager*, 5 as *developer*, 2 as *software architect*, and 12 as other business roles only mentioned once. The researchers stated mainly two research areas: 16 times *requirements engineering* and 10 times *software engineering*. 4 respondents mentioned other research areas in computer science which were only mentioned once. On average, the practitioners had 9.2 years of experience and the researchers 7.4 years.

Attitudes Towards Video: Of the 64 respondents, 38 had a positive, 25 a neutral and 1 a negative attitude towards video as a medium in RE. 59 respondents stated that videos have the potential to improve RE. 34 respondents mentioned threats of video for RE. Table 1 summarizes the previously described findings. All respondents stated at least one strength and one weakness of video.

Table 1. Video as a medium in RE: attitudes, potential, and threats

	Attitude towards Videos			Potential for RE?		Threats for RE?	
	Positive	Neutral	Negative	Yes	No	Yes	No
Researcher	21	9	0	28	2	17	13
Practitioner	17	16	1	31	3	17	17
Total	**38**	**25**	**1**	**59**	**5**	**34**	**30**

Figure 1 shows the Coding Frequencies (CF) for the open-ended questions about the strengths, weaknesses, opportunities, and threats of videos in RE.

Strengths: Videos are most appreciated for their *richness* (CF: 42) of detailed and comprehensive information such as gestures, facial expressions, emotions, and rationales. This information can be used and understood fast and easily due to the *simplicity* (CF: 32) of videos. The respondents emphasized the *accuracy* (CF: 27) of videos since they capture exact statements and visualize concrete examples, problems, and solutions. Videos have an increased *reusability* (CF: 26) for later analyses or sharing due to their long-term accessibility and persistence.

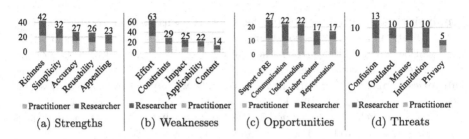

Fig. 1. Coding Frequencies (CF) of the open-ended questions

The visualization of videos is less ambiguous than textual descriptions wherefore videos are an *appealing* (CF: 23) medium.

Weaknesses: The most mentioned weakness of videos is the high *effort* (CF: 63) in terms of costs and time for planning, producing, watching and processing a video. The technical *constraints* (CF: 29) of videos such as file format, size, or required equipment are a further problem. Videos may have a negative *impact* (CF: 25) on people with different effects, e.g. too high expectations, intimidation, or low acceptance. The respondents also stated the *applicability* (CF: 22) of videos as difficult. Besides legal and privacy issues, videos are not suitable for every kind of content and context. Additionally, the information *content* (CF: 14) of videos is difficult since a video needs to include the right amount of detailed and relevant information.

Opportunities: The most mentioned opportunity of video is the *support of RE* (CF: 27) in terms of improving activities (elicitation, interpretation, validation, and documentation) and techniques (interview, workshop, focus group, and observation). Especially, the respondents think that videos can improve *communication* (CF: 22) and *understanding* (CF: 22) of all involved parties in RE. According to our respondents, videos can provide a *richer content* (CF: 17) than textual descriptions due to their increased information content with more detailed and comprehensive information. Videos also allow an improved *representation* (CF: 17) of workflows, interactions, environments, and scenarios due to a better description by visualization.

Threats: The most mentioned threat of videos is their *confusion* (CF: 13) since they contain a lot of unstructured data. Thus, it is challenging to identify the right, important, and meaningful content. The management of videos is also cumbersome since frequent changes are difficult to handle and can easily lead to *outdated* (CF: 10) information. The *misuse* (CF: 10) of videos is a further threat since they should not be used as a single medium to convey information. Videos may cause *intimidation* (CF: 10) of people. The respondents stated that the use of video can lead to a changed behavior and untrue statements by persons who feel uncomfortable or do not want to appear in a video. Some respondents mentioned *privacy* (CF: 5) concerns with respect to the misuse of recorded information or the violation of privacy.

3.2   Threats to Validity

Construct Validity: The single use of a questionnaire causes a mono-method bias. All collected data is based on a single source and thus only allows restricted explanations of our findings. The respondents' rationales and thoughts behind their answers remain unknown. The findings might also be affected subjectively since the author performed the coding and analysis on his own. This threat was mitigated by using *in vivo coding* to adhere closely to the respondents' actual language found in the qualitative data. We published the questionnaire and all collected data online to increase the transparency of our results [11].

External Validity: According to the respondents, all of them were software professionals from industry and academia. Thus, we expect that they belong to the target population. The survey, however, was accessible to anyone to achieve heterogeneity in the respondents' attitudes. We also cannot foreclose that respondents made false statements. However, there was no financial reward and thus little incentive to participate in the survey without giving honest answers.

Internal Validity: Two important threats to internal validity are maturation and instrumentation. The time taken to complete the survey is crucial. In case of too many questions, respondents may be affected negatively and abort. We refined carefully the questionnaire design to improve the instrumentation (see Sect. 3). In case of an abort, all entered data was deleted to increase the respondents' trust in our research.

Conclusion Validity: The validity of any scientific evaluation highly depends on the reliability of measures. A good question wording, instrumentation, and instrumentation layout are crucial for the results of a survey. We followed survey guidelines and used LimeSurvey, which is a professional survey software, to ensure these aspects. We consciously decided on the respondents' heterogeneity to increase the external validity. However, the variation in knowledge and background might affect the findings and thus restricts the conclusion validity.

4   Discussion

We investigate the assumption that software professionals' perceive video as a medium that can contribute to RE. Despite 35 years of research on integrating videos in RE, this medium is still not an established documentation option. We focus on the attitudes of software professionals towards video to achieve insights whether they fundamentally reject videos in RE or not. Our findings substantiate the assumption, but also indicate crucial concerns in terms of weaknesses and threats that impede the application of videos in RE.

Software professionals generally have a positive attitude towards videos. 59 out of 64 respondents stated that videos have the potential to improve RE by supporting multiple RE activities and techniques and by providing a richer content as well as a better representation than textual descriptions. The mentioned strengths of videos (*richness*, *simplicity*, *accuracy*, *reusability*, and *appealing*ness) underline the benefits of video as a powerful, simple, and appealing documentation option. Especially, the top-3 opportunities (*support of RE*, improved *communication*, and improved *understanding*) emphasize the suitability of video as a medium in RE for requirements communication.

However, the respondents stated weaknesses and threats that are crucial concerns which impede the application of videos in RE. Especially, the perceived high *effort* to plan, produce, watch, and process videos is the most frequently identified code overall. Besides this primary weakness, further mentioned weaknesses and threats of videos are i.e. technical *constraints*, negative *impact*, *misuse*, and an improper information *content*. All of them indicate a lack of knowledge of software professionals on how to produce and use good videos that are suitable for RE. As an answer to our research question, we can summarize:

Answer: Software professionals' attitudes towards video as a medium in RE are mostly positive. They do not fundamentally reject videos in RE. However, besides clear strengths and opportunities, there are crucial weaknesses and threats that impede the application of videos in RE.

These findings coincide with the conclusions of different researchers [6,17] and the argumentation in our position paper [13]. "The important thing is to know how to visually communicate" [17, p. 80]. Previous approaches focused on the use of videos in RE but omitted the details about how to produce them [13]. So far, little research encountered the challenge of enabling software professionals with the required knowledge to produce and use good videos for visual communication [13]. This emphasizes the need for research that focuses on the production of effective videos to establish them as a communication tool in RE practice [6].

We want to encounter this challenge of enabling software professionals to produce and use good videos on their own at moderate costs, yet sufficient quality. For this, software professionals need to understand what constitutes the quality of a good video. As proposed in our position paper [13], our future work focuses on developing a quality model for videos since such a model allows (1) to evaluate the quality of existing videos and (2) to guide the video production and use process. Software professionals can use this quality model as an orientation for planning, shooting, post-processing, and viewing videos in RE.

5   Conclusion

Despite its low communication richness and effectiveness, a written specification is the most common medium for requirements communication. In contrast, videos allow a richer knowledge transfer. Although several researchers suggested applying videos in RE by proposing corresponding approaches, this medium is still not an established documentation option. We conducted a survey to explore software professionals' attitudes towards video as a medium in RE in order to achieve insights if they fundamentally reject videos.

Based on our findings, software professionals do not fundamentally reject videos. However, this medium still has a neglected potential. The identified strengths and opportunities underline the benefits of video as a documentation option for communication. Nevertheless, videos are also associated with multiple weaknesses and threats that impede their application in RE. We consider our findings as further indicators that substantiate a lack of knowledge of software professionals on how to produce and use good videos for visual communication. Thus, we follow our proposed future work of developing a quality model for videos to encourage and enable software professionals to produce and use effective videos for RE on their own at moderate costs, yet sufficient quality.

Acknowledgment. This work was supported by the Deutsche Forschungsgemeinschaft (DFG) under ViViReq, Grant No.: 289386339, (2017–2019).

References

1. ISO/IEC/IEEE 29148:2011: Systems and Software Engineering - Life Cycle Processes - Requirements Engineering (2011)
2. Abad, Z.S.H., Noaeen, M., Ruhe, G.: Requirements engineering visualization: a systematic literature review. In: 24th IEEE International Requirements Engineering Conference (2016)
3. Al-Rawas, A., Easterbrook, S.: Communication problems in requirements engineering: a field study (1996)
4. Baum, T., Leßmann, H., Schneider, K.: The choice of code review process: a survey on the state of the practice. In: Felderer, M., Méndez Fernández, D., Turhan, B., Kalinowski, M., Sarro, F., Winkler, D. (eds.) PROFES 2017. LNCS, vol. 10611, pp. 111–127. Springer, Cham (2017). https://doi.org/10.1007/978-3-319-69926-4_9
5. Brill, O., Schneider, K., Knauss, E.: Videos vs. use cases: can videos capture more requirements under time pressure? In: Wieringa, R., Persson, A. (eds.) REFSQ 2010. LNCS, vol. 6182, pp. 30–44. Springer, Heidelberg (2010). https://doi.org/10.1007/978-3-642-14192-8_5
6. Carter, L.R., Karatsolis, A.: Lessons from trying to develop a robust documentation exemplar. In: Proceedings of the 27th ACM International Conference on Design of Communication (2009)
7. Creighton, O., Ott, M., Bruegge, B.: Software cinema - video-based requirements engineering. In: 14th IEEE International Requirements Engineering Conference (2006)
8. Feeney, W.: Documenting software using video. In: IEEE Workshop on Software Engineering Technology Transfer (1983)
9. Fricker, S., Glinz, M.: Comparison of requirements hand-off, analysis, and negotiation: case study. In: IEEE 18th International Conference on Requirements Engineering (2010)
10. Fricker, S.A., Grau, R., Zwingli, A.: Requirements engineering: best practice. In: Fricker, S.A., Thümmler, C., Gavras, A. (eds.) Requirements Engineering for Digital Health, pp. 25–46. Springer, Cham (2015). https://doi.org/10.1007/978-3-319-09798-5_2
11. Karras, O.: Survey data - attitudes towards video as a medium in requirements engineering (2018). https://doi.org/10.5281/zenodo.1404742

12. Karras, O., Kiesling, S., Schneider, K.: Supporting requirements elicitation by tool-supported video analysis. in: 24th IEEE International Requirements Engineering Conference (2016)
13. Karras, O., Schneider, K.: Software professionals are not directors: what constitutes a good video? In: 26th IEEE International Requirements Engineering Conference Workshops (2018)
14. Karras, O., Unger-Windeler, C., Glauer, L., Schneider, K.: Video as a by-product of digital prototyping: capturing the dynamic aspect of interaction. In: 25th IEEE International Requirements Engineering Conference Workshops (2017)
15. Klünder, J., Karras, O., Kortum, F., Schneider, K.: Forecasting communication behavior in student software projects. In: 12th International Conference on Predictive Models and Data Analytics in Software Engineering (2016)
16. Lethbridge, T.C., Singer, J., Forward, A.: How software engineers use documentation: the state of the practice. IEEE Softw. **6**, 35–39 (2003)
17. Owens, J., Millerson, G.: Video Production Handbook, 5th edn. Focal Press, Oxford (2011)
18. Robson, C., McCartan, K.: Real World Research. Wiley, Hoboken (2016)
19. Saldaña, J.: The Coding Manual for Qualitative Researchers. Sage, London (2015)

Do Developers Really Worry About Refactoring Re-test? An Empirical Study of Open-Source Systems

Stev Counsell[1(✉)], Stephen Swift[1], Mahir Arzoky[1],
and Giuseppe Destefanis[2]

[1] Department of Computer Science, Brunel University, London, UK
steve.counsell@brunel.ac.uk
[2] Department of Computer Science, University of Hertfordshire, Herts, UK
g.destefanis@herts.ac.uk

Abstract. In this paper, we explore the extent to which a set of over 12000 refactorings fell into one of four re-test categories defined by van Deursen and Moonen; the 'least disruptive' of the four categories contains refactorings requiring only minimal re-test. The 'most disruptive' category of refactorings on the other hand requires significant re-test effort. We used multiple versions of three open-source systems to answer one research question: Do developers prefer to undertake refactorings in the least disruptive categories or in the most disruptive? The simple answer is that they prefer to do both. We provide insights into these refactoring patterns across the systems and highlight a fundamental weakness with software metrics trying to capture the refactoring process.

Keywords: Refactoring · Test · Taxonomy · Metrics · Open-source

1 Introduction

Since Fowler's seminal text on refactoring [3] and earlier work by Opdyke [7], the field of refactoring has, even conservatively speaking, spawned hundreds of studies [2, 4]. One facet of refactoring we know little about empirically, however, is the re-test implications of refactoring. Re-testing after refactoring is a necessary, yet time-consuming and potentially error-prone process and is heavily dependent on the type of refactoring being performed. One question that could inform our understanding of developer productivity, code quality and developer habits and which motivates this research is whether developers opt to undertake refactorings with a high re-test burden, *vis-à-vis* those that have only limited re-test requirements. An earlier paper by van Deursen and Moonen (vD&M) [9] explored Fowler's seventy-two refactorings and attached a test severity category to each. Their work was motivated by the fact that a refactoring should: "*not change its* [the code's] *observable behaviour. Ideally, this is verified by ensuring that all the tests pass before and after a refactoring. In practice, it turns out that such verification is not always possible: some refactorings restructure the code in such a way that tests can only pass after the refactoring if they are modified*". We used refactoring data extracted in a previous study by Bavota et al. [1] to

M. Kuhrmann et al. (Eds.): PROFES 2018, LNCS 11271, pp. 159–166, 2018.
https://doi.org/10.1007/978-3-030-03673-7_12

carry out our analysis. The data was drawn from multiple versions of three open-source systems and is made available as a free download from [10]; it comprises 12046 refactorings extracted using Ref-Finder, a tool capable of extracting fifty-four of Fowler's seventy-two [8]. The same work by Bavota et al. investigated whether refactorings had been applied to code for which quality metrics (e.g., for size, coupling and cohesion) indicated the need for refactoring. A key result was that the metrics did *not* show a clear and obvious relationship with refactoring, suggesting that they cannot be used to identify classes that might need refactoring. Table 1 (taken from [1]) summarizes the three systems used, the versions analyzed and the ranges in classes and KLOC for each system. We note that in the original paper [1], a refactoring *and* code smell analysis was also undertaken; for the purpose of our study we used just the refactoring data giving rise to the 12046 refactorings.

Table 1. System summary (taken from [1])

System	Period	Releases	Classes	KLOC
Apache	Jan 2000–Dec 2010	18	87–1191	8–255
Xerces	Oct 2002–Dec 2011	23	777–1519	362–918
ArgoUml	Nov 1999–Nov 2010	11	181–776	56–179

2   vD&M's Test Taxonomy

In their paper, vD&M [9] describe four separate categories into which the seventy-two refactorings of Fowler can be placed. Initially, five categories (A-E) were described in their paper. However, Category A refactorings were dropped from their analysis on the basis that they were simply an amalgam of smaller refactorings. The four remaining categories (B-E) are defined in increasing levels of re-test burden as:

1. Compatible (Category B refactorings): do not change the original interface.
2. Backwards Compatible (Category C refactorings): change the original interface and are inherently backwards compatible, since they extend the interface.
3. Make backwards compatible (Category D refactorings): change the original interface and can be made backwards compatible by adapting the old interface. For example, the 'Move method' refactoring that moves a method from one class to another can be made backwards compatible through the addition of a 'wrapper' method to retain the old interface.
4. Incompatible (Category E refactorings): change the original interface and are not backwards compatible because they may, for example, change the types of classes involved making it difficult to wrap the changes (e.g., Move field).

So, in theory Category B refactorings should present less of a re-test burden than those in Category C and those in Category C less than in Category D etc. Table 2 shows the seventy-two refactorings of Fowler when placed into each of the four categories (B-E) as detailed by vD&M.

Table 2. The four vD&M categories and refactorings in each [9]

Category/Set of refactorings
Category B: Change Bi-directional Association to Unidirectional, Replace Magic Number with Symbolic Constant, Replace Nested Conditional with Guard Clauses, Consolidate Duplicate Conditional Fragments, Replace Conditional with Polymorphism, Replace Delegation with Inheritance, Replace Inheritance with Delegation, Replace Method with Method Object, Remove Assignments to Parameters, Replace Data Value with Object, Introduce Explaining Variable, Replace Exception with Test, Change Reference to Value, Split Temporary Variable, Decompose Conditional, Introduce Null Object, Preserve Whole Object, Remove Control Flag, Substitute Algorithm, Introduce Assertion, Extract Class, Inline Temp
Category C: Consolidate Conditional Expression, Replace Delegation with Inheritance, Replace Inheritance with Delegation, Replace Record with Data Class, Introduce Foreign Method, Pull Up Constructor Body, Replace Temp with Query, Duplicate Observed Data, Self Encapsulate Field, Form Template Method, Extract Superclass, Extract Interface, Push Down Method, Push Down Field, Extract Method, Pull Up Method, Pull up Field
Category D: Change Unidirectional Association to Bi-directional, Replace Parameter with Explicit Methods, Replace Parameter with Method, Separate Query from Modifier, Introduce Parameter Object, Parameterize Method, Remove Middle Man, Remove Parameter, Rename Method, Add Parameter, Move Method
Category E: Replace Constructor with Factory Method, Replace Type Code with State/Strategy, Replace Type Code with Subclasses, Replace Error Code with Exception, Replace Subclass with Fields, Replace Type Code with Class, Change Value to Reference, Introduce Local Extension, Replace Array with Object, Encapsulate Collection, Remove Setting Method, Encapsulate Downcast, Collapse Hierarchy, Encapsulate Field, Extract Subclass, Hide Delegate, Inline Method, Inline Class, Hide Method, Move Field

2.1 Category Analysis

We first detail the number of refactorings found in each category according to the data of Bavota et al. Table 3 shows, for each of the three open-source systems, (1) the number of refactorings applied across the four categories (B, C, D and E), (2) the percentages that this represents and, (3) the totals for each category and each system. For example, in Apache, 673 refactorings were applied from Category B. This represents 52.21% of the total of 1289 refactorings undertaken in the entire system. Equally, 17.41% is the corresponding proportion of 3865 Category B refactorings that 673 represents. For Apache, Category D was only the second highest in terms of refactorings (exceeded by the number in Category B). Table 3 also shows that the highest number of refactorings for Xerces and ArgoUml was in Category D (3663 and 1505 refactorings, respectively). This category accounted for 46.41% of the total number of refactorings across the three systems. For Xerces, 48.83% of all refactorings were in Category D and 65.52% of Category D refactorings were attributable to the same system (bolded in the table). The lowest number of refactorings in all systems was for Category C, accounting for just 807 (6.70%) of the total 12046.

Table 3. Number of refactorings in each category (all systems)

System	Category B		Category C		Category D		Category E		Total
Apache	673		105		423		88		1289
	52.21	17.41	8.15	13.01	32.82	7.57	6.82	10.90	
Xerces	2056		499		3663		1284		7502
	27.41	53.20	6.65	61.83	48.83	**65.52**	17.11	**72.01**	
ArgoUml	1136		203		1505		411		3255
	34.90	29.39	6.24	25.15	46.24	26.92	12.63	23.05	
Total	3865 (32.09)		807 (6.70)		5591 (46.41)		1783 (14.80)		**12046**

While Category B accounted for a significant proportion of the total (32.09%), it was Category D that seems to dominate the overall set. At the other extreme, Category E accounted for just 1783 (14.80%) of total number of refactorings; finally, Xerces accounted for 72.01% of all Category E refactorings (value bolded in the table).

Result Summary

From the data presented, it is evident that developers did undertake many low test impact refactorings. Category B accounts for nearly a third of all refactorings. However, nearly 50% of the total number of refactorings across all systems were drawn from Category D. This propensity for Category D refactorings was a surprising and revealing result and contrary to our intuition. We might have expected developers to prefer to undertake Category B and C refactorings because they are simpler in a re-test sense (in fact Category C actually saw the lowest number of refactorings). This does not seem to be the case, however from the data.

2.2 Refactoring Analysis

One relevant question is which refactorings were applied most frequently across the four categories? That might help us understand why the result of the previous section was found. For Apache, three refactorings stood out in Category D, namely: Add parameter, Remove parameter and Rename method. These three refactorings accounted for 30.72% of all refactorings applied in the system. The most frequent was Rename method, whose motivation is described by Fowler [3] as: "*The name of a method does not reveal its purpose*". The solution is to: "*Change the name of the method*". In Category B, most of the refactorings related to the low-level manipulation of conditional logic in the code. For example, 314 of the 673 refactorings were attributable to the: Replace magic number with symbolic constant (RMNwSC) refactoring. The motivation for this refactoring [3] is: "*You have a literal number with a particular meaning*". The solution is to: "*Create a constant, name it after the meaning, and replace the number with it.*" The example in [3] to illustrate is as follows:

```
double potentialEnergy(double mass, double height) {
  return mass * height * 9.81;
}
```

After the refactoring, this code becomes:

```
double potentialEnergy(double mass, double height) {
  return mass * GRAVITATIONAL_CONSTANT * height;
}
static final double GRAVITATIONAL_CONSTANT = 9.81;
```

For Xerces, three refactorings stood out in Category D. These were Rename method (in keeping with Apache), Move method and Add parameter (again, the same as Apache) with 1061, 1183 and 929 refactorings, respectively. In addition, a significant number of Move field refactorings (Category E) were also found (1183). In terms of Category B refactorings, the RMNwSC refactoring again stood out with 597 refactorings. Another noticeable Category B refactoring was Consolidate conditional duplicate fragments (CDCF) with 474 instances. The motivation for CDCF according to Fowler [3] is: *"The same fragment of code is in all branches of a conditional expression"*. The solution is to: *"Move it outside of the expression"*. The following example illustrates this refactoring [3]:

```
if (isSpecialDeal()) {
  total = price * 0.95;
  send();
}
else {
  total = price * 0.98;
  send();
}
```

After being refactored, the code without the duplicated method send() becomes:

```
if (isSpecialDeal())
  total = price * 0.95;
else
  total = price * 0.98;
send();
```

In ArgoUml, the same core set of refactorings seemed to arise. In Category D, the Add parameter, Remove parameter and Rename method refactorings again featured as those most applied with 491, 427 and 261 refactorings, respectively. Together, these three accounted for 1179 of the 1505 D category refactorings (i.e., 78.33%). For the B and C categories, only two refactorings stood out. The Replace method with method object refactoring (Category B) accounted for 367 refactorings. The purpose of this refactoring is to turn a method into its own object so that the local variables it uses become fields on that object. Equally, the Remove control flag (RCF) refactoring accounted for 224 of the total number of refactorings. The motivation for RCF is when *"You have a variable that is acting as a control flag for a series of boolean expressions"*. The solution is to: *"Use a break or return instead"*. Finally, the RMNwSC refactoring again featured with 145.

Result Summary

A small subset of refactorings therefore dominates the total set of refactorings across all three systems. In Category B, refactorings that manipulated low-level program logic accounted for the majority e.g., Replace magic number with symbolic constant' and, correspondingly, in Category D, where Add Parameter, Remove parameter and Rename method accounted for the majority. This result confirms Bavota et al.'s conclusion with respect to metric applicability. Very few current, popular metrics seem to capture low-level code logic constructs (i.e., that of conditionals, nesting, flag manipulation). Many of these refactorings manipulate low-level code (e.g., RCF, RNCwGC and RMNwSC etc.) and so it goes without saying that such metrics will be unlikely to provide insights into refactoring behaviour. Metrics that capture coupling, cohesion and size etc therefore largely miss the point of refactoring. It is no surprise that Bavota et al. found no relationship between metrics and refactoring.

2.3   Evolutionary Analysis

One aspect of the data that might further inform our analysis is whether, over the course of time, the trend in application of refactorings changes. We therefore looked at whether developers tended to undertake less of the Category D and E refactorings and more in the B and C categories on an evolutionary basis. The premise of this analysis is that, as systems age, they become more difficult to maintain as they erode and developers will therefore undertake refactorings with less complexity and with less of a test burden than others. To answer this question, we ordered the set of refactorings according to the version they were applied in Figs. 1a, 1b and 1c show the distribution of the four categories across versions for the three systems. The x-axis is the version number (we have simply numbered these starting from 1) and the y-axis the number of refactorings in each of the four types.

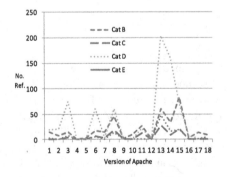 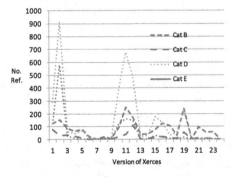

Fig. 1a. Refactorings in Apache   **Fig. 1b.** Refactorings in Xerces

Figure 1a shows the data for Apache. Most pronounced from the figure are the peaks in Category D refactorings which occur throughout the course of the versions studied, but are particularly evident in versions 13, 14 and15. The same is true to a lesser extent for Category B with a number of peaks, particularly in later versions. Version 15 stands out with 80 refactorings in this sense. The other two categories remain relatively static in numbers apart from one peak for Category E in version 13 with 47 refactorings. However, for this system, there does not appear to any less inclination to undertake Category D refactorings as the system ages (Category E showed very few refactorings overall anyway). On the other hand, there does seem to be an increase in the number of Category B refactorings as the Apache system evolves given by the relatively large peaks in version 13 onwards. Figure 1b shows the same data for Xerces. Again, the presence of peaks in the first and middle versions for Category D is notable. Category E also shows extremes in version 2 and to a lesser extent 11. As for Apache, Category D is relatively erratic in nature with peaks and troughs throughout the versions studied. The same is true of Category B. For Category D, peaks in version 2 and 11 can be seen and the same for Category B in versions 11 and 19. The pattern of erratic refactorings for Xerces is similar to Apache. Again, however there does not appear to any less inclination to undertake Category D refactorings as the system ages. Finally, Fig. 1c shows the data for ArgoUml. The peaks, particularly in Categories B, D and E are noticeable from the graph. For Categories B and D, there are large peaks in version 5 (a lesser peak for Category D is also evident in version 2). Category E also features some peaks in versions 2, 5 and 8. While the number of Category D refactorings in later versions is less pronounced, there is still little evidence that developers avoided test-intensive refactorings in later versions of the system.

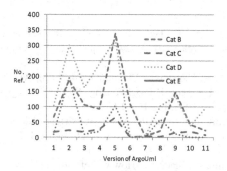

Fig. 1c. Refactorings in ArgoUml

Across all three systems, there does not seem to be a reduction in Category D and E refactorings or a dramatic rise in Category B and C refactorings.

3 Conclusions and Further Work

In this paper, we explored the extent to which a set of over 12000 refactorings fell into one of four re-test categories previously defined by van Deursen and Moonen. We explored whether developers would prefer to carry out refactorings with a low test burden rather than those where significant re-test might be involved (Category B and C refactorings versus D and E). The analysis showed as a primary result that open-source developers seem to apply refactorings largely irrespective of the test category and hence the re-test burden. Clearly, developers do not really care about refactoring re-test or, if they do, this does not affect their choice of refactoring. No trends in that direction were found on an evolutionary basis either. Of course, we have no information on whether developers used tools to assist in the refactoring process or whether they were manually performed. We have also only studied three open-source systems and limited versions of those systems. However, in defence of this threat, various other studies of developer habits suggest that developers generally prefer to refactor manually, rather than using tools. In one study by Murphy-Hill et al. [5] approximately 90% or all refactorings were applied manually. In another study by Negara et al. [6], experienced developers were found to apply 11% more manual refactorings than automatic, especially in renaming operations. A secondary and more wide-ranging result of the research was that current metrics seem to capture OO class features well, but they are not at the right level for analysing refactoring; this was a key result of Bavota et al. [1] and on which our research is based. This effectively means that OO metrics are largely redundant for indicating the need for refactoring. One avenue of future work is to encourage fresh metric initiatives to establish those that do – and these should be targeted at conditional nested code constructs. In addition, it would be interesting to explore whether, using data mining techniques, certain refactorings were always applied together.

References

1. Bavota, G., De Lucia, A., Di Penta, M., Oliveto, R., Palomba, F.: An experimental investigation on the innate relationship between quality and refactoring. J. Syst. Soft. **107**, 1–14 (2015)
2. Demeyer, S., Ducasse, S., Nierstrasz, O.: Finding refactorings via change metrics. In: ACM Conference on Object Oriented Programming Systems Languages and Applications (OOPSLA), Minneapolis, USA, pp. 166–177 (2000)
3. Fowler, M.: Refactoring: improving the design of existing code (1999)
4. Mens, T., Tourwe, T.: A survey of software refactoring. IEEE Trans. Softw. Eng. **30**(2), 126–139 (2004)
5. Murphy-Hill, E., Parnin, C., Black, A.: How we refactor, and how we know it. IEEE Trans. Softw. Eng. **38**(1), 5–18 (2012)
6. Negara, S., Chen, N., Vakilian, M., Johnson, R.E., Dig, D.: A comparative study of manual and automated refactorings. In: Castagna, G. (ed.) ECOOP 2013. LNCS, vol. 7920, pp. 552–576. Springer, Heidelberg (2013). https://doi.org/10.1007/978-3-642-39038-8_23
7. Opdyke, W.: Refactoring OO frameworks, Ph.D. thesis, University of Illinois (1992)
8. Prete, K., Rachatasumrit, N., Sudan, N., Kim, M.: Template-based reconstruction of complex refactorings. In: International Conference on Software Maintenance, Timisoara, Romania, pp. 1–10 (2010)
9. van Deursen, A., Moonen, L.: The video store revisited - thoughts on refactoring and testing. In: International Conference on eXtreme Programming and Flexible Processes in Software Engineering XP 2002, Sardinia, Italy (2002)
10. https://figshare.com/articles/An_Experimental_Investigation_on_the_Innate_Relationship_between_Quality_and_Refactoring/1207916

Moving Beyond the Mean: Analyzing Variance in Software Engineering Experiments

Adrian Santos[1]([✉]), Markku Oivo[1], and Natalia Juristo[2]

[1] M3S (M-Group), ITEE University of Oulu, Oulu, Finland
{adrian.santos.parrilla,markku.oivo}@oulu.fi
[2] Escuela Técnica Superior de Ingenieros Informáticos,
Universidad Politécnica de Madrid, Madrid, Spain
natalia@fi.upm.es

Abstract. Software Engineering (SE) experiments are traditionally analyzed with statistical tests (e.g., t-tests, ANOVAs, etc.) that assume equally spread data across groups (i.e., the homogeneity of variances assumption). Differences across groups' variances in SE are not seen as an opportunity to gain insights on technology performance, but instead, as a hindrance to analyze the data. We have studied the role of variance in mature experimental disciplines such as medicine. We illustrate the extent to which variance may inform on technology performance by means of simulation. We analyze a real-life industrial experiment on Test-Driven Development (TDD) where variance may impact technology desirability. Evaluating the performance of technologies just based on means—as traditionally done in SE—may be misleading. Technologies that make developers obtain similar performance (i.e., technologies with smaller variances) may be more suitable if the aim is minimizing the risk of adopting them in real practice.

Keywords: Experiments · Analysis · Variance
Test-Driven Development

1 Introduction

SE experiments are traditionally analyzed with statistical tests (e.g., t-tests, ANOVAs, etc. [1]) that assume equally spread data across groups (i.e., the homogeneity of variances assumption [2]). Perhaps inadvertently, and as a consequence of just relying on traditional statistical tests' results, researchers judge the performance of software technologies solely with regard to their mean performances. Not just differences across mean performances are relevant when deciding on the suitability of a new technology. Variation of technologies' scores, for example, may also be relevant if the aim is minimizing the risk of adopting such technologies in real-life contexts.

© Springer Nature Switzerland AG 2018
M. Kuhrmann et al. (Eds.): PROFES 2018, LNCS 11271, pp. 167–181, 2018.
https://doi.org/10.1007/978-3-030-03673-7_13

For example, let us suppose that two development processes (let us say Method A and Method B) perform similarly 'on-average' (and thus, that the estimation of the *means* of Method A and Method B are similar) on a certain outcome of interest (e.g., quality in a percentage scale) in an experiment where two independent groups of developers apply each a different development process (i.e., an AB between-subjects experiment [3,4]). Let us further suppose that albeit both groups achieve similar means, the spread of the scores in each group are different (e.g., Method A's quality scores are clumped together close to the mean, and Method B's quality scores are largely dispersed along the 0–100% interval). Even though Method A and Method B perform similarly 'on-average' (i.e., in terms of means), developers' quality scores with Method B are more spread than those with Method A. A traditional statistical test (e.g., a t-test [2]) applied on such data will not detect any difference between the means of both methods (as after all, 'on-average' both methods perform similarly, and t-tests just compare means [2]). Does this imply that Method A and Method B are equally suitable in all circumstances? If we had to make a decision and choose a technology for a group of developers, which one would we prefer?

It depends. If we were a risk-averse manager, choosing Method A (i.e., the less variable method) over Method B may be beneficial. After all, as all developers are expected to obtain similar quality scores with Method A, it is possible to make precise predictions on the quality to be achieved in a new software product being developed. On the contrary, if we were an enthusiastic developer, choosing Method B (i.e., the most variable method) may be beneficial. Indeed, it might be the case that we obtain large benefits with it, certainly not a thing to expect with Method A—as all developers obtain quality scores close to the mean.

Along this work we aim to answer a main **research question**:

- Is it worth it investigating variance in SE experiments?

To answer this research question we first perform a simulation to illustrate the extent to which different variances across technologies—even if their means are identical—may determine their suitability. Then, we analyze a real-life industrial experiment on TDD where a similar circumstance may have materialized. In particular, by analyzing the data just with traditional statistical tests (i.e., the t-test) as it is commonly done in SE experiments, both technologies seem to perform similarly. To what extent is it so? Along this research we found:

Key findings

- Not just differences between means are relevant when judging technology's performance: differences between variances may be relevant also.
- Failing to detect real differences across treatments' variances does not mean that technologies have identical variances: statistical tests may be under-powered to detect real differences across variances given SE experiments' small sample sizes.

The main **contributions** of this paper are a *a call to analyze variance in SE experiments* and a reminder *that other statistical points rather than means (e.g., variances) may also serve to inform about technology performance.*

Along this study we argue that as SE experiments are commonly analyzed by means of traditional statistical tests, perfectly suitable technologies may have passed unnoticed due to their perhaps similar mean performances. In addition, as individual experiments in SE are generally small to detect real differences between means [1], the same may hold for detecting differences between variances [5]. In view of this, we suggest:

Actionable results

- Variance should be investigated in SE experiments and considered when judging technology performance.
- Effect sizes quantifying the difference between technologies' variances should be provided with the aim of easing the interpretation of results.

Paper Organization. In Sect. 2 we report the background of this research. In Sect. 3 we outline the research method followed along this study. We analyze a toy-experiment to show the extent to which variation of quality scores may pass unnoticed in SE experiments in Sect. 4. We analyze a real-life industrial experiment on Test-Driven Development in Sect. 5. We discuss our findings in Sect. 6. We outline the threats to validity of this study in Sect. 7. Finally, we show the conclusions of this study in Sect. 8.

2   Background

SE experiments' results are usually conveyed in terms of effect sizes, p-values and confidence intervals (CIs) [2,6]. Effect sizes quantify the relationship between two groups (or more generally, between two variables: the dependent and the independent variable [7]). Effect sizes can be provided in either *standardized units* (e.g., Cohen's d that conveys the difference between the means of two groups divided by a pooled standard deviation [7]) or in *unstandardized units* (e.g., t-tests' estimates that convey the difference between the means of two groups in natural units [7]). p-values quantify the probability of achieving such effect size— or a larger one—given that a certain *null hypothesis* (generally stating that there is no relationship between the dependent and independent variable) is true [6]. If the p-value is lower than a certain threshold (typically lower than 0.05 [8]), then it is claimed that the effect size is *statistically significant*. If the effect size is statistically significant, then the relationship between the dependent and independent variable can be claimed to be different from 0—at least given the evidence collected from the experiment's data. Confidence intervals include the range of effect sizes compatible with the data at a certain probability threshold [9]. Confidence intervals (CIs) are commonly used as a measure of *precision* of the effect size [6]: the narrower the confidence interval at a certain threshold (e.g., 95%), the larger the accuracy of the effect size and viceversa.

Traditionally used statistical tests—as well as traditionally used effect sizes such as Cohen's d [10]—depend upon certain *statistical assumptions* to provide reliable results [2]. For example, they depend upon the normality assumption and more critically, on the *homogeneity of variances* assumption—when the groups are *independent* [2].[1] In view of this, SE researchers routinely apply statistical tests (such as the Levene test, etc. [2]) to check the homogeneity of variances assumption and thus, being able to interpret the results of their experiments.

Unfortunately, obtaining a non-significant p-value by means of a statistical test such as the Levene test, and thus claiming that the data are compatible with the homogeneity of variances assumption, *does not* imply that the effects of the technologies in the *population* are equally sparse [5]. In particular, such misleading result may have just emerged as a consequence of the low statistical power of statistical tests in small sample sizes—as those common in SE experiments [1]—and thus, the failure of the statistical test to detect differently sparse data across groups.

Among the many statistical tests that can be used due to check differences across groups' variances (e.g., Barlett's, Hartley's, Levene's test, etc. [5]), along this study we illustrate the Brown-Forsythe test [12] due to its robustness to departures from normality and its intuitiveness: it is just an ANOVA test performed on the deviations of each data point to the median of its group. The Brown-Forsythe test checks the *null hypothesis* that the variances of all groups are identical. If the Brown-Forsythe test is statistically significant, then, there is enough evidence to claim that *at least one* of the groups has a different variance [12]. Not just statistical tests shall be run to identify differences across groups' variances: effect sizes quantifying the differences between them shall be also provided with the aim of easing the interpretation of results [13].

Various effect sizes such as the *lnCVR* are starting to be used to assess treatments' variances in ecology and medicine [13–16]. The lnCVR is more suitable than the difference between standard deviations for evaluating variances, specially in small sample sizes (as the sampling distribution of the standard deviation may not follow normality [13]). The lnCVR stands for the *natural logarithm (ln)* of the *ratio between the coefficients of variation (CVR)* of two groups. The coefficient of variation (CV) of each group can be simply obtained by dividing its standard deviation by its mean (i.e., *sd/mean*). Large coefficients of variation (CVs) indicate large variance over small mean effects. On the contrary, small CVs indicate small variance over large mean effects. In SE parlance, a technology has a large CV if all developers perform wildly different to each other and perform to the minimum. On the contrary, a technology has a small CV if all developers perform similarly to each other and perform to the maximum. Thus, when obtaining the ratio between two CVs (i.e., obtaining the CVR), if

---

[1] Even though other statistical tests allowing for unequal variances across groups are also available (e.g., the Welch's t-test, Generalized Least Squares, etc. [11]), they are rarely used to analyze SE experiments [1], and thus, left out of our study.

the technology in the numerator is *less variable* than that in the denominator, the natural logarithm of the CVR (i.e., the lnCVR) tends to a negative number. The larger the *magnitude* of the lnCVR, the larger the difference between the variances of both technologies.

For example, if we run an experiment to compare the performance of two technologies with regard to their variances (let us say Method A and Method B) and the CV of Method A is equal to 1, and the CV of Method B is equal to 2, this implies that Method A scores are *half as variable* as those of Method B. When dividing their CVs and taking the natural logarithm (i.e., calculating the lnCVR), a negative number is obtained (i.e., $ln(1/2) = -0.30$). The larger the magnitude of the lnCVR (i.e., the more negative the number is), the larger the difference between the variances of both technologies. The lnCVR effect size is defined as follows [13]:

$$lnCVR = ln\left(\frac{CV_t}{CV_c}\right) + \frac{1}{2*(n_t - 1)} + \frac{1}{2*(n_c - 1)}$$

where CV_t and CV_c are $s_t/\bar{x}_t$ and $s_c/\bar{x}_c$, for the treatment and control group, respectively.

3   Research Method

We conducted a literature review on the role of variance in ecology and medicine after realizing that variance is starting to be evaluated to assess the performance of new treatments in such disciplines [13–16]. In addition, from our experience at conducting and analyzing SE experiments, and after looking at SE experiments' reports included in Dyba et al. [1], we noticed that variances are rarely assessed in SE but to be able to interpret traditional statistical tests' results (e.g., the results of t-tests or ANOVAs [1]).

With the aim of motivating the relevance of variance on technology performance, and illustrating visually why SE experiments' small sample sizes may not be able to detect differences across them, along this article we rely on simulation. In particular, we first simulate the performance of two hypothetical technologies in a continuous outcome (lets us say quality in a percentage scale) in an *imaginary population* of developers (e.g., the population of all Finnish developers). We simulate the performance of each technology by means of a Beta distribution [17]. Even though the shape of these distributions in the *population* may never be known (unless, eventually after an infinite number of experiments, all the developers within the population had been sampled), by means of simulation *we can act as if we knew the real distribution* of quality scores of each technology in the population, and then, simulate experiments just by sampling from these distributions (i.e., obtaining random data-points, each representing a different developer).

Beta distributions are a family of continuous probability distributions defined in the interval $[0, 1]$ with a shape governed by two parameters: α and β [17]. Both α and β parameters define the shape (and thus, the mean and variance) of beta distributions [17]. The relationship between means, variances, α and β parameters follows:

$$Mean = \frac{\alpha}{\alpha + \beta}$$

and

$$Variance = \frac{\alpha * \beta}{(\alpha + \beta)^2 * (\alpha + \beta + 1)}$$

Thus, obtaining Beta distributions with identical means and different variances (or standard deviations) is straightforward by selecting appropriate α and β parameters. As an example, Fig. 1 shows the *Beta(12,18)* distribution (with $M = 0.4$; $SD = 0.09$) and the *Beta(2,3)* distribution (with $M = 0.4$; $SD = 0.2$). For illustrative purposes, let us suppose that the *Beta(12,18)* distribution plays the role of the quality scores achieved with Method A in *a certain population* of developers, while the *Beta(2,3)* distribution plays the role of the quality scores achieved with Method B in *that same population*.

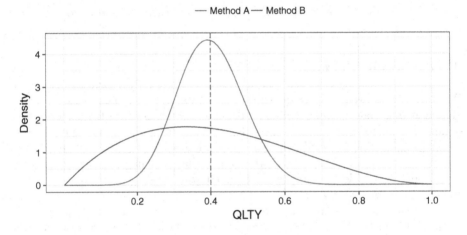

Fig. 1. Beta distributions. (Color figure online)

As it can be seen in Fig. 1, Method A quality scores are clumped together around 0.4 (i.e., 40%). In SE terms, most developers using Method A obtain quality scores around 40%. On the other hand, developers using Method B obtain sparse quality scores (ranging between 0 and 100%). Thus, according to the simulation parameters, both means are identical (see the overlapping dashed red and blue lines in $M = 0.4$), even though the spread of the scores in Method B double those of Method A. Even though the means of Method A and B are identical, can we assume that both methods would perform similarly in a software project? Should a manager just look at means when deciding which technology to adopt in his company?

With the aim of portraying the insights that may be obtained in a prototypical SE experiment, we sample 15 data-points from each distribution (each data-point representing a different imaginary developer). This way, we obtain a *simulated AB between-subjects experiment* [3] with a sample size of 30 (a common sample size in SE experiments according to Dyba et al. [1]). Then, we analyze the experiment with the statistical test usually performed in such circumstances in SE [3,4]: an independent *t*-test. The independent *t*-test relies on the normality and the homogeneity of variances assumptions [2]. We assess the normality assumption by means of the Shapiro-Wilk test. Then we check the homogeneity of variances assumption by means of the Brown-Forsythe test [18]. With the aim of easing the interpretation of results we calculate the Hedge's g effect size and the lnCVR effect size [13].

Finally, we analyze the results of a *real-life industrial experiment* evaluating the performance of TDD on quality. We follow an identical procedure to that followed for analyzing the simulated experiment, but this time, we analyze the data with a dependent *t*-test instead (as the experiment uses an AB within-subjects design instead of an AB between-subjects design—see below). The dependent *t*-test relies on the normality assumption [2]. As in the case of the independent *t*-test, we assess the normality assumption by means of the Shapiro-Wilk test. Instead of stopping there and interpreting results as usual, *we go a step further* and assess the differences between the variances by means of the Brown-Forsythe test. Finally, we complement the statistical analyses with their respective effect sizes. Did this last step reveal any extra insight on the performance of TDD?

4   Simulated Experiment

Figure 2 shows the violin-plot and box-plot corresponding to a simulated AB between-subjects experiment comparing the performance of Method A and B. The data of each group have been simply obtained by sampling 15 different points from each of the two Beta distributions previously presented in Fig. 1 (Sect. 3). Table 1 shows the descriptive statistics of quality in each group.

As it can be seen in Fig. 2, and as expected, most subjects applying Method A obtained quality scores clumped around 0.4, while subjects applying Method B obtained more sparse quality scores. By looking at Table 1, it can also be seen that the ratio between the means of both groups is almost 1:1 ($M = 0.413$ divided by $M = 0.398$). On the contrary, the ratio between the standard deviations of both groups seems much larger (i.e., a ratio of 1:1.5 where Method B's standard deviation is larger than that of Method A).

Table 1. Descriptive statistics.

Treatment	N	Mean	SD	Median
A	15	0.413	0.115	0.424
B	15	0.398	0.173	0.359

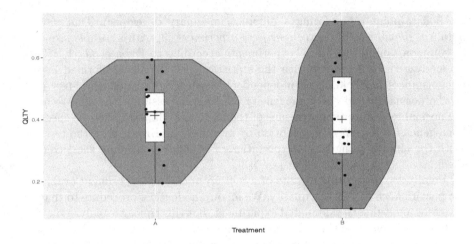

Fig. 2. Method A vs. Method B: violin-plot and box-plot.

We run an independent t-test to analyze the data. The independent t-test requires the data to meet the normality assumption and the homogeneity of variances assumption. We used the Shapiro-Wilk test to check the normality assumption. According to the Shapiro-Wilk test, both distributions can be assumed to be normally distributed (p-value $= 0.92$ and p-value $= 0.92$, for Method A and B, respectively). We used the Brown-Forsythe's test to check the homogeneity of variance assumption. According to the Brown-Forsythe's test's results, the homogeneity of variance assumption is met, and then, both distributions can be assumed to be similarly sparse (p-value $= 0.147$). Thus, despite having introduced different variances in the population by means of simulation, *the Brown-Forsythe's test was unable to detect the difference between variances due to the small sample size* of the experiment. Thus, as the Brown-Forsythe's test says that the homogeneity assumption is met, the Shapiro-Wilk test says that the normality assumption is met, and if this was a real experiment we would have no idea about the shape of the distributions in the population, we proceed as usual and interpret the results of our experiment according to the results of an independent t-test. Table 2 shows the results of the independent t-test.

Table 2. Independent t-test for quality: Method A vs Method B.

Coeff.	Estimate	t-statistic	p-value
Diff	−0.015	−0.276	0.784

As it can be seen in Table 2, the difference in performance between Method A and B is small ($M = -0.015$) and non-statistically significant (p-value $= 0.784$). In addition, *Hedge's g* is equal to $M = -0.0982$ (i.e. a small effect size according to rules of thumb [7]). Thus, according to the results of the t-test—and the Hedge's g magnitude—*the difference between the means of both methods in the population* (i.e., the dashed red and blue lines in Fig. 1) *is almost negligible*—as it was expected according to the parameters of the simulation. In SE parlance, *Method A and Method B seem to perform similarly.*

Finally, the $lnCVR$ is equal to $M = 0.445$. Back-transforming the lnCVR to natural scale (i.e., $exp(lnCVR) = 1.504$), Method B's scores seem to be around 50% (i.e., 1.504-1) more variable than those of Method A -as it was expected according to the parameters of the simulation. Thus, *the scores of each method in the population seem differently spread according to the lnCVR.* However, and despite the large difference between the variances of both groups, *the Brown-Forsythe's test was unable to detect the real difference between both methods' variances* (see above) due to the small sample size of the experiment.

5   Real Experiment

We run an experiment at a telecommunications company in 2014 with the aim of assessing the performance of TDD on external quality. The independent variable within the experiment is **development approach**, with TDD and ITL—the reverse-order methodology of TDD following Erdogmus et al. [19]—as treatments. We measured external quality as the percentage of test cases that successfully passed from a battery of test cases that we built to test participants' solutions. Specifically, QLTY was measured as:

$$QLTY = \frac{\#Test\ Cases(Pass)}{\#Test\ Cases(All)} * 100$$

5.1   Experimental Settings

Table 3 summarizes the settings of the experiment.

Table 3. Experimental settings.

Aspect	Values
Factors	Development Approach
Treatments	TDD vs ITL
Response variables	QLTY
Design	AB Within-subjects
Training	TDD seminar
Training duration	3 days/6 h
Experiment Duration	2.25 h
Environment	C++, Eclipse, Boost Testing
Number of subjects	20

5.2 Data Analysis

Figure 3 shows the violin-plot and box-plot of the data gathered. Table 4 provides the corresponding descriptive statistics.

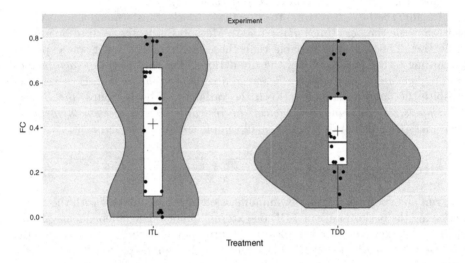

Fig. 3. ITL vs. TDD: violin-plot and box-plot.

As it can be seen in Fig. 3, ITL's quality scores look clumped either at the top or at the bottom of the distribution. In addition, TDD's quality scores seem grouped around the mean of the distribution (i.e., around 40%).

Table 4. Descriptive statistics.

Treatment	N	Mean	SD	Median
ITL	20	0.416	0.317	0.508
TDD	20	0.383	0.225	0.333

As it can be seen in Table 4, the ratio of the means is around 1:1 (i.e., ITL and TDD means are similar). However, the ratio of standard deviations is close to 1:1.4. In particular, TDD's quality scores seem less spread than those of ITL.

As usual in SE, we conduct a dependent t-test to analyze the data. The dependent t-test requires the difference of the quality scores between both groups to be normally distributed [2]. We check the normality assumption by means of the Shapiro-Wilk test. According to the Shapiro-Wilk test the difference between the quality scores of both groups is normally distributed (p-value $= 0.133$). In view of this, we can interpret the results of the dependent t-test safely. Table 5 shows the results of the dependent t-test.

Table 5. Dependent t-test for QLTY: ITL vs. TDD.

Coeff.	Estimate	t-statistic	p-value
Diff	−0.033	−0.387	0.703

As it can be seen in Table 5, the difference in performance between ITL and TDD is small ($M = -0.033$) and non-statistically significant (p-value = 0.703). In addition, the *Hedge's g* is equal to $M = -0.119$ (i.e., a small effect size according to rules of thumb [7]). In view of these results, *TDD does not offer any advantage over ITL on quality.*

However, in this occasion we go a step further than usual when analyzing SE experiments: instead of just interpreting the results of the dependent t-test and finalizing the data analysis, we go ahead and study the differences between the variances of ITL and TDD by means of the Brown-Forsythe's test. According to the Brown-Forsythe's test, the difference between the variances is statistically significant (p-value = 0.04). In addition, the *lnCVR* is equal to $M = -0.260$. Back-transforming the lnCVR to natural scale (i.e., $exp(lnCVR) = 0.77$), TDD scores are 33% ($1-0.77$) less variable than those of ITL. Thus, *subjects with TDD seem to achieve more consistent quality scores than with ITL.* In view of this, *TDD does offer advantages over ITL* (see below).

6   Discussion

As we have seen in the simulated experiment, meeting the homogeneity of variances assumption according to a statistical test (e.g., Levene, Brown-Forsythe, etc.) *does not* imply that technologies have identical variances: the presence of small sample sizes—as it is common in SE experiments [1]—makes statistical tests under-powered to detect real differences [5]. Besides, as we have seen in the industrial experiment that we analyzed, not needing to check the homogeneity of variances assumption (as in the dependent t-test [2]) *does not* imply that variances should be overlooked when judging the performance of new technologies: technologies with identical means may turn to be more—or less—beneficial depending upon their variances.

In the particular case of the industrial experiment that we analyzed, TDD seemed to provide less sparse quality scores than ITL—despite their similar means. If we had relied just on traditional statistical tests' results—as it is commonly done in SE—not much could have been said: ITL seemed to perform similarly to TDD. However we went a step further: instead of solely relying on the results of the dependent t-test to judge the performance of TDD, we also analyzed the data to uncover differences across variances by means of the Brown-Forsythe's test. According to its results, TDD provided significantly less sparse quality scores than ITL. In SE terms, *the quality scores achieved with TDD seemed less dependent upon developers' characteristics than those achieved with ITL* (as TDD quality scores resemble much more to each other than those of ITL regardless of the developers' characteristics). This has also some implications at the management level: if an hypothetical manager selects ITL for her group of developers, *the quality scores of her developers can be hardly predicted* (as they may be either low or high quality scores). In turn, in such group of developers, some developers may achieve large quality scores (perhaps those assigned to develop some part of a software product) and some others may achieve small quality scores (perhaps those assigned to other part of a software product). Depending upon the assignment of developers to functionality, *this may be detrimental to the construction of a new software product* (e.g., when the developers achieving the worse quality scores are assigned unknowingly to develop the core functionality of the software product). On the contrary, if the manager had selected TDD for her group of developers, the quality scores of all developers may have resembled more to each other and thus, the quality of the whole software product may have been more similar across its functionalities.

Notice that even though we were able to identify real differences across technologies variances in the industrial experiment that we conducted, this may not be the case in most SE experiments due to their typical small sample sizes [1]. We could see this in the simulated experiment, where despite different variances were *designed* within the population, it was not possible noticing the difference between them in the experiment. Thus, we suggest, as well as effect sizes such as Cohen's d are commonly provided for quantifying differences across treatment means, variance effect sizes such as lnCVR should also be provided to eventually ease the identification of real differences across treatment variances [13].

The main message of this article is that variance can be a differentiating element when assessing the performance of new technologies. Technologies with large variances may imply unpredictable performances and "developer-dependent" characteristics (e.g., skills, background etc.) impacting results. On the contrary, technologies with small variances may imply predictable performances and "robustness" to developers' characteristics. In view of this, we suggest to analyze variance in SE experiments to uncover perhaps "hidden" strengths—or weaknesses—of the technologies under assessment.

Finally, we want to highlight than whenever an experiment is being analyzed by means of a traditional statistical test such as the *t*-test, what is being compared is not the performance of the two technologies in general, but instead, the difference *between the means* of the two technologies. Put differently, sample-to-population inferences are being made on *statistical points* (e.g., differences between means) and not on the distribution of the data. In view of this, not just differences between means may be of interest to judge technology's performance: differences between variances, medians or even quantiles may be also of interest. Even though this article was just a call to analyze variance in SE experiments, by using more advanced statistical methods such as Bootstrap [5], it is also possible to assess differences between variances, medians, quantiles or even customized statistical points. Are we going to just rely on means to judge the performance of new technologies? After all, now we may be at the verge of assessing the performance of new technologies under perspectives never thought before.

7   Threats to Validity

Just one experiment, how generalizable are our results? We acknowledge the limitations of our study with regard to the use of a single experiment. However, we have complemented the results of the real-life experiment with those of a simulation. In particular, we used this simulation to illustrate that similar circumstances to that of the real experiment may materialize unknowingly, and that just relying on traditional statistical tests' results to judge technology performance may be misleading. Both the sample size of the simulation and the sample size of the industrial experiment are representative of SE experiments according to Dyba et al. [1]. Under this point of view, we expect our results to be representative for SE experiments.

Parametric tests and effect sizes, are there any threats to their application? Along this study we just relied upon *parametric* tests and effect sizes to analyze the data. Even though they may be unsuitable to analyze non-normal data—as that common in SE experiments [20]—we relied on them as they allow to provide inferences in terms of differences between *statistical parameters* (e.g., means, variances, etc.) and *not in terms of ranks* (as non-parametric tests such as the Wilcoxon or U-Mann Whitney do) [2], they are usually recommended to analyze SE experiments [3,4], they have been the most used to analyze SE experiments [1], and they are robust to departures from normality—even in smaller data-sets than those typical in SE experiments [21,22].

Just one statistical test per statistical assumption, how limited are the findings? Along this study we just used the Shapiro-Wilk test to check the normality assumption and to the Brown-Forsythe test to check the homogeneity of variances assumption. Even though we could have also used other tests such as the Kolmogorov-Smirnov test to check the normality assumption [2], we used the Shapiro-Wilk test just for illustrative purposes. Besides, we used the Brown-Forsythe test as it is more suitable than the Levene test when data departs from normality [12] (and thus, may be more suitable to analyze SE experiments). As an aside, in the simulated experiment and the real-life experiment that we analyzed both tests for normality and for homogeneity of variances provided similar results. Thus, results seem consistent regardless of the statistical test used.

8   Conclusion

Commonly applied statistical tests to analyze SE experiments (e.g., *t*-test, ANOVA etc. [3,4]) rely on the homogeneity of variances assumption to provide sample-to-population inferences [2]. As a consequence, different variances across groups in SE are not seen as an opportunity to provide insights on technology's performance but instead, as a hindrance towards the analysis of the data [20,23]. Perhaps inadvertently, and as a consequence of just relying on traditional tests results, SE technologies are only assessed with regard to their mean performance.

Along our study we showed that meeting traditional statistical assumptions (e.g., homogeneity of variances) does not imply that the underlying data distributions are equally sparse. Instead, this may be a sign that a larger sample size is required to find statistical significant differences across technologies' performances. In addition, not needing to meet the homogeneity of variances assumption does not imply that variance should be overlooked when judging technology performance.

Instead of considering variance as a hindrance, we suggest, variance should be considered in SE experiments as a valuable source of knowledge—as it is already being done in other disciplines such as medicine or biology [13–15]. In particular, technologies with similar means may not be equally desirable if variances are largely dissimilar, specially if it is aimed at lowering the risk of adopting them in real practice. Under this point of view, technologies that make subjects resemble to each other may be more desirable than those technologies that do not (as not much deviation from the 'average' performance is expected with their use). Are you going to continue judging the relevance of technologies just in terms of means? Or are you going to move beyond them? After all, now you are a few extra statistical tests and effect sizes away from obtaining new insights on technology's performance.

Acknowledgments. This research was developed with the support of the Spanish Ministry of Science and Innovation project TIN2014-60490-P.

References

1. Dybå, T., Kampenes, V.B., Sjøberg, D.I.: A systematic review of statistical power in software engineering experiments. Inf. Softw. Technol. **48**(8), 745–755 (2006)
2. Field, A.: Discovering Statistics Using IBM SPSS Statistics. Sage, London (2013)
3. Wohlin, C., Runeson, P., Höst, M., Ohlsson, M.C., Regnell, B., Wesslén, A.: Experimentation in Software Engineering. Springer Science & Business Media, New York (2012)
4. Juristo, N., Moreno, A.M.: Basics of Software Engineering Experimentation. Springer Science & Business Media, New York (2001)
5. Quinn, G.P., Keough, M.J.: Experimental Design and Data Analysis for Biologists. Cambridge University Press, Cambridge (2002)
6. Cumming, G.: Understanding the New Statistics: Effect Sizes, Confidence Intervals, and Meta-analysis. Routledge, New York (2013)
7. Borenstein, M., Hedges, L.V., Higgins, J.P., Rothstein, H.R.: Introduction to Meta-Analysis. Wiley, New York (2011)
8. Cohen, J.: The earth is round (p $<.05$). American Psychologist (1994) 997–1003
9. Kruschke, J.K., Liddell, T.M.: The bayesian new statistics: hypothesis testing, estimation, meta-analysis, and power analysis from a bayesian perspective. Psychon. Bull. Rev. **25**(1), 178–206 (2018)
10. Fritz, C.O., Morris, P.E., Richler, J.J.: Effect size estimates: current use, calculations, and interpretation. J. Exp. Psychol. Gen. **141**(1), 2 (2012)
11. Bates, D., Mächler, M., Bolker, B., Walker, S.: Fitting linear mixed-effects models using lme4. arXiv preprint arXiv:1406.5823 (2014)
12. Sheskin, D.J.: Handbook of Parametric and Nonparametric Statistical Procedures. CRC Press, Boca Raton (2003)
13. Nakagawa, S., et al.: Meta-analysis of variation: ecological and evolutionary applications and beyond. Methods Ecol. Evol. **6**(2), 143–152 (2015)

14. Senior, A.M., Gosby, A.K., Lu, J., Simpson, S.J., Raubenheimer, D.: Meta-analysis of variance: an illustration comparing the effects of two dietary interventions on variability in weight. Evol. Med. Public Health **2016**(1), 244–255 (2016)
15. Stevens, S.L., et al.: Blood pressure variability and cardiovascular disease: systematic review and meta-analysis. bmj 354 (2016) i4098
16. Senior, A., Nakagawa, S., Raubenheimer, D., Simpson, S., Noble, D.: Dietary restriction increases variability in longevity. Biol. Lett. **13**(3), 20170057 (2017)
17. Gelman, A., Carlin, J.B., Stern, H.S., Rubin, D.B.: Bayesian Data Analysis. vol. 2. Taylor & Francis, Boca Raton (2014)
18. Brown, M.B., Forsythe, A.B.: Robust tests for the equality of variances. J. Am. Stat. Assoc. **69**(346), 364–367 (1974)
19. Erdogmus, H., Morisio, M., Torchiano, M.: On the effectiveness of the test-first approach to programming. IEEE Trans. Softw. Eng. **31**(3), 226–237 (2005)
20. Kitchenham, B., Madeyski, L., Budgen, D., Keung, J., Brereton, P., Charters, S., Gibbs, S., Pohthong, A.: Robust statistical methods for empirical software engineering. Empir. Softw. Eng. **22**(2), 579–630 (2017)
21. Vickers, A.J.: Parametric versus non-parametric statistics in the analysis of randomized trials with non-normally distributed data. BMC Med. Res. Methodol. **5**(1), 35 (2005)
22. Norman, G.: Likert scales, levels of measurement and the laws of statistics. Adv. Health Sci. Educ. **15**(5), 625–632 (2010)
23. Dieste, O., Fernández, E., Garcia Martinez, R., Juristo, N.: Comparative analysis of meta-analysis methods: when to use which? In: 15th Annual Conference on Evaluation & Assessment in Software Engineering (EASE 2011), IET, pp. 36–45 (2011)

An Activity and Metric Model for Online Controlled Experiments

David Issa Mattos[1]([✉])(iD), Pavel Dmitriev[2], Aleksander Fabijan[3],
Jan Bosch[1](iD), and Helena Holmström Olsson[3](iD)

[1] Department of Computer Science and Engineering, Chalmers University of
Technology, Hörselgången 11, 412 96 Gothenburg, Sweden
{davidis, jan.bosch}@chalmers.se
[2] Outreach, 1441 North 34th Street, Seattle, WA 98103, USA
pavel.dmitriev@outreach.com
[3] Department of Computer Science and Media Technology, Malmö University,
Nordenskiöldsgatan, 211 19 Malmö, Sweden
{aleksander.fabijan, helena.holmstrom.olsson}@mau.se

Abstract. Accurate prioritization of efforts in product and services development is critical to the success of every company. Online controlled experiments, also known as A/B tests, enable software companies to establish causal relationships between changes in their systems and the movements in the metrics. By experimenting, product development can be directed towards identifying and delivering value. Previous research stresses the need for data-driven development and experimentation. However, the level of granularity in which existing models explain the experimentation process is neither sufficient, in terms of details, nor scalable, in terms of how to increase number and run different types of experiments, in an online setting. Based on a case study of multiple products running online controlled experiments at Microsoft, we provide an experimentation framework composed of two detailed experimentation models focused on two main aspects; the experimentation activities and the experimentation metrics. This work intends to provide guidelines to companies and practitioners on how to set and organize experimentation activities for running trustworthy online controlled experiments.

Keywords: Data-driven development · A/B tests
Online controlled experiments

1 Introduction

Prioritizing the development of software features and services that deliver value to customers is critical for the success of every company. One way to accurately discover what customers value is to evaluate the assumptions of the company by means of experiments. These experiments, commonly called A/B tests, provide a framework for companies to establish causal relationships between modifications on their systems and changes in metrics. Running experiments allows companies to continuously update their assumptions on their user behavior and preferences, along with many other benefits [1].

© Springer Nature Switzerland AG 2018
M. Kuhrmann et al. (Eds.): PROFES 2018, LNCS 11271, pp. 182–198, 2018.
https://doi.org/10.1007/978-3-030-03673-7_14

Several publications and reports from companies such as Microsoft, Facebook, Google, and LinkedIn, among many others [2–5], report the competitive advantage that online controlled experiments, such as A/B testing, deliver [1]. Data-driven organizations make use of relevant collected data to drive decisions and directions for the organization, and experiments are one of the key techniques used by these organizations. However, the support and evolution of experimentation practices is far from simple, and several pitfalls can invalidate experiments and lead to incorrect conclusions [6].

Different models proposed in the literature [7–9] provide a general structure for data-driven development and experiment processes. Although these models can be used as a starting point for companies to move to an iterative experiment-driven development process, previous research [6, 10–15] also describes pitfalls, techniques to provide scaling of the experimentation process and techniques to ensure trustworthiness in the experimentation process that are not captured in or represented by the higher level of abstraction provided in these models. Because these models do not capture this level of detail, instantiating these models directly from a higher level of abstraction can lead to the limitations in the scalability and trustworthiness of the experimentation's activities already identified by previous research. Additionally, it can lead to multiple experimentation initiatives inside an organization and lack of rigor in the process, resulting in non-comparable tests and untrustworthy results.

To address this gap, this research provides a framework that captures specific experimentation details and necessary steps for running trustworthy online controlled experiments. The framework divides the experimentation process into two main interconnected models: the set of activities that organizations should support to run trustworthy experiments, and the role of metrics and how they align experiments with long-term business goals. The proposed framework is based on an inductive case study in collaboration with the Analysis and Experimentation team at Microsoft.

The contribution of this paper is twofold. First, we present the new findings from the case study. These findings represent important characteristics of the experimentation process that were not captured in previous models and reinforces the need of a new experimentation process model. Second, we present a framework composed of two models for an experimentation process that covers the two main aspects: (1) the experimentation activities and (2) the experimentation metrics. The framework provides a detailed process which aims to help companies scale their experimentation organization with a trustworthy experimentation process.

The rest of the paper is organized as follows. Section 2 provides a background in controlled experiments and related work. Section 3 describes the research process of this case study. Section 4 presents new findings from the case study that reinforce the need for a new experimentation process model. Section 5 presents the two main aspects of the developed experimentation process framework. Section 6 concludes this paper.

2   Background and Related Work

Although there are many different techniques for learning about customer preferences and using them to evaluate ideas (e.g. interviews, focus groups, observational studies, prototypes and mock-ups) [16], online controlled experimentation is gaining significant momentum in software companies [17]. Controlled experiments are a group of tech- niques where users are randomly assigned to two or more variants of a product: the control (e.g. the current system) and the treatments (the system with change X). The change could be the addition of a new feature or the modification of existing func- tionality. The system is instrumented and key metrics of the user's behavior are computed. After a pre-determined period of time, the metrics are analyzed. If the only consistent difference between the experiment variants is the change X and external factors are spread out evenly between the two variants, the differences in the metrics are due to the change X. Based on this statistical analysis, companies can make data-driven decisions. Kohavi et al. [15] provide a detailed guide on running controlled experi- ments on the web.

Gupta et al. [18] describe the software architecture of the Microsoft ExP Platform, the design decisions made while designing the platform, and its main components. This platform and its components capture essential steps and activities that enable trust- worthy experiments on a large scale. Kevic et al. [19] analyzed the results of over 20,000 experiments at Bing, providing an empirical characterization of the experi- mentation process in a product-running experiment at scale. This characterization shows that the average experimentation process takes forty-two days and includes multiple iterations to minimize the likelihood of hurting users or the business due to issues with the change that is being tested.

However, not all companies and products have the capacity to run experiments at the same scale as Microsoft Bing. Experimentation in software companies typically evolves from a few independent experiments towards a mature stage where several teams run many trustworthy experiments at the same time. Fabijan et al. [20] provide guidance on how to evolve into a data-driven company, exploring the technical, organizational and business evolution. The evolution of experiments in products is divided into four levels of maturity (crawl, walk, run, fly) across three dimensions (the technical, organizational and business). Additionally, the study presents steps and experimentation activities which are commonly used during the evolution of experi- mentation. One of the key challenges in controlled experiments is how to decide which metrics should be used in the Overall Evaluation Criteria (OEC). The OEC is the experiment objective, which should ideally capture the long-term interests of the company. Determining a good OEC is hard as it captures abstract concepts that are difficult to validate and compare with other metrics [21]. If the OEC metric captures long-term goals or represent value, true movements of the metric represent the aggregated value that a variant is bringing to the system.

Deng and Shi [22] provide an extensive discussion on metrics for online experi- ments, classifying the types of metrics, the qualities and characteristics of good metrics, and how to evaluate and select metrics. Dmitriev and Wu [21] discuss a metric eval- uation framework at Bing using an offline historical experiment dataset called exper- iment corpus. The experiment corpus helps to evaluate new metric sensitivity and alignment with user value. This framework helps to select suitable OEC metrics for experiments.

Previous research has provided different models and frameworks that capture and provide guidance on how to develop experiment-driven software. The QCD model (Quantitative/qualitative Customer-driven Development) [9] is an inductive model based on a generalization of approaches used by companies to guide their collection of customer feedback throughout the development process. Experimentation explores the notion of continuous validation of customer value, in contrast to the traditional up-front specification of requirements. The QCD explores this notion by treating requirements as hypotheses that need customer validation at the beginning of the development process. New hypotheses are based on business strategies, customer feedback, innovation strategies and previous hypothesis cycles. Qualitative feedback (surveys, interviews, focus groups and mock-ups), together with quantitative data (feature usage, customer behavior and support data), allows the evaluation of hypotheses. Hypotheses that are not confirmed through any of the selected customer feedback techniques are abandoned while validated hypotheses can be refined into a more detailed hypothesis or can be implemented and deployed. This model provides a general framework for evaluating hypotheses with customer feedback. This model can incorporate online experiments at a higher level of abstraction. However, it does not provide detailed clear steps and activities for instantiating an online experiment in software systems.

Olsson and Bosch [8] present the HYPEX (Hypothesis Experiment Data-Driven Development) model as an alternative development process for companies to compress the customer feedback loop. This model advocates for an iterative and incremental development approach, rather than spending engineering effort on larger quantities of functionalities without customer validation. The HYPEX model is composed of six steps: (1) the generation of a feature backlog from customer needs or business goals. (2) Feature selection and specification (what is the intended behavior, what is the gap it addresses, and multiple implementation alternatives). (3) The implementation and instrumentation of a minimum viable feature (MVF). (4) Analyzing whether the measured behavior of the MVF addresses the gap or not. (5) Generation of hypotheses that explain the feature behavior and why the gap was/wasn't addressed. If the gap was addressed new features are selected as in the second step. (6) If the gap was not addressed, alternative implementations can be made (step 3) or a decision to abandon the feature can be made. The HYPEX model is a general model for data-driven development and running product experiments, but it does not provide specific steps for running online controlled experiments.

Fagerholm et al. [7] present the RIGHT (Rapid Iterative value creation Gained through High-frequency Testing) model for continuous experimentation. The goal of this model is to provide a systematic framework for developing experiment-based software. This is achieved by establishing a series of building blocks that act as preconditions for running experiments. These blocks are divided into two main parts: the RIGHT process model and the RIGHT infrastructure architecture model. The RIGHT process model follows the Lean Startup methodology cycle [23]: build, measure, learn. The goal of this cycle is to achieve the vision of the company (which is connected to the business model). This is operationalized through hypotheses generated due to uncertainties in how to execute the vision through the business model and strategy. The set of generated hypotheses is prioritized with the learning of previous iterations. The selected hypothesis is implemented through an instrumented minimum viable feature or product (MVF). The collected data from the MVF is analyzed and used to update the assumptions of the business strategy and abandon the tested hypothesis or the data is used to further iterate with the hypothesis by changing or optimizing it. The RIGHT infrastructure architecture model sketches the infrastructure needed to run experiments and specifies the roles and tasks, the technical infrastructure, and the information artefacts consumed and generated during the experimentation process. The RIGHT model was created in a startup environment by two companies starting to run their first online experiments, and it takes the approach of abstracting the underlying details of a continuous experimentation system, in order to be generalizable to a range of different experiments that can be conducted in a startup environment.

The discussed models can be used as a starting point for companies to systematically move to an iterative experiment-driven development process, providing a higher level of abstraction of the experimentation process and describing general activities. However, previous research [6, 10–15] describes pitfalls, techniques to provide scaling of the experimentation process and techniques to ensure trustworthiness in the experimentation process that are not captured and represented by the higher level of abstraction provided in the discussed models. Instantiating these models directly from a higher level of abstraction can lead to the limitations in the scalability and trustworthiness of the experimentation's activities already identified by previous research.

3   Research Method

To help companies develop and support their experimentation process and infrastructure models we conducted an inductive case study [24] in collaboration with the Analysis and Experimentation team at Microsoft.

Data Collection: The collected empirical data consists of interview notes, whiteboard drawings, quotes and shared supporting data from nine semi-structured interviews with an average and median length of thirty-two minutes each. At the time of the data collection, the second author was working with the Analysis and Experimentation team and was the main contact person for the other researchers during the data collection and analysis phases. All the interviews were conducted in the premises of the company by the first author, who was accompanied by the second author when possible. The interviewees were selected by the second author and represent a diverse selection of software engineers and data scientists working both within the experimentation platform and as users of the platform in different product groups.

The interviews were based on a questionnaire containing eight open-ended questions, starting with a short introduction and explanation of the research. The participants were asked to describe their experimentation process and how it is conducted in each product they work with. Next, the participants were asked to compare their own experimentation process and infrastructure with the existing models in the literature and point out similarities and differences. Next, they were asked about what experimentation activities they performed, the time spent on these activities, their relative impact on the experiment reliability, and the other main activities performed by other people in an experiment lifecycle (from hypothesis generation to decision). We organized the interviews by products and by an approximation of the number of experiments the interviewees ran each year. This allowed us to differentiate experiences from products that run experiments on a large scale from products that start and run experiments on a small scale.

Data Analysis: Thematic coding was used to analyze the grouped data [25]. Recurring codes, drawings of the experimentation process and references to different parts of the platform architecture and activities helped to formalize the new findings and derive the proposed experimentation framework. For example: descriptions of different tests and analysis to ensure the experiment was properly configured were grouped in the "Pre-quality checks" while the different techniques used to evolve a metric were divided between "Online evaluation" and "Offline validation". We grouped the different experimentation activities in the development, execution and analysis categories. Based on the thematic coding and the reported activities, we compared them with the existing experimentation models to identify the differences from existing models and propose the activity and metric model. Our analysis is based only on data reported by more than one interviewee, and when available in the development of the models we triangulate the data with other research reports by the Analysis and Experimentation team at Microsoft, available at the weblink: https://exp-platform.com/.

Validity Considerations: To improve the construct validity of the study, and prior to the data collection stage, the semi-structured interview guide was applied to a group of two developers from a Brazilian company with experience in A/B testing, known to the first author, and two Ph.D. students in software engineering. This helped to identify potential problems, such as ambiguity in the questions and the explanations. Regarding the external validity process, although our work was conducted with only one case company, our empirical data was collected from experiences of several different products which are running trustworthy experiments at scale as well as only a few experiments per year. This helped to identify and compare trustworthy experimentation processes at different stages of maturity. Therefore, we believe that our results can be generalized for companies that want to scale their experimentation organization with a trustworthy experimentation process.

4   Findings

In this section, we describe new findings obtained from the empirical data that are not presented in previous research. Together with the description of the experimentation process collected during the interviews, these findings reinforced our motivation to develop the experimentation process framework presented in the next section.

1 - Customer Feedback is an Important Source of Experimentation Ideas
The first finding from the empirical data is that experimentation ideas, which are later synthesized into experimentation hypotheses, are often inspired by customer feedback, instead of high-level business goals. In this research, we differentiate experiment ideas from experiment hypotheses. Experiment ideas are the first source of potential changes that can be made to systems, and they represent the potential value of a modification. However, often experiment ideas do not represent real value and therefore need to be tested in experiments [26]. Experiment hypotheses synthesize ideas into concrete experimentation scenarios, addressing what the change is, and how it can be imple- mented and evaluated. Ideas are synthesized into an experiment hypothesis by experiment owners. An experiment hypothesis, after deployment, can measure the real

value of the synthesized idea. Developers and product owners often collect experiment ideas using different qualitative feedback collection techniques. Experiment ideas are refined, developed, prioritized and synthesized based on the experiment owners (developers, product owners and data scientists) being convinced of the positive impact for the user and for the key metrics. Another source of customer feedback ideas are differentiator features and user feedback in competitors' open channels. Although experiment ideas can come from business strategies, often they influence the prioritization process of experiments by influencing the metrics.

"It is very rare that an experiment comes from the business. Most experiments come from a group of engaged developers willing to code new ideas and run the experiments [...] The ideas for the new features and their experiments are almost always inspired by customers and competition" – Principal Data Scientist

Existing models such as the HYPEX and the RIGHT model propose that the business goals impose outcomes for experiments, but do not explicitly represent how hypotheses are identified and prioritized. The QCD model proposes business strategies, innovation initiatives, customer feedback and previous experiments as the source of new ideas. However, it does not consider differences between experiment ideas and experiment hypotheses and how they can be further developed in a concrete experiment hypothesis. This insight reinforces the direct and indirect customer feedback as the drivers of new experiment ideas. However, experiment ideas still need to be prioritized and synthesized into experiment hypothesis by experiment owners and engineers.

2 - Metrics Guide Experiments Towards Long-Term Goals and Help Prioritize Hypotheses

The second finding refers to the role of metrics in learning and in hypothesis prioritization. Experiments are launched with the goal of validating a change in the system or learning more about user behavior. Both the validation of a change and the outcomes of an experiment are closely related to the validity of the metric, whether it measures its concept correctly, and whether it reflects the business strategy of the company. If a metric is misaligned with the business strategy of the company, changes and knowledge gained from experiments will also be misaligned with the strategy. However, correctly chosen metrics incentivize teams to take actions which are aligned with the long-term goals of the company [21]. Good metrics will help them prioritize experiments that can have a positive impact on the long-term goals.

"If our decisions to ship are based on these metrics, these metrics have a big impact on the development and evolution of the product. They guide the teams to develop and focus their work to improve these metrics" – Principal Data Scientist

The existing experimentation models do not describe or emphasize how metrics impact hypothesis prioritization and long-term company goals. When metrics are considered only part of the instrumentation system, they do not reflect the bidirectional influence on the business strategy of the company.

3 - Metrics Evolve and Capture the Experiment Assumptions

As discussed in the second finding, metrics can guide the long term-goals of the company and help prioritize the hypotheses. Additionally, metrics also capture uncertainty and experiment assumptions. As metrics often represent abstract and subjective concepts [21] such as satisfaction and engagement, they contain assumptions about what constitutes these concepts. These assumptions should be tested and validated during the experimentation process and should be constantly iterated in order to maintain alignment with the business strategy. This constant update and validation of the assumptions based on the results of an experiment leads to a metric evolution process. Metrics can start as low level signals, and then evolve to capture more complex concepts that are more closely aligned with the business strategy. Additionally, the evolution of metrics also reflects the evolution of the business strategy and the product focus over time. As the company changes its strategies, metrics should be updated to align with these changes.

Existing models describe the presence of uncertainty and assumptions in the business strategy and in the role of the business analyst, as they are responsible for hypothesis prioritization. However, these models do not describe or discuss how the metrics evolution and the business strategy influence each other and impact the product.

5   The Experimentation Process Framework

In the previous section, we discussed the findings and compared them to previous research. Previous research did not capture all the identified characteristics from the findings nor present specific experimentation details, or the necessary steps to take when running trustworthy online controlled experiments. This led to the motivation and the need to develop a new framework that incorporates these findings. The framework is based on the collected empirical data, including descriptions and drawings of the process, comparison with other processes and the characteristics identified in the new findings and in the different components represented in the Microsoft ExP Platform described in [18]. During the data collection, the researchers asked the interviewees to describe their experimentation process and compare it with existing models. This discussion, together with findings from previous research, led to the development of this framework, which consists of the two main aspects of the experimentation process: (1) the experimentation activities, and (2) the experimentation metrics. These aspects are related to the business long-term strategies as represented in Fig. 1. This diagram

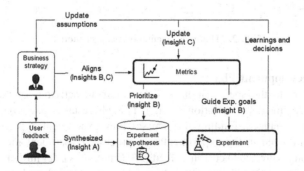

Fig. 1. The relationship between the two main aspects (in bold), their relation with the business strategy, and how the findings connect them.

represents how the two main aspects of experimentation used in this work relate to each other and to the business, and how they connect to the findings discussed in the previous section. Next, we detail these two aspects in two separate models, the experimentation activity model, and the metric model. These models were developed based on the collected empirical data and previous research.

5.1   The Experimentation Activity Model

The experimentation activity model describes the different activities which comprise a single experiment iteration, from the experiment ideas, to the experiment analysis necessary for the running of trustworthy online experiments. The arrows correspond to sequential connected activities. For example, when the experiment is launched pre-quality checks are run followed by ramp-up procedures before the experiment data is collected from a larger user base. Furthermore, our model divides the experimentation process into three sequential phases: *the experiment development phase, the experiment execution phase,* and *the experiment analysis phase.* We illustrate the experimentation activity model in Fig. 2 and describe the three phases in greater detail.

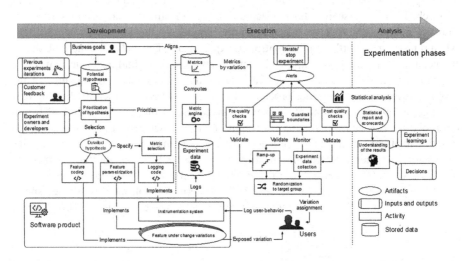

Fig. 2. The experimentation activity model

Experiment Development Phase

This phase refers to the specification and development activities of the experiment necessary to implement the variation change. This phase takes place before users are exposed to any variations. Finding A discusses how experiment hypotheses are generated and synthesized in the experimentation process. Experiment ideas are usually derived from four sources: (1) customer feedback (Finding A), (2) further iteration from previous experiments iterations [19], (3) need to understand and model the user behavior, and (4) less often through higher-level business goals (dashed line). The hypotheses are prioritized based on the experiment owners' prior analysis of how the hypotheses can impact the OEC. This analysis can be based on historical data from the feature, insights from other market segments (e.g. a feature that shows success in the US market might be prioritized for launch in another market or globally), or on experience gained from similar previous experiments or other products.

Following prioritization of the hypothesis a detailed hypothesis is elaborated. This includes specification of the experiment type (A/B, A/B/n, MVT etc.), how many variants are going to be present, cohorts or market segmentation, experiment duration and metrics to be used. Additionally, it covers the feature/change specification, including the area of functionality, actual and expected behavior, and implementation alternatives and considerations.

In addition, the detailed hypothesis specifies the target metrics that are expected to have impact and movements. The specification of the experiment metrics is closely related to the metrics used to prioritize the experiment itself. This includes lower-level signals that measure user-specific behaviors, guardrail metrics that indicate whether an experiment is within the allowed experiment conditions, and the leading metrics [1] that guide the experiment analysis. The metric selection is related to logging capabilities. The logging code represents the instrumentation of the system that interacts with the experimentation system. The logging code collects lower-level user behavior signals that can be used to compose complex metrics in the experimentation system. It is worth noting that the logging code should comply with the same standards (e.g. deployment, testing, code review, and integration pipeline) as any other product code.

Depending on the type of detailed specification of the hypothesis, the change in the system at the product level can happen in two ways, or a combination of the two. The first is through coding of the modification. This method is common when the experiment specification requires coding of a new feature or extensive modification of existing ones. The experiment set-up is a comparison of the current system with the change (treatment) and the system without the change (control). The second way in which the change can be done is by parametrizing an existing functionality and running experiments to modify these parameters. In this case the functionality already exists but appears to have suboptimal performance. The parameters of this functionality are configured during the experiment execution and are assigned to users. Although this might require a larger overhead in supporting and setting up a configuration manager, it reduces the effort and time spent on each experiment.

Experiment Execution Phase
After the experiment is properly designed, the metrics selected, the change coded and instrumented, the experiment moves to the experiment execution phase. Here, users are randomized and are assigned to the experiment variations of the feature under change. The user behavior is logged, and the initial metrics are computed per variation using the metric engine and initial statistical analysis are computed using the statistical analysis tool. The metric engine is responsible for collecting and transforming raw data into experiment metrics. These metrics are consumed by the statistical analysis tool in order to run quality checks, check for guardrail-metrics and generate scorecards. The metrics, as discussed in the metric model, align the experiment goals with the business strategy and serve as input in the prioritization of experiment hypotheses.

The assignment of the users to the different variations can happened in two general ways (other methods used for websites are described in [15]). The first is to use a feature toggling system. In this case, the change in the system is parametrized using a variable, and the users are assigned to feature variations that the parameter activates (treatment group) or deactivates (control group). The second method is through traffic routing, where multiple instances of the system are run in parallel and the assignment system redirects the user to one of the multiple instances. The randomization refers to how users are assigned to a specific variation of the experiment during the execution phase. The randomization usually targets a specific group of users at the beginning and then generalizes to a larger audience. This target is specified in the detailed hypothesis. Although randomization might look intuitive, there are several techniques available to ensure that the randomization is not biased towards any variation [15, 27]. Then the instrumentation system captures the user behavior and logs the experiment data for use in statistical analysis.

The first step in the execution phase is to have confidence that the experiment will yield trustworthy results.

"A lot of effort goes into making sure the experiment passes the (pre-) quality checks. This is an essential step that gives us confidence in the experiment, so that we will not go to the next steps only to discover we did something wrong at the beginning"
– Principal Data Scientist

Before running experiments and exposing users to different variations, pre-quality tests are run to check for common pitfalls. Examples of pre-quality tests are: A/A or null tests, sample ratio mismatching, randomization checks, and offline testing. The A/A test assigns the users to the same variant A (the system without the change) with the aim of testing the experimentation system and assessing variability in the collected data [15]. The sample ratio mismatch (SRM) [10] is considered a critical diagnosis tool for online experiments. The SRM checks the percentage allocation of the users. This allows the experiment owners to detect bias (that would invalidate the experiment results) towards any variation as well as check performance considerations. Randomization checks are tests which identify whether the randomization procedure is biased or has any patterns and checks the consistency of the randomization between sessions (to ensure that recurring users see the same variations). Offline testing uses historical data to assess the impact of the changes in the system and estimate confidence intervals [28].

After the pre-quality checks the activities that take place in the experiment execution phase are: the ramp-up, guardrail boundaries and experiment data collection. Ramp-up is a procedure where the treatment variations are initially launched to a small percentage of users. This is useful because critical errors can be detected early while exposing only a small number of users to the treatment variations. Large effect sizes in key metrics are mostly related to experiment errors [29], therefore fewer users' needs will be exposed to the change while identifying such errors. As the experiment runs without severe degradations, the percentage of users exposed to the treatment can be continuously increased until each variation has equal allocation, so that the experiment power is maximized [15]. A ramp-up procedure should be implemented together with an automated alerting capability with different significant levels and configurable actions. By checking guardrail metrics and experiment boundaries, such as key metrics that the experiment should not alter or deteriorate, the alerting system will alert experiment owners if something unusual is happening. In extreme cases, it will shut down an experiment with a significant negative impact if no action was taken. This allows organizations to invest in innovative and bold changes while reducing the risk of exposing users to bad ideas and errors [15].

After the main experiment execution, post-quality tests can be run to ensure that the experiment is valid and the data is reliable. Common post-quality checks are (1) checking for experiment invariant metrics, (2) learning effects, (3) A/A tests, (4) interaction effects with other overlapping experiments, and (5) novelty effects [20]. Experiment invariant metrics are metrics that are not expected to change within the scope of the experiment. If there is a statistically significant movement in those metrics during the experiment execution, either the assumptions about the impact of the experiment are wrong or the implementation of the experiment is wrong. In both cases, it is worth exploring the reasons for these unexpected results. Other quality checks that are beyond the scope of this paper can be seen in [2, 10, 20]. The statistical analysis tool supports the whole experiment execution, computing guardrail tests and quality checks. Following the post-quality checks, the statistical analysis tool generates reports and scorecards for the key metrics of the experiment. Qualitative data collected from feedback boxes and other consumer feedback channels (if available) can be used together with the quantitative analysis to help explain the result.

Experiment Analysis Phase

The analysis phase follows both the data collection and the conclusion of the experiment execution. The analysis phase consists of developing an understanding of the statistical output of the experimentation system in the context of assumptions about user behavior.

Understanding of the results is an activity that analyzes the results from the statistical analysis in order to generate evidence about customer preferences and behavior and thus facilitate the decision-making process. It is important to reinforce that as the complexity of the experiment increases and there is not a standard OEC, key metrics can move in opposite directions, behave differently in different markets and in different user segments. In such scenarios, it is important to understand why different markets or user segments behaved differently. Not only does this generate meaningful knowledge which can be used to update assumptions about user behavior, but it also facilitates the process of decision-making and helps the evolution of the metrics and their alignment with the business strategy. Based on the results of this activity, the company can make decisions (such as ship or not ship the change) and update their assumptions and the metrics.

5.2   The Experiment Metric Model

A key component of the experimentation process described above is the metrics. Metrics guide hypothesis prioritization, the instrumentation required in the system, and the understanding of the results, and reveal whether the experiment results can be trusted. The experiment metric model that we discuss in this section characterizes two aspects of metrics: metric lifecycle and metric type. These two aspects are related to the findings B and C. These findings reinforce the central role that metrics play in the experiment design and execution. The metric lifecycle is divided into four main phases: creation, evolution, maturity and phase-out. The metric type is based on the four metric types identified in previous research [10]: OEC metrics, data-quality metrics, guardrail metrics and local feature and diagnostic metrics. The metric model is represented in Fig. 3.

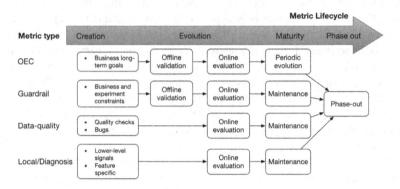

Fig. 3. The metric model

The arrow in the metric model refers to the different stages in a metric lifecycle. In the creation phase, a first prototype of a metric is created. In this step, the metric consists of either aggregated lower-level signals (such as usage time, clicks, etc.), or modifications of existing metrics (such as linear combination or proportions).

The evolution phase consists of refining the metric and aligning it with the metric goal. During this process additional metrics can be combined with the original one to better capture more complex concepts. The refinement process can also impact the sensitivity of the metric. Offline validation and online evaluation are two techniques used to assess and support the evolution of a metric. The offline validation process analyses the metric directionality and sensitivity. Directionality refers to the direction of positive impact. The sensitivity of a metric refers to how well a metric is capable of moving due to the treatment. Techniques for offline validation of metrics can be found in [21, 22]. Online evaluation refers to analyzing the metric during an experimental run. This includes computing the metric with live users. The evaluation can be done through the comparison of the new metric with other existing metrics and through degradation experiments. Degradation experiments refer to the degrading of the user experience to find the directionality and sensitivity of metrics in the absence of an experiment corpus or analogous metrics for comparison. Strange movements of metrics during the experiment execution and quality tests can indicate instrumentation problems.

The maturity phase represents a period where the metric has been evaluated or validated and does not go through extensive modifications. For some metrics, the maturity phase represents a phase where they are updated in pre-established periods with learnings from multiple experiments or updated to accommodate changes in the business strategy of the company or the product, or only when issues arise in a maintenance process.

The last phase is the phase-out. In this phase, older metrics can be replaced with newer metrics, and metrics specific to an experiment or feature are deactivated after the experiment or feature lifecycle is over. It is worth noting that each metric might reach the different stages during different time frames. Metrics designed to be used only in one experiment can go through the creation to the phase-out process in only one experiment cycle. Metrics specific to features go through many experiment cycles, until the feature is only maintained or it is abandoned. OEC metrics that cross several features and even products can last many experimental cycles and years.

The second aspect of the metric model that we describe refers to the type of metric. Overall Evaluation Criteria (OEC) metrics guide the experiment outcomes and are a measure of the experiment's success. They represent and capture assumptions about business strategies and long-term company goals. OEC metrics are used across experiments and their evolution depends on the inputs from multiple experiments and the alignment with business goals. The evolution of OEC metrics affects multiple experiments and therefore is only updated periodically. The update of such metrics goes through offline validation and online evaluation.

Data-quality metrics are used in quality checks and inconsistency checks, such as implementation bugs, synchronization errors, and telemetry loss. Some of these metrics are feature specific, such as checking for data quality in experiments specific for a feature, while others are used in multiple experiments during pre-quality checks, such as the Sample Ratio Mismatch and checks for randomization imbalance during A/A tests. These metrics are evaluated online and their evolution and update occur when feature-specific modifications require updates or when issues arise.

Guardrail metrics are metrics that are not used as an indicator of success but instead serve as boundaries for the experiment. Negative movements of guardrail metrics might be an indicator that experiment conditions were violated, generating alerts. These metrics, although they do not represent business directions as the OECs do, can represent business constraints on the OEC movement. These metrics evolve periodically in order to align with changing business restrictions. When updated, guardrail metrics go through offline validation and online evaluation.

Local feature and diagnosis metrics are metrics used in individual functionalities of products. They do not impact other experiments and serve as diagnostic indicators used to understand the movement of OECs and guardrail metrics. Diagnosis metrics represent lower-level signals and serve as debug metrics for understanding unexpected movements of OEC and guardrail metrics. Local feature and diagnosis metrics are usually constrained to the experiment or feature lifecycle. Due to their short lifecycle these metrics are only evaluated online. To support the creation, evolution, maturity and phase-out phases of the different types of metrics, the experimentation team should support a metric management platform. This type of system prioritizes important metrics, constrains metrics to specific features and keeps track of inactive phased-out metrics for comparison and offline validation between older and newer experiments.

6 Conclusions

Online controlled experiments have become the standard practice for evaluating ideas and prioritizing features in most large web-facing software-intensive companies [1, 3–5]. Although companies can rely on models to start their experimentation organization and data-driven practices they might struggle to establish a trustworthy experimentation process as they scale their experimentation organization. Previous research provides models and processes for starting an experimentation organization based on higher-level descriptions of the experimentation process. However, these models do not capture all details and techniques that allow companies to scale and to ensure trustworthiness in the experimentation process [6, 10–15]. Based on a case study research with multiple product teams responsible for running online controlled experiments at Microsoft, we provide an experimentation framework composed of two detailed experimentation models focused on two main aspects; the experimentation activities and the experimentation metrics. This model discusses granular aspects of the experimentation process that can help companies and practitioners to scale their experimentation activities into a trustworthy experimentation process.

In future research, we plan to validate this experimentation process in other companies, to compare how the different activities map onto their experimentation process and analyze other aspects of the experimentation process, such as how the organization roles change during the evolution of the experiment.

Acknowledgments. This work was partially supported by the Wallenberg Artificial Intelligence, Autonomous Systems and Software Program (WASP), funded by the Knut and Alice Wallenberg Foundation. The authors would like to thank Microsoft's Analysis and Experimentation team for the opportunity to conduct this study with them.

References

1. Fabijan, A., Dmitriev, P., Olsson, H.H., Bosch, J.: The benefits of controlled experimentation at scale. In: Proceedings of the 43rd Euromicro Conference on Software Engineering and Advanced Applications, SEAA 2017, pp. 18–26 (2017)
2. Kohavi, R., Deng, A., Frasca, B., Longbotham, R., Walker, T., Xu, Y.: Trustworthy online controlled experiments. In: Proceedings of the 18th ACM SIGKDD International Conference on Knowledge Discovery and Data Mining, KDD 2012, p. 786 (2012)
3. Bakshy, E., Eckles, D., Bernstein, M.S.: Designing and deploying online field experiments. In: Proceedings of the 23rd International Conference on World Wide Web, WWW 2014, pp. 283–292, September 2014
4. Gui, H., Xu, Y., Bhasin, A., Han, J.: Network A/B testing. In: Proceedings of the 24th International Conference on World Wide Web, WWW 2015, pp. 399–409 (2015)
5. Tang, D., Agarwal, A., O'Brien, D., Meyer, M.: Overlapping experiment infrastructure. In: Proceedings of the 16th ACM SIGKDD International Conference on Knowledge Discovery and Data Mining, KDD 2010, p. 17 (2010)
6. Dmitriev, P., Frasca, B., Gupta, S., Kohavi, R., Vaz, G.: Pitfalls of long-term online controlled experiments. In: Proceedings of the 2016 IEEE International Conference on Big Data, Big Data 2016, pp. 1367–1376 (2016)

7. Fagerholm, F., Sanchez Guinea, A., Mäenpää, H., Münch, J.: The RIGHT model for continuous experimentation. J. Syst. Softw. **123**, 292–305 (2017)

8. Olsson, H.H., Bosch, J.: The HYPEX model: from opinions to data-driven software development. In: Bosch, J. (ed.) Continuous Software Engineering, pp. 155–164. Springer, Cham (2014). https://doi.org/10.1007/978-3-319-11283-1_13

9. Olsson, H.H., Bosch, J.: Towards continuous customer validation: a conceptual model for combining qualitative customer feedback with quantitative customer observation. In: Fernandes, J.M., Machado, R.J., Wnuk, K. (eds.) ICSOB 2015. LNBIP, vol. 210, pp. 154–166. Springer, Cham (2015). https://doi.org/10.1007/978-3-319-19593-3_13

10. Dmitriev, P., Gupta, S., Dong Woo, K., Vaz, G.: A dirty dozen: twelve common metric interpretation pitfalls in online controlled experiments. In: Proceedings of the 23rd ACM SIGKDD International Conference on Knowledge Discovery and Data Mining, KDD 2017, pp. 1427–1436 (2017)

11. Crook, T., Frasca, B., Kohavi, R., Longbotham, R.: Seven pitfalls to avoid when running controlled experiments on the web. In: Proceedings of the 15th ACM SIGKDD International Conference on Knowledge Discovery and Data Mining, KDD 2009, p. 1105 (2009)

12. Kluck, T., Vermeer, L.: Leaky abstraction in online experimentation platforms: a conceptual framework to categorize common challenges (2017)

13. Chen, R., Chen, M., Jadav, M.R., Bae, J., Matheson, D.: Faster online experimentation by eliminating traditional A/A validation, pp. 1635–1641 (2017)

14. Kaufman, R.L., Pitchforth, J., Vermeer, L.: Democratizing online controlled experiments at Booking.com. http://arxiv.org/abs/1710.08217. Accessed 23 Oct 2017

15. Kohavi, R., Longbotham, R., Sommerfield, D., Henne, R.M.: Controlled experiments on the web: survey and practical guide. Data Min. Knowl. Discov. **18**(1), 140–181 (2009)

16. Fabijan, A., Olsson, H.H., Bosch, J.: Customer feedback and data collection techniques in software R&D: a literature review. In: Fernandes, J.M., Machado, R.J., Wnuk, K. (eds.) ICSOB 2015. LNBIP, vol. 210, pp. 139–153. Springer, Cham (2015). https://doi.org/10.1007/978-3-319-19593-3_12

17. Kohavi, R., Thomke, S.: The surprising power of online experiments. Harv. Bus. Rev. **95**, 74 (2017)

18. Gupta, S., Bhardwaj, S., Dmitriev, P., Ulanova, L., Raff, P., Fabijan, A.: The anatomy of a large-scale online experimentation platform. In: International Conference on Software Architecture, ICSA 2018, May 2018

19. Kevic, K., Murphy, B., Williams, L., Beckmann, J.: Characterizing experimentation in continuous deployment: a case study on bing. In: Proceedings of the 2017 IEEE/ACM 39th International Conference on Software Engineering: Software Engineering in Practice Track, ICSE-SEIP 2017, pp. 123–132 (2017)

20. Fabijan, A., Dmitriev, P., Olsson, H.H., Bosch, J.: The evolution of continuous experimentation in software product development. In: Proceedings of the 39th International Conference on Software Engineering, ICSE 2017 (2017)

21. Dmitriev, P., Wu, X.: Measuring metrics. In: Proceedings of the 25th ACM International on Conference on Information and Knowledge Management, CIKM 2016, pp. 429–437 (2016)

22. Deng, A., Shi, X.: Data-driven metric development for online controlled experiments. In: Proceedings of the 22nd ACM SIGKDD International Conference on Knowledge Discovery and Data Mining, KDD 2016, pp. 77–86 (2016)

23. Ries, E.: The Lean Startup: How Today's Entrepreneurs Use Continuous Innovation to Create Radically Successful Businesses (2011)

24. Runeson, P., Höst, M.: Guidelines for conducting and reporting case study research in software engineering. Empir. Softw. Eng. **14**(2), 131–164 (2009)

25. Robson, C., McCartan, K.: Real World Research, 4th edn. John Wiley & Sons Ltd., New York (2016)
26. Kohavi, R., Deng, A., Frasca, B., Walker, T., Xu, Y., Pohlmann, N.: Online controlled experiments at large scale. In: Proceedings of the 19th ACM SIGKDD International Conference on Knowledge Discovery and Data Mining, KDD 2013, p. 1168 (2013)
27. Deng, A., Lu, J., Litz, J.: Trustworthy analysis of online A/B tests. In: Proceedings of the Tenth ACM International Conference on Web Search and Data Mining, WSDM 2017, pp. 641–649 (2017)
28. Bottou, L., et al.: Counterfactual reasoning and learning systems. J. Mach. Learn. Res. **14**, 3207–3260 (2013)
29. Kohavi, R., Deng, A., Longbotham, R., Xu, Y.: Seven rules of thumb for web site experimenters. In: Proceedings of the 20th ACM SIGKDD International Conference on Knowledge Discovery and Data Mining, KDD 2014, pp. 1857–1866 (2014)

Influential Factors of Aligning Spotify Squads in Mission-Critical and Offshore Projects – A Longitudinal Embedded Case Study

Abdallah Salameh[(✉)] and Julian Bass

University of Salford, 43 Crescent, Salford M5 4WT, UK
{a.salameh,j.bass}@salford.ac.uk

Abstract. Changing the development process of an organization is one of the toughest and riskiest decisions. This is particularly true if the known experiences and practices of the new considered ways of working are relative and subject to contextual assumptions. Spotify engineering culture is deemed as a new agile software development method which increasingly attracts large-scale organizations. The method relies on several small cross-functional self-organized teams (i.e., a squads). The squad autonomy is a key driver in Spotify method, where a squad decides what to do and how to do it. To enable effective squad autonomy, each squad shall be aligned with a mission, strategy, short-term goals and other squads. Since a little known about Spotify method, there is a need to answer the question of: *How can organizations work out and maintain the alignment to enable loosely coupled and tightly aligned squads?*

In this paper, we identify factors to support the alignment that are actually performed in practice but have never been discussed before in terms of Spotify method. We also present *Spotify Tailoring* by highlighting the modified and newly introduced processes to the method. Our work is based on a longitudinal embedded case study which was conducted in a real-world large-scale offshore software intensive organization that maintains mission-critical systems. According to the confidentiality agreement by the organization in question, we are not allowed to reveal detailed description of the features of the explored project.

Keywords: Spotify · Alignment · Large-scale agile development
Agile transformation · Mission-critical system · Longitudinal case study

1 Introduction

Since the introduction of the agile manifesto, several agile methods have been developed and introduced. The introduction of those methods shows a fundamental shift in how organizations try to cope with encountered complexity and volatility issues [11]. Thus, no wonder why agile methods are increasingly

© Springer Nature Switzerland AG 2018
M. Kuhrmann et al. (Eds.): PROFES 2018, LNCS 11271, pp. 199–215, 2018.
https://doi.org/10.1007/978-3-030-03673-7_15

becoming attractive for many software development organizations of different sizes [4,6,28]. It is important to mention that agile methods have some common share techniques such as iterative and incremental development, communication, coordination, collaborative development, acceptance of the uncertainty, etc. [35]. However, each method has its specific techniques [35], strengths and weaknesses [28].

Large-scale contexts show particular challenges as several teams should work closely together to release a single software product while large groups of people need to collaborate and coordinate [7,16,21]. Spotify engineering method, as an agile method, is increasingly attracting the practitioners. The substantial notion of the method is to create autonomous yet collaborative squads. However, an observed challenge of this method is how to get the balance right between squads autonomy and effective collaboration among them. Due to the lack of scientific research related to the Spotify method [17–19], there is no insightful data through which we can deduce *how organizations can work out and maintain the alignment in order to enable loosely coupled and tightly aligned squads.*

In this paper, we adopt a longitudinal embedded case study in large-scale offshore software intensive organization which maintains mission-critical systems. We conduct direct observation over 19 months and 9 semi-structured practitioner interviews to find out how the alignment is actually performed. We identify four influential factors to the alignment, which are actually performed in practice. To the best of our knowledge, these four factors have not been identified before in terms of Spotify method. We also present "Spotify Tailoring" by highlighting the modified and newly introduced processes to the method.

The rest of this paper is organized as follows: in the next section, we present the background. Section 3 describes our research method. Section 4 discusses threats to validity. In Sect. 5, we present our findings. In Sect. 6 we discuss those findings. Finally, we conclude and provide future directions in Sect. 7.

2   Background

2.1   Large-Scale Agile Development

The suggested definitions of "large-scale project" are wide-ranging and reflect the various types and contexts of large-scale projects. Dingsøyr et al. [9] defined large-scale agile development as *"agile development efforts that involve a large number of actors, a large number of systems and interdependencies, which have more than two teams"*. This is in line with Rolland et al. definition [31]. Whereas, a very large-scale agile development is defined as *"the agile development efforts with more than ten teams"* [9]. Similarly, while Large Scale Scrum (LeSS) is applied to up to 10 Scrum teams (of seven people), LeSS Huge is applied to a few thousand people working on one product [22]. Some authors refer to very large-scale agile as *"Enterprise Agile"* [1,13]. Also, Dingsøyr et al. [7] provided a standard taxonomy of agile development scale and associated this scale to the some employed coordination approaches. In this paper, "large-scale project" means a project that has at least two teams working on the same product.

Agile methods (such as LeSS [22], Scaled Agile Framework (SAFe) [23] and Spotify [19]) are increasingly used in large-scale software development. Dingsøyr et al. summarized some of the discussions on research challenges in large-scale agile development [8]. Also, the challenges and the success factors in large-scale agile transformations have been reported [6].

2.2   Inter-team Coordination

Coordination among teams helps transparent participation of all stakeholders, and enables rules and standards that would overcome possible difficulties which might hinder the large-scale projects. Scaled agile has been a hot research topic in the agile community for some years now, where Inter-team coordination is one of important topics that have been pointed out in large-scale agile [26].

In the last two decades, large-scale development has faced coordination challenges. The setup of team of teams has been used because of the increasing dependencies, complexity and uncertainties [2,20,34]. As projects increase in size and complexity, the number of inter-team dependencies tends to increase as well [6,24]. Hence, more coordination effort is needed to deal with these dependencies so that the goals of the teams and the overall goals of the project are achieved [20,29,34]. Also, as the requirement specifications might change over time, large-scale projects come with more uncertainties that also affect the coordination due to the unpredictability of required tasks [20].

Eckstein [12] identifies self-organizing teams as a difficulty in a large-scale agile and suggested a model to help in resolving it. Although inter-team coordination is characterised as non-agile in nature where teams are supposed to be self-organized and be empowered, there is inevitable need for the teams to coordinate with each other. If inter-team coordination is weak, it can contribute to integration failure. Hence, scaled agile also need different practices and processes to become more efficient and to overcome the challenges of large-scale agile [3].

2.3   Spotify

The Spotify method has been developed to utilize agile development with hundreds of developers over 30 teams across 3 cities [19]. The overall structure consists, mainly, of Squads, Chapters, Guilds and Tribes [17–19]. Spotify has numerous squads which are loosely coupled and tightly aligned [18], self-organized and use their own preferable agile methods. Each squad is autonomous and has two types of missions (1) a long-term mission, which is based on the product strategy, and (2) a short-term mission that is quarterly renegotiated [18]. Squads autonomy is presented in the ability for bypassing layers of management and acting upon the decisions that the members have taken together. The Squads are encouraged to implement some Lean Startup principles such as Minimum Viable Product (MVP) where a feature is not finished until the impact is analysed [19]. While a squad leader is responsible for communicating what problem needs to be solved and why, Squads' job is to collaborate with each other to find the best solution [17,18]. A Squad has access to a coach who is in charge of improving squads' ways of working [19]. Also, each squad has a Product Owner (PO) who is responsible for prioritising the work and for matching product backlog for each squad [19]. Moreover, it is the responsibility of the POs as whole to maintain a high-level roadmap that shows where the organization is heading [19].

A Tribe is a collection of co-located squads that is designed to be smaller than 100 people and aims to promote collaboration and to minimize dependencies that can slow or obstruct a squad. A gathering is arranged regularly within a Tribe to show what have worked on and delivered so that others can learn [19]. Within the same tribe, there are small groups of people (i.e. Chapters) that have similar skills and working within the same competency area. People within a Chapter meet regularly to help in solving the problems. Chapters are considered the glue that sticks the company together without sacrificing too much autonomy [19]. While Chapters are always located within a Tribe, there are groups of people (i.e. Guilds) who are wide-reaching with a desire to share knowledge, tools, code, and practice across the whole organization [19].

The alignment of squads refers to the extent of which the organization strategy and goals are proudly understood and undertaken by having focused team interactions rather than tactics. Each Squad has autonomy to decide what to build, how to build it, and how to work together while building it. Though, squads need to be aligned with the squad's mission, product strategy, and short goals. Thus, squads should be autonomous, but don't sub-optimize and cross-pollination is better than standardization [18]. Also, due to the alignment on the product-level, the developers become experts in specific areas [19]. However, since "squads share products instead of owning them" [18], collective code ownership is adopted to encourage all squads to contribute [28].

Despite the inevitable dependencies between them, squads should have no blocking dependencies [19]. Hence, the Spotify method adopts some continuous discussions to find ways to eliminate the problematic dependencies [19]. In Scrum-of-scrums, a synchronization meeting is continuously conducted between ambassadors to report completions, next steps and impediments on behalf of the teams they represent [29]. However, it is considered beneficial to have smaller and focused inter-team meetings with only participants of similar interests [29]. In Spotify, conducting a meeting for the sake of synchronization is only allowed on demand to coordinate the squads involved [19]. Spotify tries to minimize handoff to scale without having dependencies and coordination. It achieves this by permitting the working on other squads' tasks when facing conflicting priorities [18]. Thereby, the other squad can review the code [18]. This indicates the existence of possible contradicted situations that require inter-team coordination.

3   Research Design and Methodology

In order to understand how the alignment is maintained in a Spotify Engineering Culture, we conduct a qualitative research comprising a longitudinal embedded case study over two years period [32]. This qualitative research is based on a case study on a large-scale offshore mission-critical services provider, that last

19 months. During the case study, approximately 200 ceremonies were observed from 5 project teams, and 9 semi-structured interviews have been conducted. A Grounded Theory (GT) approach is adopted to analyse the collected data.

3.1 Research Site

Our case study is carried out in a real-world company. The company employs approximately 650 staff members in its software development organization including support and management staff in 60 markets. It processes around 60 billion EUR per year. Our study focus only on managing mission-critical autonomous online services. These autonomous systems are collection of connected sub-systems which operate under the control of one administrative online system that presents a common and clearly defined management policy to the service.

The Spotify method is tailored and the developers are co-located in the headquarter. Besides the developers who are distributed into 6 squads, there are 1 architect, 5 POs, 2 agile coaches and 1 test lead.

3.2 Data Collection

The research draws on direct observation of over 200 ceremonies. The observed ceremonies include daily stand-ups, planning sessions, backlog grooming and retrospectives. The team meetings are usually conducted weekly during active periods. One advantage of direct observation is that it provided a deep understanding of the phenomenon that is studied. Another advantage is that it prevents any kind of suspected deviation between "semi-structured interviews" view of matters and the "real" case [30]. Nine semi-structured interviews are conducted for data collection [27]. Open-ended interview guide approach was used to provide interviewees with the opportunity to raise any other issues outside the scope of the semi-structured interview. The questions were revised after the second interview. Each interview was recorded, continued for around 45 min and transcribed verbatim for detailed analysis in a continuous basis.

3.3 Data Analysis

GT aims to generate a theory while having an absence of up-front clear research problem or hypothesis and by harnessing a constant comparison of data at increasing levels of abstraction [5]. Hence, the researcher tries to uncover the research problem as the main concern of the participants. In this paper we employ the classic approach (Glaserian approach).

These data have been analysed using the GT [5]. In essence, this is a process of continuous undertaking of data collection, coding and analysis, memoing, sorting and constant comparison of the collected data, and theoretical saturation. Initially, the audio interview and associated written transcript were carefully reviewed to ensure consistency. The interpretive process of open coding broke down the data analytically and generated categories and concepts. A few questions, suggested by Glaser [15], were asked when conducting open coding: "what is this data a study of?", "what category does this incident indicate?", "what is actually happening in the data?", "what is the main concern being faced by the participants?" and "what accounts for the continual resolving of this concern?". Answering these questions allowed us to continue coding effectively without feeling overwhelmed by the data. Due to the limited ways in which we could organize and interact with the data by using NVivo 10, we settled for using print-outs of the transcripts and physically coded along the margins. A constant comparison was used to refine and sharpen the categories emerging from data, which are free from any prior assumptions held by the researchers. Furthermore, we analyzed the observations and compared them to the concepts derived from the interviews. We found our observations did not contradict but rather supported the data provided in interviews.

4   Threats to the Validity

Threats to the validity are discussed as described by Runeson and Höst [32]:

Construct validity refers to the extent of which the employed research methodology captures studied concepts and what is investigated according to the research questions [32]. Therefore, the interview protocol was tested during two pilot interviews and minor revisions were made. Also, a GT research study produces a "mid-ranged" theory [14]. This implies that the theory is not claimed to be universally applicable, but it can be modified by having constant comparison to accommodate more data from new contexts [14]. However, a key contribution of a GT study is the focus on conceptualization and the production of modifiable concepts that interrelate to generate an abstract theory, which explains the main concerns of the participants in a substantive area [5].

Internal validity refers to the risk of interference in causal relations within the research [32]. Since this study is of empirical nature, incorrect data is a validity threat. However, this is a longitudinal study that involves repeated observations of the same variables over long periods of time which gave a chance to further validate the findings [32]. In case of the interviews, the written extensive notes, continuous observation and the recordings assured the correct data.

External validity refers to the extent of which the findings of the research can be generalized and of interest to other cases [32]. This case study includes interviews with different roles and squads to brace the external validity of this research. The generalizability is affected negatively because the interviews are performed at one company. However, the purpose of qualitative studies puts more emphasis on describing and recognizing a contemporary phenomenon and less emphasis on generalizing the findings. Nevertheless, results from this case study may benefit the investigation of phenomena within similar contexts.

Conclusion validity refers to the extent of which the data and the analysis are dependent on the specific researchers. In this case study, the conducted semi-structured interviews was tested through two pilot interviews and subsequently followed by a revised version. We adopts a longitudinal embedded case study in which the observations of the same variables were repeated to confirm the findings, and GT is used to analyze the collected data. Also, we aim to conduct a comparative study to validate and generalize the results.

5 Findings

A synergy has been observed between the following categories, which are depicted in Fig. 1, and strengthening the alignment among the squads. In this section, we will ignore the *"adaptive structure with more focus on communities"* category since it has been covered already in the literature [17–19] yet it is discussed in the context of this case study.

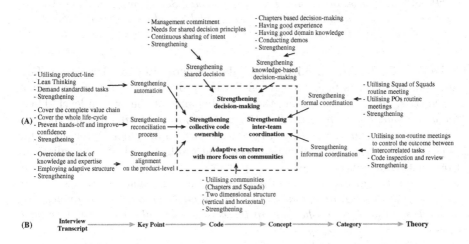

Fig. 1. (A) Emergence of the categories, (B) Levels of data abstraction (GT)

5.1 Strengthening Collective Code Ownership

Collective Code Ownership Requires Alignment over the Product-Level. The squads are provided the freedom to do the required software development on different associated systems due to the realization of collective code ownership. However, it has been realized that sharing products instead of owning them causes a waste of time and resources. This is because of either the lack of knowledge and expertise on the product-level or due to the insufficient ownership.

> *"Handling maintenance or improvement tasks associated to the product-line by other squads is considered as time consuming and will likely require relearning to be able to take the right action"*–P1, Agile Coach and Architect

> *"There should be someone or a team in charge of the bigger picture... A bit more structure around the ownership based on the missions and verticals, and by considering a long-term road map"*–P6, PO and Key Account Manager

Having many discrete tasks affects knowledge sharing and causes a waste of time and resources and this will raise the need of employing a relearning process. *"The nature of maintenance tasks requires having discrete tasks where each developer works alone"*–P1, Agile Coach and Architect. This case is mostly for those user stories with maintenance nature. Thus, *"code review and inspection are considered crucial to ensure the continuity of deploying successful releases and for the sake of knowledge sharing"*–P1, Agile Coach and Architect. Thereby, the squads should be aligned with the product-level to support collective code ownership and to facilitate the process of knowledge sharing and mastering.

> *"People might abuse the freedom that agile provides. Sometimes, they do not take care of things that they don't like. The responsibility and commitment should be a central part of the work."*–P7, PO and Key Account Manager

Collective Code Ownership Demands a Reconciliation Process. Handling shared products requires a reconciliation process between the key associated parties, and before adopting the desired change at the system level. Thus, *"the development team may need, sometimes, to discuss their proposed solution with their peers, management team or architecture"*–P3, Senior Developer. This is because of either a lack of expertise at the product-level or the realization of product as a service where the complete value chain and the whole lifecycle need to be taken into account. Without having a reconciliation process, *"...the task might get blocked or a waste of resources might be a result of implementing inefficient solution or shortage in the commitment of management or third parties"*–P3, Senior Developer.

The developers tend to be, sometimes, unconfident when working on a shard product that is not within their expertise regardless of having communities (Chapters and Squads). For instance, in case of having an incident where a hot-fix is requested, the reviewers, who are either from other squads and possess expertise or from the same squad, were hesitant to handle the situation. This is mostly because of either the complexity of such tasks or being uninformed about the low-level details which requires knowledge transformation and relearning.

> *"A Hot-Fix is requested in case of facing incident after having a new release. If not, the release is rolled-back. Mostly, the developer who owns this task is requested to solve it with some support..."*–P6, PO and Key Account Manager

Constantly adjusting the plan by utilising a Kanban board for each customer satisfies their needs and guarantees having aligned strategy while progressing toward their goals. Providing a visual control through the Kanban board results in an effective mechanism and low coordination overhead. As a result, better management decisions are taken at the right time in a continuous basis. Thus, all squads follow a standardized operational process that is controlled by Kanban board in a routine base because of having a strong culture of cross-pollination. This routine is depicted through the definition of "Done" which indicates the completion of the implementation of tasks and rules the overall process flow (includes: backlog management, task selection, implementation, peer review, testing, integration, packaging, deployment and feedback). Thus, POs will be able to insure the alignment of the organizational strategy.

> *"Continuously maintaining the practices, such as the definition of 'DONE', helps the customers in gaining a strong competitive advantage due to the rapid response in a highly disciplined manner... Constantly, adjusting the plan through Kanban board satisfies them and guarantees the alignment of the strategy while progressing toward their goals"*–P6, PO and Key Account Manager

The Automation of Standardized Tasks Strengthens Collective Code Ownership. Adopting a product-line (PL) requires task standardization to streamline the process of working within the same squad and aids other squads when working on related aspects. Since the organization is providing a service that manages autonomous systems, it adopts a PL way of working in order to integrate the system into the external sub-systems. Figure 2 illustrates the lifecycle of the PL. A task standardization, which is a key principle in Lean Thinking (eliminating the waste), is depicted through predefined checklists. These predefined checklists are utilized to facilitate planning, estimation, documentation, technical details such as security check-list, code review, knowledge sharing, etc. This process helps the organization to speed up the process and to eliminate possible issues. However, these checklists need to be enhanced further and other potential areas need to be covered.

> *"Code review results, sometimes, missing important aspects due to the weakness of coverage in the current predefined checklist of the PL. Enhancing the existing ones and creating new ones to cover other important task types could be beneficial"*–P2, Senior Developer

> *"We should have efficient check-lists to provide wider coverage in the PL and to have things go smoothly"*–P6, PO and Key Account Manager

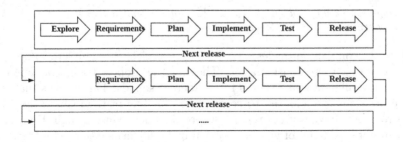

Fig. 2. Product-line lifecycle

Despite the fact that Spotify way of working results in a very little standardization because of having loosely coupled squads that are tightly aligned, it was realized that whole organization tends to be leaner due to the strong culture of cross-pollination besides being transformed from Lean. The organization implements a number of Lean principles such as; Kanban board, continuous process (Lean Thinking), documentation for the software development process (value stream mapping), and automation whenever possible. The organization *"tries to automate the processes whenever is possible by utilising DevOps through continuous integration, delivery, deployment, testing and release"*–P4, Senior Developer. Also, Lean thinking is depicted through the adoption of continuous processes. This includes continuous backlog monitoring, prioritization and feedback, integration, delivery, deployment, release, testing, refactoring, verification and inspection.

> *"We have instructions to (1) setup the system for developers, (2) build unit tests, (3) access and deploy, (4) fix release configuration, (5) follow the processes, and (6) do a code implementation and validation using a predefined checklist for the PL"*–P9, Senior Developer

5.2 Strengthening Decision-Making

Having autonomous squads demands an ability of taking right decisions without relying on others. Having a continuously communicated and shared intent facilitates decision-making. *"We should be familiar with how the GOOD should be look like in all areas associated to the provided service!"*–P6, PO and Key Account Manager. Also, P8, Senior Developer, confirms this need. Obstacles to decision making emerged from lacking shared decision principles. Thus, embracing the principles of having good shared decisions requires having policies and principles that are explicitly and regularly communicated.

Tackling business associated decisions and developing a functionality that can be utilized by all portfolios are considered important aspects when providing a service that manages autonomous systems. In fact, decision-making is, mostly, shifted from a domain independent approach, which relies on routine decisions, to a knowledge-based approach, which relies on the experience and knowledge.

> *"Taking a decision about which solution to adopt is time consuming for the developers with no good knowledge in this domain and makes it hard to work independently"*–P1, Agile Coach and Architect

Since the company provides a product as a service, the complete value chain needs to be taken into consideration. Thereby, the proposed solutions might be tackled with different stakeholders from different squads. This implies that non-routine decisions are adopted to control the outcome of the tasks rather than to control the behavior of the process where the uncertainty is high. However, a more conventional point of view is depicted by highlighting the needs of having a routine meeting between the POs. This meeting is needed to ensure the alignment between squad's missions and the overall road map of the organization. Also, it ensures the ownership of the product itself while the customers, in B2B contexts, are mainly enthusiastic about how to use the service in their own way.

> *"We do not have a product management team. POs should ensure the continuous alignment between them in respect to the road map and be in charge of the bigger picture"*–P6, PO and Key Account Manager

5.3 Strengthening Inter-team Coordination

The Engineering Culture of Spotify does not directly cover inter-team coordination practices and processes since it tries to speed up the process by having autonomous teams instead of relying on managers. However, the existence of possible contradicted situations requires inter-team coordination to resolve conflicted priorities between the teams and to take into consideration the complete value chain and the whole lifecycle. Thus, *"we need to have a team spirit in order to have the work done and not by only working independently. The harmony of the used processes should be high"*–P2, Senior Developer.

Inter-team coordination is essentially depicted in two routine meetings; (1) Squad of Squads meeting and (2) POs meeting. In Squad of Squads meeting, POs provide brief information about what their teams are determined to do by sharing their intents and obstacles (if any) instead of reporting work status. In POs meeting, they arrange between themselves to ensure (1) the alignment between squads' missions, (2) the ownership of the product itself, and (3) the alignment for the overall road map of the organization. Moreover, non-routine inter-team coordination process is utilized between the associated squads' members to control the outcome of the tasks and to overcome the high-level of uncertainty (aforementioned in Sect. 5.2).

> *"We start our week by having a meeting for all squads. In this meeting the POs highlight on what obstacles they are facing and the work they determine to do"*–P6, PO, Key Account Manager

> *"We have regular meetings between the POs to tackle important tasks in the upcoming iteration(s). Also, POs meet up to discuss and prioritize intersected tasks to aligned between the squads"*–P4, Senior Developer

Exposing the adopted coordination processes and providing rules would streamline inter-team coordination. This exposure will level up the alignment and thereby it will become a matter of nature and people will start to behave naturally in different circumstances to achieve the desired goals.

> *"Explaining the values behind the followed processes besides making them obvious are considered crucial. By making them explicit for the teams, we will know what to do and when to do it."*–P5, PO

> *"I do know whom to contact internally and why for each part of the system... This makes my life easier to coordinate, extract the requirements, and to take the right decisions quickly"*–P7, PO and Key Account Manager

Since external parties are involved in the PL, it is crucial to have close collaboration and coordination to carry on the software development. Otherwise, the process of integrating the system into external sub-systems might get blocked and consequently the organization will be behind the anticipated due dates.

"Some tickets get blocked for some time in the PL due to the needs of having feedback from third parties. This affects the planning, thereby the customers get informed about the situation by the POs"–P4, Senior Developer

6   Discussion

The Spotify method is increasingly attracting the industry as a result of tailoring several agile and lean practices together. The key principle the Spotify method is that it is driven by creating autonomous squads. Autonomy is important to have motivated and innovative teams that can deliver quickly while reducing possible mistakes caused by handoffs. However, autonomy can not be precisely defined since the squads are still involved in the same project and there is a common share interest among them. Hence, there should be alignment between the squads and the overall product goals and plans. In spite of Spotify awareness of alignment and their significant roles for the method, there is no adequate guidelines about how to build and maintain the alignment.

Building the alignment is subject to several contextual factors, where the size of the organization is one of them [4]. In this section, we discuss the outcomes of our case study which reveal the factors that influence the way by which the alignment is maintained in a real-world large-scale organization. Also, we present the "Spotify Tailoring".

One of the important reasons for the organization under discussion to transform to the Spotify method is the need of having loosely coupled, yet tightly aligned teams while adopting different agile methods. Since the organization adopts LSD whilst the Spotify method encourages the implementation of Lean Startup principles such as MVP, there was a common ground through honouring product perfection (i.e., maximizing customer value). Moreover, the organization continues to employ Lean Thinking with more emphasis on PL. Hence, the divergence from LSD to Spotify did not impose a considerable challenge.

Based on our findings, we identify four main influential factors of aligning the Squads. Table 1 presents them and shows the applicability of the underlying concepts of these factors within the Spotify method and the case study.

Spotify introduces an adaptive structure based on a matrix of two dimensions, (1) vertical (i.e. Squads and Tribes) and (2) horizontal (i.e. Chapters and Guilds) [19], to build communities around them. This adaptive structure empowers the squads and inspires their innovation. The organization, utilizes the communities of squads and chapters to establish the alignment. However, it does not benefit from the Guilds and Tribes due to the small size of software development teams compared to the size of the teams in Spotify organization itself (P6, P9). Furthermore, the case study indicates that the Guilds and their

Table 1. The influential factors to the alignment in Spotify

Factor	Concept	Spotify	Case Study
Adaptive structure with more focus on communities	Utilizing vertical and horizontal dimensional structure	Yes	Yes
	Utilizing communities (Chapters and Squads)	Yes	Yes
	Utilizing communities (Guilds and Tribes)	Yes	No
Collective Code Ownership	Alignment on the product-level	Yes	Yes
	Reconciliation process	N/A	Yes
	Automation process	N/A	Yes
Facilitating decision-making	Shared decision-making	N/A	Yes
	Knowledge-based decision-making	N/A	Yes
Inter-team coordination	Formal coordination	No	Yes
	On demand coordination	Yes	Yes
	Informal coordination	Unknown	Yes

meetings pose unnecessary time consuming efforts. Consequently, the organization replaces the Guild communities by arranging demo sessions and non-routine meetings between the members who share the same interest.

Since the Spotify method is more about sharing than owning the product, collective code ownership is adopted implicitly. However, there is a link between the degree of autonomy and the shift from code ownership towards collective code ownership, where less autonomy leads to the latter. This link is perceived, in this case study, through the ability of making decisions in an entrepreneurial climate without too much interference from the management. In fact, the Spotify method makes an alignment over the product level, which is beneficial in long-term missions. For the organization in question, however, product level alignment impacts the performance of the squads when it encounters conflicting priorities. This impact is caused due to the lack of knowledge of other product levels. To avoid wasting time and resources, the organization realized the importance of having a reconciliation process between the involved squads. The importance of such a process is because of: (1) not considering the complete value chain and the whole lifecycle in terms of a product as a service, (2) the lack of knowledge of other product levels, or (3) not providing common solutions. Another way that the organization has adopted to streamline the process of working on shared products is the automation of standardized tasks, which is mostly related to the PL by employing Lean Thinking.

The Spotify method does not prescribe how the alignment is maintained when it comes to decision-making. In fact, Kniberg [18] highlights the importance of getting things into production easily rather than knowing who is making the decision. The autonomy of the squads, in our case study, is influenced by decision-making related obstacles (after the transformation). The two determined obstacles are (1) unwillingness to commit to decisions due to a poor alignment on the product-level, and (2) facing conflicted priorities that results in tackling the tasks by another squad who lacks the expertise on the product-level. These two obstacles are in line with what Drury et al., found [10] where they cause a lack of ownership. As a result, the organization adopts shared decision principles and continuous sharing of intent at different strategic, tactical, and operational levels that are explicitly and regularly communicated. This adoption facilitates the process of shared decision-making and strengthens the alignment between the squads. In turn, the alignment of shared decisions strengthens the commitment and ownership, and builds a culture of providing quick help to other squads, which eventually supports the notion of *"we are all in this boat all together"*. The principle of shared decisions becomes a matter of culture where their policies are implicitly followed and adapted by time. Sharing of intent, on the other hand, clarifies how the GOOD should look like and strengthens squads' autonomy. By continuously sharing the intent, decision-making is shifted from a domain independent approach to a knowledge-based approach that facilitates decision-making and removes the dependencies.

The organization encounters other challenges in terms of shared decision-making which also match the findings of Moe et al., [25]. These challenges are: (1) insufficient alignment of strategic product plans, (2) insufficient allocation of development resources, and (3) performing development and maintenance tasks within the teams. As for the first challenge, conducting non-routine meetings between the involved squads' members are useful to control the outcome of the tasks that have high level of uncertainty. Thereby, non-routine decisions are conducted (bounded rational decision-making [25]). Also, utilizing a routine decision-making (aka rational decision-making [25]) by having meeting between the POs is deemed as crucial for the sake of ensuring (1) the alignment between squads' missions, (2) the ownership of the product itself, and (3) the alignment of the overall road map of the organization. However, decision-making is mostly shifted from a domain independent approach, which relies on routine decisions, to a knowledge-based approach (naturalistic decision-making [25]), which relies on the experience of the team members. This knowledge-based approach is oriented by having "Chapters" besides the alignment at the product-level.

Since the Spotify method intends to speed up the process by having autonomous teams, it does not formally support inter-team coordination processes but only on demands. As projects in larger scale software development increase in size, complexity, dependencies and uncertainties [2,20,24,34], more coordination effort is needed to achieve teams' goals and project's overall goal [20,21,29,34]. Hence, large-scale software development needs to use standards and structures [33] by embracing and exposing inter-team coordination process [3,12]. For instance, the teams are synchronized and coordinated in Scrum-of-Scrums through (1) inter-team Sprint Planning meetings, (2) inter-team Daily Scrums, (3) inter-team Product Refinements, and (4) inter-team Sprint Reviews. In our case study, two essential routine coordination meetings are determined: (1) Squad of Squads meeting and (2) POs meeting. Also, non-routine inter-team coordination process is used between the involved squads' members to (1) control the outcome of tasks, which is inline with the findings of Paasivaara et al., [29], (2) overcome uncertainties, and (3) share interesting expertise.

7   Conclusion and Future Research

In this paper, we have explored the alignment among the squads in the Spotify method to uncover the empirical evidence of how the alignment is maintained among the squads. Our work is based on a longitudinal embedded case study which was conducted in a real-world large-scale offshore software intensive organization that maintains mission-critical systems. The analysis revealed the influential factors to the alignment among the squads that are actually performed in practice. We also present "Spotify Tailoring" by highlighting the modified and newly introduced processes to the Spotify method.

Our work in this paper contributes to identify influential factors for aligning Spotify squads and presents "Spotify Tailoring" with respect to a specific case study. In order to gain more confidence in the presented results of our work, we strongly believe that future work should focus on conducting more comparative studies to further investigate the influential factors. We also encourage further exploration of "Spotify Tailoring" through studying the observed divergence between the authentic Spotify method by the Spotify organization and the tailored Spotify method by other organizations and practitioners.

References

1. Bass, J.M.: How product owner teams scale agile methods to large distributed enterprises. Empir. Softw. Eng. **20**(6), 1525–1557 (2015)
2. Bick, S., Scheerer, A., Spohrer, K.: Inter-team coordination in large agile software development settings: five ways of practicing agile at scale. In: Proceedings of the Scientific Workshop Proceedings of XP2016, XP 2016 Workshops, USA (2016)
3. Bjørnson, F.O., Vestues, K.: Knowledge sharing and process improvement in large-scale agile development. In: Proceedings of the Scientific Workshop Proceedings of XP2016, XP '16 Workshops, pp. 7:1–7:5. ACM, New York (2016)
4. Campanelli, A.S., Parreiras, F.S.: Agile methods tailoring - a systematic literature review. J. Syst. Softw. **110**, 85–100 (2015)
5. Corbin, J., Strauss, A., Strauss, A.L.: Basics of Qualitative Research, 4th edn. Sage, Thousand Oaks (2014)
6. Dikert, K., Paasivaara, M., Lassenius, C.: Challenges and success factors for large-scale agile transformations: a systematic literature review. J. Syst. Softw. **119**, 87–108 (2016)
7. Dingsøyr, T., Fægri, T.E., Itkonen, J.: What Is large in large-scale? *a taxonomy of scale for agile software development.* In: Jedlitschka, A., Kuvaja, P., Kuhrmann, M., Männistö, T., Münch, J., Raatikainen, M. (eds.) PROFES 2014. LNCS, vol. 8892, pp. 273–276. Springer, Cham (2014). https://doi.org/10.1007/978-3-319-13835-0_20
8. Dingsøyr, T., Moe, N.B.: Research challenges in large-scale agile software development. ACM SIGSOFT Softw. Eng. Notes **38**(5), 38–39 (2013)
9. Dingsøyr, T., Moe, N.B., Fægri, T.E., Seim, E.A.: Exploring software development at the very large-scale: a revelatory case study and research agenda for agile method adaptation. Empir. Softw. Engg. **23**(1), 490–520 (2018)

10. Drury, M., Conboy, K., Power, K.: Obstacles to decision making in agile software development teams. J. Syst. Softw. **85**(6), 1239–1254 (2012). Special Issue: Agile Development
11. Dybå, T., Dingsøyr, T.: Empirical studies of agile software development: a systematic review. Inf. Softw. Technol. **50**(9), 833–859 (2008)
12. Eckstein, J.: Sociocracy: an organization model for large-scale agile development. In: Proceedings of the Scientific Workshop Proceedings of XP2016, XP 2016 Workshops, pp. 6:1–6:5. ACM, New York (2016)
13. Fitzgerald, B., Stol, K.J.: Continuous software engineering: a roadmap and agenda. J. Syst. Softw. **123**, 176–189 (2017)
14. Glaser, B.: "Naturalist inquiry" and grounded theory. Forum : Qual. Soc. Res. **5**(1), 114–133 (2004)
15. Glaser, B.G.: Doing Grounded Theory: Issues and Discussions. Sociology Press, Mill Valley (1998)
16. Hildenbrand, T., Rothlauf, F., Geisser, M., Heinzl, A., Kude, T.: Approaches to collaborative software development. In: 2008 International Conference on Complex, Intelligent and Software Intensive Systems, pp. 523–528, March 2008
17. Kniberg, H.: Spotify squad framework - part ii, April 2014. https://medium.com/project-management-learnings/spotify-squad-framework-part-ii-c5d4b9398c30
18. Kniberg, H.: Spotify squad framework - part i, January 2014. https://medium.com/project-management-learnings/spotify-squad-framework-part-i-8f74bcfcd761
19. Kniberg, H., Ivarsson, A.: Scaling agile spotify with tribes, squads, chapters & guilds, October 2012. https://blog.crisp.se/wp-content/uploads/2012/11/SpotifyScaling.pdf
20. Kraut, R.E., Streeter, L.A.: Coordination in software development. Commun. ACM **38**(3), 69–81 (1995)
21. Larman, C., Vodde, B.: Practices for Scaling Lean & Agile Development: Large, Multisite, and Offshore Product Development with Large-Scale Scrum, 1st edn. Addison-Wesley Professional, Boston (2010)
22. Larman, C., Vodde, B.: Scaling agile development. CrossTalk **9**, 8–12 (2013)
23. Leffingwell, D.: SAFe 4.0 Reference Guide: Scaled Agile Framework for Lean Software and Systems Engineering, 1st edn. Addison-Wesley Professional, Boston (2016)
24. Melo, C., Cruzes, D., Kon, F., Conradi, R.: Interpretative case studies on agile team productivity and management. Inf. Softw. Technol. **55**, 412–427 (2013)
25. Moe, N.B., Aurum, A., Dybå, T.: Challenges of shared decision-making: a multiple case study of agile software development. Inf. Softw. Technol. **54**(8), 853–865 (2012)
26. Moe, N.B., Olsson, H.H., Dingsøyr, T.: Trends in large-scale agile development: a summary of the 4th workshop at XP2016. In: Proceedings of the Scientific Workshop Proceedings of XP2016, p. 1. ACM (2016)
27. Myers, M., Newman, M.: The qualitative interview in is research: examining the craft. Inf. Organ. **17**(1), 2–26 (2007)
28. Nerur, S.: Acceptance of software process innovations the case of extreme programming. Eur. J. Inf. Syst. **18**(4), 344–354 (2009)
29. Paasivaara, M., Lassenius, C., Heikkilä, V.T.: Inter-team coordination in large-scale globally distributed scrum: do scrum-of-scrums really work? In: Proceedings of the 2012 ACM-IEEE International Symposium on Empirical Software Engineering and Measurement, pp. 235–238, September 2012
30. Robinson, H., Segal, J., Sharp, H.: Ethnographically-informed empirical studies of software practice. Inf. Softw. Technol. **49**(6), 540–551 (2007)

31. Rolland, K.H., Fitzgerald, B., Dingsoyr, T., Stol, K.J.: Problematizing agile in the large: alternative assumptions for large-scale agile development. In: ICIS 2016 PROCEEDINGS : 37 International Conference on Information Systems (2016)
32. Runeson, P., Hőst, M.: Guidelines for conducting and reporting case study research in software engineering. Int. J. **14**(2), 131–164 (2009)
33. Saeeda, H., Arif, F., Minhas, N.M., Humayun, M.: Agile scalability for large scale projects: lessons learned (report). J. Softw. **10**(7), 893 (2015)
34. Scheerer, A., Hildenbrand, T., Kude, T.: Coordination in large-scale agile software development: a multiteam systems perspective. In: 2014 47th Hawaii International Conference on System Sciences, pp. 4780–4788, January 2014
35. Sutharshan, A., Maj, S.: An evaluation of agile software methodology techniques. Int. J. Comput. Sci. Netw. Secur. **10**(12), 68–71 (2010)

Testing

Test-Driving FinTech Product Development: An Experience Report

Anders Sundelin[1,2]([✉]), Javier Gonzalez-Huerta[1]([✉]), and Krzysztof Wnuk[1]([✉])

[1] Blekinge Institute of Technology, Karlskrona, Sweden
[2] Ericsson AB, Karlskrona, Sweden
anders.sundelin@ericsson.com,
{javier.gonzalez.huerta,krzysztof.wnuk}@bth.se

Abstract. In this paper, we present experiences from eight years of developing a financial transaction engine, using what can be described as an integration-test-centric software development process. We discuss the product and the relation between three different categories of its software and how the relative weight of these artifacts has varied over the years. In addition to the presentation, some challenges and future research directions are discussed.

Keywords: Test-driven development · Software craftsmanship
Testing architecture

1 Introduction

Software and software products are the critical elements of the Financial Technology (FinTech) [9] revolution that reshape the way how individuals and financial institutions save, borrow, make payments, and manage risk [7]. Software is enabling societal change in our relationship with money, especially in developing economies where alternative financial services are more customer focused and allow more people to have access to finance without the need of a bank [3]. Ericsson has seen the opportunity that FinTech offers as early as 2010 and decided to create a financial product for developing economies that provides access to payment services to users without credit card or bank account. Ericsson developed the product considering market demands and requirements such as *security, auditing, correctness, performance, availability, flexibility, fast time to market* and *development efficiency.*

In this paper, we discuss experiences on how Ericsson tackled the problem of crafting a software product for the financial sector not only migrating to a modern programming language and with a Service Oriented Architecture, but also using modern ways of developing the software such as *test-driven development, integration tests, continuous integration, clean code, learning by doing, mandatory solution review* and *simple communication.* Several studies analyze

Research supported by Ericsson AB and PLEng School.

M. Kuhrmann et al. (Eds.): PROFES 2018, LNCS 11271, pp. 219–226, 2018.
https://doi.org/10.1007/978-3-030-03673-7_16

the effects that TDD has on code quality and defect rate [10,12], though few studies analyze the long-term effects that TDD might have in the project, regarding the number of defects and the size of the test base as compared to the code base. Moreover, there is a lack of longitudinal experience reports of developing Fintech products for global markets.

2 Background and Related Work

Although it has earlier roots in the Smalltalk community, the term Test-Driven Development was popularized in the late 1990s and described as part of the Extreme Programming process, [1,2]. Several scientific studies have analyzed the effects of TDD e.g., [5,10,12].

In an experiment described in [6], the authors compare TDD with the alternative iterative test-last (ITLD) process, concluding that the claimed benefits of TDD arise not from its test-first approach, but from the fine-grained, steady steps, with fast feedback that improve focus and flow. Our paper supports this conclusion, adding aspects of product development over eight years.

One of the first public tools to support automated acceptance tests was the Framework for Integrated Tests (Fit)[1]. The acceptance-test-driven development (ATDD) process [13] was studied in [8,11].

Most of the studies of TDD have focused on shorter timescales, from some weeks, up to a few years worth of software development. This paper adds experiences from eight years of building a product from scratch using rigorous testing methodologies, and the effects that this has had on the code base.

3 Case Description and Analysis Method

The system under study forms part of a FinTech global product that enables access to financial services via mobile phones and the Internet. It is typically installed in a high-availability configuration, with geographical redundancy, to meet service uptime requirements. The system is a transaction-intensive application, with incoming and outgoing interfaces, a database, and scheduled tasks such as the sending of notifications. As it is a financial application, security has played a central role in its development.

The studied system consists of the financial core of the application, containing the core business logic, such as the financial transaction management. The core exposes its services via a set of *requests*, similar in spirit to the system calls of the Unix kernel. There are other components in the product, such as user interfaces, both graphical and textual, but these are not studied in this report. All other components use the services of the core in order to perform their tasks. The system is built in Java, using EJB 3[2] principles and is deployed using a custom, light-weight EJB container, also exempt from this study.

---

[1] http://fit.c2.com/.

[2] http://download.oracle.com/otndocs/jcp/ejb-3.1-pfd-oth-JSpec.

One of the guiding principles when developing this application was intensive test automation. Testing should take place in different layers, with the bulk of the tests in the lower layers (unit tests), and progressively fewer tests the higher the abstraction level. This follows the principles outlined in the testing pyramid [4].

3.1   Studied Artifacts

We analyzed the production code and test artifacts developed by the *development team* during feature development. Ericsson also has dedicated *testing teams*, focusing on testing the complete system, including all required special hardware, such as hardware cryptography modules and application firewalls, but these activities are not studied in this report.

The studied software is classified according to the following three categories:

- *Production code* - which is deployed at the customer site, and perform some useful action in live deployed systems.
- *Unit test code* - which is developed alongside the production code, typically by the same developer.
- *Integration test code* - using the externally visible interfaces of the system, typically describing the use cases that the application shall provide. Integration tests are developed by the same team and at the same time as the production code, though typically by different developers.

In addition to these three categories, the system also contains small amounts of other software and configurations files, such as installation support software, test enablers that aid integration testing, and system test code for testing the entire software system.

The number of authors of the studied software has varied over time, due to business and organizational changes. For the production and unit test code, the number of authors has been between 9 and 74, with a median of 35. The integration tests have a slightly wider span, between 8 and 79 authors, also with a median of 35. The majority of developers (median: 29.5) has developed both production code and integration tests.

3.2   Tools

We use the common open-source tools cloc[3] and Git[4] in order to calculate statistics for the above-mentioned categories. We collected statistics for every feature-enhancing release made of the product, plus three initial "pre-releases", denoted P01, P02, P03, before the first commercial release, denoted R01, in mid-2012. On average, 81 days have passed between releases, with a median of 62.5 days and an IQR of 55.5 days. There have also been other releases made of the software, both for error corrections, and candidates meant for internal testing.

---

[3] https://github.com/AlDanial/cloc.

[4] https://git-scm.com/.

4   Results and Discussion

4.1   Size of the Code Base

Table 1 lists the mean and median lines per file and Fig. 1 illustrates the number of lines of code per category, for each studied release. The last studied release, R32, consists of about 5000 files of production code, and about half as many unit test files. The number of integration test files is more than double the number of production files, about 12000.

Table 1. Mean and median number of lines per file.

File type	Mean lines/file	Median lines/file
Production code (Java)	90	55
Unit test code (Java)	228	163
Integration test (XML)	133	97

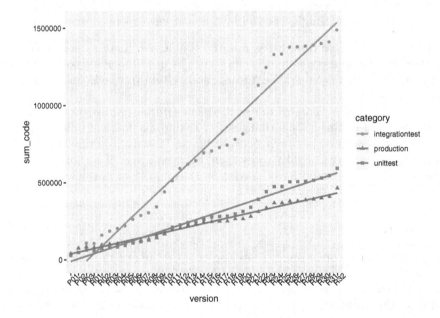

Fig. 1. Lines of code for each category, per release, P01, P02 and P03 are initial prereleases and R01 is the first commercial release. (Color figure online)

Figure 1 shows a linear growth, with integration test code (red) dominating over production code (green). While the production code has grown from about

42 kLOC in 583 files in the first preliminary release, to about 460 kLOC in 5166 files in the last studied release, the number of lines of integration tests has grown to 1488 kLOC, in 11211 files. The first two preliminary releases contained no integration tests but were tested using other tools, later discarded due to lack of productivity. To enable efficient integration testing, the developers chose to develop an XML-based testing tool. The tool was first used in the P03 release, which comprised of 110 kLOC integration test code lines, distributed in 622 files.

Regarding the unit test code (blue), we see that starting from release R11, the number of lines of unit test code exceeds the number of lines of production code. In the latest studied release, there are about 30% more lines of unit test code than of production code. Thus, the unit test code base is also growing faster than the production code, though not as fast as the integration tests. The fact that the typical unit test file is larger than the typical production code file supports the notion that the tests are mostly concrete code, in the typical *Arrange*, *Act*, *Assert* fashion, whereas the production code consists of a higher number of interfaces and abstract classes.

We can conclude that this is a product where test code, both unit tests, and integration tests, make up the bulk of the software. As the growth rate of both the unit tests and the integration tests are higher than for production code, it becomes a necessity to manage this growth, for instance by reducing duplication and increasing modularity and reusability. The importance of this increases as the product ages and grows.

4.2   Defect Prevalence

Figure 2 shows the number of corrected defects per release. The upper (red) line is the total number of corrected defects, the middle (green) line is the number of defect corrections that are new to the release, and the lower (blue) line is the ratio between the defects new to the release and the size in kLOC of the production code base.

The defects in this statistic include those found by customers in the field, internal testing organizations during system verification, and those found by the developers after the release of a feature. Defects found by developers during the development of a feature are not included. No goals or penalties related to the number of found defects in the product have been used by the organization, though goals related to the defect response time have been used. Thus, it is unlikely that developers have refrained from issuing defect reports in order to fulfill some target objective.

It is quite evident from the picture that the ratio of defects was higher at the beginning of the product lifecycle when there were few lines of production code, and none or few integration tests. It is also quite evident that some releases contain more corrections than others. There are two reasons for this: Some releases (e.g. R24 and R26) contained many corrections from customer branches, which was then integrated into the main branch. Some releases (e.g. R25) was made very close in time to the prior release, causing it to contain fewer changes. Further analysis of the defect origin is deferred to another paper.

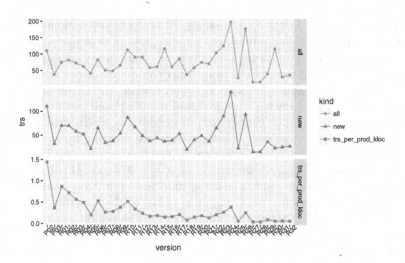

Fig. 2. Number and ratio of corrected defects for different versions. (Color figure online)

4.3 Changes to the Code Base

By using *git diff* to analyze files changed in each version, it is possible to get an overview of the changes in the code base. It should be noted that this is only the "net change", as this statistic does not capture files that have changed multiple times between versions. Also, lines are reported regardless of whether it is a code or comment line, and a changed line is counted as both an added line and a removed line.

On average, between versions, production code have added 28372 lines and removed/changed 14535 lines in 884 files, unit tests have added 32891 lines and removed/changed 12934 lines in 565 files, and integration tests have added 75005 lines and removed/changed 39424 in 2530 files. This is another way of illustrating that changes to the integration tests dominate over the production and unit test code.

4.4 Guiding Principle: Test Fast, Test in Layers

While the ATDD and TDD processes were encouraged, explained and exercised during onboarding of new developers, it was still up to each developer to do their tasks in the order they preferred. Thus, it is likely that some developers followed other processes, such as Incremental Test-Last (ITL) [6]. The common ground between these two processes is that tests should be developed as close (organizational and temporal) to the production code as possible, and refactorings should be performed when all tests succeed. This is in contrast to a more traditional "Design-Implement-Test" approach, where typically the tests are developed once all, or most functionality is implemented.

The organization actively required that tests were developed as the requirements were implemented. No feature was allowed into the product without having the required supporting test base. Also, there were continuous discussions among developers, how a feature should best be verified, and what things that were the most important to verify. As is shown in the defect statistics, Fig. 2, the integration test base helped limit the number of defects as the product has grown. One of the consequences of this principle is that the amount of test code will grow, in parallel with the growth of the production code. We see in the reported statistics that both the unit tests and the integration tests grow faster than the production code.

Both the number of files and the number of lines of integration tests is much greater than the corresponding metrics for production and unit testing code. In part, this stems from the use of XML as a specification language for the integration tests.

One obvious benefit of having a separate language for integration tests is that it is possible to enforce certain rules, by only implementing wanted features in the language executor. For instance, in the current integration test language, there is no support for conditional branches and only limited support for iterative loops. Another benefit is that developers specifying the integration tests have a clear line between the production code/unit tests and the integration tests. They can safely ignore the Java syntax and features in the Java language.

The most severe disadvantage of the separate integration test language is that the lack of effective module support causes the number of lines of integration tests to grow faster than the production code and unit test code. Another disadvantage is that there is no IDE support, such as code completion, refactoring or debugging support, out of the box. Thus, trivial transformations or reports such as *rename method*, or *find usages* becomes difficult for developers not well versed in file system and text processing tools such as *find*, *grep*, *awk* or *perl*. Due to the lack of code completion, there is also the risk of longer development times, and developers being unaware of similar functions for setting up the scenarios.

5   Implications for Research and Practice

As can be devised from the statistics shown in Sect. 4, the product currently consists of considerably more lines of test code than production code. In order to be able to work efficiently and develop with speed, it is imperative that this test code is kept clean and undergoes a similar refactoring scheme as the production code. A design principle used when developing test cases is that each test should be "self-contained", and "self-specified". Each test case should specify its required state, and asserts should reference this state, and not obscure references to other "magic numbers". The disadvantage of "the self-containment principle" is that naive developers may copy code, instead of extracting sections into methods or modules.

Care has to be taken when refactoring test code. In particular, it is important that the principles of *Arrange, Act, Assert* continues to hold for each test. Also, each test case should continue asserting everything it asserted before the refactoring, to avoid causing the refactored test case to be more lenient than the original one. The *Arrange* phase, however, should be as lenient as possible, only specifying the minimal state required to make the test succeed. Different initial states are typically referred to as fixtures, and to avoid undue repetition, it is important to keep track of which fixtures that are already available when writing new test cases.

A solution to the test refactoring problem is to introduce known errors in the production code while refactoring the test code, checking that both the old and new test cases catch the introduced errors. Once a satisfactory refactoring has been completed, the new, refactored test case is committed, and the introduced errors reverted, leaving the original (non-faulty) production code. This field should be studied more thoroughly, e.g., whether the refactoring validation process can be automated, or if some static rules could be devised.

References

1. Beck, K.: Extreme Programming Explained: Embrace Change. Addison-Wesley Longman Publishing Co., Inc., Boston (1999)
2. Beck, K.: Test Driven Development: By Example. Addison-Wesley Longman Publishing Co., Inc., Boston (2002)
3. Blakstad, S., Allen, R.: FinTech Revolution. Springer, Cham (2018). https://doi.org/10.1007/978-3-319-76014-8. https://books.google.se/books?id=0_VeDwAAQBAJ
4. Cohn, M.: Succeeding with Agile: Software Development Using Scrum, 1st edn. Addison-Wesley Professional, Boston (2009)
5. Erdogmus, H., Morisio, M., Torchiano, M.: On the effectiveness of the test-first approach to programming. IEEE Trans. Soft Eng. **31**(3), 226–237 (2005)
6. Fucci, D., Erdogmus, H., Turhan, B., Oivo, M., Juristo, N.: A dissection of the test-driven development process: does it really matter to test-first or to test-last? IEEE Trans. Softw. Eng. **43**(7), 597–614 (2017). https://doi.org/10.1109/TSE.2016.2616877
7. Gai, K., Qiu, M., Sun, X.: A survey on FinTech. J. Netw. Comput. Appl. **103**, 262–273 (2018). https://doi.org/10.1016/j.jnca.2017.10.011
8. Haugset, B., Hanssen, G.K.: Automated acceptance testing: a literature review and an industrial case study. In: Agile 2008 Conference, Toronto, Canada, pp. 27–38 (2008)
9. Lee, I., Shin, Y.J.: Fintech Ecosystem, business models, investment decisions, and challenges. Bus. Horiz. **61**(1), 35–46 (2018). https://doi.org/10.1016/j.bushor.2017.09.003. http://www.sciencedirect.com/science/article/pii/S0007681317301246
10. Maximilien, E.M., Williams, L.: Assessing test-driven development at IBM. In: 25th International Conference on Software Engineering, Portland, OR USA, vol. 6, pp. 564–569 (2003)
11. Melnik, G.I.: Empirical analyses of executable acceptance test driven development. Ph.D. thesis, University of Calgary, Calgary, Canada (2007)
12. Nagappan, N., Maximilien, E.M., Bhat, T., Williams, L.: Realizing quality improvement through test driven development: results and experiences of four industrial teams. Empir. Soft Eng. **13**(3), 289–302 (2008)
13. Pugh, K.: Lean-Agile Acceptance Test Driven Development : Better Software Through Collaboration. Addison-Wesley, Boston (2010)

Does the Performance of TDD Hold Across Software Companies and Premises? A Group of Industrial Experiments on TDD

Adrian Santos[1]([✉]), Janne Järvinen[2], Jari Partanen[3], Markku Oivo[1], and Natalia Juristo[4]

[1] M3S (M-Group), ITEE University of Oulu, Oulu, Finland
{adrian.santos.parrilla,markku.oivo}@oulu.fi
[2] F-Secure, Oulu, Finland
janne.jarvinen@f-secure.com
[3] Bittium, Oulu, Finland
jari.partanen@bittium.com
[4] Escuela Técnica Superior de Ingenieros Informáticos,
Universidad Politécnica de Madrid, Madrid, Spain
natalia@fi.upm.es

Abstract. Test-Driven Development (TDD) has been claimed to increase external software quality. However, the extent to which TDD increases external quality has been seldom studied in industrial experiments. We conduct four industrial experiments in two different companies to evaluate the performance of TDD on external quality. We study whether the performance of TDD holds across the premises of the same company and across companies. We identify participant-level characteristics impacting results. Iterative-Test Last (ITL), the reverse approach of TDD, outperforms TDD in three out of four premises. ITL outperforms TDD in both companies. The larger the experience with unit testing and testing tools, the larger the difference in performance between ITL and TDD (in favour of ITL). Technological environment (i.e., programming language and testing tool) seems not to impact results. Evaluating participant-level characteristics impacting results in industrial experiments may ease the understanding of TDD's performance in realistic settings.

Keywords: Experiment · Industry · Quality
Test-Driven Development · Company

1 Introduction

TDD is an agile development approach that enforces the construction of software systems by means of short and iterative testing-coding cycles—contrary to traditional approaches, where coding is usually performed before testing, coding and

M. Kuhrmann et al. (Eds.): PROFES 2018, LNCS 11271, pp. 227–242, 2018.
https://doi.org/10.1007/978-3-030-03673-7_17

testing are rarely interleaved, and testing is commonly performed after the whole system has been developed [1]. These short and iterative testing-coding cycles are, according to its proponents [1], the main reason behind TDD's superiority over traditional approaches (e.g., Waterfall) with regard to software quality. Even though the performance of TDD on various software quality attributes [2] has been studied before [3–9], external quality seems to be the most investigated so far. External quality is usually considered in the TDD literature as the proportion of test cases that successfully pass from a battery of tests specifically built for testing the software system under development.[1]

Several industrial case studies and surveys support the superiority of TDD over traditional approaches with regard to external software quality [3–6]. However, the extent to which TDD outperforms control approaches with regard to external quality varies largely from study to study [10,11]. This may be due to the technological environments on which studies are run or due the characteristics of the subjects participating in the studies (e.g., professional experience, skills, background, etc.). Unfortunately, despite the alleged benefits of industrial experiments (e.g., making causality claims on technology performance in realistic settings [12,13], increasing internal validity compared to industrial case studies or surveys [14], etc.), only two of the studies conducted so far on TDD— evaluating external quality—are industrial experiments (i.e., [15,16]). Unfortunately, in none of them it is possible isolating the effects of TDD on external quality. This led Munir et al. to claim in one of the latest secondary studies conducted on TDD [3]: *"strong indications are obtained that external quality is positively influenced, which has to be further substantiated by industry experiments..."*.

Along this article we aim to answer the following **research questions** with regard to the performance of TDD on external quality:

- Does TDD outperform control approaches in industrial experiments as in case studies and surveys?
- Does the performance of TDD hold across premises within the same company and across companies?

To answer these questions we conduct a group of four industrial experiments evaluating the effects of TDD and ITL on external quality. We run three experiments at F-Secure—a multinational security and digital privacy company [17]—and one at Bittium—a multinational telecommunications company. We first analyze all the experiments individually, and then, we combine their results by means of meta-analysis [18]. Finally, we assess the extent to which results hold across premises within the same company and across companies and identify participant-level characteristics that may be behind the variability of results observed. Throughout this research, we made several **findings**:

---

[1] For simplicity's sake, along the rest of the article we refer to external quality and quality interchangeably.

Key findings

- According to our results, ITL outperforms TDD for novices on TDD. Results hold across the two companies that we have studied.
- The extent to which ITL outperforms TDD looks dependent upon participant-level characteristics. In particular, the larger the experience with unit testing and testing tools, the larger the difference in performance between ITL and TDD (in favour of ITL).
- ITL outperforms TDD in our group of industrial experiments. This is contrary to what has been previously claimed in case studies and surveys. This difference of results may have emerged due to the lack of previous familiarity of our participants with the TDD process.

The main **contributions** of this paper are a *comparison of the results achieved in four industrial experiments on TDD* and *the first assessment of participant-level characteristics impacting the performance of TDD across software industries*. As a secondary contribution we offer a compilation of the primary studies that evaluate the effects of TDD on external quality in industry and a comparison of F-Secure and Bittium's results with those.

Along this study we argue that despite the long years of research on TDD, almost none of the available studies has evaluated the effects of TDD on quality in industrial experiments. Industrial experiments not only allow to assess the effects of TDD on quality in realistic environments, but also, the effect of practitioners' characteristics on TDD's performance. In view of this, we suggest:

Actionable results

- The impact of *participant-level characteristics* (e.g., experience with programming, unit testing, etc.) should be studied to learn about the practitioners' characteristics that impact TDD's performance.
- As industrial experiments' sample sizes tend to be small, *replications* shall be conducted and analyzed jointly to detect participant-level characteristics impacting results.
- Participants' previous familiarity with more traditional development approaches (e.g., ITL) may distort the evaluation of TDD's performance. In view of this, we suggest to assess the performance of TDD in further occasions in industrial *between-subjects experiments*—being the subjects in each group either experts in TDD, or experts in ITL, respectively.

Paper Organization. In Sect. 2 we portray the related work of this study. In Sect. 3 we outline the characteristics of our group of experiments. In Sect. 4 we conduct the analysis of our group of experiments. Then, in Sect. 5 we discuss the results of our group of experiments and put them in perspective. Finally, in Sect. 6 we outline the threats to validity of our study, and then in Sect. 7 the conclusions.

2   Related Work

To gather a list of primary studies evaluating the effects of TDD on external quality in industrial settings, we go over the secondary studies conducted so far on TDD [3–9]. Table 1 shows the list of the primary studies that we identified, their research methods (i.e., case studies, surveys or controlled experiments following Wohlin et al. definitions [14]) and their results (i.e., the difference in performance between TDD and the control approach).

Table 1. TDD effects on quality in industrial studies.

Method	Reference	Result
Case study	[10, 11, 19–29]	+
Survey	[30, 31]	+
Experiment	[15]	+
	[16]	?

As it can be seen in Table 1, all studies—but one experiment [16]—report positive results (i.e., TDD is superior to the control approach).

Even though all the *case studies* report that TDD outperforms control approaches with regard to quality, wildly heterogeneous improvements with TDD over control approaches are claimed [3–9]: ranging from improvements as low as 18% [10], to improvements as high as 50% [11,25]. Such heterogeneity of results may have emerged due the different technological environments where case studies were run or the characteristics of the participants involved: from environments where JUnit and Java were used to develop systems from scratch by accountants, lecturers or expert programmers [10] to environments where C++ and CUnitTest were used to increase the functionality of legacy systems by groups of intermediate and novice developers [21].

With regard to the evidence obtained in *surveys*, one found that TDD outperformed industry averages on quality [31] and another found that TDD helps to achieve greater quality than control approaches [30]. Again, participants' characteristics varied largely across studies: from largely experienced practitioners [31] to developers with almost no previous experience in programming [30]. Despite their advantages for obtaining preliminary evidence [14], case studies and surveys are usually included within the lowest positions in hierarchies of evidence [32,33] due to their inability to prove causality. This is so because in such empirical studies other elements rather than the technologies themselves may be the cause of results (e.g., external factors in case studies or personal opinions in surveys). This is where experiments have their natural fit [14].

From the two *experiments* conducted so far in industry [15,16], the first experiment [16] reports inconclusive results (as all subjects are able to achieved the maximum quality regardless of the development approach being applied).

The second experiment [15] evaluated the effects of TDD and pair-programming together and thus, the effects of TDD cannot be isolated from those of pair-programming (i.e., TDD and pair-programming effects are confounded).

As a summary of the evidence collected so far on TDD with regard to external quality in industrial settings, most studies are either surveys or case studies. In those, a large heterogeneity of results materialized: either due to differences across technology environments or participants' characteristics. Besides, in the pair of experiments available, certain shortcomings did not allow to assess the extent to which TDD affects quality. In turn, the question of how does TDD influence quality in industrial experiments is still unanswered, since the only type of empirical study able to prove causality are experiments [14].

We previously ran a series of *identical experiments* at F-Secure [17] and got opposite results to those obtained in industrial case studies and surveys. In particular, according to the results obtained at F-Secure, ITL outperformed TDD. However, F-Secure's experiments are just the first-step towards proving causality. In particular, F-Secure's experiments' results may be artifactual (i.e., caused by the technological environment of the experiment) or have occurred just by chance [34]. Thus, in this study we run a replication of F-Secure's experiment at a different company (i.e., Bittium) changing the technological environment to validate our previous results. In addition, we meta-analyze their results together with the aim of increasing the reliability of the joint findings and study the differences of results across companies.

3   Group of Experiments

We conducted a total of four experiments to evaluate the effects of TDD on quality. Three *exact replications* were run at F-Secure (each one at a different location: Helsinki, Kuala-Lumpur and Oulu). Differences across F-Secure's experiments' results and the participant-level characteristics that may have led to such differences were not investigated before. We conducted a *close replication* at Bittium. We introduced as few changes as required by Bittium's managers (i.e., changes in the programming language and the testing tool) with the aim of minimizing the risk of confounding effects across experiments. Thus, Bittium's experiment is a *close replication* of F-Secure's. This should increase the reliability of the joint findings, ease the comparison of results across companies, and at the same time, facilitate the elicitation of practitioners' characteristics impacting TDD's performance across software industries.

3.1   Dependent and Independent Variables

The independent variable across all the experiments is **development approach**, with TDD and ITL as treatments. ITL was defined as the reverse-order approach of TDD following Erdogmus et al. [35].

The dependent variable across all the experiments is **external quality**. As commonly done in the TDD literature, we measure external quality as the *percentage* of test cases that successfully pass from a battery of tests that we specifically built for testing participants' solutions. Specifically, we measure external quality as:

$$QLTY = \frac{\#Test\ Cases(Pass)}{\#Test\ Cases(All)} * 100$$

3.2 Experimental Settings

Seminars on TDD were conducted at each site. An experiment was embedded within each seminar. Table 2 summarizes the settings of the experiments conducted at F-Secure and Bittium (changes across companies' settings in *italics*).

Table 2. Experiments' settings: F-Secure and Bittium.

Aspect	Values
Factors	Development approach
Treatments	TDD vs ITL
Response variables	QLTY
Design	AB repeated-measures
Training	TDD course
Training duration	3 days/6 h
Experiment duration	2.25 h
Programming language	F-Secure: *Java*; Bittium: *C++*
Unit testing tool	F-Secure: *JUnit*; Bittium: *GTest*

The trade-off assessment of the experimental design, the specification of the instruments and the experimental tasks, and an in-depth discussion of the threats to validity of F-Secure's experiments can be found elsewhere [17].

3.3 Subjects

Subjects were handed a survey some days before the experiment. The survey contained a series of ordinal-scale (i.e., inexperienced, novice, intermediate and expert) self-assessment questions with regard to their experience with programming, unit testing and the programming language and testing tool used during the experiment.[2] Table 3 shows the mean—and standard deviations—of the participants' experiences with programming, the programming language, unit testing and the testing tool used within the experiment (1–4, for inexperienced, novice, intermediate and experts, respectively).[3]

---

[2] The survey and its results were published elsewhere [36].

[3] For simplicity's sake, we consider the variables measured along the survey as continuous. This approach is commonly followed in other disciplines [37].

Table 3. Mean and standard deviation of experiences across experiments.

Experiment	N	Programming	Prog. language	Unit testing	Testing tool
F-Secure H	6	3.67 (0.52)	2.33 (1.21)	2.17 (0.98)	2.17 (1.17)
F-Secure K	11	2.91 (0.7)	1.82 (0.87)	1.64 (0.5)	1.27 (0.47)
F-Secure O	7	3.29 (0.76)	2.71 (1.11)	2.71 (0.76)	2 (0.82)
Bittium	9	3 (0.87)	2.89 (0.93)	1.67 (0.87)	1 (0)

To ease the interpretation of the data presented in Table 3, we provide in Fig. 1 a profile-plot showing the mean of the experiences of the participants in each experiment.

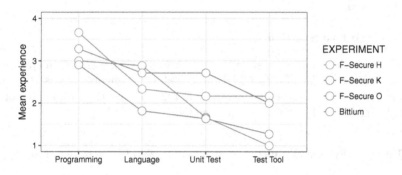

Fig. 1. Profile-plot for experiences across experiments.

As it can be seen in Fig. 1, F-Secure H's participants are the most experienced with programming. Besides, F-Secure O and Bittium's participants seem the most experienced with the programming language used during the experiment. Finally, subjects across all experiments have lower experiences with unit testing and testing tools than with programming or the programming language used during the experiment. In general, those with the higher experience in unit testing and testing tools tend to be the most senior professionals. Overall, our group of experiments is formed by *an heterogeneous population of TDD novices with relatively low experience in unit testing and testing tools.*

3.4 Analysis Approach

First, we provide the *descriptive statistics* (i.e., number of data-points, mean, median and standard deviation) of ITL and TDD across the experiments. Then, we provide a profile plot for easing the understanding of the data.

Afterwards, we analyze each experiment *individually* with an identical statistical test: a repeated measures analysis of variance (RM ANOVA) [38]. The

RM ANOVA assumes that the residuals are normally distributed [38]. We check the normality assumption by means of the Shapiro-Wilk test [38].

Then, with the aim of providing a *joint result*, we combine the results of the RM ANOVAs jointly by means of a random-effects meta-analysis following the steps outlined by Burke et al. [39]. We also perform a *sub-group meta-analysis* [18] to assess the extent to which results hold across companies (i.e., F-Secure vs. Bittium).

Finally, with the aim of identifying participant-level characteristics influencing results, we perform a series of "post hoc" analyses—one per experience variable (i.e., programming experience, programming language experience, unit testing experience and testing tool experience). We follow Fisher et al.'s guidelines [40] to identify participant-level characteristics impacting results.

4 Analysis

4.1 Descriptive Statistics

Table 4 shows the descriptive statistics (i.e., sample size, mean, standard deviations and medians) for ITL and TDD across all experiments. To ease the interpretation of the data presented in Table 4, Fig. 2 shows the profile-plot of the means for ITL and TDD across experiments.

Table 4. Descriptive statistics for quality: ITL vs TDD across experiments.

Experiment	Treatment	N	Mean	SD	Median
F-Secure H	ITL	6	30.71	36.58	24.16
	TDD	5	18.48	7.30	16.67
F-Secure K	ITL	11	22.17	20.44	17.98
	TDD	11	13.98	10.21	13.64
F-Secure O	ITL	7	16.05	20.81	7.87
	TDD	7	16.99	15.08	19.70
Bittium	ITL	9	15.45	18.52	5.75
	TDD	9	2.47	0.26	2.38

As it can be seen in Table 4, TDD's mean scores go from as high as $M = 18.48$ in F-Secure H to as low as $M = 2.47$ in Bittium. Bittium's participants achieved the lower ITL's mean scores ($M = 15.45$) while F-Secure H obtained the largest ($M = 30.71$). Moreover, while F-Secure H, F-Secure K and Bittium's participants showed lower mean performance with TDD than with ITL (i.e., negative slope in Fig. 2), F-Secure O participants show an almost similar performance with TDD and ITL (even though TDD slightly outperforms ITL).

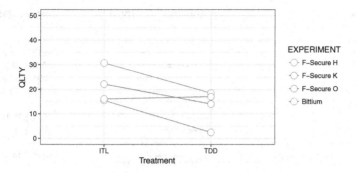

Fig. 2. Profile-plot for ITL and TDD across experiments.

4.2   Individual Analyses

Table 5 shows the results of analyzing each experiment with a RM ANOVA.[4]

Table 5. Results across experiments.

Experiment	N	Estimate	SE	t-value	p-value	Significance
F-Secure H	5	−14.12	14.17	−0.99	0.345	✗
F-Secure K	11	−8.18	5.98	−1.37	0.186	✗
F-Secure O	7	0.93	5.68	0.16	0.871	✗
Bittium	9	−12.98	6.20	−2.09	0.053	✗

As it can be seen in Table 5, ITL outperforms TDD in three out of four experiments (as treatment estimates are negative in F-Secure H, F-Secure K and Bittium). In addition, the difference in performance between them is not statistically significant in any experiment (even though Bittium's is almost statistically significant).

4.3   Joint Result and Sub-group Meta-analysis

After analyzing each experiment individually, we aggregate their results by means of a random effects meta-analysis [18]. Figure 3 shows the results of the meta-analysis performed (and the results of the sub-group meta-analysis performed for each company).

According to the joint result (see the black diamond at the bottom of Fig. 3), *ITL outperforms TDD to a small* ($M = −6.96$; $95\%CI = (−14.47, 0.54)$) and *non-statistically significant extent* (as the 95% CI crosses 0). Besides, Bittium's

---

[4] The normality assumption is met in all experiments according to the Shapiro-Wilk test [38].

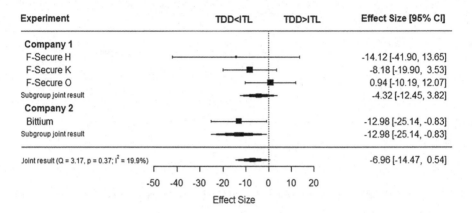

Fig. 3. Forest-plot: TDD vs ITL.

results seem within the realm of those of F-Secure (as Bittium's effect size is even smaller in *magnitude* than that of F-Secure H). In addition, notice how F-Secure's joint effect size ($M = -4.32$; $95\%CI = (-12.45, 3.82)$) overlaps with that of Bittium ($M = -12.98$; $95\%CI = (-12.45, 3.82)$). In view of this, *results hold across companies: TDD does not increase quality (compared to ITL) in none of the companies.* In turn, as results hold across companies, we conclude, *technological environment* (e.g., Java and JUnit at F-Secure and C++ and GTest at Bittium) *seems not to impact results.*

Finally, even though results hold across companies, *heterogeneity emerged* when aggregating results together ($I^2 = 19.9\%$). As heterogeneous results emerged even among the identical experiments conducted at F-Secure (see that F-Secure O's results are observably different that those of F-Secure H and K), we hypothesize, *participant-level characteristics* (i.e., experience with programming, programming languages, unit testing or testing tools) *may be behind the heterogeneity of results detected.*

4.4   Post-hoc Analysis: Developers' Characteristics

We performed four different RM ANOVAs (one per experience variable) to assess the effects of participant-level experiences on results. Table 6 shows the estimates and standard errors provided by the RM ANOVAs fitted to assess the effects of the experience variables on results.

Table 6 can be read as the impact of one unit increase in experience on the performance achieved with TDD *beyond the performance achieved with ITL.* For example, per each unit increase in experience with the testing tool used (see the row "Testing Tool" in Table 6), the performance with TDD decreases in $M = -6.80$; $SE = 5.66$ units. Thus, the larger the experience with the testing tool (ranging between 1 to 4), the lower the performance with TDD in comparison with the performance achieved with ITL. Notice how in comparison with the joint result of our group of experiments (i.e., $M = -6.96$ according to the results

Table 6. Participant-level characteristics impact on TDD's performance.

Factor	Estimate	SE	t-value	p-value	Significance
Programming	0.74	5.32	0.13	0.89	✗
Language	0.78	3.94	0.19	0.84	✗
Unit testing	−3.54	5.09	−0.69	0.49	✗
Testing tool	−6.80	5.66	−1.19	0.24	✗

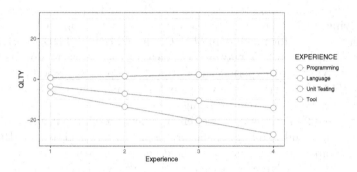

Fig. 4. Participant-level characteristics impact on TDD's performance.

achieved in the previous section), the decrease in quality per unit increase in experience with the testing tool seems considerable (i.e., almost a 1:1 ratio). Thus, experience with the testing tool seems to be a relevant *moderator* of the effects of TDD. With the aim of easing the understanding of results, Fig. 4 shows the regression lines corresponding to the estimates of Table 6.[5]

As it can be seen in Fig. 4, the experience with programming or programming languages seems not to impact results (as lines seem flat along all the experience levels). However, *the larger the experience with unit testing or the testing tool, the lower the performance with TDD* in comparison with the performance achieved with ITL (as the lines have a downward slope).

5   Discussion

ITL outperformed TDD in three out of four experiments (i.e., F-Secure H, F-Secure K and Bittium). Besides, after aggregating their results together, still ITL slightly outperformed TDD. The results of our group of experiments cannot be compared with those of any other industrial experiment (as the couple of experiments published so far do not allow to isolate the effects of TDD on quality). However, our results can be compared with those of industrial case studies and surveys [3–9]. Long story short, our results are opposite to those

---

[5] The regression lines for "Programming" and "Language" partially overlap and thus, only that of "Language" is visible.

of case studies and surveys: while we observed a slight decrease in the performance achieved with TDD over ITL, surveys and case studies reported large improvements with TDD over control approaches. These opposite results may have emerged as our participants had no previous experience on TDD, and in turn, this may have lowered their performance with TDD in comparison with more "traditional" approaches such as ITL.

Our results also suggest that the larger the experience with unit testing and testing tools (and thus, the potentially larger the experience with more traditional approaches including testing such as ITL), the larger the drop in quality when applying TDD (the recently learned development approach). In view of this, we suggest that for making an objective evaluation of TDD's performance in industrial experiments, it may be necessary to run between-subjects experiments with two similarly experienced treatment groups (e.g., experts in TDD vs. experts in ITL). Otherwise, the development approach in which the participants are more experienced may end up being favoured.

Finally, the different technological environments used in our group of experiments (i.e., Java and JUnit for F-Secure, and C++ and GTest for Bittium), seem not to impact results (as results hold across companies). In view of this, and also in view of the large heterogeneity of results observed across case studies and surveys, we hypothesize, participant-level characteristics may be behind the large heterogeneity of results observed in literature.

6   Threats to Validity

Conclusion validity concerns the statistical analysis of results [14]. We used commonly applied statistical techniques to analyze the data (i.e., RM ANOVA [38] and random-effects meta-analysis [18]). In addition, the required data assumptions (i.e., normality assumption [38]) were assessed before interpreting the results of the RM ANOVA. In view of this, we do not expect any threat to conclusion validity to impact our results.

Internal validity is the extent to which the detected effects are caused by the treatments and not by other variables beyond researcher's control [14]. There is a potential maturation threat: seminars were offered as a three-day training course on TDD and contained multiple exercises and experimental laboratories. Thus, factors such as tiredness or inattention might have materialized. In order to minimize this threat we ensured that subjects were given enough breaks. Treatment leakage may have influenced results: subjects might have increased their performance with TDD because they learned something (i.e., slicing) in the previous session while applying ITL. However, treatment leakage seems not to have materialized: ITL outperformed TDD in three out of four experiments.

Construct validity refers to the correctness in the mapping between the theoretical constructs under investigation and the operationalizations of the variables in the study. As usual in SE experiments, the study suffers from the mono-operation bias (as only test cases were used to measure external quality). Conformance to the development approaches is one of the notorious threats to validity in most SE experiments. This threat was minimized by encouraging subjects to adhere as closely as possible to the development approaches taught during the seminar. We complemented such encouragement with visual supervision.

External validity relates to the possibility of generalizing results beyond the objects and subjects involved in the study [14]. As usual in SE experiments, it was not possible to obtain random samples from the population under study: convenience sampling was used in all experiments. Experiments were conducted with toy-tasks. This may limit the generalizability of the findings. However, we expect results to be representative for professionals who are starting to learn the TDD process coding toy-tasks.

7   Conclusion

TDD has been claimed to increase external quality over traditional approaches in industrial case studies and surveys [3–9]. However, the extent to which TDD performs in industrial experiments has been seldom studied. Industrial experiments allow to assess not just the performance of TDD in realistic settings, but also the effects of participant-level characteristics on TDD's performance.

We conducted a group of four industrial experiments with TDD novices to assess the extent to which TDD performs in industrial settings. ITL slightly outperformed TDD in three out of four experiments. When aggregating their results together by means of meta-analysis, ITL still slightly outperformed TDD. Our results are opposite to those found in industrial case studies and surveys. These different results may have emerged due to the lack of previous familiarity of our experiments' participants with the TDD process.

Finally, results held across the two companies that we studied. In view of this, companies' technological environments seemed not to impact results. However, the extent to which ITL outperformed TDD looked dependent upon participants' characteristics (as heterogeneity materialized even across identical experiments). According to our results, the larger the experience with unit testing and testing tools (and thus, the potentially larger experience with more traditional approaches), the larger the drop in performance with TDD over the performance achieved with ITL. In view of this, we suggest, the development approach in which subjects are more experienced may end up being favoured in controlled experiments. With the aim of tackling this shortcoming, we suggest to run between-subjects experiments evaluating the performance of TDD and control approaches with similarly experienced subjects across groups.

Once again in SE [41], a large number of elements seem to impact the performance of a technology (in this case TDD) in realistic settings. In this research we want to make a call to run experiments in industry and to assess not just the effects of TDD, but also, disentangle the characteristics of the participants that make TDD more or less desirable. Unfortunately, as SE industrial experiments tend to be small, individual experiments may be under-powered for detecting participant-level characteristics impacting results [42]. In view of this, multiple replications may be required to be conducted and analyzed jointly (as access to the raw-data is a requirement to elicit participant-level characteristics [43]). Are we still going to think that one size fits all? Or instead, are we going to learn about the characteristics that make practitioners more prone to benefiting from the application of TDD? After all, we are still at the beginning of understanding how TDD works in industrial settings [44].

Acknowledgments. This research was developed with the support of the Spanish Ministry of Science and Innovation project TIN2014-60490-P.

References

1. Beck, K.: Test-Driven Development: By Example. Addison-Wesley Professional (2003)
2. ISO: ISO/IEC 25010:2011 (2011)
3. Munir, H., Moayyed, M., Petersen, K.: Considering rigor and relevance when evaluating test driven development: a systematic review. Inf. Softw. Technol. **56**(4), 375–394 (2014)
4. Rafique, Y., Mišić, V.B.: The effects of test-driven development on external quality and productivity: a meta-analysis. IEEE Trans. Softw. Eng. **39**(6), 835–856 (2013)
5. Bissi, W., Neto, A.G.S.S., Emer, M.C.F.P.: The effects of test driven development on internal quality, external quality and productivity: a systematic review. Inf. Softw. Technol. **74**, 45–54 (2016)
6. Kollanus, S.: Test-driven development-still a promising approach? In: Seventh International Conference on the Quality of Information and Communications Technology (QUATIC), pp. 403–408. IEEE (2010)
7. Shull, F., Melnik, G., Turhan, B., Layman, L., Diep, M., Erdogmus, H.: What do we know about test-driven development? IEEE Softw. **27**(6), 16–19 (2010)
8. Causevic, A., Sundmark, D., Punnekkat, S.: Factors limiting industrial adoption of test driven development: a systematic review. In: IEEE Fourth International Conference on Software Testing, Verification and Validation (ICST), pp. 337–346. IEEE (2011)
9. Mäkinen, S., Münch, J.: Effects of test-driven development: a comparative analysis of empirical studies. In: Winkler, D., Biffl, S., Bergsmann, J. (eds.) SWQD 2014. LNBIP, vol. 166, pp. 155–169. Springer, Cham (2014). https://doi.org/10.1007/978-3-319-03602-1_10
10. McDaid, K., Rust, A., Bishop, B.: Test-driven development: can it work for spreadsheets? In: Proceedings of the 4th International Workshop on End-User Software Engineering, pp. 25–29. ACM (2008)
11. Maximilien, E.M., Williams, L.: Assessing test-driven development at IBM. In: Proceedings of the 25th International Conference on Software Engineering, pp. 564–569. IEEE (2003)
12. Sjoberg, D.I., et al.: Conducting realistic experiments in software engineering. In: Proceedings of the International Symposium on Empirical Software Engineering, pp. 17–26. IEEE (2002)
13. Sjøberg, D.I.K., et al.: Challenges and recommendations when increasing the realism of controlled software engineering experiments. In: Conradi, R., Wang, A.I. (eds.) Empirical Methods and Studies in Software Engineering. LNCS, vol. 2765, pp. 24–38. Springer, Heidelberg (2003). https://doi.org/10.1007/978-3-540-45143-3_3

14. Wohlin, C., Runeson, P., Höst, M., Ohlsson, M.C., Regnell, B., Wesslén, A.: Experimentation in Software Engineering. Springer, Heidelberg (2012). https://doi.org/10.1007/978-3-642-29044-2
15. George, B., Williams, L.: A structured experiment of test-driven development. Inf. Softw. Technol. **46**(5), 337–342 (2004)
16. Geras, A., Smith, M., Miller, J.: A prototype empirical evaluation of test driven development. In: Proceedings of the 10th International Symposium on Software Metrics, pp. 405–416. IEEE (2004)
17. Tosun, A., et al.: An industry experiment on the effects of test-driven development on external quality and productivity. Empir. Softw. Eng. **22**(6), 2763–2805 (2017)
18. Borenstein, M., Hedges, L.V., Higgins, J.P., Rothstein, H.R.: Introduction to Meta-analysis. Wiley, Chichester (2011)
19. Bannerman, S., Martin, A.: A multiple comparative study of test-with development product changes and their effects on team speed and product quality. Empir. Softw. Eng. **16**(2), 177–210 (2011)
20. Siniaalto, M., Abrahamsson, P.: Does test-driven development improve the program code? Alarming results from a comparative case study. In: Meyer, B., Nawrocki, J.R., Walter, B. (eds.) CEE-SET 2007. LNCS, vol. 5082, pp. 143–156. Springer, Heidelberg (2008). https://doi.org/10.1007/978-3-540-85279-7_12
21. Bhat, T., Nagappan, N.: Evaluating the efficacy of test-driven development: industrial case studies. In: Proceedings of the 2006 ACM/IEEE International Symposium on Empirical Software Engineering, pp. 356–363. ACM (2006)
22. Ynchausti, R.A.: Integrating unit testing into a software development teams process. In: XP 2001, pp. 84–87 (2001)
23. Damm, L.-O., Lundberg, L.: Quality impact of introducing component-level test automation and test-driven development. In: Abrahamsson, P., Baddoo, N., Margaria, T., Messnarz, R. (eds.) EuroSPI 2007. LNCS, vol. 4764, pp. 187–199. Springer, Heidelberg (2007). https://doi.org/10.1007/978-3-540-75381-0_17
24. Nagappan, N., Maximilien, E.M., Bhat, T., Williams, L.: Realizing quality improvement through test driven development: results and experiences of four industrial teams. Empir. Softw. Eng. **13**(3), 289–302 (2008)
25. Damm, L.O., Lundberg, L.: Results from introducing component-level test automation and test-driven development. J. Syst. Softw. **79**(7), 1001–1014 (2006)
26. Lui, K.M., Chan, K.C.C.: Test driven development and software process improvement in China. In: Eckstein, J., Baumeister, H. (eds.) XP 2004. LNCS, vol. 3092, pp. 219–222. Springer, Heidelberg (2004). https://doi.org/10.1007/978-3-540-24853-8_27
27. Williams, L., Maximilien, E.M., Vouk, M.: Test-driven development as a defect-reduction practice. In: 14th International Symposium on Software Reliability Engineering, ISSRE 2003, pp. 34–45. IEEE (2003)
28. Dogša, T., Batič, D.: The effectiveness of test-driven development: an industrial case study. Softw. Qual. J. **19**(4), 643–661 (2011)
29. Slyngstad, O.P.N., Li, J., Conradi, R., Rønneberg, H., Landre, E., Wesenberg, H.: The impact of test driven development on the evolution of a reusable framework of components-an industrial case study. In: The Third International Conference on Software Engineering Advances, ICSEA 2008, pp. 214–223. IEEE (2008)
30. Aniche, M.F., Gerosa, M.A.: Most common mistakes in test-driven development practice: results from an online survey with developers. In: Third International Conference on Software Testing, Verification, and Validation Workshops (ICSTW), pp. 469–478. IEEE (2010)

31. Sanchez, J.C., Williams, L., Maximilien, E.M.: On the sustained use of a test-driven development practice at IBM. In: Agile Conference (AGILE), pp. 5–14. IEEE (2007)
32. Dybå, T., Dingsøyr, T.: Strength of evidence in systematic reviews in software engineering. In: Proceedings of the Second ACM-IEEE International Symposium on Empirical Software Engineering and Measurement, pp. 178–187. ACM (2008)
33. Guyatt, G.H., et al.: Grade: an emerging consensus on rating quality of evidence and strength of recommendations. BMJ (Clinical research ed.) **336**(7650), 924–926 (2008)
34. Gomez, O.S., Juristo, N., Vegas, S.: Understanding replication of experiments in software engineering: a classification. Inf. Softw. Technol. **56**(8), 1033–1048 (2014)
35. Erdogmus, H., Morisio, M., Torchiano, M.: On the effectiveness of the test-first approach to programming. IEEE Trans. Softw. Eng. **31**(3), 226–237 (2005)
36. Dieste, O., Aranda, A.M., Uyaguari, F., Turhan, B., Tosun, A., Fucci, D., Oivo, M., Juristo, N.: Empirical evaluation of the effects of experience on code quality and programmer productivity: an exploratory study. Empir. Softw. Eng. **22**(5), 2457–2542 (2017)
37. Norman, G.: Likert scales, levels of measurement and the laws of statistics. Adv. Health Sci. Educ. **15**(5), 625–632 (2010)
38. Field, A.: Discovering Statistics Using IBM SPSS Statistics. Sage (2013)
39. Burke, D.L., Ensor, J., Riley, R.D.: Meta-analysis using individual participant data: one-stage and two-stage approaches, and why they may differ. Stat. Med. **36**(5), 855–875 (2017)
40. Fisher, D., Copas, A., Tierney, J., Parmar, M.: A critical review of methods for the assessment of patient-level interactions in individual participant data meta-analysis of randomized trials, and guidance for practitioners. J. Clin. Epidemiol. **64**(9), 949–967 (2011)
41. Briand, L., Bianculli, D., Nejati, S., Pastore, F., Sabetzadeh, M.: The case for context-driven software engineering research: generalizability is overrated. IEEE Softw. **34**(5), 72–75 (2017)
42. Kraemer, H.C.: Pitfalls of multisite randomized clinical trials of efficacy and effectiveness. Schizophr. Bull. **26**(3), 533 (2000)
43. Cooper, H., Patall, E.A.: The relative benefits of meta-analysis conducted with individual participant data versus aggregated data. Psychol. Methods **14**(2), 165 (2009)
44. Offutt, J.: Why don't we publish more TDD research papers? Softw. Test. Verif. Reliab. **28**(4), e1670 (2018)

Test Case Prioritization Using Test Similarities

Alireza Haghighatkhah[(✉)] , Mika Mäntylä , Markku Oivo ,
and Pasi Kuvaja

M3S Research Unit, University of Oulu, P.O. Box 3000, 90014 Oulu, Finland
{alireza.haghighatkhah,mika.mantyla,markku.oivo,pasi.kuvaja}@oulu.fi

Abstract. A classical heuristic in software testing is to reward diversity, which implies that a higher priority must be assigned to test cases that differ the most from those already prioritized. This approach is commonly known as similarity-based test prioritization (SBTP) and can be realized using a variety of techniques. The objective of our study is to investigate whether SBTP is more effective at finding defects than random permutation, as well as determine which SBTP implementations lead to better results. To achieve our objective, we implemented five different techniques from the literature and conducted an experiment using the defects4j dataset, which contains 395 real faults from six real-world open-source Java programs. Findings indicate that running the most dissimilar test cases early in the process is largely more effective than random permutation (Vargha–Delaney A [VDA]: 0.76–0.99 observed using normalized compression distance). No technique was found to be superior with respect to the effectiveness. Locality-sensitive hashing was, to a small extent, less effective than other SBTP techniques (VDA: 0.38 observed in comparison to normalized compression distance), but its speed largely outperformed the other techniques (i.e., it was approximately 5–111 times faster). Our results bring to mind the well-known adage, "don't put all your eggs in one basket". To effectively consume a limited testing budget, one should spread it evenly across different parts of the system by running the most dissimilar test cases early in the testing process.

Keywords: Test case prioritization · Regression testing
Test diversity · Test similarity

1 Introduction

The software industry is moving toward an agile, continuous delivery paradigm in which software changes are released more frequently and considerably faster than before [29]. This development paradigm has brought many benefits but posed several challenges, particularly regarding software quality [25,29]. To ensure software correctness, software developers employ regression testing (RT), which involves running a dedicated regression test suite after each revision to verify

© Springer Nature Switzerland AG 2018
M. Kuhrmann et al. (Eds.): PROFES 2018, LNCS 11271, pp. 243–259, 2018.
https://doi.org/10.1007/978-3-030-03673-7_18

that recent changes have not negatively impacted the software's functionality [4]. Industrial software-intensive systems often comprise many test cases, and the execution of these test cases require several hours or even days. For example, the JOnAS Java EE middleware requires running 43,024 test cases to verify all of its 16 configurations [21]. To improve RT processes, the software engineering literature has proposed many solutions [34]. Test case prioritization (TCP) [30] is one of these solutions; it is concerned with the ideal ordering of test cases to maximize desirable properties (i.e., early fault detection). From the fault detection viewpoint, TCP seems to be a safe approach because it does not eliminate test cases and simply permutes them within the test suite.

To increase the likelihood of detecting faults, one potential strategy is spreading the testing budget evenly across different parts of the system [11,18,23], and realizing this strategy involves utilizing a diverse set of test cases. To devise a diverse test suite, one needs to measure similarities among the test cases. The notion of similarity measurement is a subject of interest for many applications. The degree to which two objects share characteristics is called similarity, and the degree to which they differ is termed distance. In the software testing literature, a point of particular interest is quantifying similarities among test cases. For example, in coverage-based testing, coverage information has been used as a proxy to measure the similarities among test cases [18]. More recently, several other properties have been described in the literature i.e., the overlap between test paths and their coverage in model-based testing [3,12], as well as the source code of test cases [23], test input and output [16], topic models extracted from test scripts [32], and even English document of manual test cases [15].

The main intuition is that *test cases that capture the same faults tend to be more similar to each other, and test cases that capture different faults tend to be more dissimilar* [11,18,23]. The number of published empirical studies that support this intuition are growing (e.g., [1,5,7,13,15,32]). The implication for TCP is that a higher priority must be assigned to test cases that are most dissimilar to those already prioritized. This can be realized by maximizing the distances among test cases ordered in the test suite. Similarity-based test prioritization (SBTP) is a black-box static technique (i.e., it does not require the source code and execution of the system under test) that can potentially be applied, for example, where code instrumentation is too costly or impossible.

The natural question that arises is whether running the most dissimilar test cases early in the testing process improves the test suite's fault-detection capability. SBTP can be implemented in a variety of ways, such as applying different similarity metrics. Thus, a follow-up question that arises is which implementation yields the best results. A similar objective was pursued by Ledru et al. [23] in 2012. The authors conducted a comprehensive experiment on the Siemens test suite and evaluated four classical string metrics using a pairwise algorithm. This study extends prior research by investigating the effectiveness and performance of five different SBTP techniques (4 additional in comparison to Ledru et al.). These techniques rely on different similarity metrics and were selected from the literature based on the results of recent experimental studies [5,6,14,23,26].

The ultimate objective of our study is to detect regression faults early in the testing process, allowing software developers to perform RT more frequently and continuously. To achieve this objective, we conducted an experiment using the defects4j dataset [20], which contains 395 real faults from 6 real-world open-source Java programs. Findings from our study indicate that:

- When their average percentage of faults detected (APFD) are compared, test suites ordered by SBTP are largely more effective than random permutation (VDA: 0.76–0.99 observed using normalized compression distance [NCD] across all subjects), which means running the most dissimilar test cases early in the testing process improves the test suite's fault-detection capability.
- Of the 5 SBTP implementations investigated, no technique was found to be superior with respect to the effectiveness. Locality-sensitive hashing (LSH) was, to a limited extent, less effective than other SBTP techniques (VDA: 0.38 observed in comparison to NCD), but its speed largely outperformed the other techniques (i.e., it was approximately 5–111 times faster).

Our findings yield important academic and practical implications. From the academic perspective, we provide empirical evidence that supports test diversity and its impact on TCP. From the of practitioners' perspective, our results bring to mind the well-known adage, "don't put all your eggs in one basket". To effectively consume a limited testing budget, one should spread it evenly across different parts of the system by running the most dissimilar test cases early in the process. The remainder of the paper is organized as follows. Section 2 discusses the background and related works. Section 3 describes the research methodology, and Sect. 4 presents answers to the research questions. The findings are discussed in Sect. 5, and conclusions are discussed in Sect. 6.

2   Background and Related Work

2.1   Background

Figure 1 presents a general model of RT techniques. Let P be a program, P' be a modified version of the program, and T be a test suite developed for P. In the transition from P to P', a previously verified behavior of P may have become faulty in P'. RT seeks to capture regressions in P' and verify that changes to the system have not negatively impacted any previously verified functionalities. During RT, several techniques may be employed. One of the techniques is test suite minimization; it seeks to identify and permanently eliminate obsolete or redundant test cases from the test suite. Another technique, regression test selection, aims to select only the subset of test cases affected by the recent changes. TCP is concerned with the ideal ordering of test cases to maximize desirable properties (i.e., early fault detection), while test suite augmentation aims to identify newly added source code and generate new test cases accordingly.

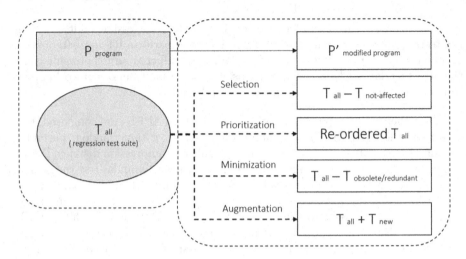

Fig. 1. General model of RT techniques

2.2 Related Work

A similarity metric, which is also known as similarity/distance function, is a metric that measures the similarity or distance (i.e., inverse similarity) between two objects. Similarity metrics have been widely applied in the literature (e.g., classification problems, plagiarism detection, sequence and image analysis).

In software engineering, particularly in software testing, similarity metrics have been applied. For instance, Shahbazi and Miller [31] conducted a large empirical study on black-box automated test-case generation using several string metrics. Their results indicate that superior test cases can be generated by controlling the diversity and length distribution of the string test cases. Hemmati et al. [13] proposed a similarity-based test case selection technique that selects the most diverse subset of test cases among those generated by applying a coverage criterion on a test model. Feldt et al. [5] proposed the test set diameter (TSDm) technique, which was developed based on NCD for multisets. Their results indicate that test selection using TSDm leads to higher structural and fault coverage than random selection. NCD multisets, which provides similarity measurement at the level of entire sets of elements rather than between pairs, have also been applied in the TCP literature recently [16].

To implement SBTP, the distances among test cases must be measured using a specific metric, and this information must then be leveraged to perform TCP. Ledru et al. [23] conducted a comprehensive experiment on the Siemens test suite and evaluated four classical string metrics for TCP purposes (i.e., Cartesian, Levenshtein, Hamming, and Manhattan distance). Their findings indicated that TCP using string metrics is more effective than random prioritization, and on average, Manhattan distance yields better results than the other investigated metrics. To calculate the distance between a test case t and set of test cases T',

Ledru et al. proposed the following function, which uses distance measure d:

$$distance(t, T', d) = min\{d(t, t_i) | t_i \in T', t_i \neq t\}$$

Ledru et al. used the min operation because an empirical study by Jiang et al. [18] showed that maximize-minimum is more efficient than maximize-average and maximize-maximum. Ledru et al. also proposed an algorithm (Algorithm 1) that iteratively picks the most dissimilar test case (i.e., having the greatest distance from a set of already prioritized test cases).

Algorithm 1. Similarity-based TCP Using a Pairwise Algorithm

Data: Test Suite TS
Result: Prioritized Suite PS
1 Find $t \in TS$ with the maximum $distance(t, TS)$;
2 Append t to PS and remove from TS;
3 **while** TS *is not empty* **do**
4 | Find $t \in TS$ with the maximum $distance(t, PS)$;
5 | Append t to PS and remove from TS;
6 **end**

Using SBTP with a pairwise algorithm comes with the cost of pairwise comparison, and its performance becomes inefficient as the test suite becomes larger. The underlying issue in SBTP can be defined as a similarity search problem, which involves searching within a large set of objects for a subset of objects that closely resemble a given query object. One popular approach to solving similarity search problems is LSH, which was originally introduced by Indyk and Motwani [17] in 1998. LSH hashes input items so that similar items map to the same buckets with high probability [24]. LSH is widely used in the literature (see the many references in Google Scholar to [17]) but is only occasionally applied to software engineering problems (e.g., clone detection [19] and test generation [31]). More recently, Miranda et al. [26] proposed an approach based on LSH, which provides scalable SBTP in both white-box and black-box fashion.

The purpose of our study is to investigate whether SBTP is more effective at finding defects than random permutation and which SBTP implementations yield the best results. A similar objective was pursued by Ledru et al. [23] in 2012. In comparison to their work, we have investigated five different techniques with respect to their effectiveness and performance. These techniques rely on different similarity metrics and were selected from the literature based on the results of recent experimental studies [5,6,14,23,26]. The rationale behind their selection and details about their implementation is described in Sect. 3.3. The Siemens test suite, which was used by Ledru et al., is a classical dataset and widely used in the software testing literature. However, its representative character has been debated for several reasons (e.g., in [27], which was also acknowledged by Ledru et al. in [23]). In this work, we report an experiment conducted on the defects4j dataset [20], which contains 395 real faults from 6 open-source Java programs.

3   Research Method

In this section, the study's objective and research questions, study subject, study design, and evaluation methods are discussed.

3.1   Objective and Research Questions

The main objective of our study is to catch regression faults early in the testing process, allowing software developers to perform RT more frequently and continuously. The research questions and their rationales are as follows:

RQ1: Is prioritization by similarity-based TCP more effective at finding defects than random permutation? This research question is designed to investigate whether running the most dissimilar test cases early in the testing process improves the test suite's fault-detection capability in comparison to random ordering.

RQ2: Which similarity-based TCP technique is the most effective and has the best performance? This research question is designed to compare the effectiveness and performance of investigated SBTP implementations. The rationale behind the investigated techniques' selection and details about their implementation are described in Sect. 3.3.

3.2   Subjects Under Study

To answer our research questions, we conducted an experiment using the defects4j dataset [20], which contains 395 real faults from 6 real-world open-source Java programs. The subject's characteristics are presented in Table 1. Each analyzed subject's name is presented in the first column, while the second column shows the number of versions analyzed for each program. The third and fourth columns present the median number of test classes and test cases, and the range is in parentheses. The last two columns show the source's size (kilo line-of-code) and test code for the most recent version, as reported by SLOC-Count[1].

3.3   Study Design

To answer RQ1, we compared the effectiveness of SBTP with random permutation. SBTP does not use a system under test; thus, it can hardly be more effective than TCP techniques, which use code coverage criteria [23]. Thus, like Ledru et al., we used random permutation as the baseline of our experiment. For the sake of a sanity check, we also included a TCP approach in which we minimize the diversity (i.e., maximize similarity among test cases). The rationale behind our sanity check is if diversity is valuable in TCP, then minimizing

---

[1] SLOCCount is a suite of programs used to count lines of code: https://www.dwheeler.com/sloccount/.

Table 1. Subject characteristics

Project	Versions	Test classes	Test cases	S-LOC	T-LOC
JFreeChart (Chart)	26	323 (301–356)	1789 (1591–2193)	123.527	37.396
Closure Compiler (Closure)	133	216 (118–235)	7389 (2595–8443)	251.855	85.138
Apache Lang (Lang)	65	89 (81–111)	1760 (1540–2291)	45.609	28.199
Apache Math (Math)	106	253 (91–385)	2319 (817–4378)	22.738	12.238
Mockito	38	237 (128–268)	1233 (704–1388)	38.914	10.638
Joda-Time (Time)	27	122 (120–123)	3906 (3749–4041)	176.965	41.536

diversity should, in turn, negatively affect the test suite's fault-detection capability [16]. Effectiveness was measured using APFD, which is a commonly used metric in the TCP literature and elaborated on in Sect. 3.4.

To answer RQ2, we presented the aggregated the investigated techniques' performance and effectiveness within and across studied subjects. Using the aggregated values, we can determine which technique achieved the best effectiveness and performance on average. The five SBTP techniques presented in Table 2 were selected from the literature and investigated in this experiment. To calculate the distances, we automatically downloaded the source code for all studied versions and used the source code behind the test classes at their exact version.

Table 2. TCP techniques investigated

Name (Acronym)	Objective	Reference
Random Permutation (RND)	Baseline	-
Manhattan Distance (MNH)	Maximize diversity	Ledru et al. [23]
Jaccard Distance (JAC)	Maximize diversity	Hemmati and Briand [14]
Normalized Compression Distance (NCD)	Maximize diversity	Feldt et al. [6]
Sanity Check (SC) using NCD	Maximize similarity	-
NCD Multisets (NCD-MS)	Maximize diversity	Feldt et al. [5]
Locality Sensitive Hasing (LSH)	Maximize diversity	Miranda et al. [26]

We implemented the Manhattan, Jaccard, NCD, and NCD Multisets using the pairwise algorithm proposed by Ledru et al. [23]. The Manhattan distance between two objects is the sum of the differences of their corresponding components. To calculate the Manhattan distance, the source code is converted to a vector of numbers. In practice, each character should be replaced with their ASCII code (or any other numerical coding). The Jaccard similarity between two sets x and y is defined as $JS(x,y) = |x \cap y|/|x \cup y|$, and their distance is $JD(x,y) = 1 - JS(x,y)$. To calculate the Jaccard distance, the source code is converted to a set of k-shingles (e.g., any substring of length k found within the text). In our study, we used $k = 5$, which is commonly used in the analysis of relatively short documents [24].

NCD and NCD Multisets both rely on a compressor function C, which calculates the approximate Kolmogorov complexity and returns the length of the input string after its compression, using a chosen compression program. In this study, we used LZ4, which is a high-speed lossless data compression algorithm[2]. The difference between NCD and NCD Multisets is that the latter performs similarity measurement at the level of entire sets of elements rather than between pairs. For the NCD Multisets, we adapted the pairwise algorithm so that at each iteration, we pick a test $t \in TS$ that has maximum Kolmogorov complexity when compressed with the entire set of the already prioritized suite PS. This means that the candidate test has less mutual information with PS and is more different than any other $t \in TS$.

Furthermore, we implemented LSH using the MinHash technique to rapidly estimate Jaccard similarity. In our implementation, we followed the instructions provided by [24], which are also described here. To estimate the Jaccard similarity, we converted the source code to a set of 5-shingles. However, their size is often large, and it is impractical to use them directly. Using MinHashing technique, we replaced these sets with a much smaller representation (e.g., a signature) while preserving the Jaccard similarity between them. Given a hash function h and an input set S, we hashed all elements in the set using the hash function and picked the minimum resulting value as MinHash of S. This process was repeated P times (i.e., the number of permutations) using different hash functions to calculate the signature of a set (e.g., a sequence of MinHashes). Thereafter, the Jaccard similarity of two sets can be estimated using the fraction of common MinHashes in their signature. Using MinHashing, we were able to compress large sets into a small signature; similarity searches among large numbers of pairs is inefficient.

LSH works with a signature matrix (e.g., MinHash signatures as column) and divides it into b bands consisting of r rows each. For each band, LSH takes vectors of numbers (e.g., the portion of one column within that band) and hashes them to the buckets using a hash function. The more similar two columns are, the more likely they collide into some bands. When two items fall into the same bucket, it means a portion of their signature agrees, and they will be added to the candidate set. The candidate set returned by an LSH query only contains a subset of items that are more likely similar (e.g., having Jaccard similarity over a certain threshold). An approximation of this threshold is defined as $ST = (1/b)^{(1/r)}$.

Typically, LSH is configured with a high ST so that the candidate set only contains closely similar items. However, in our context, we are interested in items with a maximum distance from the LSH query. Thus, like Miranda et al. [26], we configured LSH so that we achieved an approximately 0.1 similarity threshold[3], and the candidate set CS would contain almost all test cases, and the distant set DS would include a small number of remaining items with high Jaccard distance.

---

[2] The LZ4 compression algorithm and details regarding its implementation are available at http://lz4.github.io/lz4/.

[3] Permutations: 10; bands: 10; rows: 1.

To employ LSH for TCP purpose, we implemented an algorithm (Algorithm 2) proposed by Miranda et al. [26].

Algorithm 2. Similarity-based TCP Using Locality-Sensitive Hashing

---

Data: Test Suite TS
Result: Prioritized Suite PS
1 $signatures \leftarrow$ MinHashSignature(TS);
2 LSH.Index ($signatures$);
3 $query \leftarrow$ MinHashSignature($\emptyset$);
4 **while** $signatures$ is not empty **do**
5 | $CS \leftarrow$ LSH.Search($query$);
6 | $DS \leftarrow signatures - CS - PS$;
7 | Find $i \in DS$ with the maximum JD (estimate) to PS;
8 | Append i to PS and remove from $signatures$;
9 | $query \leftarrow$ Update cumulative MinHash signature of PS;
10 **end**

3.4 Evaluation

To compare the investigated TCP techniques, effectiveness and performance are both important. Performance was measured using average method execution time (AMET) in seconds. AMET includes both the preparation time (i.e., calculating the distance matrix or LSH initialization) and the prioritization algorithm itself. To assess effectiveness, we used an APFD metric that was originally introduced by Rothermel et al. [30] and is widely used in the literature [22]. Let T be an ordered test suite containing n test cases and F be a set of m faults detected by T; then TF_i indicates the number of test cases executed in T before capturing fault i. APFD indicates the average percentage of faults detected and is defined as follows:

$$APFD = 100 * (1 - \frac{TF_1 + TF_2 + ... + TF_M}{nm} + \frac{1}{2_n})$$

To properly compare the investigated TCP techniques, we performed statistical analyses. A Mann–Whitney U test [2], which is a non-parametric significance test, was applied to determine whether the difference between two techniques is statistically significant, using $p < 0.05$ as the significance threshold. The null hypothesis of this test indicates that there is no significant difference between the effectiveness of the techniques under evaluation. This test was selected because the studied data may not follow a normal distribution. The Mann–Whitney U test indicates whether there is any difference between techniques but does not show the degree of difference between them. Thus, we used a VDA measure [2], which is a non-parametric effect size. A VDA measure is a number between 0 and 1. When $VDA(x, y) = 0.5$, it indicates the two techniques are equal. When $VDA(x, y) > 0.5$, it means x outperformed y and vice versa. To compare the investigated techniques across the subject programs, we presented the mean for the analyzed variables, and a 95% non-parametric confidence interval (CI) based on 1000 bias-corrected and accelerated bootstrap replicates. Furthermore, when comparing TCP techniques, we also provided violin plots to visualize the distribution of APFDs.

4   Findings

This section is structured to address the research questions and includes the aggregated results of all execution rounds (see the number of versions presented for each subject in Table 1). The experiments were conducted on a computer with an Intel 2.7 GHz Xeon E5-2680 CPU and 16 GB installed RAM. To accelerate the performance of investigated TCP techniques, we parallelized all techniques.

4.1   RQ1: Is Prioritization by Similarity-Based TCP More Effective at Finding Defects Than Random Permutation?

Table 3 presents the effect sizes for differences between analyzed SBTP techniques and random permutation. The analyzed SBTP techniques' effectiveness varies among subjects. However, one can observe that SBTP is largely more effective in finding defects than random permutation (VDA 0.76–0.99 observed using NCD across all subjects). These differences are also statistically significant in nearly all cases, which indicates running the most dissimilar test cases early in the testing process (maximizing the diversity) increases the test suite's fault-detection capability. This was also verified by our sanity check (SC) where the inverse approach was employed. The sanity check indicated maximizing similarities among tests would decrease the test suite's fault-detection capability, and as expected, it was less effective than random ordering (VDA: 0.03–0.34). Figure 2 shows the violin plots for the investigated TCP techniques within the studied subjects.

Table 3. VDA effect size - TCP technique vs. RND permutation

Project	MNH	JAC	NCD	NCD-MS	LSH	SC
Chart	0.87	0.81	0.81	0.91	0.76	0.21
Closure	0.89	0.8	0.87	0.87	0.71	0.12
Lang	0.79	0.75	0.77	0.76	0.69	0.25
Math	0.84	0.82	0.84	0.84	0.76	0.16
Mockito	0.58	0.74	0.76	0.6	0.67	0.34
Time	0.96	0.99	0.99	0.96	0.9	0.03
VDA range	0.58–0.96	0.74–0.99	0.76–0.99	0.60–0.96	0.67–0.90	0.03–0.34

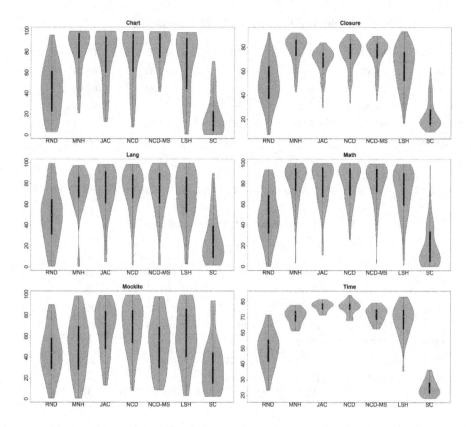

Fig. 2. Effectiveness (APFD) comparison - violin plots

4.2 RQ2: Which Similarity-Based TCP Technique Is the Most Effective and Has the Best Performance?

For a TCP approach to be applicable in a real-world environment, effectiveness (measured by APFD) and performance (measured by AMET) are both critical. Table 4 compares the effectiveness of the investigated techniques within and across the studied subjects. However, Table 5 compares the investigated techniques' performance within and across the studied projects. One can observe that all SBTP techniques except LSH achieved very close mean APFD scores across all subjects (72.69–75.44). LSH achieved the lowest effectiveness (66.79), but had the best performance and scored a very low AMET across all subjects (1.24 s). Overall, on average and across all subjects, no technique was found to be superior with respect to the effectiveness. LSH was, to a small extent, less effective than other SBTP techniques (VDA: 0.38 observed in comparison to NCD), but its speed largely outperformed the other techniques (i.e., it was approximately 5–111 times faster).

Table 4. Effectiveness (APFD) comparison

Project	MNH	JAC	NCD	NCD-MS	LSH
Chart	81.89	75.72	77.3	84.32	69.94
Closure	77.47	68.24	74.41	74.84	63.65
Lang	74.26	72.14	73.16	72.69	66.85
Math	80.39	78.81	80.37	80.32	72.21
Mockito	51.69	67.09	67.58	53.82	59.52
Time	70.39	76.95	75.99	71.8	68.06
Mean APFD (95% CI)	75.05 (72.90–76.87)	72.69 (70.84–74.47)	75.44 (73.83–77.28)	74.35 (72.51–76.26)	66.79 (64.64–68.81)

Table 5. Performance (AMET) comparison

Project	MNH	JAC	NCD	NCD-MS	LSH
Chart	138.22	25.02	15.65	102.99	2.84
Closure	230.15	15.05	5.85	89.99	1.32
Lang	33.18	2.76	0.58	7.22	0.29
Math	142.64	17.22	10.01	97.69	1.62
Mockito	41.54	7.14	5.63	14.32	1.04
Time	56.78	5.88	1.27	18.24	0.39
Mean AMET (95% CI)	138.21 (130.50–146)	12.88 (12.14–13.57)	6.41 (5.87–6.95)	67.11 (61.85–73.29)	1.24 (1.15–1.33)

5   Discussion

5.1   Overview of Findings, Their Implications, and Future Works

The ultimate objective of our study was to detect regression faults early in the testing process, allowing software developers to perform regression testing more frequently and continuously. To achieve our objective, we conducted an experiment using the defects4j dataset [20].

Test suites ordered by SBTP were largely more effective at finding defects than random permutation (VDA: 0.76–0.99 observed using NCD across all subjects). This indicates running the most dissimilar test cases early in the testing process (maximizing the diversity) increases the test suite's fault-detection capability. This is also verified by our sanity check where the reverse approach was applied (VDA: 0.03–0.34). Of the 5 SBTP implementations investigated, no technique was found to be superior with respect to the effectiveness. LSH was, to a small extent, less effective than other SBTP techniques (VDA: 0.38 observed in comparison to NCD), but its speed largely outperformed the other techniques (i.e., it was approximately 5–111 times faster). From practical perspective, NCD seems to be the best choice because it achieved high effectiveness with relatively low average method execution time. Yet, LSH is more practical when the prioritization time is critical.

Findings from our study bring to mind the well-known adage "don't put all your eggs in one basket". To effectively consume a limited testing budget, one should spread it evenly across different parts of the system by running the most dissimilar test cases early in the testing process. The underlying intuition is that *test cases that capture the same faults tend to be more similar to each other, and test cases that capture different faults tend to be more different* [11,18,23]. In comparison to other TCP techniques, SBTP requires minimal information (i.e., only the required information is encoded in the test suite) and has potential applications. SBTP can be applied in different contexts and during initial testing where no information about the system under test is available (e.g., code coverage or historical data). SBTP is an especially interesting approach when code instrumentation is too costly or impossible (e.g., in automotive system testing where source-code is not always available [8,10]). SBPT can also be applied in a complementary fashion and combined with other TCP techniques (e.g., history-based diversity proposed in our previous work [9]).

To realize SBTP in practice, one must measure the similarities among test cases. This similarity measurement can be performed using string metrics and on different properties (i.e., the source code, documentation, or any other information about the test cases). As acknowledged by Ledru et al. [23], string metrics are based on lexicographic information and do not necessarily capture the semantics behind the test cases. Two test cases might consequently be considered similar, although they are distant and correspond to different execution paths. Future works are required to investigate possible approaches that precisely measure the semantic similarities among test cases. The candidate approach should not come with a high overhead; otherwise, its application remains in theory.

Once similarity measurement has been performed, this information should be leveraged to perform TCP. One can argue that diversification is perhaps the best strategy when no strong clues about fault-revealing test cases are available. Test diversity is a classical heuristic in the literature and has been applied previously [1,5,7,11,13,15,18,23,32]. The opposite viewpoint is the intensification strategy, where the testing budget is consumed by and around the most probable fault-revealing test cases. Theoretically, both strategies can be applied simultaneously (i.e., intensify where it is necessary and diversify the remaining budget). However, making decisions about when and how to apply these strategies, either individually or combined, remains a challenge. To the best of our knowledge, the application of these strategies, as well as their relevance and impact, have not been widely investigated in the literature. The only exception we are aware of is the recent study by Patrick and Jia [28] wherein the authors investigated the trade-off between diversification and intensification in adaptive random testing.

Regardless of which strategy is chosen, a TCP algorithm needs to iteratively find the most (dis)-similar item to the set of already prioritized test cases. This can be done using different search techniques. TCP using a pairwise algorithm does not scale, and its performance becomes inefficient as the test suite's size increases. In this work, we have investigated LSH as one popular solution to the similarity search problem. There are other solutions proposed in the literature. Future work should also investigate the effectiveness and performance of candidate solutions.

5.2   Threats to Validity

In empirical software engineering, validity threats can be grouped into four distinct classes: construct validity, internal validity, external validity, and reliability [33]. In the present context, construct validity relates to the use of right measures. To assess the investigated TCP techniques' effectiveness, we used the APFD metric, which is widely used in the literature (see the latest systematic literature review on TCP by Khatibsyarbini et al. [22]). Internal validity concerns the relationship between the constructs and the proposed explanation. This corresponds to the potential faults in our implementation. Our implementation was piloted on a small sample before running the actual experiment. Furthermore, the implementation and results were discussed and reviewed in regular meetings, which were held among the co-authors of this study.

External validity relates to the generalizability of the study and whether the subjects of our study are real-world projects. Our experiment was conducted on the defects4j dataset [20], which contains 395 real faults from 6 real-world open-source Java programs. Our conclusions are drawn based on ex-post analysis of software artifacts. This motivates our future work to replicate our experiment in industry and to larger systems. Reliability concerns the repeatability and reproducibility of the research procedure and conclusions. This required access to the analyzed subjects and a throughout report of the experiment. The data that we used is publicly available, and detailed information about our experiment and its implementation were presented in this paper.

6   Concluding Remarks

The ultimate objective of our study was to detect regression faults early in the testing process, allowing software developers to perform regression testing more frequently and continuously. To achieve this objective, we conducted an experiment using the defects4j dataset, which contains 395 real faults from 6 real-world open-source Java programs. In summary, the results from our experiments suggest the following:

(1) Test suites ordered by SBTP were largely more effective at finding defects than random permutation (VDA: 0.76–0.99 observed using NCD across all subjects), which means running the most dissimilar test cases early in the testing process improves the test suite's fault-detection capability; (2) Of the 5 SBTP implementations investigated, no technique was found to be superior with respect to the effectiveness. LSH was, to a small extent, less effective than other SBTP techniques (VDA: 0.38 observed in comparison to NCD), but its speed was faster than the other techniques studied (approximately 5–111 times faster).

Taken together, these results bring to mind the well-known adage "don't put all your eggs in one basket". To effectively consume a limited testing budget, one should spread it evenly across different parts of the system by running the most dissimilar test cases early in the process. Our study contributes to the literature by providing empirical evidence in support of test diversity and its impact on TCP.

References

1. Arafeen, M.J., Do, H.: Test case prioritization using requirements-based clustering. In: 2013 IEEE Sixth International Conference on Software Testing, Verification and Validation (ICST), pp. 312–321. IEEE (2013)
2. Arcuri, A., Briand, L.: A practical guide for using statistical tests to assess randomized algorithms in software engineering. In: 2011 33rd International Conference on Software Engineering (ICSE), pp. 1–10. IEEE (2011)
3. Cartaxo, E.G., Machado, P.D., Neto, F.G.O.: On the use of a similarity function for test case selection in the context of model-based testing. Softw. Test. Verif. Reliab. **21**(2), 75–100 (2011)
4. Engström, E., Runeson, P.: A qualitative survey of regression testing practices. In: Ali Babar, M., Vierimaa, M., Oivo, M. (eds.) PROFES 2010. LNCS, vol. 6156, pp. 3–16. Springer, Heidelberg (2010). https://doi.org/10.1007/978-3-642-13792-1_3
5. Feldt, R., Poulding, S., Clark, D., Yoo, S.: Test set diameter: quantifying the diversity of sets of test cases. In: 2016 IEEE International Conference on Software Testing, Verification and Validation (ICST), pp. 223–233. IEEE (2016)
6. Feldt, R., Torkar, R., Gorschek, T., Afzal, W.: Searching for cognitively diverse tests: towards universal test diversity metrics. In: IEEE International Conference on Software Testing Verification and Validation Workshop, ICSTW 2008, pp. 178–186. IEEE (2008)
7. Flemström, D., Potena, P., Sundmark, D., Afzal, W., Bohlin, M.: Similarity-based prioritization of test case automation. Softw. Qual. J., 1–29 (2017). https://doi.org/10.1007/s11219-017-9401-7
8. Haghighatkhah, A., Banijamali, A., Pakanen, O.P., Oivo, M., Kuvaja, P.: Automotive software engineering: a systematic mapping study. J. Syst. Softw. **128**, 25–55 (2017)
9. Haghighatkhah, A., Mäntylä, M., Oivo, M., Kuvaja, P.: Test prioritization in continuous integration environments. J. Syst. Softw. (2018). https://doi.org/10.1016/j.jss.2018.08.061, http://www.sciencedirect.com/science/article/pii/S0164121218301730
10. Haghighatkhah, A., Oivo, M., Banijamali, A., Kuvaja, P.: Improving the state of automotive software engineering. IEEE Softw. **34**(5), 82–86 (2017)
11. Hemmati, H., Arcuri, A., Briand, L.: Reducing the cost of model-based testing through test case diversity. In: Petrenko, A., Simão, A., Maldonado, J.C. (eds.) ICTSS 2010. LNCS, vol. 6435, pp. 63–78. Springer, Heidelberg (2010). https://doi.org/10.1007/978-3-642-16573-3_6
12. Hemmati, H., Arcuri, A., Briand, L.: Empirical investigation of the effects of test suite properties on similarity-based test case selection. In: 2011 IEEE Fourth International Conference on Software Testing, Verification and Validation (ICST), pp. 327–336. IEEE (2011)

13. Hemmati, H., Arcuri, A., Briand, L.: Achieving scalable model-based testing through test case diversity. ACM Trans. Softw. Eng. Methodol. (TOSEM) **22**(1), 6 (2013)
14. Hemmati, H., Briand, L.: An industrial investigation of similarity measures for model-based test case selection. In: 2010 IEEE 21st International Symposium on Software Reliability Engineering (ISSRE), pp. 141–150. IEEE (2010)
15. Hemmati, H., Fang, Z., Mäntylä, M.V., Adams, B.: Prioritizing manual test cases in rapid release environments. Softw. Test. Verif. Reliab. **27**(6), e1609 (2017)
16. Henard, C., Papadakis, M., Harman, M., Jia, Y., Le Traon, Y.: Comparing white-box and black-box test prioritization. In: 2016 IEEE/ACM 38th International Conference on Software Engineering (ICSE), pp. 523–534. IEEE (2016)
17. Indyk, P., Motwani, R.: Approximate nearest neighbors: towards removing the curse of dimensionality. In: Proceedings of the Thirtieth Annual ACM Symposium on Theory of Computing, pp. 604–613. ACM (1998)
18. Jiang, B., Zhang, Z., Chan, W.K., Tse, T.: Adaptive random test case prioritization. In: Proceedings of the 2009 IEEE/ACM International Conference on Automated Software Engineering, pp. 233–244. IEEE Computer Society (2009)
19. Jiang, L., Misherghi, G., Su, Z., Glondu, S.: Deckard: scalable and accurate tree-based detection of code clones. In: Proceedings of the 29th International Conference on Software Engineering, pp. 96–105. IEEE Computer Society (2007)
20. Just, R., Jalali, D., Ernst, M.D.: Defects4j: a database of existing faults to enable controlled testing studies for Java programs. In: Proceedings of the 2014 International Symposium on Software Testing and Analysis, pp. 437–440. ACM (2014)
21. Kessis, M., Ledru, Y., Vandome, G.: Experiences in coverage testing of a Java middleware. In: Proceedings of the 5th International Workshop on Software Engineering and Middleware, pp. 39–45. ACM (2005)
22. Khatibsyarbini, M., Isa, M.A., Jawawi, D.N., Tumeng, R.: Test case prioritization approaches in regression testing: a systematic literature review. Inf. Softw. Technol. **93**, 74–93 (2017)
23. Ledru, Y., Petrenko, A., Boroday, S., Mandran, N.: Prioritizing test cases with string distances. Autom. Softw. Eng. **19**(1), 65–95 (2012)
24. Leskovec, J., Rajaraman, A., Ullman, J.D.: Mining of Massive Datasets. Cambridge University Press, New York (2014)
25. Mäntylä, M.V., Adams, B., Khomh, F., Engström, E., Petersen, K.: On rapid releases and software testing: a case study and a semi-systematic literature review. Empir. Softw. Eng. **20**(5), 1384–1425 (2015)
26. Miranda, B., Verdecchia, R., Cruciani, E., Bertolino, A.: Fast approaches to scalable similarity-based test case prioritization. In: 2018 IEEE/ACM 40th International Conference on Software Engineering (ICSE). IEEE (2018)
27. Orso, A., Rothermel, G.: Software testing: a research travelogue (2000–2014). In: Proceedings of the on Future of Software Engineering, pp. 117–132. ACM (2014)
28. Patrick, M., Jia, Y.: KD-ART: should we intensify or diversify tests to kill mutants? Inf. Softw. Technol. **81**, 36–51 (2017)
29. Rodríguez, P., et al.: Continuous deployment of software intensive products and services: a systematic mapping study. J. Syst. Softw. **123**, 263–291 (2017)
30. Rothermel, G., Untch, R.H., Chu, C., Harrold, M.J.: Prioritizing test cases for regression testing. IEEE Trans. Softw. Eng. **27**(10), 929–948 (2001)
31. Shahbazi, A., Miller, J.: Black-box string test case generation through a multi-objective optimization. IEEE Trans. Softw. Eng. **42**(4), 361–378 (2016)
32. Thomas, S.W., Hemmati, H., Hassan, A.E., Blostein, D.: Static test case prioritization using topic models. Empir. Softw. Eng. **19**(1), 182–212 (2014)

33. Wohlin, C., Runeson, P., Host, M., Ohlsson, C., Regnell, B., Wesslén, A.: Experimentation in Software Engineering: An Introduction. Kluwer Academic Publishers, Norwell (2000)
34. Yoo, S., Harman, M.: Regression testing minimization, selection and prioritization: a survey. Softw. Test. Verif. Reliab. **22**(2), 67–120 (2012)

Measurement and Monitoring

Feature Crumbs: Adapting Usage Monitoring to Continuous Software Engineering

Jan Ole Johanssen[1]([✉]), Anja Kleebaum[2], Bernd Bruegge[1], and Barbara Paech[2]

[1] Technical University of Munich, Munich, Germany
{jan.johanssen,bruegge}@in.tum.de
[2] Heidelberg University, Heidelberg, Germany
{anja.kleebaum,paech}@informatik.uni-heidelberg.de

Abstract. Continuous software engineering relies on explicit user feedback for the development and improvement of features. The frequent release of feature increments fosters the application of usage monitoring, which promises a broad range of insights. However, it remains a challenge to relate monitored usage data to changes that were introduced by an increment and thereby to a particular specific of a feature.

We introduce *Feature Crumbs*, a lightweight, code-based concept to specify a feature's run-time characteristics. This enables monitored usage data to be allocated to a feature increment. In addition, we analyze the implications for the overall development process. We outline the reference implementation of a platform for collecting, managing, and assessing feature crumbs. We report an evaluation of both the feature crumb concept and the reference implementation in a university capstone course.

Feature crumbs and their changes to the development process contribute to the product quality; they enable feature increment assessment in combination with additional knowledge sources, such as decision knowledge.

Keywords: Feature crumb · Usage data · User · Usage monitoring Process · Agile development · Continuous software engineering

1 Introduction

User feedback is pivotal for software evolution. Continuous software engineering (CSE) [2,7] acknowledges this by relying on early and frequent releases—even with immature prototypes [1]—to retrieve explicit feedback, such as written reviews, from users. This feedback is then turned into change requests for a feature under development. However, this approach is time consuming and dependent on humans [14], leading to a discrete, rather than continuous, source of feedback.

Frequent software releases foster implicit user feedback, namely the application of usage monitoring, enabling a broad research field [17]. Implicit feedback

© Springer Nature Switzerland AG 2018
M. Kuhrmann et al. (Eds.): PROFES 2018, LNCS 11271, pp. 263–271, 2018.
https://doi.org/10.1007/978-3-030-03673-7_19

can be collected continuously, without interfering with users, and supports developers in reasoning about how to improve a feature [14]. In contrast to explicit user feedback, which provides the ability for application feature extraction [9], usage data maps to the entire implementation, shown as (B) in Fig. 1. Therefore, one challenge remains in relating usage data to the feature increment specifics.

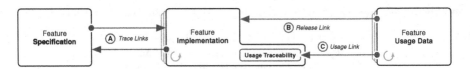

Fig. 1. Different link types: feature **specifications** are codified in a feature **implementation** while *trace links* (A) can be established using feature tags [18]. The implementation is frequently delivered to users who produce **usage data**. Usage data can be mapped to the entire implementation based on a *release link* (B). Represented by feature crumbs, a *usage link* (C) enables actual **usage traceability**, which allows to create a relationship between usage data and implementation specifics.

We introduce the *Feature Crumbs* concept, which allows the allocation of usage data to a feature increment. Similar to requirements traceability, as described by Gotel & Finkelstein [8], feature crumbs create a *usage traceability*, which links usage data to code in a backward direction, shown as (C) in Fig. 1. Feature crumbs represent software sensors that are manually seeded into the application source code to describe the user-centric structure of a feature. Feature crumbs facilitate a detailed evaluation of features; they form the basis for deriving run-time information, such as whether users (a) started, (b) canceled, or (c) finished usage of a feature. Additional information may be recorded at run-time to enrich the assessment of a feature. For example, users' behavioral characteristics aligned with detected feature crumbs might precisely reveal situations in which users are confused. Likewise, decision knowledge regarding the implementation of a feature can be related to the monitored usage data of this feature; such a relationship can be used to assess previous decisions. Ultimately, usage data collected using the feature crumb concept may lead to the discovery of additional requirements or to the refinement of existing requirements.

Along with the introduction of the feature crumb concept, the adaption of usage monitoring to CSE affects multiple parts of the software development process. Thus, we elaborate on new developer capabilities, such as designing run-time feature representations, considerations regarding development artifacts, such as working with branches, and arising needs for additional tool support.

This paper is structured as follows. Section 2 describes requirements for the adaption of usage monitoring to CSE. Section 3 introduces the feature crumb concept and its implications for the software development process. In Sect. 4, we outline a reference implementation of feature crumbs and report its initial evaluation. We situate our concept in related work in Sect. 5 and conclude the paper by providing a summary, discussion, and future work in Sect. 6.

2   Requirements

Similar to the integration of decision knowledge into CSE [12], we elicited the following six requirements for the adaption of usage monitoring to CSE. These requirements form the basis for the crumbs concept introduced in Sect. 3.

R1: **Feature Assessment.** Usage monitoring during CSE shall enable developers to assess whether a feature under development was employed by the user. This allows them to only consider usage data produced by a user who actually used a particular feature. Furthermore, performance indicators, such as the cancelation rate of a feature, enable the feature to be assessed.

R2: **Usage Data Allocation.** Feature usage usually involves multiple elements, such as a sequence of buttons that users tap to achieve a goal. A usage monitoring approach shall allow the allocation of observed usage data to a specific step within a feature. This enables precise feature analyses, such as studying time frames between feature steps or relationships to other knowledge sources.

R3: **Feature Flexibility & Comparability.** CSE promotes frequent and rapid releases of new software increments. This requires a usage monitoring concept that allows for a simple extension and flexible replacement of new functional additions to the feature under development. Notably, the concept shall take into consideration that usage data from consecutive feature increments are comparable. This is important to enable the investigation of a feature's evolution.

R4: **Application Range.** The applicability of a concept shall be independent of the product: as CSE is often used in the domain of mobile interactive systems, the concept shall be applicable to graphical user interfaces, but also to computationally intensive code. At the same time, the concept shall be applicable to new user interfaces, such as voice, and consider server-side operations.

R5: **Environment Compatibility.** Development environments are a heterogeneous composition of management approaches, software processes, tools, and platforms. The concept shall be compatible with existing environments and not impose an additional burden upon developers. For example, it should make no difference whether a project organizes features with user stories or scenarios.

R6: **Effort & Learnability.** Usage monitoring shall be easy for developers to learn and apply. In particular, the concept shall impose a minimal cognitive load upon developers responsible for adding and maintaining the means for usage monitoring to guarantee its seamless and continuous application.

3   Feature Crumb Concept

Following the above-mentioned requirements, we present an object model of the feature crumb concept in Sect. 3.1 and describe its implications for the development process in Sect. 3.2. Thereby, we highlight its lightweight character.

3.1   Object Model

The major entities and their relations are depicted in Fig. 2. A `Feature` has a `name` and a `description`. A `Path` is uniquely defined for every feature.

It consists of a sequence of **steps**, which represents a sorted array of **Crumbs** to specify the flow of crumbs needed to complete a feature. As a feature is extended or updated, crumbs can be **added** to or **removed** from a path. If the introduced changes are major, both activities increment the path **version**.

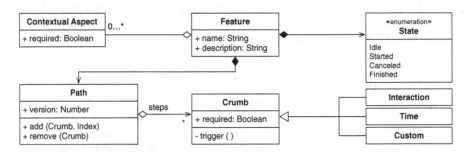

Fig. 2. Object model representing the feature crumb concept as a UML class diagram.

If a feature is composed of optional steps, the respective crumb's attribute **required** might be set to *false*. We distinguish between different classes of crumbs, which all share the capability to **trigger** an event, each under a certain condition: an **Interaction** crumb might be triggered by any interaction or event that can occur during the run-time of an application. A **Time** crumb defers its trigger call until a specified time frame is passed. **Custom** crumbs await any individually-designed conditions, such as the input of a pre-defined string into a text field, before triggering an event. A feature's **State** relates to its observed execution. Based on the recorded events triggered by crumbs and given the feature path, we distinguish the following feature states: (a) *Idle*, if the feature has never been initiated by the user; (b) *Started*, if the first crumb of the feature path sequence was detected; (c) *Canceled*, if the assessment of a path is stopped due to a certain criterion; or (d) *Finished*, if all crumbs that are part of the sequence were detected sequentially. Eventually, **Contextual Aspects** describe conditions that need to be met to start the feature path observation. These may be pre- or post-conditions, such as an external event or the availability of certain user data. Contextual aspects can be optional. An informal representation of the feature crumb concept is sketched in Fig. 3 to illustrate objects shown in Fig. 2.

3.2   Implications for the Development Process

The introduction of feature crumbs and the adaption of usage monitoring to CSE impacts the overall development process. This is because usage monitoring is situated at the end of a development cycle as it verifies the product. In Fig. 4, we outline the major capabilities required by developers, resulting artifacts, and supportive tools when cycling through a software development process.

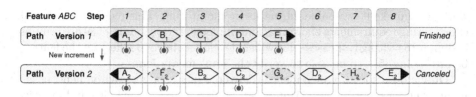

Fig. 3. A `Feature` entitled *ABC* that was improved once. Thus, `Path` was updated with a new `version` number. Version *1* consists of five feature `Crumbs`, which are depicted as a hexagon while black corners signal either the first or last crumb of a `steps` sequence. Version *2* introduces three new crumbs (dashed, green border) that occupy steps that were previously allocated to other crumbs. The red antenna signals the call of the `trigger` method; while this means for version 1 that the feature has been executed properly (*Finished*), version 2 was *Canceled*, since C_2 was triggered before B_2. (Color figure online)

Phases	Requirements Elicitation	Implementation	Testing	Deploying	Usage Monitoring
Capabilities	Elicit and implement requirements, design run-time feature representation *		Design and assess test cases, analyze crash reports		Evaluate monitored data *
Artifacts	User Story, Scenario *	Branches and Commits *	Test Cases	Crash Reports	Feature Crumbs *
Tools	Issue & Knowledge Management System	Version Control System	Integration System	Delivery and Distribution System	User Understanding System *

Fig. 4. Outline of major capabilities, artifacts, and tools across the phases of a software development process; partially drawn and combined from [2] and [3]. Individual entries are interweaved and may be based on their predecessor. This is relevant for the entries related to usage monitoring, which are written in red font and followed by a star (*). (Color figure online)

A software development process depends upon the elicitation and management of requirements for a feature. A feature might be described as a use case or as a scenario, while the latter represents a concrete instance of this use case [3]. Given their lightweight character, feature crumbs fit into different concepts of how a feature is designed, managed, or tracked during design-time. Notably, given the similar structure of subsequent events, feature crumbs promote scenarios, highlighting their usefulness for collecting and analyzing usage data [15].

The selection of a branching strategy affects the work with feature crumbs: we propose relying on a branching model that uses feature branches for implementation work [13] to allow the integration of knowledge into CSE [11]. Feature crumbs can be added only to feature branches to maintain feature atomicity and to avoid interference with the development of other features.

During requirements elicitation and feature implementation, developers need to be able to design a run-time representation of the feature on which they are working to make it evaluable during usage monitoring. This requires additional effort during requirements elicitation and implementation: adding feature crumbs is similar to writing test cases—for which developers have to reflect on the feature before coding [5]—to be able to verify the implementation.

Only after a software increment is delivered into a target environment, usage monitoring based on feature crumbs can be performed. To manage and analyze usage data, tool support in the form of a user understanding system is required. We provide one aspect of such as system—with a focus on the collection, management, and assessment of feature crumbs—in the following Sect. 4. This enables developers to evaluate monitored data and reflect upon the product quality.

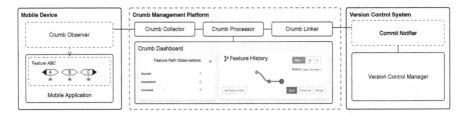

Fig. 5. The reference implementation including the major systems. Dashed, red borders indicate components created or added to enable the feature crumb concept. (Color figure online)

4   Reference Implementation and Initial Evaluation

We developed a **reference implementation** for the feature crumb concept to demonstrate its feasibility. In Fig. 5, we outline the three major systems: First, a framework for *Mobile Devices* allows developers to integrate crumbs for a feature. This framework also includes a *Crumb Observer* that reports triggered crumbs during application run-time. Second, we developed a *Crumb Management Platform*, which is the main interaction point for developers to work with the crumbs. It receives crumbs from applications via a *Crumb Collector*. The *Crumb Processor* is in charge of connecting received crumbs and the feature path information. The result, i.e., the feature state, is visualized on a *Crumb Dashboard* which further enables developers to define a feature path for a specific software increment that is released to users. The *Crumb Linker* is in charge of creating a relationship between a feature and a release that is uniquely identified by a code commit. The commit information is provided by a *Commit Notifier*, which represents the third aspect of the implementation. Based on a webhook system, this component informs the crumb management platform about new commits.

We ran an **initial evaluation** of the feature crumb concept and the reference implementation according to two variables of the technology acceptance model: the *perceived usefulness* (U) and the *perceived ease-of-use* (E) [6]. As a sample of prospective users, we relied upon nine students, each performing a usability representative role in a project within a university capstone course in which up to 100 students work on real industry projects [4] over the course of two months. Regarding U, all projects were able to define one or more features, including a feature path and crumbs. Users reported useful aspects, such as being able to *determine the repetition of a feature* to detect important steps, or to *assess if a customer was able to complete a feature* to detect if a navigational path might be unclear. At the same time, one user reported that their *app did not include much user interaction*, which limits the usefulness of feature crumbs; still, they would have been able to measure implementation internals. Regarding E, we obtained diverse feedback: the initial manual addition of commits was perceived as inconvenient, which led to the development of the commit notifier. Some users reported that the registration of a feature path was cumbersome and error-prone. One user emphasized *increased effort to integrate crumbs into code*.

5   Related Work

The feature crumb concept forms a lightweight task model to describe user interactions and shares similarities with the *ConcurTaskTrees* specification [16], which introduces four task types: a *user*, an *abstract*, an *interaction*, and an *application* task. Given their manifestation in code, feature crumbs do not distinguish *who*, e.g., the system or user, triggered them. Therefore, in Fig. 3, we apply the same symbol—the hexagon, which is used for application tasks in [16]—for all classes of feature crumbs (Fig. 2). Generally, feature crumbs focus on applications developed during fast-cycled processes, such as CSE. Moreover, they depict a linear path, rather than hierarchies or logical relationships.

To implement actual run-time observation, development environments[1] rely on code additions, similar to feature crumbs, that enable developers to create success and cancel paths. These concepts are, however, for debugging and profiling applications. Platforms[2] that apply such concepts for usage monitoring only address single events and do not promote the addition of other knowledge types.

There exist various approaches that utilize usage data for software evolution. For instance, UI-Tracer [10] supports developers in comprehending a software system by automatically identifying source code that is related to user interface elements. Similarly, feature crumbs can be understood as traces that relate user elements with their implementation; however, our concept is not limited to user interface elements. Furthermore, feature crumbs describe features to collect usage data, which can be linked to other knowledge types, such as decision knowledge.

6   Conclusion

In this paper, we have presented feature crumbs, a lightweight, code-based concept to describe a feature with the goal of adapting usage monitoring to CSE. We

---

[1] https://developer.apple.com/videos/play/wwdc2018-405/?time=1097.

[2] https://docs.microsoft.com/en-us/appcenter/analytics/event-metrics.

have summarized six requirements and implications for the development process. We have outlined a reference implementation to demonstrate the feasibility of collecting, managing, and assessing feature crumbs. We have reported an initial evaluation of both the concept and the implementation in a university context.

Discussion. The implementation and evaluation have indicated that feature crumbs promote usage monitoring in CSE. Now, we face two major areas for discussion. First, the focus of a feature: while we provide the means for feature definition and tracking, we observed that it is difficult to decide where to seed crumbs, i.e., the first crumb. We consider providing a guideline to developers. Second, the platform usability: developers need different functionalities. Discussion is required to select important ones and make them easily accessible.

Future Work. We plan to improve the feature crumb management platform towards a comprehensive user understanding system and to continue evaluating it to investigate developers' acceptance. A long-term goal is to add multiple knowledge sources that can be better assessed when relying on feature crumbs.

Acknowledgments. This work was supported by the DFG (German Research Foundation) under the Priority Programme SPP1593: Design For Future – Managed Software Evolution. We thank Jan Philip Bernius and Lara Marie Reimer for their excellent work on the development of the reference implementation and the participants of the university capstone course for their feedback.

References

1. Alperowitz, L., Weintraud, A.M., Kofler, S.C., Bruegge, B.: Continuous prototyping. In: 3rd International Workshop on Rapid Continuous Software Engineering, pp. 36–42 (2017)
2. Bosch, J.: Continuous software engineering: an introduction. In: Bosch, J. (ed.) Continuous Software Engineering, pp. 3–13. Springer, Cham (2014). https://doi.org/10.1007/978-3-319-11283-1_1
3. Bruegge, B., Dutoit, A.H.: Object-Oriented Software Engineering Using UML, Patterns, and Java, 3rd edn. Prentice Hall Press, Upper Saddle River (2010)
4. Bruegge, B., Krusche, S., Alperowitz, L.: Software engineering project courses with industrial clients. ACM Trans. Comput. Educ. **15**(4), 17:1–17:31 (2015). https://doi.org/10.1145/2732155
5. Crispin, L.: Driving software quality: how test-driven development impacts software quality. IEEE Softw. **23**(6), 70–71 (2006). https://doi.org/10.1109/MS.2006.157
6. Davis, F.D., Bagozzi, R.P., Warshaw, P.R.: User acceptance of computer technology: a comparison of two theoretical models. Manag. Sci. **35**(8), 982–1002 (1989). https://doi.org/10.1287/mnsc.35.8.982
7. Fitzgerald, B., Stol, K.J.: Continuous software engineering: a roadmap and agenda. J. Syst. Softw. **123**, 176–189 (2017). https://doi.org/10.1016/j.jss.2015.06.063
8. Gotel, O.C.Z., Finkelstein, C.W.: An analysis of the requirements traceability problem. In: Proceedings of IEEE International Conference on Requirements Engineering, pp. 94–101 (1994). https://doi.org/10.1109/ICRE.1994.292398
9. Guzman, E., Maalej, W.: How do users like this feature? A fine grained sentiment analysis of app reviews. In: IEEE 22nd International Conference on Requirements Engineering, pp. 153–162 (2014). https://doi.org/10.1109/RE.2014.6912257

10. Hebig, R.: UI-tracer: a lightweight approach to help developers tracing user interface elements to source code. In: Software Engineering and Software Management, pp. 225–236 (2018)
11. Johanssen, J.O., Kleebaum, A., Bruegge, B., Paech, B.: Towards a systematic approach to integrate usage and decision knowledge in continuous software engineering. In: Proceedings of the 2nd Workshop on Continuous Software Engineering, pp. 7–11 (2017)
12. Kleebaum, A., Johanssen, J.O., Paech, B., Bruegge, B.: Tool support for decision and usage knowledge in continuous software engineering. In: Proceedings of the 3rd Workshop on Continuous Software Engineering, pp. 74–77 (2018). https://doi.org/10.11588/heidok.00024186
13. Krusche, S., Alperowitz, L., Bruegge, B., Wagner, M.O.: Rugby: an agile process model based on continuous delivery. In: Proceedings of the 1st International Workshop on Rapid Continuous Software Engineering, pp. 42–50 (2014). https://doi.org/10.1145/2593812.2593818
14. Maalej, W., Happel, H.J., Rashid, A.: When users become collaborators: towards continuous and context-aware user input. In: Proceedings of the ACM SIGPLAN Conference Companion on Object Oriented Programming Systems Languages and Applications, pp. 981–990 (2009). https://doi.org/10.1145/1639950.1640068
15. Nielsen, J.: Scenarios in discount usability engineering. In: Carroll, J.M. (ed.) Scenario-based Design, pp. 59–83. Wiley (1995)
16. Paterno, F., Mancini, C., Meniconi, S.: ConcurTaskTrees: a diagrammatic notation for specifying task models. In: Howard, S., Hammond, J., Lindgaard, G. (eds.) Human-Computer Interaction INTERACT '97. ITIFIP, pp. 362–369. Springer, Boston, MA (1997). https://doi.org/10.1007/978-0-387-35175-9_58
17. Ros, R., Runeson, P.: Continuous experimentation and A/B testing: a mapping study. In: 4th International Workshop on Rapid Continuous Software Engineering, pp. 35–41 (2018). https://doi.org/10.1145/3194760.3194766
18. Seiler, M., Paech, B.: Using tags to support feature management across issue tracking systems and version control systems. In: Grünbacher, P., Perini, A. (eds.) REFSQ 2017. LNCS, vol. 10153, pp. 174–180. Springer, Cham (2017). https://doi.org/10.1007/978-3-319-54045-0_13

Software Process Measurement and Related Challenges in Agile Software Development: A Multiple Case Study

Prabhat Ram$^{(\boxtimes)}$, Pilar Rodriguez, and Markku Oivo

M3S, University of Oulu, 90014 Oulu, Finland
{prabhat.ram,pilar.rodriguez,markku.oivo}@oulu.fi

Abstract. Existing scientific literature highlights the importance of metrics in Agile Software Development (ASD). Still, empirical investigation into metrics in ASD is scarce, particularly in identifying the rationale and the operational challenges associated with metrics. Under the Q-Rapids project (Horizon 2020), we conducted a multiple case study at four Agile companies, using the Goal Question Metric (GQM) approach, to investigate the rationale explaining the choice of process metrics in ASD, and challenges faced in operationalizing them. Results reflect that companies are interested in assessing process aspects like velocity, testing performance, and estimation accuracy, and they prefer custom metrics for these assessments. Companies use metrics as a means to access and even capitalize on the data, erstwhile inaccessible due to technical or process constraints. However, development context of a company can hinder metrics operationalization, manifesting primarily as unavailability of the data required to measure metrics. The other challenge is the uncertain potential of metrics to help derive actionable inputs to facilitate decision-making. Essentially, development context has a strong influence over a company's choice of process metrics, rationale, and challenges to operationalize these metrics.

Keywords: Process metrics · Agile Software Development · GQM

1 Introduction

Software measurement enables understanding of cost and quality of software development [1], and it supports in planning, monitoring, controlling, and evaluating software processes [2]. The increasing popularity of Agile Software Development (ASD) [3, 4] makes understanding of software metrics in agile context more relevant. Research recognizes the need for agile organizations to use metrics, but empirical research on metrics in industrial ASD remains scarce [3, 5].

Existing studies discuss use of metrics in ASD for planning and tracking software development [5], estimating effort [6], understanding development performance and product quality [3], and reporting ASD progress and quality to stakeholders not involved in the actual development [7]. These studies propose metrics focused on specific quality improvement goals, but most of them present initial emerging results that have not been evaluated within larger industrial context. Kupiainen et al. [5] conducted a systematic literature review to investigate the reasons and actual use of

M. Kuhrmann et al. (Eds.): PROFES 2018, LNCS 11271, pp. 272–287, 2018.
https://doi.org/10.1007/978-3-030-03673-7_20

metrics in ASD, and drew a similar conclusion that there is a lack of empirical studies in industrial context. There is also a need to investigate metrics that can influence process improvement in ASD, how they are operationalized [5], and the accompanying challenges. These gaps motivate the following research questions (RQ):

- **RQ1:** What metrics are software-intensive companies interested in to assess their ASD processes, and the rationale behind them?
- **RQ2:** What are the challenges faced by software-intensive companies in operationalizing the metrics to assess their ASD processes?

We conducted our research in the context of the Q-Rapids[1] project, a Horizon 2020 (H2020) project, involving three research organizations and four ICT companies. The goal of the project is to develop an agile-based, data-driven, quality-aware rapid software development framework [8]. Building on top of the project progress [9], we used Goal Question Metric (GQM) to collect data at the four case companies, and facilitate the multiple case study to help answer the research questions. We conducted 12 GQM workshops (three with each case company), involving a total of 19 practitioners. These case companies have several years of experience in ASD, are of different size, and focus on diverse industrial domains. Differences in development contexts at the four case companies enabled rich data collection and comparative analysis of our findings.

In comparison to existing literature, our study contributes in the following ways:

- We present empirical evidence on the metrics that software-intensive companies use to assess their ASD process.
- We identify and discuss aspects that influence their choice of metrics.
- We draw a metric-centric comparison among the four case companies, and discuss the challenges faced in operationalizing these metrics.

The remainder of the paper is structured as follows: Sect. 2 covers background and related work on the topic. Section 3 describes the research methodology, followed by the multiple case study findings in Sect. 4, and discussion in Sect. 5. Section 6 presents the threats to validity to our paper, followed by conclusion and future research directions in Sect. 7.

2 Background and Related Work

Software measurement in ASD is different from traditional software development methods, primarily because of the differences in processes in these methods [5, 10]. Some of the metrics defined for ASD include velocity, software size estimation, burndown chart, cumulative flow, etc. [10]. Systematic reviews have investigated the state of the art on the use and impact of ASD metrics in industry [5], to provide an overview of metrics on effort estimation [11], as well as effort estimation practices in agile, iterative, and incremental software development [12]. Although the scientific literature

---

[1] http://www.q-rapids.eu/.

has discussed the role metrics play in ASD, there is still insufficient empirical evidence on that role in industrial context, especially in view of large companies [13].

The systematic review by Kupiainen et al. [5] investigated the state of the art on the industry use of metrics in ASD, rationale, and the consequent impact. The authors argue that the use of metrics in ASD and traditional software development companies is similar, as the emphasis in both appear to be on planning and monitoring. In addition to the metrics described in Agile literature, companies also use custom metrics to measure aspects such as business value, defect count, and customer satisfaction. Kupiainen et al. [5] call for more empirical studies to investigate rationales behind metrics use in ASD.

Most primary studies (case studies) in Kupiainen et al. [5] investigate the impact of using Agile in a software company, and use metrics as a tool to measure that impact. Very few studies have enquired the role of metrics in ASD, as used by practitioners. For example, Dubinsky et al. [14] reported on the experience of using software metrics program at an XP development team of the Israeli Air Force. The authors found that using metrics to measure the amount, quality, pace, and work status could lead to accurate and professional decision-making. However, authors focused mainly on the impact of metrics use, and not on the challenges in operationalizing them. A similar approach was followed by Díaz-Ley et al. [15], where a measurement framework, customized for SMEs, was applied in an industrial context. One key benefit the authors reported was being able to define better measurement goals that align with the company's maturity. However, similar to [14], the authors did not discuss the challenges of operationalizing metrics. Furthermore, the focus on process metrics was also missing from these studies.

The research gaps identified in the systematic review conducted by Kupiainen et al. [5] serve as the foundation for the research questions we address in our paper. Similar to [15], we adopted GQM approach to gather empirical evidence about process metrics from diverse companies using Agile development practices, and identify rationales and challenges in operationalizing these metrics. The Goal-Question-Metric (GQM) approach establishes a mechanism to define and interpret software measurement driven by organizational goals. GQM helps specify a goal to be measured, refined into a set of quantifiable questions. These questions, in turn, help define a set of metrics and data for collection [16]. All of this information is recorded on an "abstraction" sheet to provide a structured approach [17] in data interpretation. An abstraction sheet is a tool used to record interviews in the GQM approach. Essentially, GQM approach helps trace a goal to the data that can define that goal operationally, and provide a framework to interpret that data with respect to the goal [3]. Linking data (metrics answering the questions) to goals ensures that relevant metrics are collected, allowing for control over what is collected and its quality [16, 18].

3   Research Methodology

Following the case-study guidelines by Runeson et al. [19], this paper reports a multiple case study involving four case companies. We used GQM for data collection, followed by thematic synthesis [20] for analyzing the results and construct themes to answer the research questions.

3.1 Research Context

Table 1 presents the development context for the four case companies. The development context is distinguished across company size, software development method, and development team composition involved in our case study.

Table 1. Case study context

Company & Size	Product	Development method	Development team
A – Medium	Production testing software framework	Scrum	One team with 6–7 members
B – Large	Software platform	Scrum	Eight globally distributed sub-teams
C – Large	Software modeling tool	Ad-hoc process following Agile principles	One team with 9 members
D – Small	"R" project	ScrumBan & Scrumbut	10 members with same core team

Company A is a medium-size company (over 600 employees) that develops secure communication and connectivity solutions for multiple industry domains. In a bid to achieve efficiency and shorten time-to-market, the company moved to agile and lean software development about 10 years ago. The company aims to develop metrics to measure ASD process to introduce high-level transparency, and a more data-driven and evidence-based decision-making process. The software development process is mainly Scrum-based. For our study, we worked with one of the software teams developing a hardware-testing framework, used internally to test secure solutions that Company A develops.

Company B is a large-size company (over 100,000 employees) developing distributed systems in telecommunication networks. The company aims to have a standardized way of working and tools to identify, analyze, manage, and implement quality requirements right until individual product releases. The software development method, at team level, is Scrum-based. The company's development unit is divided into multiple teams, which are further divided into sub-teams. We focused on the metrics the eight sub-teams will use to develop a software platform, which will be used to build other products.

Company C is a large-size company (over 900 employees) that develops a modeling tool used by developers for model driven development. The product is mature, with multiple releases already in the market. Company C wants to improve quality of the ASD process through early detection of anomalies in development. The company does not follow any formalized method like Scrum, but uses different software development methods that adhere to agile principles. Thus, the company has defined their own agile way of working. They engage in iterative development, but do not have any pre-defined sprint cycles, as they focus more on current issues.

Company D, a small company, is engaged in developing independent software products for multiple industrial domains. The company is targeting for metrics that allows its developers to anticipate design issues, security issues, and platform limitations. The core development team remains the same, but other team members may change from project to project. The software development process is Scrum-based, but with some exceptions. Here, the company uses a pre-software development process to acquire functional and quality requirements. Initial mock-ups and user stories collected during this process serves as the basis for the implementation process. The company develops software in iterations, and uses Kanban board to monitor the status of backlog items.

3.2   Data Collection

We collected data by conducting 12 GQM workshops, three with each case company. The GQM goal driving the workshops was, *"to analyze the agile/rapid software development process for the purpose of monitoring with respect to process performance/quality from the viewpoint of the process users in the context of the company case"*. Based on this generic goal, questions were devised during the GQM workshops, and metrics to provide answers to those questions were elicited. We requested that individuals (stakeholders) involved in process management activities attend these workshops. Taking together all the four case companies, a total of 19 practitioners participated in the workshops. Participants included project managers, product owners, quality managers, and developers. Table 2 shows the details of these workshops:

Table 2. GQM workshops

Sessions	Parameters	Company A	Company B	Company C	Company D
Session 1	Role (# participants)	Quality Lead, Developers (2), Requirement & Process Lead	Quality Manager (2), Project Manager, Developer (3) Development Manager (2)	Architect/Developer, Project Manager, R&D Manager, CEO/Product Owner	Product Owner, Project Manager, System Designer
	Data Collection	Documented	Both	Both	Documented
	Length (hrs)	3.5	3.5	3	3
Session 2	Role (# participants)	Quality Lead, Developers (2), Requirement & Process Lead	Quality Manager, Project Manager, Developer (2) Development Manager	Architect/Developer and R&D Manager	Product Owner, Project Manager
	Data Collection	Both	Both	Both	Documented
	Length (hrs)	2.5	2	1	1.5
Session 3	Role (# participants)	Quality Lead, Developers (2), Requirement & Process Lead	Quality Manager, Project Manager, Developer (2)	Architect/Developer	Project Manager
	Data Collection	Both	Both	Documented	Documented
	Length (hrs)	2.5	1	0.5	1.5

Instead of starting from scratch, we built on top of a preliminary set of process metrics that were already identified by the case companies during earlier project tasks [9]. One of the first tasks in the project was to develop a 'Quality Model' that helps the case companies better define their understanding of quality [8, 9]. Software quality workshops were held to define this Quality Model, consisting of application of GQM+Strategies™, Quamoco, and GQM. Metrics were classified as either 'product factors' or 'process factors' based on whether they signified product or process characteristics [9]. Some process metrics emerged as relevant during these workshops, conducted between December 2016 and February 2017. However, only the metrics that could help the case companies assess and improve product quality were developed further, as that was the focus of the project's tasks. The process metrics that remained became the preliminary set to start the subsequent GQM workshops, conducted as part of this multiple case study between November 2017 and January 2018.

From the preliminary set, case companies chose the process metrics they considered relevant to their development context. Similarly, they discarded metrics from the preliminary set that they considered irrelevant for measuring Agile process performance and quality, and added new metrics that particularly focus on assessing their ASD processes. While eliciting metrics, we enquired participants to focus on details such as why the metric was relevant, how the metric would be measured (e.g. formula to measure the metric), data sources needed to obtain the data, and ways to operationalize the metric.

Wherever possible, we recorded or documented the workshops extensively. Three researchers participated in the kick-off workshop with each case company. Two researchers participated in the subsequent workshops, where one conducted the workshop and the other documented it.

3.3   Data Analysis

Data collected during the GQM workshops consisted of the metrics recorded in GQM abstraction sheets [17], recordings, and supporting notes. Data was analyzed incrementally. At the end of every GQM session, one researcher analyzed the documentation/recording, and shared the analysis with the other researcher for corroboration. Next, before the following session in a case company took place, the analysis was shared with the individual case company for validation and feedback. This analysis helped answer the first part of RQ1 (choice of process metrics).

We used thematic synthesis to analyze the data (recordings, meeting minutes, and feedback) generated from the GQM workshops to answer the second part of RQ1 (metrics rationale) and RQ2 (operationalization challenges). One researcher performed line-by-line coding of the data and recorded concepts focusing on metrics rationale, and on concepts related to operationalization challenges. The researcher further analyzed the inductively coded concepts at a higher abstraction level to develop descriptive themes. Themes help transform large number of codes into a smaller analytical unit. Next, the researcher mapped these descriptive themes based on their interrelationships to develop higher-order analytical theme(s) for metrics rationale and for operationalization challenges. The thematic synthesis framework and the resulting themes were discussed with other researchers and refined further.

4 Results

Overall, we found that case companies targeted very similar process aspects, but adopted custom metrics to assess those process aspects. They also share very similar rationale and challenges in operationalizing these metrics.

4.1 RQ1: What Metrics Are Software-Intensive Companies Interested in to Assess Their ASD Processes, and the Rationale Behind Them?

A total of 132 metrics were elicited from the workshops (including metrics from the software quality workshops), available in Appendix A (https://goo.gl/nf1WLJ). For brevity, we present our results in Table 3 from factors' point of view, further elaborated in Appendix B (https://goo.gl/8zbScQ). 'Factors' here is a generalization of 'product factors' and 'process factors', and our focus is on the latter.

Table 3. Metrics and Rationale

Factors	Measures...	Rationale
Testing Performance**	...testing phase performance aspects like execution time	Track improvements & bottlenecks
Issues' Velocity**	... capability to fulfil issues planned for a sprint	Assess & improve planning capability, Identify bottlenecks, Knowledge sharing
Code Quality*	... impact of code changes in source code quality	Knowledge sharing
Issues' Estimation Accuracy**	...difference between effort estimated and actual effort invested for an issue	Resource planning
Testing Status*	....unit test success density	Process improvement
Blocking Code*	...number of files not violating quality rule, which otherwise may block the flow of other coding activities	Identify bottlenecks
Delivery Performance***	....capability for on-time delivery, considering resource management	Identify bottlenecks
External Quality***	...quality of a product from customer standpoint	Process improvement
Development Speed***	...daily build progress	Data availability
Quality Issues' Specification*	...amount of issues entering backlog in an incomplete state	Traceability

* - Factors identified and completely defined in the software quality workshops [9]
** - Factors identified during the software quality workshops [9], but metrics elicited/refined in the GQM workshops
*** - New factors identified and defined in the GQM workshops

A total of 10 factors were identified, of which seven make clear references to process aspects (*Testing Performance, Issues' Velocity, Issues' Estimation Accuracy, Testing Status, Delivery Performance, Development Speed,* and *Quality issues' specification*). *Code Quality* [9] and *External Quality* can be argued as more product-oriented factors. However, case companies argued that improvement in these factors can indicate good process, and so should also be considered from process-improvement standpoint.

We describe the results for RQ1 further based on the degree of commonality in choice of factors (and in extension, metrics) among the case companies.

Factors Common to All Companies. At factors level, all the case companies were interested in assessing *Testing Performance, Issues*[2] *Velocity, Code Quality,* and *Issues' Estimation Accuracy.* For assessing *Testing Performance,* companies preferred mostly custom metrics. Aiming to track improvements in testing process and bottlenecks in review phases, Company A defined metrics like 'Error leakage' and 'Average number of iterations in the code-review phase', respectively. Targeting code-review phase, Company B defined metrics like 'Actual feedback time from CI to developers' to assess *Testing Performance.* Similarly, Company C defined metrics like '% errors identified during a validation for a given release', but with the objective of learning what went wrong in testing and why, evident from the following quote: "At the end of the project…we may have to have an analysis about how the [development] process goes…what went wrong, or good, and why". Company D was interested in metrics that could meet three distinct objectives of informing developers about their progress, assisting Product Owner in development team management, and informing the management about the overall project status. The objective of keeping developers in the loop, in addition to tracking bottlenecks in testing, is reflected in their choice of custom metrics like 'No. of tickets that are pending tests' and 'No. of tickets in the "Ready" column' to assess *Testing Performance.*

For assessing *Issues' Velocity,* case companies A and C use several common process metrics like 'Average speed to resolve issues' and 'No. of issues/tickets/story points at start of the sprint'. These metrics will help Company A access the data their system is already producing, and even assess sprint planning capability. The latter rationale is reflected in one of the stakeholders' quote, "Do we allocate too much story points to a sprint?" For Company C, these metrics can help identify bottlenecks in releasing on time, reflected in the following quote, "…[focus was] not the performance of the process but the efficiency of the process. And the idea is to have products or projects on time with acceptable quality". Both Company B and C relied mainly on custom metrics to assess *Issues' Velocity.* Company B defined 11 custom metrics like 'No. of issues/tickets at start of the sprint' and 'No. of done issues at the end of the sprint' to track its sprint progress. Similarly, Company D defined nine custom metrics like 'No. of Ready issues', and 'No. of issues that are delayed' to learn if their sprint planning needs improvement.

---

[2] A JIRA terminology that could represent a software bug, a project task, a helpdesk ticket, etc. - https://goo.gl/vNQGJE.

As described in [9], in assessing *Code Quality*, three case companies used largely the same set of metrics. The metric of 'Complexity' was the only common metric for all the case companies. In contrast, Company D preferred mainly custom metrics like 'Code reliability', 'Code maintainability', 'Code security', etc. to assess *Code Quality*. Although not process oriented, these metrics can be used to measure process performance, as good quality process results in good quality code.

Lastly, all the case companies were interested in assessing *Issues' Estimation Accuracy*. The common rationale was to measure the accuracy with which a case company plans the effort (man-days) required to implement an issue. The fundamental metrics like 'Estimated effort of an issue/story point' and 'Real invested effort of an issue/story point' were common to all the case companies. However, they expressed difficulties when enquired about their plans to operationalize these metrics, which we elaborate upon in Sect. 4.2.

Factors Common to Three or Two Case Companies. *Testing Status* was common to three case companies (Company C being the exception). Only Company A and Company B shared similarities at metrics level, while Company D relied exclusively on custom metrics to assess this process factor.

Blocking code was common to Company B and C, and was assessed using the only metric '% files without critical/blocker quality rules'. This process factor refers to the condition where a particular file violates a predefined quality rule, which could block other coding activities [9]. A clear rationale could not be gathered for this metric, but it appears to satisfy Company C's aim to identify causes for delays in product releases.

Custom Factors. The factors of *Delivery Performance* and *External Quality* were exclusive to Company C, thereby requiring custom metrics to assess them. Based on the principle that process dictates product quality, *External Quality* comprises metrics that highlight product-related concerns resulting from process inefficiencies. Company C is interested in recording product quality related issues raised by the end users, map these to corresponding development processes, and improve upon them for subsequent product releases. Metrics under the *Delivery Performance* factor align well with the case company's aim to identify reasons for delay in releases.

Company A's interest in process metrics for assessing *Development Speed* was driven by the need to retrieve data from its Continuous Integration/Development (CI/CD) engine to measure their daily build performance. This decision finds support in their rationale of accessing and using the rich data, erstwhile inaccessible due to lack of appropriate retrieval mechanisms, which their system is producing.

Only Company B expressed interest in assessing *Quality Issues' Specification*, using the only metric '% issues completely specified'. The metric refers to the issues that have been completely specified in the backlog, and can, hence, commence implementation. Company B works on large-size features, with implementation spanning multiple teams and sub-teams using diverse tools. A given feature may be specified differently in different tools, making it a time-consuming task to trace these different specifications back to the original feature. It is this traceability that the chosen metric is expected to help with, by linking feature information across different tools with different specifications.

Overall, the four case companies were interested in measuring same factors (*Testing Performance, Issues' Velocity, Code Quality,* and *Issues' Estimation Accuracy*). Despite the commonality at factor level, these companies preferred mainly custom metrics for assessing them. This decision was dictated by the development context, especially the technical infrastructure available and the existing software development process.

The distinct rationales of planning, tracking improvements and bottlenecks, knowledge sharing, traceability, and process improvements were possible because the data for relevant metrics were available to support these objectives. At a higher abstraction level, these rationales evolve into the descriptive themes of Data availability, Planning and bottleneck tracking, Information consistency, and Visibility. The last three rationales are the companies capitalizing on the data that is now available and accessible in the desired form due to the metrics. Therefore, further analysis of the four descriptive themes lead to the higher-order analytical theme of *Data Capitalization,* presented in Appendix C (https://goo.gl/Dtr5nx). Specifically, companies want to use the metrics data to create *awareness* about project activities by keeping relevant stakeholders in the loop, and improving transparency across the organization. Secondly, the metrics data could help companies identify bottlenecks in resource planning, testing, and review phase, enabling them to exercise *control* over these processes as a measure of improvement.

4.2   RQ2: What Are the Challenges Faced by Software-Intensive Companies in Operationalizing the Choice of Metrics to Assess Their ASD Processes?

From the GQM workshops, we identified some common and some unique challenges concerning operationalization of the elicited metrics. We categorized these challenges in three groups, as presented in the following Table 4:

Table 4. Challenges in operationalizing metrics

Challenge	Description
Lack of data or appropriate tools to produce that data	Development practices and processes at a company does not produce the data needed to measure a metric, or the company is not aware what data they can retrieve, or they are not using the tool(s) needed to measure a metric
Existing process inhibiting change	Existing development process does not result in the data needed to measure the metric a company is interested in
Difficulty in deriving actionable inputs	Data to measure a metric is available, but a company is uncertain about that metric's potential in providing actionable inputs

Lack of Data or Appropriate Tools to Produce That Data. Lack of data and lack of appropriate tools are closely interlinked. For example, despite interest in several metrics, Company A did not have suitable tools to produce the data needed for these metrics, as reflected in the following quote: "It's not available, because we are not using Gerrit [in the case concerned] just yet". Similarly, for Company C, availability of data depended on how easily it could be retrieved, as highlighted in the comment: "...if we could track this, we could explain a lot of other phenomenon in the development... and this is never done. It's difficult to collect, but useful to know". Data unavailability can also stem from unawareness of what data could be retrieved from a certain tool. The following comment supports this claim: "We don't know what information in this specific tool is available".

Existing Process Inhibiting Change. Specific development practices and processes can pose a problem in operationalizing some metrics. For instance, identification of bugs is not made explicit during sprints for Company A. To use metrics that require such information, company will need to change its development process, which is a challenge as indicated in the quote: "That's a process change. We should then change our process. Everybody write everything to JIRA, and I know that nobody will do this...This will waste developer's time hugely". Similarly, another case company believed that it is theoretically possible to measure the metric 'Ticket Size', but in practice, it would require an additional task on their part, which they do not encourage. The same challenge was identified even in case of assessing *Issues' Estimation Accuracy* process factor. This particular challenge could manifest in many ways like case companies do not have a formal practice in place to collect the data for the metrics, or the management is not interested in assessing this process factor, or the metric is not compatible with the development practice followed. Overall, in order to measure some of these metrics, a change in existing software development process or practice is required. However, such a change may run the risk of compromising the agile aspect of their software development process.

Unavailability of data can be seen as a consequence of lack of relevant tools that produce the needed data, or lack of supporting development process, or both. Analysis of the above-discussed two specific challenges produced the higher-order theme of *Data Unavailability*, as the common underlying challenge in metrics operationalizing. The analysis is available in Appendix D (https://goo.gl/KRUZBX). One of the common manifestations identified for this challenge is *process inertia*, which can be viewed as a condition where development process related aspects obstruct a case company from operationalizing their choice of metrics.

Difficulty in Deriving Actionable Inputs. A company may have the right tool and the supporting development process to collect the necessary metric data. However, application of that data within a larger strategic context poses a challenge. Company B illustrated this challenge as follows: "...we have plenty of data and tools to collect metrics, but we have shortcomings for efficiently and smartly utilizing the collected data". A similar supporting inference was drawn from the following comment made by a stakeholder of Company C: "It has to add value to the measure...what I'd like to have is 'green' or 'red' light about my project. That's enough. I don't want hundreds of measures, curves, and pie-chart, and so on".

Analysis of the above challenge produced a higher-order theme of *Lack of Actionable Input* (in Appendix D - https://goo.gl/KRUZBX) representing the second challenge in metrics operationalization in our study. Essentially, case companies expect their chosen metrics to facilitate decision-making, or at least add enough value to stimulate actions toward improving their development process. Extraction of such actionable inputs from metrics is difficult, as expressed by one of the case companies.

5 Discussion

In this section, we discuss the multiple case study's results and address the two RQs. In comparison to existing literature, we find that the study's results reinforce and even extend existing knowledge, particularly in case of RQ2.

5.1 RQ1: What Are the Metrics Software-Intensive Companies Interested in to Assess Their ASD Processes, and the Rationale Behind Them?

We found that the case companies are interested in assessing processes related to implementation (*Issues' Velocity,* and *Development Speed*), testing (*Testing Performance* and *Testing Status*), and planning (*Issues' Estimation Accuracy* and some metrics under *Issues' Velocity*). Research suggests that interest in such process factors indicates the need to plan and track sprints and projects [5]. *Issues' Velocity* metrics like 'No. of issues/ticket at the start of the sprint' and 'No. of issues/ticket at the end of the sprint' point to the need to assess sprint-planning capability. Similarly, by identifying bottlenecks by assessing *Delivery Performance* process factor, a company could learn if there is a need to plan their releases better. Such metrics suggest that agility imparted by ASD does not make a company immune to concerns associated with traditional software development [5]. Moreover, metrics assessing sprint or project velocity align with the third Agile principle of delivering working software in shorter cycles [21]. Similarly, factors like *Blocking Code* and *Quality Issues' Specification* reflect the Agile principle of continuous attention to technical excellence and good design [5, 21, 22]. Compliance to Agile principles indicates that the case companies selected metrics that stayed true to the tenets of ASD.

Variations in development context may not fully affect what process factors a company is interested in (4/10 factors are common), but it certainly influences how they are used. This is apparent in assessment of factors like *Testing Performance, Issues' Velocity, Code Quality, Testing Status,* and even *Blocking Code* to some extent. In addition to common metrics, case companies defined several custom metrics that aligned with their development context. Current literature [5] identifies company size and project characteristics as the development context aspects that can influence a company's choice of metrics, and our findings further reinforces this claim. For instance, Company D (small company) mostly preferred low-level metrics (specific measurement like 'No. of issues that are delayed') to high-level metrics (complex measurement like 'Average time to fix an error'). In addition, a typical project at Company D lasts for around four months. This further reinforces their interest in low-level metrics, as such metrics can help them gather insights at a lower granularity. The opposite was true for Company B (large company), where low-level process metrics proved to be inadequate at measuring process aspects for the large-size features the company implements. Furthermore, a typical project at Company B can take years, involving development of large features by a team of thousands. Hence, process insights at the lowest granular level may be insufficient at assessing development processes supporting development of large-scale product. Instead, higher-level metrics can provide the relevant insights to Company B in a condensed format. Existing research argues that company size and project characteristics determine adoption of ASD. Based on our findings, we argue that these determinants can also influence adoption of certain process metrics in ASD.

Rationales like identifying bottlenecks, tracking improvements, knowledge sharing find support in [5]. However, *Data Capitalization* is the overarching rationale that ties these disparate rationales together. Case companies want to use metrics to derive insights from the large amount of data produced by their systems and processes, and communicate this knowledge across the organization to enhance visibility (create *awareness*). Subsequently, the companies want to use this knowledge to exercise control in an effort to improve planning, track progress, and manage information integrity. The need to create awareness among stakeholders and use controlling measures to induce improvements is also reflected in current literature [23, 24]. Exercising control is in contrast to the tenets of Agile, but research argues that successful software companies tend to plan and estimate projects accurately [25], even in case of ASD [5].

5.2   RQ2: What Are the Challenges Faced by the Software-Intensive Companies in Operationalizing the Choice of Metrics to Assess Their ASD Processes?

In contrast to the fundamental rationale of data availability, data unavailability is one of the two fundamental challenges to obstruct metrics operationalization. *Process Inertia* was identified as a manifestation of this challenge. Ideally, to overcome such a challenge, an existing development process needs to be changed, but this is not always considered a feasible alternative. Such challenges are in line with the requirement that metrics in ASD should adhere to a company's development context [26, 27], be lightweight, and not hinder normal development activities [28]. The incompatibility between some of the process metrics chosen by the case companies and their development context appears to be the cause of process inertia, further translating into one of the two main challenges of *Data Unavailability*.

The second challenge of *Lack of Actionable Input* is supported by the concerns raised by some case companies that metrics should ideally reflect or stimulate actionable inputs, geared towards decision-making. The case companies expected their chosen metrics to help them in producing actionable inputs to support their decision-making. This philosophy resembles that of *actionable analytics*, where practitioners derive actionable inputs from the predictive capacity of the collected data [29]. In the absence of such information, a metric may not benefit a company in ways it expects it to. It is also required that a company be able to extract actionable input from a metric, and utilize it in an efficient and even strategic ways. However, the case companies were skeptical if use of metrics' would indeed lead to actionable inputs. Furthermore, they indicated that extracting actionable inputs from a metric can be a struggle.

6   Threats to Validity

Potential misinterpretation of GQM goal and the questions can be a threat to our study's construct validity. By explicating the GQM goal, questions, and having the findings and analyses validated by the case companies helped mitigate the threat to construct validity.

Internal validity concerns examination of causal relations free of influences unknown to the researcher [19]. The primary source of threat to our study's internal validity could be the selection of participants for the GQM workshops, as these could lead to elicitation of metrics that are irrelevant from ASD process standpoint. A company champion helped us identify stakeholders that are responsible for taking process related decisions in each case company, thereby mitigating the said threat. Next, two researchers executed and analyzed the data collected from the GQM workshops, which were shared with the case companies for feedback. This also helped mitigate threat to the study's internal validity.

Generalizability (external validity) of our multiple case study findings is limited only to the contexts of the four case companies that participated in the study. However, analysis and integration of other similar cases could extend our results, and companies with context similar to any of the case companies may find our findings applicable.

Reliability is related to the extent to which the data and the analysis are dependent on a researcher [19]. Multiple researchers participated in both data collection and data analysis, as a measure to enhance the study's reliability.

7   Conclusion and Future Work

Existing scientific literature focuses on the impact of using metrics in industrial ASD, but the associated rationales and challenges remain underexplored. Using the GQM approach, we conducted a multiple case study, involving four case companies, to address this research gap.

The case companies were interested in similar process factors like *Issues' Velocity, Testing Performance, Issues' Estimation Accuracy,* and *Code Quality.* Depending on individual requirements, case companies also wanted to measure exclusive process factors like *Development Speed, Delivery Performance,* and *External Quality.* Rationales such as data availability, tracking planning and bottlenecks, traceability, and knowledge sharing support the selection of metrics. However, being able to capitalize on the data to create awareness and exercise control over development processes appear to be the fundamental rationales. Data unavailability, a consequence of prevailing development context like limiting technical infrastructure or inhibiting development process, underlie several individual challenges that can obstruct metrics operationalization. For a company to extract actionable input from a metric to seek value addition or facilitate decision-making is another challenge that deserves further attention.

Our paper is part of the larger research project to help companies make data-driven (informed) decisions in Agile and rapid software development. The case companies are in the process of operationalizing the metrics reported in this study. Our future scientific studies will be about observing the influences these metrics have on ASD process at the case companies, and how they translate these metrics into actionable inputs.

Acknowledgment. This work is a result of the Q-Rapids Project, which has received funding from the European Union's Horizon 2020 research and innovation programme, under grant agreement No. 732253.

References

1. Gopal, A., Krishnan, M.S., Mukhopadhyay, T., Goldenson, D.R.: Measurement programs in software development: determinants of success. IEEE Trans. Softw. Eng. **28**, 863–876 (2002)
2. Briand, L.C., Morasca, S., Basili, V.R.: An operational process for goal-driven definition of measures. IEEE Trans. Softw. Eng. **28**, 1106–1125 (2002)
3. Tarhan, A., Yilmaz, S.G.: Systematic analyses and comparison of development performance and product quality of incremental process and agile process. Inf. Softw. Technol. **56**, 477–494 (2014)
4. Rodríguez, P., Markkula, J., Oivo, M., Turula, K.: Survey on agile and lean usage in finnish software industry. In: Proceedings of the ACM-IEEE International Symposium on Empirical Software Engineering and Measurement, ESEM 2012, p. 139 (2012)
5. Kupiainen, E., Mäntylä, M.V., Itkonen, J.: Using metrics in agile and lean software development - a systematic literature review of industrial studies. Inf. Softw. Technol. **62**, 143–163 (2015)
6. Tanveer, B., Guzmán, L., Engel, U.M.: Understanding and improving effort estimation in Agile software development. In: Proceedings of the International Conference on Software and Systems Process, ICSSP 2016, pp. 41–50 (2016)
7. Tamburri, D.A., Lubsen, Z.,, Boerman, M.P., Visser, J.: Measuring and monitoring agile development status. In: Proceedings of the Sixth International Workshop on Emerging Trends in Software Metrics, pp. 54–62. IEEE Press (2015)
8. Franch, X., et al.: Data-driven requirements engineering in agile projects: the Q-rapids approach. In: Proceedings of the 2017 IEEE 25th International Requirements Engineering Conference Workshops, REW 2017, pp. 411–414 (2017)
9. Martínez-Fernández, S., Jedlitschka, A., Guzmán, L., Vollmer, A.-M.: A quality model for actionable analytics in rapid software development. In: Euromicro SEAA 2018 (2018, in press)
10. Javdani, T., Zulzalil, H., Ghani, A.: On the current measurement practices in agile software development. Int. J. Comput. Sci. Issues **9**, 127–133 (2013)
11. Usman, M., Mendes, E., Weidt, F., Britto, R.: Effort estimation in agile software development: a systematic literature review. In: ACM International Conference Proceeding Series, pp. 82–91 (2014)
12. Nguyen-Cong, D., Tran-Cao, D.: A review of effort estimation studies in agile, iterative and incremental software development. In: The 2013 RIVF International Conference on Computing & Communication Technologies - Research, Innovation, and Vision for Future (RIVF), pp. 27–30. IEEE (2013)
13. Radjenović, D., Heričko, M., Torkar, R., Živkovič, A.: Software fault prediction metrics: a systematic literature review. Inf. Softw. Technol. **55**, 1397–1418 (2013)
14. Dubinsky, Y., Talby, D., Hazzan, O., Keren, A.: Agile metrics at the Israeli air force. In: Agile Development Conference (ADC 2005), pp. 12–19. IEEE Computer Society (2005)

15. Díaz-Ley, M., García, F., Piattini, M.: Implementing a software measurement program in small and medium enterprises: a suitable framework. IET Softw. **2**, 417 (2008)
16. Basili, V.R.: Software modeling and measurement: the Goal/Question/Metric paradigm (1992)
17. Van Latum, F., Van Solingen, R., Oivo, M., Hoisi, B., Rombach, D., Ruhe, G.: Adopting GQM-based measurement in an industrial environment. IEEE Softw. **15**, 78–86 (1998)
18. Basili, V., Heidrich, J., Lindvall, M., Münch, J., Regardie, M., Trendowicz, A.: GQM+Strategies - aligning business strategies with software measurement. In: Proceedings of the 1st International Symposium on Empirical Software Engineering and Measurement, ESEM 2007, pp. 488–490 (2007)
19. Runeson, P., Höst, M.: Guidelines for conducting and reporting case study research in software engineering. Empir. Softw. Eng. **14**, 131–164 (2009)
20. Cruzes, D.S., Dyba, T.: Recommended steps for thematic synthesis in software engineering. In: 2011 International Symposium on Empirical Software Engineering and Measurement, pp. 275–284 (2011)
21. Beedle, M., et al.: Manifesto for agile software development, pp. 2–3 (2001)
22. Patel, C., Lycett, M., Macredie, R., De Cesare, S.: Perceptions of agility and collaboration in software development practice. In: Proceedings of the 39th Annual Hawaii International Conference on System Sciences (HICSS 2006), pp. 1–7 (2006)
23. Grady, R.B.: Successfully applying software metrics. Computer (Long. Beach. Calif.) **27**, 18–25 (1994)
24. Pulford, K., Kuntzmann-Combelles, A., Shirlaw, S.: A Quantitative Approach to Software Management: The Ami Handbook. Addison-Wesley, Reading (1996)
25. Jones, C.: Applied Software Measurement: Global Analysis of Productivity and Quality. McGraw-Hill Education Group, New York (2008)
26. Hartmann, D., Dymond, R.: Appropriate agile measurement: using metrics and diagnostics to deliver business value. In: AGILE 2006, pp. 126–134 (2006)
27. Gregory, P., Barroca, L., Taylor, K., Salah, D., Sharp, H.: Agile challenges in practice: a thematic analysis. In: Lassenius, C., Dingsøyr, T., Paasivaara, M. (eds.) XP 2015. LNBIP, vol. 212, pp. 64–80. Springer, Cham (2015). https://doi.org/10.1007/978-3-319-18612-2_6
28. Layman, L., Williams, L., Cunningham, L.: Motivations and measurements in an agile case study. J. Syst. Archit. **52**, 654–667 (2006)
29. Yang, Y., Falessi, D., Menzies, T., Hihn, J.: Actionable analytics for you. IEEE Softw. **35**, 51–53 (2018)

Emperor's New Clothes: Transparency Through Metrication in Customer-Supplier Relationships

Christian R. Prause[1(✉)] and Alfred Hönle[2]

[1] German Aerospace Center, Bonn, Germany
christian.prause@dlr.de
[2] OHB System AG, Weßling, Germany
alfred.hoenle@ohb.de

Abstract. Space projects, and development of software embedded in these systems, are complex, sometimes costing hundreds of millions of Euros and involving several tiers of suppliers. An important means of improving mutual understanding is to increase transparency of the development status between customers and suppliers. We raise the problem of transparency in complex projects to the reader's attention, and, relying on results of a small survey of practitioners, propose to use ECSS software metrics/KPIs as a mitigation. We present our metrication infrastructure, and describe issues to be considered when implementing an early metrication programme in a real-world, industry space project.

Keywords: Software metrication · Management
Customer-supplier transparency · Embedded software · Aerospace
ECSS · KPI

1 Introduction

You software guys are too much like the weavers in the story about the Emperor and his new clothes. When I go out to check on a software development the answers I get sound like, "We're fantastically busy weaving this magic cloth. Just wait a while and it'll look terrific." But there's nothing I can see or touch, no numbers I can relate to, no way to pick up signals that things aren't really all that great. And there are too many people I know who have come out at the end wearing a bunch of expensive rags or nothing at all.[1] The situation today might be not as dramatic as provocatively stated almost 50 years ago. But since the early days of the *software crisis* and *software engineering*, size and complexity of software have kept increasing. The ratio of costs for all hardware and software of 10:1 reversed to 1:2 in US missions. The embedded flight software alone accounts for up to 20% of satellite costs. It allows more challenging missions and to reply to increasingly demanding user requirements [1, 12, 15, 25]. Although

---

[1] Statement by an Air Force decision maker as reported by [6].

© Springer Nature Switzerland AG 2018
M. Kuhrmann et al. (Eds.): PROFES 2018, LNCS 11271, pp. 288–296, 2018.
https://doi.org/10.1007/978-3-030-03673-7_21

a metrication standard exists, not much attention has yet been paid to it in practice. *RQ: Are ECSS[2] metrics a practicable way to improve transparency of software development in customer-supplier relationships of space missions?*

- We describe our practitioners' view on transparency in the pervasive customer-supplier relationship of European space projects (Sect. 2),
- survey industry and agency practitioners whether they wish for improved transparency, and if they expect benefits from software metrics (Sect. 3),
- present the software architecture of the AENEAS metrication infrastructure and define a data protocol for delivering the data (Sect. 4), and
- identify early lessons from implementing and using metrication (Sect. 5).

Finally, we conclude (see Sect. 6).

2 Background: Transparency and Software Metrics

Many spacecraft are one-of-a-kind devices with uncommon and custom-built hardware and software. An identical unit is rarely built. If the mission goal is not reached, for whatever reason, there is no second chance. In these systems, software fulfills more and more critical functions. A single failure, in the worst case, can mean that the spacecraft and its mission are lost (cf. [22]). While most software can be updated in flight, fixing bugs in decades old software (without introducing new ones) is challenging. Preparing a mission, which includes making of the spacecraft and its ground support equipment, may take more than ten years. Its cost can be the hundreds of millions of Euros. What adds to project complexity is that there are many stakeholders like the final customer, prime contractor(s), several tiers of suppliers, scientific users, and potentially material providers on some other contractual basis. Space systems are similar to other large, one-of-a-kind things like airports or nuclear power plants; and likewise, as opposed to buying off-the-shelf, contract partners need visibility or *transparency*. Customers get involved in the development (process) so that problems can be identified early and reacted upon in a timely manner [8] (see also [22]). Donaldson and Siegel [8] note: "Successful software development is first and foremost an ongoing exercise in effective communication between the customer and the seller throughout a software project."

Transparency through customer involvement is a major motivator for agile development. However, it is not considered as a home ground for high-reliability products, and there are some issues with contract design and public offer bidding [7,10,14,18,19]. Successful ways to improve transparency are (i) *stages* with extensive[3] reviews at system and subsystem levels, which are a key element in

---

[2] The European Cooperation for Space Standardization (ECSS) is a cooperative effort of ESA, national space agencies, and industry to develop and maintain a single, coherent set of standards for hardware, software, and other activities ([12], cf. [22]).

[3] Stages are central to ECSS (cf. [11]). Yet, if conducted only half-heartedly, they cannot satisfy transparency needs and should then be considered a waste of time [8].

ECSS standards, and (ii) *measurements* of software process and product [8]. Hence, for us, *software metrics* are not only typical source code metrics like cyclomatic complexity, but also other Key Performance Indicators (KPI).

Software engineering is "a systematic, disciplined, quantifiable approach to the development, operation, and maintenance of software; that is the application of engineering to software" [16]. Unsurprisingly, metrication has a long history in software engineering. Ebert and Dumke [9] point out that the more mature an engineering discipline is, the more measurements are used, that one can only control what can be observed and measured, and that in the global market organizations cannot be successful without paying attention to their performance (including quality). Without metrication, different understandings of process goals and progress may become apparent late, leading to discussion, disappointment, rework, and/or contractual adjustments; e.g., regarding unit test coverage (cf. [24]). In software development, many of the relevant artifacts to be measured are already stored in information systems. Once interfaces are set up, metrication incurs practically no additional cost. Metrication reduces risks for suppliers by reducing room for misinterpretation, misunderstandings and speculation, and may promote timely dealing with certain customer expectations. The customer benefits from reduced risks for the business partners (e.g., promoting Deming's ideal of long-term partnership, lower risk surcharges, etc.), better adherence to plans, and confidence to get the desired project result (cf. [12]).

Metrication in space projects. In space projects, obtaining highly dependable and high quality software within time and budget is a priority objective. Measurements are the only way to quantitatively assess the quality of a process or product, to know what to do better, and what to look at to understand where lessons learned can support improvement. Metrication provides a management tool for keeping the project on track and achieve the intended product quality. It is used to *characterize* existing processes and product status, to *evaluate* project status to detect deviations and regain control, to *predict* by gaining an understanding of process-product relationships, and to *improve* product quality and process performance [12]. The main software standards in the ECSS are ECSS-E-ST-40C [11] and ECSS-Q-ST-80C [13]. They both lay the foundation for metrication by specifying respective metrication requirements.

ECSS-Q-HB-80-04A is based on ISO-15939 adapted to space software projects and describes metrication as part of the project [12,17]. It covers topics like selecting metrics, metrication planning, interfaces with other processes, data collection aspects, feedback from metrics into process and product, continuous improvement through metrics. Most of the document is an appendix with 40+ process, product and object-oriented metrics listing details like the addressed quality characteristics, owner/producer, target audience, evaluation method, calculation formula, and in which phases and to software of what criticality the metrics are applicable. After defining a project's quality model, the metrics shall be tailored to the model, and to company culture and experience [12].

Related Work. Basili et al. [5] used metrics successfully to introduce improvements at NASA, and advance software engineering as a whole. An ecosystem of tools evolved alongside computer-assisted software measurement and evaluation (CAME) [9]. Current studies of tools often focus on code metrics, e.g., [20,26], which are the basis of software visualization (e.g., [27]). Practitioners in applied research projects mostly use metrics like lines of code, code coverage, or cyclomatic complexity; however, over 50% of projects use no metrics at all [23].

An earlier (unpublished) project to implement ECSS metrics used SQuORE (cf. [2]). Yet only few of its generic data providers fitted to space processes, and would have had to be developed anew for AENEAS. Data export, and deliveries between customer and supplier were not inherent features, and vendor lock-in impended. With respect to this, the open-source platform Alambic might become a suitable alternative [3].

3 Pre-Test Survey of Need for Metrics

In order to better understand the issue of transparency of software development in space systems development, we organized a small-scale survey based on a no-more-than-ten-minutes questionnaire. Table 1 shows the questionnaire design. We invited key personnel from industry and a space agency via email, providing a paper version for anonymous answering but participants could also respond via email. Participation was voluntary, with a response rate of ≈40%.

Table 1. Questionnaire design. Responses: SC/MC = single/multiple choice, FT = free text, 5Ls = 5-point Likert-scaled (1 = fully disagree, ..., 5 = fully agree).

Question	Type	Question (abbreviated), response options
D-Role	MC, FT	What are your roles? (Engineer, project manager, product/quality assurance, team/department head, ...)
D-Sw	SC	Is your main job in the area of software? (yes/no)
D-CuSu	MC	Do you act mainly as customer or supplier?
D-Size	FT	Estimated annual average total cost of projects where you fulfill your role(s)?
Q-i	5Ls	Do you agree to the statement about software and the emperor's new clothes?
Q-ii	5Ls	Do you wish for more transparency of software development?
Q-iii	5Ls	Would regular delivery of ECSS metrics (some examples given) help you fulfill your role?

Survey participants (N = 23) see themselves as customer (12) and supplier (13), as PA/QA (6), and as software people (13), they fulfill engineering (11) and more management-heavy roles (12). The average survey participant fulfills his roles in projects with an annual budget of 70M EUR. Figure 1a shows that

292   C. R. Prause and A. Hönle

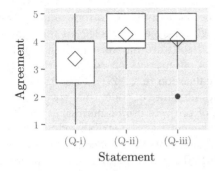

Subj. attribute	Q-i	Q-ii	Q-iii
D-Size	0.49	0.45	0.57*
D-Role	0.31	0.15	-0.03
Is Customer	0.43*	0.21	-0.07
Is PA/QA	0.36	0.07	0.16
Is Software	-0.49*	-0.01	0.28

(*) = Statistical significance at $p <$ 0.05. Note: Failed significance tests may be due to small N, and not necessarily mean there is no effect.

(a) Boxes go from lower to upper quartile. Diamond shows mean. Horizontal line marks median. Median of 3.5/4.5 results from responses"3.5"/"4.5"in an email.

(b) Influence factors for agreement to questions Q-i, Q-ii and Q-iii as Pearson correlation coefficients r.

Fig. 1. Analysis of survey participants' responses to Q-i, Q-ii, and Q-iii. N = 23.

average respondent (rather) approves all three questions. However, in particular the statement regarding software and the weavers of the emperor's new clothes is polarizing. The responses range from full agreement and to full disagreement, with both extremes not being outliers. Wishes for more transparency and perceptions of usefulness of metrics are clearly present. Figure 1b investigates the effects of personal attributes on opinions. Being involved in larger projects leads to more agreement (positive correlation) with all questions. Participants working in management-heavy roles[4], tend to see software development as more problematic but differences diminish regarding the wish for transparency and usefulness of metrics. Similar, but stronger, is this effect for customers as compared to suppliers; PA/QA personnel seem to value metrics more. Interestingly, for software people the effect is inverted: they rather reject Q-i, do not have transparency needs different from others, but might tend to see more value in metrics.

Limitations. The survey was designed to be small-scale, i.e., we only had few question items, and invited few participants from two organizations only. Consequently, N = 23 is small, with implications on statistical significance. Also, respondents with management- and software-heavy roles are not evenly distributed across customer and supplier roles, leading to bias in influence factor results.

4   AENEAS Project: Implementation and Field-Trial

We designed a metrication infrastructure which consists of two major components (see Fig. 2): The supplier's *Collector* collects metrics data through *Data Providers* that, following UNIX philosophy, are implemented as standalone

---

[4] We transformed D-Role responses to a 1–5 score, e.g., engineers (1), system engineers (2), project and PA managers (3), team leaders (4) and C-level managers (5).

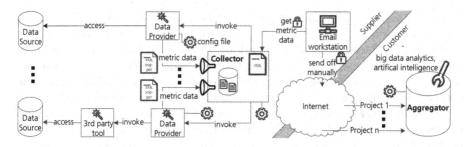

Fig. 2. Software architecture overview of the metrication infrastructure

```
<?xml version="1.0" encoding="utf-8"?>
<xml> <Format version="1.0" />
 <Project name="DemoSat"> <Component name="FlightSW">
  <Delivery milestone="PDR" supplier="OHB-OPF" date="2018-07-16T14:30:36+0200">
   <metric version="1.0" id="A.3.3.01" created="2018-07-16T14:30:36+0200">
    <row> <!--Metric: ECSS-Q-HB-80-04A A.3.3.01 Requirement allocation-->
     <cell description="SSS/TS Requirements traced from SRS">97</cell>
     <cell description="SSS/TS Requirements Total">128</cell>
     <cell description="SRS Requirements traced from SDD">207</cell>
     <cell description="SRS Requirements Total">256</cell>
    </row> ... </metric> ... </Delivery> </Component> ... </Project> </xml>
```

Fig. 3. Data format example of a machine-readable metrics deliverable

programs/scripts that directly access data sources, or rely on other programs. They generate metric data snippets, and return it in a standardized XML format (see Fig. 3). The *Aggregator* component is a database that ingests delivered metric data packages. Data packages can be inserted, analyzed, exported, and, if needed, removed. There is not necessarily a 1:1-relationship between Collector and Aggregator: typically, a customer can collect data from more than one supplier, and can forward the data to higher-tier customers and other stakeholders. Suppliers can run additional own company-internal Aggregators. Data delivery is not designed as automatism but is done manually through encrypted data in (encrypted) email messages so that deliveries can be officially authorized, and senders have control over their sensitive data. Also, using email infrastructure does not require changes to corporate IT-infrastructure/firewalls. AENEAS is currently deployed in one major project, and scheduled to provide data for 18 months, in order to evaluate the concept, the infrastructure and to collect lessons learned. Deployment in a second project is planned.

5   Lessons for Early Metrication Programmes

The following lessons are based on our early experiences with the metrication programme. When introducing metrication, concede anonymity to early projects to mitigate fears of bad consequences. Metrics are hard measurements available to a wider audience that not necessarily understands how to interpret the data, and do not have appropriate background information of the project. Also, initial data is needed to calibrate baselines, and learn how to deal with the data.

ECSS-Q-HB-80-04A metrics definitions appear immature and it is unclear, whether they have been used in practice before. Many descriptions are from our point of view imprecise, ambiguous, or incomplete, although they seem quite detailed. We had to create our own specification to further detail metrics.

Space industry's information system landscape is far from being standardized. So, the main cost driver is adapting Data Providers to data sources for each project. In our experience, effort for implementing data providers can be many times over what is originally planned. An anecdote may exemplify the problems: Projects are long running (10+ years until launch) and distributed across sites, while parts of the development environment already have heritage of 20 years. For metric *SPR/NCR*[5] *Trend Analysis*, three data providers (instead of one) had to be implemented because of different SPR/NCR information systems.

The price of enabling a metric varies strongly, so efforts are hard to calculate. ECSS-Q-HB-80-04A recommends situation-specific tailoring, taking into account benefits, experience or implementation cost (cf. [4]). Yet, on the other hand, big data analytics works best when generating unexpected hypotheses [21] from collected data, and so speaks against tailoring. This is a strategic decision.

6   Conclusion

Metrication is the foundation of engineering disciplines, and an important part of controlling development. The pressure of modern global economy forces organizations to focus on their performance, be it with respect to quality of products and processes, efficiency, effectiveness, or other attributes. In this world, as Clive Humby noted, "data is the new oil." Although metrics alone are not a universal remedy, they can serve as an early warning system, and, at large, allow the employment of big data analytics and artificial intelligence to improve processes and cooperation for the benefit of involved partners and the industry as a whole.

The AENEAS effort aims to improve mutual understanding in customer-supplier relationships in space projects by increasing the transparency of the software development status through metrication. The 50-year old provocative comparison of "software guys" to the weavers in the tale The Emperor's New Clothes, was found to still have some—polarizing—truth in it. So, practitioners expressed a wish for more transparency, and deemed software metrics/KPIs according to ECSS-Q-HB-80-04A as a viable, partial mitigation.

The presented AENEAS infrastructure consists of two parts that collect metrics data from suppliers and aggregate the delivered data on customer sides. While the AENEAS project has not yet completed its evaluation, we presented some lessons regarding the technical implementation and its use in a real-world, major space project. In the future, with larger amounts of data, we want to be able to answer questions what benefits and costs (individual) metrics have

---

[5] SPR: Software Problem Report; a mere bug report. NCR: Non-Conformance Report, a severe form with PA/QA and possibly customer involvement.

in customer-suppliers relationships. Data may be utilized to enhance metrics, to improve reasoning and planning, to increase cost efficiency, to better tailor metrics to project needs, and to advance process and product quality.

Acknowledgments. The AENEAS project is contracted by the German Aerospace Center on behalf of the German Ministry of Economics and Energy (BMWi) under FKZ 50PS1602. We thank the project teams and participants of our survey.

References

1. Apgar, H.: Cost estimating. In: Space Mission Engineering: The New SMAD (STL vol. 28), pp. 289–324. Space Technology Library, Microcosm Press (2011)
2. Baldassari, B.: SQuORE: a new approach to software project quality measurement. In: International Conference on Software & Systems Engineering and their Applications (2012)
3. Baldassari, B.: Alambic: an open-source platform for software engineering data management. the case of embedded software development. In: ICSSEA (2016)
4. Basili, V.R., Lindvall, M., Regardie, M., et al.: Linking software development and business strategy through measurement. Computer **43**(4), 57–65 (2010)
5. Basili, V.R., McGarry, F.E., Pajerski, R., Zelkowitz, M.V.: Lessons learned from 25 years of process improvement: the rise and fall of the NASA Software Engineering Laboratory. In: 24th International Conference on Software Engineering, pp. 69–79. ACM (2002)
6. Boehm, B.: Software and its impact: a quantitative assessment. Technical report (1972)
7. Boehm, B.: Get ready for agile methods, with care. Computer **35**, 64–69 (2002)
8. Donaldson, S.E., Siegel, S.G.: Successful Software Development. P.-Hall (2001)
9. Ebert, C., Dumke, R.: Software Measurement: Establish-Extract-Evaluate-Execute. Springer Science & Business Media, Heidelberg (2007). https://doi.org/10.1007/978-3-540-71649-5
10. ECSS-E-HB-40-01A: Space engineering - agile software development handbook. Standard, ECSS Secretariat, ESA ESTEC (2018, to appear)
11. ECSS-E-ST-40C: Space engineering - software. Standard, ECSS Secretariat (2009)
12. ECSS-Q-HB-80-04A: Space product assurance - software metrication programme definition and implementation. Standard, ECSS Secretariat, ESA ESTEC (2011)
13. ECSS-Q-ST-80C: Space product assurance - software product assurance. Standard, ECSS Secretariat, ESA ESTEC (2009)
14. Gennen, K.: Auswirkungen hybrider projektvorgehensmethoden auf den softwareerstellungsvertrag. In: Engstler, M., et al. (eds.) PVM. GI, Bonn (2016)
15. Greves, D., Schreiber, B., Maxwell, K., et al.: The ESA initiative for software productivity benchmarking and effort estimation. ESA Bull. **87**, 84–88 (1996)
16. IEEE standard glossary of software engineering terminology (1990)
17. ISO/IEC 15939: Software engineering - software measurement process. Standard, International Organization for Standardization (2007)
18. Klünder, J., et al.: Towards understanding the motivation of german organizations to apply certain software development methods. In: 3rd HELENA. Springer (2018)
19. Kuhrmann, M., et al.: Hybrid software and system development in practice: waterfall, scrum, and beyond. In: International Conference on Software and System Process. IEEE (2017)

20. Lincke, R., Lundberg, J., Löwe, W.: Comparing software metrics tools. In: International Symposium on Software Testing and Analysis, pp. 131–142. ACM (2008)
21. Müller, I.: Big data analytics. Lecture, OpenHPI, November 2017
22. Prause, C.R., Bibus, M., Dietrich, C., Jobi, W.: Managing software process evolution for spacecraft from a customer's perspective. Managing Software Process Evolution, pp. 137–163. Springer, Cham (2016). https://doi.org/10.1007/978-3-319-31545-4_8
23. Prause, C.R., Reiners, R., Dencheva, S.: Empirical study of tool support in highly distributed research projects. In: International Conference on Global Software Engineering ICGSE. IEEE (2010)
24. Prause, C.R., Werner, J., Hornig, K., Bosecker, S., Kuhrmann, M.: Is 100% test coverage a reasonable requirement? lessons learned from a space software project. In: Felderer, M., Méndez Fernández, D., Turhan, B., Kalinowski, M., Sarro, F., Winkler, D. (eds.) PROFES 2017. LNCS, vol. 10611, pp. 351–367. Springer, Cham (2017). https://doi.org/10.1007/978-3-319-69926-4_25
25. Rechtin, E.: Reducing the costs of space science research missions. In: Proceedings of a Workshop, pp. 23–29. National Academy Press (1997)
26. Reddy, V.R.: Software metrics tool. Master's thesis (2016)
27. Scheibel, W., Weyand, C., Döllner, J.: EvoCells - a treemap layout algorithm for evolving tree data. In: International Joint Conference on Computer Vision Theory and Applications (2018)

Global Software Engineering and Scaling

Global Software Development: Practices for Cultural Differences

Marcelo Marinho[1,3(✉)], Alexandre Luna[2], and Sarah Beecham[3]

[1] Department of Computer Science (DC),
Federal Rural University of Pernambuco (UFRPE), Recife, PE, Brazil
marcelo.marinho@ufrpe.br
[2] Informatics Center (CIn), Federal University of Pernambuco (UFPE),
Recife, PE, Brazil
ajhol@cin.ufpe.br
[3] Lero, the Irish Software Research Centre University of Limerick, Limerick, Ireland
sarah.beecham@lero.ie

Abstract. Drivers for globalization are significant where today's organizations look for cheaper and faster ways to develop software as well as ways to satisfy quality and investment requirements imposed by customers, shareholders, and governments. Given these needs, Global Software Development (GSD) has become a "normal" way of doing business. Working in GSD often require teams of different cultures to work together. A poor understanding of cultural differences can create barriers to trust or missed opportunities. The literature on culture in GSD is either outdated or disparate, requiring practitioners to read many papers to get an overview of how to manage multi-cultural teams. In this study, we aim to highlight how to increase cultural awareness within teams, avoid potential conflict and harness differences for improved team spirit. To answer our research question, "How should cultural differences be managed, identified and communicated to a GSD team?", we conducted a systematic literature review of the GSD literature. A synthesis of solutions found in nineteen studies provided 12 distinct practices that organizations can implement, to include, "provide a cultural knowledge base", "understand and make team members aware of cultural differences" and "plan responses to mitigate occurrences of cultural misunderstandings". These implementable cultural practices go some way to providing solutions to managing multi-cultural development teams, and thus to support one of the problem dimensions in GSD and embrace cultural differences.

Keywords: Global Software Development · Global teams
Culture · Systematic literature review

1 Introduction

Software development is a human-centric and socio-technical activity. The complex interaction of different values, attitudes, behavioural patterns, beliefs and

M. Kuhrmann et al. (Eds.): PROFES 2018, LNCS 11271, pp. 299–317, 2018.
https://doi.org/10.1007/978-3-030-03673-7_22

communication approaches of members of a project can give rise to misunderstanding and misinterpretation of intent. This misunderstanding can result in conflict, mistrust and under-utilisation of expertise [4].

Globalisation implies cultural heterogeneity [29] requiring organisations to develop high cross-cultural understanding, intercultural communication skills and management competencies. Global organisations that take the cultural context of their teams into account generally experience greater project success [32]. Global software development (GSD) is an established field of application and research. Developing software offshore, in different parts of the world, amongst other economic benefits, gives access to skills and knowledge over and above those available in the local environment [5].

GSD is widespread, and therefore it is important to have a good understanding of the effects of cultural differences within multi-site teams. Culture will have a strong bearing on how individuals are motivated and therefore needs to be taken into account when managing, interacting with and rewarding individual software engineers [4]. The implications of such cultural factors are amplified within global teams increasing project risk and uncertainty [24].

In managing GSD projects, differences between various dimensions of team members' cultures can lead to increased conflict, reduced quality of cooperation and increased effort required to obtain trust [29]. Cultural diversity is shown to be an issue in GSD, leading to a significant amount of research on how to manage cultural differences, in fact culture is one of the mature research areas in Global Software Engineering research [15].

The existing GSD literature also suggests that many software GSD organisations have the potential benefits, resulting in project delays [28]. For this reason, several studies have looked at methods for improving the results of GSD. Although there has been a significant growth in GSD practice and agile scalability frameworks [31], this particular strand of research is generally focussed on technical problems and often overlooks cultural difference issues.

Richardson et al. [32] developed a global teaming model (GTM) that presented a set of practices for effective management of software teams in GSD scenarios. Although the GTM addresses the need to acknowledge cultural differences and provides some relevant recommendations, the model is focussed on general practices in GSD and does not present clear implementable practices for solving problems arising from cultural differences.

This paper contributes to the GSD the body of knowledge by presenting a set of practices for managing culture in distributed teams. These cultural practices are the result of a systematic synthesis of recommendations found in the related GSD. We present 12 distilled best practices that address how global practitioners can manage cultural differences in GSD. These practices are aligned with Scaled Agile Framework (SAFe) roles [22].

This paper is organized as follows: in Sect. 2, we introduce the background to the problem and define our research questions. Section 3 describes the method we apply. Sections 4 and 5, present the results, their implications and limitations, respectively. Finally, in Sect. 6 presents conclusions and future research directions.

2 Background

2.1 Global Software Development - GSD

GSD involves the use of teams located in scattered locations worldwide to develop commercially viable software [5]. The GSD approach allows companies to leverage development benefits in terms of time, cost and access to appropriate and a wider set of resources [5]. In developed countries, there is an increasing interest in using GSD to benefit from cost disparities with developing-country labour markets; and some organisations have adopted GSD found a reduction in software development costs and increased product quality as objectives [28].

However, cultural differences associated with geographically distributed teams and the need to work across different time zones are problematic for GSD-based projects [29], and several key GSD challenges have been identified, namely, lack of customer involvement, lack of knowledge transfer, hidden costs and communication problems [28]. Certainly cost advantages are not guaranteed with evidence pointing to increased communication overhead as a costly problem [34].

The GTM [32] has been proposed as a solution to problems in GSD. The GTM was developed as a mechanism for guiding project managers in a global context based on recommendations for addressing time, culture and geographic problems.

2.2 Global Teaming Model - GTM

The GTM is a global software engineering model with a particular emphasis on the organisation, governance and management of globally distributed development teams. The specific practices are further elaborated into sub-practices that are used to provide one or more recommendations for implementing detailed actions. Overall, GTM comprises five specific practices, twenty sub-practices and sixty-four recommendations, all of which have been validated against real industrial scenarios [3,4].

Based on their empirical studies, Richardson et al. [32] further recommended that "Cultural differences should be identified and communicated to the management and team members". However, GTM does not specify how, or by whom, practices should be implemented.

2.3 Cultural Differences in GSD

Culture, the sum of the learned values and behaviours shared by a group of people, plays a vital role in guiding how a person performs his/her work through their individual patterns of thinking, feeling and acting [23]. Given that global virtual team members have diverse national, organisational, professional and cultural backgrounds, cultural diversity is inherent in GSD [32]. Studies have shown that cultural diversity can be beneficial in increasing creativity and innovation, which are essential to the knowledge-intensive work of software development [32]. Nevertheless, cultural diversity can also become a barrier to communication, coordination and knowledge-sharing and transference, adding difficulties to the management of GSD [27–29].

3   Method

In carrying out this study, we took a systematic yet focussed approach to examining the relevant literature. Our goal was not to uncover all recorded practices but to select a sufficient collection of studies to enable the identification of recurring themes.

Established systematic review guidelines [20] recommend that a reviewer carry out the following steps: (i) identify the need for a systematic literature review; (ii) formulate review research question(s); (iii) carry out a search for relevant studies. (iv) assess and record the quality of included studies; (v) classify the data needed to answer the research question(s); (vi) extract data from each included study; (vii) summarise and synthesise study results (meta-analysis); (viii) interpret results to determine their applicability; and (ix) write up the study results as a report.

The need for this review was established through an examination of the software engineering literature, which revealed no comprehensive survey addressing the research question regarding practices with respect to managing, identifying and communicating cultural differences in GSD projects.

We therefore sought to answer the following research question: *How should cultural differences be managed, identified and communicated to a GSD team?*

We used the following boolean search string to ensure that we captured a wide variety of papers: *(((Global OR distributed) AND ("software engineering" OR "software development")) AND "cultural differences")*.

We used this string to search the metadata relating to journals and conference proceedings in the IEEEXplore, ACM Digital Library, Elsevier ScienceDirect and Scopus bibliographic databases.

3.1   Document Selection

The search produced 451 references (IEEE = 73; ACM = 58; Scopus = 72; and Science = 248). The idealised selection process had two components: (sp1) an initial selection of research results that could reasonably satisfy the selection criteria (outlined next) based on a reading of the articles' titles and abstracts; followed by (sp2) a final selection against these criteria from the initially selected list of papers based on a reading of their introductions and conclusions.

Inclusion/Exclusion criteria: The following criteria guided the selection of papers that helped us address the research questions.

We *included*: (i) complete, peer reviewed, published articles; and (ii) empirical studies that fully or partially addressed one or more of our research questions. Texts had to be (iii) published between January 2007 and February 2018. (The start date relates to the year that the Scaled Agile Framework (SAFe) [22] was introduced, and limited the number of studies down to a manageable size).

We *excluded*: (i) texts not published in English; (ii) lacking in proven scientific relevance; (iii) incomplete papers; and (iv) articles that not clearly related to the research questions.

Before accepting a paper into the final set for review, we checked to ensure that there was no replication. For example, if a given study was published in two different journals with a different order of primary authors, only one study would be included in the review; this would usually be the most comprehensive or recent study. Besides, we checked to ensure that there was no duplication. For example, the same paper listed in more than one database, only one study would be included in the review.

We identified 21 duplicate articles and none replication. After excluding duplicated results from the dataset, we identified 430 articles for inclusion in the initial selection (sp1). Of these, 31 were passed on to the sp2 stage, in which a further twelve were eliminated and nineteen were passed on to the data extraction and data synthesis phase.

3.2 Study Quality

The quality assessment criteria adopted for our study are based on principles and good practices established for driving empirical research in software engineering [14], are briefly summarised as follows. We answered the following questions using *Yes, No, Partially*: (i) Is there a clear definition of the study objectives?; (ii) Is there a clear definition of the justifications of the study?; (iii) Is there a clear definition of how the research was carried out?; (iv) Is validity threat addressed in the study discussion?; and (v) Are the findings of the research clearly stated?

3.3 Data Extraction

We examined each selected publication to extract the following elements: (i) study aim or research question; (ii) identified practices for addressing cultural diverse in GSD teams; (iii) other results relevant to the study; and (iv) potential themes emerging from the study's conclusions.

We synthesised the data by first identifying each paper's recommendation as to how to identify and communicate cultural differences to the GSE team. We then generated a summary showing the number of papers mentioning each practice (see Table 2). As we gave each occurrence the same weight, the frequencies presented simply reflect how many papers mention a given practice; frequencies therefore reflect prevalence of a theme and not its potential importance.

4   Results

Of the initial 451 papers examined, 19 met the criteria established in Sect. 3 as sources for this study; these are listed in Table 1. Analysis of these papers with respect to our research questions revealed practices for identifying and communicating cultural differences in GSD.

Table 1. Paper accepted for analysis.

Author(s)	Title	Ref
Ayed et al.	Agile Cultural Challenges in Europe and Asia: Insights from Practitioners	[1]
Bannerman et al.	Scrum Practice Mitigation of Global Software Development Coordination Challenges: A Distinctive Advantage?	[2]
Breth and Drechsler	Toward an Integrative Model of Influence Factors for Success of Global software development projects	[7]
Boden et al.	Knowledge Management in Distributed Software Development Teams - Does Culture Matter?	[6]
Casey	Leveraging or Exploiting Cultural Difference?	[8]
Chang and Búrca	An Investigation into how Small Companies in London and the South East UK Engage in IT Offshore Outsourcing and the Impact of Culture on this Phenomenon	[9]
Cramton and Hinds	An Embedded Model of Cultural Adaptation in Global Teams	[10]
Deshpande et al.	Culture in Global Software Development - A Weakness or Strength?	[12]
Dorairaj et al.	Bridging Cultural Differences: A Grounded Theory Perspective	[13]
Giuffrida and Dittrich	A Conceptual Framework to Study the Role of Communication Through Social Software for Coordination in Globally-Distributed Software Teams	[16]
Holtkamp et al.	Soft Competency Requirements in Requirements Engineering, Software Design, Implementation, and Testing	[18]
Huang and Trauth	Cultural Influences on Temporal Separation and Coordination in Globally Distributed Software Development	[19]
Mishra and Mishra	Cultural Issues in Distributed Software Development: A Review	[26]
Spohrer et al.	Global Sourcing of Information Systems Development - Explaining Project Outcomes based on Social, cultural, and Asset-Related Characteristics	[35]
Schloegel et al.	Age Stereotypes in Distributed Software Development: The Impact of Culture on Age-Related Performance Expectations	[33]
Tugrul et al.	Exploring the Communication Breakdown in Global Virtual Teams	[11]
van Marrewijk	Situational Construction of Dutch–Indian Cultural Differences in Global IT Projects	[25]
Zaghloul et al.	Communication in Firm-Internal Global Software Development with China	[36]
Zeid	Using Simulation Games to Teach Global Software Engineering Courses	[37]

Each study was assessed independently by two researchers according to five possible quality criteria (see Sect. 3.2). Only one studies [19] received the maximum score. The other papers were evaluated on the following scales: 12 between 4,5-4,0; 3 between 3,5-3,0 and 3 less or equal 2,5 points.

4.1   Understand and Be Aware of Cultural Differences

Project managers must recognise and understand the cultural needs of their global teams with respect to their differing organisational, geographic, national, religious, gender and power relations [26].

Table 2. Practices to deal with cultural differences in GSD

Practice	Citations
Understand and be aware of cultural differences	[7–9, 11, 13, 19, 25, 26, 37]
Make onsite visits	[6, 9, 12, 13, 19, 33, 37]
Standardise skills required for global team members	[1, 10, 12, 19, 33, 35, 37]
Identify and establish the cultural context of each global team	[8, 10, 11, 16, 19, 33, 35]
Provide cultural training	[2, 8, 12, 19, 33, 35]
Look out for cultural misunderstanding in Requirement	[7, 9, 18, 19, 26, 35]
Develop and maintain cultural knowledge base	[7, 10, 19, 33, 37]
Assign a local manager with the skills needed for a global team	[6, 9, 12, 18, 19]
Offer English language training sessions	[12, 19, 33, 36]
Plan how to mitigate issues caused by cultural misunderstanding	[2, 6, 12, 13]
Prepare for distributed meetings	[13, 36, 37]
Project managers should take into account cultural differences during group exercises	[9, 19]

Understanding the challenges associated with cultural differences at an early stage can help workgroups in more effectively managing their cross-cultural communication and conflict management techniques [37].

To address problems in software development while maintaining an atmosphere of mutual respect and team spirit, a global team needs to be aware of its members' respective cultural norms. To develop a better understanding of cultural differences, it is important to consider the personal experiences of team members [13]. In developing an understanding of the subtleties of cultural influence on GSD development, it is also important to draw upon the subjective experience and understanding of the participants [19, 25].

Because certain activities and types of behaviour that are acceptable in one culture might be unacceptable in another, project managers and participants seeking more effective interaction must understand the multiple individual historical, political, economic, social and cultural contexts of team members [8].

The first step to bridging cultural differences is stimulating cultural awareness [13], and GSD project team members should be prepared for intercultural collaboration by raising an initial awareness of cultural differences [7, 11, 19, 25].

Cultural awareness helps global teams in collaborating efficiently to achieve the goals and visions of projects [13]. Team members should have an understanding of other members' cultural backgrounds to enable an atmosphere of mutual respect in the software development process [9, 13].

4.2   Make Onsite Visits

Another useful practice is conducting face-to-face meetings at remote sites to provide socialisation opportunities that enhance trust-building [19].

Some studies [6,9,12,13,19] have reported that onsite visits help team members to improve mutual understanding, resolve issues and become familiar with others' work practices, priorities and environments. The results of time spent at outside sites have revealed that personal, face-to-face contact plays a significant role in knowledge exchange [6,19].

In addition to building trust in the skills of remote team members, personal meetings play an essential role in learning how to approach offsite personnel. Such face-to-face meetings constitute an essential basis for building social ties, which are reinforced by informal exchange of personal information online [6,37].

As building an understanding of different values and norms takes some time, management should, despite the additional cost, consider sending team members abroad for more extended periods or even maintaining mixed-cultural teams at project locations [33].

4.3   Standardise Skills Required for Global Team Members

Spohrer et al. [35] suggested that success on a project level is contingent on the quality of the relationship between both the partner organisations and the respective employee teams.

Team members and managers encounter cultural differences in terms of expectations, meanings and norms that are stubbornly anchored in local institutions, societies and contexts. By applying an embedded view of cultural adaptation, project managers can become more aware of and effective in responding to the challenges team members face as they bridge worlds [10,33].

Understanding the subtleties of cultural influence on a global project requires drawing on the subjective experiences and understandings of the global virtual team members who are engaged in the work [19].

Attributes to be considered in understanding other team members include: the language used for communication, which is essential to the interpretation of discussion and communication; gender, which is crucial in identifying the role of female participants as team members while managing cultural diversity [12]; geography, i.e., where the team members are located; age, as age stereotypes and problems in a GSD context can create considerable barriers to the complex task of software development [33]; Hofstede cultural measures [17], which can help in gaining insight to differing national cultures [1,12,33,37]; and, finally, skills in terms of identifying requirements, developing designs, implementation, testing, leadership and knowledge of other cultures [10,37].

4.4 Identify and Establish the Cultural Context of Each Global Team

Culture has many interacting layers that cannot be examined in isolation. Virtual partners can differ in terms of organisational culture, resulting in work practice differences that impact project success [11,35].

Different cultures often have different values, attitudes, beliefs, behavioural norms and approaches to communication and problem-solving; these differences can lead to, on one hand, creativity and innovation and, on the other hand, misunderstandings and conflict in the GSD process [8,10,33,35].

Spohrer et al.'s [35] literature and practice investigation revealed that differences in terms of modes of thinking and acting can affect the quality of the relationship between teams. The authors commented that high variance in habits can in some cases be traced back to differences in culture. However, standardised procedures, working practices and roles could decrease misunderstanding and disagreement as to responsibilities.

Huang and Trauth [19] reported on a global project in which members discussed the effects of organisational culture on values and norms and the effects of bridging some of these cultural differences on time estimation, commitment and adherence to schedule. The project established and promoted global value procedures to leverage its diverse talents and enhance the synergies amongst different company sites. Team members reported that they felt that the organisation valued local cultural diversity while striving to develop a global culture that could serve as a sensemaking device to guide and shape the behaviours of its global workforce.

Identifying and establishing the cultural context of a global team based on respective social customs can help in understanding organisational categorisations, establishing practices in new distributed teams and re-negotiating practices in established teams [16].

4.5 Provide a Cultural Training

Culture and language differences in particular can quickly lead to misunderstandings and/or offense, alienating people and resulting in cooperation barriers [2].

In [35], a global project with Indian and German teams had an Indian manager at its German site who had been living in Germany for three years. According to the report, this cultural experience provided the manager with an improved understanding of the differences in terms of culture, behaviour and work practices between the two teams.

Training can aid in the education of team members from different cultures or with different religious values and in the interpretation of the behaviours of geographically distinct team members and clients, resulting in an enhanced level of understanding [8,12,19,35].

Schloegel et al. [33] identified cultural training in a GSD context as one of the most important best practices for global teams and posited that it is an economically efficient route to achieving better understanding amongst project participants and, therefore, improved prospects for project success. As a result, cultural diversity training for global team members has become a commonly used strategy for promoting cultural awareness [19].

4.6 Look Out for Cultural Misunderstanding in Requirements

In the early phases of the software development process, many projects must cope with volatile and ambiguous requirements or specifications that can only be resolved through communication amongst all stakeholders. These early phases are, consequently, the most critical of the GSD process [7], and it is necessary that a sufficient understanding of specifications be reached on the vendor side before technical specification of the system begins [26].

Chang and Búrca [9] reported a case study in which there was a misunderstanding of delivery obligations as a result of cultural issues. Following this, the project members worked together to establish social criteria for the delivery of requirements.

In complement, Spohrer et al. [35] and Huang and Trauth [19] reinforce the role of national cultural mindset for the "problem solving processes", which in turn, is an essential element of requirements engineering "to decode the meanings behind each other's language" about "business needs", and transform those needs in software requirements. Hence, Holtkamp et al. [18] point out that "intercultural competences seem to be specifically important in tasks with a high level of communication".

4.7 Develop and Maintain a Cultural Knowledge Base

During the team-building phase, GSD project members require ample time to get to know each other and to reflect on culture-specific communication and collaboration behaviours [7].

Although culturally driven divergences in terms of modes of communication are common, consultation or attempts to obtain more information on other cultures leads to improvements in communication among project members [10,37]

Different cultural backgrounds in GSD projects lead to different team member experiences and knowledge bases; increasing the similarity of the knowledge bases and the extent of a shared understanding will lead to less ambiguity and more successful exchange between project members [7].

Schloegel et al. [33] explained that team members from different national cultures have different communication and problem-solving processes, leading to problems in creating collective knowledge, a shared mental model, social ties and trust, all of which can negatively impact the product quality.

It is therefore vital to create a technical knowledge-base for decoding the meanings behind each member's language, develop a protocol for sharing information and apprising the team of cultural differences and the use of the knowledge-base [19].

4.8   Assign a Local Manager with the Skills Needed for a Global Team

Onsite managers can help manage cultural diversity in GSD [12]. Local project managers play a critical role in temporal coordination through their responsibility for evaluating available resources, setting realistic goals, monitoring processes, making resource and schedule adjustments when needed and communicating and coordinating with other remote sites concerning changes and progress [19].

Boden and Liam [6] found that people with relevant technical and domain knowledge who can connect between cultures make natural facilitators for managing and mediating communication. Similarly, Huang and Trauth underlined the necessity of educating qualified local GSD project managers [18,19].

Chang and Búrca [9] presented a case in which the local manager became essential to the coordination of cultural challenges. Their finding suggests the importance to the overall GSD process of having a local manager to mediate communication issues and conduct project activities.

4.9   Offer English Language Training Sessions

In situations in which team members do not share a common English language proficiency, training can be provided to enhance language skills [12]. Such language training can be essential to promoting cultural understanding and facilitating communication [19].

English language training is best facilitated through the provision of training sessions to all virtual teams with a focus on business terms used in the industry [36]. Creating mutual understanding by increasing contact in various ways is even more critical when projects face cultural differences [33].

4.10   Plan How to Mitigate Issues Caused by Cultural Misunderstanding

Teams with frequent contact and mutual development in which a good professional working relationship is fostered among teams tend to outperform disconnected teams [2,12].

The project manager should plan responses in the form of shared artefacts and repositories that can mitigate problems caused by cultural differences [6]. Additionally, the establishment of backup teams at various geographical locations can help international GSD project managers address unforeseen or surplus events that arise as a result of cultural differences [12]. Global teams should also develop shared work practices to strengthen their team relationships [13].

4.11   Prepare for Distributed Meetings

Clear meeting agendas and minutes must be written and disseminated early enough to provide team members with the chance to prepare for meetings [37]. Using minutes, team members can write down issues that they wish to discuss during the meeting, enabling them to express themselves clearly and be better understood by other team members [13].

In general, managers and participants should not provide simple "yes" or "no" answers. In some cultures it is a common practice for respondents to write up a document outlining their opinions following important sessions.

It is essential that the project manager repeatedly underline the importance of open conversation and to be understanding of reporting mistakes during projects [36].

4.12   Project Managers Should Take into Account Cultural Differences During Group Exercises

Cultural differences can occur even when teams share a common language and/or nationality, as differences in "corporate culture" can lead to conflicting approaches to problem-solving and communication, which in turn might be misinterpreted as rudeness or incompetence [9].

Such "clashes of cultures" in the form of misunderstandings and schedule delays are common occurrences in global projects. It is therefore necessary to foster an open atmosphere and establish trust relationships at the team level to make team members more willing to raise issues, express concerns and seek and offer help [9,19]. The project manager should repeatedly convey the importance of open conversation. This process can be abetted through the use of a progress-tracking system in which a developer updates the status of his/her task each day to avoid late notifications [19].

5   Discussion

In this study, we extracted practices for managing, identifying and communicating cultural differences amongst GSD team members. From a directed search of the literature, we have isolated and identified 12 practices that help to align cultural differences amongst members operating in across multi-site and multi-cultural teams. Research suggests that implementing these practices are important to the success of global software development projects. Such practices can be used in the context of GSD teams that adopt specific approaches by combining well-structured comprehensive methods (traditional) or flexible agile practices or yet the combination between traditional and Agile, a hybrid approach [21]; for instance, they can be used in the context of scaling Agile [31]. We believe that this would represent a successful contribution to the Scaled Agile Framework (SAFe). Although SAFe focusses on large enterprises and takes a scaled approach to Agile adoption, it does not currently represent practices with a cultural difference focus.

To help implement our set of identified practices, we convert each practice into a pattern. We replicate this *patternizing* of a practice method as introduced in Noll et al. [30]. Patterns break down a process into: goals, inputs and outputs, artefacts, and suggested steps. Steps are defined by an action and a role (*who -*

a person responsible for carrying out the action (s)). We have defined these roles according to those delineated under SAFe [22]: Development Team (DT); Scrum Master (SM); Release Train Engineer (RTE); Solution Train Engineer (STE); Product Owner (PO); Product Management (PM); and Solution Management (SM).

Understand and Be Aware of Cultural Differences *Goal*: Understand and raise awareness of cultural differences. *Who*: SM; RTE; STE; *Inputs*: Preliminary understanding of cultural differences; *Outputs*: Preliminary understanding is conveyed to the teams.

1. Foster awareness of other cultures to enable problem solving in the software development process for mutual respect and team spirit;
2. Prepare team members (DT) for intercultural collaboration by making them aware of cultural differences;
3. Develop an understanding of the subtleties of cultural influences;
4. Encourage mutual respect of differences to create an environment in which everyone can voice their opinions;
5. Enable team members to think through the lens of other cultural perspectives.

Make On-Site Visits *Goal*: Provide socialisation opportunities for trust building. *Who*: SM; RTE; STE; *Input*: Initial familiarity with other team members; Project initial understanding and knowledge gained; *Output*: Integration amongst team members.

1. Send team members (DT) abroad for more extended periods;
2. Arrange face-to-face meetings at remote sites.

Standardise Skills Required for Global Team Members *Goal*: Establish guidelines for recruiting and selecting team members who compliment the global team culture. *Who*: PO; PM; SM; *Input*: Organisational guidelines; Project needs; Current profiles of team global members; *Output*: Mapping of team members' skills.

1. Identify all global team members in terms of skills, knowledge, experience and behaviours;
2. Explain to each project team member what is expected from him/her and assess the individual's personal circumstances, motivations, interests and goals.

Identify and Establish the Cultural Context of Each Global Team *Goal*: Establish procedures for each global team. *Who*: SM; RTE; STE; *Input*: Cultural information from all involved remote teams; *Output*: Guide for valuing cultural differences and directions for the global project.

1. Standardise procedures, working practices and roles;
2. Identify and establish the cultural context and communication style of each global team based on knowledge of their social customs;
3. Explain that team members from dierent national and cultural contexts use different communication and problem-solving approaches;
4. Ensure that cultural differences are valued while developing a global culture that can serve as a sensemaking device to guide and shape the behaviours of the global workforce.
5. Establish how each team member is motivated according to the cultural identity.

Provide Cultural Training *Goal*: Ensure cultural diversity in the context of the project is well understood by all stakeholders. *Who*: SM; RTE; STE; *Input*: Cultural information from all involved remote teams; *Output*: Ability to interact with different cultures.

1. Create openness based on mutual respect among all individuals and group representatives involved with the project;
2. Educate team members on cultural and religious value differences to enable mutual interpretation of the behaviour of geographically dispersed team members to attain a required level of understanding.
3. Explain to individuals that some cultures are more direct than others (e.g. English can be indirect and over-polite when asking someone to do a task, whereas Americans will just tell people what to do and can appear abrupt to some people).

Look Out for Cultural Misunderstanding in Requirements *Goal*: Define requirements, according to customer expectations and acceptance criteria. *Who*: PO; PM; SM; *Input*: Cultural information from all remote teams; *Output*: Establishment correct set of requirements and expectations.

1. Identify the national cultural mindset of each global team for improvements to communication in requirements;
2. Clearly and unambiguously define the project results (objectives, deliverables) expected for all parties;
3. Be aware of the "mum" effect dominant in some cultures (hesitation to share bad news).
4. Be explicit as to which stakeholders' expectations will not be part of the project objectives and the various results or deliverables to be produced.
5. Be aware of "false friends" (words that appear in two languages but have different meanings (for example English magazine and French magasin "shop").

Develop and Maintain Cultural Knowledge Base *Goal*: Establish a system that captures cultural diversity. *Who*: SM; RTE; STE; *Input*: Cultural information from all involved remote teams; *Output*: Structured information on the varying cultures of project teams.

1. Collect and register types of behaviour that might be acceptable in one culture but unacceptable in another;
2. Collect and register technical knowledge to be used at different sites;
3. Collect information on the interests of the respective parties associated with the project and assess its reliability on a personal and working level;
4. Incorporate prevailing societal values (as influenced by political opinion, group pressure, interested parties, etc.) that can affect the project;
5. Develop a protocol for sharing information and making the team aware of cultural differences and the use of the knowledge base.

Assign a Local Manager with the Skills Needed for a Global Team
Goal: Help manage and be responsible for cultural diversity. *Who*: RTE; STE; *Input*: A team member with relevant technical, domain knowledge and people skills; *Output*: Designation of this person as a local leader.

1. Designate a team member as a leader (referred to as a coach or scrum master) for bridging cultures.

Offer English Language Training Sessions : *Goal*: To promote cultural understanding and facilitate communication. *Who*: SM; RTE; STE; *Input*: English Language fluency levels of all members in global team; *Output*: Improvement in the linguistic skills of team members.

1. Promote English training to enhance team member language skills;
2. Promote English training with a focus on business terms used in the industry;
3. Standardise jargon and vocabulary to be used within the project.

Plan How to Mitigate Issues Caused by Cultural Misunderstanding
Goal: Minimise misunderstanding due to cultural differences and reduce likelihood of problems arising from cultural differences in the future. *Who*: DT; SM; RTE; STE; PO; PM; SM; *Input*: Cultural information from all involved remote teams; *Output*: Set of responses for mitigating identified occurrences.

1. Get feedback from stakeholders on how they would like to deal with cultural misunderstanding;
2. Plan responses for mitigating circumstances that occur due to cultural differences;
3. Establish backup teams at various geographical locations;
4. Develop work practices and share these with all team members.

Prepare for Distributed Meetings *Goal*: Enable each team member to express themselves clearly and for the other team members to understand what they convey. *Who*: SM; RTE; STE; *Input*: Cultural information from all involved remote teams; *Output*: Improvements in communication and in the relationship among team members.

1. Consider the factual arguments around particular issues;
2. Prepare a presentation that includes rebuttals to possible counter-arguments;
3. Assess the people who will be involved in the discussion and their likely points of view, interests and relationships;
4. Prepare an agenda for the meeting in which the issues will be discussed;
5. Express thanks to the meeting participants for their interest and show appreciation for their input;
6. Cultivate sustainable relationships with interested parties;
7. Continuously learn from the experience and apply this learning in the future.

Project Managers Should Take into Account Cultural Differences During Group Exercises : *Goal*: Avoid misunderstandings and scheduling delays arising from cultural differences. *Who*: SM; RTE; STE; PM; *Input*: Cultural information from all involved remote teams; *Output*: Establishment of estimated normalised according to cultural differences.

1. Standardise a set of norms for communication and conflict management, for a shared team identity and shared performance expectations;
2. Create opportunities to stimulate openness amongst the team;
3. Learn from each situation and continue to improve methods for retaining openness;
4. Constantly follow verbal and non-verbal cues passed along by the team;
5. Provide feedback and encourage people to listen.

5.1 Limitations

Our search string was intentionally constructed to produce a highly focussed set of candidate papers for review. By including additional terms in the search string (by, for example, adding "diversity") and searching additional libraries, we might have produced a larger initial pool of candidates. IEEEXplore, ACM, Science Direct and Scopus comprise a broad array of literature from conferences and journals, ensuring that our findings represent a cross-section of available results. Although our search was focussed, it revealed multiple studies discussing each of the practices for addressing our identified cultural differences in GSD. Although broadening either the set of search terms or target libraries might have revealed additional practices; in our current corpus of papers we started to reach saturation (where on further reading no new themes emerged), and we therefore believe that a larger candidate pool would more likely have only produced additional evidence in support of the practices we have already identified.

6   Conclusions

It is necessary to take into account many technical, organisational and temporal issues in the interactive and cooperative delivery of GSD solutions, a requirement that is enhanced in situations involving increased team sizes, structures involving teams of teams and more complex management structures.

In such settings, cultural difference can be seen as an enriching factor in which different bodies of knowledge are brought together; it can also lead to severe misunderstanding and conflicts.

As the existing literature did not adequately address particular approaches to successfully implementing practices for managing cultural differences in GSD, we performed an SLR of existing studies to extract specific practices.

Our analysis of these practices revealed a number of actions that organisations can apply in their development processes. In future studies, we will apply the practices identified in this study to a specific organisation with the goal of identifying relevant changes to be taken to enhance the organisation's intercultural effectiveness.

Acknowledgment. This work was supported, in part, by Science Foundation Ireland grant no. 13/RC/2094.

References

1. Ayed, H., Vanderose, B., Habra, N.: Agile cultural challenges in Europe and Asia: insights from practitioners. In: Proceedings of the 39th International Conference on Software Engineering: Software Engineering in Practice Track, pp. 153–162. IEEE Press (2017)
2. Bannerman, P.L., Hossain, E., Jeffery, R.: Scrum practice mitigation of global software development coordination challenges: a distinctive advantage? In: 2012 45th Hawaii International Conference on System Science (HICSS), pp. 5309–5318. IEEE (2012)
3. Beecham, S.: Motivating software engineers working in virtual teams across the globe. In: Ruhe, G., Wohlin, C. (eds.) Software Project Management in a Changing World, pp. 247–273. Springer, Heidelberg (2014). https://doi.org/10.1007/978-3-642-55035-5_10
4. Beecham, S., Noll, J.: What motivates software engineers working in global software development? In: Abrahamsson, P., Corral, L., Oivo, M., Russo, B. (eds.) PROFES 2015. LNCS, vol. 9459, pp. 193–209. Springer, Cham (2015). https://doi.org/10.1007/978-3-319-26844-6_14
5. Beecham, S., Richardson, I., Noll, J.: Assessing the strength of global teaming practices: a pilot study. In: IEEE 10th International Conference on Global Software Engineering (ICGSE), pp. 110–114 (2015)
6. Boden, A., Avram, G., Bannon, L., Wulf, V.: Knowledge management in distributed software development teams-does culture matter? In: 4th IEEE International Conference on Global Software Engineering, (ICGSE), pp. 18–27 (2009)
7. Breth, S., Drechsler, A.: Toward an integrative model of influence factors for success of global software development projects. In: Twentieth Americas Conference on Information Systems. Association for Information Systems (2014)
8. Casey, V.: Leveraging or exploiting cultural difference? In: 4th International Conference on Global Software Engineering (ICGSE), pp. 8–17 (2009)
9. Chang, J., de Búrca, C.: An investigation into how small companies in London and the South East UK engage in IT offshore outsourcing and the impact of culture on this phenomenon. Procedia Comput. Sci. **100**, 611–618 (2016)

316   M. Marinho et al.

10. Cramton, C.D., Hinds, P.J.: An embedded model of cultural adaptation in global teams. Organ. Sci. **25**(4), 1056–1081 (2014)
11. Daim, T.U.: Exploring the communication breakdown in global virtual teams. Int. J. Project Manag. **30**(2), 199–212 (2012)
12. Deshpande, S., Richardson, I., Casey, V., Beecham, S.: Culture in global software development-a weakness or strength? In: 5th IEEE International Conference on Global Software Engineering (ICGSE), pp. 67–76. IEEE (2010)
13. Dorairaj, S., Noble, J., Malik, P.: Bridging cultural differences: a grounded theory perspective. In: Proceedings of the 4th India Software Engineering Conference, pp. 3–10. ACM (2011)
14. Dyba, T., Dingsoyr, T., Hanssen, G.K.: Applying systematic reviews to diverse study types: an experience report. In: 1st International Conference on Empirical Software Engineering and Measurement (ESEM) 2007, pp. 225–234. IEEE (2007)
15. Ebert, C., Kuhrmann, M., Prikladnicki, R.: Global software engineering: evolution and trends. In: 2016 IEEE 11th International Conference on Global Software Engineering (ICGSE), pp. 144–153 (2016)
16. Giuffrida, R., Dittrich, Y.: A conceptual framework to study the role of communication through social software for coordination in globally-distributed software teams. Inf. Softw. Technol. **63**, 11–30 (2015)
17. Hofstede, G.: Cultures and Organizations: Intercultural Cooperation and its Importance for Survival. Software of the Mind. Mc Iraw-Hill, London (1991)
18. Holtkamp, P., Jokinen, J.P., Pawlowski, J.M.: Soft competency requirements in requirements engineering, software design, implementation, and testing. J. Syst. Softw. **101**, 136–146 (2015)
19. Huang, H., Trauth, E.M.: Cultural influences on temporal separation and coordination in globally distributed software development. In: ICIS 2008 Proceedings (2008)
20. Kitchenham, B., Charters, S.: Guidelines for performing systematic literature reviews in software engineering. Technical report, EBSE Technical Report EBSE-2007-01 (2007)
21. Kuhrmann, M., et al.: Hybrid software and system development in practice: waterfall, scrum, and beyond. In: Proceedings of the 2017 International Conference on Software and System Process, pp. 30–39. ACM (2017)
22. Leffingwell, D.: Scaling Software Agility: Best Practices for Large Enterprises. Pearson Education, London (2007)
23. MacGregor, E., Hsieh, Y., Kruchten, P.: The impact of intercultural factors on global software development. In: Canadian Conference on Electrical and Computer Engineering, pp. 920–926. IEEE (2005)
24. Marinho, M., Sampaio, S., Moura, H.: Managing uncertainty in software projects. Innov. Syst. Softw. Eng. **14**(3), 157–181 (2018)
25. van Marrewijk, A.: Situational construction of Dutch-Indian cultural differences in global it projects. Scand. J. Manag. **26**(4), 368–380 (2010)
26. Mishra, A., Mishra, D.: Cultural issues in distributed software development: a review. In: Meersman, R. (ed.) OTM 2014. Lecture Notes in Computer Science, vol. 8842, pp. 448–456. Springer, Heidelberg (2014). https://doi.org/10.1007/978-3-662-45550-0_45
27. Monasor, M.J., Vizcaíno, A., Piattini, M.: Cultural and linguistic problems in GSD: a simulator to train engineers in these issues. J. Softw. Evol. Process **24**(6), 707–717 (2012)
28. Niazi, M., et al.: Challenges of project management in global software development: a client-vendor analysis. Inf. Softw. Technol. **80**, 1–19 (2016)

29. Noll, J., Beecham, S., Richardson, I.: Global software development and collaboration: barriers and solutions. ACM Inroads 1(3), 66–78 (2010)
30. Noll, J., Richardson, I., Beecham, S.: Patternizing GSD research: maintainable decision support for global software development. In: IEEE 9th International Conference on Global Software Engineering (ICGSE), pp. 110–115 (2014)
31. Razzak, M.A., Noll, J., Richardson, I., Canna, C.N., Beecham, S.: Transition from plan driven to SAFe®: periodic team self-assessment. In: Felderer, M., Méndez Fernández, D., Turhan, B., Kalinowski, M., Sarro, F., Winkler, D. (eds.) PROFES 2017. LNCS, vol. 10611, pp. 573–585. Springer, Cham (2017). https://doi.org/10. 1007/978-3-319-69926-4_47
32. Richardson, I., Casey, V., Mccaffery, F., Burton, J., Beecham, S.: A process framework for global software engineering teams. Inf. Softw. Technol. 54(11), 1175–1191 (2012)
33. Schloegel, U., Stegmann, S., van Dick, R., Maedche, A.: Age stereotypes in distributed software development: the impact of culture on age-related performance expectations. Inf. Softw. Technol. 97, 146–162 (2018)
34. Ŝmite, D., Wohlin, C.: A whisper of evidence in global software engineering. IEEE Softw. 28, 15–18 (2011)
35. Spohrer, K., Kramer, T., Heinzl, A.: Global sourcing of information systems development - explaining project outcomes based on social, cultural, and asset-related characteristics. In: Kotlarsky, J., Oshri, I., Willcocks, L.P. (eds.) Global Sourcing 2012. LNBIP, vol. 130, pp. 212–233. Springer, Heidelberg (2012). https://doi.org/ 10.1007/978-3-642-33920-2_13
36. Zaghloul, B., Riehle, D., Zhou, M.: Communication in firm-internal global software development with China. In: Fernandes, J.M., Machado, R.J., Wnuk, K. (eds.) ICSOB 2015. LNBIP, vol. 210, pp. 132–138. Springer, Cham (2015). https://doi. org/10.1007/978-3-319-19593-3_11
37. Zeid, A.: Using simulation games to teach global software engineering courses. In: 2015 IEEE Frontiers in Education Conference (FIE), pp. 1–9. IEEE (2015)

Exploring Cross-Site Networking
in Large-Scale Distributed Projects

Aivars Sablis[1]([✉]), Darja Smite[1,2], and Nils Brede Moe[1,2]

[1] Blekinge Institute of Technology, 371 33 Karlskrona, Blekinge, Sweden
{aivars.sablis,darja.smite}@bth.se
[2] SINTEF, Trondheim, Norway
Nils.B.Moe@sintef.no

Abstract. Context: Networking in a distributed large-scale project is complex because of many reasons: time zone problems can make it challenging to reach remote contacts, teams rarely meet face-to-face which means that remote project members are often unfamiliar with each other, and applying activities for growing the network across sites is also challenging. At the same time, networking is one of the primary ways to share and receive knowledge and information important for developing software tasks and coordinating project activities.

Objective: The purpose of this paper is to explore the actual networks of teams working in large-scale distributed software development projects and project characteristics that might impact their need for networking.

Method: We conducted a multi-case study with three project cases in two companies, with software development teams as embedded units of analysis. We organized 20 individual interviews to characterize the development projects and surveyed 96 members from the total of 14 teams to draw the actual teams networks.

Results: Our results show that teams in large-scale projects network in order to acquire knowledge from experts, and to coordinate tasks with other teams. We also learned that regardless of project characteristics, networking between sites in distributed projects is relatively low.

Conclusions: Our study emphasizes the importance of networking. Therefore, we suggest that similar companies should pay extra attention for cultivating a networking culture in the large to strengthen their cross-site communication.

Keywords: Large-scale · Distributed · Software development
Knowledge networks · Coordination networks

1 Introduction

Large-scale distributed software development has shown a strong growth rate the last years. However, still, the success of organizing distributed work has been varying a lot [14]. The key reasons for varying success are the challenges with

M. Kuhrmann et al. (Eds.): PROFES 2018, LNCS 11271, pp. 318–333, 2018.
https://doi.org/10.1007/978-3-030-03673-7_23

communication and coordination in distributed development [11], and managing dependencies in large-scale projects [8].

Large-scale software development means working with a product that has millions of lines of code, multiple subsystems, and very long product lifecycles. No single developer or even a development team possess all the expertise needed for conducted for solving their development tasks [14]. Further, the necessity to divide development work between several teams in large-scale development creates dependencies between teams. Therefore, teams need to rely on their network within the project to solve dependencies and to solve complex tasks. "Who you know" affects "what you know", and a large network is more likely to help to solve development problems and handle dependencies between teams faster. As a consequence, networking - the exchange of tacit or explicit information and knowledge between project members, is of paramount importance [6]. At the same time, wrong assumptions about network and decision structure could lead to poorly made decisions impacted by a lack of necessary knowledge and even to devastating results [10] in extreme scenarios.

In a distributed large-scale project networking is complex, because time zone issues makes it hard to reach the remote partner or team, and growing the network across sites is problematic. In distributed projects, teams rarely meet face-to-face, and the lack of familiarity makes networking across sites challenging. Lack of familiarity with other sites means that, in practice, remote locations often work in isolation, especially when following modularized ways of working with a clear split of responsibilities. But what happens when work tasks are interdependent, or knowledge needed to complete a task resides at a remote location in another timezone? To the best of our knowledge, little is known about the importance of networking in large-scale distributed projects, including how teams rely on their networks, and the important actors in these networks. In-depth empirical cases of networking and coordination in large-scale distributed projects, in which work is shared and not modularized, are scarce. Motivated by the importance of knowledge networks in large-scale distributed software development we suggest the following research question:

RQ: What characterizes networking in large-scale distributed projects?

The remainder of the paper is organized as follows. Section 2 outlines related work. In Sect. 3, we describe our research methodology. In Sect. 4, we present our findings from the cases and cross-case analysis, which are further discussed in Sect. 5. Finally, Sect. 6 concludes the paper.

2   Related Work

In this section, we describe related research on need of networking in large-scale projects and how project members share task-related product knowledge and how coordinate the tasks with others.

2.1 Networking Needs in Large-Scale Distributed Projects

Networking needs in large-scale distributed software development is affected by formidable challenges mainly in two fronts - scale and distribution.

First, large-scale software projects are challenging because of the challenges of managing portfolios and customer requirements, while at the same time coordinating and distributing work to many teams [7]. Because of the scale, many tasks such as systems management, verification and validation, integration etc. are centralized and performed by specialized support roles. This creates task interdependencies between teams and supporting roles, requiring task coordination and alignment to deliver the final product [20]. Similarly, the development tasks may have interdependencies, requiring teams to mutually coordinate.

Second, sheer expertise needed to do quality work in the product [14] is huge and often leads to knowledge fragmentation and necessity for coordination. Large-scale software development means working with a product that has millions of lines of code, multiple subsystems, and often a very long product lifecycle. That often will lead to the point where a single developer or even a development team does not possess all the expertise needed for their task [7,14]. To address this need for task knowledge, inevitably networks of knowledgeable contacts are created between different teams and roles in the project. The importance of these networks grows along with the growth of the product.

To successfully develop tasks, software developers have to rely on both their own and their team members knowledge and the knowledge and information pulled from their social network outside the team [19]. Well-connected members have efficient access to valuable knowledge and coordinate task dependencies with others more effectively.

The complexity of large-scale distributed software projects has been traditionally minimized by chunking the work into manageable pieces (moduls) and minimizing the interaction between the teams and sites [13]. This often results in knowledge differentiation, which reduces the burden of knowing everything. Experiences show that modularization is insufficient since modules are rarely isolated and cross-module interfaces require cross-team and cross-site interaction [5].

2.2 Experts in Networks

Networking - the exchange of knowledge and coordination between project members, is of paramount importance in large-scale projects. Research on organizational learning has demonstrated the implications of knowledge and information coordination on performance [1], and the importance of social relationships when acquiring such information [4]. We know that social network perspective can help understand collective information exchange in organizations [1].

Networks similar to those in large-scale distributed development, in which some know more than others, have also been previously addressed. Social capital has been often discussed together with social networks. Social capital is described as "advantages that individuals or groups have because of their location in social network" [4]. Current research on social capital determines that those who are better positioned or active in a network are able to solve tasks with better quality and also influence others [4,15]. These are usually more senior contacts, or formal and informal experts, and are recognized as contacts that are sought by the teams in software development [19]. Similarly, certain project members have to be more active in networking due to the necessity to coordinate task-related dependencies. In the large-scale distributed environment there might be hundreds of people, thus understanding how to establish and cultivate valuable contact networks is both challenging and of paramount importance. Also, not all information and knowledge plays the same role. While two persons in a network might be connected, it is critical for them to exchange relevant information about a task for their connection to be beneficial (the one to capitalize upon) [4]. Finding the right experts and creating connections with them in the network requires time and effort [15].

3   Methodology

Since in-depth empirical cases of networking and coordination in large-scale distributed projects are scare, we used an exploratory approach in our research study [16] to understand to what characterizes networking in large-scale distributed projects. We conducted an embedded case multi-case study where the unit of analysis was a development team in large-scale distributed software development project [16]. In our exploratory research we relied on theoretical sampling to select cases. We have studied large-scale software development projects in two companies, Company A (Project A and Project B) and Company B (Project C), and we selected projects with overlapping and complementary characteristics for the case study to explore what characterizes networking in large-scale software development projects.

3.1   Data Collection

Qualitative data was collected through individual interviews with project members in each of the companies. Interviews followed a structured guide, where management representatives and persons occupying supporting roles were asked directly about project characteristics to clarify team responsibilities, and the type and complexity of team tasks in the studied projects. All interviews in the three projects were recorded and later transcribed. Most interviews were organized on onshore sites, but in two Project A and Project C also in offshore sites. Most of the interviews were organized face-to-face, and all held in English. In total, we organized 20 individual interviews, see Table 1.

Quantitative data was collected using a questionnaire. We decided to use a survey as it is a common method for empirical evidence in social network analysis [12] and also is recognized in software engineering [18] as a means of systematic relation data collection [12]. We conducted a survey with 14 teams. The respondents were asked to report their knowledge sharing network in a free recall manner. We have specifically inquired to identify persons whom the respondents transfer the project-related knowledge to, or retrieve the knowledge from, as well as the nature and content of the knowledge transferred or retrieved. This survey instrument is described in detail in [19]. The survey responses were collected in two ways: with the help of a web-based tool (Project A onshore site, Project B offshore site) and manually using paper printouts (Project A offshore site, Project B onshore site, Project C onshore sites and offshore site). Participants in paper-based surveys were given around 30 min to fill in responses for as many contacts as they felt needed in free-recall format. Participants in the web-based survey were given two days to fill in responses for as many contacts as they felt needed in a free-recall format. Longer time was required due to the need of the participants to allocate time in their daily work schedule. We completed the list of recalled contacts and clarified these with company representatives to clarify the roles of the reported contacts in the company and their office location. In total members of 14 teams participated in the study for a total of 96 participants, see see Table 1. Actual team sizes ranged from 5 to 18.

Table 1. Data collection

Activity	Location	Time	Participants	Researchers
Company A - Project A				
Survey	Sweden	Apr2014	3 development teams, 16 participants	A1, A2, A3
	China	Mar2014	3 development teams, 19 participants	A1, A2, A3
Interviews	Sweden	Aug2013	7 interviews	A2, A3
Company A - Project B				
Survey	Sweden	Nov2014	2 development teams, 17 participants	A1, A3
	China	Nov2014	2 development teams, 12 participants	A1, A3
Interviews	Sweden	Nov2014	4 interviews	A2, A3
Company B - Project C				
Survey	Sweden1	Feb2014	2 development teams, 9 participants	A1, A2, A3
	Sweden2	Feb2014	1 development teams, 5 participants	A1, A2, A3
	India	Jul2014	1 development group, 18 participants	A1
Interviews	Sweden1	Aug2013	6 interviews	A2, A3
	Sweden2	Feb2014	3 interviews	A1, A2

* This column refers to the authors participation in the data collection;
the first author is A1, the second author is A2, and so forth.

3.2   Data Analysis

To understand what characterizes networks in large-scale projects, we seek an understanding of networking in terms of contacts and connections, and the content flowing through the network. In particular, we want to know who are the key contacts in the network in two categories, those who share task-related product knowledge with others and those who help coordinate the tasks with others.

Project Characteristics: We use data gathered in interviews to classify different project characteristics. Each of these characteristics have potential influence on the way information exchange is done in projects social networks.

Networks: All reported connections were classified into three categories based on the reported content: task-related product knowledge, task coordination (coordination of task interdependencies and alignment-related coordination) and administrative information (the rest of connections). We calculated the number of connections between project sites and within each site. Further, we created graph diagrams to visualize connection categories, surveyed team members, their reported contacts and their affiliation with onshore or offshore sites.

Key Contacts in Network: We used multiple social network analysis measures to understand who the key contacts in network are. We did this, because there is no single measure that would precisely determine the central contacts in a network, because centrality can be attributed to different aspects [2]. Thus, our aim is to combine multiple measures and therefore triangulate different aspects of network "centrality". We calculate three measures - Degree, Betweenness and Centrality [9].

- **Degree (Degr.)** measures the number of connections each contact has. The more connection a contact has, the larger the degree. In our case, for Task knowledge we are using Out Degree capturing contacts transferring knowledge to others. The more knowledge a contact transfers, the greater is the value of that contact in the network [3,9].
- **Closeness centrality (Clos.)** - measures how many steps are required to access every other vertex (in this case: contact) from a given vertex. Larger closeness centrality measures might indicate that the contact is in a relatively central position in the network, which increases the chance of exchanging the information in a timely manner [3,9].
- **Betweenness (Betw.)** - measures the number of geodesics (shortest paths) going through a vertex. Larger betweenness scores might indicate that the contact holds a relatively unique position in the network in relation to the ability to transfer knowledge to different sub-groups in that network, which creates opportunities for information control benefits [3,9].

We rank each of these three measures and aggregate them in the final score and are calculated separately for task-related product knowledge and task coordination connections. Role-wise, we classified all network contacts according to a previously defined schema [17] into five different categories: Line Management (LM), Product Management (PM), Feature Product Development (FDS) and Development Support (DS) and Developers and Testers from teams (OD).

4   Results

In this Section, we start with a presentation of the three cases. Then we visualize the networks and present the main network measures and share the key findings related to overall structures of project networks. Lastly, we present our findings of key contacts in each of the cases.

4.1   Project Cases

All three selected projects are large-scale projects delivering complex software-intensive sub-systems or entire systems, all development efforts are distributed across two or more sites. The main characteristics, similarities and differences between the projects are described in Table 2.

Table 2. Project cases

	Project A	Project B	Project C
Product type, maturity	Sub-system of a large software product	Sub-system of a large software product	A software solution
Methodology	Agile	Agile	V-model
Size and complexity	Very complex, contains several millions LOC	Very complex, contains several millions LOC	Large, safety-critical and very complex embedded software system
Product architecture	Contains multiple components, layered architecture, interacts with other sub-systems	Contains multiple components, layered architecture, interacts with other sub-systems	Contains multiple interrelated modules
Project distribution	5 teams in Sweden, 8 teams in China, 2 homeshore teams in China, 2 teams in Korea	4 teams in Sweden and 5 teams in China	6 teams in the main site in Sweden, 1 team in the secondary Swedish location, 1 group in India
Team setup	Cross-functional agile feature teams	Cross-functional agile feature teams	Disciplined component teams

4.2   Networks

Project A network is visualized in Fig. 1. In Table 3 we have calculated all connections by type within and between sites. Results show that in Project A site networks are clustered. Most of the knowledge and task coordination

Table 3. All connections between and within sites - Project A

From	To	Know.	Know. %	Coord.	Coord. %	Admin.	Admin. %	Total
Sweden	Sweden	32	27.40	57	48.70	28	23.90	117
Sweden	China	11	57.90	7	36.80	1	5.30	19
China	Sweden	2	18.20	8	72.70	1	9.10	11
China	China	61	45.50	40	29.90	33	24.60	134

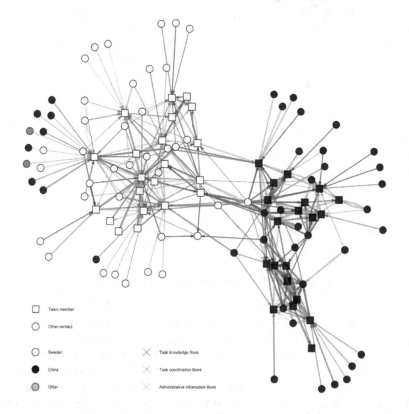

Fig. 1. Visualization of project A network flows

connections is done within sites. Further results show that compared to onshore teams, offshore teams with less experience have more knowledge connections (45.5% of all reported connections, as seen in Table 3), thus indicating that offshore teams are pulling the knowledge necessary for task completion. When it comes to task coordination, these primarily occur among the onshore teams and supporting roles (48.7% of all reported connections).

Project B network is visualized in Fig. 2. In Table 4 we have calculated all connections by type within and between sites. Results show that in Project B site networks are also clustered. Both knowledge and task coordination connections

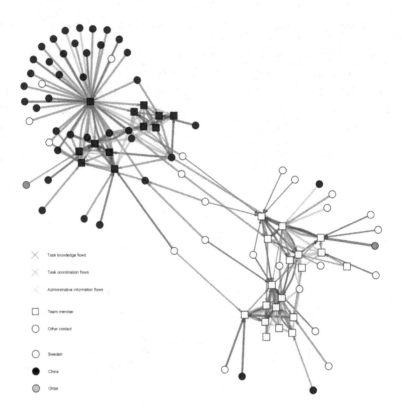

Fig. 2. Visualization of project B network flows

occur within a site. Further, the results show that the Swedish site has equal distribution of communication for both knowledge exchange and task coordination, reported at 37.1% and 39.0% respectively. While the results show that task coordination scores high in the offshore site (48.2% of all reported connections), it is largely tunneled by a single key contact, as discussed in next section.

Project C network is visualized in Fig. 3. In Table 5 we have calculated all connections by type within and between sites. Results show that similarly to other projects, site networks in Project C are clustered, and there is a low number of connections between sites. There are more connections between the two Swedish locations, while the offshore site in India is connected via few connections apart, primarily tunneled through one key contact. In one of the Swedish locations (1) and the offshore site the largest percentage of classified connections are knowledge connections.

4.3   Key Contacts in Networks

Key Contacts in Project A Network: Results show that the main role categories for transferring knowledge are Product Management (six contacts)

Table 4. All connections between and within sites - Project B

From	To	Know.	Know. %	Coord.	Coord. %	Admin.	Admin. %	Total
Sweden	Sweden	39	37.10	41	39.00	25	23.80	105
Sweden	China	1	10.00	9	90.00	0	0.00	10
China	Sweden	1	25.00	2	50.00	1	25.00	4
China	China	29	26.40	53	48.20	28	25.50	110

Table 5. All connections between and within sites - Project C

From	To	Know.	Know. %	Coord.	Coord. %	Admin.	Admin. %	Total
India	India	36	53.70	25	37.30	6	9.00	67
India	Sweden1	1	100.00	0	0.00	0	0.00	1
India	Sweden2	0	0.00	2	100.00	0	0.00	2
Sweden1	India	7	70.00	3	30.00	0	0.00	10
Sweden1	Sweden1	34	45.30	26	34.70	15	20.00	75
Sweden1	Sweden2	5	38.50	3	23.10	5	38.50	13
Sweden2	India	1	50.00	1	50.00	0	0.00	2
Sweden2	Sweden1	2	40.00	3	60.00	0	0.00	5
Sweden2	Sweden2	7	29.20	12	50.00	5	20.80	24

and Feature Development Support (one contact), listed in Table 6 In this project, all Technical Experts/Architects are designated and formally appointed roles. Further, three key contacts are from the onshore site and four from the offshore site. Results show that the knowledge that is transferred by the key contacts are the knowledge about the architecture and design of the product and other related sub-systems. In a few cases, key contacts are also experts in other, related sub-systems and then key knowledge transferred is about the other sub-system.

Our results show that the main role categories for task coordination are developers from teams and development support roles, listed in Table 7. Further, five key contacts are from the onshore site and two key contacts are from offshore site. Results show that designated team members are responsible for task coordination with different supporting roles regarding responses to team development task proposals, progress of testing and test results, test environment tools and coordinating progress.

Key Contacts in Project B Network: Results show that the main role categories for transferring knowledge are Product Management (three contacts) and Developers from teams (three contacts), listed in listed in Table 6. While in this project Technical Experts-Architects are designated and formally appointed roles, this role is only one of many responsibilities without clear dedicated time and complained about being overloaded. Interestingly, all key contacts for task coordination that are reported are from onshore site. Results show, that the

Table 6. Top 7 key contacts for knowledge in each project

	id	Role	Role cat.	Location	Degr.	Rank	Betw.	Rank	Clos.	Rank	Total rank
Project A	s56	Technical Expert/Architect	PM	China	9.00	2	0.17	3	24.88	2	1
	s51	Technical Expert/Architect	PM	Sweden	10.00	1	0.00	13	29.19	1	2
	s84	Technical Expert/Architect	PM	Sweden	3.00	9	0.47	1	19.98	8	3
	s59	System Manager	FDS	China	9.00	2	0.00	13	23.22	3	4
	s38	Technical Expert/Architect	PM	China	9.00	2	0.00	13	22.69	4	5
	s05	Technical Expert/Architect	PM	China	7.00	5	0.06	11	20.39	6	6
	s80	Technical Expert/Architect	PM	Sweden	5.00	6	0.00	13	20.39	6	7
Project B	s57	Technical Expert/Architect	PM	Sweden	4.00	1	0.00	14	21.22	1	1
	s56	Technical Expert/Architect	PM	Sweden	3.00	2	0.31	7	20.38	8	1
	s07	Developer	OD	Sweden	2.00	5	0.00	14	20.73	3	3
	s06	Developer	OD	Sweden	2.00	5	0.00	14	20.69	4	4
	s48	System Manager	FDS	Sweden	3.00	2	2.55	1	19.97	21	5
	s05	Developer	OD	Sweden	2.00	5	0.69	5	20.32	16	6
	s58	Technical Expert/Architect	PM	Sweden	2.00	5	0.00	14	20.36	9	6
Project C	s20	Developer	OD	Sweden2	3.00	5	1.17	11	24.48	5	1
	s14	Team Leader	OD	Sweden1	4.00	3	0.56	14	24.19	7	2
	s36	Expert	PM	Sweden1	3.00	5	0.00	19	24.71	3	3
	s28	Developer	OD	Sweden1	4.00	3	0.00	19	24.21	6	4
	s25	Developer	OD	Sweden1	3.00	5	5.87	1	23.45	23	5
	s15	Developer	OD	Sweden1	6.00	2	1.63	9	23.69	20	6
	s57	Technical Coordinator	FDS	India	8.00	1	5.83	2	19.99	29	7

knowledge that is transferred by the key contacts is about product behavior, legacy, system-specific and testing-related knowledge.

Our results also show that in this project, task coordination is done by a variety of roles, including Technical Expert/Architects, Scrum Masters and Developers from teams, listed in Table 7. However, all of these key contacts are a part of teams, being part-time members. Further, five key contacts are from the onshore site and, two key contacts are from the offshore site. Results show that the key contacts coordinate information related to testing and test results, troubleshooting progress, tips and tricks. Also, in this project, two of the key contacts appear in both categories.

Key Contacts in Project C Network: Results show that the main role categories for transferring the knowledge are experienced developers from teams or team leaders (five contacts), while also showing that formally recognized experts (Expert and Technical Coordinator) are the key contacts, listed in Table 6. Further, five key contacts are from prime location site, one key contact is from another Swedish site, and one is from offshore site. Main knowledge transferred

Table 7. Top 7 key contacts for coordination in each project

	id	Role	Role cat.	Location	Degr.	Rank	Betw.	Rank	Clos.	Rank	Total rank
Project A	s06	Developer	OD	Sweden	14.00	1	1.10	1	15.15	8	1
	s42	Developer	OD	China	8.00	6	0.49	3	19.81	2	2
	s34	Test Support Specialist	DS	China	11.00	3	0.13	5	15.61	7	3
	s104	Developer	OD	Sweden	6.00	8	0.62	2	16.89	5	4
	s21	Developer	OD	Sweden	12.00	2	0.00	13	18.13	3	5
	s76	Tester	OD	Sweden	9.00	5	0.15	4	14.08	10	6
	s87	Developer	OD	Sweden	10.00	4	0.00	13	17.49	4	7
Project B	s45	Scrum Master	LM	China	25.00	1	17.35	1	35.35	15	1
	s48	System Manager	FDS	Sweden	6.00	4	1.81	10	70.97	3	2
	s12	Developer	OD	Sweden	4.00	6	2.45	7	40.22	9	3
	s03	Developer	OD	Sweden	4.00	6	1.38	13	56.70	5	4
	s57	Technical Expert/Architect	PM	Sweden	3.00	9	10.51	4	36.63	13	5
	s77	Tester	OD	China	10.00	2	1.84	9	34.77	16	6
	s07	Developer	OD	Sweden	3.00	9	1.70	11	44.35	7	7
Project C	s63	Developer	OD	India	5.00	4	2.10	6	47.52	2	1
	s62	Developer	OD	India	4.00	5	1.54	7	47.33	3	2
	s23	Developer	OD	Sweden2	7.00	2	5.32	3	32.66	11	3
	s57	Technical Coordinator	FDS	India	4.00	5	6.17	1	32.55	12	4
	s76	Developer	OD	India	7.00	2	0.83	12	47.24	4	5
	s25	Developer	OD	Sweden1	10.00	1	0.00	15	42.15	6	6
	s15	Developer	OD	Sweden1	4.00	5	4.26	4	24.34	16	7

from key contacts are specific issues with a respective module, such as framework architecture, protocols, and module functionality.

Our results show that the main role categories for task coordination are developers from teams or team leaders (five contacts). Interestingly, four of key contacts are from the offshore site, listed in Table 7. Reported coordination content from these contacts is code reviews, testing procedures, and general process related issues, while contacts from both Swedish sites reported work coordination and coordination about specific issues.

Also, in this project, three key contacts appear in both categories, showing that experienced developers from teams are both key contacts for task knowledge and task coordination.

5 Discussion

We have studied three large-scale distributed projects and explored the importance of networking in this context, including the content of network connections, and the important actors in these networks. Establishing and cultivating valuable contact networks is both challenging and of paramount importance for enabling team coordination [20] and knowledge exchange [14] in large-scale distributed projects, in which networks consist of hundreds of people spread across multiple geographic locations. In the following, we discuss three cases in the light of our research question:

What characterizes networking in large-scale distributed projects?

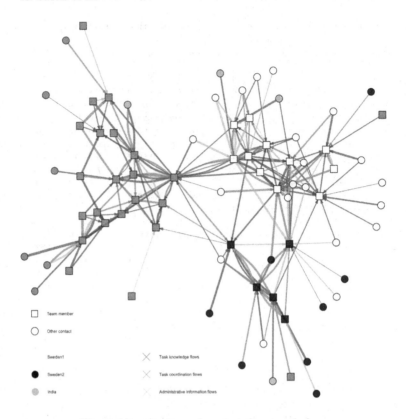

Team member
Other contact

Sweden1   Task knowledge flows
Sweden2   Task coordination flows
India   Administrative information flows

Fig. 3. Visualization of project C network flows

5.1 Networking in Large-Scale Distributed Projects

Our work contributes to the debate on how to set up communication and coordination in large-scale distributed projects [11,13] which argues that cross-site coordination is challenging and that information is likely to circulate within one physical location. Our findings from studying networks in three large-scale distributed development efforts confirms that networking between sites is relatively low (see Tables 3, 4, 5) and site networks are clustered (illustrated in Figs. 1, 2, 3). In all three companies, despite the differences in project characteristics, cross-site coordination was limited. This was intentional. In Projects A and B, the company intended to assign interdependent feature tasks within the same location, and make tasks allocation across site as independent as possible. In Project C teams were responsible for components, and relatively interdependent components were assigned to teams within a short distance (separate floors or cities within the same country). Evidently, cross-site coordination between the two Swedish site was relatively high, even though lower than within the same location. Our results indicate that sameshore networking is thus possible, and in Project C was fostered by extensive traveling and face-to-face visits, and a long history of mutual collaboration. When it comes to knowledge exchange, we found that remote offshore locations in all three cases depended on the onshore competence, which was the main purpose for cross-site networking. In Project A dedicated experts were found to share their knowledge with teams from all sites. In Project B, where formally recognized experts were assigned to this role as only one of many of responsibilities, knowledge exchange between sites was very limited. In Project C, knowledge exchange was tunneled by a technical expert, who was familiar with the Swedish contacts due to his long history in the company, and accumulated contact network during onsite visits.

Finally, we suggest that software companies have to be aware that because cross-site knowledge exchange and task coordination are challenging, they require dedicated resources, extensive travel and time to bridge the geographical and temporal distances. Similarly to our case companies, software companies may decide whether to invest in networking or use approaches that limit the need for cross-site communication and coordination. In our cases, companies tried to minimize dependencies, and this was confirmed in the results. However, to realize such a structure and still ensure even knowledge levels in all sites and coordination across sites the experts are important. When software companies decide to invest in networking, it is the experts that require dedicated time and need to be available for all sites. The companies need enough experts, so the experts do not become a bottleneck or become vulnerable if an expert leaves.

5.2 Key Contacts in Network

Finding the right contacts and creating valuable connections in large-scale projects takes time and effort [15]. Previous research suggests that some contacts excel in networking more than others, and thus may gain a better position in a network [4]. Based on our analysis of the key contacts (summarized in Tables 6 and 7), we suggest that key contacts for knowledge exchange are either dedicated formal experts or informal experts (experienced team members). In Project A and B, there were dedicated technical experts to connect the offshore sites (i.e. the Swedish sites with the offshore sites in China), while the knowledge exchange across the two Swedish locations in Project C was done by very experienced team members who have visited each other often or have a long history of working together.

When it comes to task coordination, the network is not as centralized and instead is more evenly connected. At the same time, in all cases, we have observed coordination champions, i.e. few team members with a large network of contacts with whom they coordinate teams task dependencies, including supporting roles and contacts from other teams.

Interestingly, in Projects B and C, we found that some of the contacts appear as key for both knowledge exchange and coordination. This might be because few people actually traveled across sites, and established remote connections. Furthermore, when discussing our findings with the cases, the project representatives revealed that these emerging contacts, who once gained the key position in the project network, remain acting as the key cross-site coordinators, and often complain about being overloaded. We, therefore, suggest that software companies shall be aware of the actual needs for knowledge exchange and coordination across sites, and actively support the teams by dedicating a sufficient number of experts and coordination champions and give them time to network.

5.3 Implications and Limitations

One may wonder what can we expect in other large-scale distributed projects? The generalizability of our work is, of course, impacted by our sampling strategy and the cases included in our investigation. We studied networks in three large-scale development projects in two companies, different in project structure and characteristics. We suspect that the intensity of the networks and the key positions in each individual case will depend on the various project characteristics, such as the task allocation approach, modularization initiatives, formal choice of technical experts and coordination champions. At the same time, we can with large certainty say that cross-site coordination on a large distance in the majority of such cases will be limited, as also shown in previous research [6,7,11]. In our work we have specifically distinguished between knowledge exchange flows and coordination flows, which helped us gain a better understanding of the content and the needs for coordination in a large-scale project. Our results show that the importance of one or the other type of connections can be impacted by the maturity of sites and teams, ways of working (including project methodology) and project architecture and distribution. However, further research is needed to establish better explanations of the underlying reasons and causality. Specifically, we would like to suggest looking finding more cases to compare networking in agile versus non-agile projects.

6   Conclusions

In this paper, we shared the findings from an exploratory study of the role of networking in three large-scale distributed development projects. In response to our research question (What characterizes networking in large-scale distributed projects?), we identified limited cross-site networking, and that networks in large-scale distributed projects are geographically clustered in all three cases. At the same time, we learned that cross-site networking can be established, if the geographic distance is not large, and the sites have a long history of collaboration. We also found that knowledge networks are centered around formal and informal experts, while coordination networks are more equally connected and are performed by mutual coordination among the teams. Further research is needed to better understand the impact of networking on team performance in large-scale projects.

References

1. Borgatti, S.P., Cross, R.: A relational view of information seeking and learning in social networks. Manag. Sci. **49**(4), 432–445 (2003)
2. Borgatti, S.P., Everett, M.G.: A graph-theoretic perspective on centrality. Soc. Netw. **28**(4), 466–484 (2006)
3. Borgatti, S.P., Jones, C., Everett, M.G.: Network measures of social capital. Connections **21**(2), 27–36 (1998)
4. Burt, R.S.: The network structure of social capital. Res. Organ. Behav. **22**, 345–423 (2000)
5. Cataldo, M., Bass, M., Herbsleb, J.D., Bass, L.: On coordination mechanisms in global software development. In: Second IEEE International Conference on Global Software Engineering, ICGSE 2007, pp. 71–80. IEEE (2007)
6. Dingsøyr, T., Moe, N.B.: Research challenges in large-scale agile software development. ACM SIGSOFT Softw. Eng. Notes **38**(5), 38–39 (2013)
7. Dingsoyr, T., Smite, D.: Managing knowledge in global software development projects. IT Prof. **16**(1), 22–29 (2014)
8. Flyvbjerg, B.: What you should know about megaprojects and why: an overview. Proj. Manag. J. **45**(2), 6–19 (2014)
9. Freeman, L.C.: A set of measures of centrality based on betweenness. Sociometry, 35–41 (1977)
10. Garner, J.T.: It's not what you know: a transactive memory analysis of knowledge networks at nasa. J. Tech. Writ. Commun. **36**(4), 329–351 (2006)
11. Herbsleb, J.D., Mockus, A.: An empirical study of speed and communication in globally distributed software development. IEEE Trans. Softw. Eng. **29**(6), 481–494 (2003)
12. Marsden, P.V.: Survey methods for network data. In: The SAGE Handbook of Social Network Analysis, vol. 25, pp. 370–388 (2011)
13. Mockus, A., Weiss, D.M.: Globalization by chunking: a quantitative approach. IEEE Softw. **18**(2), 30–37 (2001)
14. Moe, N.B., Šmite, D., Hanssen, G.K., Barney, H.: From offshore outsourcing to insourcing and partnerships: four failed outsourcing attempts. Empir. Softw. Eng. **19**(5), 1225–1258 (2014)
15. Nahapiet, J., Ghoshal, S.: Social capital, intellectual capital, and the organizational advantage. In: Knowledge and Social Capital, pp. 119–157. Elsevier (2000)
16. Runeson, P., Host, M., Rainer, A., Regnell, B.: Case Study Research in Software Engineering: Guidelines and Examples. Wiley, Hoboken (2012)
17. Šāblis, A., Šmite, D.: Agile teams in large-scale distributed context: isolated or connected? In: Proceedings of the Scientific Workshop Proceedings of XP2016, p. 10. ACM (2016)
18. Sjoberg, D.I., Dyba, T., Jorgensen, M.: The future of empirical methods in software engineering research. In: Future of Software Engineering, FOSE 2007, pp. 358–378. IEEE (2007)
19. Šmite, D., Moe, N.B., Šāblis, A., Wohlin, C.: Software teams and their knowledge networks in large-scale software development. Inf. Softw. Technol. **86**, 71–86 (2017)
20. Van de Ven, A.H., Delbecq, A.L., Koenig Jr, R.: Determinants of coordination modes within organizations. Am. Sociol. Rev. 322–338 (1976)

Benefits and Challenges of Adopting the Scaled Agile Framework (SAFe): Preliminary Results from a Multivocal Literature Review

Abheeshta Putta[1]([✉]), Maria Paasivaara[1,2], and Casper Lassenius[1,3]

[1] Department of Computer Science, Aalto University, Espoo, Finland
{abheeshta.putta,casper.lassenius}@aalto.fi
[2] IT University of Copenhagen, Copenhagen, Denmark
mpaa@itu.dk
[3] Simula Research Laboratory, Oslo, Norway

Abstract. Over the past few years, the Scaled Agile Framework (SAFe) has been adopted by a large number of organizations to scale agile to large enterprises. At the moment, SAFe seems to be the most predominant agile scaling framework. Despite the current popularity of SAFe in the software intensive industry, there exists surprisingly little scientific research on the benefits and challenges of SAFe adoption. To collect the existing knowledge on this topic, we conducted a multivocal literature review, which includes both peer-reviewed and non-peer reviewed case studies and experience reports on organizations that have adopted SAFe. We identified 52 unique organisations adopting SAFe, five from the scientific literature and 47 from the grey literature.

The most salient benefit categories were: transparency, alignment, productivity, predictability and time to market. The most frequently mentioned challenge categories were: change resistance, challenges with the first program increment planning and moving away from agile.

Keywords: Agile software development
Large-scale agile software development · Scaled agile framework · SAFe

1 Introduction

Agile development methods have become highly popular in software organizations since the early 2000. The principles and practices of agile development were originally designed for small and co-located teams [5]. To leverage the potential benefits also in larger enterprises, the agile practices have to be scaled [8,33]. Large-scale agile transformations has been a burning topic [8,26], with increased concerns for additional coordination mechanisms and integration of non-development units, such as finance and human resource management [8]. To support scaling, new frameworks such as the Scaled Agile Framework (SAFe)

© Springer Nature Switzerland AG 2018
M. Kuhrmann et al. (Eds.): PROFES 2018, LNCS 11271, pp. 334–351, 2018.
https://doi.org/10.1007/978-3-030-03673-7_24

[25], Large Scale Scrum (LeSS) [24], and Disciplined Agile Delivery (DAD) [3] have been proposed by agile consultants. International workshops on large-scale agile organized at XP2016 [27] and XP2017 [26] have highlighted the importance and need for research into the adoption of scaling frameworks [26].

According to the 12th State of Agile Survey, which Version One conducts yearly, SAFe continues to be the most popular scaling framework in large enterprises [29]. Moreover, a recent survey on software development approaches indicated the predominance of SAFe over LeSS and DAD [23]. As the number of organizations adopting scaling frameworks is increasing [29], this provides opportunities for researchers and software practitioners to accumulate knowledge on the usage of these frameworks through case studies, technical reports and experience reports. To our knowledge, no secondary studies on the benefits and challenges of the scaling frameworks or their adoption process have been published. This is striking, given their importance in the industry. In this paper, we start filling this gap by summarizing the benefits and challenges of adopting the SAFe framework in the form of a multi-vocal literature review.

2 Related Work

2.1 Scaled Agile Framework (SAFe)

The Scaled Agile Framework was designed by Dean Leffingwell to scale agile to large enterprises [1,36]. It incorporates practices from Scrum, Extreme Programming, Kanban and Lean. It offers four levels: the *Team, Program, Portfolio and Value stream* levels. The team level comprises the agile teams. Agile Release Trains (ART's) are introduced to scale a large number of teams and individuals at the program level. ART's follow HIP (Hardening, Innovation, Planning) iterations to develop Potential Shippable Increments (PSI) or Program Increments (PI). PI's are planned during the release planning days. SAFe introduces additional roles such as the Agile Release Train Engineer, system teams, release management team and portfolio management team. The core values of SAFe are: *build in quality, transparency, alignment and program execution* [16]. Figure 1 gives on overview of the SAFe framework.

2.2 Secondary Studies on Large-Scale Agile

Secondary studies on large-scale agile have explored topics such as challenges and success factors of large-scale agile transformations [8], organizational, managerial and cultural aspects [32], scalability and adoptability [22], inter-team coordination [14], architectural roles [35] and quality requirements practices [2]. However, systematic literature reviews on scaling frameworks have not been found in the literature. The only review found on scaling frameworks, compares a few scaling frameworks based on team size, practices and organization type [1]. Neither that review, nor other previous reviews on large-scale agile have included the grey literature, e.g. case studies or experience reports published on the homepages of

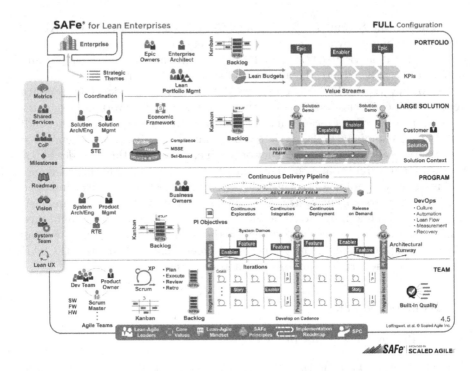

Fig. 1. Scaled agile framework, version 4.5 [19]

the frameworks. While there are inherent problems with case studies published by the proponents of a particular framework, completely eliminating such studies from literature reviews unnecessarily excludes the voice of the practitioners on the usage of scaling frameworks and implementation of agile at scale. Thus, in particular given the lack of scientific literature, we consider it important to study such cases, fully understanding the related problems, further discussed below.

3   Research Method

We conducted a multivocal literature review on the adoption of the SAFe framework to answer the following research questions:

RQ1: What are the reported benefits of adopting SAFe?
RQ2: What are the reported challenges of adopting SAFe?

3.1   Multivocal Literature Review

Systematic literature reviews and systematic mapping studies have been popular in the field of software engineering. They help to summarize the existing studies reported in a specific research domain [11]. According to the widely adopted systematic literature review guidelines [21], a *"fully systematic literature review"* should include both the grey and the peer reviewed literature. Grey literature is defined as, *"(the literature), produced on all levels of government, academics, business and industry in print and electronic formats, but which is not controlled by commercial publishers, i.e., where publishing is not the primary activity of the producing body"* [11].

However, most SLRs published in the software engineering literature have not included the grey literature [12]. Including the grey literature is challenging, and the search strategy for grey literature has not been systematically addressed in the SLR guidelines [21]. This is unfortunate, as excluding this literature will eliminate the voice and opinions of the practitioners who do not publish in the academic forums [4,12]. It has been evident that most of the software practitioners do not publish in academic fora [13].

The situation seems to be slowly changing for the better. Recent literature reviews including both peer reviewed literature, as well as grey literature from blogs, websites, and white papers, have popularized the term *"multi-vocal literature reviews"*, or MLRs [12]. Several such reviews have been conducted in software engineering to bridge the gap between the voice of practitioners and academics [4,12,28,34].

The inclusion of grey literature can also be considered as a threat, as the information reported is based on the opinions and experiences of the practitioners rather than systematic data collection procedures and analysis [10]. Thus, there are severe issues with, e.g., author and publication bias that needs to be accounted for when analyzing such literature. However, several SLRs published in the SE literature have already included peer-reviewed experience reports, written by consultants and practitioners, and that rely on experiences rather than systematic data collection and analysis (e.g., [8,9,31]).

Table 1. Search strings

Database	Search strings	# matches
Scopus	("safe" AND "scrum") OR "Scaled agile framework"	33
Web of science	("safe" AND "scrum") OR "Scaled agile framework"	16
ACM	(+safe +(scrum)) OR "Scaled agile framework"	6
IEEEXplorer	("safe" AND "scrum") OR "Scaled agile framework"	8
Total		**63**

3.2 Study Selection

Databases: For identifying the peer-reviewed literature we searched scientific databases by formulating keywords. The number of matches and the search strings are given in Table 1.

The main source for the grey literature was the official SAFe website [19]. We included the case studies, including backlinks, published there. We used this source, as it currently is the most notable source of SAFe studies available. The case studies are based on a defined review and data collection procedure. Organizations initially answer a questionnaire [17] and thereafter, the *"scaled agile team"* reviews the answers and supplements provided by the organizations. The team contacts organizations for interviews with key members responsible during the SAFe implementation to gather background information [18]. Drafts are written with the help of case study specialists. These are reviewed and approved by the organizations before being published on the website. The aim is to publish reports of mature SAFe organizations, i.e., the reports should reflect the situation no earlier than after 18–24 months into the SAFe implementation [18].

The main benefits of this material are the standard format and questionnaire used giving some opportunity for cross-case analysis. However, the review process is likely built not only to guarantee the quality of the published case studies, but also to ensure that the SAFe framework is put in a good light. Therefore, the publication bias is extremely strong, and it can be questioned whether case studies providing negative results would make it through.

Inclusion Criteria: We used the following inclusion criteria:

1. Only articles related to the Scaled Agile Framework.
2. Only primary evidence: experience reports, case studies, action research.
3. Publication type: Conference papers, journal papers, workshop papers, white papers from the Scaled Agile Framework's homepage.

Search Procedure: During the keyword search from scientific databases 63 matches from four databases were identified. After removing the duplicates, we had a total of 41 papers. These were filtered based on the titles and abstracts by two authors resulting in eight includes and 33 excludes. After full-text filtering, six scientific papers were selected for the analysis. Finally, we selected *five papers*, eliminating one paper, as the same case was published both as a conference and a journal paper: we included only the journal paper. We backward searched by snowballing through the references of selected five papers and also forward searched by snowballing the citations. In the forward search we found one primary study meeting the inclusion criteria. Thus, in total, we included six primary studies from peer-reviewed sources.

Grey Literature: For identifying the grey literature, we manually searched the SAFe homepage [19] and identified 48 white paper reports. In addition, we used backlinks and gathered additional supplements supporting the case studies, such as downloadable presentations and external links published within each white paper report (e.g.: John Deere [G11, G12, G13, G14, G80][1]). We gathered 46

---

[1] **G** denotes non peer-reviewed sources or grey literature sources.

case study reports published on the SAFe homepage, seven downloadable reports, sixteen presentations and thirteen links *(8 internal and 5 external)*. In total, we included 82 reports from the grey literature.

Search Results: In total, we selected 88[2] documents: 82 gathered from the grey literature and six from the scientific databases. When the same organization was described in multiple documents, we treated it as one case only if the documents described an adoption in the same organizational unit. If the adoptions were separate, e.g., coming from different organizational units of the the same company (e.g., AVL Gmbh: $D^3$6 and D7) they were treated as different *cases* coming from the same *organization*. When the same paper described multiple cases (e.g., adoption in different units at different time frames), they were separated as different cases (e.g., Comptel [P3][4]: D3 and D4). Altogether, we got 54 unique SAFe adoption *cases* from 52 *organizations* (see Table 2).

3.3 Analysis

The qualitative data from both peer-reviewed and non-peer reviewed sources was imported into the coding tool NVivo 11 [20]. We followed the coding guidelines presented in [6]. The analysis started with open coding. The open codes were constantly compared to each other based on similarities and differences observed between them. They were grouped into higher code categories, called axial codes. Both axial and open codes formed were thoroughly discussed by the three authors constantly during the coding process that was performed by the first author. We identified 23 codes[5] for the benefits and 15 codes for the challenges of SAFe adoption. We clustered the benefits according the core values of the SAFe framework: *alignment, build in quality, transparency*, as they are the elementary beliefs that are claimed to be of primary importance for the effective SAFe implementation [16]. We clustered the challenges into *organizational and cultural, roles, practices, as well scaled and distributed*. Regarding each benefit and challenge, we mention the number of cases to express the predominance across organizations. However, we did not make any other quantitative analysis, like ranking the benefits and challenges according to the most important and least important, as even though very interesting, that was not possible with this qualitative data.

4 Results and Discussion

We identified only six peer-reviewed primary studies on SAFe. The focus areas of these studies were: assessing the maturity of SAFe adoption [P6], SAFe self-assessment [P5], the SAFe framework in testing [P2], a real-world example on

---

[2] Due to space limitations, all the primary sources can be found using this link: https://figshare.com/s/6be7337493b080ed70b6.

[3] D represents a peer reviewed case.

[4] **P** denotes peer-reviewed sources or scientific literature sources.

[5] More detailed analysis of the code categories will be presented in the journal version.

key elements of SAFe [P1], the adoption of SAFe in a globally distributed organization [P3] and one partially focused on the challenges [P4]. Only three studies focused on the adoption and usage of SAFe [P4, P3, P5]. We identified 47 unique cases (82 documents) from the SAFe homepage. These reports focused on the adoption reasons, transformation steps, and benefits of SAFe. Neither the peer-reviewed nor the grey literature had an explicit focus on the adoption challenges. The grey literature provided deeper insights on the SAFe adoption and usage compared to the peer-reviewed literature.

A total of 54 unique cases from 52 organizations (Table 2), were identified. Out of 54 cases, seven[6] were identified from the peer-reviewed literature[7] and 47 cases[8] were identified from the grey literature. Organizations from various domains have adopted SAFe such as financial (12 cases), software (9 cases), manufacturing (6 cases), and telecommunications (6 cases). The most prominent domain was the financial services. Moreover, SAFe has been popular in globally distributed organizations.

4.1 Benefits of Adopting SAFe

The reported benefits achieved by adopting SAFe are summarized in Table 3. The most common benefits identified are: *transparency* (22 cases), *alignment* (19 cases), *quality* (17 cases), *time to market* (17 cases), *predictability* (16 cases) and *productivity* (15 cases). The benefits marked by a star (*) in Table 3, are common to both the peer-reviewed and the non-peer reviewed studies.

The core values of SAFe are: build in quality, alignment, program execution and transparency [16]. A large proportion of the cases mentioned they had gained these benefits by adopting SAFe. We compared our findings to the 12th state of agile survey. 29% of respondents of that survey had adopted SAFe [29]. This survey reported similar benefits of agile in general as our study found regarding SAFe, visibility (66%), productivity (61%), alignment (65%), morale (61%), predictability (49%), quality (47%), and time to market (62%).

According to our results, practitioners seem to think that SAFe can help to bring several business benefits, such as improved time to market, and faster and more frequent deliveries. Surprisingly, none of the business benefits were reported in the peer-reviewed studies, but the majority of non-peer reviewed studies have attributed their business success to the SAFe framework. This difference could be due to the Scaled Agile Team insisting for business benefits, *"most importantly, we look for specific business results, which may include time-to-market, productivity, quality, and employee engagement"* [18]. Moreover, non-peer reviewed studies are more inclined towards presenting the benefits of the SAFe framework compared to peer-reviewed studies, e.g., only 8 (marked by *) out of 24 benefits were reported by peer-reviewed studies.

---

[6] * marked in Table 2.
[7] marked with D in Table 2.
[8] marked with C in Table 2.

Table 2. Domain of the case organizations

Domain	Organizations and cases
Financial Services (12)	Standard Bank: C1 [G55], Capital One: C2 [G45], Northwestern Mutual: C3 [G54], Nordea: C4 [G77, G23], SEI: C5 [G5, G6, G7], Tradestation: C6 [G28], Westpac: C7 [G43, G68], Simcorp*: D1 [P4], Vantiv: C8 [G56], Fannie Mae: C9 [G48], Edge Verve: C10 [G57, G63], Seamless Payments: C11 [G65, G64],
Electronics (4)	Thales: C12 [G44], Intel: C13 [G20, G82], Fitbit: C14 [G49], TomTom: C15 [G42, G60]
Software (9)	Sony PlayStation: C16 [G26], Amdocs: C17 [G36], HP: C18 [G39], Anonymous: C19 [G31, G76], BMC Software: C20 [G16, G78], Mitchells: C21 [G21, G66], Censhare: C22 [G47], Accenture: C23 [G32, G1], X company*: D2 [P6]
Telecommunications (6)	Comptel*: D3 and D4 [P3], Amdocs: C17 [G36], Swisscom: C24 [G41], Telstra: C25 [G27, G3, G69], Big IT: C26 [G15, G70, G71, G72, G73, G74]
Retail and Distribution (3)	Kantar Retail: C27 [G50], Travis Perkins: C28 [G79, G29, G75], DiscountTire: C29 [G18]
Medical and Pharma (4)	NHS: C30 [G53], Philips: C31 [G40], Elekta: C32 [G33, G62], AstraZeneca: C33 [G37]
Media and Marketing (2)	Valpak: C34 [G30], Sproutland: C35 [G59]
Agriculture (1)	LIC: C36 [G52]
Manufacturing (6)	Cisco: C37 [G38], TomTom: C15 [G42, G60], SK Hynix: C38 [G25, G61], Lego: C39 [G51, G10], JohnDeere: C40 [G11, G12, G13, G14, G80], Ocuco*: D5 [P5]
COT's (1)	RMIT University: C41 [G4, G34, G9, G35]
Customer Care (1)	CSG: C42 [G17]
Outsourcing (1)	Infogain: C43 [G19]
Government IT (2)	PoleEmploi: C44 [G8, G24, G2], Australian Postal Services: C45 [G67, G46]
Maritime IT (1)	NAPA: C46 [G22, G81]
Automobile (2)	AVL Gmbh* (2): D6 [P1] and D7 [P2]
Aviation (1)	Air France KLM: C47 [G58]

According to our results, practitioners clearly think that SAFe has brought benefits, however, it is also important to look into how the organizations measured these benefits. Unfortunately, not much information is given related to this. Only one study in the peer-reviewed literature focused on SAFe metrics [P5]. Most grey literature cases attributed all the mentioned benefits to the

SAFe adoption. However, it would be interesting to learn, e.g., which practices of SAFe brought the benefits. Only few cases had done that. Moreover, most of the benefits mentioned were similar to the general benefits from implementing agile. In the future it would be interesting to study what the unique benefits provided by SAFe practices, such as Agile Release Trains, PI planning meetings and value streams are.

4.2 Challenges of Adopting SAFe

The reported challenges of adopting SAFe are summarized in Table 4. The most commonly mentioned challenges are: *resistance to change* (10 cases), *moving away from agile* (7 cases), *First PI planning* (7 cases), controversies with the framework (6 cases), *Agile Release Train challenges* (6 cases), *staffing roles* (5 cases), and *GSD challenges* (4 cases). Change resistance, GSD challenges, integration of the non-development units and test automation challenges found in our review, were also mentioned in the *Systematic Literature Review on Challenges and Success Factors for Large-scale Agile Transformations* [8]. Further, *change resistance*, could be supported by the results from the 12th state of agile survey, *general resistance* [29].

11 out of 15 challenges were common both for the peer-reviewed and non-peer reviewed studies (marked by * in Table 4). It is notable that the majority of the peer-reviewed studies reported challenges during the SAFe adoption, while very few non-peer reviewed studies mentioned challenges.

Even though SAFe is a framework for scaling agile to large enterprises, several organizations felt they were *moving away from agile*. This challenge is supported by the arguments of several "agilists", for example, Ken Schwaber (co-creator of Scrum), says that *"SAFe is based on RUP, rather than Scrum"* [15], Ron Jeffries (co-founder of XP) sees issues in centralized approaches and planning in the framework [15] and Stephen Denning (board of directors of Scrum Alliance), finds SAFe to enforce the horizontal ideology of agile into vertical structures by saying [7] *"they run the risk that the firm will emerge back in the unproductive vertical world of hierarchical bureaucracy"* [7]. Pancholi and Grover [30] argue that SAFe *"murders the spirit of agile development"* and claim that SAFe is sold to large organizations that fear change, but would like to increase their productivity and reduce defects. According to them the framework portrays an *"agile fairy illusion"* [30].

Both organizations previously using traditional methods, as well as those having agile already in use, have shown resistance towards accepting SAFe. There is also a need to draw attention towards the specific challenges of SAFe, such as the challenges related to PI planning, value streams and agile release trains. Some faced controversies within the framework itself, like overhead, and story point normalization. Unlike the benefits, challenges have been mentioned only by 40% of the cases. Consequently, there is a need for more research into the challenges of the SAFe framework adoption and usage, as well as ways to overcome those challenges.

Table 3. Benefits of adopting SAFe

Benefit	Description	# cases
Build in Quality		
Quality	Improved product quality [G36, G37, G44, G56, G41, G28, G33, G39, G50, G18, G40, G17, G55, G58][a], higher quality releases [G78, G39], higher code quality [G5, G7, G59]	17
Defect Reduction	Drop in the defect rate [G18, G25, G61, G22, G21, G39, G27, G66, G43, G52, G48], reduction of the patches [G22], increase in the defect removal efficiency, reduction in quality assurance defects [G38] and escaped defects [G57, G63], warranty expenses down [G11], bug fixes reduced [G31, G76]	14
Continuous Improvement*	Focus on continuous improvement [G16, G39, G60, G67, G7, P4, P5][b]	7
Waste elimination	Less duplicated work [G51], reduced rework [G51, G44], negligible waste [G42, G60], reduced waste [G79, G73]	5
Alignment		
Alignment*	Increased alignment teams [G32, G1, G51, G7, G23, G41, G56, G43, P1, G59], management and development teams [G47, G33, G23], solved problems of misaligned teams [G51], alignment of business [G7], customer expectations [G36], alignment between IT and business units [G30, G59], client and vendor teams [G19], alignment towards organizational goals [G56], processes and projects [G37, G2, G40], tools [G40], products [G45, G57] and priorities [G19]	19
Collaboration*	Enhanced collaboration [G9, G44, G80, P3, G6, G35], greater collaboration between team members [G57, G23], multiple teams [G23] international teams [G38, P5], diverse working groups [G44], different units (IT, Business) [G30, G19, G58, G6], cross site and cross functional collaboration [G33]	14
Dependencies*	Improved dependency management [G26, G47, G55, G52, P5], dependencies across trains are addressed [G24], less dependency problems [G10, G2]	7
Vision	Established shared vision [G50, G47, G38], shared goals [G10] broader view on company wide strategies [G49, G26]	6

(continued)

Table 3. (*continued*)

Benefit	Description	# cases
Transparency		
Transparency*	Enhanced transparency [G67, G25, G61, G22, G26, G44, G42, G31, G56, G5, G7, G35, G58, G48], process transparency [G33, G30, G50, G9, G23, G10, G56, G19], cross team dependencies are transparent [G47, P1], transparency in communication [G20]	22
Visibility*	Improved visibility [G73, G30, G49, G82, G30, G20, G50, P4, G9, G26, G35, G57, G59, G48]	11
Organizational Benefits		
Productivity	Improved productivity [G16, G17, G18, G67, G28, G55, G57, G58, G48], increase in productivity across teams and employees [G50, G30], increased delivery of number of products, variants and capabilities [G49, G56, G20, G26]	15
Team Autonomy*	More empowered teams [G67, G16, G47, G30, G10, G23, G5, G48, G59], self managing teams [G60, G52], self organizing teams [G30, G6, P5], improved morale [P4, G45, G30], ownership [G42, G58], control of own commitments [G60] and own code [G60]	13
Engagement	Improved employee engagement [G16, G45, G67, G49, G11, G13, G56, G43, G44, G52, G59], improved employee retention [G45, G21], decrease in attrition [G56, G50]	12
Employee Satisfaction*	Improved employee satisfaction [G67, G47, G38, P3, G58], happier teams [G15, G73, G27, G31, G76], happy employees [G31, G76]	8
Predictability	Greater predictability in the product delivery [G36, G25, G61, G82, G22, G26, G42, G50, G45, G55, G56, G7, G67, G58, G52, G59, G48]	16
Feedback	Faster feedback from customers [G36, G16, G50, G48] and greater feedback mechanisms [G56]	5

(*continued*)

Table 3. (*continued*)

Benefit	Description	# cases
Business Benefits		
Cost	Financial benefits [G37], reduced costs [G16, G55], controlled costs [G39], reduced cost per epic [G50, G57], reduced cost point size [G44], decreased infrastructural costs [G67], decrease in delivery costs [G15, G27], reduced quality costs [G32]	11
Frequent Deliveries	Increase in release frequency [G78, G44, G27, G34, G80, G39], frequent deliverable's [G45, G30, G36, G52, G48, G58] and value [G30], increased deployments [G55]	13
Faster Deliveries	Faster deliveries [G37, G45, G39, G44, G34], faster feature delivery [G78, G38], quick releases [G30, G80, G78], decrease in feature cycle time [G40, G54] and release cycle down [G40, G43, G38, G34]	12
On time delivery	On time delivery [G15, G50, G39, G49, G56, G48], no missing dates [G30] and schedule slips [G20]	8
Responsiveness	More responsive towards market needs [G50] and customer needs [G56] and decrease in time to respond to customer requests [G21, G50]	4
Time to market	Improved time to market [G36, G37, G45, G47, G18, G30, G31, G39, G11, G13, G50, G55, G41, G56, G58, G57, G52, G66]	17
Customer Satisfaction	Increase in the customer satisfaction [G36, G45, G31, G50, G41, G56, G6, G5, G67, G2, G58, G57] delighted [G36] and happy customers [G76]	13

[a]**G** denotes non peer-reviewed sources or grey literature sources
[b]**P** denotes peer-reviewed sources or scientific literature sources

5 Limitations

This section presents the threats to validity [37] and the steps that have been taken to mitigate those threats.

Selection Bias. This occurs during the selection of primary studies based on the interpretation of inclusion and exclusion criteria. We mitigated this by involving all authors in designing the criteria and two researchers filtered the abstracts and titles of peer-reviewed articles independently. Regarding the non-peer reviewed literature, we included all the case studies published on the homepage of the Scaled Agile Framework, which mitigated the threat of selection bias.

Table 4. Challenges of adopting SAFe

Challenge	Description	# cases
Organizational and cultural		
Change resistance*	Resistance [G39, G45, G58, G52, G59] towards accepting change, experiencing change as negative [P3], initial hesitation from teams [G56], individuals choose to leave [G54], teams reject to take part in ART [G60], initial resistance towards ART [G45] and reject the common ways of working, strong change resistance from teams towards lack of SAFe knowledge and need to change [P3]	10
Mindset*	Difficult to implement agile mindset [P4, G72]	2
Autonomy*	Teams lacked autonomy [P3, G45]	2
Plan driven or traditional culture*	Struggles to become iterative from fixed delivery cycles [P2, G4, G34], struggle to shift from waterfall culture [G54, G34, G4]	3
Roles		
Resistance for new roles*	Resistance from traditional project managers roles during adoption of SAFe [G44], challenges with change of roles [P4]	2
Staffing roles	Trouble to find the Product Owners [G72, G14, G28, G6, G53] and challenging to find someone with both technical and industrial experience [G28]. Product ownership is complex across universities [G9]. Staffing scrum master was also difficult [G6]	6
Practices		
Value streams	Defining values streams [G62, G6, G14]	3
First Program Increment Planning*	Lack of knowledge on importance about PI [P3], chaotic event [P3, G48], people were uncomfortable during PI [P3] and considered it as unpleasant [G72], clash of time slots to fix PI planning [P3], surprises during PI planning [P3], hard to focus on PI [G10] and ambiguity about time allocation to event [G50], lack of technical knowledge (how to code) during first PI [G50], fail to implement effective PSI and find PSI cadence [G72], teams resist towards PI [P3], feature shaping to PSI was difficult [G72], logistic challenges [G53], technical dependencies in PI's [G8] and management reviews were chaotic [G10]	7
Backlog Management and feature shaping	Feature grooming [G72] and backlog prioritization challenges [G33], not finding right backlog [G9], feature prioritization did not involve every one, mostly a *solo effect* (only product manager) [G43], feature shaping clashed with deployment requirements [G72]	4

(*continued*)

Table 4. (*continued*)

Challenge	Description	# cases
Test automation*	Automated unit tests could not be applied to legacy systems [P2], automated testing was challenging [G4, P5]	3
Controversies with framework*	More complex [G10, P6] and risky [P6], confusion with the way of working [P4], framework as overhead [P3], controversies regarding story point normalization [G72], difficulties with release management in SAFe framework [G33], separation of deployment cycle from PSI cycle was challenging [G72], framework not suitable for organizations working on multiple products [G51]	6
Agile Release Train*	Failure demand of ART's due to ineffective PSI [G72], integration of teams with less dependencies into agile release trains [P1], handling cross team dependencies across the ART's [P1], rearrangement of trains for distributed teams [G33], rejection to take part into ART [G60], difficulties to define ART in organizational context [G8, G14]	6
Moving away from agile*	Moving to SAFe feels like moving back to plan driven methods (such as waterfall and RUP like) [P6, P3, G72, G59], fixed increments [P3], centralized planning [P6], not really incremental [G9], loss of incremental and iterative development [G60], too much detail [G10]	7
Scaling and distribution		
Large and distributed settings	Challenges of full scaling of agile to whole organization [P4] and global organization [P2], integrating non development units such as IT, HR and sales and marketing [P4]	2
GSD*	Collaborative planning meeting and critical gatherings were difficult due to distributed teams [P2], deriving global priorities [G33], different time zones [G33] [G4], scaling agile to global organization [P2], rearrangement of ART's was challenging due to geographic distribution [G33], release planning challenges due to distributed teams [P6]	4

Subjective Bias. This threat occurs during the coding of qualitative data. Coding was performed by the first author very meticulously. Coding was iterative, and all authors had several discussions during the coding process regarding the naming of the axial codes and categorization of the open codes into axial codes. The process is traceable.

Restricted Time Span. In the database search, we included primary studies published in the selected databases until November 2017. For the non-peer reviewed literature, we included all case studies published by May 4th, 2018.

Publication Bias. Including grey, non-peer reviewed, literature can be seen as a limitation. Non-peer reviewed articles usually present positive results [37]. This was also evident from our study, as majority of these cases gave attention to the benefits of the framework. In addition, the Scaled Agile team reviewed all case studies reported by the organizations. There might be a possibility for them to influence the organizations to present only the positive elements of the SAFe adoption process. However, out of 82 documents from grey literature 26 documents came directly from the organizations and other online websites, as additional supplements. These supplements (e.g.: presentations) reported the same information as was published under the case studies on the website. This threat of bias was partially mitigated by comparing the benefits from peer-reviewed primary studies, identified in this MLR (6 studies) and the State of Agile survey [29]. The challenges of adopting SAFe were compared to the findings of the SLR on challenges of large-scale agile transformations [8] as well as to the State of Agile survey [29]. However, to establish scientific evidence there is a strong need for more empirical research on benefits and challenges of SAFe.

Information Loss. The codes with only a few quotes and cases (3 cases or less for benefits, 1 case for challenges) were not reported. The keyword search could have missed some studies. We mitigated this by going through the references and citations of all 5 selected studies. We found one additional case study [P5] from the citations of already selected papers [P3].

6   Conclusions and Future Work

The number of organizations adopting scaling frameworks has increased tremendously during the recent years. A few studies have given insights on agile usage in large organizations, however, the literature on the adoption and usage of scaling frameworks has not been systematically reviewed. Moreover, systematic literature reviews on large-scale agile, have not included the grey literature. This means that most published information about the scaling frameworks has been excluded, giving an incomplete picture, as current research literature on them is very limited. Therefore, we included also grey literature in this multivocal literature review.

We analyzed 54 peer and non-peer reviewed cases on the adoption of the Scaled Agile Framework. The most salient benefit categories were: *transparency, alignment, productivity, predictability and time to market.* The most frequently mentioned challenge categories were: *change resistance, challenges with the first program increment planning and moving away from agile.* The most important difference between the peer-reviewed and grey literature was the bias in reporting benefits, especially with respect to business benefits received from the usage of the framework. These benefits were mentioned only in the grey literature.

This emphasizes the need for validation of the claimed benefits reported in the grey literature. The majority of the challenges were common for both the peer-reviewed and grey literature.

Apart from the challenges related to scaling agile, SAFe has brought in new challenges with respect to practices such as PI planning, value streams, and Agile Release Trains. Empirical research on how the SAFe framework is addressing the existing challenges, that have been reported in the *agile in the large* literature, could be interesting for practitioners. Moreover, finding solutions for the challenges reported in this MLR, would help organizations to address these challenges.

We identified only six peer reviewed primary studies on SAFe since the introduction of the framework (year 2011). Literature lacks in-depth primary studies on the usage and adoption of SAFe. Some of the non-peer reviewed cases published at the SAFe home page had deep insights on the rationale behind the SAFe adoption, transformation steps, implementation of practices, as well as the benefits of the adoption. Unfortunately, both peer-reviewed and grey literature lack extensive information on challenges and the negative traits of SAFe in large enterprises, as there likely is an inherent positive bias in the cases published at the SAFe home page. Hence, it is crucial to conduct more in-depth primary studies on SAFe adoptions to establish scientific evidence on the SAFe framework usage in large scale.

References

1. Alqudah, M., Razali, R.: A review of scaling agile methods in large software development. Int. J. Adv. Sci. Eng. Inf. Technol. **6**(6), 828–837 (2016)
2. Alsaqaf, W., Daneva, M., Wieringa, R.: Quality requirements in large-scale distributed agile projects – a systematic literature review. In: Grünbacher, P., Perini, A. (eds.) REFSQ 2017. LNCS, vol. 10153, pp. 219–234. Springer, Cham (2017). https://doi.org/10.1007/978-3-319-54045-0_17
3. Ambler, S.W., Lines, M.: Disciplined Agile Delivery: A Practitioner's Guide to Agile Software Delivery in the Enterprise. IBM Press, Indianapolis (2012)
4. Ampatzoglou, A., Ampatzoglou, A., Chatzigeorgiou, A., Avgeriou, P.: The financial aspect of managing technical debt: a systematic literature review. Inf. Softw. Technol. **64**, 52–73 (2015)
5. Boehm, B., Turner, R.: Management challenges to implementing agile processes in traditional development organizations. IEEE Softw. **22**(5), 30–39 (2005)
6. Corbin, J.M., Strauss, A.L.: Basics of Qualitative Research: Techniques and Procedures for Developing Grounded Theory, 3rd edn. Sage Publications Inc., Los Angeles (2008). http://www.loc.gov/catdir/toc/ecip0725/2007034189.html
7. Denning, S.: Agile: its time to put it to use to manage business complexity. Strat. Leadersh. **43**(5), 10–17 (2015)
8. Dikert, K., Paasivaara, M., Lassenius, C.: Challenges and success factors for large-scale agile transformations: a systematic literature review. J. Syst. Softw. **119**, 87–108 (2016)
9. Dybå, T., Dingsøyr, T.: Empirical studies of agile software development: a systematic review. Inf. Softw. Technol. **50**(9–10), 833–859 (2008)

10. Garousi, V., Felderer, M., Mäntylä, M.V.: The need for multivocal literature reviews in software engineering: complementing systematic literature reviews with grey literature. In: Proceedings of the 20th International Conference on Evaluation and Assessment in Software Engineering, p. 26. ACM (2016)
11. Garousi, V., Felderer, M., Mäntylä, M.V.: Guidelines for including the grey literature and conducting multivocal literature reviews in software engineering. arXiv preprint arXiv:1707.02553 (2017)
12. Garousi, V., Mäntylä, M.V.: When and what to automate in software testing? A multi-vocal literature review. Inf. Softw. Technol. **76**, 92–117 (2016)
13. Glass, R.L.: Software Creativity 2.0. developer.* Books (2006)
14. Gustavsson, T.: Assigned roles for inter-team coordination in large-scale agile development: a literature review. In: Proceedings of the XP2017 Scientific Workshops, p. 15. ACM (2017)
15. van Haaster, K.: Agile in-the-large: getting from paradox to paradigm
16. Scaled Agile Inc.: Core Values. http://www.scaledagileframework.com/safe-core-values/
17. Scaled Agile Inc.: Questionnaire for safe adopters. https://www.scaledagile.com/resources/submit-a-case-study/
18. Scaled Agile Inc.: Review process. https://www.scaledagile.com/case-study-faqs/
19. Scaled Agile Inc.: Scaled Agile Framework. http://www.scaledagileframework.com/case-studies/
20. QSR International: Coding Tool for Qualtitaive Analysis. http://www.qsrinternational.com/nvivo/support-overview/downloads
21. Keele, S., et al.: Guidelines for performing systematic literature reviews in software engineering. In: Technical report, Ver. 2.3 EBSE Technical Report. EBSE. sn (2007)
22. Khalid, H., Ahmed, M., Sameer, A., Arif, F.: Systematic literature review of agile scalability for large scale projects. Int. J. Adv. Comput. Sci. Appl. (IJACSA) **6**(9), 63–75 (2015)
23. Kuhrmann, M., et al.: Hybrid software and system development in practice: waterfall, scrum, and beyond. In: Proceedings of the 2017 International Conference on Software and System Process, pp. 30–39. ACM (2017)
24. Larman, C., Vodde, B.: Practices for Scaling Lean & Agile Development: Large, Multisite, and Offshore Product Development with Large-scale Scrum. Pearson Education, London (2010)
25. Leffingwell, D.: Scaling Software Agility: Best Practices for Large Enterprises. Pearson Education, Boston (2007)
26. Moe, N.B., Dingsøyr, T.: Emerging research themes and updated research agenda for large-scale agile development: a summary of the 5th international workshop at xp2017. In: Proceedings of the XP2017 Scientific Workshops, p. 14. ACM (2017)
27. Moe, N.B., Olsson, H.H., Dingsøyr, T.: Trends in large-scale agile development: a summary of the 4th workshop at xp2016. In: Proceedings of the Scientific Workshop Proceedings of XP2016, p. 1. ACM (2016)
28. Myrbakken, H., Colomo-Palacios, R.: DevSecOps: a multivocal literature review. In: Mas, A., Mesquida, A., O'Connor, R.V., Rout, T., Dorling, A. (eds.) SPICE 2017. CCIS, vol. 770, pp. 17–29. Springer, Cham (2017). https://doi.org/10.1007/978-3-319-67383-7_2
29. One, V.: State of Agile Survey. https://explore.versionone.com/state-of-agile/versionone-12th-annual-state-of-agile-report
30. Pancholi, A., Grover, S.: Scaled agile framework: a blight. Int. J. Innov. Res. Dev. **3**(5) (2014)

31. Rafi, D.M., Moses, K.R.K., Petersen, K., Mäntylä, M.V.: Benefits and limitations of automated software testing: systematic literature review and practitioner survey. In: Proceedings of the 7th International Workshop on Automation of Software Test, pp. 36–42. IEEE Press (2012)
32. Razavi, A.M., Ahmad, R.: Agile development in large and distributed environments: a systematic literature review on organizational, managerial and cultural aspects. In: 2014 8th Malaysian Software Engineering Conference (MySEC), pp. 216–221. IEEE (2014)
33. Rolland, K.H., Fitzgerald, B., Dingsøyr, T., Stol, K.J.: Problematizing agile in the large: alternative assumptions for large-scale agile development (2016)
34. Tom, E., Aurum, A., Vidgen, R.: An exploration of technical debt. J. Syst. Softw. **86**(6), 1498–1516 (2013)
35. Uludağ, Ö., Kleehaus, M., Xu, X., Matthes, F.: Investigating the role of architects in scaling agile frameworks. In: 2017 IEEE 21st International Enterprise Distributed Object Computing Conference (EDOC), pp. 123–132. IEEE (2017)
36. Vaidya, A.: Does dad know best, is it better to do less or just be safe? Adapting scaling agile practices into the enterprise. In: PNSQC. ORG, pp. 1–18 (2014)
37. Zhou, X., Jin, Y., Zhang, H., Li, S., Huang, X.: A map of threats to validity of systematic literature reviews in software engineering. In: 2016 23rd Asia-Pacific Software Engineering Conference (APSEC), pp. 153–160. IEEE (2016)

Industry Talks

Threat Analysis in Practice – Systematically Deriving Security Requirements

Markus Fockel[(✉)], Sven Merschjohann, and Masud Fazal-Baqaie

Software Engineering and IT Security, Fraunhofer IEM, Paderborn, Germany
{Markus.Fockel,Sven.Merschjohann,Masud.Fazal-Baqaie}@iem.fraunhofer.de

Abstract. With the growing number of incidents, the topic security gains more and more attention across all domains. Organizations realize their lack of state-of-the-art security practices, however, they struggle to improve their software lifecycle in terms of security. In this talk, we introduce the concept of security by design that implements security practices within the whole software lifecycle. Based on our practical experience from industry projects in the regulated industrial automation and unregulated classical IT domain, we explain how to perform a threat analysis and how to integrate it into the software lifecycle.

Keywords: Threat analysis · Security by design · IEC 62443

1 Introduction

Across all domains cyber-security gains more and more attention as the number of reported incidents is increasing. Due to the growing degree of software within products and services, the potential attack surface increases while at the same time attacks are getting more professional. In order to counter this disturbing trend, organizations across all domains need to improve on their security measures. Indeed, in our daily practice, we often observe the lack of state-of-the-art security practices and thus a lot of potential for improvement. Some industries react by establishing security standards to enforce the use of proper security practices. For example, the standard IEC 62443 [2] regulates the security for industrial automation and describes process requirements for security. But also in the classical IT domain where no such standard exists the awareness for the lack of security practices is growing. In this talk, we introduce the concept of "security by design" that integrates security practices within the whole software lifecycle (Sect. 2). We highlight "threat analysis" as its first step to identify security requirements. Based on our practical experience from industry projects in the industrial automation and classical IT domain, we explain how to perform threat analysis and how to integrate its results into the software lifecycle for reaching security by design and compliance with standards (Sect. 3). We demonstrate the threat assessment based on STRIDE [3], and explain that adjusting

M. Kuhrmann et al. (Eds.): PROFES 2018, LNCS 11271, pp. 355–358, 2018.
https://doi.org/10.1007/978-3-030-03673-7_25

the used tools to the context of the organization ensures an efficient analysis and process workflow. We conclude the talk with our assessment of the benefits of threat analysis (Sect. 4).

2   Security by Design

In order to systematically develop secure products and services, security must be emphasized throughout the whole software lifecycle, such that the results are secure by design. Thus, every step of a common software lifecycle is enhanced with security practices as illustrated in Fig. 1. The shown high-level process can be further tailored and refined towards specific domains and system classes [1] and many aspects also correlate with security standards for specific domains, e.g., IEC 62443 for industrial automation.

The very first security practice is the *threat analysis*. It is used to identify the system's assets, its security objectives, threats to it and associated risks. Using these results of the threat analysis a *secure design* can be created, which specifically targets the identified threats with appropriate countermeasures on an architectural level. This ensures that the risk of the threats is reduced to an acceptable level and the product design is secure. However, the realization can still introduce vulnerabilities, e.g., due to flaws in the code like buffer overflows. Therefore, *code analysis* and code reviews need to be applied to ensure secure code. In addition, each identified threat should be the basis for a test case, such that its mitigation can be verified. In practice, many vulnerabilities are caused by faulty deployments. Hence, the process demands the *enforcement* of secure configurations. Lastly, the process also needs to cover the long-term security by implementing a functional *patch management*, in order to quickly fix vulnerabilities after the product or service has been released.

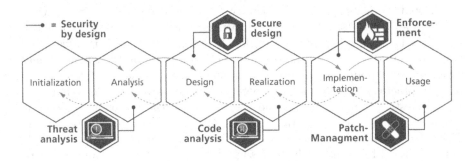

Fig. 1. Security by design: security practices throughout the whole software lifecycle

3   Security Practice: Threat Analysis

As a first step towards security by design, we apply threat analysis and integrate it into existing development processes. We integrate it, for example, by integrating the tool used for threat modeling with existing application lifecycle management (ALM) tools. Consequently, identified and modeled threats can be refined as and traced to requirements and test cases in the ALM tooling. In the following, we illustrate the five steps of threat analysis and provide practical advice based on several projects across various domains.

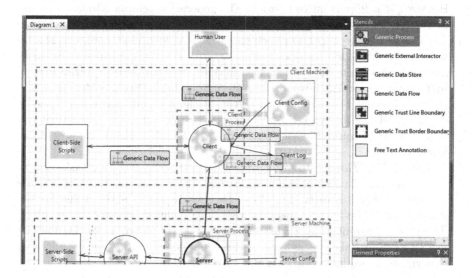

Fig. 2. A threat model in the threat modeling tool (color figure online)

1. *Specify System and its Security Context.* In our projects, we often use the Microsoft Threat Modeling Tool (TMT) as tool support[1] to specify the system under development as illustrated in Fig. 2. Here, elements within the system (circles) and external to the system (rectangles) as well as different zones of trust (denoted by red, dashed borders) define the system boundaries and which elements are more trustworthy than others. In addition, it is important to specify assumptions about security measures that are provided by the system's context (the so-called security context). The more security measures are taken by the system's context, the less measures need to be provided by the system itself. For instance, if we can rely on the operating system's user management, we do not need to develop our own login mechanism. It is crucial to document the assumptions about the security context.
2. *Determine Assets and Security Objectives.* In the second step, the assets of the system are identified. For all elements it is determined what security objectives need to be achieved and what needs to be safeguarded, e.g., "confidentiality of customer data in the database" or "availability of the server".

---

[1] https://www.microsoft.com/en-us/download/details.aspx?id=49168.

3. *Identify and Localize Threats.* In this step, possible threats for the parts of the system are identified. We use STRIDE [3] for categorization and systematically go through all communication flows that cross zones of trust to brainstorm about possible threats. While performing this step in workshops with system experts, it is helpful to have a list of possible threats as a starting point to foster discussions. TMT has an automated threat generation feature. However, it is important to customize its generation template to avoid superfluous generated threats, ultimately leading to frustrated participants.

4. *Define Countermeasures.* For each threat that is identified, countermeasures have to be defined. This does not necessarily lead to implemented security mechanisms within the system. Countermeasures can also be taken care of by the system context beyond the system boundaries. Stakeholders may also choose to accept the risk by open threats without countermeasures. There is a n-to-m relation between threats and countermeasures, e.g., one threat can require a set of countermeasures to reduce the residual risk to an acceptable level.

5. *Assess Risk of Threats.* In order to prioritize threat mitigation tasks and to assess the effectiveness of countermeasures, the risk associated with threats is assessed. For instance, IEC 62443 requires to assess a risk value for the unmitigated threat and a residual risk once countermeasures are in place. There are different ways to assess risk, for early threat prioritization, we use Protection Poker [4] as part of threat modeling workshops with system experts, as it produces quick results with low effort.

4   Conclusion

In order to counter the growing trend of security incidents, organizations need to improve their security measures. As illustrated, this can be achieved by systematically integrating security practices within the software lifecycle, thus achieving security by design. Based on the practical experience from various industry projects, we explained how to perform threat analysis as the first security practice in the process and how to integrate it into the lifecycle for compliance with standards.

References

1. Geismann, J., Gerking, C., Bodden, E.: Towards ensuring security by design in cyber-physical systems engineering processes. In: International Conference on Software and System Process (ICSSP 2018), May 2018
2. International Electrotechnical Commission (IEC): IEC 62443-4-1:2018: Security for industrial automation and control systems - Part 4–1: Secure product development lifecycle requirements, Jan 2018
3. Shostack, A.: Threat Modeling: Designing for Security. Wiley, Indianapolis (2014)
4. Williams, L., Meneely, A., Shipley, G.: Protection poker: The new software security "game". IEEE Secur. Privacy **8**(3), 14–20 (2010)

Process Evolution and Product Maturity: From Prototype to Product

Tilman Seifert[✉]

QAware GmbH, München, Germany
`tilman.seifert@qaware.de`
`https://www.qaware.de`

Abstract. Processes cannot just be judged as "good" or "efficient"—
they must be appropriate for the type of project. As the type of a
project changes over time, the processes must adjust in order to stay efficient and appropriate. We accompanied the transformation of a large and
fast-growing project, using agile development methods and cloud-native
technologies, from the very first steps of a prototype to the development
of a customer-ready product. This experience report shows patterns we
found on the way. It argues that systematic process evolution can be
done without documentation overhead or relying on questionable process KPIs. We only used information which is available anyway; this
includes our archive of sprint retro boards which allows to create a clear
picture of the project's evolution, regarding both the process and the
product quality.

1 Situation and Challenges

The case-study we report here develops a novel kind of entertainment system. It's
a cloud-native based backend system with a number of micro services, which also
integrate third party services, and an individually developed client (hardware
and software). As the project matured from the first prototype steps and passed
a number of investment decision boards, the team also grew heavily. Today, two
years later, there are more than 170 people involved, working as developers,
testers, designers, scrum masters, product owners or others. The whole team is
organized in scrum teams; all of them collaborate in a "Nexus" pattern which
organizes the co-operation of scrum teams. We are responsible for one of the
sub-teams with 23 members.

After each sprint, we do a retro to identify options for technical or process
improvements. We also tried to step back and analyze the process evolution,
and check whether the process changes we applied over time accurately reflected
the needs of the project. Did they effectively address the pain points? Were the
measures applied at the right time? Does the process cater for the current team
size? This paper reports on the results of that process evolution analysis.

© Springer Nature Switzerland AG 2018
M. Kuhrmann et al. (Eds.): PROFES 2018, LNCS 11271, pp. 359–362, 2018.
https://doi.org/10.1007/978-3-030-03673-7_26

2   Approach

When we wanted to analyze the process evolution, we decided to set up the following constraints: The analysis should be reproducible; the data it is based on should be available from our project work, without adding any documentation overhead. Therefore, we used our archive of sprint retros. This works at least on a qualitative level, which is not perfect, but offers a nice effort-to-insight ratio.

The sprint retros use an online tool with the usual "glad/sad/mad" columns and the agreed tasks and measures. We took screenshots of these boards and archived them after each sprint retro. For the analysis, we first considered which process areas we want to focus on; then we wrote down hypotheses to test. The second step was to go through all sprint retros and extract any indicators related to any of these theses; we used a simple spreadsheet here. The third step was to analyze this spreadsheet, whether correlation to the theses can be found or not.

This approach has strengths and weaknesses. The data creation is not systematic in the sense that not in every retro specific questions were asked regarding the theses discussed below. It's possible that team members did not comment on a specific issue, just because they felt other issues were more pressing, or because they had mentioned them before. However, it's much more reliable than just a personal memory of the project's evolution, it's zero effort for the project team, and it's authentic information.

3   Appropriate Processes in a Changing Environment

Software development processes differ, depending on the product to build; they must be *appropriate* for the product to be developed and for the environment where this is done. Any project which starts with a prototype to evaluate a technology, and then decides to go for a customer-ready product will experience changes in appropriate processes. Processes must match team sizes, so as the team grows, processes will change over time.

The following sections present theses about four selected process areas. They highlight the differences we see between a prototype phase and product development. Note that there was never a hard cut, but rather a gradual shift in assurance that the project will make it to the market. Both the theses and the selection of process areas are opinionated. However, we present data from our analysis of the sprint retro archive which support each thesis.

3.1   Communication Structures and Tools

Teams need to share information; they need to support each other if there are questions. This may happen informally (just go and ask), via tools (e-mail, chat, etc.), or via documentation (Wiki pages, documents etc.). The informal way is often most informative—however, it does not scale with a larger team.

In a prototype phase, when the teams are small, it's important to make sure that knowledge is distributed as far as possible in order to fix things and to stimulate ideas. In product development, when teams grow, knowledge transfer and communication needs more structure.

Our data shows that with increasing time size (not only in this sub-team, but overall), the team complained about interruptions caused by support requests and questions by other teams. We agreed on measures like dedicated support channels, or dedicated support times etc. On the other hand, the team explicitly valued working phases without interruption, when the could actually "get stuff done". They also valued well-articulated questions from neighbor teams. While developers don't fancy writing documentation, they much prefer it to being interrupted by phone, e-mail, or chat for the ever-same questions. Finding the right channels for communication lead to different answers over time.

3.2 Focus: Just Let People Work

In a prototype phase, one main goal is to generate ideas; in product development, the goal shifts to develop stable components, and to integrate the solution parts of all teams; this typically requires short test and deployment cycles. At all times, demos to senior management are important to keep the sponsors' support.

Our data shows that while the team appreciated senior management's interest in the project and its improvements, it felt that often unplanned demos suddenly got higher priority than the development of required features. This implied changes, interrupting work and blocking team members. Therefore, many demos were perceived counter-productive. Measures against such obstruction include having one environment and a set of dedicated clients ready for demos at all times. This may be hard to achieve if resources are scarce. Our lesson is that proper planning for demos and sound expectation management is crucial.

Other priorities also changed too often on short notice. There was e. g. one specific system to integrate. It proved to be difficult (indicating to integrate it in a later release), but offered a high business value (being a reason to put it the first release). The decision whether it would be part of the first release or not changed an uncounted number of times. Every time the customer decides to change his goals or priorities, this information must be communicated to all scrum teams. The teams must then re-validate and maybe reorder their backlogs to match the new goals; this is a time-consuming process.

Even in an agile environment, where "embrace change" is a ubiquitous slogan, having stable goals offers security. The sprint concept is meant to provide security (i. e. to protect the team from uncontrolled change impact) while the sprint is under way. Sharing goals between all sub-teams gives the security that the current work is important and will be used soon. Our data supports this view: It's motivating for a team to find its results being used, and vice versa.

3.3 Allow to Produce Quality

Quality deficiencies of all kinds (requirements, concepts, architecture, implementation) result in re-work—which is costly. In a prototype phase, there is nothing wrong with trying, testing, judging, and changing; moving fast and learning a lot are the top-priorities. In product development, however, we experienced that the team considers too many changes in the same areas as tiresome. We saw developers who long for stable requirements, because they wish for producing high-quality, long-living code. The data shows a low level of satisfaction with re-work, especially when things were just finished. It also shows an increase in satisfaction when re-work was actively reduced (e. g. with explicit analysis and design phases, involving all relevant stakeholders, and by documenting decisions).

There are many ways to measure and achieve quality, including using quality metrics tools on code level (SonarQube, Structure101 et al.). While all of this is feasible and valuable, there is one thing which is even easier and very effective: just ask the team—and listen to their response.

3.4   Requirements Engineering

In a prototype phase, teams build what is possible to build, because learning what is possible—maybe even pushing the limits of what seems possible—is the top-goal. In product development, however, teams should build what is useful for customers, thereby generating business value. While this sounds simple, it proves to be a great mind-shift, because it introduces a completely new source of priorities.

One way to cope with this change is doing requirements engineering. This proposal has lead to disputes about whether this is a waterfall approach and must therefore be avoided. In our pragmatic experience, it's a good idea to first fully understand a feature and to actually write it down, then consider consequences for related features or services, and only then start to build it. We do so in what we call "exploration teams" which are ahead of the development teams by at least one sprint. The exploration team makes sure that all features are well-understood before implementation; they also challenge the customer's prioritization of features by mapping them to the overall goals. We opt for dedicated exploration teams to do analysis and write user stories or mini-specifications (as opposed to do so within the development teams) as these tasks require a different skill set. The data shows that the team's satisfaction rose when an exploration team was installed which introduced systematic requirements analysis.

4   Conclusion

Teams with a mature understanding of processes will change and adapt their development methods, activities, communication structures, and tools as they move from a prototype to a customer-ready product. Over time, processes change: different activities gain or lose importance, collaboration and information flow between neighboring teams changes—even if the overall process framework stays the same. Simple things like the sprint retro archive offer good insight to allow for qualitative analysis of the project's evolution and maturity, and to derive appropriate improvement measures in a lightweight, yet systematic way.

Workshops and Tutorial

Workshops and Tutorials

Jürgen Münch[1][(✉)] and Krzysztof Wnuk[2]

[1] Department of Computer Science, Reutlingen University,
Reutlingen, Germany
`juergen.muench@reutlingen-university.de`
[2] Department of Software Engineering, Blekinge University of Technology,
Karlskrona, Sweden
`krzysztof.wnuk@bth.se`

The 19th International Conference on Product-Focused Software Process Improvement (PROFES 2018) hosted two workshops and three tutorials. The workshops and tutorials complemented and enhanced the main conference program, offering a wider knowledge perspective around the conference topics. The topics of the two workshops were *Hybrid Development Approaches in Software Systems Development* (HELENA) and *Managing Quality in Agile & Rapid Software Development Processes* (QUaSD). The topics of the tutorials were *The human factor in agile transitions – Using the personas concept in agile coaching, Process Management 4.0 – Best Practices*, and *Domain-specific languages for specification, development, and testing of autonomous systems*.

The workshop organizers would like to thank all persons that organized the workshop or contributed to the workshops as well as the presenters of the tutorials. The workshops and tutorials provided interesting forums for discussing ideas, presenting novel work, learning and networking. In the following the workshop and tutorials are summarized based on the content of the respective workshop and tutorial web descriptions.

1 Workshops

3rd International Workshop on Hybrid Development Approaches in Software Systems Development (HELENA)

A software process provides a game plan for organizing project teams and running projects. Software processes have existed in many forms, over a period of decades. Yet, it is still a challenge to select the most appropriate process for a given context. A multitude of development approaches compete for the developers' favor, and there is no silver bullet serving all possible setups. Moreover, recent research as well as experience from practice show companies utilizing different development approaches to assemble the best-fitting approach for the respective company, team and project at that point in time. For instance, a more traditional process might provide the basic framework often to serve the organization, while project teams embody this framework with more agile (and/or lean) practices to leverage their flexibility.

This Workshop continued the software process community work initiated at ICSSP 2016 (Austin, Texas). The HELENA workshops accompany the HELENA study which aims at investigating the current state of practice in software and systems development. HELENA is an acronym for "Hybrid dEveLopmENt Approaches in software systems development". In particular, the study aims to determine which development

M. Kuhrmann et al. (Eds.): PROFES 2018, LNCS 11271, pp. 365–369, 2018.
https://doi.org/10.1007/978-3-030-03673-7_27

approaches (traditional, agile, mainstream, or homegrown) are used in practice and how they are combined, how such combinations are developed over time, and if and how standards (e.g., safety standards) affect the development process as such and the methods applied. With this information, the study aims to push forward systematic process design and improvement activities to allow for more efficient and lower-overhead development approaches.

The HELENA study has been planned as a 3-stage international research endeavor. The first stage initiated data collection through the building and testing of a survey instrument. The second stage enabled "mass data" collection using a revised survey instrument, available in four languages. This second stage was conducted via a large international consortium comprising more than 70 partners from more than 20 countries. Finally, the third stage will emphasize more focused research based on the outcomes of the second stage. This workshop aimed at bringing together all HELENA contributors in order to

1. Report the current state and (tentative) outcomes of the HELENA survey (from global and regional perspectives),
2. Develop a work program and define next steps within the whole community, and
3. Build working groups, to work on the selected (sub-)topics of interest.

The 3rd HELENA Workshop was a full-day event, organized for the community to meet and advance topics of interest. The program included sessions on work in progress and ongoing initiatives and the current state of the HELENA study from a global perspective. In addition, future joint initiatives were planned and the foci of the third phase of the HELENA study was presented and discussed. The 3rd HELENA workshop was organized by Paolo Tell (IT University of Copenhagen), Stephen MacDonell (Auckland University of Technology), and Sherlock Licorish (University of Otagoc).

2nd International Workshop on Managing Quality in Agile and Rapid Software Development Processes (QuASD)

The 2nd International Workshop on Managing Quality in Agile & Rapid Software Development Processes aimed at investigating product and process quality in the context of agile and rapid software development. The objective of the workshop was to exchange challenges, experiences, and solutions among researchers and practitioners in the aforementioned area to bring agile and rapid software development processes a step further to seamless integrate quality management activities into their practices.

The program started with a keynote talk by Dietmar Pfahl on the topic *Data Science for Software Quality Management – Examples and Challenges*. The following abstract summarizes the keynote: "Software has become part of our daily life: whether we drive a car, sit on a plane, use our washing machine, perform a bank transaction, or file our tax return, software is involved in all of these activities. To develop such systems, software engineers must take many decisions in their daily work. The quality of their decision-making is crucial for the success of every new software system deployed to the market. Unlike other engineers, software engineers cannot rely on the laws of nature but must base their decisions to a large extent on experience and empirically derived models. During the last decade, with the emergence of what is now called Data Science, automated approaches for managing quality in software projects and products have come into the focus of research and practice, often using techniques from the realms of Artificial Intelligence and Machine Learning (ML)." The talk provided (a) two examples of using ML in the context of software quality management, (b) a discussion of some of the associated challenges, and (c) a list of questions that should be answered when using automated approaches to software quality management.

The workshop accepted the following articles

- Simon Andre Scherr, Frank Elberzhager and Lisa Müller. Quality Improvement of Mobile Apps – Tool-supported Lightweight Feedback Analyses
- Raquel Ouriques, Krzysztof Wnuk, Richard Svensson and Tony Gorschek. Thinking Strategically about Knowledge Management in Agile Software Development
- Nuno Santos, Jaime Pereira, Nuno Ferreira and Ricardo-J. Machado. Modeling in agile software development: decomposing use cases towards (logical) architecture design
- Philipp Hohl, Sven Theobald, Martin Becker, Michael Stupperich and Jürgen Münch. Mapping Agile to Automotive Software Product Line Concerns
- Marcus Ciolkowski and Florian Lautenschlager. Making Runtime Data Useful for Diagnosis

The 2nd QuASD workshop was organized by Claudia Ayala (Universitat Politècnica de Catalunya), Silverio Martínez-Fernández (FhG), and Pilar Rodríguez (University of Oulu).

2   Tutorials

The Human Factor in Agile Transitions – Using the Personas Concept in Agile Coaching

Any agile transition would be simple if there were not people involved. Unfortunately, we will not just come upon ideal personalities for the agile transition in real world. As agile leader and coach, we must support every single person and lead all team members to use their skills efficiently for the agile transition. The team should have a common understanding of how to work. The Personas (lat. mask) concept is an effective analytical approach used in human-computer-interaction to identify so called "personas". A persona is a prototype for a group of users. It is described with specific characteristics and user behavior. The concept offers excellent guidelines for the design and development of the desired software. In this tutorial we want to apply the personas concept to people involved in the agile transition process and gather answers to the following questions: Which personas do we know? What are their characteristics? How do we empower them to do the right things for the team effort? Together with the tutorial participants we want to identify suitable personas who represent a certain group of people in the agile transition. These are described with specific characteristics and behavior. Together we want to find ways to empower, promote and challenge these personas in the sense of coaching and leading teams in agile transitions.

This presenters of this tutorial are Markus Seiwert (Bank Deutsches Kraftfahrzeuggewerbe) and Stefan Hilmer (Acando)

Process Management 4.0 – Best Practices
The tutorial provides best practice methods and techniques for all areas of process management that were accrued in more than 15 years of experience in which Method Park performed worldwide process audits at more than 700 engineering organizations. As a participant, you will benefit from (a) a 360° view with which you will be able to identify the potential for optimization in the process management of organizations, (b) the tools with which you can initiate appropriate improvements or carry them out yourself. The tutorial covers the following topics:

- Motivation
  - What do digitalization and Industry 4.0 mean for process management?
  - Process modeling instead of process description and what it facilitates
- Setting objectives
  - How process management can support business objectives and why it should
  - How can one derive meaningful metrics from the objectives?
- Analysis of the current state
  - Dimensions of the analysis of the current state (process capability) and why we have to consider it for process management (influencing factors)
- Process architecture
  - Techniques for process reuse for modularization or variant creation
  - The value chain as an architectural founder
  - Architectural challenges of engineering processes
- Process definition
  - Process-collection techniques
  - Modeling guidelines
  - The RASIC model of the responsibility of roles in the process
  - Compliance with norms, standards and maturity models
- Process implementation (process roll-out)
  - Methods and aspects of process introduction
- Process management
  - Roles and structural organization of process management
  - The process of process management
  - Feedback-, change- and release management

The presenter of this tutorial is Oliver Hammrich (Method Park).

Domain-specific Languages for Specification, Development, and Testing of Autonomous Systems
Autonomous systems become more and more integrated in the workplace, taking over a wide range of tasks from providing product support, to automated credit decisions, to autonomous driving functions in modern cars. Guaranteeing the safety and correctness of such systems is of utmost importance since their actions can have severe consequences. Two key aspects for assessing the safety of these systems is understanding the domains they operate in and making their decisions comprehensible in the language of a domain – found in requirements. One big challenge is bridging the gap between

informal specifications and system implementation. Domain-specific languages can close this gap. Domain-specific languages (DSLs) are programming languages that are less expressive than general-purpose programming languages and provide vocabulary for specific domains (e.g., for describing situations an autonomous system can encounter). After being an active field of research and development for many years, frameworks for developing DSLs have become reliable and stable tools in the toolbox of software engineers. Today's vision is so-called language-driven development of systems, where domain engineering and accompanied DSL development become an integral part of the early phases of software projects, closing the gap between requirements and system by enabling system implementation in a domain-specific language. Languages and frameworks for smart executable contracts are one instance of this new paradigm that received a lot of attention in the recent past. The tutorial consists of two parts:

1. An introductory lecture that provides a brief introduction to the state of the art in the area of domain-specific languages and testing.
2. A tutorial in which participants can work on a small domain-specific language for development and testing of an autonomous system.

The demonstrated tools have been used successfully in numerous industrial projects. The presenters of this tutorial are Falk Howar, Stefan Naujokat and Bernhard Steffen (Dortmund University of Technology).

November 2018

Jürgen Münch
Krzyszstof Wnuk

Workshop: QuASD 2018

2nd QuASD Workshop: Managing Quality in Agile and Rapid Software Development Processes

Claudia Ayala[1]([✉]) [iD], Silverio Martínez-Fernández[2] [iD],
and Pilar Rodríguez[3] [iD]

[1] GESSI Group, Universitat Politècnica de Catalunya (UPC) - BarcelonaTech,
Barcelona, Spain
cayala@essi.upc.edu
[2] Fraunhofer Institute for Experimental Software Engineering IESE,
Kaiserslautern, Germany
Silverio.Martinez@iese.fraunhofer.de
[3] M3S Group, University of Oulu, Oulu, Finland
pilar.rodriguez@oulu.fi

Abstract. The QuASD workshop aims at investigating product and process quality in the context of agile and rapid software development. The objective of the workshop is to exchange challenges, experiences, and solutions among researchers and practitioners to bring agile and rapid software development processes a step further to seamless integrating quality management activities into their practices. In this second edition of the workshop we expect to foster the exchange of ideas between researchers and industry and consolidate a research agenda and collaborations.

Keywords: Quality · Agile software development
Rapid and continuous software development

1 Introduction

Welcome to the Second International Workshop on Managing Quality in Agile and Rapid Software Development Processes (QuASD).

The QuASD workshop aims at investigating the current challenges that companies using agile software development and rapid release cycles face when integrating quality management activities into their practices. The objective of the workshop is to exchange experiences and solutions to bring agile and rapid software development processes a step further towards seamless integration of quality management activities into their practices. To strengthen this objective, QuASD 2018 is held in the context of one of the top-recognized software development and process improvement conferences: the International Conference on Product-Focused Software Process Improvement (PROFES 2018) on November 28, 2018, in Wolfsburg, Germany.

© Springer Nature Switzerland AG 2018
M. Kuhrmann et al. (Eds.): PROFES 2018, LNCS 11271, pp. 373–377, 2018.
https://doi.org/10.1007/978-3-030-03673-7_28

2 Keynote: Data Science for Software Quality Management – Examples and Challenges

The keynote focuses on the application of data science for managing quality in software projects. As we know, software has become part of our daily life: whether we drive a car, sit on a plane, use our washing machine, perform a bank transaction, or file our tax return, software is involved in all of these activities. To develop such systems, software engineers must take many decisions in their daily work. The quality of their decision-making is crucial for the success of every new software system deployed to the market. Unlike other engineers, software engineers cannot rely on the laws of nature but must base their decisions to a large extent on experience and empirically derived models. During the last decade, with the emergence of what is now called Data Science, automated approaches for managing quality in software projects and products have come into the focus of research and practice, often using techniques from the realms of Artificial Intelligence and Machine Learning (ML). In this keynote, Dietmar Pfahl (a) presents two examples of using ML in the context of software quality management, (b) discusses some of the associated challenges, and (c) lists questions that should be answered when using automated approaches to software quality management.

Dietmar Pfahl earned his Master (1986) and PhD (2001) degrees in Germany, at the Universities of Ulm and Kaiserslautern, respectively. Before joining the University of Tartu in 2013 as an Associate Professor, he worked eight years in industry (Siemens AG, Germany), and held appointments with the University of Calgary, Canada, the Lund University, Sweden, and the University of Oslo, Norway. He also worked for the German Aerospace Research Establishment near Munich, Germany, the Fraunhofer IESE in Kaiserslautern, Germany, and the Simula Research Laboratory near Oslo, Norway. He was the founder and director of Pika Research, Inc., Claresholm, Canada, from 2009 to 2015. Since 2008, he is Adjunct Professor with the Schulich School of Engineering at the University of Calgary, Canada. In spring 2017, he was appointed Professor of Software Engineering at the University of Tartu, Estonia.

3 Industry Talk: The Q-Rapids Approach from the Bittium Perspective

Bittium (www.bittium.com) is a Finnish company specialized in the development of reliable, secure communications and connectivity solutions leveraging its 30-year legacy of expertise in advanced radio communication technologies. Bittium provides innovative products and services, customized solutions based on its product platforms and R&D services. Complementing its communications and connectivity solutions, Bittium offers proven information security solutions for mobile devices and portable computers. Bittium also provides healthcare technology products and services for biosignal measuring in the areas of cardiology, neurology, rehabilitation, occupational health and sports medicine. The company is characterized by its continuous looking for more efficient ways to work and shorten the time to market (release time), starting to use Agile methods more than a decade ago.

The industry talk focuses on their experience on the Q-Rapids approach (http://www.q-rapids.eu/) to improve quality in agile software development processes. The Q-Rapids approach consolidates the developer tool chains to a modern way of working to manage nonfunctional and functional requirements. They will highlight how the Q-Rapids approach is integrated to a company systems and development as well as data visualization tool chains is introduced.

The presentation will bridge good developer practices like Developer Continuous Integration into proper software development life-cycle management, modern software tool chains and up to non-functional requirements management. In particular, the talk focuses on how Bittium has been developing the Lean and Agile Way of Working (WoW) to be able to adapt the models for Continuous Deployment from software developer point of view. To be able to introduce faster pace of development several experiments have been executed. These experiments include finding common company level models for Continuous Integration, experimenting and deploying the model across the product and solutions areas, developing the Way of Working from developers point of view by introducing Developer Continuous Integration and introducing models of DevOps to just name a few. These highlight also how the requirements from the functional and non-functional point of view have been managed in a context of more than 10 teams working for the same scope.

4 Accepted Papers

After a revision process by at least three members of the Program Committee, five papers were accepted for this second edition of the workshop. These works address issues on quality in agile software development from different perspectives. The effort and dedication of the Program Committee and the additional reviewers who collaborated in the revision process were outstanding and deserve recognition (see Sect. 5).

The accepted papers composing the QuASD workshop program are:

- **3 technical papers** (12 pages long) describing beyond-state-of-the-art methods, tools, or techniques in support of the management of quality in agile and rapid software development and continuous software development contexts:
  - Simon Andre Scherr, Frank Elberzhager and Lisa Müller: "*Quality Improvement of Mobile Apps – Tool-supported Lightweight Feedback Analyses*".
  - Nuno Santos, Jaime Pereira, Nuno Ferreira and Ricardo-J. Machado: "*Modeling in agile software development: decomposing use cases towards (logical) architecture design*".
  - Philipp Hohl, Sven Theobald, Martin Becker, Michael Stupperich and Jürgen Münch: "*Mapping Agile to Automotive Software Product Line Concerns*".
- **1 experience report paper** (9 pages long) describing first-hand experience and lessons learned related to the management of quality in agile and rapid software development:
  - Marcus Ciolkowski and Florian Lautenschlager: "*Making Runtime Data Useful for Incident Diagnosis: An Experience Report*".

- **1 vision paper** (6 pages long) providing arguments for new directions to follow in managing quality in agile and rapid software development:
  - Raquel Ouriques, Krzysztof Wnuk, Richard Svensson and Tony Gorschek: *"Thinking Strategically about Knowledge Management in Agile Software Development"*.

5 Program Committee

The program committee was composed of prominent researchers from several universities and the industrial sector.

- Jan Bosch, Chalmers University of Technology, Sweden
- Michal Choras, ITTI Ltd., Poland
- Javier Criado, University of Almería, Spain
- Oscar Franco-Bedoya, Universidad Nacional de Colombia, Colombia
- Matthias Galster, University of Canterbury, New Zealand
- Juan Garbajosa, Universidad Politécnica de Madrid, Spain
- Lidia Lopez, Universitat Politècnica de Catalunya, Spain
- Paulo Motta, Numina, Brazil
- Elisa Nakagawa, University of São Paulo, Brazil
- Anh Nguyen Duc, University College of Southeast Norway, Norway
- Marc Oriol Hilari, Universitat Politècnica de Catalunya, Spain
- Paulo Sérgio Santos, PESC/COPPE/UFRJ, Brazil
- Martin Solari, Universidad ORT Uruguay, Uruguay
- Davide Taibi, Tampere University of Technology, Finland
- Dan Tofan, Digital Science & Research, Romania
- Guilherme Travassos, COPPE/UFRJ, Brazil
- Anna Maria Vollmer, Fraunhofer, Germany
- Agustin Yague, Universidad Politécnica de Madrid, Spain

6 Activities

The workshop aims to promote discussions and interchange of ideas among participants from both industry and academia sectors. Thus, the keynote and industry talks are expected to shake the audience and foster fruitful discussions. In addition, the presentations of the accepted papers in various sessions will focus the discussions on their specific topics. In the last session, we will organize an open brainstorming space through a wall of ideas, where the participants will post their key messages on particular topics, followed by a plenary discussion on the hottest emerging topics.

All these activities are aimed to:

- Scope the current state of quality management in agile and rapid software development in both research and practice.
- Compile success and failure experiences.

- Continue on the research agenda from the previous edition.
- Establish a community to foster long-term collaboration.

We hope that the workshop participants will enjoy the topics presented here and perhaps find the inspiration to push the field a step further, or open the door for new collaborations.

Finally, we would like to acknowledge all the people who have enabled the organization of QuASD 2018: the authors, who submitted their papers; the Program Committee members, who made possible the conference program; the invited speakers for the keynote and the industry talk for being willing to share their experiences on quality and quality requirements in the context of agile and rapid software development; and the organizing committee members, who handled all the complexity of arranging an event such as PROFES 2018 and the associated workshops.

Claudia Ayala
Silverio Martínez-Fernández
Pilar Rodríguez
QuASD 2018 Organizers

Quality Improvement of Mobile Apps – Tool-Supported Lightweight Feedback Analyses

Simon André Scherr[✉], Frank Elberzhager, and Lisa Müller

Fraunhofer IESE, Fraunhofer Platz 1, Kaiserslautern, Germany
{simon.scherr, frank.elberzhager,
lisa.mueller}@iese.fraunhofer.de

Abstract. Mobile apps have penetrated the market and are used everywhere. The success of apps also depends on user feedback as this enables users to influence other potential customers and provides new opportunities for identifying features. An efficient development process including quality assurance is obligatory for app-developing companies. However, developers also face challenges, such as short time to market, many release cycles, or low budgets for quality assurance. Therefore, we present a lightweight approach that considers textual feedback from users and a corresponding tool chain. With this, quality can be monitored and development and quality assurance decisions for upcoming sprints can be made fast and easily. Furthermore, examples of such textual analyses show how the approach can provide information to improve apps.

Keywords: User feedback · Product improvement · Software release planning
Quality monitoring · User experience

1 Introduction

Mobile apps are nowadays part of our daily lives. They are used in various ways in our private lives, but there are also more and more business apps. Currently app stores are offering millions of different apps [1]. The challenges for developers are increasing continuously. Time to market is often short, but quality needs to be at a level that users are satisfied with the apps. If not, users often provide feedback in stores or via other channels, which can have a great influence on other users in terms of whether they want to use this app or not, depending on the actual feedback.

In order to support app developers, we created the Opti4Apps approach and analyzed to which extent this approach fits common agile practices, i.e., how strong the invasiveness and the benefits of our approach are [2]. Basically, the approach considers feedback from users and derives suggestions on what to improve in the next development cycles of a mobile app [3].

In this article, we will show how to operationalize the Opti4Apps approach further and will provide a tool chain that offers concrete support to quality engineers or product owners during quality monitoring. To do so, we focus on textual feedback, notably on

© Springer Nature Switzerland AG 2018
M. Kuhrmann et al. (Eds.): PROFES 2018, LNCS 11271, pp. 378–388, 2018.
https://doi.org/10.1007/978-3-030-03673-7_29

emojis. Emojis can reflect the emotions of app users with a sufficiently high level of validity in order to identify issues encountered with a mobile app. We show our flexible crawling infrastructure that enables us to gather textual feedback from several sources, our analytics backend and present our dashboard, which includes specific analyses enabling product owners or quality engineers to plan and make decisions for the next development cycles. Furthermore, we provide examples of such app analyses in order to show what kind of results can be expected from the approach.

Section 2 provides some background and explains what kinds of textual feedback are included. Section 3 elaborates the textual analysis process and the tool chain, and Sect. 4 concludes our article.

2   Background

2.1   Demand for Lightweight Analyses

User feedback analyses enable companies to adapt products to the needs of the users. This leads to a higher product acceptance. Special for mobile apps are fast iterations within product development. Making use of user feedback therefore does not only require reliable analyses, the results must also be available within short time to allow the company to use them within upcoming sprints. Current methods for analyzing natural language are often not mature enough to yield results that can be used in these environments. For example, many approaches rely on analyzing sentiment by considering the text. However, these analyses are challenging [4]. Ribeiro et al. [5] compare state-of-the-art approaches and conclude that "existing methods vary widely regarding their agreement". Hogenboom et al. [6] capture another problem of sentiment analysis: They argue that results cannot be compared across languages, because methods do not perform equally between languages. Dashtipour et al. [7] say that the reason is a lack of lexical resources in many languages.

Nevertheless, feedback offers huge potential for product improvement and quality assurance. We put our focus on lightweight analyses that do not require a deep understanding of the language. The goal is to get solutions that can support fast innovation and development cycles and that require neither a huge amount of time nor a deep understanding of natural language.

2.2   Using Emojis to Analyze Textual User Feedback

According to ISO 9241-210, emotion is one of the key aspects of user experience [8]. One way to analyze emotions included in feedback, is to consider the emojis used in it. Emojis are colorful symbols that can represent faces, objects, or activities, like 😊, ;-) or 🔥. They are used to express emotions or at least sentiment. Emojis occur at important places [9] and are used to clarify or highlight the meaning of a text.

We collected 612 emojis that can be used to express emotions. In order to use them for text analysis, we built an emotion model to classify them. We investigated emotion models such as those by Ekman [10], Lazarus [8], and Plutchik [11] to build a suitable model for emojis. Our model has the two dimensions *Sentiment* and *Emotion*. We built the mapping between emojis and *Sentiment* and *Emotion* by performing a survey [12]. The evaluation showed that people perceive most emojis in the same way, as we could assign a sentiment to 591 of the 612 emojis. An emotion could be assigned to 512. People perceive emojis similar independent of age or gender [12].

To check the practicability of using emojis for analyzing user feedback, we compared the analysis of emojis to star ratings. We considered 178.848 feedback entries from different apps and correlated the 5-star ratings and sentiment value of the emojis. This resulted in high correlation, as explained in [13]. Due to this correlation, emojis are a reasonable tool for analyzing user feedback.

3 Feedback-Driven Quality Process and Tool Chain

We have developed a detailed process to make use of user feedback as a tangible and detailed instantiation of Opti4Apps [3]. To keep the effort as low as possible for developers, we are currently developing automation support for this process.

3.1 Process and Supporting Toolchain

The concepts and ideas for Opti4Apps were detailed into a fine-grained process for improving software quality considering textual user feedback (see Fig. 1). While keeping the effort for using the process low, the results must allow to improve the product substantially. Our solution aims on enabling product managers to make fast and well-grounded decisions.

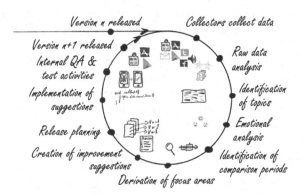

Fig. 1. Process for quality improvement by detecting trends in user feedback

Overview of the Process. The key driver of the process is to collect and analyze feedback continuously. The process contains twelve steps, which are categorized into three phases: (1) feedback collection, (2) data analysis, and (3) product improvement.

Feedback Collection. After a version of a product is released, feedback data collectors start collecting data from various different data sources, such as app stores, social media, bulletin boards, or customer support data.

Data Analysis. During this phase, the raw data analysis calculates how much feedback was captured per data source and per period and analyzes any existing rating indicators like star ratings, likes, or votes. In the third step, the approach identifies topics. A topic could be, for example, single features, errors, use cases, or screens of the app. The goal of the topic identification step is to create a better understanding of the aspects on which the users focus. The next step is the detection of emotions by using emojis within the text. To detect emotions, we use the results of our previous work described in Sect. 2.

Having identified the topics, the feedback is analyzed from a temporal perspective. This includes relating feedback from the current product version to the previous version and relating new feedback data to the data used for the analysis before. Depending on the topic, other suitable comparison periods are selected. This allows detecting mood trends, mood changes, as well as changes in the amount of feedback. In addition, it is also checked how topics and emotions have developed over time.

The next step is to derive focus areas for the product manager. A focus area is a subset of the feedback requiring attention. Focus areas themselves are neutral, as they might contain positive or negative aspects. For instance, a focus area could be the fact that a topic that has historically been more negative has changed into something positive due to a well-received change.

Product Improvement. The product improvement phase of the process starts with the derivation of improvement suggestions. These suggestions are created based on the focus areas derived in the previous step, but also by using heuristics. A suggestion might lead to a bug fix, a new feature, or a change request. Once these suggestions have been derived, each of them is prioritized.

Based on the improvement suggestions and their prioritization, each of them is incorporated into the product's release plan. After the implementation phase, the product is subjected to quality assurance, which is done in the traditional way by systematically checking the improvement suggestions implemented for this version. If the version fulfills the desired quality standard, an update is published. As soon as the improved product is released, the process starts again with the collection step. This enables long-term product improvement by consistently including user feedback.

Automating the Process with Tool Support. To achieve a holistic approach for collecting and analyzing textual user feedback, we developed a flexible data model and infrastructure that is able to handle various types of different feedback data sources. Our goal is to include all these different types of data within one single solution to make it easier to use. In general, we have (1) a crawling infrastructure for accessing the data sources, (2) an analysis backend for performing the analyses, and (3) a web-based dashboard that gives insights on the user feedback to the quality manager. The current focus regarding automation is on acquiring feedback from heterogeneous data sources and automating the first analysis steps of the process presented above.

Crawling Infrastructure. The data collection relies on automated crawlers. To make our work independent of data sources, we built a generic data model for feedback. This model can be found in Fig. 2. The data model abstracts from the actual data being retrieved and clusters it into different entities. First of all, we have *Projects*, which might contain one or multiple *Products*. Related to the products are the data sources that are getting crawled. The textual feedback is stored along with meta-data in the element review. In order to also provide support for different types of ratings, such as five-star rating, we built a flexible data type for ratings. As some data sources also provide information on how accurate or good a review of a product is, we store this information in the form of our *Confidence* entity.

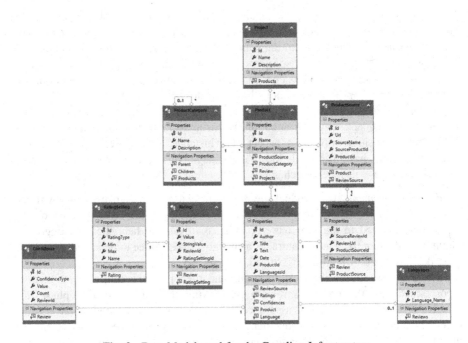

Fig. 2. Data Model used for the Crawling Infrastructure

This data model enables us to build a flexible crawling infrastructure. In addition, we have developed an API that crawlers have to use (see Fig. 3). This allows us to add new data sources to our existing solutions while still maintaining compatibility with other data sources. Besides that crawler have to follow the API, they have to use the data model explained above and must provide certain events when crawling. The *IReveiwCrawlerPlugin* requires a brief description of the crawler plugin as well as trigger methods to start crawling, and an event for informing about updates of the crawling process. *ReviewCrawlerResult* contains the final result after the crawl has completed, like status reports, failures, and the identified reviews. The reviews themselves are modeled according to our data model in Fig. 2. *ReviewCrawlerUpdate* contains periodic status updates for the system about the crawling process. When a new

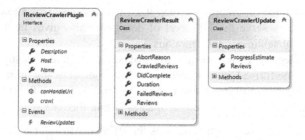

Fig. 3. API for Crawlers

data source is needed a new plugin for the data source is written and integrated into our infrastructure. This enables holistic support for feedback data sources.

Currently, we can automatically crawl data from: Amazon Market Place, Apple App Store, Google+ Google Play Store, Instagram, and Twitter. A crawler for Facebook is currently under development, as well as a solution for accessing YouTube video content. In addition, we can manually add feedback not captured by our crawlers. This is used, for instance, to manually add customer support requests. The variety of possible data sources within one single infrastructure allows us to tailor the feedback acquisition directly to the behavior of the respective users.

To reduce the complexity of feedback analysis in practice, the crawling infrastructure supports delta updates on feedback data. This requires, on the one hand, the ability to update data with newer feedback data sets, and, on the other hand, the possibility to add or remove data sources. As data sources are exchangeable for us, the crawling states have to be maintained for each data source and not for the entire product.

Analysis Backend. The analysis backend accesses the crawled raw data and continues the processing of the data with the raw data analysis. The analysis backend is built using the asp.net web API and provides a REST API.

To make further steps easier, we apply text processing techniques that are commonly used. First of all, the texts get a lemmatized representation using LemmGen [14], which is an open source lemmatizer capable of working with twelve languages. This results in getting the root forms of the words. Based on the lemmatization, we remove typical filler words. Furthermore, we use dictionaries to replace Internet slang terms with their common equivalents, e.g. "coz" would be replaced by "because". The analysis continues with the creation of a so-called n-gram model of the text. We use unigrams and bigrams for our further analysis steps. Unigram models are based on pure words, while bigram models consider a word as well as the next word.

Afterwards, we perform the topic identification by making use of the n-grams created before. They are further processed into so-called bag-of-words models. Such a model basically counts how often words occur in a text. The bag-of-words model and the n-grams of a review are further processed to identify the topics of a review.

The emotion analysis using emojis is implemented in two ways. We perform an analysis based on the entire product. This is followed by an analysis for each topic. Similar to the bag of words for topic generation, we use a bag-of-emojis approach here.

After having identified all emojis, we map them to emotions. This allows us to view specific emojis to preserve the full level of detail, but also gives us the aggregated version in terms of sentiment and emotions.

The process steps following the emotion analyses are currently mostly expert-based and have to be performed in our front-end. Like our crawling infrastructure, the backend was built with changing data in mind. This means that all the analyses have to support multiple data sources as well as updates within the data sets.

Dashboard. The web-based dashboard uses the REST-API of our backend to get the data. The dashboard contains a landing page listing all the products available. Within one product, we distinguish between three major tabs: *Overview*, *Data*, and *Results*. *Overview* presents key insights and data on the product and serves as a form of executive summary. The *Data* tab allows digging deeper into the raw data being captured. Both tabs provide insights about the distribution of the ratings, as well as how many ratings were received in which time period and what the average rating was (see Fig. 4). These analyses can be viewed in total or per data source.

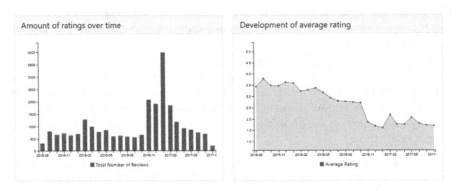

Fig. 4. Amount of Ratings over Time and Development of average Rating for the App Uber

To support decision-making based on feedback, the *Results* tab is the most crucial aspect as it shows the outcome of our analysis. The landing page of this area gives a summary of all results. From here, one can access subpages to get detailed reports about certain analyses or aspects. The landing page prominently shows a word cloud (see Fig. 5) that gives insights on the most frequently identified topics during the topic identification step. Besides, we also have a prominently displayed overview of the detected emotions. These results can be restricted to the desired timeframes.

Clicking on an item in the word cloud shows detailed information on the corresponding topic, like where and when the reviews were identified, and about their context, like surrounding words and elements. We also provide insights on the development of the topic over time in terms of emotions, amount of feedback, and rating development. To get an even deeper understanding, it is possible to read the actual feedback items related to the topic.

Fig. 5. Word Cloud for Uber in January 2017

3.2 Examples and Discussion

We used our current implementation of the toolchain for an evaluation of our process, including the creation of focus areas. We investigated user feedback from the Apple App Store for different apps. For many apps, abrupt drops in the average ratings over time or sudden increases in the number of ratings for certain time periods can be seen.

Uber, for example, shows an outstanding peak in the amount of user feedback in January 2017. The number of reviews increased from 1,903 in December 2016 to 3,984 in January 2017 and then again decreased to 1,840 reviews one month later. Also, the average rating over time was at a minimum of 1.6 in January (see Fig. 4). The results in our dashboard show intensive use of the topic "delete" (see Fig. 5) in reviews from this month. In fact, many users were very upset about the cooperation of Uber's CEO with a politician. As a consequence, Uber lost many users. After the CEO resigned in February [15] due to these events, the average rating increased from 1.6 to 2.2. We also observed that Uber is often compared to its competitor Lyft. At the time people decided to delete Uber, many people claim to have switched to Lyft. Feedback mentioning switches to lift or comparing Uber to lift has an average rating of 1.28 stars and contains mostly negative emotions. This example shows that user feedback gives insights on the relationship between the user and the company's reputation and direction as well as insights into competing products.

Pinterest experienced a decrease in the average rating from 3.7 to 3.0 when they removed the "like" button from the app [16]. In June 2017, there was a total of 722 reviews containing the word "button" and many users were complaining about the missing button. The identified emotions are mostly negative, with sad being the most prominent one. A potential improvement suggestion that should be investigated would be to bring back the "like" button.

Our implementation also detected a problem for Tinder in March 2018, when the average rating decreased by 0.8 to 2.5. In this month, the number of reviews was more than three times as high as in the previous month. Our analysis shows high usage of the topics "profile" and "fake" during that month and most of the user feedback containing one of these two was given in March 2018. Furthermore, in many reviews, "fake" was combined with "profile". Indeed, there was a huge amount of user feedback where users complained about too many fake profiles on Tinder. The corresponding improvement suggestion would be to investigate how a feature could be implemented that reduces the number of fakes or that acts as a fake check. Alternatively, a feature could be developed that shows "verified profiles". In the following months, the number of reviews containing "fake" evidently decreased.

In April, the ratings for Tinder faced an abrupt drop to 2.3 stars. Prominent topics leading to this situation were "login", "logout", and "account". This was related to an issue caused by Facebook changing the way third-party developers can use their API. Tinder was not able to issue an update before the changes became effective and people were logged out of Tinder and could not successfully log in again [17]. The issue correlated with a decline in positive emojis and an increase in negative emojis, especially those connected with "sad" and "angry" emotions.

These examples show that user feedback immediately reflects changes in a product or problems experienced by the users. This makes feedback analysis a factor that enables huge contributions to product improvement. It reveals which problems the users experience and allows checking how well updates are accepted by the user base. High update frequency is related to rapid changes in user feedback. This finding allows adapting release plans and implementations quickly and adjusting a product within a short amount of time without losing a larger user base.

3.3   Future Work

A major part of our future work will be to increase the degree of automation, especially the derivation of focus areas and suggestion. For the focus areas, this means having a better preselection of time periods. Currently, this is mostly expert-based. Certain aspects in the feedback might be related to changes within the last update. Inclusion of the change log in our implementation might enable relating issues directly to changes made by the team. In addition, certain aspects, such as an immediate increase in feedback items, a deviation between Android and iOS ratings, or changes in the most frequently used topics might also give insights into focus areas and suggestions.

We plan to automate focus areas as well as improvement suggestions with the help of event detection within the data. The difference between a detected focus area and a detected improvement suggestion is that the latter is a focus area with a concrete interpretation of what to do next.

One idea is to use the derivative to detect differences in the number of feedback items, ratings, and emotions. This would allow us to monitor changes within the topics. Combined with our average values for the complete data set, we could define thresholds for the product that alert the product manager about changes in the derivatives. Another solution we are implementing is the modeling of feature vectors within user feedback. These feature vectors should represent the collected data and allow us to see whether the current feedback is more similar to feedback that represents an event or to feedback that does not. This would also allow us to compare the data not only over the entire period, but also over shorter periods of data.

This event detection will be implemented for each app, each data source for the product, each topic, and each data source of a topic. In the first step, this will reduce the manual effort required to derive focus areas. In the second step, it will be combined with heuristics and artificial intelligence to allow more automation for the creation of improvement suggestions.

In addition, we envision that a collection of failure patterns can be used for the detection of suggestions. If the analysis is trained to detect a failure pattern as the result of the presence of several keywords, it would be possible to label the feedback items with the failure pattern. These failure patterns could lead to a repository of issues suffered by apps or experienced by a specific app in the past. If a pattern occurs often, the suggestions should contain a call to action to investigate this failure pattern in more detail.

As we have successfully applied our process and tools in form of post-mortem analyses of data we plan to perform case studies with actual app developer teams. This will give us additional insights how the approach acts in the second half of the process when it comes to prioritizing suggestions and tracking user feedback issues over multiple product iterations

4 Conclusion

As part of Opti4Apps, we identified the need for lightweight methods for feedback analysis. For this purpose, we defined a quality assurance process. The focus of the process is on practical applicability for product owners and quality assurance engineers. One core aspect is the analysis of emojis contained in feedback items and fast detection of trends represented by focus areas. These results are used to derive suggestions for product improvement. The suggestions aim on easing planning and decision making for the upcoming development iterations.

We have shown and explained our process for analyzing textual feedback. The central requirements for the process as well as for the implementation were that it must be possible to perform the feedback analysis without much additional effort and that it must be suitable for highly iterative product development environments. Our process does this by applying lightweight measures. Within the execution of each process iteration product and quality managers get insights about potential problems of the product, new feature ideas and how recent changes have improved the quality of the product from a user's perspective.

To establish the goals of our process in practice, the process needs to be automated. Therefore, we developed a flexible crawling infrastructure that can handle various different data sources by maintaining a single data structure. In addition, this infrastructure supports changing the data sources as well as updating the data from a data source. We have also shown how subsequent steps of the process are currently automated by our tool chain and how we can increase the automation of our process. Currently, the process is fully automated as far as emotion analysis is concerned.

We used our solutions to perform an analysis with examples from apps that show that user feedback provides valuable information for product development. Even short events have a significant impact on user feedback. This shows that fast and continuous analysis of user feedback is necessary, and making use of this information gives developers the ability to quickly react to emerging trends. Even though we only evaluated our approach in the context of mobile apps, the approach itself is not restricted to that. The next steps we are planning in terms of tool support include further automation in the areas of focus areas and improvement suggestions, which are currently mostly expert-based.

Acknowledgments. The research described in this paper was performed in the project *Opti4Apps* (grant no. 02K14A182) of the German Federal Ministry of Education and Research (BMBF). We thank Sonnhild Namingha for proofreading.

References

1. statista: Number of apps available in leading app stores as of 1st quarter 2018. https://www.stati sta.com/statistics/276623/number-of-apps-available-in-leading-app-stores/. Accessed 2018
2. Elberzhager, F., Holl, K., Karn, B., Immich, T.: Rapid lean UX development through user feedback revelation. In: PROFES 2017: Product-Focused Software Process Improvement (2017)
3. Scherr, S., Elberzhager, F., Holl, K.: An automated feedback-based approach to support mobile app development. In: Proceedings - 43rd Euromicro Conference on Software Engineering and Advanced Applications, SEAA 2017, Vienna (2017)
4. Hussein: A survey on sentiment analysis challenges. Journal of King Saud University - Engineering Sciences (2016)
5. Ribeiro, F., Araújo, M., Gonçalves, M., Benevenuto, F.: SentiBench - a benchmark comparison of state-of-the-practice sentiment analysis methods. EPJ Data Sci. **5**(1) (2016). https://doi.org/10.1140/epjds/s13688-016-0085-1
6. Hogenboom, A., Bal, M., Frasincar, F., Bal, D.: Towards cross-language sentiment analysis through universal star ratings. Adv. Intell. Syst. Comput. **172**, 69–79 (2013)
7. Dashtipour, K., Poria, S., Hussain, A., Cambria, E., Hawalah, A., Gelbukh, A., Zhou, Q.: Multilingual sentiment analysis: state of the art and independent comparison of techniques. Cogn. Comput. **8**, 757–771 (2016)
8. Lazarus, R.: Emotion & Adaptation (1991)
9. Provine, R., Spencer, R., Mandell, D.: Emotional expression online. J. Lang. Soc. Psychol. **26**(3), 299–307 (2007)
10. Ekman, P., Friesen, W.: Constants across cultures in the face and emotion. J. Pers. Soc. Psychol. **17**(2), 124–129 (1971)
11. Plutchik, R.: A general psychoevolutionary theory of emotion. In: Theories of Emotion, pp. 3–33 (1980)
12. Scherr, S., Polst, S., Müller, L., Holl, K., Elberzhager, F.: The perception of emojis for analyzing app feedback. Int. J. Interact. Mob. Technol. (accepted)
13. Scherr, S., Elberzhager, F., Meyer, S.: Listen to your users - quality improvement of mobile apps through lightweight feedback analyses. In: International Conference on Software Quality (2019)
14. Jozef Stefan Institute: LemmaGen. http://lemmatise.ijs.si. Accessed 2010
15. Wong, J.: Uber CEO steps down from Trump advisory council after users boycott. https://www.theguardian.com/technology/2017/feb/02/travis-kalanick-delete-uber-leaves-trump-council. Accessed 3 Feb 2017
16. O., K.: Goodbye, Like button. https://newsroom.pinterest.com/en/post/goodbye-like-button. Accessed 20 Apr 2017
17. Fingas, J.: Tinder suffers sign-in problems following Facebook's privacy changes. https://www.engadget.com/2018/04/04/tinder-sign-in-problems-following-facebook-changes/. Accessed 04 Apr 2018

Thinking Strategically About Knowledge Management in Agile Software Development

Raquel Ouriques[1]([✉]), Krzysztof Wnuk[1], Richard Berntsson Svensson[2], and Tony Gorschek[1]

[1] Blekinge Institute of Technology, Karlskrona, Sweden
{raquel.ouriques,krzysztof.wnuk,tony.gorschek}@bth.se
[2] Department of Computer Science and Engineering,
Chalmers — University of Gothenburg, Gothenburg, Sweden
richard.berntsson.svensson@gu.se

Abstract. Agile methodologies gave teams more autonomy regarding planning tasks and executing them. As a result, coordination gets more flexible, but much relevant knowledge remains undocumented and inside teams' borders, due to informal communication and reduced development documentation. Since knowledge plays an essential role in software development, it is important to have effective knowledge management (KM) practices that contribute to a better knowledge resource allocation. Several KM practices have been reported in empirical studies in Agile Software Development (ASD). However, these practices are not evaluated regarding its effectiveness or how do they affect product quality. Besides, the studies do not demonstrate connections between the KM practices in the project level and the strategic level. The lack of connection between these levels can result in deviations from the company's corporate strategy, wasted resources and irrelevant knowledge acquisition. This paper discusses how the strategic management can contribute to an integrated approach to KM in ASD; considering the organizational structure and the corporate strategy. Based on this discussion, we propose research areas that may help with planning KM strategies that can have their effectiveness measured and contribute to product quality.

Keywords: Knowledge Management · Product quality
Agile Software Development

1 Introduction

The knowledge of individuals is a well-known competitive resource, and has been philosophically discussed and validated by several researchers within the strategic management field [6,8,9,17]. Knowledge Management (KM) strategies, which are based on knowledge needs and organizational characteristics [4,13],

M. Kuhrmann et al. (Eds.): PROFES 2018, LNCS 11271, pp. 389–395, 2018.
https://doi.org/10.1007/978-3-030-03673-7_30

help with effective knowledge resources management. Successfully employing the knowledge resource contributes to product and company growth [1].

Software development is significantly dependent on exploiting the knowledge resources [10,13]. However, the Agile Software Development (ASD) empirical literature seems to give more attention to descriptive studies that report the use of tools and practices for knowledge sharing, rather than their effectiveness and impact on the software development [10,20].

We identified in our previous study that the KM practices reported in empirical studies in ASD context have low or no connection with the strategic level of the companies, which has negative implications for traceability between the development practices and the company strategy, and measurement of successful implementation of these strategies [20].

Treating knowledge as a resource implies that it needs to be managed with a logical and structured approach [9,13]. We conjecture that the lack of integration of KM practices with the strategic level, together with the adoption of informal KM practices adds low value to the companies that adopt ASD, and hinders unlocking the full potential that ASD brings.

Based on the recent results of our literature review on empirical studies [20] and on KM theories from the strategic management domain, we discuss future research implications of considering knowledge as a resource in ASD.

2   Knowledge Management in Strategic Management Domain

The rationale behind using theories is the glue that connect the explanatory factors [21]. Therefore, we base our discussion on concepts originated in underlying theories of the strategic management domain.

The theoretical literature in the referred domain states that the knowledge embedded in organizational routines contributes to company's effort to achieve its goals, by creating and delivering value to its customers [5,7]. The value created can be product value as well as organizational competence in solving problems and addressing customer needs.

The value creation process has social and cognitive relationships for enhancing individual's abilities for production. Therefore, organizations arrangements tend to change regarding hierarchical aspects, varying from the factory model to flat organizations. In these different structures, activities are more or less knowledge-intensive, which influence how individuals create value [11].

Several companies perceive the strategic relevance of knowledge as the main competitive resource, especially in knowledge-intensive environments. However, building and maintaining the competitive advantage based on the knowledge resource, requires a strategic plan that integrates the long-term vision with the knowledge resources [12].

Companies are often affected by changes in the external environment, e.g., suppliers, market, laws and customers' requirements. In this changing environment, companies need to adapt themselves in order to be more responsive and monitor current and future knowledge needs.

In previous work, we envisioned a conceptual framework (refer to Fig. 1), that displays a high-level perspective of the integration between the corporate strategy and the project level of ASD. The KM strategy reflects the corporate strategy, and promotes, through practices, one or more knowledge processes (KC - knowledge creation, KA - knowledge application, KT - knowledge transfer, KS - knowledge storage) through the company's levels.

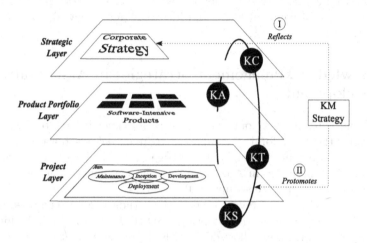

Fig. 1. KMS-ASD [20]

The corporate strategy guides how a company acquires and distributes its resources, e.g., if the company aims for product innovation, which investments in technology and knowledge should be made. In each level, KM strategies might influence different knowledge processes, depending on knowledge needs and their sources [20].

In a study in the manufacturing and services sectors, Ferraresi et al. [14] provided empirical evidence that the business performance is positively impacted by KM strategies only when these strategies are connected to a strategic orientation. Product quality is also affected by KM. Lee et al. [23] investigated in several industry sectors how KM is linked to product quality. They found that product quality is significantly affected by how process management moderates customer knowledge acquisition and the participation of employees in KM activities.

KM effectiveness seems to have a relation to the management encouragement. The rationale behind a KM implementation involves an internal analysis of the company's resources and its needs. Then, the decision regarding which tools and methods to use to achieve the selected goals need to be made [4].

The literature gathers three common approaches for conceiving KM strategies: The rational approach - considers an analysis of the companies resources and need, and external environment of the company, such as market and competitors. The emergent approach - developed based on the employees' daily activities, for example, their methods of problem-solving and their knowledge needs.

The integrated approach, which is the combination of both rational and emergent approaches - it is a dynamic interaction where the strategic level provides guidance with the company's general vision, supported by inputs from the lower level [4].

In any of the three common approaches, we notice that the connection with the corporate strategy of the company is recurrent. Another important aspect that should be considered is the domain where the KM strategies will be executed, by reason of companies size and hierarchy, and knowledge intensiveness of the activities.

3 Knowledge Management Strategies in Agile Software Development

Most of the software development activities are knowledge-intensive [18,19], which evoke the need for the companies to make efforts towards leveraging individuals' competence throughout the organizational layers. However, when it comes to KM practices in ASD, there is a lack of connection between these practices and the corporate strategy [20].

In a previous literature review on empirical studies [20], we mapped the KM practices in software companies adopting ASD (Refer to Fig. 2) and which type of strategy these practices follow. Most of KM practices in ASD are focused on personalization strategies, which focus on human interaction to communicate knowledge, and the majority of them are established in the project layer.

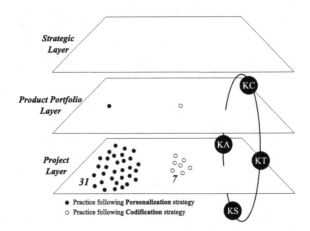

Fig. 2. Distribution of KM practices in organizational layers through KMS-ASD [20]

Moreover, there is a tendency of isolation regarding agile teams when it comes to KM, see Fig. 2. Most of the KM practices might work well inside the teams; however, these practices are informal and occasional. The lack of connection between KM practices and the corporate strategy can result in deviations from the core vision, wasted resources and irrelevant knowledge acquisition that adds no value to the company [9,13,22].

The corporate strategy guides the resources allocation for achieving organizational aims [4,20]. In the resource-based view of the firm, Barney [9] emphasizes that the means of how a company allocates and uses its resources confers the competitive advantage that differentiates the company from its competitors.

Knowledge is an asset that requires comprehensive and logical management to obtain benefits, since, together with skills, it is the main resource of software development organizations [13,15]. Steen [3] argue that in software development, the product quality phenomenon is heavily dependent on knowledge and skills, however, few research explores this relation.

Santos et al. [16] observed, in an empirical study, that in an ASD context, knowledge sharing effectiveness has relation to purposeful practices, organizational conditions and the stimuli that individuals have to share.

Similarly, goal-modeling may be used in the beginning of software projects to align the system to the organizational goals, which also might indicate that goal-oriented practices are a positive approach to further effectiveness measures for KM; why the practices are needed for; how do them connects to corporate strategy and customer needs.

Both empirical findings and theoretical dialogue connect our discussion, within which the strategic management aspects of having knowledge as a resource, have implications for KM strategy planning.

3.1 Potential Research Opportunities

Since 2010, publication related to KM in ASD gained diversity regarding KM focus, e.g., practices, challenges, and theories. Despite that, the state of the research remains far from the KM mainstream in strategic management studies.

We highlight the following research opportunities for exploring KM in ASD:

- *Strategic KM.* Concerns regarding KM effectiveness were raised in previous studies in software engineering [10,20]. Knowing that KM practices produce the desired results might be crucial to a company on deciding to invest in KM. The two essential aspects to consider in planning KM strategies for a company are the connection between the corporate strategy with the organizational arrangement; and the long-term goals of the KM strategy [4]. Illustrating these elements in ASD contexts, we could explore: how KM strategies comply with coordination? what adaptations are necessary? Could goal-oriented KM practices facilitate KM effectiveness measurement in ASD?

- *Product quality.* A KM resource remains valuable to the extent that it can deliver value to the customer, and also contributes to achieving enhanced performance [1]. Empirical research has shown that the degree of participation of an employee in activities related to knowledge dissemination impacts the quality of new products significantly [2]. Steen [3] found that software product quality cannot be entirely formalized, but rely on, to a great extent, the practical knowledge, and experience of individuals. Since knowledge is the main resource for software development, future research should keep attention on how to manage the knowledge resource, in ASD context, in a way that it provides superior customer value. What KM activities result in better product quality? In what context? How these activities affect quality in the software development process, such as requirements, implementation, testing, validation and verification?

4   Conclusion

In this vision paper, we discuss the potential research opportunities of KM perspective in ASD. Our inference is that we have reached a degree where the research demands investigations that go beyond mapping the companies actions against the KM theories, to real planned interventions with companies. Knowledge is socially created and translated into processes and products, representing unique characteristics that every company has. Future research should aim to gather more empirical evidence regarding effectiveness, and substantial impacts of KM strategies in coordination and other aspects, such as software quality.

Acknowledgements. The work is partially supported by a research grant for the ORION project (reference number 20140218) from The Knowledge Foundation in Sweden.

References

1. Teece, D.J.: Strategies for managing knowledge assets: the role of firm structure and industrial context. Long Range Plan. **33**(1), 35–55 (2000)
2. Yang, J.: Managing knowledge for quality assurance: an empirical study. Int. J. Qual. Reliab. Manag. **25**(2), 109–124 (2008)
3. Steen, O.: Practical knowledge and its importance for software product quality. Inf. Softw. Technol. **49**, 625–636 (2007)
4. Bolisani, E., Bratinau, C.: Knowledge strategy planning: an integrated approach to manage uncertainty, turbulence, and dynamics. J. Knowl. Manag. **21**(2), 233–253 (2017)
5. Kogut, B., Zander, U.: Knowledge of the firm, combinative capabilities and the replication of technology. Organ. Sci. **3**, 383–97 (1992)
6. Nonaka, I., Takeuchi, K.: The Knowledge Creating Company: How Japanese Companies Create the Dynamics of Innovation. Oxford University Press, Oxford (1995)
7. Porter, M.E.: Competitive Advantage: Creating and Sustaining Superior Performance. The Free Press, New York, NY (1985)
8. Davenport, T.H., Prusak, L.: Working Knowledge: How Organizations Manage What They Know. Harvard Business School, Boston (2000)
9. Barney, J.B.: Firm resources and sustained competitive advantage. J. Manag. **17**(1), 99–120 (1991)
10. Bjørnson, F.O., Dingsøyr, T.: Knowledge management in software engineering: a systematic review of studied concepts, findings and research methods used. Inf. Softw. Technol. **50**(11), 1055–1068 (2008)

11. Mahesh, K., Suresh, J.K.: Knowledge criteria for organization design. J. Knowl. Manag. **13**(4), 41–51 (2009)
12. Halawi, L.A., McCarthy, R.V., Aronson, J.E.: Knowledge management and the competitive strategy of the firm. Learn. Organ. **13**(4), 384–397 (2006)
13. Rus, I., Lindvall, M.: Knowledge management in software engineering. IEEE Softw. **19**(3), 26–38 (2002)
14. Ferraresi, A.A., Quandt, C.O., Dos Santos, S.A., Frega, J.R.: Knowledge management and strategic orientation: leveraging innovativeness and performance. J. Knowl. Manag. **16**(5), 688–701 (2012)
15. Annosi, M.C., Magnusson, M., Martini, A., Appio, F.P.: Social conduct, learning and innovation: an abductive study of the dark side of agile software development. Creat. Innov. Manag. **25**(4), 515–535 (2016)
16. Santos, V., Goldman, A., de Souza, C.R.: Fostering effective inter-team knowledge sharing in agile software development. Empir. Softw. Eng. **20**, 1006–1051 (2015)
17. Penrose, E.T.: The Growth of the Firm. Wiley, NewYork (1959)
18. Ryan, S., O'Connor, R.V.: Development of a team measure for tacit knowledge in software development teams. J. Syst. Softw. **82**, 229–240 (2009)
19. Dingsøyr, T., Bjørnson, F.O., Shull, F.: What do we know about knowledge management? Practical implications for software engineering. IEEE Softw. **26**(3), 100–103 (2009)
20. Ouriques, R.A.B., Wnuk, K., Svensson, R.B., Gorschek, T.: Knowledge management strategies and processes in agile software development: a systematic literature review. Int. J. Softw. Eng. Knowl. Eng. (in press)
21. Whetten, D.: What constitutes a theoretical contribution? Acad. Manag. Rev. **14**, 490–495 (1989)
22. Bolisani, E., Scarso, E.: Strategic planning approaches to knowledge management: a taxonomy. Edited by Constantin Bratianu, Assoc. Prof. E, P.VINE, vol. 45, no. 4, pp. 495–508 (2015)
23. Lee, C.C., Yang, J., Yu, L.M.: The knowledge value of customers and employees in product quality. J. Manag. Dev. **20**(8), 691–706 (2001)

Modeling in Agile Software Development: Decomposing Use Cases Towards Logical Architecture Design

Nuno Santos[1,2(✉)] ⓘ, Jaime Pereira[1,2] ⓘ, Nuno Ferreira[2,3] ⓘ, and Ricardo J. Machado[1,2] ⓘ

[1] CCG/ZGDV Institute, Guimarães, Portugal
nuno.santos@ccg.pt
[2] ALGORITMI Centre, School of Engineering, University of Minho, Guimarães, Portugal
[3] i2S Insurance Knowledge, Porto, SA, Portugal

Abstract. **[Context and motivation]** There are a plethora of agile practices that relate to management (e.g., Sprints, Scrum ceremonies), development (e.g., pair programming, TDD, BDD, DevOps) or strategy (e.g., Lean Startup), **[Question/problem]** but lack a comprehensive description on how its adoption influences requirements modeling and *"You Aren't Gonna Need It"* (YAGNI) features. **[Principal ideas/results]** This paper presents Agile Modeling Process for Logical Architectures (AMPLA), an Agile Modeling (AM) oriented process composed by UML diagrams (namely, Sequence, Use Cases and Component). **[Contributions]** AMPLA uses agile practices in order to deliver small increments (of a requirements package) and to promote continuous customer feedback. The proposed AM process also includes a candidate architecture and further requirements refinement in parallel with a software increment delivery.

Keywords: Agile modeling · Agile RE · UML use cases Logical architectures

1 Introduction

Agile software development (ASD) is nowadays composed with a mashup of practices and industry coins (e.g., Scrum, XP, BDD, MVP, DevOps, large-scale agile, Squads/Tribes, Management 3.0, and many others) that cover all software and application lifecycle. Although none of this practices specifically relate to requirements engineering (RE) discipline, performing these practices into an ASD process has direct implications on how RE practices are performed and how artifacts are built. Agile modeling (AM) [1] addresses requirements through modeling in ASD contexts.

This work was developed within the project UH4SP: Unified Hub 4 Smart Plants (Project ID 017871), under Portuguese National Grants Program for R&D projects (P2020 – SI IDT), COMPETE: POCI-01-0145-FEDER-007043 and FCT – Fundação para a Ciência e Tecnologia within the Project Scope: UID/CEC/00319/2013.

M. Kuhrmann et al. (Eds.): PROFES 2018, LNCS 11271, pp. 396–408, 2018.
https://doi.org/10.1007/978-3-030-03673-7_31

In plan-driven approaches (e.g., Waterfall), tasks related to RE discipline are traditionally managed in a phase separated in time from design and development. In change-driven approaches, like ASD, RE discipline – also called *"Agile RE"* – are executed continuously [2], and takes an iterative discovery approach [3]. Elicitation, analysis, and validation are present in all ASD processes [4].

ASD widely use User Stories [5] as items in the backlog for "reminders of a conversation" about a functionality. However, using only User Stories, without attached requirements specifications or models, may be insufficient to assure a common understanding or, in case of multi-teams, to clearly define inter-systems interaction. Additionally, requirements modeling need an AM approach in order to prevent unnecessary efforts in *"You Aren't Gonna Need It"* (YAGNI) features.

Applying AM should start by enabling a first iteration of requirements modeling, which is then the basis for further refinements and emerges, as the software increments are being delivered throughout the Sprints [6]. The inception, like the pregame phase or Sprint zero in Scrum, aims providing a shared understanding of the project and the required information for the development phase. In the same line of reasoning, Ambler presents an evolution and emerge-oriented approach for using models in ASD, called "Agile Model-Driven Development" (AMDD) [7], where the starting point is "just-enough" requirements and architecture, which are updated alongside Delivery Cycles.

This paper presents Agile Modeling Process for Logical Architectures (AMPLA), a process for model derivation applicable in an Agile RE and AM context. Inspired by a V-Model approach [8] based in successive model derivation, namely referring to sequence, use case and components diagrams, this process aims modeling the same artifacts however using agile practices such as Lean Startup, Design Thinking, Domain-driven Design (DDD), Behaviour-driven Development (BDD), and others. The model derivation follows typical agile feedback loops, encompassing discovery and exploration, learning from feedbacks and adjusting posterior loops. It also addresses AM so requirements emerge from these loops, by including only core and high-level requirements in early phase of projects, use them for deriving a UML components diagram using the Four-Step-Rule-Set (4SRS) method [8], and further incremental refinements within development cycles (e.g., Scrum Sprints). AMPLA seeks preventing waste in modeling YAGNI features.

This paper is structured as follows: Sect. 2 presents the main concepts on *"Agile RE"* and the artifacts present in the referred agile practices; Sect. 3 presents AMPLA's artifacts, phases and milestones; Sect. 4 presents the applicability of the process; and Sect. 5 describes the conclusions and future work.

2   Main Concepts

2.1   RE Discipline in ASD

In ASD contexts, RE activities (like elicitation, analysis and documentation) are still in a relatively early phase of development [9]. However, their timings and how they are used do change [9]. In ASD frameworks, like Scrum, XP, Kanban, SAFe, LeSS, Scrum@Scale or Nexus, the requirements are included in a product backlog, which then drives the development process, thus most of the RE activities are performed earlier.

Models are not included in most ASD frameworks. XP uses Themes, Epics and User Stories for addressing requirements. Scrum and Kanban only prescribe using work items in the Product Backlog regardless the form (however commonly these items are in form of User Stories). Test Driven Development (TDD), Acceptance Test Driven Development (ATDD), BDD and Specification by Example (SBE), - cf. Sect. 2.4 - use testable scenarios as input for the software development. The Disciplined Agile Delivery (DAD) framework uses the AM approach, which is independent from a modeling format. Approaches like the V+V model [10], the Agile Unified Process (AUP) [11], Jacobson's "Use Case 2.0" [12], or others like [13–15] use UML models in ASD projects. Despite the ASD context, the UML models result from upfront RE activities. In the Agile Product Line Architecting (APLA) approach [16], RE activities were also performed upfront, however using feature models. Golra *et al.* [17] use free modeling for gathering client requirements.

The Agile Extension to the BABOK® Guide [9] lists a variety of requirements artifacts and activities present in these ASD frameworks and gives a comprehensive description of RE approaches and techniques to use them within the software lifecycle. Leftingwell presents the associations between the types of requirements information in product backlogs [18]. In fact, AMPLA is inspired by both works to define how backlog items may be proposed to teams [19].

2.2 Lean Startup

The first introduced practice is the Lean Startup [20]. It is a hypothesis-driven approach, where a "Build-Measure-Learn" cycle is the basis for supporting product development adequate to the market. It is also worth referring that this cycle is inspired by the "Plan-Do-Check-Act" (PDCA) from Lean Manufacturing. The agile scaling framework DAD also encompasses an "Exploratory lifecycle" that uses the "Build-Measure-Learn" cycle from Lean Startup.

With Lean Startup, the following concepts arose: (i) Minimal Viable Product (MVP), (ii) Minimal Marketable Feature (MMF), (iii) Minimal Marketable Release (MMR), and (iv) Minimal Marketable Product (MMP). (i) An MVP is a version of a new product that is created with the least effort possible to be used for validated learning about customers. A development team typically deploys an MVP to the market to test a new idea, to collect data about it, and thereby learn from it. (ii) An MMF is the smallest piece of functionality that can be delivered that has value to both the organization delivering it and the people using it. An MMF is a part of an MMR or MMP. (iii) An MMR is the release of a product that has the smallest possible feature set that addresses the customers current needs. (iv) An MMP is the first deployment of a MMR.

2.3 Design Thinking

Another agile practice introduced is Design Thinking [21]. It addresses understanding the customer need through systematic exploration. The objective is to understand the right product to develop. This approach encompasses "Empathize", "Define", "Ideate", "Prototype" and "Test" phases.

2.4   Behaviour-Driven Development (BDD)

BDD [22] is an agile practice that consists in defining increments of software behavior and their delivery. Similarly, there is also TDD, ATDD and SBE. All these have in common to start by defining development based in scenarios and use the "Given, When, Then" (gherkin language). Although different, for the sake of this paper, these practices are referred conjunctly, since the definition of scenarios (cf. Sect. 3.1) is shared between them.

2.5   Domain-Driven Design

DDD [23], as the name suggests, is an approach that proposes the division of concepts by domains, or sub-domains, if applicable. This separation of domains is useful for defining clearly the scope of application for a given requirement. DDD has gained some attention as greatly applied in microservices development, because it promotes each teams to work independently inside their bounded contexts.

3   The AMPLA Process

This section presents the AMPLA approach that is the process for candidate architecture design, based on successive and specific artifacts generation. AMPLA is composed by discovery and exploration of user needs, *A–type sequence diagrams* [8], use case models, a software logical architecture diagram, feedbacks from customers and issues identification, and the consequent software delivery. All these artifacts are properly described in further sections of the paper. The generated artifacts and the alignment between the explored needs and modeled software requirements can be represented by a V-Model (Fig. 1). In our proposed V-Model, the artifacts are generated based on the rationale and in the information existing in previously defined artifacts, i.e., *A-type sequence diagrams* are based on discovered and explored scenarios, use case model is based on *A-type sequence diagrams*, the logical architecture is based on the use case model, and finally feedback from customers based in the logical architecture. After the feedback and consequent learning and adjustments (if needed), the approach ends with the candidate logical architecture, which is then used as input for defining the required backlog items for delivering the software [19]. When software delivery begins, the process is performed in typical cycles, whether in Scrum, Kanban, or other frameworks.

AMPLA is composed by artifacts, phases and milestones (Fig. 1). AMPLA's successive model derivation is performed in iterative cycles, easing the execution of agile feedback loops and hence contributing to the process' agility. These loops encompass phases of (1) Do; (2) Learn; and (3) Adjust. Each loop may include all phases of AMPLA, or just a subset of them. The artifacts should be modeled incrementally, where the ideal is to have short cycles to have design prototypes ready for

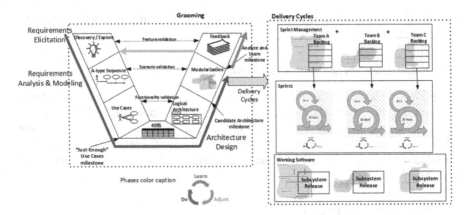

Fig. 1. AMPLA approach

customer analysis and feedback. It is better to deliver small portions of models and quickly validate with customers that the right product is being developed, rather than deliver bigger portions of models and realize that they do not reflect customer needs. Hence, the path encompassing "Discovery/Explore", "*A–type sequence diagrams*", "use cases", "4SRS" and "logical architecture" relate to (1) Do phase. "Feedback" from customers relate to the (2) Learn. Finally, the (3) Adjust is reflected in new, changed or eliminated artifacts output during the (1) Do phase. It has three established phases: (i) Requirements Elicitation (cf. Sect. 3.1); (ii) Requirements Analysis & Modeling (cf. Sect. 3.2); (iii) Architecture Design (cf. Sect. 3.2); and (iv) Delivery Cycles (cf. Sect. 3.3). For milestones, besides the checkpoints before passing from one phase to another, there are additional ones within phases that aim promoting agility. In Requirements Analysis & Modeling, the use cases refinement are validated for having "just-enough" detail before executing the 4SRS method (cf. Sect. 3.2). The execution of the 4SRS outputs a candidate version of the logical architecture, which is the first system model prototype that is presented to stakeholders for feedback (cf. Sect. 3.3). The analyze and learn milestone relates to the feedback gathered from the architecture, where issues and adjustments are identified before passing on to Delivery Cycles phase.

3.1   Requirements Elicitation and Discovery

This section relates to the elicitation and discovery phase of AMPLA. This phase relates to eliciting customer needs, exploring alternatives, discover new requirements, all aligned with current agile practices from ASD frameworks, techniques and philosophies. In AMPLA, this phase outputs a set of scenarios, i.e., processes and activities performed using the solution under development. These scenarios are documented in a stereotyped version of UML Sequence Diagrams, called *A-type sequence diagrams*, firstly introduced in [8]. *A-type sequence diagrams* are a stereotyped version of UML sequence diagrams that only include actors and use cases. At this stage, the use cases included in these diagrams are not yet composing part of the Use Case model from the next stage. Rather, they are classified as candidate use cases, because they relate to specific activities and tasks that a given actor performs (in software or not) within a given scenario. The flows between actors and candidate use cases relate to the actions performed. The use of these diagrams, instead of UML Activity diagrams, BPMN, or any other process–oriented language, relates to the use of candidate use cases, which help to construct the model in the next stage, because the candidate use cases are input for the use case model.

Applying agile practices in this phase influences:

- In **Lean Startup**, stakeholders define scenarios with the experiment mindset in mind. At this point, stakeholders have decided which features to include/experiment in the MVP. The scenarios for such features are elicited with the knowledge to date, where is not the purpose to have detailed technical description of how the solution will support such scenarios, but rather to define the referring processes. The remaining features may be refined afterwards. It is not the purpose of AMPLA to define how to reach minimum features (typically using 'bespoke RE' or 'market-driven RE' techniques), but rather to use the resulting business need as input for scenario modeling.
- In **Design Thinking**, the customer's desires and expectations are included in the scenarios, but the idea is also to discover and explore scenarios with different solutions and processes rather than only address what customers dictate. *A-type sequence diagrams* represent as many tasks as the scenarios are discovered and explored (Fig. 2).
- In **BDD** (or TDD, ATDD or SBE), the requirements discipline is addressed in the discovery and definition of scenarios (in gherkin language format). This format is mapped in *A-type sequence diagrams*, where "Given" contextualize each sequence diagram, "When" relates to a main sequence, or alternatively optional or exception sequence (if existing), and "Then" relate to the flows within the diagram.

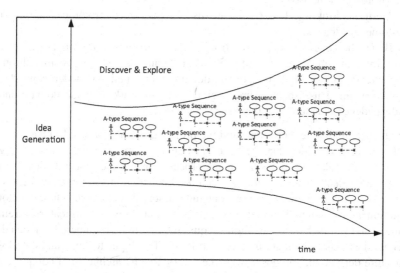

Fig. 2. Discovery and exploration of the scenarios

These scenarios, right or wrong (have in mind this is an exploration phase) are modeled in *A-type sequence diagrams*. These diagrams are the first visual prototype where customers are able to provide feedback.

3.2   Requirements Modeling

This section describes the following phase of AMPLA, which aims modeling a UML Use Cases diagram. Using as input the elicited scenarios, namely the model artifacts relating to *A-type sequence diagrams*, the Use Cases diagram is built and each Use Case refined. The gathering from the sequence diagrams are based in a set of decisions, which are aligned with agile practices as Design Thinking and DDD.

In this phase, candidate use cases from *A-type sequence diagrams* will give origin to "typical" use cases, i.e., formal software functional requirements. The idea is to use the gathered information and use it to model Use Cases and their refinements. The gathered information allows identifying detailed information about a requirement, which correspond to a use case functionally decomposed in refined use cases. Cruz *et al.* [24] and Azevedo *et al.* [25] present such refinement by sub-domains that compose a domain or by splitting a process. They model use case refinement in decomposition trees, and so does this approach. The candidate use cases from *A-type sequence diagrams* are grouped in a logical way, typically grouping them to the scenario from *A-type sequence diagrams* that originated them.

Applying agile practices in this phase influences:

- In **Lean Startup**, as customers define which scenarios to include in MVP/MMR/MMP, they are expressed in more detail rather than the scenarios that are left out at this phase. Thus, there is more context to define the models that will compose MMF, which result in more decomposition of those use cases. The remaining requirements that are not refined for the MMF are identified however not afterwards decomposed.
- In **Design Thinking**, Use Cases are used as designed prototypes aiming firsts customer feedbacks.
- In **BDD**, the candidate use cases from *A-type sequence diagrams* are grouped in domains and sub-domains. The refinement "branches" of the decomposition tree hence relate to a single domain or sub-domain, which define bounded contexts for a (sub-)domain. This aspect assures a given team to work on a sub-domain and the independence is assured by the bounded context.

If all stakeholders' expectations and the project goals are included in the Use Case model, one may consider that we have "just-enough" requirements for enabling the product design. Like in any requirements process, one of the first critical tasks is to identify all projects stakeholders, as well as the solution's interacting actors. By mapping stakeholders to the use cases, one must assure that every stakeholder/actor has a requirement related to it, or else it is a sign that there are critical requirements missing. Having all the "just-enough" requirements elicited, gathered, modeled and validated, these Use Cases are now able to be used as input for the candidate logical architecture derivation, composed with the "just-enough" architectural components.

The 4SRS method supports the functional decomposition of requirements (using UML use cases) and, based on them, derives a logical architecture composed by UML components that relate to each functionality [8]. The 4SRS method is composed by four steps: Component Creation; Component Elimination (divided in seven micro-steps); Packaging and Aggregation; and Component Associations. The first step regards the creation of software architectural components. In the second step, components are submitted to elimination tasks according to pre-defined rules. In the third step, the components are grouped in packages of semantically consistent components. The final step refers to the associations between components. Hence, the architectural diagram is composed by the components remaining after step 2, grouped in packages as defined after step 3, and with information flows between them as defined in the associations after step 4. Further details of the 4SRS method can be found in [8].

3.3   Software Delivery Kick-off Phase and Learning from the Models

The derivation of models described so far is performed before the Sprints cycles. Only then there is context for deriving backlog items. The transformation of the artifacts in backlog items may be performed before or during a Sprint 0 cycle, where no software was delivered. Then, the process is structured in Scrum Sprints. The main difference is that, in parallel with delivering a software increment, other team members are responsible for refining requirements not yet included in the backlog, and that are planned to be implemented in further Sprints (Fig. 3).

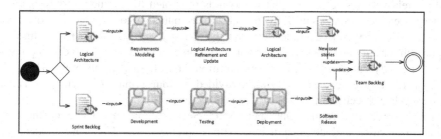

Fig. 3. Parallel tasks within Sprints in SPEM diagram

Requirements and Analysis tasks are performed in iterative cycles and incrementally, always synchronized with the development and deployment during the Sprints, in a sense that what is elicited, gathered and modeled in use cases during a cycle is then ready to be implemented in next cycles. They originate a new increment of the 4SRS method, deriving additional components to the logical architecture under refinement. These models require validation from customer before being ready to be included in the Team Backlog. Then, requirements and the 4SRS address the functionalities to be implemented in the next or in ahead Sprints.

4   Modeling Requirements Within the UH4SP Research Project

In this section, AMPLA is evaluated in a case study depicting the applicability of the process in a software project [26]. The method is evaluated by describing some modeling outputs from a research project called Unified Hub for Smart Plants (UH4SP), and to depict how agile practices influenced the resulting models.

The UH4SP project aims developing a platform for integrating data from distributed industrial unit plants, allowing the use of the production data between plants, suppliers, forwarders and clients. The consortium was composed with five different entities for software development where each had specific expected contributes, from cloud architectures to industrial software services and mobile applications. The solution is based in the Industry 4.0 paradigm, and IoT and cloud computing technologies. The entities are geographically distributed, but each entity had a single located team. An analysis team composed with elements from each entities, aiming to define the initial requirements, conducted the requirements phase. Since they belong to different entities, they had to schedule on-site meetings to perform requirements workshops (cf. Sects. 3.1 and 3.2). Only when beginning the software delivery cycles, after boundaries were clear, each team was responsible for refining their requirements (cf. Sect. 3.3).

The requirements elicitation (cf. Sect. 3.1) started by listing a set of stakeholder expectations towards the product roadmap, encompassing the entire product but only MVP features were detailed. The expectations list of the project included 25 expectations, categorized by environment, architecture, functional and integration issues, which relate to business needs that afterwards promoted the discussion of scenarios. These scenarios were elicited by the customer, but also to explore and discover alternatives. The project's objectives that were stated referred to: (1) to define an approach for a unified view at the corporate (group of units) level; (2) to develop tools for third-party entities; (3) in-plant optimization; and (4) system reliability. This task output 15 *A–type sequence diagrams*, divided in four groups of scenarios. These groups relate directly to the project's four objectives.

Afterwards, the requirements analysis (cf. Sect. 3.2) included gathering the candidate use cases and defining the decomposition tree. The Use Case model was composed by 37 use cases after the refinement. Figure 4 is not zoomed since the objective is to present the refinement levels, their inclusion in the MVP and the identification of DDD's bounded contexts, rather than the details of the Use Cases of the project.

The impacts of these agile techniques in modeling the use cases:

- **By applying DDD**, Use Cases are grouped by the domains and sub-domains. This means that each of the tree's "branches" relate only to a given domain, which also assures that the contexts are properly bounded. Each bounded context is represented like in Fig. 4. The identified domains relate directly to the four scenario groups. Two of them, "tools for third-party entities" and "system reliability", were afterwards divided in two and three domains, respectively, hence making a total of seven. Two of the "system reliability" bounded context are not depicted due to MVP decisions.

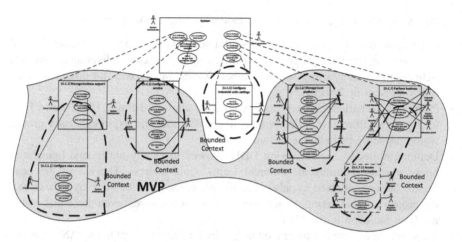

Fig. 4. Use case decomposition tree of UH4SP, the Use cases from MVP features and for further releases (Lean Startup), and the domain's and sub-domain's bounded contexts (DDD)

- **By applying Lean Startup**, the features defined to be included in the MVP are identified in the model by having refined use cases, while the remaining were just identified in the first-level. Use cases *{UC.3}* and *{UC.4}* relate to features not addressed in the MVP, hence were not object of further decomposition. The remaining use cases were included in the MVP, where, namely, *{UC.1}* was decomposed in five use cases, *{UC.2}* was decomposed in eight use cases, *{UC.5}* was decomposed in two use cases, *{UC.6}* was decomposed in five use cases, and *{UC.7}* was decomposed in ten use cases.

The UH4SP logical architecture had as input 37 use cases and, after executing 4SRS method, was derived with 77 architectural components that compose it. Figure 5 depicts the logical architecture diagram, with focus in *"unified view at the corporate level"* bounded context, namely four logical components ({C1.1.1.i}, {C1.1.1.i2}, {C1.1.1.c} and {C1.1.1.d}) derived from use case *{UC1.1} Configure users account*.

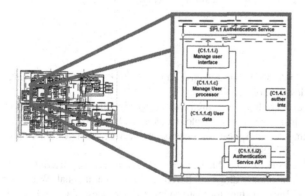

Fig. 5. UH4SP logical architecture derived after 4SRS execution.

Applying AMPLA affected use case modeling with the following advantages:

- Overall, the use of agile practices per se did not make the process agile, but allowed specifying agilely the right product for the customer's needs. Delivering the product right is promoted by using Scrum, Kanban, XP, SAFe or LeSS, for instance, which is also present in AMPLA.
- Promoting scenarios discovery and exploration allowed defining 15 scenarios from four groups (from the project's objectives). Without the exploring, each groups would probably include one or two scenarios.
- Defining bounded contexts using DDD allowed to clearly understand boundaries between what requirements different teams could address. The use of the Lean Startup strategy allowed to only refine the use cases from the MVP hypothesis that the project aim validating, rather than refining all use cases, even those that would not been included in the MVP.
- These practices ease customer feedback, which is fundamental in any ASD process.

However, AMPLA proposes additional activities and artifacts in agile RE methods and may require dedicated teams for RE, which may be perceived as a disadvantage. A threat to validity is that AMPLA was only applied by the method's designers.

5   Conclusions and Future Work

This paper presents AMPLA, an AM process that promotes successive model derivation, as well as it is suitable to be executed within small agile feedback loops. If ASD frameworks enable the right development of products, then agile RE practices – aligned with agile practices such as Design Thinking, DDD, BDD, and Lean Startup - provide the tools so the delivered product is the right product. Models are incrementally refined in parallel with ASD frameworks such as Scrum, XP or Kanban.

The process was tested in a project where a requirements team was responsible for eliciting the initial requirements and, afterwards, each team was responsible for refining their assigned modules. AMPLA will be validated in the future in contexts where each team starts defining requirements from the beginning. Additionally, AMPLA will be formalized in a process-oriented notation (e.g., SPEM, ESSENCE).

References

1. Ambler, S.: Agile Modeling: Effective Practices for Extreme Programming and the Unified Process. Wiley, Hoboken (2002)
2. Grau, B.R., Lauenroth, K.: Requirements engineering and agile development - collaborative, just enough, just in time, sustainable. Int. Requir. Eng. Board (2014)
3. Cao, L., Ramesh, B.: Agile requirements engineering practices: an empirical study. IEEE Softw. 25, 60–67 (2008)
4. Paetsch, F., Eberlein, A., Maurer, F.: Requirements engineering and agile software development. In: Proceedings of Twelfth IEEE International Workshops on Enabling Technologies: Infrastructure for Collaborative Enterprises (WET ICE 2003). IEEE (2003)

5. Cohn, M.: User Stories Applied: for Agile Software Development. Addison-Wesley, Boston (2004)
6. Santos, N., Pereira, J., Morais, F., Barros, J., Ferreira, N., Machado, Ricardo J.: An agile modeling oriented process for logical architecture design. In: Gulden, J., Reinhartz-Berger, I., Schmidt, R., Guerreiro, S., Guédria, W., Bera, P. (eds.) BPMDS/EMMSAD -2018. LNBIP, vol. 318, pp. 260–275. Springer, Cham (2018). https://doi.org/10.1007/978-3-319-91704-7_17
7. Ambler, S.W.: Agile model driven development is good enough. IEEE Softw. **20**(5), 71–73 (2003)
8. Ferreira, N., Santos, N., Machado, R.J., Fernandes, J., Gasević, D.: A V-model approach for business process requirements elicitation in cloud design. In: Bouguettaya, A., Sheng, Q., Daniel, F. (eds.) Advanced Web Services, pp. 551–578. Springer, New York (2014). https://doi.org/10.1007/978-1-4614-7535-4_23
9. IIBA: Agile Extension to the BABOK Guide (2017)
10. Costa, N., Santos, N., Ferreira, N., Machado, Ricardo J.: Delivering user stories for implementing logical software architectures by multiple scrum teams. In: Murgante, B., et al. (eds.) ICCSA 2014. LNCS, vol. 8581, pp. 747–762. Springer, Cham (2014). https://doi.org/10.1007/978-3-319-09150-1_55
11. Ambler, S.: The Agile Unified Process (AUP). Ambysoft (2005)
12. Jacobson, I., Spence, I., Bittner, K.: Use Case 2.0: The Definite Guide. Ivar Jacobson International (2011)
13. Santos, N., et al.: Using scrum together with UML models: a collaborative university-industry R&D software project. In: Gervasi, O., et al. (eds.) ICCSA 2016. Lecture Notes in Computer Science, vol. 9789. Springer, Cham (2016). https://doi.org/10.1007/978-3-319-42089-9_34
14. Cho, J.: A hybrid software development method for large-scale projects: rational unified process with scrum. Issues Inf. Syst. **10**, 340–348 (2009)
15. Durdik, Z.: Towards a process for architectural modelling in agile software development. In: Proceedings of ACM SIGSOFT QoSA-ISARCS on Quality of Software Architectures, New York, p. 183. ACM Press (2011)
16. Díaz, J., Pérez, J., Garbajosa, J.: Agile product-line architecting in practice: a case study in smart grids. Inf. Softw. Technol. **56**, 727–748 (2014)
17. Golra, F.R., Beugnard, A., Dagnat, F., Guerin, S., Guychard, C.: Using free modeling as an agile method for developing domain specific modeling languages. In: ACM/IEEE 19th International Conference on Model Driven Engineering Languages and Systems – MODELS, New York, USA, pp. 24–34. ACM Press (2016)
18. Leffingwell, D.: Agile Software Requirements: Lean Requirements Practices for Teams, Programs, and the Enterprise. Addison-Wesley, Upper Saddle River (2010)
19. Santos, N., Pereira, J., Morais, F., Barros, J., Ferreira, N., Machado, R.J.: An experience report on using architectural models within distributed Scrum teams contexts. In: XP 2018 Workshops (in press), Preprint version available in. https://bit.ly/2nPpgeG. ACM (2018)
20. Ries, E.: The Lean Startup: How Today's Entrepreneurs use Continuous Innovation to Create Radically Successful Businesses. Crown Books, Largo (2011)
21. Brown, T.: Change by Design: How Design Thinking Transforms Organizations and Inspires Innovation. Harper Collins, New York (2009)
22. Smart, J.F.: BDD in Action: Behavior-driven Development for the Whole Software Lifecycle. Manning Publications, New York (2015)
23. Evans, E.: Domain-driven Design: Tackling Complexity in the Heart of Software. Addison-Wesley, Boston (2004)

24. Cruz, E.F., Machado, R.J., Santos, M.Y.: On the decomposition of use cases for the refinement of software requirements. In: 2014 14th International Conference on Computational Science and its Applications, pp. 237–240. IEEE (2014)
25. Azevedo, S., Machado, R.J., Braganca, A., Ribeiro, H.: The UML «include» relationship and the functional refinement of use cases. In: 36th EUROMICRO Conference on Software Engineering and Advanced Applications (SEAA), pp. 156–163. IEEE (2010)
26. Kitchenham, B., Pickard, L., Pfleeger, S.: Case studies for method and tool evaluation. IEEE Softw. **12**, 52–62 (1995)

Mapping Agility to Automotive Software Product Line Concerns

Philipp Hohl[1]([✉]), Sven Theobald[2], Martin Becker[2], Michael Stupperich[1], and Jürgen Münch[3]

[1] Daimler AG, Research and Development, Ulm, Germany
{philipp.hohl,michael.stupperich}@daimler.com
[2] Fraunhofer Institute for Experimental Software Engineering IESE, Kaiserslautern, Germany
{sven.theobald,martin.becker}@iese.fraunhofer.de
[3] Reutlingen University, Reutlingen, Germany
juergen.muench@reutlingen-university.de

Abstract. Context: Software product lines are widely used in automotive embedded software development. This software paradigm improves the quality of software variants by reuse. The combination of agile software development practices with software product lines promises a faster delivery of high quality software. However, the set up of an agile software product line is still challenging, especially in the automotive domain. **Goal:** This publication aims to evaluate to what extend agility fits to automotive product line engineering. **Method:** Based on previous work and two workshops, agility is mapped to software product line concerns. **Results:** This publication presents important principles of software product lines, and examines how agile approaches fit to those principles. Additionally, the principles are related to one of the four major concerns of software product line engineering: Business, Architecture, Process, and Organization. **Conclusion:** Agile software product line engineering is promising and can add value to existing development approaches. The identified commonalities and hindering factors need to be considered when defining a combined agile product line engineering approach.

Keywords: Software product line · Agile · Agility
Automotive software development · Commonalities · Hindering factors

1 Introduction

The automotive domain is recently in a disruptive change. Vehicles are no longer isolated, but connected to the environment [1]. The uprising complexity has to be addressed for the development of new car generations. A lot of innovation is nowadays addressed in software. According to Oliveira [2], 85% of the functionalities in cars are realized with software running on electronic control units. The amount of software has evolved from zero to tens of millions of lines of code

© Springer Nature Switzerland AG 2018
M. Kuhrmann et al. (Eds.): PROFES 2018, LNCS 11271, pp. 409–421, 2018.
https://doi.org/10.1007/978-3-030-03673-7_32

[3], distributed on more than 70 electronic control units [4,5]. In 2006, Broy [6] already identified the increasing amount of software. He stated that the amount of software in the car has increased exponentially in the last decades [6]. McCaffery et al. [7] expect that the quantity of software grows continuously. They further emphasize that software must be developed faster and in a more cost effective way, but still in a high quality [7].

The reuse of software parts is necessary to keep pace with the high amount of different variants, while simultaneously maintaining the quality of the software. Software product lines are a paradigm for systematic software reuse [8]. This paradigm is particularly important for the automotive domain to meet different requirements across multiple markets [9]. According to Wozniak et al. [10], the automotive domain is the most challenging environment for systems and software product line engineering. Millions of different software variants exist, whereby each one of them comprises a large complexity [10]. The complexity is based on the large number of variation points within the product [10,11]. There exist several variant management approaches, methods and processes to handle variants [12]. However, it is important to ensure that the approach is suitable for the automotive domain. The consistency and reliability of systems has to be ensured at all times [8] and must be compliant to valid norms and restrictions given by the law.

Traditional working structures make it difficult to deliver the required high amount of software fast enough [6], because the development processes are too slow to keep pace with the fast changing market [13,14]. Since 2001, agile software development methods promise a fast delivery of high-quality products. Furthermore it is possible to react dynamically on changing requirements from customers and market demands, due to close customer collaboration and incremental development. The adoption of agile practices within the automotive domain is therefore a possible way to keep pace with fast changing market demands [15].

However, the combination of agile software development and software product lines for software development is assumed to be difficult [15]. Agile methods and practices are primarily designed for short development cycles in small development teams. For larger teams, agile methods are scaled up to approaches for large organizations, such as the Scaled Agile Framework or Scrum of Scrums. In the automotive domain, software product lines are used to manage the software development, by "intra-organisational reuse through the explicitly planned exploitation of similarities between related products" [9, p. 531].

Various combinations of agile software development and plan-driven development approaches are already present within parts of the automotive domain. These hybrid approaches are often very specific to the context they are used and rarely consider a strategic software reuse [16]. In order to ensure the quality of a agile software product lines processes, the aim of this paper is to identify competing and aligned goals for the combination of agile elements and software product lines. Considering the goals, it is possible to define a development process to maintain long-term productivity, efficiency, and profit (cf. [17])

The remainder of this paper is structured as follows. Section 2 discusses related work. Section 3 describes the research approach. Section 4 presents the key findings and Sect. 5 discusses these findings. Finally, Sect. 6 summarizes the paper and gives an outlook on future work.

2   Related Work

This section investigates publications for a combination of software product lines and agile software development in the automotive domain.

2.1   Agile Software Product Lines in Automotive

The published literature does not provide significant information or approaches on how to adapt existing agile software development approaches to software product line development in the automotive domain.

Thiel et al. [9] analyze the combination of agile and plan-driven processes. This combination could be seen as a typical characteristic of current automotive software development. They emphasize that a combination is beneficial under certain conditions, such as rigid quality and safety requirements [9]. They further suggest to introduce selected agile practices and methods to automotive systems engineering [9]. This suggestion follows as well from the "Agile in Automotive Survey" from Kugler and Maag [18]. The survey identifies that many companies only introduce single agile elements into existing and proven development cycles. In addition, the use of Scrum as defined in [19] is often not applicable due to the context factors and the development environment. In most cases, Scrum is tailored to the specific context [20].

Schlosser et al. [21] define an imminent challenge for automotive software development. They mention the necessity of shorter development time for multiple software variants by considering constraints of a high cost pressure. They further argue that more incremental software deliveries in a shorter time are necessary. With the incremental approach, a quick response from customers could be achieved, which leads to a shorter development time and saves money [15,21].

In addition, the agile element of *Continuous Integration* is seen as a key component for agile automotive development. Continuous Integration provides a quick response with respect to functional aspects [21–23].

In order to integrate further agile elements into the automotive domain, different models and processes are introduced, such as the *Feedback Loop Model* and the *Mega Scale Software Product Line Engineering*.

The concurrent *Feedback Loop Model* introduces feedback loops for different organizations to enable cooperation [24]. The cooperation (including communication) between different organizations is managed by a new architect role to shorten the development time. The reduction of time is validated in a case study. Furthermore, the *System Architecture Virtual Integration* (SAVI) initiative helps to improve the agile development. In SAVI, Continuous Integration is concurrently operated within the software development process. Integration starts with

412   P. Hohl et al.

the earliest available system models into a virtual integration environment. With a virtual integration strategy vendors are more closely tied to the project [1].

In order to handle the complexity, the *Mega Scale Software Product Line Engineering* (MS-SPLE) approach is introduced. This approach is applied for large product sets with complex products and complex feature variations like the automotive domain. MS-SPLE is a possibility to manage, e.g., calibration parameters for the software variation mechanism and the complexity management. However, agile software development is not taken into account within MS-SPLE [10].

In total, four different trends could be identified.

- Adopting agile software development in the automotive typically concentrates only on selected agile practices such as Continuous Integration or Pair Programming. The published literature does not show any recommendations to use a comprehensive set of agile elements and practices together in the automotive domain.
- The majority of the published literature suggests that agile models and processes should get customized to the specifics of the automotive domain before they are implemented in practice.
- Agile models and processes that are already customized to the specifics of the automotive domain are proposed in the published literature. An example is the *Feedback Loop Model* that especially considers the collaboration between different organizations (such as OEMs and suppliers).
- Combination approaches include interesting new concepts such as virtual integration on the system level.

3   Research Approach

The research presented in this publication is guided by the question:
Which commonalities and hindering factors need to be considered when combining software product lines and agile development? This question identifies how well both approaches can be combined. It further examines incompatibilities which need special attention for setting up a combination.

3.1   Research Design

Hohl et al. conducted a qualitative interview study [25], a literature review [26] and gave some recommendations on the combination of agile development and software product lines in the automotive domain. Our research is based on these publications and on two workshops. These expert workshops aimed at achieving a common understanding how to combine agile software development and software product lines in the automotive domain. We combined the experience of the authors due to the active involvement of Researcher 1 (P. Hohl) and Researcher 4 (M. Stupperich) in the automotive software development and the experience of Researcher 2 (S. Theobald) regarding agile practices. Furthermore, we included the experience of Researcher 3 (M. Becker) in software product lines and the knowledge of Researcher 5 (J. Münch) in software engineering. The workshops were held at the "Fraunhofer Institute for Experimental Software Engineering" (IESE) in Kaiserslautern, Germany. In both workshops, researchers from Fraunhofer IESE attended the workshop as additional participants. Each participant was invited by Researcher 1 and Researcher 3 to participate in the workshop due to their experience in agile development practices and the use of software product lines.

The first workshop took place in September 2017. This one day workshop was divided into two sessions of 3 h each. Industrial participation was given by Researcher 1 and Researcher 4 working at the Daimler AG. Furthermore, four participants (including Researcher 2 and Researcher 3) from the departments of embedded systems engineering and process engineering from the Fraunhofer IESE participated in the workshop. In the first session, each of the six participants gave a short presentation about their experience on the topic. Researcher 1 presented his thoughts on assessment models for agile software product line engineering.

The second session was a discussion round to identify common ground, to interconnect the knowledge of the participants and link agile practices and software product line techniques together. Within the workshop, the "Business (B), Architecture (A), Process (P) and Organization (O) (BAPO)" Model was identified as the basis for a discussion to evaluate agile principles according to the major concerns of software product line engineering [27]. The end of the session was the identification of topics for discussion in the follow-up meeting.

Researcher 3 prepared a list of product line engineering principles and categorized them according to the BAPO Model. Researcher 1 and Researcher 2 reviewed the categorization and completeness of the principles prior to the follow-up meeting. Researcher 3 prioritized the principles from the software product line view and Researcher 2 rated the importance of those principles for supporting the agile way of working. Researcher 1 reviewed the combined results.

The follow-up workshop took place in January 2018 with 4 participants from the first workshop (including Researcher 1, Researcher 2 and Researcher 3). It consists of two sessions of 3 hours each. In the first session the results which were generated between the workshops were presented and discussed. In the second session, the results were presented to an independent researcher. The subsequent discussion provided feedback to the categorization.

3.2 Threats to Validity

Threats to the validity are described and a mitigation strategy for each threat is given.

Bias may be introduced by the researchers, which were also the workshops participants. The completeness and correctness of the mapping could be influenced by the experience of the workshop participants. However, we limit this threat by including researchers from different fields and several review iterations.

Furthermore, the categorization was reviewed by an independent researcher. With this approach, a balanced view on the combination was possible.

The categorization into the four major concerns of software product line engineering: Business (B), Architecture (A), Process (P) and Organization (O) [27] could influence the result for the identification of commonalities and hindering factors. We addressed this threat by a review process and a discussion with an independent and unbiased researcher from the Fraunhofer IESE in the second session of the follow-up workshop.

4   Results and Analysis

Which commonalities and hindering factors need to be considered when combining software product lines and agile development?

To identify the potential combination we introduced a list with a comparison of agile and software product line approaches. Each list item is related to one of the four major concerns of software product line engineering: Business (B), Architecture (A), Process (P) and Organization (O) [27] and organized in two categories. The categorization is based on the Family Evaluation Framework (FEF) proposed by van der Linden [27,28], which has been developed in the CAFÉ/Families EU projects. It provides the four dimensional evaluation scheme to assess the readiness or maturity of product line adoption within an organization. Commonalities and hindering factors are identified (cf. Fig. 1).

The mappings are denoted as *"X-Description"*, whereas *"X"* defines one of the four dimensions (B,A,P,O) and *"Description"* names the identified principle.

4.1   Aligned Goals

This subsection presents the aligned goals. The principles were denoted as aligned if both approaches show the same trend (cf. Fig. 1).

B-Know Feature Cost, B-Know Feature Value. Agile development focuses on individual single-system products. The costs for each features are estimated. A prediction of the overall costs cannot be done precisely at the start. The economic justification for introducing product line engineering is the reduction of costs [29]. The concept of software reuse is simple. Reuse already implemented software parts saves the cost of designing, writing and testing new code [30]. Budget steering is essential to balance reuse on the one hand and to foster customer orientation on the other hand [31]. Benefits of a reuse program must always be considered in the long term [30].

B-Know Company Goals, B-Aligned Strategies, B-Plan Feature Roadmap/Evolution. In agile development, it is helpful to consider the company goals and align with company strategies, but not always needed, e.g., a single team can develop a product for a customer independently of the rest of the organization. In software product line engineering the company goals are defined for the long term and considered to direct the evolution of the software product line.

P-Predictable Quality. In product line engineering, all features are extensively tested and a higher quality is achieved by using the core assets in multiple products. In agile development, short iterations and continuous testing help to avoid a big-bang integration. The learning loop about the maturity of the software is shorter and failures in the software are detected earlier in the development process. High qualitative software is mandatory for automotive software. Long lasting software tests and tests with real cars help to achieve a high software quality and to be compliant with the restrictions given by the law [25].

O-Share Domain Knowledge. Agile methods and Product line engineering aim at including experts to share their domain knowledge. The ideal agile team follows the one-room principle to center the cross-functional team. In product line engineering, domain experts are systematically involved to identify common parts in the scoping process. The development processes in the automotive domain are organized in a hierarchical structure. Coordination of the worldwide distributed software development requires to share domain knowledge to avoid a diverge of the common software baseline [25].

4.2   Competing Goals

This subsection presents the identified competing goals based on the BAPO model for product line engineering [27]. The principles were denoted as competing if one approach fosters (Helpful, Needed) and the other one hinders (Hampering, Impending) an agile software product line (cf. Fig. 1).

A-Ease Customization. Agile development is customer-oriented. The use of agile methods enables the development to react on customers' needs and changing requirements [32]. Customer oriented development focuses on a specific problem within a standalone solution. The idea of the software product line is to develop different products from one core asset base (also called a platform) [33]. Pohl et al. [29] mention the platforms used for mass-customization in their definition of software product line engineering. For software customization, customer-specific product variants can be generated using parts from the platform and customize it to fulfill customers' demands [31].

A-Share Architecture, A-Share Assets, P-Manage Interdependencies. In product line engineering, it is important to manage the traceability between requirements, architecture, code and tests [31]. Small changes in core assets can have an effect on multiple systems. The complex interdependencies between variants in a product line need special attention and require strategic long-term

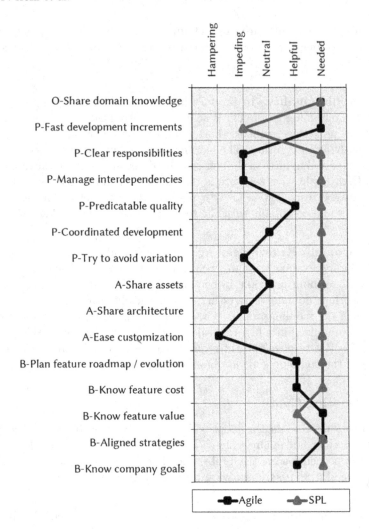

Fig. 1. Commonalities and hindering factors for the combination of agile and software product line approaches according to the four major concerns of software product line engineering: Business (B), Architecture (A), Process (P) and Organization (O) [27].

planning [34]. In contrast, agile development focuses on single product development and changes in the code or architecture only affect the single product. The software development in the automotive domain requires a coordination that addresses the interdependencies with other parties such as suppliers, in-house development, mechanical and hardware development.

P-Try to Avoid Variation. Agile methods and practices do not explicitly address the development of several similar products at the same time. Therefore, a structured reuse of software between several products for different customers is not considered. The development often follows a so called "clone and own" approach. In contrast, the software product line supports the structured development of different software variants. Members of a product family, addressing the same domain, are developed together. The reusability of domain assets is one success factors of the software product line [34]. The reusable assets are assembled into customer-specific software systems [35]. However, the software product line requires strategic long-term planning [34]. This is competing with the flexible planning fostered by agile methods. In the automotive domain, it is still challenging to plan in the long term, but equally important to be able to react on changing market demands in the short term.

P-Clear Responsibilities, P-Coordinated Development. Blau and Hildenbrand [31] point out that it is necessary to manage the development process and to identify possible reusable software parts, called core assets, to avoid redundant development [31]. Complex interdependencies between individual products in the product line require coordination and defined responsibilities for the development process. In agile methods, the concept of collective code ownership gives the responsibility to the team. However, current organizational hierarchy in the automotive domain likely keeps responsibility in higher management levels.

P-Fast Development Increments. Agile development focuses on customer demands and allows for small iterations where product increments are produced. Changes in requirements are welcomed and thus changes happen regularly based on the feedback collected at the end of each iteration. In product line engineering, new requirements and changes in the planned core assets cannot be addressed ad-hoc, since the impact to the whole product line has to be evaluated first.

5 Discussion

The categorization into the four major concerns of software product line engineering: Business (B), Architecture (A), Process (P) and Organization (O) [27] resulted in commonalities and hindering factors.

On a high-level view (cf. Fig. 1), our comparison shows alignment on business (B) and organizational (O) level. The aligned goals show that a combination is possible with a low effort. In the comparison, both approaches (agile software development and software product line engineering) show the same trend to address issues such as feature cost, feature value, and software quality. This confirms our understanding that both approaches follow similar goals.

However, guidelines are needed to combine both approaches in a structured way. This is even more important for the competing goals, as they are impeding a combination. Differences occur on the level of architecture (A) and processes (P). Maintaining a shared architecture to address the large amount of different software variants is challenging. The interdependencies of variants need special attention regarding the development process. The competing goals need to be considered carefully to combine agile development and software product lines successfully.

An assessment model is expected to be beneficial to guide the combination of agile software development with software product line engineering in order to shorten time to market and maintain long-term productivity, efficiency, and profit [17]. Hohl et al. [36] present an assessment model that could support the combination, by comprising the identified compatibility of both approaches. Furthermore, such an assessment model shall be aligned to existing standards, such as ASPICE [37] and comprises the major concerns of software product line engineering.

Existing literature [21–23] introduce agile elements into plan-driven processes. However, none of the mentioned publications provides a recording of the actual situation concerning product lines and agile development processes.

6 Conclusion

This publication identifies whether agility fits to the presented product line engineering principles. We identify commonalities and hindering factors of agile elements and software product lines. Therefore, we categorized the important characteristics to the four major concerns of software product line engineering: Business (B), Architecture (A), Process (P) and Organization (O) [27].

The results show that both approaches can be successfully combined. Aligned goals support a combination with low effort, because both approaches follow the same goal. Competing goals must be considered carefully.

The results motivate the development of an adjusted assessment model to support a successful introduction. An in-depth process knowledge and management of software variants can make a difference for success in the case of reuse based software development. An assessment model can foster the combination by reinforcing the implementation of the aligned goals and supporting an effective management program by explicitly including important areas to consider. Other domains that apply software product lines may benefit from the assessment model, while assessing the possibilities of combining agile software development with the existing software product line.

For future work, we plan to extend and validate the factors for a successful combination, by including other standards of software product line engineering. Further, the mapping of both approaches will be refined in a more granular way, to get a better understanding of the conflicts and synergies. Especially, the agile view will be considered more extensively.

References

1. Taiber, J., McGregor, J.D.: Efficient engineering of safety-critical, software-intensive systems. In: 2014 International Conference on Connected Vehicles and Expo (ICCVE), pp. 836–841
2. Oliveira, P., Ferreira, A.L., Dias, D., Pereira, T., Monteiro, P., Machado, R.J.: An analysis of the commonality and differences between ASPICE and ISO26262 in the context of software development. In: Stolfa, J., Stolfa, S., O'Connor, R.V., Messnarz, R. (eds.) EuroSPI 2017. CCIS, vol. 748, pp. 216–227. Springer, Cham (2017)
3. Pretschner, A., Salzmann, C., Schätz, B., Staudner, T.: Fourth International Workshop on Software Engineering for Automotive Systems (SEAS 2007): Proceedings, ICSE 2007 Workshops, 20–26 May 2007, Minneapolis ICSE 2007. IEEE, Piscataway (2007)
4. Contag, M., et al.: How they did it: an analysis of emission defeat devices in modern automobiles. In: 2017 IEEE Symposium on Security and Privacy (SP), pp. 231–250. IEEE (2017)
5. Münch, J., Schmid, K., Rombach, H.D.: Perspectives on the Future of Software Engineering: Essays in Honor of Dieter Rombach. Springer, Heidelberg (2013). https://doi.org/10.1007/978-3-642-37395-4
6. Broy, M.: Challenges in automotive software engineering. In: Proceedings of the 28th International Conference on Software Engineering, ICSE 2006, pp. 33–42. ACM (2006)
7. McCaffery, F., Pikkarainen, M., Richardson, I.: Ahaa-agile, hybrid assessment method for automotive, safety critical smes. In: Schäfer, W. (ed.) Companion of the 30th International Conference on Software Engineering, p. 551. ACM (2008)
8. Leitner, A., Mader, R., Kreiner, C., Steger, C., Weiß, R.: A development methodology for variant-rich automotive software architectures. e & i Elektrotechnik und Informationstechnik **128**(6), 222–227 (2011)
9. Thiel, S., Babar, M.A., Botterweck, G., O'Brien, L.: Software product lines in automotive systems engineering. SAE Int. J. Passeng. Cars Electron. Electr. Syst. **1**(1), 531–543 (2009)
10. Wozniak, L., Clements, P.: How automotive engineering is taking product line engineering to the extreme. In: Schmidt, D.C. (ed.) Proceedings of the 19th International Conference on Software Product Line, pp. 327–336. ACM (2015)
11. Galster, M., Avgeriou, P.: Supporting variability through agility to achieve adaptable architectures. In: Agile Software Architecture, pp. 139–159. Elsevier (2014)
12. Hohl, P., Münch, J., Stupperich, M.: Forces that support agile adoption in the automotive domain. In: Software Engineering (2017)
13. Bosch, J., Bosch-Sijtsema, P.M.: Introducing agile customer-centered development in a legacy software product line. Softw. Pract. Exp. **41**(8), 871–882 (2011)
14. Eliasson, U., Heldal, R., Lantz, J., Berger, C.: Agile model-driven engineering in mechatronic systems - an industrial case study. In: Dingel, J., Schulte, W., Ramos, I., Abrahão, S., Insfran, E. (eds.) MODELS 2014. LNCS, vol. 8767, pp. 433–449. Springer, Cham (2014). https://doi.org/10.1007/978-3-319-11653-2_27
15. Katumba, B., Knauss, E.: Agile development in automotive software development: challenges and opportunities. In: Jedlitschka, A., Kuvaja, P., Kuhrmann, M., Männistö, T., Münch, J., Raatikainen, M. (eds.) PROFES 2014. LNCS, vol. 8892, pp. 33–47. Springer, Cham (2014). https://doi.org/10.1007/978-3-319-13835-0_3

16. Hohl, P., Stupperich, M., Münch, J., Schneider, K.: Die variantenvielfalt agil managen: agile software-produktlinien im automobilsegment. In: Tagungsband - Embedded Software Engineering Kongress 2016 : 28. November bis 2. Dezember 2016, Sindelfingen, pp. 427–433 (2016)

17. Martini, A., Pareto, L., Bosch, J.: Communication factors for speed and reuse in large-scale agile software development. In: Jarzabek, S. (ed.) Proceedings of the 17th International Software Product Line Conference, p. 42. ACM, New York (2013)

18. KUGLER MAAG CIE GmbH: Agile in automotive - state of practice 2015, April 2015

19. Schwaber, K., Sutherland, J.: The Scrum Guide (2001)

20. Diebold, P., Ostberg, J.-P., Wagner, S., Zendler, U.: What do practitioners vary in using scrum? In: Lassenius, C., Dingsøyr, T., Paasivaara, M. (eds.) XP 2015. LNBIP, vol. 212, pp. 40–51. Springer, Cham (2015). https://doi.org/10.1007/978-3-319-18612-2_4

21. Schloßer, A., Schnitzler, J., Sentis, T., Richenhagen, J.: Agile processes in automotive industry – efficiency and quality in software development. In: Bargende, M., Reuss, H.C., Wiedemann, J. (eds.) 16. Internationales Stuttgarter Symposium. Proceedings, pp. 489–503. Springer, Wiesbaden (2016). https://doi.org/10.1007/978-3-658-13255-2_35

22. Valade, R.: The big projects always fail: Taking an enterprise agile. In: Agile 2008 Conference, pp. 148–153 (2008)

23. Antinyan, V., et al.: Identifying risky areas of software code in agile/lean software development: an industrial experience report. In: 2014 Software Evolution Week - IEEE Conference on Software Maintenance, Reengineering and Reverse Engineering (CSMR-WCRE), pp. 154–163 (2014)

24. Hayashi, K., Aoyama, M., Kobata, K.: A concurrent feedback development method and its application to automotive software development. In: 2015 Asia-Pacific Software Engineering Conference (APSEC), pp. 362–369 (2015)

25. Hohl, P., Münch, J., Schneider, K., Stupperich, M.: Forces that prevent agile adoption in the automotive domain. In: Abrahamsson, P., Jedlitschka, A., Nguyen Duc, A., Felderer, M., Amasaki, S., Mikkonen, T. (eds.) PROFES 2016. LNCS, vol. 10027, pp. 468–476. Springer, Cham (2016). https://doi.org/10.1007/978-3-319-49094-6_32

26. Hohl, P., Ghofrani, J., Münch, J., Stupperich, M., Schneider, K.: Searching for common ground: existing literature on automotive agile software product lines. In: Bendraou, R., Raffo, D., LiGuo, H., Maggi, F.M. (eds.) Proceedings of the 2017 International Conference on Software and System Process - ICSSP 2017, pp. 70–79. ACM Press (2017)

27. van der Linden, F.: Family evaluation framework overview & introduction, 29 August 2005

28. van der Linden, F., Schmid, K., Rommes, E.: Software Product Lines in Action. Springer, Heidelberg (2007). https://doi.org/10.1007/978-3-540-71437-8

29. Pohl, K., Böckle, G., Linden, F.: Software Product Line Engineering: Foundations, Principles, and Techniques. Springer, Heidelberg (2005). https://doi.org/10.1007/3-540-28901-1

30. Wentzel, K.D.: Software reuse—facts and myths. In: Proceedings of the 16th International Conference on Software Engineering, ICSE 1994, pp. 267–268. IEEE Computer Society Press (1994)

31. Blau, B., Hildenbrand, T.: Product line engineering in large-scale lean and agile software product development environments - towards a hybrid approach to decentral control and managed reuse. In: 2011 Sixth International Conference on Availability, Reliability and Security (ARES), pp. 404–408 (2011)
32. Black, S., Boca, P.P., Bowen, J.P., Gorman, J., Hinchey, M.: Formal versus agile: survival of the fittest. Computer **42**(9), 37–45 (2009)
33. Buckle, G., Clements, P.C., McGregor, J.D., Muthig, D., Schmid, K.: Calculating roi for software product lines. IEEE Softw. **21**(3), 23–31 (2004)
34. International Organization for Standardization: Software and systems engineering – reference model for product line engineering and management, 01 December 2015
35. Tian, K.: Adding more agility to software product line methods: a feasibility study on its customization using agile practices. Int. J. Knowl. Syst. Sci. **5**(4), 17–34 (2014)
36. Hohl, P., Stupperich, M., Münch, J., Schneider, K.: An assessment model to foster the adoption of agile software product lines in the automotive domain
37. VDA QMC Working Group 13/Automotive SIG: Automotive spice process assessment/reference model, 01 November 2017

Making Runtime Data Useful for Incident Diagnosis: An Experience Report

Florian Lautenschlager[✉] and Marcus Ciolkowski[✉] [iD]

QAware GmbH, Aschauer Str. 32, 81549 Munich, Germany
{florian.lautenschlager,marcus.ciolkowski}@qaware.de
http://www.qaware.de

Abstract. Important and critical aspects of technical debt often surface at runtime only and are difficult to measure statically. This is a particular challenge for cloud applications because of their highly distributed nature. Fortunately, mature frameworks for collecting runtime data exist but need to be integrated.

In this paper, we report an experience from a project that implements a cloud application within Kubernetes on Azure. To analyze the runtime data of this software system, we instrumented our services with Zipkin for distributed tracing; with Prometheus and Grafana for analyzing metrics; and with fluentd, Elasticsearch and Kibana for collecting, storing and exploring log files. However, project team members did not utilize these runtime data until we created a unified and simple access using a chat bot.

We argue that even though your project collects runtime data, this is not sufficient to guarantee its usage: In order to be useful, a simple, unified access to different data sources is required that should be integrated into tools that are commonly used by team members.

Keywords: DevOps · Cloud · Monitoring · Runtime quality

1 Introduction

Existing definitions and metrics of technical debt tend to focus on static properties of software artifacts, in particular on code measurement. However, many critical aspects of technical debt often surface at runtime only and are difficult to measure statically [5].

Dynamic aspects of technical debt often surface as incidents in productive software systems; that is, as defect reports (e.g., bug tickets) or runtime problems (e.g., anomalous resource consumption, or sporadic failures due to synchronization problems). Once incidents surface, they typically need to be resolved quickly. Such *incident diagnosis* has a high need for runtime data. In this paper, incident diagnosis means detecting and analyzing the root cause of incidents to identify affected components and fix the underlying defects. Such root cause analysis requires that runtime data are available (e.g., traces, log files, and metrics) and that they can be accessed for analysis.

© Springer Nature Switzerland AG 2018
M. Kuhrmann et al. (Eds.): PROFES 2018, LNCS 11271, pp. 422–430, 2018.
https://doi.org/10.1007/978-3-030-03673-7_33

Today, means for collecting many types of runtime data exist. However, doing a proper incident analysis is difficult to do with these, since a set of tools is necessary to cover different types of runtime data. In particular, since modern cloud applications are highly distributed and their components run in their own isolated containers, their runtime data need to be brought together. For example, one can use Zipkin [21] for collecting and analyzing distributed traces, Elasticsearch [7] in combination with Fluentd [9] and Kibana [8] to analyze log files and Prometheus [18] with Grafana [11] to visualize metrics. Every one of the tools has their very own specialized interfaces (e.g., query language, dashboard concepts). As a result, it is hard to combine and correlate runtime data for a target-oriented incident diagnosis [14]. Consequently, root cause analysis often takes a long time and causes high effort (e.g., everyone asks the few people who are knowledgeable).

In this paper, we present an experience from a cloud application development project where we learned that ease of use is a critical success factor for make use of runtime data for incident diagnosis: Without an acceptable ease of use, you may spend considerable effort to collect runtime data that will not be used. We report our experiences from implementing a simplified access to runtime data based on a chat bot. We believe that the approach is sufficiently generic and can be applied to other projects, regardless of the tools used to collect the runtime data.

2   Project Context

We are working on a software project that implements a cloud application within Kubernetes [13] on Azure [2]. More precisely, the project builds a platform for speech processing that includes voice hardware clients as well as the skills themselves (i.e., commands triggered by speech). The development process is loosely based on Scrum.

About 100 IT experts from four countries (Germany, France, Spain, Romania) and from different companies work in eight different teams on the software project. Five of the teams are organized according to the system architecture (see Fig. 1): The voice client (*Client-Team*) sends the voice command to the platform (*Platform-Team*), which processes the command and calls the corresponding skill (*Skills-Team*) that offers the actual functionality (e.g., reading out a cooking recipe). The software system is designed in a microservice architecture, whereby each service is executed in its own Docker [6] container in Openshift [17] (supported by a *DevOps* [3]-*Team*), which runs in the Azure environment (operated by a *Operations-Team*).

Furthermore, there are three cross-cutting teams: The *QA-Team* verifies that a new release passes all tests, fulfills data privacy terms, etc.; the *ML-Team* optimizes voice processing using machine learning approaches, and the *Product Design-Team* optimizes the usability and the design of the hardware client.

The technologies employed are diverse: The software system is realized using industry–standard open source frameworks and libraries; for example, Spring

Boot [20] in the platform services, Python [19] to realize the skills, Go [10] for operational building blocks like ETL-Jobs, Lua [15] in the API gateway and C++ [4] to build the hardware client software. In addition, there are mobile applications for Android [1] and iOS [12].

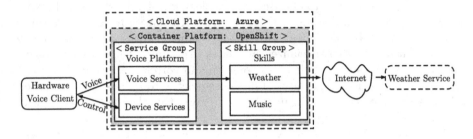

Fig. 1. Overview of the software system.

3   Problem: Root-Cause Analysis of Runtime Incidents

Obviously, developers in this project work in a distributed mode and have diverse sets of skills and expert knowledge (e.g., voice processing, machine learning, programming languages, system operation and monitoring). Therefore, there is a high need for communication, especially when different teams are necessary to understand the cause of an error at runtime.

For a given runtime incident (e.g., a bug report), the challenge is to quickly identify the root cause, at least the affected component. For example, a speech command may not provide the expected result in a specific situation. Some of the potential causes are that the microphone may have been switched off too early, that the speech recognition may have been faulty, that the command or the intent may not have been correctly identified, or there may have been a problem with a background service. As the customer's expectation with DevOps is that problems are quickly detected and corrected, root-cause analysis of incidents is time-critical. However, since many different, distributed teams are involved, it is also potentially resource-intensive, and therefore expensive. In particular, it may involve experts from different teams, as well as for technologies and environment-dependent configurations. Therefore, some form of automated support is needed.

4   Providing Runtime Data

For a root-cause analysis of incidents and runtime problems, one needs to gather runtime data showing the runtime behavior of the software system that helps understanding the issue. One critical support for root-cause analysis is, therefore, to provide sufficient runtime data.

4.1   Setting up a Tool Chain for Data Collection

We built up a tool chain to collect necessary runtime data that every single service produces: metrics (i.e., numeric values measured at regular intervals like memory usage), log events (i.e., information provided by logging) and traces (i.e., information to understand how a request was processed). Each of them is collected, stored and analyzed in a separate tool (see Fig. 2): We use Prometheus with Grafana for metrics; Fluentd, Elasticsearch and Kibana for log events; and Zipkin for distributed traces.

To be able to combine and correlate runtime data from these separate sources, the application's components need to share conventions for providing runtime data. For example, naming conventions (e.g., metric names for outgoing calls) or a common log file structure to ensure that log events are comparable across components. Furthermore, each data point needs to be enriched with appropriate information: traces and logs both share the same context (e.g. userId to identify specific users, traceId to identify a specific service call); metrics are labeled with comparable context information. In addition, all types of runtime data have a notion of time; typically, a timestamp of their creation.

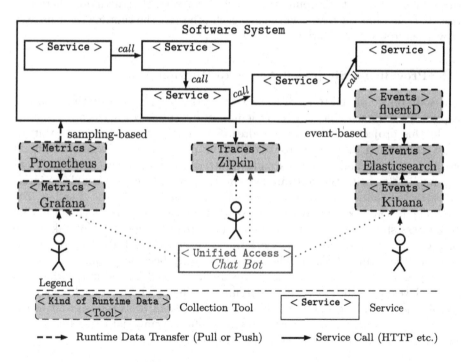

Fig. 2. Overview of the tools to collect and to analyze runtime data.

However, combining information from these separate sources is still not trivial. For example, metrics are sampling-based, while log events and traces are collected based on events. Hence, to combine metrics (sampling-based) with traces and logs (event-based), one needs to use means such as a timeline (e.g., based on proximity of time stamps) or context information (e.g., a specific service call). Analyzing incidents and problems thus requires to query all different data sources separately, knowing which key to use to find the desired information; that is, it requires knowing specific query syntaxes of the different tools and knowing which method for combining information to use in which case.

Consequently, despite of the availability of runtime data, most team members relied on asking the few available analysis experts. Thus, for nearly all incident analyses, these experts had to answer simple questions and gradually became first-level support for runtime analysis concerns. For example, if a runtime error was detected by the QA-Team, they issued a ticket with some sparse information based on their observation (e.g. what they did, the observed error message). They felt unable to provide more diagnosis information and felt unable to trace the error to a specific service, component or line of code. Therefore, each of the different teams had to analyze the ticket, ask for more detailed information from the QA-team, and they had to work together by analyzing separately their runtime data. This is a slow, time consuming and expensive process with lot of wasted effort, since most teams would do the same analysis steps and come to the conclusion that their component worked correctly. Furthermore, there is a risk that the different teams will blame each other for the runtime error instead of working towards a solution.

4.2 Providing a Simplified Access to Runtime Data

The solution we picked to lower the access barrier to become a runtime analysis expert by offering simple access to the important and necessary runtime data.

In this project, all teams were already using the same chat tool (Mattermost [16], see Fig. 3), for example to talk about problems, new features or general project news. We had already extended Mattermost with a chat bot to facilitate communication with the software system; that is, a developer is able to interact with the software system by addressing text messages to the chat bot. For example, he can ask for a joke or the weather forecast (Fig. 3) instead of having to address speech commands through a microphone. The chat bot takes care of the authentication and message formats (e.g., special HTTP headers) and provides the returned result. The chat bot quickly became a standard tool for developers of the different teams; for example, for testing the integration of a newly developed skill in the test environment. That's why it seemed obvious to enable the chat bot to interact with our runtime data tools too, so that in the case of an error, the chat bot can provide useful runtime data (see Fig. 4). We enhanced the chat bot with several integrations:

1. **Traces in Zipkin:** For every interaction with the software system that fails at runtime, the chat bot provides the error message as well as a link that points to Zipkin and shows the trace of the issued request using the traceId. This allows one quickly to see how the request was processed and in which service or component the error occurred.

Fig. 3. The chat bot is a textual interface to interact with the software system.

2. **Log Events in Kibana:** The chat bot links to the log events for the given request. As mentioned above, log events and traces share the same context. Hence, we can use the `traceId` of the trace to define the context (i.e., the request) to correlate log events. Therefore, the link points to Kibana that shows the log events of all involved services ordered by time that share the same `traceId`.

3. **Metrics in Prometheus:** It is not easy to correlate a single request with metrics, due to the different collection strategies (event-based vs. sampling-based). However, since metrics are still an important source of runtime data, we also integrated Prometheus into the chat bot. Instead of showing the metrics for a specific request, one can ask the chat bot for the overall status of the software system; for example, which services are up and running, whether the end-to-end tests run successfully, etc.

We have observed that this simplified access to the runtime data of the software system has been consistently accepted by all teams. As a result, it leads to numerous improvements, for example

– **Clear tickets:** Especially the QA-team is now able to provide the unique context of a request in incident tickets, often already identifying which component is responsible for a runtime error and which team is assigned to the ticket. This also facilitates in-depth analysis by the teams, since the ticket already provides meaningful context information.

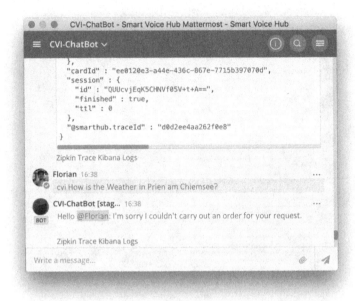

Fig. 4. In case of an error, the chat bot provides two links (to Zipkin and Kibana) that serve as entry points for the runtime data analysis.

- **More efficient cross-team communication:** Due to the possibility to search for errors independently, the teams no longer have to communicate so intensively with each other. The context is also used for clear and more efficient communication between the teams, in cases where discussion is still necessary.
- **Higher motivation understanding the behavior:** The different team members show an increased willingness to solve their problems independently. This reduces the workload for the analysis experts, who are able to concentrate on their other roles.
- **Higher attention to runtime characteristics:** Software is an intangible good. Therefore, it is difficult to create a suitable and understandable representation of it. Metrics, log events and traces provide a good representation of runtime aspects of the software system. This chat bot approach enables non-analysis experts to understand the runtime behavior of the software system and its effects and increases their awareness to observe runtime behavior.

5   Discussion and Conclusions

We found out that utilizing runtime data (such as data from a monitoring tool chain) requires a simplified and easy-to-use means of access in order to be usable in practice.

We implemented a chat bot to integrate runtime data from different sources into the usual communication of the teams, which was already based on a chat tool. We believe that such an approach can be implemented in many typical project contexts: We used standard tools for cloud applications to collect runtime data, and chat tools are common in many software development projects.

The feedback within the project is outreaching across the teams involved so far, and now spread to the operations team, who also wants to integrate the concepts into their custom first-level support application.

Integrating access of runtime diagnosis data into the chat bot improves and reduces the cross-team communication at the same time (e.g., between backend and frontend developers, testers) by providing a unique, meaningful context (e.g., the `traceId` of an erroneous request) that can be used by all teams for further detailed analysis. For example, it has become a standard practice in the project that incident/bug ticket issuer always provide the `traceId`, with which the developers can easily understand the software system's behavior in terms of logs and traces. This has improved ticket quality as well as reduced effort for analysis. In result, the costs for understanding runtime incidents are decreasing.

Further, providing a simple form of access has improved everyone's skills in analyzing as well as their awareness of existing runtime data: For example, every team member is now able to correlate and combine runtime data, which used to be restricted to a few experts in query syntax of the tools.

In future, we plan to enhance the chat bot further. One idea is that the chat bot might also provide a link to directly create a ticket for a discovered runtime incident (instead of just providing information required to write a ticket). The chat bot may pre-fill the ticket with all the necessary runtime data, which in result leads to less effort for creating tickets and to a higher standardization and quality of incident/bug tickets. Another idea is to integrate the runtime data with the first-level support tool (i.e., the support that interacts with customers directly), so that the first-level support is able to provide detailed information for incident analysis. For example, the chat bot may collect information based on a customer's unique identifier instead of an approximate description of observed failure symptoms only.

Acknowledgments. We thank Robert Hoffmann from Deutsche Telekom for his support.

References

1. Android. https://www.android.com/. Accessed 26 July 2018
2. Azure. https://azure.microsoft.com/de-de/. Accessed 26 July 2018
3. Bass, L., Weber, I., Zhu, L.: DevOps: A Software Architect's Perspective. Addison-Wesley Professional, Boston (2015)
4. C++. https://isocpp.org/. Accessed 26 July 2018
5. Ciolkowski, M., Guzmán, L., Trendowicz, A., Vollmer, A.M.: Challenges in assessing technical debt based on dynamic runtime data, pp. 442–445, Prague, August 2018. https://doi.org/10.1109/SEAA.2018.00078

6. Docker. https://www.docker.com/. Accessed 26 July 2018
7. Elastic, Inc.: Elasticsearch. https://www.elastic.co/de/products/elasticsearch/. Accessed 26 July 2018
8. Elastic, Inc.: Kibana. https://www.elastic.co/de/products/kibana/. Accessed 26 July 2018
9. Fluentd. https://www.fluentd.org/. Accessed 26 July 2018
10. Go. https://golang.org/. Accessed 26 July 2018
11. Grafana. https://grafana.com/. Accessed 26 July 2018
12. iOS. https://www.apple.com/de/ios/. Accessed 26 July 2018
13. Kubernetes. https://kubernetes.io/. Accessed 26 July 2018
14. Lautenschlager, F., Philippsen, M., Kumlehn, A., Adersberger, J.: Chronix: long term storage and retrieval technology for anomaly detection in operational data. In: Proceedings of the 15th USENIX Conference on File and Storage Technologies (FAST 2017), pp. 229–242 (2017)
15. Lua. https://www.lua.org/. Accessed 26 July 2018
16. Mattermost. https://mattermost.com/. Accessed 26 July 2018
17. Openshift. https://www.openshift.com/. Accessed 26 July 2018
18. Prometheus. http://prometheus.io/. Accessed 26 July 2018
19. Python. https://www.python.org/. Accessed 26 July 2018
20. Spring Boot. https://spring.io/projects/spring-boot/. Accessed 26 July 2018
21. Zipkin. https://zipkin.io/. Accessed 26 July 2018

Workshop: HELENA 2018

3rd Workshop on Hybrid Development Approaches in Software System Development

Paolo Tell[1]([⊠]), Stephen MacDonell[2], and Sherlock A. Licorish[3]

[1] IT University of Copenhagen, Copenhagen, Denmark
pate@itu.dk
[2] Auckland University of Technology, Auckland, New Zealand
stephen.macdonell@aut.ac.nz
[3] University of Otago, Dunedin, New Zealand
sherlock.licorish@otago.ac.nz

Abstract. Evidence shows that software development methods, frameworks, and even practices are seldom applied in companies by following the book. Combinations of different methodologies into home-grown processes are being constantly uncovered. Nonetheless, an academic understanding and investigation of this phenomenon is very limited. In 2016, the HELENA initiative was launched to research hybrid development approaches in software system development. This paper introduces the 3rd HELENA workshop and provides a detailed description of the instrument used and the available data sets.

1 Introduction

A software process is the game plan to organize project teams and run projects. Even though a multitude of development methods and frameworks have been proposed over the years, the daunting statement that "there is no silver bullet" [3] serving all possible setups still holds strong. Given the context of a company, project, or team, the selection of the appropriate development approach or the creation of an ad-hoc combination is still a challenge. Recent research as well as experience from practice shows companies utilizing different development approaches to assemble the best-fitting approach for the respective company.

After West identified in 2011 [10] the presence of what he labelled water-scrum-fall—the ad-hoc combination of different software process philosophies into home-grown instances to fit the different organizational needs of a company—several researchers investigated this phenomenon. In 2015, a systematic review to reveal the current state of practice in software process use revealed a considerable imbalance between the research understanding of practice and practice itself [9]. Consequently, the HELENA initiative was born.

In the remainder of this paper we describe in more details the HELENA project (Sect. 2) and the third instance of the yearly HELENA workshop (Sect. 3). Section 4 concludes this paper by providing a summary of future activities.

M. Kuhrmann et al. (Eds.): PROFES 2018, LNCS 11271, pp. 433–440, 2018.
https://doi.org/10.1007/978-3-030-03673-7_34

2   The HELENA Study

HELENA is an international exploratory multistage survey-based study on the use of "**H**ybrid d**E**ve**L**opm**EN**t **A**pproaches in software systems development". In [7], we defined *hybrid software development approaches* as any combination of agile and traditional (plan-driven or rich) approaches that an organizational unit adopts and customizes to its own context needs (e.g., application domain, culture, processes, project, organizational structure, techniques, technologies, and other factors).

The Team and its Organization

After three years, the HELENA project now involves about 80 researchers from (currently) 25 countries. Besides the member role, the structure of the project comprises a core group tasked with ensuring the progression of activities, and a main representative for each of the 25 countries responsible for maximising local coordination. The project aims to investigate the current state of practice in software and systems development; in particular: which development approaches (traditional, agile, main-stream, or home-grown) are used in practice and how they are combined, how such combinations were developed over time, as well as if and how standards (e.g., safety standards) affect the development process as such and the methods applied. With this information, we aim to push forward systematic process design and improvement activities to allow for more efficient and reduced-overhead development approaches.

Table 1. Detailed overview of the HELENA instrument structure. ([**n**]: number of available options; **FT**: free text; **SC**: single choice, **MC**: multiple choice; **RT**: rating; **LIex**: Likert scale including "don't know" option.

Additional information on the options provided for each question including details on the Likert scales and rating variables are publicly available at https://goo.gl/yoA1m4)

Page	Questions	Code	Type
1	*Introduction*	I001	
2..14	*Main questionnaire (see Table 2)*		
15	• Do you have any further comments or issues not addressed so far?	C001	FT
	• If you want to be informed about the study's outcomes and possible future iterations (with in-depth interviews), please leave your e-mail address here:	C002	FT
	• In future iterations, we plan to complement this survey with in-depth interviews. Would you be willing to participate in these interviews?	C003	SC[2]
	• Have you already participated in stage 1 of the HELENA survey?	C004	SC[2]
	• Have you filled in the questionnaire more than once (i.e., for more than one project/product)?	C005	SC[2]
	• How did you learn about this survey/how were you contacted?	C008	SC[5]+FT
16	• For which company/organization do you work?	C006	FT
	• Are we allowed to name your company in the list of participants?	C007	SC[3]+FT
17	*Closing*	I004	

Table 2. Detailed overview of the HELENA instrument questions and variables. ([**n**]: number of available options; **FT**: free text; **SC**: single choice, **MC**: multiple choice; **RT**: rating; **LIex**: Likert scale including "don't know" option.
Additional information on the options provided for each question including details on the Likert scales and rating variables are publicly available at https://goo.gl/yoA1m4)

Page	Questions	Code	Type
2	• What is your companys size in equivalent full-time employees (FTEs)?	D001	SC[5]
	• What is the main business area of your company?	D002	MC[7]+FT
3	• Please describe the project or product your answer is related to in a few words (less than 100), or provide an acronym.	D008	FT
	• What is the size of the project or product to which your answer is related?	D009	SC[5]
	• Is the project or product your answer refers to carried out in a (globally) distributed manner?	D003	SC[4]
	• In which country are you personally located?	D004	SC[241]
	• What is the major role you have in this project or product?	D007	SC[11]+FT
	• How many years of experience do you have in software and systems development?	D010	SC[5]
4	• What is the target application domain of the project or product your answer is related?	D005	MC[19]+FT
	• In the project or product you refer to, a software failure conceivably can: <criticality>	D006	MC[9]+FT
5	• Does your company define a company-wide standard process for software and system development?	PU01	SC[3]
	• How was your project-specific development approach defined?	PU08	SC[6]+FT
	• Do you intentionally deviate from defined policies?	PU11	SC[2]+FT
6	•Which of the following frameworks and methods do you use?	PU09	RT[24]
	• Do you use further frameworks and methods?	PU14	FT
7	• Which of the following practices do you use?	PU10	RT[36]
	• Do you use further practices?	PU15	FT
8	• Do you combine different development approaches in the development of one project or product?	PU04	SC[2]
9	• For the following standard activities in the project or product development, please indicate to which degree you carry out these activities in a more traditional or more agile manner.	PU05	LIex[11]
10	• How were the combinations of development frameworks, methods, and practices in your company developed?	PU07	MC[3]+FT
	• What are the overall goals that you aim to address with your selection and combination of development approaches?	PU12	MC[18]
	• Is there a further/other motivation to combine the different development frameworks, methods, and practices?	PU06	FT
11	• To what degree did the combination of approaches help you to achieve your goals?	PU13	RT[18]
12	• Do you implement external standards in your company?	PS01	SC[2]+FT
13	• Why have you implemented the aforementioned standards?	PS02	MC[3]+FT
	• How is the compliance of the development process assessed?	PS03	MC[5]+FT
	• Does agility challenge the implementation of the standards you have to apply?	PS04	SC[2]+FT
	• Is the project or product your answer relates to also subject to certification?	PS05	SC[2]+FT
14	• Based on your personal experience, please rate the following statements:	EX01	LIex[8]
	• Based on your personal experience, please specify any problems that have arisen regarding your current process and your current application domain.	EX02	FT

The Data Collection Instrument

To achieve these goals the project is designed to collect data through a survey, which has been refined over several iterations. After being successfully tested within Europe in project stage one [7], the HELENA project is reaching the end of stage two, during which the survey has been conducted globally in more than 25 countries. A third and final stage will conclude the project. In stage three, focus groups will perform in depth research on community-defined topics of interest based on the results of stage two. The form and coverage of the questionnaire that has been used in stage two can be seen in Tables 1 and 2. These tables not only show the question and answer types, but also the arrangement of questions into questionnaire pages, which is an important piece of information when it comes to understanding the different data sets that have been created for data analysis. These are discussed in the remainder of this section together with a selection of descriptive results.

The Data Sets
The survey instrument was accepting responses between May and November 2017. The survey was promoted through personal contacts of the 75 participating researchers, through posters at conferences, and by posts to mailing lists, social media channels (Twitter, Xing, LinkedIn), professional networks and websites (ResearchGate and researchers (institution) home pages).

In total, 1467 data points were collected, of which 691 are complete. As a first step, given the discrepancy between the two sets, the data was analyzed by two members of the core team to investigate the level of completeness, which yielded the identification of a third set that was deemed complete enough to pursue the majority of the investigations planned. The constraints applied during this process were mainly based around the presence of core questions (see Table 2):

PU09: used frameworks and methods,
PU10: used practices,
PU04: self-awareness regarding the use of hybrid approaches, and
PU05: self-assessment of philosophies followed with respect to the general project-related activities listed in the Guide to the SWEBoK [1].

Following this rationale and to avoid bias, rather then applying filters to the data set on the presence of answers—as participants were given the option to skip questions—we identified page #9 of the questionnaire as the marker that had to be reached for a data point to be accepted to the third data set. This set comprises the data points that are considered usable for the majority of the investigations that the HELENA project planned to research, for the main objective is eventually to explore hybrid development approaches in software system development. Therefore, as visually represented in Fig. 1, members of the HELENA team were given access to three data sets[1]:

Full: comprising 1467 data points. Members were discouraged from using this set.

---

[1] Only the core team has access to the survey instrument given that page #16 contained confidential information that the instrument tool collected separately.

Suggested: comprising 732 data points[2] selected according to the process described above.

Completed: comprising 691 data points of participants that answered the questionnaire in its entirety.

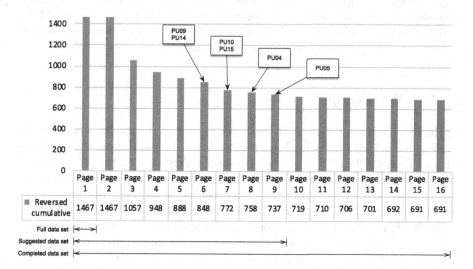

Fig. 1. Overview of response rate per page detailing the size of the three data sets.

Selected Results from the Suggested Dataset

The remainder of this section presents some selected results from the *Suggested dataset* to showcase the richness of the information collected through the survey.

D001 - **Company size** (n = 732) Five categories were provided to choose from: *micro* (<10 employees) (11.6%), *small* (11–50 employees) (13.0%), *medium* (51–250 employees) (24.9%), *large* (251–2499 employees) (27.0%), *very large* (>2500 employees) (23.1%). Among the respondents, 0.4% did not answer this question. An interesting aspect about this distribution lies in the fact that, after merging the micro and small categories, the groups become extremely balanced in size.

D009 - **Product/Project size** (n = 732) Again five categories were provided: *very small* (<2 person weeks) (2.2%), *Small* (2 person weeks - 2 person months) (3.8%), *medium* (2 person months - 6 person months) (15.0%), *large* (6 person months - 1 person year) (18.7%), *very large* (>1 person year) (60.2%). All respondents answered.

D010 - **Experience** (n = 732) Among the respondents, the majority reported more than 10 years of experience (59.8%). Following, 18.3% reported 6–10 years experience, 14.1% between 3 and 5 years, 5.1% 1–2 years, and only 2.7% stated less then one year.

---

[2] Five data points were additionally dropped due to the instrument marking such entries as inconsistent.

D003 - **Distribution** (n = 732) Given the significant implications, an interesting aspect of software system development regards whether teams are physically co-located. Respondents were asked to describe the level of distribution of their product/project. Also for this variable, the distribution appears to provide good sample sizes. In particular, of the products/projects: 37.6% are *co-located*, 24.6% are *distributed nationally (within the same country)*, 11.9% are *distributed regionally (within the same continent)*, and 25.8% are *globally distributed*. One respondent (0.1%) did not answer.

3   The Workshop

Continuing along the tradition of yearly meetings and the community work initiated at ICSSP 2016 (Austin, Texas), ICSSP 2017 (1st workshop, Paris, France [8]), and Profes 2017 (2nd workshop, Innsbruck, Austria [6]), the 3rd HELENA workshop focuses on discussing results from Stage 2 of the HELENA project.

In this workshop, we aim to bring together all (academic) contributors and further interested people to: (i) report the current state and (tentative) outcomes of the HELENA survey (from a global and regional perspective); (ii) develop a work program and define next steps within the whole community; and, (iii) build working groups to research on selected (sub-)topics of interest.

Workshop Organization
The 3rd HELENA workshop is a 1-day workshop aimed at bringing together all members of the HELENA project to network and work together around selected topics. An overview of the schedule is provided in Table 3. We will start by providing an overview of the current state of the project including the main objectives that have been achieved and chief results that have been found. Ample space will then be given to the presentation of submitted articles and reports from ongoing activities. In this regard, two pieces of work have been accepted to the workshop:

1. Using Institutional Theory as a lens, the author models the tension between traditional software engineering and agile software development of today's software engineering, allowing a better understanding of how and why hybridisation comes about in software organisations. The paper provides an ideal ground for an engaged discussion at the workshop. [2]
2. A second paper reports on the potential relationship between institutional goals and the adoption of certain software development methods in German organisations. Ultimately, it finds that no such relationships exist at a broad level—the most often cited goals are common irrespective of methods used. The paper succeeds in presenting open possibilities for strengthening the analysis, and the investigation relating criticality of the product with the level of agility presented in the paper represents indeed an interesting discussion topic for the workshop. [4]

The second segment of the event will focus on the presentation of major topics that have been identified through the project and that will lead to further

Table 3. Overview of the workshop topics and schedule

Duration	Topic
15'	Introduction (organizers)
15'	HELENA: report of the current state from a global perspective
40'	Presentation of submitted articles (20' per presentation)
60'	Reports from ongoing initiatives (10' to 20' per presentation)
Break	
10'	Presentation of major topics under investigation
10'	Discussion on further topics that should be considered for inclusion
90'	Working groups on major topics and newly created ones (if any)
60'	Plenary session based on outcomes from working groups
Break	
60'	Presentation and discussion of the foci for the third phase of HELENA
30'	Refinement of the HELENA Agenda and next steps
15'	Closing session

endeavours. Active sessions will be run to critically scrutinize such topics and, if relevant, identify new ones. The segment will close with a plenary session to consolidate the outcomes. Finally, the third segment will revolve around the discussion and refinement of the next steps of the HELENA project—chiefly Stage three.

4 Conclusion and Future Work

Over a small timeframe, the work conducted by the HELENA community has managed to provide significant evidence highlighting the importance of this topic. Several pieces of work have already been published in highly relevant venues (e.g., Profes [9], ICSSP [7], IEEE Software [5]). Insofar, we have shown that hybrid development approaches in software system development are a reality that affect companies regardless of size and industry sector. We have also, in several instances, characterized the evidence based on different regions.

Current activities within the HELENA community are investigating, inter alia, (i) the impact of the strategies used to devise hybrid development approaches on the ability to achieve set goals, and (ii) the alignment of software and system development frameworks, methods, and practices taught in higher education with those used in industry. Through more thorough and rigorous analysis of the large collections of data, we are now uncovering an increasing number of results that not only constantly strengthen past results, but allow us to push forward systematic process design and improvement activities geared towards more efficient and reduced-overhead development approaches.

Acknowledgments. We want to thank Profes 2018 organization board for providing us with the opportunity to hold the third HELENA workshop in conjunction with Profes 2018. We look forward to continuing such fruitful collaboration with the Profes community.

References

1. Bourque, P., Fairley, R.E.: Guide to the Software Engineering Body of Knowledge (SWEBOK(R)): Version 3.0. IEEE Computer Society Press, Washington, D.C. (2014)
2. Doležel, M.: Possibilities of applying institutional theory in the study of hybrid software development concepts and practices. In: Kuhrmann, M., et al. (eds.) PROFES 2018. LNCS, vol. 11271, pp. 441–448. Springer, Cham (2018)
3. Fraser, S., Mancl, D.: No silver bullet: software engineering reloaded. IEEE Softw. **25**(1), 91–94 (2008). https://doi.org/10.1109/MS.2008.14
4. Klünder, J., et al.: Towards Understanding the Motivation of German Organizations to Apply Certain Software Development Methods. In: Kuhrmann, M., et al. (eds.) PROFES 2018. LNCS, vol. 11271, pp. 449–456. Springer, Cham (2018)
5. Kuhrmann, M., et al.: Hybrid software development approaches in practice: a European perspective. IEEE Softw., 1 (2018). https://doi.org/10.1109/MS.2018.110161245
6. Kuhrmann, M., Diebold, P., MacDonell, S., Münch, J.: 2nd workshop on hybrid development approaches in software systems development. In: Felderer, M., Méndez Fernández, D., Turhan, B., Kalinowski, M., Sarro, F., Winkler, D. (eds.) PROFES 2017. LNCS, vol. 10611, pp. 397–403. Springer, Cham (2017). https://doi.org/10.1007/978-3-319-69926-4_28
7. Kuhrmann, M., et al.: Hybrid software and system development in practice: waterfall, scrum, and beyond. In: Proceedings of the 2017 International Conference on Software and System Process, ICSSP 2017, pp. 30–39. ACM, New York (2017). https://doi.org/10.1145/3084100.3084104, http://doi.acm.org/10.1145/3084100.3084104
8. Kuhrmann, M., Münch, J., Tell, P., Diebold, P.: Summary of the 1st international workshop on hybrid development approaches in software systems development. ACM SIGSOFT Softw. Eng. Notes **42**(4), 18–20 (2018)
9. Theocharis, G., Kuhrmann, M., Münch, J., Diebold, P.: Is *Water-Scrum-Fall* reality? On the use of agile and traditional development practices. In: Abrahamsson, P., Corral, L., Oivo, M., Russo, B. (eds.) PROFES 2015. LNCS, vol. 9459, pp. 149–166. Springer, Cham (2015). https://doi.org/10.1007/978-3-319-26844-6_11
10. West, D., Gilpin, M., Grant, T., Anderson, A.: Water-scrum-fall is the reality of agile for most organizations today. Forrester Research, Cambridge (2011)

Possibilities of Applying Institutional Theory in the Study of Hybrid Software Development Concepts and Practices

Michal Doležel(✉) (iD)

University of Economics, Prague, W. Churchill Sq. 4, 130 67,
Prague, Czech Republic
michal.dolezel@vse.cz

Abstract. Nowadays, hybrid software development approaches represent an important trend. By creatively combining various software development methods and techniques, companies seek to benefit from an increased flexibility in their software-intensive domains. This conceptual paper has two goals. First, it attempts to extend the concept of hybridity beyond the visible aspects of software development. Second, it introduces the concept of "institutional logic" as a cornerstone adopted from institutional theory. I propose to use this theory as a lens to improve our understanding of the waterfall/agile type of hybridity, i.e. when the logic of Traditional Software Engineering and the logic of Agile Software Development are concurrently adopted in an organization. Also, a relation between institutional logics and organizational cultures is proposed. The seeds of theory presented in this paper lead to a further theory building effort that will hopefully result in a better characterization of adoption motives and strategies related to hybrid software development.

Keywords: Institutional theory · New institutionalism · Institutional logic
Development methods · Organizational culture · Agile culture
Theory building

1 Introduction

"Culture eats strategy for breakfast" [1] is a famous, widely used phrase originated by Peter Drucker. The wisdom behind the phrase, in essence, teaches managers to maintain the congruence between material (or visible) and non-material (or invisible) aspects related to professional activities within their organizations. Research and practice in the area of Software Engineering (SE) originally leaned toward the former. By contrast, from the inception of agile methods by a group of "organizational anarchists" [2], a central position in software development has been given to people [3, 4]. Similarly, a number of industry experts have recognized the importance of resolving "soft" issues in order to achieve "true agility". Mainly thanks to this belief, it is not uncommon to hear anecdotal arguments similar to the following one. "To be successful, we need to start thinking about Agile as a culture and not as a product or family of processes" [5]. Similarly, the difference between "Doing Agile" and "Being Agile" [6, 7] is frequently brought to discussion by consultants who claim the latter as a way to magically "unlock

© Springer Nature Switzerland AG 2018
M. Kuhrmann et al. (Eds.): PROFES 2018, LNCS 11271, pp. 441–448, 2018.
https://doi.org/10.1007/978-3-030-03673-7_35

200–300%" [8] productivity improvement. Given that there has been little scientific evidence that would support such claims, it appears imperative to explore the power of the non-material aspects (especially of culture) in a deeper manner.

First and foremost, a critically minded researcher may wonder: What sort of culture is "agile culture", really [9]? Can be such cultures easily replicated between organizations [7]? And how to integrate this culture- or mindset-centric view with engineering people's understandable tendencies to focus on visible practices and artifacts [6]? To answer some of these questions, researchers have previously explored the cultural implications of Agile software development. Specifically, they have connected our understanding of agility with the concept of organizational culture presented as an iceberg with both visible and invisible layers [6, 9].

Moving forward, their ideas could be extended to the arena of hybrid software development. For the purpose of this paper, *hybrid software development* is used as an umbrella term to label diverse organizational approaches (e.g. methods, techniques, and processes) that combine elements of multiple software development logics. Clearly, hybrid software development is increasingly popular [10]. Although there are many possible combinations of software development methods, one of them seems to be of particular importance; that is Water-Scrum-Fall. While previous research provides certain important insights into this particular trend [10], it says relatively little about the effects of Water-Scrum-Fall on the deeper (i.e. invisible) levels of organizational culture's iceberg. In other words, we do not know whether the values and ideals exemplified in the Agile manifesto *suffer* or *thrive* in real software organizations who follow the path of hybrid software development. Interestingly, we know that the mere execution of certain organizational practices may result in a significant change in organizational culture [11]. It thus appears reasonable to take a closer look on the potential impact of invisible elements of organizational culture. So, my first intention with this paper is to *extend the concept of hybridity beyond the visible software development elements of organizational cultures*, i.e. to "dive under the surface" [6].

However, what would be still missing after this extension is a *connection between the micro and macro levels*, i.e. between organizational cultures and social forces that shape them (cf. [12]). The latter may be represented, for example, by the activities of consultants or professional associations acting in a given (macro) organizational field. In essence, to establish such a link means to better understand the adoption processes related to ideas and ideals adopted by particular organizations, including in such ideas and ideals also software development methods. Hence, my second intention with this paper is to propose a conceptual grounding which can help to *problematize the connection between the micro and macro organizational worlds*. Based on my interest in organizational theory, which has been driven by my previous IT management experience, I introduce here a central concept from *new institutional theory*. Such an aim builds on a general premise that we need more theory-driven work that would ground the basic software development concepts [13, 14].

This conceptual paper proceeds as follows. Section 2 briefly reviews the existing body of knowledge related to (neo) institutionalism. Section 3 introduces a conceptual framework proposed for further elaboration. Finally, Sect. 4 concludes the paper.

2   Applying Institutional Theory in Software Engineering

(New) institutional theory is a broad area of research spanning sociology and management studies. Rather than a coherent and "neat" theory, it should be viewed as a loosely coupled body of knowledge, which has been accumulated in several distinct streams of research [15, 16]. The conceptual broadness causes that institutional research may appear somewhat "messy" and over-complicated from the view of scholars from other disciplines. Interestingly, institutional concepts have been applied in areas as diverse as the rebirth of French cuisine that resulted in French chefs' identity shift [17], or U.S. drug court negotiations interpreted from the perspective of different actors working in that environment [18]. In the area of computing, previous work involving institutional theory was typically conducted within the information systems discipline. However, very little of these contributions deal specifically with software development activities and processes (cf. [19]), or with the influence of agile methods on the software engineering profession.

A notable exception is the work [20], where the authors identified three unique logics (i.e. entrepreneurial, consulting profession, managerialist). Highlighting the context-rooted differences between these logics, their work offers an interesting explanation for the observed diversity in agile adoption patterns across various fields and company types (e.g., a small social-media start-up vs. a consulting company). However, rather than being software process-centric, their perspective highlights the importance of the industrial context in which a particular company operates.

Given the purpose stated above, my starting position in this paper is different. Below I use the hybridity of software development methods as a central concept, which I view as resulting from two distinct institutional logics related to two distinct segments of the software engineering profession (i.e. Traditional Software Engineering and Agile Software Development). While both the theory-focused positions (i.e. their and mine) are quite divergent, they are not necessarily in conflict. Note that one possible use of theories is to provide a lens for understanding the phenomena under interest from different theoretical perspectives [21]. Based on the above introduction, my starting argument is that institutional theory offers a promising repertoire of analytical tools applicable in the SE domain, especially when one is interested in a people-centered perspective that would connect micro and macro levels of analysis. Space constrains do not allow to present a comprehensive literature review here. Hence, to present only some seeds of theory, I take below a very pragmatic perspective.

The central element of institutional research is represented by **institutions**, which are diverse societal and professional entities (mostly virtual in their nature) such as family, religion, economy or peer groups. Institutions are not the same as organizations. The former can be simply defined as "the rules of the game in a society" or community, or more formally, as "humanly devised constraints that shape human interaction" [22]. Organizations, by contrast, are formalized entities officially represented by their administrators, who direct them towards a goal (e.g., profit generation in case of business organizations). To give an example: education is an institution, whereas a concrete university is an organization.

Institutional logics are defined by sociologists as "the socially constructed, historical patterns of material practices, assumptions, values, beliefs, and rules by which individuals produce and reproduce their material subsistence, organize time and space, and provide meaning to their social reality" [16]. An illustrative example follows. If we take *national economy* as an example of institution, a common institutional logic in the West is capitalism. In other parts of the world, however, the prevailing institutional logic may be different, for example Communism. Interestingly, in some institutional orders, two or more logics may be present. For example, in the first few years after removal of the Iron Curtain, the ex-Communist countries in Central Europe certainly experienced both the mentioned (conflicting) logics.

Generally speaking, researchers who are already familiar with the concept of organizational culture [23] may argue that institutional logics seem to be just old wine in new bottles. To be clear, there is definitely some overlap between the two concepts. However, this overlap should be rather perceived as an opportunity than as a deficiency [24]. As already discussed, organizational cultures can be seen and interpreted as patterns of both behavior and meaning [23]. Similarly, a "key assumption of an institutional logics perspective is that each of the institutional orders in society has both material and... [non-material] characteristics" [16]. Hence, it is crucial to consider that both material *and* non-material aspects of software development activities in organizations are important for our understanding of the practice of software engineering. By contrast, software processes, as previously conceptualized in SE research, *cover only the material part of both organizational culture and institutional logic concepts* [6].

3 Proposed Conceptual Framework

The central assumption articulated in this paper is that the practice of software engineering can be conceptualized as a professional institution that codifies two core institutional logics: (i) the logic of Traditional Software Engineering (TSE) and (ii) the logic of Agile Software Development (ASD).

3.1 The Logic of Traditional Software Engineering

In line with Boehm and Turner [25], and with relevant research in computing history [26], I trace the conceptual foundations of the logic of Traditional Software Engineering to the period of "disciplining" software development activities in the United States during 1970s. Resulting in software development standards such as MIL-STD-1679, DOD-STD-2167 and MIL-STD-498, the military efforts of that period effectively transformed the area of military software development from "black magic" and "art form" into an engineering discipline [26]. This process has had important consequences. Not only that such transformation fulfilled the expectations of army officials; it also delineated the key paradigmatic values of software engineering as an academic discipline studied and researched at higher education institutions [25].

The logic of Traditional Software Engineering can be characterized as rooted primarily in rigorous discipline and engineering values. Leaving aside other important characteristics, I propose the upfront planning and production of documentation as key activities satisfying the desire of independent control from outside [26]. Organizationally, the logic of Traditional Software Engineering has been underpinned by the values of scientific management of F.W. Taylor (i.e. Taylorism).

3.2   The Logic of Agile Software Development

In sociological terms, the advent of Agile manifesto can be seen as emergence of an identity movement. "Identity movements arise when activists construct institutional gaps by showing how the existing logic cannot be an effective guide for action" [17]. In reading the Agile manifesto, such creating of gaps is quite obvious, for example, from the diction "*We are uncovering better ways of developing software*". In a similar vein, by introducing a new terminology for existing concepts (e.g., "user stories" instead of requirements, "sprints" instead of iterations etc. [14]), SCRUM (an agile framework) clearly distances itself from the underpinning logic of Traditional Software Engineering.

The logic of Agile Software Development can be characterized as rooted in humanism and creativity. The philosophy of engineering has been replaced by the philosophy of craftsmanship ([5], see also http://manifesto.softwarecraftsmanship.org/). Organizationally, the logic stems from the ideas of flat and networked organizations.

3.3   The Adoption of Hybrid Methods as a Reaction to Conflicting Logics

I offer the following conceptual framework (Fig. 1) to briefly discuss few theses. The two institutional logics portrayed can be viewed as macro forces active on the level of software engineering profession. In line with [15] I see them as "macro-level meaning structures that become embedded in local practice through a process of translation". *Translation*, is, in turn, "a process of adapting, adjusting or interpreting institutional models and practices to fit local needs and circumstances" (ibid.). Depending on a particular organizational reality, the local needs and circumstances may be related either to whole organization, or to a department, a team (i.e. an entity). For the sake of simplicity, this fact is not explicitly showed in Fig. 1 (but see [19] with regard to the differentiation).

I believe that our increased understanding of the nature of the translation process is key for a better understanding of adoption motives that commonly drive hybridization. A crucial idea is that translation does happen with a varying quality. This quality largely depends on the particular level of abstraction associated with a concept, and also on the quality of communication channels used [27]. In general, simple ideas, such as concrete XP or SCRUM practices, translate easily. By contrast, complex ideas, such as the elements of the "agile culture" [7], may experience a sort of communication noise (see the red "distortion" marks in Fig. 1) that affects the translation process. Such a noise may be one reason for unintended hybridization. Preferably, however, logics are translated with no or minimal distortion when the destination context is "fitting". This fit could be defined in terms of the level of mutual "ideological compatibility" between the logic and destination context (Fig. 1, I and III). This understanding explains an initial hostility towards agile methods in regulated environments (I), and, by contrast, a natural affinity towards agile methods in open organizational cultures (III) [7].

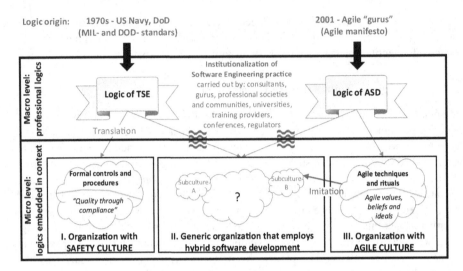

Fig. 1. Institutional logics and their embedding in organizational cultures

The spread of hybrid software development methods may be seen as a result of the influence of two conflicting macro SE logics, of which the latter has recently increased in popularity. Here, the logics' conflict should not be understood negatively; it is reasonable to expect that some companies are very happy with their hybridized processes. On the other hand, some adoption strategies may, perhaps, outgrow into unproductive organizational behaviors (e.g., when adoption is *forced* by the management [11]). In theory, there are very diverse scenarios that would principally deserve discussion here. For example, is the organization/its entity unsuccessfully trying to replace the previous logic (unintended hybridization), or rather to carefully combine both the logics (intended hybridization)? Has a significant level of consensus regarding the adoption goals been reached across the organization? If not, is this a forced adoption from the top, a rebellious adoption from the bottom, or a middle management experiment? And so on.

Also, there may be a special form of translation, which is called *Imitation* here. This is basically a 1:1 copying process between organizations while bypassing the macro mechanism of institutional logics. Imitation may happen when organizations try to adopt agile development methods due to seeing them as a sort of salvation device (e.g., they follow a "me too" strategy based on a management fashion). See also [28].

4   Conclusion and a Way Forward

My personal interest in theorizing about hybrid software development has been motivated by my previous professional experience. Being in a position to closely observe tensions between the two aforementioned conflicting logics (as being *both* simultaneously translated into a *single* organizational reality) provided me with quite a unique opportunity. In this particular case, the level of organization-wide consensus regarding the adoption goals was relatively low. The basic structure of the conceptual framework as presented here is a result of long-term thought exercise connected with the above context. I believe, however, that the framework will be similarly useful for theorizing about the implementations of hybrid software development that were undertaken elsewhere.

Before concluding, I must reiterate that the goal of the present paper was not to present revolutionary ideas. In fact, I assume that many professionals and researchers intuitively perceive certain paradigmatic differences between the traditional SE and the Agile SE worldviews (i.e. institutional logics). Hence, this paper was rather to propose: (i) how these philosophical differences can be *named* and *explored*, putting on a lens borrowed from sociology and management studies, (ii) that the invisible part of organizational and institutional realities cannot be omitted. The perspective sketched here paves the way towards a deeper understanding of motives behind hybrid development methods adoption, which is a much needed task [29]. In essence, my primary motivation was to find a connection between the micro and macro organizational forces, i.e. between the concept of organizational culture (which consists of both material and non-material elements [9]) and macro institutional forces (which carry also both such classes of elements). *Hybridized software development practices can be in turn conceptualized as the visible elements of organizational cultures, in which they got embedded thanks to the influence of institutional logics.*

In sum, the paper is meant as a work in progress report that shows the direction towards a full-fledged theory building exercise. My hope is that such exercise will result in an increased understanding of the driving forces behind the wide adoption of hybrid software development methods.

References

1. Culey, S.: Leadership and culture: part 1 - the case for culture. Eur. Bus. Rev. (May–June), 2–7 (2012)
2. Fowler, M., Highsmith, J.: The agile manifesto. Dr. Dobb's J. (2001). http://www.drdobbs.com/open-source/the-agile-manifesto/184414755
3. Fontana, R.M., Fontana, I.M., Da Rosa Garbuio, P.A., Reinehr, S., Malucelli, A.: Processes versus people: how should agile software development maturity be defined? J. Syst. Softw. 97, 140–155 (2014)
4. Biddle, R., Meier, A., Kropp, M., Anslow, C.: MyAgile: sociological and cultural effects of agile on teams and their members. In: CHASE (2018)
5. Sahota, M.: An Agile Adoption and Transformation Survival Guide: Working with Organizational Culture (2012)
6. Gren, L.: The systems approach to change and the agile software development context. In: Psychology of Programming Interest Group Workshop (PPIG) (2016)
7. Küpper, S., Kuhrmann, M., Wiatrok, M., Andelfinger, U., Rausch, A.: Is there a blueprint for building an agile culture? In: Vorgehensmodelle (2017)
8. Lots of "doing Agile", not much "being Agile,". https://www.equinox.co.nz/blog/lots-doing-agile-not-much-being-agile

9. Tolfo, C., Wazlawick, R.S., Ferreira, M.G.G., Forcellini, F.A.: Agile methods and organizational culture: reflections about cultural levels. J. Softw. Maint. Evol. **23**, 423–441 (2011)

10. Kuhrmann, M., et al.: Hybrid software development approaches in practice: a European perspective. IEEE Softw. (2018, in press)

11. Canato, A., Ravasi, D., Phillips, N.: Coerced practice implementation in cases of low cultural fit: cultural change and practice adaptation during the implementation of Six Sigma at 3M. Acad. Manag. J. **56**, 1724–1753 (2013)

12. Gren, L.: On gender, ethnicity, and culture in empirical software engineering research. In: CHASE (2018)

13. Dittrich, Y.: What does it mean to use a method? Towards a practice theory for software engineering. Inf. Softw. Technol. **70**, 220–231 (2016)

14. Clarke, P., O'Connor, R.V., Yilmaz, M.: In search of the origins and enduring impact of agile software development. In: ICSSP, pp. 142–146 (2018)

15. Pallas, J., Fredriksson, M., Wedlin, L.: Translating institutional logics: when the media logic meets professions. Organ. Stud. **37**, 1661–1684 (2016)

16. Thornton, P.H., Ocasio, W.: Institutional logics. In: The SAGE Handbook of Organizational Institutionalism. Sage, London (2008)

17. Rao, H., Monin, P., Durand, R.: Institutional change in Toque Ville: Nouvelle cuisine as an identity movement in French gastronomy. Am. J. Sociol. **108**, 795–843 (2003)

18. McPherson, C.M., Sauder, M.: Logics in action: managing institutional complexity in a drug court. Adm. Sci. Q. **58**, 165–196 (2013)

19. Rowlands, B.: Institutional aspects of systems development. In: ACIS (2008)

20. Berente, N., Hansen, S.W., Rosenkranz, C.: Rule formation and change in information systems development: how institutional logics shape ISD practices and processes. In: Proceedings of the Annual Hawaii International Conference on System Sciences (2015)

21. Gregor, S.: The nature of theory in information systems. MIS Q. **30**, 611–642 (2006)

22. North, D.: Institutions, Institutional Change and Economic Performance. Cambridge University Press, Cambridge (1990)

23. Schein, E.H.: Organizational Culture and Leadership. Jossey-Bass, San Francisco (2010)

24. Zilber, T.B.: The relevance of institutional theory for the study of organizational culture. J. Manag. Inq. **21**, 88–93 (2012)

25. Boehm, B., Turner, R.: Balancing Agility and Discipline. Addison Wesley, Boston (2003)

26. McDonald, C.: From art form to engineering discipline? A history of US military software development standards, 1974–1998. IEEE Ann. Hist. Comput. **32**, 32–45 (2010)

27. Lillrank, P.: The transfer of management innovations from Japan. Organ. Stud. **16**, 971–989 (1995)

28. Cram, W.A., Newell, S.: Mindful revolution or mindless trend? Examining agile development as a management fashion. Eur. J. Inf. Syst. **25**, 154–169 (2016)

29. Kuhrmann, M., et al.: Hybrid software and system development in practice: waterfall, scrum, and beyond. In: SCCP, pp. 30–39 (2017)

Towards Understanding the Motivation of German Organizations to Apply Certain Software Development Methods

Jil Klünder[1], Philipp Hohl[2], Steffen Küpper[3]([✉]), Stephan Krusche[4], Pernille Lous[5], Masud Fazal-Baqaie[6], and Christian R. Prause[7]

[1] Leibniz Universität Hannover, Hanover, Germany
jil.kluender@inf.uni-hannover.de
[2] Daimler AG, Ulm, Germany
philipp.hohl@daimler.com
[3] Technische Universität Clausthal, Clausthal-Zellerfeld, Germany
steffen.kuepper@tu-clausthal.de
[4] Technische Universität München, Munich, Germany
krusche@in.tum.de
[5] IT University of Copenhagen, Copenhagen, Denmark
pelo@itu.dk
[6] Fraunhofer-Institut für Entwurfstechnik Mechatronik IEM, Paderborn, Germany
masud.fazal-baqaie@iem.fraunhofer.de
[7] German Aerospace Center, Cologne, Germany
prause@acm.org

Abstract. The motivation to apply and to integrate agile methods into established development processes can be seen all over the world. However, the motivation for applying agile methods is not well understood as different objectives are possible: some organizations address the constantly changing market and customer demands, others are doing "agile" as the presumed best practice. This publication aims towards a better understanding of the motivation to apply the chosen development methods in Germany. We present preliminary results based on the data collection of the "Hybrid dEveLopmENt Approaches in software systems development" (HELENA) study. Further, we exemplary look at the role of criticality for choosing agile or traditional development methods. The results indicate that the six development methods applied most in Germany are Scrum, Kanban, DevOps, Waterfall, V-Model, and Iterative Development. However, a particular method is not necessarily chosen due to a specific goal. This indicates that as future work other influencing factors, e.g., the criticality of the final product, need to be identified and taken into account for analysis.

Keywords: Agile methods · HELENA study
Hybrid software development

M. Kuhrmann et al. (Eds.): PROFES 2018, LNCS 11271, pp. 449–456, 2018.
https://doi.org/10.1007/978-3-030-03673-7_36

1   Introduction

More and more organizations are adopting agile development approaches for the application in various domains [7]. The wide distribution is associated with the presumed advantages of adopting agile approaches, such as a reduced time to market or a better customer satisfaction [9]. However, there are organizations that do not pursue specific goals, but consider agile approaches just as state of the practice for modern software engineering [11]. Latest research revealed that practitioners most likely adopt agile approaches by combining agile and traditional software development methods in a pragmatic manner to an individually constructed software development approach [13].

In this paper, we strive towards an overview of the distribution of software development methods applied in Germany and discuss whether specific goals drive the application of certain development methods. We aim at providing further guidance for the selection and construction of software development approaches. For understanding the motivation to apply certain development methods, we want to answer the following research question:

Which goals do German organizations pursue with the application of the selected development methods?

We present preliminary results based on data obtained in the HELENA study[1]. Our findings are two-fold. First, we could identify goals that seem to be independent from the software development approach: an improved productivity as well as improved planning and estimation. Second, some goals seem to be strongly associated with agile or traditional development methods. Therefore, we consider the criticality of the system under development as one candidate aspect influencing the agility.

2   Related Work

Nowadays, agile and lean practices are considered some of the most promising approaches to improve the working process in industry [4]. This includes improving delivery speed and code quality, better collaboration and team dynamics within a software development team [5]. Additional possible benefits from agile development are improved communication, collaboration and control within the team and a shared code ownership [5,9].

Eklund et al. [6] reported further goals of implementing agile methods. They conducted a two-year case study involving six different large scale companies and analyzed their goals of adopting agile approaches. The companies strived for, e.g., combining different disciplines in one team and continuous releases [6].

A survey conducted with participants of a major software engineering conference identifies the "essence of agile development" [3]. Most interviewees of the

---

[1] https://helenastudy.wordpress.com.

study agree that the essence of agile development is the "adjustment to changing requirements" (65% agreed), "series of short term subprojects" (57% agreed), "a working product at the end of each iteration" (57% agreed), and "customers can see and try evolving software" (43% agreed) [3].

Klünder et. al. [10] identified the distribution of agile, plan-driven, and hybrid development approaches in Germany. The results indicate a high popularity of hybrid development approaches in Germany. Further, they point out that among global organizations, it has become widely accepted to adopt Scrum over traditional methods such as the waterfall process [10]. Scrum as one of the agile frameworks includes specific project management practices to simplify project control, increase team engagement, and improve the communication with the client [2]. Holmström et al. [8] present two case studies. One of the observed companies implements Scrum and the other one practices Extreme Programming. The identified goals of the companies are the alleviation of problems regarding communication, coordination, and control. Extreme Programming was beneficial for technical and coding aspects. Furthermore, the team achieved a higher quality of the code. Scrum evoked the feeling of being united as one team despite the team's distribution throughout the practice of daily stand-ups [8].

3 Data Analysis

The survey distributed at the second stage of the HELENA study [13] resulted in 732 suitable data points. In this publication, we consider the 127 data points provided by German respondents. Each data point contains a respondent's answers to up to 38 questions about demographics, process use, and standards as well as the respondent's experience. Table 1 lists the questionnaire items used for the preliminary analysis in this paper.

Table 1. Overview of the used questionnaire items of the HELENA study (separated into single choice/multiple choice question)

Single choice questions

Variable	Content	Possible Answers
D001	Company size	[micro, small, medium, large, very large]
D003	Global distribution	[no, nationally, regionally, globally]

Multiple choice questions

Variable	Content	Number of predefinded answers	Possible Answers
PU05	Agility degree	11	[fully traditional, mainly traditional, balanced […], mainly agile, fully agile]
PU09	Methods	24	[do not know the method, do not know if we use it, we never use it, we rarely use it, we sometimes use it, we often use it, we always use the method]
PU12	Goals	18	[yes/no]
D006	Criticality	10	[yes/no]

For data analysis, we clustered the identified development methods according to their application in German organizations (Variable PU09, cf. Table 1) and we analyzed the goals the organizations addressed when applying these methods (PU12). A method was defined to be applied by an organization, if the respective item in PU09 has been aligned to "We often use it" or "We always use the practice". The goal addressment was given by the yes/no-answer to PU12.

In order to investigate the influence of criticality on agility, we defined two new constructs: *Agility Score* (AS) and *Criticality Score* (CS). AS captures "how agile" the development process is. It is the mean of eleven "agility" assessments for different software process areas, e.g., *Project Management* or *Implementation and Coding*. For each of the process areas, the survey provided a question with a 5-point response scale ($PU05_j$) that captures how "agile" the process implementation is.

Criticality describes how fatal, in the worst case, a software failure can be. For each of the ten consequences such as "threaten human health or life" respondents stated whether a failure in the software they develop ($D006_k$) could result in such a consequence. For example, if a failure may "threaten human health or life" it can be considered extremely critical; a failure that may cost the company money might be considered less critical. We therefore defined four criticality classes and assigned weights to them: *Fatal* (weight 3), *Severe* (weight 2), *Major* (weight 1), and *Minor* (weight 0). We then assigned each of the ten consequences to one of the classes in such a way that we have a slight normal distribution. The assignment can be found in Table 2. The CS is defined to be the highest weight of any of the failure consequences that can result from a software failure.

Table 2. Consequences of software failures assigned to the criticality

Minor	Major	Severe	Fatal
financial loss	system degradation	loss of system	threaten human health or life
impact reputation	criminal law consequences	impact on the environment	legal consequences
	impact business	Other	

4 Preliminary Results

127 participants from German organizations participated in the HELENA study. 44 participants work in a very large company (more than 2500 employees) (34.6%), 37 participants work in a large company (251–2499 employees) (29.1%), and 27 work in a medium company with more than 50 and less then 250 employees (21.3%). 19 participants work either in a micro (less than 10 employees) (12; 9.4%) or in a small (11–50 employees) (7; 5.5%) company.

All participants are team members of projects which are distributed differently, 29 projects are nationally (i.e. same country), 20 are regionally (i.e. same continent), 30 are globally distributed, and 48 projects are not distributed at all.

As visualized in Fig. 1, the six methods applied the most are Scrum (54.3 %), iterative development (42.5 %), Kanban (27.6 %), the classic waterfall process (23.6 %), DevOps (20.5 %), and the V-model (20.5 %)[2]. Three of the six mostly applied methods are agile: Scrum, Kanban, and DevOps.

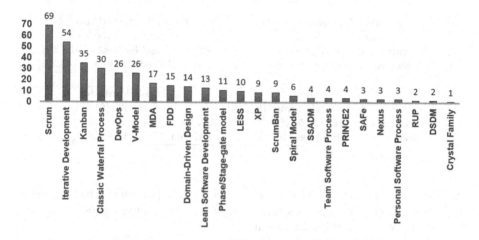

Fig. 1. Applied development methods in German organizations

We considered the addressed goals to analyze the motivation for applying at least one of these methods. Table 3 summarizes the top-3 goals that most of the organizations strived for, separately for each of the six methods applied most (and probably other ones). The results indicate that a certain method is not necessarily chosen due to a specific goal, since the goals do not vary that much: Productivity, client involvement, the frequency of delivery, external product quality as well as planning and estimation shall be improved. All six methods address at least two of these five goals.

Organizations applying these methods strive towards an improved productivity and improved planning and estimation. Especially for agile methods, frequency of delivery and the client involvement are relevant goals. External product quality is an important issue as well – in particular, when applying methods that are not agile. Irrespective thereof, it seems both, agile and traditional methods, are applied with comparable addressed goals. This leads to the presumption that the chosen development approach is not necessarily connected to any specific goals. However, there are some notable deviations between the waterfall model and Scrum, and between the V-Model and Scrum.

An observation in Table 3 is that none of the agile development methods has "external product quality" in its Top-3 (left column). As opposed to this, "external product quality" is a motive for all three traditional methods. This seems congruent with Boehm's observation [1] that there are different home

---

[2] Due to the nature of this question with multiple answers, we have more than 100%.

454   J. Klünder et al.

Table 3. Top-3 of the addressed goals by method

Top-3 Scrum	Top-3 Iterative Development
Frequency of Delivery to Customer (50.7%)	Planning and Estimation (48.1%)
Productivity (49.3%)	Productivity (48.1%)
Client Involvement (46.4%)	External Product Quality (46.3%)

Top-3 Kanban	Top-3 Waterfall model
Productivity (60.0%)	Productivity (56.7%)
Planning and Estimation (54.3%)	Planning and Estimation (53.3%)
Project Monitoring and Controlling (51.4%)	External Product Quality (43.3%)

Top-3 DevOps	Top-3 V-model
Frequency of Delivery to Customer (57.7%)	Productivity (61.5%)
Client Involvement (50.0%)	Adaptability and Flexibility (57.7%)
Planning and Estimation (46.2%)	External Product Quality (50.0%)

grounds for agile and traditional development, and, in particular, that the more fatal a software failure is, the more "conservative" development gets. Therefore, we further investigate this relationship.

Some respondents did not provide agility assessments of their processes. In the remaining 95 respondents, the average AS is 3.1 (SD = 0.9). 33 respondents stated a criticality score of 3, 13 stated a score of 2, 45 of 1 and 4 of 0.

We fitted a multiple linear regression (MLR) model to AS as the dependent variable, $D006_k$ being the independent variables. Then $R^2_{AS} = 0.19$ is the percentage of variance of the Agility Score that can be explained through criticality. Similarly, a MLR with CS as dependent variable and $PU09_j$ as independent variables gives us $R^2_{CS} = 0.14$. The Pearson correlation between CS and AS is $r_{CS,AS} = -0.32$.

5 Discussion

Based on our preliminary results, we cannot identify a trend of German organizations to apply agile or traditional methods. Considering the six mostly applied methods, we find agile, traditional, and hybrid ones. The reasons why companies choose a certain method may be different, even if they all strive for, e.g., productivity. One explanation may be that productivity is defined differently and in fact, it is used differently in traditional and agile models.

The top-3 goals are identified for all participating organizations in Germany. As one of the top-3 goals of the traditional approaches, i.e. the waterfall model and the V-Model, we identified the external product quality, which is not a major goal for agile methods, e.g. Scrum and Kanban.

However, our results should not be overgeneralized, since there are some threats which need to be avoided in further analysis. First of all, the performed analysis is coarse grained. We only considered the six mostly applied methods based on a data set with 127 data points. Another issue is the data aggregation. We considered all the goals addressed by all German organizations which apply at least one of the methods. Hence, we cannot ensure that the organizations strive to, e.g., increase the delivery to the customer using Scrum. We can only state that many organizations that apply Scrum want to improve the frequency of the delivery to the customer. Consequently, there is some follow-up analysis required in order to sharpen the statements. Half of the organizations applying Scrum want to improve the frequency of delivery to the customer, but they do not necessarily apply Scrum in order to achieve this goal.

Finding correlations between the applied methods and the addressed goals requires further analysis. Nonetheless, our preliminary results suggest that there is no generalizable relation between the methods and the goals. The chosen methods do not seem to depend on the addressed goal. However, research provides further factors, but seems to be of philosophical nature, i.e., collecting and naming success factors, and collecting lessons learned from specific cases. [12]. Yet, knowledge on the cause-effect relation and evaluation of the impact of these factors is rare. Hence, there are other influence factors existing; that should be subject for future work.

Analysis of the MLRs and the correlation between CS and AS has three implications: Firstly, the interpretation of the strength of a correlation (R^2) depends highly on the context. Sciences with immediate effects of variables usually find high correlation values. However, if outcomes have more than a single cause, a strong relation of two variables is unlikely. Certainly, the forming of projects' software processes depends on many different factors (such as many different humans), and also including undeliberate ones. Secondly, as $R^2_{AS} > R^2_{CS}$, AS depends more on CS than vice versa, the direction of the effect is probably Criticality $\rightarrow$ Agility. Thirdly, if we compute the Pearson correlation between CS and AS, we obtain $r_{CS,AS} = -0.32 < 0$, i.e., there is a negative relationship between CS and AS. The higher CS, the lower AS. So, indeed, potential software failures seem to lead to more traditional processes. However, these first results may not be over-generalized. Further analysis is required in order to achieve more reliable results.

6   Conclusion

The preliminary results presented in this publication point out that most German organizations aim at improving the productivity, the customer's perceived product quality, planning and estimation as well as the frequency of delivery to the customer. No explicit relationship between the goals pursued and the specific method applied could be identified. However, we could find indications that the criticality might have an influence.

Based on these results, it might be interesting to further investigate the influences of criticality, different characteristics (e.g., company size, distribution of the team, and project size) as well as additional success factors. We want to compare the German results with the motivation of organizations worldwide to apply certain development methods. In addition, we want to include the chosen development practices in our analysis.

We encourage other researchers and practitioners to participate in the analysis and to introduce new directions or ideas.

Acknowledgments. We want to thank Marco Kuhrmann and the core team of HELENA for their endless efforts in the HELENA projects.

References

1. Boehm, B.: Get ready for agile methods, with care. Computer **35**, 64–69 (2002)
2. Cristal, M., Wildt, D., Prikladnicki, R.: Usage of scrum practices within a global company. In: IEEE International Conference on Global Software Engineering, ICGSE 2008, pp. 222–226. IEEE (2008)
3. Durdik, Z., Prause, C.R.: ESEC/FSE 2011 PWG report – group 4: Agile software development. Technical report Research Center for IT (2012)
4. Dybå, T., Dingsøyr, T.: Empirical studies of agile software development: a systematic review. Inf. Softw. Technol. **50**(9–10), 833–859 (2008)
5. Ebert, C., Kuhrmann, M., Prikladnicki, R.: Global software engineering: evolution and trends. In: 2016 IEEE 11th International Conference on Global Software Engineering (ICGSE), pp. 144–153. IEEE (2016)
6. Eklund, U., Berger, C.: Scaling agile development in mechatronic organizations-a comparative case study. In: 2017 IEEE/ACM 39th International Conference on Software Engineering: Software Engineering in Practice Track (ICSE-SEIP), pp. 173–182. IEEE (2017)
7. Fitzgerald, B., Stol, K.J., O'Sullivan, R., O'Brien, D.: Scaling agile methods to regulated environments: an industry case study. In: Notkin, D. (ed.) 2013 35th International Conference on Software Engineering (ICSE), pp. 863–872. IEEE, Piscataway (2013). https://doi.org/10.1109/ICSE.2013.6606635
8. Holmström, H., Fitzgerald, B., Ågerfalk, P.J., Conchúir, E.Ó.: Agile practices reduce distance in global software development. Inf. Syst. Manag. **23**(3), 7–18 (2006)
9. Holmström Olsson, H., Bosch, J., Alahyari, H.: Customer-specific teams for agile evolution of large-scale embedded systems. In: 2013 39th EUROMICRO Conference on Software Engineering and Advanced Applications (SEAA), pp. 82–89 (2013). https://doi.org/10.1109/SEAA.2013.43
10. Klünder, J., et al.: HELENA study: reasons for combining agile and traditional software development approaches in german companies. In: Felderer, M., Méndez Fernández, D., Turhan, B., Kalinowski, M., Sarro, F., Winkler, D. (eds.) PROFES 2017. LNCS, vol. 10611, pp. 428–434. Springer, Cham (2017). https://doi.org/10.1007/978-3-319-69926-4_32
11. Klünder, J., Hohl, P., Schneider, K.: Becoming agile while preserving software product lines: an agile transformation model for large companies. In: Proceedings of ICSSP 2018: International Conference on Software and System Processes. ACM (2018)
12. Kuhrmann, M., Diebold, P., Münch, J.: Software process improvement: a systematic mapping study on the state of the art. PeerJ Comput. Sci. **2**(1), 1–38 (2016)
13. Kuhrmann, M., et al.: Hybrid software and system development in practice: waterfall, scrum, and beyond. In: Proceedings of the International Conference on Software and System Process, ICSSP. IEEE Computer Society (2017)

Author Index

Printed in the United States
By Bookmasters